ADVANCED ACCOUNTING
A Professional Approach

The Willard J. Graham Series in Accounting

Consulting Editor Robert N. Anthony *Harvard University*

ADVANCED ACCOUNTING
A Professional Approach

JAMES E. WHEELER
Professor of Accounting
The University of Michigan

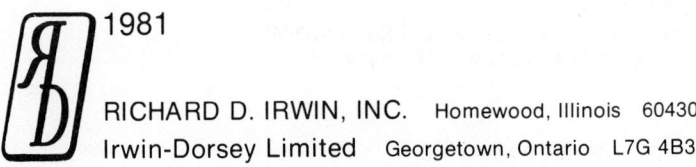

1981

RICHARD D. IRWIN, INC.   Homewood, Illinois   60430
Irwin-Dorsey Limited   Georgetown, Ontario   L7G 4B3

© RICHARD D. IRWIN, INC., 1981

All rights reserved. No part of this publication may be reproduced, stored in a retrieval system, or transmitted, in any form or by any means, electronic, mechanical, photocopying, recording, or otherwise, without the prior written permission of the publisher.

ISBN 0-256-02477-4
Library of Congress Catalog Card No. 80–82448
Printed in the United States of America

1 2 3 4 5 6 7 8 9 0 MP 8 7 6 5 4 3 2 1

Preface

It has long been the belief of this author that advanced accounting should introduce the income tax side of recorded business transactions. Indeed, the accounting for these transactions is incomplete if the income tax effects are not recorded. In addition, the history of many financial accounting problems, such as the concept of a pooling of interests, are rooted in the income tax law.

It has also been my observation that accounting for the unavoidable income tax aspects of business transactions has been one of the more difficult problem areas in accounting. It is one that students are often the least prepared to handle. The difficulty students encounter in this area when they enter practice is at least partially caused by the fact that in all of their accounting courses, including most "advanced" accounting classes, problems are solved ignoring taxes. This is obviously a false environment, perhaps acceptable in elementary accounting, but not in an advanced accounting text.

Advanced Accounting: A Professional Approach represents a substantial change by providing significant coverage of all financial accounting aspects of business transactions, including the income tax aspects. Thus, the tax effects are mentioned throughout this text and the accounting for this factor is shown. The first two chapters deal with accounting for income taxes. This material is presented first so that the student will have an appreciation for the tax aspects of corporate acquisitions, liquidations, and consolidations and for its impact on partnership activity. It should be emphasized that this is not a tax text but a financial accounting text that attempts to show the proper accounting for all factors affecting financial reporting.

The main emphasis is on accounting for corporate acquisitions and consolidations, with substantial discussion of partnerships and a brief overview of accounting for nonbusiness (primarily governmental) activity. Thus, Chapters 3 through 9 are concerned with various aspects of business combinations and consolidations. Chapter 10 covers the problems of accounting for international transactions and foreign operations. Chapters 11 and 12 deal with partnerships, and Chapter 13 is on nonbusiness accounting (sometimes called governmental accounting).

In the consolidation portions of this text (Chapters 3 through 9) the term *elimination entry* is not used. Instead, the five different forms of consolidation entries are identified by separate titles which lend more meaning to the process: substitution, deferral, restoration, offset, and advanced recognition.

Chapter 3 puts the subsequent chapters in perspective by demonstrating that consolidation is a single economic entity concept. In addition, this chapter contains one of the most complete discussions of the cost and equity methods of accounting for investments in stock of other corporations found in any text.

Chapter 4 introduces the substitution consolidation entry which replaces the investment in the subsidiary account with the net assets of the subsidiary. In many cases, this will also bring forth a minority interest. In addition, this chapter demonstrates that consolidated net earnings can be calculated without an extensive use of large work sheets. The analysis of the investment in the subsidiary equity accounts is used to accomplish this.

Chapters 5 and 6 demonstrate the accounting problems involving intercompany transactions. This discussion shows the use of deferral, restoration, offset, and advanced recognition consolidation entries and the related income tax aspects.

Chapter 7 contains a very theoretical discussion of (1) the impact of a complex capital structure within a subsidiary and (2) the effects of changes in a subsidiary's capital structure. How these problems are handled in practice is also examined.

Chapter 8 contains a discussion of tiered operations, including partnership tiers and the effects of reciprocal investments. Triangular acquisitions are examined under both the purchase and pooling concepts.

Chapter 9 concludes the discussion of consolidations and contains a discussion of planning corporate acquisitions and liquidations. The 12 rules for a pooling of interests are carefully examined and then the ITT acquisition of Hartford is used as a case analysis.

All chapters show the more general income tax aspects which often produce significant consequences in a real-world environment. Because this text reflects the entire business environment, its coverage is easily the most complete and perhaps complex in the field. It is therefore recommended for use only at schools with high-quality students. For most universities it would best fit in a master's level course in advanced accounting.

The author would like to thank Roland (Sully) Salmonson of Michigan State University; Robert N. Anthony of Harvard University; Philip M. J. Reckers of The University of Maryland; and former professor and now partner in Arthur Andersen & Co., Arthur R. Wyatt, for their extensive comments in reviewing the various drafts for this text. Special thanks also go to Howard Lowe of the University of Hawaii for allowing me to test much of this material on University of Hawaii students. I must also thank the many secretaries who did the typing for this text.

I reserve special thanks to my wife Robin and my three children, Ellen, Rebecca, and Stephen, for their endless patience and understanding.

James E. Wheeler

Contents

Chapter 1
Accounting for Income Taxes 2

Complexity in Accounting for Income Taxation. Accounting Theory and the Nature of the Income Tax. Allocation—Principal Problem in Accounting for Expenses: *Intraperiod Federal Income Tax Allocation. Intercorporate Federal Income Tax Allocation. Interperiod Federal Income Tax Allocation.* Pad for Anticipated Deficiency on Audit. Impact of Tax Credits. Sample Problem and Solution.

Chapter 2
Accounting for Income Taxes—Special Considerations 38

Some Common Additional Complexities: *Equity Method Earnings or Consolidation in Connection with Separate Tax Returns. Net Operating Losses. Some Reasons Why a Corporation May Elect Only the NOL Carryforward. Carryforwards of NOLs when There Are Deferred Tax Credits from Timing Differences. Carryforwards of Investment Tax Credits When There Are Deferred Tax Credits from Timing Differences.* Part Permanent and Part Timing (more complexity). Stock Option Complexity. Financial Disclosure of Tax Accounts: *Net-of-Tax Concept. Liability Concept. Deferral Concept. Deferred Tax Accounts in the Statement of Financial Position. Required Disclosure in the Earnings Statement.* An Evaluation of Accounting for Income Taxes: *Economic Reality as a Guideline. A Suggested Presentation.* Appendix: *Foreign Income Taxes. State and Local Income Taxes.*

Chapter 3
Accounting for Equity Investments and Asset Acquisitions 78

Business Motivations for Equity Investments. Tax Motivations for Equity Investments. Categories of Equity Investments and Accounting Methods: *Cost Method. Lower of Cost or Market. Equity Method. Consolidation Method.* Acquisition of a Corporation. Accounting Concepts on Acquisition: *Pooling of Interests. Purchase.* Illustration of the Direct and Indirect Asset Acquisition by a Corporation Using the Purchase Concept. Allocation of the Purchase Price in a Multiple Asset Acquisition: *Fair Market Value (FMV) Allocation Method. Modified FMV Allocation Method. Residual Allocation Method.* Appendix: A Summary of Accounting Requirements for Stock Investments and for the Timing Differences Created by Undistributed Earnings.

Chapter 4
Substitution of Assets and Liabilities for Capital Stock Investments in Preparing Consolidated Statements 126

Substitution under the Purchase Concept at the Date of Acquisition: *Investment at the Book Value of the Underlying Net Assets. Investment at More than the Book Value of the Underlying Net Assets. Investment at Less than the Underlying Book Value—100 Percent Acquisition. Investment at Less than the Underlying Book Value—Majority Acquisition.* Substitution under the Purchase Concept Subsequent to the Date of Acquisition: *Investment at the Underlying Book Value—100 Percent Acquisition. Investment at More than the Underlying Book Value—100 Percent Acquisition. Investment at More than the Underlying Book Value—Majority Acquisition. Investment at Less than the Underlying Book Value—Majority Acquisition.* Substitution under the Pooling of Interests Concept: *Substitution at Acquisition—with 90 Percent Minimum Ownership. Substitution Subsequent to Acquisition—with 90 Percent Minimum Ownership.* Appendix: Possible Combinations of Book Value, Fair Value, and Cost.

Chapter 5
Accounting for Intercorporate Transactions which Defer Gains or Loss Recognition 168

Effect of the Single Entity Concept. Accounting Periods and Methods. Offset, Deferral, and Restoration Entries: *Terminology. Offsets. Deferrals and Restorations.* Subsidiary Sales to Parent. A Complete Illustration. Impact on Earnings under the Equity Method when the Parent Is the Selling Affiliate.

Chapter 6
Accounting for Intercorporate Debt-Transactions Which May Advance Gain or Loss Recognition 212

Pathways for Debt Acquisition. Direct Acquisition from the Member Issuing the Debt. Disposal of Directly Acquired Debt: *Sale to an Out-*

sider. Sale to Debtor or to Another Member. Acquisition from an Outside Party. The Problem of Allocating Gains and Losses. Years Subsequent to Acquisition from an Outside Party. The Minority Interest Aspects. A Working Paper Analysis.

Chapter 7
Accounting for Complex and Changing Capital Structures within a Subsidiary 238

Complex Structures: *The Problem of Distinguishing between Debt and Owners' Equity. The Tax Incentive. The Analysis of Investments with Both Common and Preferred Stock.* Changing Ownership Interests: *Change in Ownership through Conversion of Securities. Change in Ownership through the Issuance of Shares by the Subsidiary. Change through Options. Change through New Share Issues. Change through Treasury Stock Transactions. Change through Sale of a Part or All of the Ownership Interest.*

Chapter 8
Accounting for Tiered Operations 288

Development of Tiered Structures. Acquisition with Parent Corporation Stock. Acquisition of a Chain of Corporations: *Under the Pooling Concept. Under the Purchase Concept. Indirect Acquisition of Marketable Securities under the Purchase Concept.* Reporting the Operations of a Tiered Chain of Corporations: *Reporting for Tiered Operations where the Subsidiaries Were Acquired under Pooling. Reporting for Tiered Operations where the Subsidiaries Were Acquired by Purchase.* Reciprocal Interests: *Recognition of Reciprocal Interests. Treasury Stock Treatment of Reciprocal Interests.*

Chapter 9
Planning Corporate Acquisitions and Liquidations 324

Parties to an Acquisition or Combination. Reasons for Corporate Acquisitions. Types of Acquisitions or Combinations with Stock as Compensation: *The Accounting Concept for Taxable and Purchase Acquisitions. The Accounting Concept for Tax-Free and Pooling Combinations.* Some of the Basic Requirements for a Tax-Free Exchange. Some Theoretical Aspects of Pooling: *Pooling and Prior Years. Origin of Pooling. Perfect Case for Pooling. Other Theoretical Questions for Pooling. Part Pooling and Part Purchase.* The 12 Requirements for Pooling of Interests Accounting: *Attributes of Combining Corporations. Manner of Combining Interests. Absence of Planned Transactions.* Planning the Recorded Value of Corporate Assets: *For Financial Reporting. For Tax Purposes.* Other Planning Aspects. The ITT Acquisition of Hartford Fire Insurance Company: *The Acquisition. The Tax Treatment. The Pooling of Interests Effects.* Pooling in Theoretical Perspective.

Chapter 10
Accounting for International Transactions, Investments, and Operations 366

Need for Translation. Effects of Translation: *Selling and Buying in a Foreign Market. Speculation in a Foreign Currency. Operations Located in a Foreign Country.* Summary of Current Translation Rules: *Translation of Financial Position Accounts. Translation of Earnings Statement Accounts.* Example of the Effects of Rate Changes. Some Critics. Hedging Foreign Currency Commitments or Exposed Net Asset or Exposed Net Liability Positions. Some Additional Aspects of Translation and Investments in Subsidiaries: *Translation Following a Purchase Acquisition. Translation Following a Pooling of Interests.*

Chapter 11
Accounting for Partnerships—Formation and Operation 394

Partnership Form of Business Entity: *Partnership Concept. General Income Tax Aspects of Partnerships. Partnerships as Compared to Proprietorships. Partnerships as Compared to Corporations. Partnerships as Compared to Joint Ownerships. Types of Partners. Some Types of Partnerships.* Large CPA Firms. Creating a Partnership: *Partnership Agreement. Earnings and Loss Ratios. Recording Contributed Assets and Liabilities.* Partnership Operations: *General Aspects. Corporate Partners.* Admitting New Partners: *Routes to Becoming a Partner. Premium Paid by a New Partner. Premium Paid by Old Partners. Admitting New Partners—Additional Examples. Purchasing an Existing Partner's Interest. Purchasing of Part of Each Partner's Interest.*

Chapter 12
Accounting for Partner to Partnership Transactions and Terminations 426

Partner to Partnership Transactions and Vice Versa: *Sales at Gains. Potential for Tax-Free Diversification. Sales at Losses. Impact of Contributed, Appreciated, or Depreciated Assets on Earnings and Loss Ratios.* Liabilities and Loans: *Liabilities of a Partnership. Loans from a Partner. Loans to a Partner.* Termination of a Partner's Interest: *Termination in General. Sale of a Partnership Interest.* Termination of a Partnership: *Partnership Split-Offs and Mergers. Partnership Liquidations.* Tiered Partnerships. Tax-Free Incorporation of Partnerships.

Chapter 13
An Introduction to Accounting for Governmental Operations and Certain Aspects of Other Nonbusiness Operations 454

Function of Government. Funds Concept. Standard Governmental Accounting System for a Municipality: *Governmental Group of Funds. Proprietary Group of Funds. Fiduciary Group of Funds. Self-Balancing Noncurrent Groups of Accounts.* Concept of Stewardship. Users of Governmental Reports. Development of a Fund Accounting System. Various Audit Concepts. A System for Control: *Use of Agencies. Budgeting Process. Encumbrance Accounting. Accounting Bases.* Future of Governmental Accounting. A Glance at the Federal Government: *Federal Revenues. Federal Expenditures.* A Glance at State and Local Governments: *State and Local Revenues. State and Local Expenditures.* Tax Aspects of Financing Governmental Operations: *Taxation of Investor's Earnings. Use of Industrial Development and Mortgage Bonds.* Other Nonbusiness Units Requiring Accounting and Auditing Services.

Index **483**

ADVANCED ACCOUNTING
A Professional Approach

1

Accounting for Income Taxes

Complexity in Accounting for Income Taxation
Accounting Theory and the Nature of the Income Tax
Allocation—Principal Problem in Accounting for Expenses
    Intraperiod Federal Income Tax Allocation
    Intercorporate Federal Income Tax Allocation
    Interperiod Federal Income Tax Allocation
        Differences between Pretax Accounting Income and Taxable Income
        Two Types of Permanent Differences
        Provision for Federal Income Taxes
        Reversal of Timing Differences
Pad for Anticipated Deficiency on Audit
Impact of Tax Credits
Sample Problem and Solution

Note to users: Unless you are well versed in the complexities of accounting for income taxes, you will find that much of the discussion in these first two chapters will require considerable thought and several readings.

COMPLEXITY IN ACCOUNTING FOR INCOME TAXATION

One means of judging the complexity and perhaps the importance of a topic is to ascertain how often it appears in official pronouncements. Using this yardstick, accounting for income taxation is a very complex and important topic for it appears in more pronouncements of the APB and the FASB than any other topic.[1] This frequency of appearance attests to the complexity of accounting for income taxation. Because of the very technical nature of our federal income tax system, many CPA firms now require that the auditing of a corporation's tax accrual accounts be done by a member of their tax staff rather than an audit staff member. But even where this is done, the auditor should have some knowledge of what the tax accrual accounts contain. Indeed, the client may want an explanation of what is in each of these accounts.

Given the existing complexity and the high cost of income taxation, it is the objective of the first two chapters of this text to develop (1) an understanding of the nature of the income tax and its related accounting theory, (2) knowledge of the current accounting requirements for this tax, (3) an awareness of the various accounts this accounting process creates, and (4) knowledge of the financial accounting disclosure requirements.

ACCOUNTING THEORY AND THE NATURE OF THE INCOME TAX

Official pronouncements proclaim that income taxes are an expense.[2] But when examined in depth, income tax seems to fail the principal characteristic of an expense; that is, it does not generate revenue—it is not an effort to create revenue—but the tax itself is generated because of the presence of taxable revenues in excess of tax-deductible expenses. In a strict definition, an expense is an effort or cost incurred to create revenue. This is a one-way street; an expense does not result because we have revenue in excess of other expenses. In other words, an expense generates revenue and not vice versa.

Some accounting theorists have jumped on the failure to generate revenue and thus have declared this cost to be a loss—an expiration of assets without revenue generation.

---

[1] A partial listing of the pronouncements would include *APB Opinions Nos. 1, 2, 4, 11, 23,* and *24* (where the entire opinion is devoted to income taxes), and *FASB Statement No. 9*. In addition, one or more paragraphs in many other pronouncements are devoted to tax considerations (e.g., *APB Opinion No. 10*, par. 6). This subject has also been the principal topic in several research studies.

[2] *AICPA Professional Standards, Accounting—Current Text* (New York, 1980), par. 4091.13b, reads, "Income taxes are an expense of business enterprises earning income subject to tax." Copyright (1980) by the American Institute of CPAs.

Taxes must either represent expense (the expiration of assets used in producing revenue), loss, a distribution to an equity, or an entirely distinct item which cannot be put under any general head. According to the above discussion the tax payment can best be considered a loss (which it is from the standpoint of the private owners) or a distribution in favor of the underlying equity of the state; it cannot reasonably be viewed as an expense.[3]

As noted in the above quote, some accountants have proclaimed taxation to be a profit distribution as though the government or society were a part owner. But if this were true then the government would surely be a super owner for without any direct investment it can dictate its share of the profits and limit its share of any losses. This certainly violates the idea that a profit distribution is somehow related to investment.

It seems that none of these theories really supports a definition of what an income tax actually is. Can it be that accounting theory is inadequate—that this cost can be something other than an expense, a loss, or a profit distribution? If so, this is an anomalous or distinct item which should perhaps have its own set of accounting rules.[4] But whatever the proper theory, the fact is that official bodies have declared income taxes to be expenses, and therefore the accounting principles which are applicable to expenses are employed to account for it.

ALLOCATION—PRINCIPAL PROBLEM IN ACCOUNTING FOR EXPENSES

It has been said that "every expense has been an asset even if only for a fleeting moment in time."[5] Thus, when an asset becomes an expense in different periods for book and for tax purposes, there is a problem of allocating the tax effect between accounting periods. For income taxation this is called interperiod allocation, but there are two other important types of tax allocation—intraperiod and intercompany.

---

[3] William A. Paton, *Accounting Theory* (New York: The Ronald Press Co., 1922), p. 181.

[4] For a more complete discussion of the nature of the income tax and the historical development of today's accounting rules, see James E. Wheeler and Willard H. Galliart, *An Appraisal of Interperiod Income Tax Allocation* (New York: Financial Executives Research Foundation, 1974), pp. 19–64.

[5] W. A. Paton and A. C. Littleton said essentially the same thing in the accounting classic, *An Introduction to Corporate Accounting Standards* (Sarasota, Fla.: American Accounting Association, 1977), p. 72:

"The process of applying costs incurred to revenues, . . . consists essentially of the division of charges into those to be reported in the current income sheet and those assignable to future periods. . . .

"According to the position taken here *all costs incurred prudently and in good faith are reflected at least momentarily in the total of assets*, broadly conceived, and through this avenue attach to business activity, the effort to produce revenue." (Emphasis added.)

Intraperiod Federal Income Tax Allocation

Under this form of allocation, income taxes are spread throughout the earnings statement and even taken to the statement of retained earnings (and in some fairly rare cases to paid-in capital in the statement of financial position).[6] This is a reflection of the concept that the tax effect of each transaction should be netted against that transaction. Thus, if a transaction is accounted for as a normal operating item, so is the related tax effect; and if a transaction is recorded as a sale of a segment of a business, an extraordinary item, a change in accounting principle, or a prior period adjustment, so is the related tax cost or benefit. Thus, to determine the total income tax expense, it is necessary to locate and combine all of the separately reported tax effects.

To illustrate, assume that there is a flat 40 percent tax rate and that before-tax earnings (losses) are reported as follows (all from taxable sources):

Earnings from continuing operations	$ 60,000
Loss from disposal of a segment of a business	(10,000)
Extraordinary gain	30,000
Cumulative effect of accounting changes	20,000
Net earnings before tax	$100,000
Prior period error (taken against beginning retained earnings)	$ (50,000)

Within the earnings statements these major sections and the tax effects of the transactions (at the assumed 40 percent rate) would be shown as follows:

Before-tax earnings from continuing operations	$ 60,000
Federal income tax provision	24,000
Earnings from continuing operations	36,000
Loss from disposal of a segment of a business (net-of-tax benefit of $4,000)	(6,000)
Extraordinary gain (net of tax of $12,000)	18,000
Cumulative effect of accounting charges (net of tax of $8,000)	12,000
Net earnings	$ 60,000

The prior period adjustment taken directly to beginning retained earnings would be shown as follows:

Beginning retained earnings as previously reported	xxx
Prior period error (net-of-tax benefit of $20,000)	$ (30,000)
Adjusted beginning retained earnings	xxx

---

[6] *AICPA Professional Standards,* par. 4062.17. To have any part of an expense (tax expense in this case) appear as paid-in capital is, to say the least, a rather unusual treatment for an expense. (This is discussed in more detail later in this chapter.)

Thus, the total tax provision for the year including the effects of the prior period adjustment is:

Tax charged against continuing operations	$ 24,000
Tax benefit from loss on sale of a business segment	(4,000)
Tax charged against extraordinary gain	12,000
Tax charged against the cumulative effect of accounting change	8,000
Tax benefit from error requiring a prior period adjustment	(20,000)
Total of all tax provisions recorded this year	$ 20,000

Thus, while intraperiod income tax allocation is a fairly simple concept—the tax adheres to the transaction and is reported with it—obtaining the total reported tax expense or apportioning it to the various transactions can be a more difficult task. It must be remembered that there are often three separate categories of income taxes—federal, foreign, and state and local—and the SEC requires separate disclosure of each.[7] In addition, the existence of various tax rates, different asset bases, and thus different gains (losses) between the financial reports and the tax return make this allocation more difficult than it appears.

As will be illustrated in later chapters, the existence of different book and tax bases for assets and liabilities is a fairly common situation in corporate acquisitions, where the cost of the acquired stock must be allocated to the acquired corporation's assets and liabilities in the preparation of consolidated financial statements. For example, a nondepreciable asset may have a basis of $40,000 on the financial records but have a tax basis of only $21,000 due to different methods of recording its acquisition. Thus, if this asset is sold for $30,000, the financial statements would reflect a $10,000 before-tax loss and the tax return would reflect a $9,000 gain. Assuming a 40 percent tax rate, you might expect an after-tax loss of $6,000 ($10,000 − (10,000 × 40%)), but instead this transaction would be reported as an aftertax loss of $13,600 ($10,000 + ($9,000 × 40%)). In this example the tax on the gain reported in the tax return increases the loss reported in the financial statements.

The "add-on minimum tax" on tax preferences, while technically not an income tax, can also cause problems in intraperiod allocation. This tax is currently levied at the rate of 15 percent on the total of the tax preference items, but the 15 percent is applied only after this total is reduced by an exclusion which is the greater of $10,000 or the regular corporate income tax liability.[8] Depreciation and capital gain income are but two of the items which can result in tax preferences. If there were a sale of a segment of a business which resulted in favorable capital gain treatment, then a minimum tax might be incurred; and to the extent this

---

[7] Securities and Exchange Commission, Regulation S-X, Rule 3-16(o).

[8] *Internal Revenue Code*, sec. 56–58.

tax were applicable to the sale of a business segment, it should (following the same logic as applied to an income tax) be allocated to this transaction.[9]

Intercorporate Federal Income Tax Allocation

This form of tax allocation appears whenever a consolidated tax return is prepared. While consolidation treats the consolidating entities as one corporation, they are legally and in reality separate entities, and they always need separate financial records. When a consolidated tax return is filed, there is but one tax amount to be paid to the federal government. Therefore, the tax return represents the consolidated result for many entities, and they must each be allocated their share of the tax liability. If for no other reason, this is necessary if the entities are to know whether current and future distributions are regular dividends out of earnings and profits (a tax term which is similar in many respects to retained earnings) or liquidating dividends and thus out of paid-in capital. It should be noted that the amount of "nontaxable" liquidating dividends is determined from the tax set of books. Thus, what is reported as a liquidating dividend based on the retained earnings could readily be a taxable dividend based on earnings and profits or vice versa.[10]

Suppose that we have four corporations whose entire incomes or losses *are the same for both book and tax purposes* (a most unrealistic assumption) and are in amounts as shown in Illustration 1–1.

Illustration 1–1

Corporation	Income (Loss)
A	$ 100,000
B	80,000
C	(60,000)
D	(120,000)
Before-tax book net income and taxable income	–0–

---

[9] It should be noted that the term "add-on minimum tax" is an additional tax which is added to the regular federal income tax liability; it is a minimum tax only when there is no regular federal income tax liability. There is also an "alternative minimum tax," but this does not impact on corporate taxpayers.

[10] This problem arose in 1974 for American Electric Power. They had paid dividends when their Retained Earnings account was about $450 million and thus thought the dividends were taxable to the shareholders. Like most corporations they did not keep a complete tax set of books and did not know at that time that their earnings and profits figure was negative, thus indicating "tax-free" dividends.

In this case, on a consolidated basis there would be no tax to pay to the federal government; but on a separate return basis both A and B would have had to pay, and C and D might have been able to receive a refund if they had reported taxable income in the three prior years large enough to use their losses against. Under current tax laws, C and D, on a separate return basis, can elect to carryforward their losses (net operating losses or NOLs for tax purposes) for up to seven years. Alternatively, they can elect to carry these losses back three years and then forward seven years. Suppose C and D have never had any net income and it is unlikely that they will have for many years. Should the tax savings (on a consolidated return) be given to them even though on a separate return basis they could never receive the tax benefit? If not, then the tax benefits of C's and D's losses will be retained by A and B, and this is something A and B would not have received on a separate return basis. What would be the position of the minority interest investors of C and D? Even without minority shareholders the creditors of C and D may be interested in the tax benefit asset especially if bankruptcy appears unavoidable.[11] The allocation is particularly important to minority shareholders and creditors because the accounting methods imposed on C and D by the parent corporation A (such as accelerated depreciation) may be entirely responsible for the difference between reporting a profit or a loss for federal income tax purposes.

The following quote is taken from the 1971 annual report of Norfolk and Western Railway Company.

> Operations of Dereco and its subsidiaries, EL and D&H, are included in the consolidated Federal income tax return of N&W. Because of the substantially higher tax basis of the assets of EL as compared to the amounts recorded in its accounts . . . , and also the use of different lives and methods for computing tax depreciation by both EL and D&H, their operations result in substantial losses for tax purposes. Inclusion of these companies in computations of the Federal income tax liability has reduced consolidated accruals by approximately $10.6 and $5.4 million, respectively, in 1970 and 1971. Credit through appropriate allocation of consolidated Federal income tax liability will be given EL and D&H for use of their aggregate tax losses should taxable income resulting from their operations in future years produce tax liability that could otherwise have been offset by such losses. To date, no such credits have been granted to either EL or D&H, nor is it expected that in the foreseeable future earnings of these companies will be sufficient to cause any such credits to be granted.[12]

---

[11] The trustees of Erie-Lackawanna brought suit against the parent Norfolk and Western Railway Company in an effort to obtain $74.8 million in tax benefits; see note 8 in the 1975 annual report of Norfolk and Western Railway Company.

[12] *Norfolk and Western Railway Company Annual Report 1971*, pp. 23 and 24.

The financial consolidation and the consolidated tax return often contain different corporations. The financial accounting rules as to when to consolidate are different than the tax rules. Suppose that for financial accounting we consolidate only A, B, and C and account for D under the equity method while consolidating all four corporations for income tax purposes. We must now achieve the proper allocation of the consolidated tax to D in order to pick up under the equity method the proper share of D's aftertax loss. Thus, firms reporting separately for financial accounting purposes (using the equity method) may file consolidated tax returns and firms consolidating for financial reporting may be filing separate tax returns. As an example of the former situation, AT&T for financial reporting consolidates all of its telephone subsidiaries but uses the equity method in reporting Western Electric, a 100 percent owned manufacturing subsidiary, and certain other subsidiaries, while for tax purposes all of its subsidiaries including Western Electric are consolidated.

The *Internal Revenue Code* contains three specific methods for allocating the consolidated tax among the consolidating entities.[13] None of these methods, however, would allocate any of the tax benefit to a subsidiary having losses. The *Income Tax Regulations* recognize this problem and through an election provide two modifications to the Code methods under which some or all of the tax benefit from losses can be allocated to the entity incurring the losses.[14] If a parent corporation fails to select a method, then *Code* method 1 is required and the *Regulations* modifications cannot be elected. In this case the tax law would force the tax benefits attributable to losses by some entities to be allocated to the profitable entities only. (This seems like a most unfair result to minority shareholders and creditors, especially where it would be required by law.)

This discussion has barely opened the door on the complexities involving intercorporate allocation. There are many other problems in this area which would require a more detailed tax knowledge and much more space than is available in this text.

Interperiod Federal Income Tax Allocation

The purpose of interperiod federal income tax allocation is to determine the proper total amount of income taxes for the period. In other words, interperiod income tax allocation is a concept used in apportioning the total income tax which will be paid over the life of a business into specific accounting periods. This apportionment is based on the

---

[13] *Internal Revenue Code*, sec. 1552.
[14] Income Tax Regulations, sec. 1.1502-33(d).

concept that the tax provision is related to financial accounting income as though it were an expense in generating this revenue. Thus, interperiod income tax allocation is concerned with the differences between (1) earnings for book purposes but before the impact of the income tax (often called pretax accounting income) and (2) taxable income (a specific amount as determined under the income tax law in the Internal Revenue Code). These differences are categorized in *APB Opinion No. 11* as either timing or permanent differences.[15]

Differences between Pretax Accounting Income and Taxable Income. A timing difference is an item of revenue or expense which enters into the computation of *both* pretax accounting income and taxable income but in *different* accounting periods. A permanent difference is an item generally of revenue or expense which enters into the computations of *either* pretax accounting income or taxable income but *never* enters into the computation of the other. Thus, differences between (1) pretax accounting income and (2) taxable income are called timing differences if they reverse by effecting the other in a subsequent period and permanent differences if they do not reverse thus never effecting the other or reverse by again affecting the originating side but never the other.

Illustration 1–2 demonstrates the common sources of timing differences and their effects on pretax accounting and taxable incomes.

Illustration 1–2

	Effects of Timing Differences	
	Pretax Accounting Income Exceeds Taxable Income	Taxable Income Exceeds Pretax Accounting Income
1. An expense or loss is charged against income for book purposes before it is deductible for tax purposes.		x
2. An expense or loss is deducted for tax purposes before it is charged against income for book purposes.	x	
3. Revenue or gain is recognized for book purposes before being recognized for tax purposes.	x	
4. Revenue or gain is recognized for tax purposes before being recognized for book purposes.		x
	Initial tax effect will be a deferred credit	Initial tax effect will be a deferred charge

---

[15] *AICPA Professional Standards,* par. 4091.12.

In recording federal income taxes, (abbreviated "FIT" in account titles), the liability is determined from the taxable income computation and the provision[16] is determined from the "modified" pretax accounting income figure. (The term *modified* pretax accounting income will be explained later.) Differences between these two amounts are caused by timing differences. Initially, when the tax liability exceeds the provision, then taxable income exceeds "modified" pretax accounting income and would result in the following type of journal entry:

FIT provision	x	
Deferred tax charge (prepaid tax due to initial timing differences)	x	
FIT payable		x

If initially the provision exceeds the liability, then pretax accounting income exceeds taxable income and the journal entry would appear as follows:

FIT provision	x	
FIT payable		x
Deferred tax credit (liability due to initial timing difference)		x

When a deferred tax charge or a deferred tax credit has been established and in a subsequent period the timing difference reverses, then the Deferred Tax Charge account will be credited, or if the original difference resulted in a deferred tax credit, it would be debited. These two entries would appear as follows:

FIT provision	x	
FIT payable		x
Deferred tax charge		x

(The provision exceeds the liability, but this is a reversal of timing difference, a deferred tax charge, and not an initial or originating difference which would cause a deferred tax credit to be recorded.)

FIT provision	x	
Deferred tax credit	x	
FIT payable		x

(The liability exceeds the provision, but this is the reversal of a deferred tax credit and not an originating difference requiring the recording of a deferred tax charge.)

In describing a timing difference, the term *modified* pretax accounting income was used. Certain modifications are necessary in the calculation of the tax provision to recognize the effects of permanent differences. These modifications or differences can be classified as shown in Illustration 1–3.

---

[16] As used here, provision is similar in impact to an expense, but since income taxes do not represent efforts at generating revenue the word *provision* is better terminology than expense.

Illustration 1-3

	Effects of Permanent Differences	
	Pretax Accounting Income Exceeds Taxable Income	Taxable Income Exceeds Pretax Accounting Income
1. An expense or loss is charged against accounting income but is not deductible for federal income tax purposes in any period.		x
2. An expense or loss is deducted for tax purposes but is not charged against accounting income in any period. (This difference will have an effect on the amount of tax to be paid.)	x	
3. Revenue or gain is recognized for accounting purposes but is not recognized for tax purposes in any period.	x	
4. Revenue or gain is recognized for tax purposes but is not recognized for accounting purposes in any period. (This difference will have an effect on the amount of tax to be paid.)		x

Two Types of Permanent Differences. It should be realized that there are two distinct types of permanent differences—those that have a tax effect and those which do not have a tax effect. For example, the 85 percent dividends received deduction, allowed for tax purposes but not charged against accounting income, has a tax effect. But key officer insurance expense is charged against accounting income but it is not deductible for tax purposes; thus, it does *not* have a tax effect or impact. Thus, permanent differences which *change* taxable income (items 2 and 4 of Illustration 1-3) have tax effects, and permanent differences which *do not change* taxable income (items 1 and 3) do not have tax effects. In other words, a permanent difference that has a tax effect is either (1) an expense or loss which decreases taxable income (but not pretax accounting income) or (2) revenue or gain which increases taxable income (but not pretax accounting income).

The two types of permanent differences can be illustrated by examining the definition of a permanent difference (Illustration 1-4). This is a difference which effects either pretax accounting income or taxable income but never both. Differences which impact only on pretax accounting income are permanent differences without a tax effect, and differences which impact only on taxable income are permanent differences which produce a tax effect.

Illustration 1-4

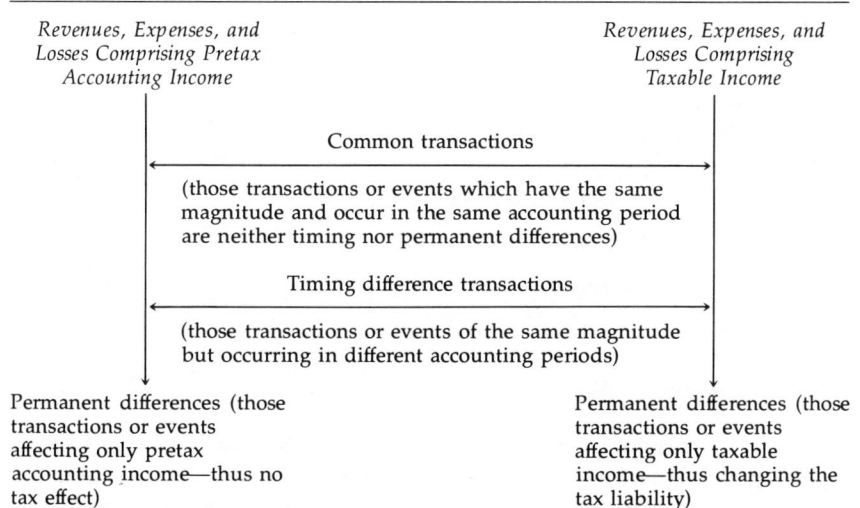

In a prior example under intraperiod income tax allocation where the book basis of an asset sold was larger than the tax basis and the sales price was an amount between the two bases, the resulting book loss was a difference without a tax effect (an item 1 difference) and the gain recognized for tax purposes was a difference with a tax effect (an item 4 difference). Thus, the book loss had no tax effect, but the gain for tax purposes increased the tax to be paid; and since this was one transaction, the tax attributable to it increased the book loss on an aftertax basis.

Provision for Federal Income Taxes. In calculating the total federal income tax provision, it is necessary first to compute the *book equivalent of taxable income* (this is the "modified" pretax accounting income). The book equivalent amount is simply the pretax accounting income plus or minus all of the permanent differences. Once this amount has been calculated, any difference between the book equivalent of taxable income and actual taxable income is due solely to timing differences.

Assume the data in Illustration 1-5 has been compiled for the Required Deferral Corporation in its first year of existence and that there is a flat 30 percent tax rate. Also assume that depreciation for tax purposes was $120,000, with the difference due to the use of accelerated depreciation for tax purposes and straight line for book purposes, and that of the accrual for product warranty only $3,000 has been actually incurred and, thus, only this amount is currently deductible for tax purposes.

Illustration 1-5

Sales		$500,000
Cost of goods sold	$300,000	
Depreciation	80,000	
Product warranty expense	10,000	
Key officer insurance expense	4,000	
Other expenses	30,000	
Dividend revenue		20,000
Interest revenue from state bonds		10,000
Totals	$424,000	530,000
		− 424,000
Pretax book net earnings		$106,000

The calculation of the book equivalent of taxable income and of actual taxable income is given in Illustration 1–6. As previously stated, the book equivalent of taxable income is simply the *pretax* book earnings plus or minus net permanent differences. Then, taxable income is simply the book equivalent of taxable income plus or minus net timing differences.

Illustration 1-6

	Book Purpose	Difference	Tax Purposes
Sales	$ 500,000	–0–	$ 500,000
Cost of goods sold	(300,000)	–0–	(300,000)
Gross margin	200,000	–0–	200,000
Depreciation	(80,000)	$(40,000) T	(120,000)
Product warranty expense	(10,000)	7,000 T	(3,000)
Key officer insurance expense	(4,000)	4,000 P	–0–
Other expenses	(30,000)	–0–	(30,000)
Dividend revenue	20,000	(17,000) P	3,000
Interest revenue from state bonds	10,000	(10,000) P	–0–
Pretax book net earnings, timing and permanent differences, and taxable income	106,000	(56,000)	50,000
Less net permanent differences	(23,000) P	(23,000) P	
Book equivalent of taxable income, net timing differences, and taxable income	$ 83,000	$(33,000) T	$ 50,000

T = timing difference; P = permanent difference.

The journal entry to record the federal income tax provision would be:

FIT provision ($83,000 × 30%)	24,900	
Deferred tax charge—product warranty ($7,000 × 30%)	2,100	
Deferred tax credit—depreciation ($40,000 × 30%)		12,000
FIT payable ($50,000 × 30%)		15,000

The permanent differences are:

1. Key officer life insurance expense of $4,000 because it is not deductible for federal income tax purposes.
2. Dividend income of $17,000 ($20,000 × 85%) because for federal income tax purposes there is an 85 percent dividends received deduction for qualifying dividends.
3. Interest income from investments in state bonds because for federal income tax purposes this income is usually excluded.

The timing differences are:

1. Depreciation of $40,000 because depreciation is deducted for tax purposes at a faster rate than it is being charged against income for book purposes; this produces a deferred tax credit (a liability account).[17]
2. Warranty expenses are deductible for tax purposes only when incurred (a cash basis application); thus, the excess accrual of $7,000 produces a deferred tax charge (an asset account).

Reversal of Timing Differences. Because initial timing differences cause deferred tax charges or deferred tax credits, their reversal in subsequent periods may result in reduction or eventual removal of the related deferred tax accounts. This creates problems because the deferrals may have been established over several years and at different tax rates and the reversal of one timing difference may be offset by originating differences on other items.

There are three concepts or methods for ascertaining the amount of the reversal. These are (1) specific identification, (2) gross change, and (3) net change. Under specific identification, the timing differences are related to each individual asset or liability. This requires very detailed record keeping and is not generally used when there are numerous items of similar assets. All methods, however, also require an assumption as to which year's differences are reversing when the deferred taxes have been established at differing rates.

To illustrate, assume a depreciable asset is acquired for $40,000 and has a 5-year useful life and no salvage value (Illustration 1–7). For book purposes, straight-line depreciation is used; and for tax purposes, double-declining balance (DDB) is used in year 1 and then a switch is

---

[17] *AICPA Professional Standards*, par. 1025.19, includes deferred tax credits from income tax allocation in the definition of liabilities and deferred tax charges from income tax allocation in the definition of assets.

Illustration 1–7

Year	Book Depreciation	Tax Depreciation	Tax Book Difference	Assumed Tax Rates by Year	Deferred Tax Credit (reversals)
1	$ 8,000	$16,000	$ 8,000	50%	$4,000
2	8,000	9,600	1,600	40	640
3	8,000	7,200	(800)	30	(x)
4	8,000	4,800	(3,200)	25	(x)
5	8,000	2,400	(5,600)	30	(x)
Total	$40,000	$40,000	–0–		–0–

made to sum-of-the-years' digits (SYD) for years 2 through 5. Also assume the tax rates change each year and that the asset is abandoned as worthless at the end of the fifth year. Note that if the reversals of the timing differences were recorded at current year rates, then the balance in the deferred tax credit account would not be zero at the end of the fifth year.

The reversals would be as shown in Illustration 1–8 for each flow assumption.

For group accounts, such as are frequently encountered with depreciation, changes in the tax deferral account are usually measured using either the gross change or the net change technique. Under the gross change method all *increases* in timing differences due to a specific item, such as depreciation, are accounted for separately from *reversals* of timing differences for that item. Tax deferrals for increases in the timing, differences are made at the current rate. Decreases in tax deferrals, because of decreases in timing differences, again introduce the need for a flow assumption whenever prior deferrals have been recorded at different rates. The gross change technique records decreases and increases separately; thus, the tax deferral account will be increased by the tax effect of originating differences and decreased by the tax effect (at whatever rate the flow assumption uses) of reversing differences. Thus, a deferred tax account, such as a deferred tax credit for depreciation, will often be debited and credited, debited for reversals and credited for originating differences.

Under the net change technique the timing differences for each type of difference, such as depreciation, are netted. A net increase in a timing difference is recorded by increasing the tax deferral at the current tax rate; a net decrease, however, would either require a flow assumption to determine which amounts are reversing when prior amounts have been recorded at different rates or arbitrary use of the current rate. In practice, when the net change method is used, the current rate is usually applied

Illustration 1–8

Deferred Tax Credit

Year	Reversal at Current Year Rates	Reversal at Historic Rates—Fifo
1	$ 4,000	$ 4,000
2	640	640
3	(240) ($800 × 30%)	(400) ($800 × 50%)
4	(800) ($3,200 × 25%)	(1,600) ($3,200 × 50%)
5	(1,680) ($5,600 × 30%)	(2,640) (($4,000 × 50%) + ($1,600 × 40%))
	$ 1,920*	–0–

* Deferred tax credit still on the books even though the asset is fully depreciated. This amount would then have to be removed when the asset is abandoned.

Deferred Tax Credit

Year	Reversal at Historic Rates—Lifo	Reversal at Historic Rates—Weighted
1	$ 4,000	$ 4,000
2	640	640
3	(320) ($800 × 40%)	(387) ($800 × 48⅓%)*
4	(1,520) (($800 × 40%) + ($2,400 × 50%))	(1,547) ($3,200 × 48⅓%)
5	(2,800) ($5,600 × 50%)	(2,706) ($5,600 × 48⅓%)
	–0–	–0–

* $4,640 ÷ $9,600 = 48⅓%.

to reversals with adjustment if necessary when assets are abandoned or sold.

The net change method is used more often than gross change, even through the gross change method is more in tune with the concept of interperiod income tax allocation, especially during periods of significant rate changes. The net change method is easier, at least for depreciation, even though after rate changes it will not be as accurate conceptually.

The timing differences due to depreciation are much larger than most persons realize. In addition to the use of accelerated depreciation methods for tax purposes, the useful lives are often only one half to one third as long as the useful lives for financial reporting. Also for tax purposes, changes in depreciation methods are often made (e.g., from double-declining balance to sum-of-the-years' digits or to straight line) in order to increase the depreciation deductions in subsequent years. With all the differences between financial reporting and tax reporting, the use of the net change method is encouraged because of its simplicity. The difference in the relevancy of the information under the net change and the gross change methods is probably nil.

To illustrate the effects of the net change and gross change methods, assume a corporation has older depreciable assets on which book depreciation exceeds tax depreciation by $20,000 and newer depreciable assets on which tax depreciation exceeds book depreciation by $50,000. Assume taxable income is $100,000 and pretax book income is $130,000 with depreciation being the only difference; also assume the tax rates had been 40 percent in all prior years but are 30 percent for the current year.

Net change method:

FIT provision ($130,000 × 30%)	39,000	
Deferred tax credit—depreciation		
(($50,000 − $20,000) × 30%)		9,000
FIT ($100,000 × 30%)		30,000

Gross change method:

FIT provision ($130,000 × 30%) −		
(($20,000 × (40% − 30%)))	37,000*	
Deferred tax credit—depreciation ($20,000 × 40%)	8,000	
Deferred tax credit—depreciation ($50,000 × 30%)		15,000
FIT payable ($100,000 × 30%)		30,000

* Or ($150,000 × 30%) − ($20,000 × 40%) = $37,000.

PAD FOR ANTICIPATED DEFICIENCY ON AUDIT

FASB Statement No. 5, "Accounting for Contingencies," has raised serious questions regarding the practice of including a "cushion or pad" for anticipated tax deficiencies. This statement allows for the recording of "probable contingencies" only if it is probable that the liability does in fact exist *and* the amount can be reasonably estimated. Some contend that the pad for future tax deficiencies does not satisfy these criteria and should not be recorded as a liability. However, the practice does continue, and in some circumstances both criteria may well be satisfied. The following discussion assumes that the pad is to be recorded.

The income tax law is exceptionally complex; and, therefore, there are often a significant number of material items where the tax treatment is in doubt. In each such case, the corporate management should file the tax return taking the most favorable position on each of these items. At the same time, however, corporate management should realize that in the event of an Internal Revenue Service (IRS) audit, they will lose on some items and, hopefully, win on others. Since a corporation's tax return is usually filed on the basis of winning every item, the anticipated loss in the event of an audit should be measured and recorded. This measurement would normally entail a listing of all potentially controversial items and amounts with each amount multiplied by a percentage probability of loss. Then, based on this analysis an anticipated additional tax liability should be recorded. This will increase both the federal income tax payable and the federal income tax provision. In addition to the tax deficiency resulting from an IRS audit, compound interest will be assessed by the IRS on the deficiency. Thus, the pad should also provide annually for the interest element but on an aftertax basis which recognizes the interest deduction.

In future years, if there is an IRS audit, the deficiency will be charged against the accrual or pad amount contained in the Federal Income Tax Liability account. If there is no audit or if the IRS agent does not contest the controversial items, the pad amount (including aftertax interest) can be left to cover items in open years. If the pad has become too large, then an amount, based on the pad for items in prior years now closed by the statute of limitations, should be removed by putting this excess amount in income of the current year.[18] (This could be done by reducing the provision applicable to the current year.) This is *not* a prior period adjustment; it is only a change in accounting estimate. Part of note 5 in the 1975 annual report for Norfolk and Western Railway Company states that:

> 1975 income taxes reflect a $6.9 million reduction representing an adjustment arising from favorable settlements of prior years income taxes. 1975 "other expenses" includes $2.9 million for interest expense on possible Federal income tax deficiencies for years not settled, but for which tax provision had been previously made.

With $2.9 million in anticipated interest (before tax) on anticipated tax deficiencies, the pad for deficiency can include the aftertax effect of interest on the anticipated but unpaid taxes. Assuming a 7 percent interest rate, the $2.9 million would represent annual interest on approximately $41.4 million of anticipated tax deficiency covering more than one year. The $2.9 million will be deductible for tax purposes when paid, thus the aftertax cost is substantially less than $2.9 million.

To illustrate this process, assume a corporation has items of potential deficiency of $500,000 in 19x1 and $300,000 and $400,000 in 19x2 with probabilities of loss as indicated in Illustration 1–9.

If these items of potential deficiency were incurred at the beginning of each year so that the potential deficiencies were for the entire year,

---

[18] An interesting example of this can be found in the AICPA, *Annual Report 1976–77*, fn. 3, p. 15, which states in part, "The Institute's unrelated business income tax returns have been settled through the year ended July 31, 1974. Accruals in prior years no longer needed in the amount of $128,000 have been credited to General Expense."

Illustration 1-9

Year of Potential Deficiency	Potential Deficiency Amounts	Percentage Chance of Losing	Anticipated Amount	Tax Rate	Potential Deficiency
19x1	$500,000	70	$350,000	40%	$140,000
19x2	300,000	80	240,000	40	96,000
19x2	400,000	20	80,000	40	32,000

then interest should also be reflected for the entire year. Assuming 7 percent interest with deductibility for tax purposes, the pad at 12/31/x1 might be $145,880 ($140,000 + ($140,000 × 7%) − (40% × ($140,000 × 7%))). If the interest element were separately reported as interest expense of $9,800 ($140,000 × 7%), then a deferred charge timing difference of $3,920 ($9,800 × 40%) would have to be reflected.

For 19x2 the pad would change as shown in Illustration 1–10.

Illustration 1-10

Year	Potential Deficiency	Interest 19x1	Tax Benefit 19x1	Tax Pad 19x1†	Interest 19x2	Tax Benefit* 19x2	Tax Pad 19x2†	Total Pad
19x1	$140,000	$9,800	$(3,920)	$145,880	$10,486‡	$(4,194)	$ 6,292	$152,172
19x2	96,000	-0-	-0-	-0-	6,720	(2,688)	100,032	100,032
19x2	32,000	-0-	-0-	-0-	2,240	(896)	33,344	33,344
	$268,000	$9,800	$(3,920)	$145,880	$19,446	$(7,778)	$139,668	$285,548

* Also a deferred tax charge for a timing difference.
† This assumes that the aftertax interest and the potential deficiency are all recorded as additional taxes and not separately recorded as potential deficiencies, interest, and deferred tax charges.
‡ ($140,000 + $9,800) × 7% = $10,486.

The entry to record all of this as part of the tax pad for 19x2 is as follows:

```
FIT provision..........................................  139,668*
Deferred tax charge—interest .........................    7,778
    FIT payable ($96,000 + $32,000 +
        $19,446 = $147,446) ..............................          147,446
```
* 145,880 from 19x1 + $139,668 from 19x2 = $285,548 total pad per Illustration 1–10.)

Recording the interest element as interest instead of taxes and the tax effect separately is as follows:

```
Interest expense ......................................   19,446
    Accrued interest payable ...........................           19,446
FIT provision..........................................  120,222
Deferred tax charge—interest ($19,446 × 40%) .........    7,778
    FIT payable ($96,000 + $32,000) ....................          128,000
```

IMPACT OF TAX CREDITS

To fully understand the complexity of accounting for federal income taxes, it is necessary to visualize the corporate tax computation formula. The formula in simplified fashion is presented in Illustration 1–11.

Illustration 1–11

Total revenue
− Exclusions
= Gross revenue (note that gross is already a net term—net of exclusions)
− Cost of goods sold
− Expenses
− Losses
− Charitable contributions
= Net income before special deductions
− Dividends received deduction
− Net operating loss deduction
− Other items
= Taxable income
× Applicable tax rates
= Gross tax liability
− Investment tax credit and energy tax credits
− Foreign tax credit
− Either the work incentive tax credit or the targeted jobs tax credit
= Tax liability

One should remember that the APB in *Opinion No. 11* defined timing and permanent differences as differences between *pretax accounting income* and *taxable income*. And based on this result the tax provision and liability for allocating within an accounting period (intraperiod) and between periods (interperiod) are to be ascertained. That this can produce only incomplete results is immediately obvious because it ignores the existence of any tax credits. The APB did attempt to produce some accounting guidelines for the investment tax credit (in *APB Opinions Nos. 2* and *4* and in the exposure draft of *Opinion No. 11*) which is the only credit we will be discussing in this section of the chapter.

Part of the problem in accounting for the investment credit results from its rather turbulent history. It was introduced by President Kennedy in 1961 and adopted by Congress after substantial modification in 1962. It was further modified in 1964, suspended in 1966, reinstated in 1967, terminated in 1969, and resurrected in 1971. And it has been modified several times since then. Initially, the APB took the position that the investment tax credit should not be recognized in the year of the tax reduction (the flow-through method) but should be recognized over the useful life of the asset for financial reporting (the deferred method). The SEC (in *Accounting Series Release No. 96* issued in January 1963) accepted either method, and this forced the APB to do the same. Thus, *APB Opinion No. 4* (issued in March 1964) replaced *Opinion No. 2* (issued in December 1962) which had only permitted deferral. But even then the maneuvering for deferral continued. The APB had been so insistent on elimination of the flow-through method and in favor of deferral of the investment tax credit that it tried to go back to the deferral position in the exposure draft of *Opinion No. 11*. In the letters the APB received in response to the exposure draft, 532 supported flow-through while only 124 supported deferral.[19]

With the legislative reenactment of the investment credit in 1971, the APB again tried to adopt the deferral method.

> It became apparent as the *Revenue Act of 1971* was being processed that the prior investment credit was going to be reinstated. As Congress was considering this legislation, the APB was drafting another exposure draft which required a spread out of the job development investment credit using the deferred method. Prior to the release of this draft, the APB had obtained a commitment from the SEC to rescind Accounting Series Release No. 96 which permitted flow-through. The fact that the SEC was prepared to rescind the prior Release may have been due to subsequent changes in the Commissioners' ranks.
>
> The Draft was released on October 22, 1971 after all opportunity for public testimony, before either the House Ways and Means Committee or the Senate Finance Committee, on this proposed accounting treatment had passed. However, the Senate Finance Committee, then in executive session, used strong language against the elimination of flow-through in the Senate Report (Senate Report 92-437). It became apparent that continued pressure to force amortization of the credit over the lives of the related assets would result in a statutory amendment. The Treasury Department indicated that it could support such an amendment:
>
>> The Treasury would prefer that the accounting profession on its own motion recognize the importance of continuing the prior practice so as not to interfere with the function of the credit to stimulate new capital investment. The Senate Finance Committee has expressed a similar view in its report.
>>
>> If it is concluded that the desired objective—optional treatment for accounting purposes—cannot be achieved by committee report language, then the Treasury Department will support a legislative resolution of this matter.[20]

---

[19] Wheeler and Galliart, *An Appraisal of Interperiod Income Tax Allocation*, p. 43.

[20] Letter from Charls E. Walker, Acting Secretary of the Treasury, to Senator Russell Long as quoted in the "Washington Report," *The Tax Adviser*, January 1972, p. 29.

The statutory amendment became necessary as proponents of amortization continued to push for the elimination of the flow-through method. Thus, accounting for the investment credit became part of the public law as Section 101(c) of the Revenue Act of 1971.[21]

Today, under federal law, corporate management can reflect the investment credit as a reduction of the tax provision in the year the tax effect is realized or it can use the APB's preferred method of deferral which gradually recognizes the tax effect (over the life of the related asset) even though the cash savings actually took place many years before recognition for accounting purposes.

It should be noted that credits, unlike deductions, reduce the tax liability dollar for dollar. Thus, they are not affected by the tax rate.

To illustrate the two methods, assume that there are no timing differences and no need for a pad for anticipated tax deficiency on audit. Then, the tax liability and the tax provision would be the same amount. Now suppose this amount were $50,000 before recognition of a $30,000 tax credit for purchase at the end of the current year of an asset with a 10-year useful life. Under the flow-through method the entry to record the tax provision would be:

```
FIT provision ..............................................  20,000
    FIT payable ...........................................           20,000
```

Under the deferral method the entry would be:

```
FIT provision ..............................................  50,000
    FIT payable ...........................................           20,000
    Deferred investment tax credit ........................           30,000
```

And then for each of the next ten years this deferral amount would be reflected as a reduction in future tax provisions by debiting the deferral account and crediting the tax provision for $3,000 each year.

SAMPLE PROBLEM AND SOLUTION

There are many more complexities than those mentioned thus far, but before going further a fairly complete problem and illustration of the solution may be useful. The solution to the problem will follow the format presented in Illustration 1–12.

For the problem, assume that the Mandated Deferral Corporation has been in operation for several years and that its current statement reflects the figures given in Illustration 1–13.

---

[21] Wheeler and Galliart, *An Appraisal of Interperiod Income Tax Allocation,* p. 35.

Illustration 1–12
FORMAT FOR ANALYSIS OF ACCOUNTING FOR DIFFERENCES BETWEEN BOOK AND TAX ACCOUNTING METHODS

Per Book Tax Provision	Types of Differences* Permanent (P) and Timing (T)	Per Tax Return Tax Liability
Gross income	P—State bond interest T—Installment sales	Gross income
Cost of goods sold Operating expenses (including taxes)	P†—Provision for federal income tax T—Accelerated depreciation	Less ordinary deductions: Cost of goods sold Operating expenses
Net income (after tax)		Net taxable income before special deductions
No special deductions	P—Net operating loss deduction P—Dividends received deduction	Less special statutory deductions
Net income (after tax) Plus or minus permanent differences	Total of all permanent differences	
Book equivalent of taxable income × Statutory rates	+/− Total of all timing differences	= Taxable income × Statutory rates
Tax provision (before credits)		Tax liability before credits
Less various credits	+/− Difference due to accounting for ITC‡ (amortization versus flow-through)	Less various tax credits
Initial tax provision	+/− Timing differences × Statutory rates +/− ITC‡ differences	= Actual tax liability
Plus/minus—change in anticipated IRS audit deficiency§		Plus/minus—change in pad for IRS audit deficiency§
Recorded tax provision	+/− Changes in all deferred tax accounts	= Recorded tax liability

* Items listed are examples, thus the list is far from complete.

† Note that this is not really a permanent or a timing difference because it does not affect either pretax book income or taxable income, but it does have some of the characteristics of a permanent difference.

‡ Investment tax credit.

§ Most large corporations maintain an anticipated tax liability account to reflect anticipated additional taxes which will be incurred when the firm is audited by the IRS.

Illustration 1–13

MANDATED DEFERRAL CORPORATION
Earnings Statement
For the Year Ended 12/31/x5

Sales	$500,000
Cost of sales	− 260,000 (1) (2) (3)
Gross earnings	240,000
Operating expenses	− 80,000 (4) (8)
Before-tax operating earnings	160,000
Other net earnings or (deductions)	+ 25,000 (5) (6) (7)
Net earnings before tax	185,000
Federal income tax provision	− 65,850 (9)
Net earnings	$119,150

Additional information:

1. The depreciation for book purposes was $30,000, and for tax purposes it was $65,000.
2. The book provision for product warranty exceeded the actual currently deductible cost by $5,000.
3. The corporation established an allowance for price changes in inventories this year and booked a $5,000 charge which is not currently deductible for tax purposes.
4. The insurance premiums on key officers exceeded the increase in cash surrender value by $2,000. This expense is never deductible for tax purposes.
5. Interest income from state and local bonds included in other income equaled $1,000. For tax purposes this income is excluded.
6. Dividends, received from investments in nonaffiliated domestic corporation shares, of $4,000 were included in other income. For tax purposes there is an 85 percent dividends received deduction.
7. Other income also included $2,000 of net long-term capital gains in excess of net short-term capital losses. The alternative tax rate on capital gains is 28 percent.
8. Excess contributions of prior years in the amount of $1,000 were deducted on the 19x5 tax return. For tax purposes there is a 5-year carryforward of certain excess contributions.
9. For book purposes the corporation amortizes the investment credit over the lives of the related assets. Under this procedure $2,000 of prior and current year investment tax credits were amortized while $3,500 of current year credits were applicable to purchases of assets in this year.
10. The regular income tax rate is 17 percent on the first $25,000, 20 percent on the second $25,000, 30 percent on the third $25,000, 40 percent on the next $25,000, and 46 percent on all over $100,000 unless the capital gain rate applies *and* is less.

Assume you are an auditor for the CPA firm of Tax and More Tax and your audit supervisor has noted that the client Mandated Deferral Corporation has already recorded a $65,850 federal income tax provision. Your supervisor *merely* wants you to reconstruct with supporting calculations the journal entry which the client used to record the federal income tax provision assuming it was correctly measured and recorded.

You immediately come up with the following entry:

FIT provision	65,850	
FIT payable		65,850

But fortunately you remember that it is not that easy; there are timing differences, permanent differences, differences in accounting for the investment tax credit, and anticipated deficiencies if audited by the IRS, and so on. You hurriedly destroy your oversimplified solution (before your supervisor sees it) and prepare the analysis and journal entry(s) given in Illustration 1–14.

Illustration 1–14

	Earning per Books	Item Number and Differences		Earnings per Tax
Sales	$ 500,000			$ 500,000
Cost of sales	(260,000)	(1)	$(35,000) T	(285,000)
		(2)	5,000 T	
		(3)	5,000 T	
Gross earnings	240,000		(25,000)	215,000
		(4)	2,000 P	
Operating expenses	(80,000)	(8)	(1,000) T	(79,000)
	160,000		(24,000)	136,000
		(5)	(1,000) P	
Other income and deductions	25,000	(6)	(3,400) P	20,600
Pretax accounting income	185,000		(28,400)	156,600
Federal income tax provision	(65,850)		65,850 P*	–0–
			Taxable	
Net earnings	$ 119,150		$ 37,450 income	$ 156,600

T = timing difference; P = permanent difference.

* This is not really a permanent difference under *APB Opinion No. 11* because it does not affect either *pretax* accounting income or taxable income.

Calculation of the actual tax liability:

Taxable income (including $2,000 of capital gain) = $156,600

Tax computation:

	$ 25,000 × 17% =	$ 4,250
	25,000 × 20% =	5,000
Capital gain	2,000 × 28% =	560
	25,000 × 30% =	7,500
	25,000 × 40% =	10,000
	54,600 × 46% =	25,116
	$156,600	52,426
Less investment tax credit		−3,500
Tax liability		$48,926

Illustration 1–14 (*continued*)

Computation of the book equivalent of taxable income and the federal income tax provision:

Net earnings		$119,150
Federal income tax provision		65,850
Pretax book earnings		185,000
Add: Key officer insurance		2,000 P
		187,000
Deduct:		
State and local bond interest	$1,000 P	
Dividends received deduction	3,400 P	−4,400
Book equivalent of taxable income		$182,600

Tax provision:		
$ 25,000 × 17%	=	$ 4,250
25,000 × 20%	=	5,000
2,000 × 28%	=	560
25,000 × 30%	=	7,500
25,000 × 40%	=	10,000
80,600 × 46%	=	37,076
$182,600		

Calculated federal income tax provision		64,386
Less the amortized tax credit		2,000
Federal income tax provision		$62,386

The Journal Entries

(1)

FIT provision	62,386	
Deferred tax charge—product warranty ($5,000 × 46%)	2,300 T	
Deferred tax charge—allowance for price change ($5,000 × 46%)	2,300 T	
Deferred tax credit—depreciation ($35,000 × 46%)		16,100 T
Deferred tax charge—contribution ($1,000 × 46%)		460 T
Unamortized investment tax credits ($3,500 − $2,000)		1,500 T*
FIT payable		48,926
(Since debits = credits, compound journal entries should be footed)	66,986	66,986

* Note this is not really a timing difference under *APB Opinion No. 11* because it does not affect either *pretax* accounting income or *taxable* income (instead of affecting both but in different periods).

(2)

You recall suddenly that the client debited the Federal Income Tax Provision account for $65,850 and your debit is only for $62,386; thus, you prepare a second entry:

FIT provision	3,464	
FIT payable		3,464
To reflect the client's audit pad accrual.		

You are satisfied with your effort and results and turn your work over to your supervisor and receive your supervisor's compliments. You are told, however, to be thankful that (1) there is no state income tax in the state the client does business in, (2) that there were no foreign operations, and (3) that the client was small. Your supervisor then tells you about the 150 separate timing differences in the tax accruals of a major client of Tax and More Tax.

You then ask if the $3,464 is not unusual for a pad amount. The supervisor tells you that this is an unusual amount, and that it appears that the client's bookkeeper did not intend to create a pad but had simply calculated the provision based on the pretax accounting income amount and had ignored the effects of permanent differences, the special capital gains tax rate, and the investment tax credit. The calculation might have been as in Illustration 1–15.

Illustration 1–15

		Tax
Pretax accounting income	$185,000	
	$ 25,000 × 17% =	$ 4,250
	25,000 × 20% =	5,000
	25,000 × 30% =	7,500
	25,000 × 40% =	10,000
	85,000 × 46% =	39,100
	$185,000	$65,850

If your client had been attempting to create an audit pad, then you should be able to verify it based on the anticipated items of conflict. Your working papers might appear as in Illustration 1–16.

In the past the IRS has made and is continuing to make attempts to obtain the CPA's working paper analyses of audit pad accounts. In one case the courts held for the CPA firms and their clients by stating that the IRS cannot have access to these specific audit working papers.[22] In most cases, however, the IRS has been successful in efforts to obtain accountant's working papers. It would obviously make the job of IRS agents easier if they had this information; in fact, it would almost do their job for them. The end result, however, might be that the CPA firms would either not audit these accounts (thus, greatly increasing their third-party liability) or at least not prepare audit working papers on these accounts.

---

[22] *U.S.* v. *Coopers & Lybrand et al.*, U.S. Court of Appeals Tenth Circuit, 550 F. 2d 615. Affirmed the decision of the U.S. District Court, District of Colorado, 75-2 USTC 9846; 36 AFTR 2d 75-6376.

Illustration 1–16

	Maximum Disallowance	Marginal Tax Rate	Maximum Tax Loss	Estimated Probability of Loss	Estimate of Deficiency
Potential conflict item 1*	$ 5,217	46%	$ 2,400	75%	$1,800
Potential conflict item 2	10,434	46	4,800	5	240
Potential conflict item 3	6,191	46	2,848	50	1,424
Maximum tax loss			$10,048		
Pad for IRS audit deficiency					$3,464

* In a real analysis each potential conflict area would be clearly identified.

In either of these cases IRS agents would not have an analysis of the potential conflicts readily available. The IRS has obtained the audit working papers from Arthur Andersen & Company for the tax accrual accounts of Good Hope Industries, Inc., pursuant to an order of the District Court for the District of Massachusetts. The IRS position was upheld on appeal to the U.S. Court of Appeals for the First Circuit. The AICPA had filed a brief Amicus Curiae in this appeal. The Supreme Court has refused to hear this case on appeal from the First Circuit.

REVIEW QUESTIONS

1. Are income taxes expenses, losses, distributions of earnings, or distinct (anomalous) items? Give a logical reason for each possibility.
2. Income tax allocation is often a difficult problem area in accounting.
    a. Identify the three general types of allocation of income taxes.
    b. Briefly define each type.
3. When a consolidated financial statement is filed and a consolidated tax return prepared, why is it absolutely necessary to allocate the consolidated tax liability?
4. Timing and permanent differences are characteristics of one type of allocation.
    a. Which type of allocation is this?
    b. Briefly define timing differences and permanent differences.
5. Accounting for timing differences can result in deferred "assets" and deferred "liabilities."
    a. What are these deferrals, and how do they arise (give an example of each)?
    b. There are also two types of permanent differences. Identify each type.

6. What frequently causes corporations to keep two "sets of books," and why is this important?
7. The Reversal Corporation had older depreciable assets on which the book depreciation exceeded the tax depreciation by $10,000 and had newer depreciable assets on which the tax depreciation exceeded the book depreciation by $30,000. The current year's tax rate is 30 percent, but the tax rate had been 40 percent in all prior years. Depreciation has been the only difference between pretax accounting income and taxable income, and pretax accounting income is $100,000.
   a. Prepare the journal entry to record the federal income tax provision assuming the net change concept is used.
   b. Prepare the same journal entry but assume the gross change concept is used.
8. Why is it often necessary to increase the federal income tax provision and federal income tax payable for an anticipated deficiency if audited by the IRS?
9. What are the two acceptable methods of accounting for the investment tax credit?
10. How is the "book equivalent of taxable income computed"?
11. What makes the "book equivalent of taxable income" significant?
12. How does "book equivalent of taxable income" differ from pretax book net earnings?
13. How does "book equivalent of taxable income" differ from taxable income?
14. Why are the investment tax credit and the federal income tax provision neither timing nor permanent differences?
15. If the federal income tax provision and the investment tax credit are neither timing nor permanent differences, what are they?
16. Why would the IRS be interested in the audit analysis of a corporation's federal income tax accounts?

PROBLEMS

Problem 1: Accelerated Corporation

Accelerated purchased a new asset for $55,000. The asset has a 10-year useful life and a zero salvage value. The treasurer of the corporation has asked you to prepare a line graph reflecting the pattern of depreciation for straight-line depreciation, SYD depreciation, and DDB depreciation. Use the following format:

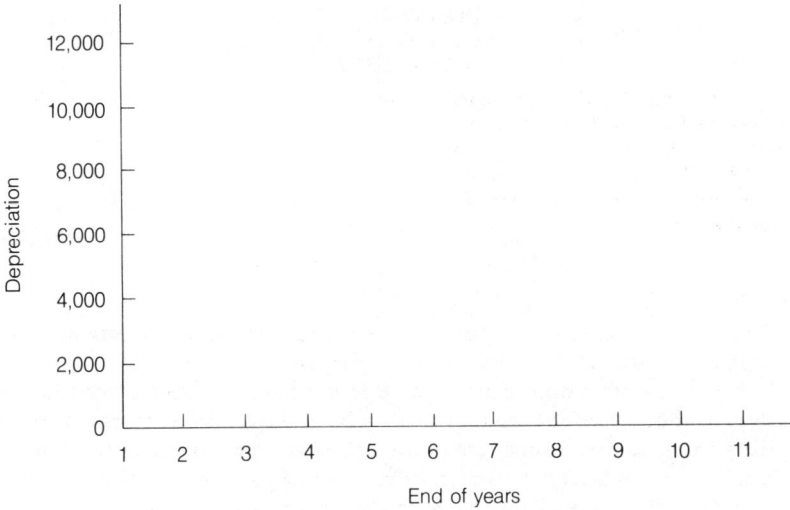

The treasurer also wants to maximize the present value of the tax savings from depreciation deductions (assuming a flat tax rate) and wants to know when to change from DDB for federal income tax purposes. The treasurer knows that you can only make one change in method (first assume a change from DDB to straight line and second from DDB to SYD).

(Note: This problem is not covered in this chapter, but you should be able to solve it based on prior knowledge.)

Problem 2: Intra Corporation

Intra Corporation's earnings statement and statement of retained earnings appear below without reflecting the total federal income tax provision of $44,000. Assume that there are no timing differences, no permanent differences, and no tax credits and that the only difference between pretax net earnings and taxable income is due to the $50,000 prior period adjustment which was taken directly to retained earnings (some might call this a permanent difference). The income tax rate has always been a flat 40 percent.

INTRA CORPORATION
Earnings Statement (Condensed)
For the Year Ended 12/31/x2

Before tax:	
Earnings from continuing operations	$200,000
Loss on disposal of a business segment	(50,000)
Extraordinary loss	(20,000)
Cumulative effect of accounting changes	30,000
Net earnings (before tax)	$160,000

INTRA CORPORATION
Statement of Retained Earnings
As of 12/31/x2

Retained earnings, 1/1/x2, as previously reported		$200,000
Prior period adjustment (before tax)		(50,000)
Adjusted retained earnings as of 1/1/x2:		
Net earnings	$ xx	xx
Dividends	(20,000)	xx
Retained earnings, 12/31/x2		xx

Required:

1. Prepare a condensed earnings statement and a statement of retained earnings on an aftertax basis for Intra Corporation.
2. If there had been a timing difference due to tax depreciation exceeding book depreciation on continuing operations by $30,000 and a reversal of timing differences because of the sale of the business segment where tax depreciation had exceeded book depreciation in prior years by $10,000—
   a. What effect would this have on the earnings statement?
   b. Prepare the journal entry to record the federal income tax provision.
3. If in addition to the timing differences in 2 above, there had been a $10,000 permanent difference due to nontaxable interest income from investments in state bonds, would this have affected net earnings? Prepare the journal entry to record the federal income tax provision.

Problem 3: Consolidated Group

Consolidated represents a group of four corporations (A, B, C, and D) that reported taxable earnings as follows:

A	$100,000
B	50,000
C	(30,000)
D	(20,000)
	$100,000

There were no timing nor permanent differences between actual taxable income and pretax book income and no tax credits (such as the investment tax credit). The federal income tax rate is a flat 40 percent, and this is the first year of operations for all four corporations. They prepare consolidated financial statements as well as federal income tax returns.

Required:

1. Prepare the journal entry(s) to record the federal income tax provision assuming that A is the parent corporation and that full benefit of loss is assigned to any company suffering losses.
2. Prepare the journal entry(s) to record the federal income tax provision assuming that A is the parent corporation and that no tax benefit from loss is assigned to any corporation suffering losses.

Problem 4: Gross, Inc.

Gross, Inc., uses the gross change method to account for depreciation timing differences. In the current year, book depreciation on older items exceeded tax depreciation by $50,000. On newer items tax depreciation exceeded book depreciation by $30,000. In prior years the timing differences were recorded at a 40 percent tax rate; the current year rate is only 30 percent. The before-tax book earnings are $100,000, and depreciation is the only difference between pretax book earnings and taxable income.

Required:
1. Prepare a schedule showing both the book equivalent of taxable income and actual taxable income.
2. Record the federal income tax provision using the gross change method.
3. Record the federal income tax provision using the net change method.

Problem 5: Contingent Credit Corporation

The following earnings statement has been prepared by the Contingent Credit Corporation:

CONTINGENT CREDIT CORPORATION
Earnings Statement
For the Year Ended 12/31/x5

Sales	$500,000
Cost of goods sold	300,000
Gross margin	200,000
Operating expenses	80,000
	120,000
Other revenue and losses	30,000
	150,000
Federal income tax provision	75,000
	75,000
Extraordinary loss (net of tax benefit of $4,000)	(4,000)
Net earnings	$ 71,000

Additional information:
1. Assume the federal income tax rate is 50 percent on ordinary income and 30 percent on capital gain.
2. Other revenue includes a $20,000 gain on sale of a capital asset; for tax purposes this was an installment sale with only one fourth or $5,000 being taxed this year.
3. A $2,000 reserve for cash discounts in accounts receivable was established this year and was recorded in the income statement as a negative sales item. For tax purposes these discounts affect taxable income only in the year they are actually taken by the customers.
4. Operating expenses include depreciation of $10,000, whereas for tax purposes the depreciation deduction was $25,000.

5. Operating expenses include a $5,000 political contribution that is not deductible for tax purposes in any year.
6. Other revenue includes $3,000 of dividends from nonaffiliated domestic corporations. For tax purposes 85 percent of this revenue is not taxed.
7. The corporation received investment tax credits of $5,000. For tax purposes this amount is an immediate reduction in tax liability. For book purposes these credits are being amortized over the related lives of the assets; thus, $500 of this year's credit and $1,500 of prior years' credits have been reflected in the federal income tax provision.

Required:

1. Calculate the book equivalent of taxable income and the actual taxable income.
2. Duplicate the journal entry(s) by which the federal income tax provision was recorded. Support and label each part of your journal entry and *do not* combine any deferred tax charges or deferred tax credits.

Problem 6: Major Corporation

The earnings statement for Major Corporation as of 12/31/x5 appears as follows:

MAJOR CORPORATION
Earnings Statement
For the Year Ended 12/31/x5

Sales	$1,000,000
Cost of goods sold	450,000
Gross margin	550,000
Operating expenses	(200,000)
Other revenues and losses	80,000
Federal income tax provision	(200,000)
Extraordinary loss (net of a tax benefit of $32,000)	(48,000)
Net earnings	$ 182,000

Additional information:

1. The federal income tax rate is a flat 40 percent on ordinary income and 25 percent on capital gain. In prior years the corporate income tax rate was a flat 50 percent on ordinary income.
2. Operating expenses includes depreciation of $30,000, whereas $60,000 in depreciation was deducted for tax purposes. On some assets book depreciation exceeds tax depreciation by $10,000, and on other assets tax depreciation exceeds book depreciation by $40,000. The gross change method is used to account for the tax effects.
3. Operating expenses also include insurance expense of $12,000 for key officer life insurance. The corporation is the beneficiary, and thus this cost is not deductible for tax purposes.
4. Other revenue includes $5,000 of interest on City of Honolulu bonds which is not taxable.

5. Other revenue also includes $10,000 of dividends from several small investments in domestic corporations. For tax purposes there is an 85 percent dividends received deduction.
6. Other revenues and losses include fines of $4,000 for overweight trucks on interstate highways. These fines are not deductible for tax purposes.
7. Investments tax credits of $10,000 were earned and used this year for tax purposes. For book purposes the investment credit is amortized over the book life of the assets, and thus only $4,000 of investment credits were recorded as used this year.

Required:
1. Beginning with net earnings compute *both* the book equivalent of taxable income and the actual taxable income. (Label your calculations!)
2. From your computations in 1 above calculate *both* the federal income tax provision and the federal income tax liability. (Label your calculations!)
3. In journal entry form duplicate the entry that the bookkeeper made (or should have made) in recording the federal income tax provision. (Record all timing differences separately.)

Problem 7: Take-a-Chance Corporation

Take-a-Chance began operations last year, in 19x2, and was immediately successful. Last year, one potentially controversial item in the amount of $400,000 was deducted in computing the income tax. There is still a 70 percent chance of losing this deduction on an IRS audit. In the current year there are two other controversial items which the corporation deducted. These amounts were $300,000 and $500,000 with an 80 percent and a 40 percent chance, respectively, of losing the deductions upon an IRS audit. The corporate income tax rate has been 40 percent for many years. Interest is charged on the potential tax assessment at 7 percent with one half year's interest being appropriate in the year of incurrence.

Required:

Compute the current year addition to the federal income tax provision for controversial items and prepare an analysis of the "pad" amount.

Problem 8: Favorable Result Corporation (Difficult problem)

The director of taxes for Favorable (a calendar-year corporation) informed the controller that in the preparation of the current year (19x4) tax return three significant and questionable items will be taken in the company's favor on the tax return. These items occurred evenly over this year. The likelihood of loss on an income tax audit are as follows:

Item	Amount Involved	Probability of Loss
1	$1,000,000	50%
2	800,000	60
3	700,000	80

The director of taxes also stated that an amount of $500,000 for a prior year's anticipation of loss on audit is no longer necessary because the IRS agent missed this item in the tax audit and that year is now closed by the statute of limitations. But on other open years the "pad" for anticipated losses still amounts to $2,000,000. In regard to the $500,000 pad item, interest on it in the amount of $200,000, after being reduced for the 46 percent tax rate, has been recorded as federal income tax payable. The corporation is in the top bracket of 46 percent, and interest at the rate of 7 percent is charged for unpaid taxes.

Required:
1. Prepare a schedule of the anticipated loss for the current year items.
2. Prepare in journal entry format all of the effects from current and prior year anticipation of losses on IRS tax audits and support all computations of amounts.

2
Accounting for Income Taxes - Special Considerations

Some Common Additional Complexities
    Equity Method Earnings or Consolidation in Connection with Separate Tax Returns
    Net Operating Losses
    Some Reasons Why a Corporation May Elect Only the NOL Carryforward
    Carryforwards of NOLs When There Are Deferred Tax Credits from Timing Differences
    Carryforwards of Investment Tax Credits when There Are Deferred Tax Credits from Timing Differences
Part Permanent and Part Timing (More Complexity)
Stock Option Complexity
Financial Disclosure of Tax Accounts
    Net-of-Tax Concept
    Liability Concept
    Deferral Concept
    Deferred Tax Accounts in the Statement of Financial Position
    Required Disclosure in the Earnings Statement
An Evaluation of Accounting for Income Taxes
    Economic Reality as a Guideline
    A Suggested Presentation
Appendix
    Foreign Income Taxes
    State and Local Income Taxes

The prior chapter presented certain concepts of accounting for income taxes and an approach to its measurement. Some of the more difficult aspects of this measurement problem and the very controversial, theoretical aspects of accounting for income taxes, however, were left for this chapter.

SOME COMMON ADDITIONAL COMPLEXITIES

Equity Method Earnings or Consolidation in Connection with Separate Tax Returns

This particular complexity is introduced here but is covered in more depth in the next chapter. Use of the equity method or consolidation for financial reporting when the cost method is used for tax purposes can result in timing differences due to undistributed earnings. These timing differences if they reverse can result in a second corporate level tax. A tax on a corporation's earnings is the first tax, and a tax on the realization of these earnings by an investor or parent corporation, through receiving dividends from undistributed prior years' earnings or by sale of the stock, is a second corporate income tax. When a *consolidated tax return* has been filed which includes (1) corporations consolidated for financial reporting or (2) accounted for under the equity method, there will not be a second corporate income tax on distributions of these prior years' earnings from the subsidiary to the parent corporation. Also there will not be a second corporate income tax if the subsidiary is a domestic corporation and owned 80 percent or more even if separate returns are filed. In this case there is a 100 percent rather than only an 85 percent dividends received deduction.

Thus, the potential for a second corporate tax, on subsidiary earnings or on earnings of an investee accounted for under the equity method, can generally occur only in the following situations:

1. The subsidiary or investee is a foreign operation. If it is a foreign operation, the dividends received deduction does not apply and generally a foreign subsidiary cannot be a party in a consolidated U.S. tax return (where intercorporate dividends of corporations included in the consolidated return are removed from taxable income and thus are not taxed).
2. When separate U.S. tax returns are filed and the domestic subsidiary is less than 80 percent owned. If the subsidiary were 80 percent or more owned, there would be no second corporate tax on distributed earnings because at this ownership level or above there is a 100 percent dividends received deduction. From ownership of one share of stock up to 80 percent ownership, there is a potential

second corporate tax on domestic corporate dividends but only on 15 percent of the distribution (in other words, there is a dividends received deduction of 85 percent of these dividends).
3. When the cost method is used in financial reporting, there is a potential second corporate tax on dividends. But in this case financial income and taxable income will generally be the same amount and reported in the same period. Thus, normally there will not be a timing difference.

The potential timing differences from undistributed earnings result from the use of the equity method or consolidation for financial reporting when separate returns (the cost method) are used for tax purposes. If all the earnings of all investees and subsidiaries were distributed, there would not be any timing difference.

When *undistributed* earnings are recorded, through consolidation or use of the equity method, *and* when a second corporate tax is possible on a later distribution of those earnings, there is the *presumption* of a timing difference requiring interperiod tax allocation. The tax to be recorded should reflect all available deductions (e.g., the dividends received deduction), credits (e.g., the foreign tax credit), and any other tax planning alternatives.

> Problems in measuring and recognizing the tax effect of a timing difference do not justify ignoring income taxes related to the timing difference.[1]

The APB in *Opinion No. 23* realized that in the case of a subsidiary under the control of the parent corporation, the presumption that undistributed earning would be distributed is refutable. Therefore, these earnings might never be distributed in such a fashion as to cause a second corporate tax.

> *Indefinite reversal criteria.* The presumption that all undistributed earnings will be transferred to the parent company may be overcome, and no income taxes should be accrued by the parent company, if sufficient evidence shows that the subsidiary has invested or will invest the undistributed earnings indefinitely or that the earnings will be remitted in a tax-free liquidation. A parent company should have evidence of specific plans for reinvestment of undistributed earnings of a subsidiary which demonstrate that remittance of the earnings will be postponed indefinitely. Experience of the companies and definite future programs of operations and remittances are examples of the types of evidence required to substantiate the parent company's representation of indefinite postponement of remittances from a subsidiary. If circumstances change and it becomes apparent that some or all of the undistributed earnings of a

---

[1] *AICPA Professional Standards, Accounting—Current Text* (New York, 1980), par. 4095.10. Copyright (1980) by the American Institute of CPAs.

subsidiary will be remitted in the foreseeable future but income taxes have not been recognized by the parent company, it should accrue as an expense of the current period income taxes attributable to that remittance; income tax expense for such undistributed earnings should not be accounted for as an extraordinary item. If it becomes apparent that some or all of the undistributed earnings of a subsidiary on which income taxes have been accrued will not be remitted in the foreseeable future, the parent company should adjust income tax expense of the current period; such adjustment of income tax expense should not be accounted for as an extra-ordinary item.[2]

The APB in *Opinion No. 24* noted that in the case of an investee, the investor does not normally have as much control over the investee as a parent has over a subsidiary.

> The Board believes that the ability of an investor to exercise significant influence over an investee differs significantly from the ability of a parent company to control investment policies of a subsidiary and that only control can justify the conclusion that undistributed earnings may be invested for indefinite periods.[3]

Without the ability to control it must be decided whether the undistributed earnings will be recognized in the future as dividend income or perhaps as capital gain on sale of the investment.

It should be realized that a future capital gain will be taxed, under existing law, at a much higher rate than if received as ordinary dividend income. The current income tax rate is 28 percent on capital gains (and with the possibility of an additional minimum tax being assessed), whereas it is only 6.9 percent (46 percent − (85% × 46%)) on qualifying dividend income due to the 85 percent dividends received deduction.

When the equity method has been used to account for an investment in a subsidiary (or an investee) incurring losses and separate tax returns have been filed, the basis for the parent's investment in a subsidiary's or investee's stock will be less for book than for tax purposes. The recognition of this loss for book purposes would normally require recognition of a related tax benefit. Because of the uncertainty of realization, the tax benefit may not be recognized in the year the loss is recorded. (This nonrecognition of tax benefits concept is discussed extensively later in this chapter under the heading of "Net Operating Losses.")

If this investment is later sold, the as yet unrecognized tax benefit of the basis difference (higher tax basis than book basis) will be realized. *FASB Interpretation No. 29* requires that the tax be recorded as part of the gain or loss on the sale of the stock rather than as a separate tax item such as an extraordinary gain.

---

[2] Ibid., par. 4095.12.

[3] Ibid., par. 4096.07.

The next chapter illustrates in more depth the complications resulting from anticipating and recording the tax on undistributed earnings. There are additional complications if an investee should become a subsidiary or if a subsidiary should become an investee through changes in stock ownership. These considerations are not covered in this text.

Net Operating Losses

A net operating loss (NOL) is strictly a tax computation. It is often totally unrelated to accounting income. In fact, some corporations have reported record high financial accounting incomes in the same years they report NOLs for tax purposes. In these cases there are large timing and/or permanent differences. One of the most striking examples of the enormous difference between two sets of records (supposedly measuring the same transactions) is found in American Electric Power Company, Inc. In the president's letter in the 1973 annual report it is stated that:

> For American Electric Power it was the best of years in one of the worst of years for our industry and our country. . . .
> Revenues, earnings and earnings per share rose to new high levels, and dividends were again increased.

These record high earnings amounted to $207,920,000 and retained earnings at 1973 year-end were also at a record high of $447,419,000. But what did the tax set of records show? This figure also was probably a record, but in this case a record loss. AEP received a $8,536,000 tax refund from NOL and investment tax credit carrybacks. And what about the increased dividends which were $144,484,000 or 69.49 percent of the record accounting earnings? Of the common dividends of $1.85 per share, only 57 cents was taxable to the shareholders and $1.28 was considered a "tax-free" return of capital or a liquidating dividend. But how can a company pay dividends with a record high (after dividend) retained earnings of $447,419,000 and have them be almost 70 percent tax free? Not only are there enormous differences in the net earnings between the two sets of records but also in the retained earnings (earnings and profits account in the tax records) amounts. Thus, while retained earnings reached an all-time high, the earnings and profits account in the tax set of books was negative after the dividend payments. This means that at a minimum there is more than $447,419,000 difference in the retained earnings and earnings and profits measurements in the two sets of records (supposedly measuring the same transactions). And to complete this bizarre comparison, it is perhaps significant to note that AEP (like most other companies) did not keep a complete set of tax books and did not know that their dividend payments were tax free because they apparently believed that with retained earnings approaching $500 million they could not be paying liquidating dividends. In fact, as their March 12, 1975, "Important Notice to Holders and Former Holders of Common Stock" letter indicates, they had been paying tax-free dividends for at least the prior three years which were still open under the statute of limitations as follows:

Year	Taxable as Dividend Income	Not Taxable as Dividend Income (return of capital)
1971	$0.29	$1.41
1972	0.29	1.47½
1973	0.57	1.28

The letter to shareholders did not mention years prior to 1971, then closed by the 3-year statute of limitations, but it did warn the shareholders to file refund claims on or before April 15, 1975. After that date year 1971 would be closed for individual shareholders.

There are some important lessons to be learned from the AEP experience. First, perhaps every company but certainly every public utility should know what its earnings and profits amount is. Second, where there are a lot of permanent and timing differences, perhaps a second and complete set of financial statements based on the tax records should be maintained. It would be unfair to criticize AEP management too much for this error because few rational persons would expect to find such enormous differences. Indeed, you may now be wondering whether you have just read some accounting literature or a fiction story. The only way to rationalize the two extreme results is to realize that Congress created the tax law from which the tax set of books must be prepared.[4]

When an NOL exists, a corporation may elect (1) to carry it back three years (to the oldest year first) and then forward seven years or (2) to carry it forward only for the 7-year period. If there is still some unused NOL after the 7-year carryforward period, it is lost. In other words, after seven, years' carryforward, an unused NOL cannot produce a tax benefit.

For financial accounting purposes and assuming no timing differences, we recognize the refund of taxes from the carryback of the NOL as income in the year the NOL arises. If there is an NOL carryforward and

---

[4] Frequently tax reformers will criticize companys such as AEP for paying little or no income tax, but except possibly for successful lobbying efforts, the full brunt of such criticism should be delivered to Congress and especially to the congressional tax committees (Senate Finance Committee and the House Ways and Means Committee) that create the tax laws.

the corporation is "assured beyond any reasonable doubt"[5] that it will create a tax benefit, an asset representing this future benefit is recorded and income (often a federal income tax provision with a credit balance) is reported in the NOL year. If the future benefit from the NOL is not assured but only anticipated or in doubt (and if there are no net deferred tax credits—this point will be discussed later), then neither the asset nor the income from the potential benefit is recorded. If a benefit from an unrecorded prior year NOL is realized, it is reported as income in the carryforward year that the NOL was used. This income is reported as an extraordinary item and not a prior period adjustment or part of normal operations if it resulted from an NOL.[6] (If it resulted from a previously unused investment tax credit when the "flow-through" method is used for financial reporting, it is usually reported as part of normal operations.)[7]

To illustrate, assume a flat and constant 40 percent tax rate and that in year 19xx there was a $100,000 NOL, and that there were pre-NOL taxable incomes and taxes paid in other years as reflected in Illustration 2–1, and that pre-NOL taxable income and pretax book income were identical amounts each year.

Illustration 2–1

Years	(Loss) Before Taxable Income an NOL Carryover	Tax Payable (Refund)	Unused NOL Carryforward	Tax Saved by Using the NOL Carryforward
19xx − 3	$ 10,000	$ 4,000	–0–	–0–
19xx − 2	20,000	8,000	–0–	–0–
19xx − 1	30,000	12,000	–0–	–0–
19xx	(100,000)	(24,000)	$(40,000)	–0–
19xx + 1	1,000	–0–	(39,000)	$ 400
19xx + 2	2,000	–0–	(37,000)	800
19xx + 3	4,000	–0–	(33,000)	1,600
19xx + 4	5,000	–0–	(28,000)	2,000
19xx + 5	8,000	–0–	(20,000)	3,200
19xx + 6	10,000	–0–	(10,000)	4,000
19xx + 7	12,000	800	–0–	4,000

The $24,000 refund would have been reflected as part of the normal operations in year 19xx, and in years 19xx+1 through 19xx+7 the tax

---

[5] *AICPA Professional Standards,* par. 4091.44. The recording of a tax benefit from an NOL carryforward is a rare event.

[6] Ibid., par. 4091.44.

[7] Ibid., pars. U4091.108 and U4094.019. Obviously, accounting theory does not support this distinction between the reporting for an NOL and an investment tax credit.

saved by applying the NOL carryforward would have been recorded as an extraordinary item of income, while a like amount would have been recorded as a tax provision in normal operations. This would be necessary in order to reflect intraperiod allocation. For years 19xx+1 and 19xx+7 this would have been recorded as follows:

19xx+1

FIT provision	400	
FIT payable (normal operations)		400
FIT payable	400	
FIT benefit (extraordinary item)		400

19xx+7

FIT provision	4,800	
FIT payable (normal operations)		4,800
FIT payable	4,000	
FIT benefit (extraordinary item)		4,000

Some Reasons Why a Corporation May Elect Only the NOL Carryforward

An NOL is a deduction in arriving at taxable income. Thus, an NOL carryback, if it is large enough to eliminate the taxable income, would preclude the application of tax credits. If these credits could no longer be carried forward (or back), they could expire without being used. An investment credit not used in the year it arises can be carried back three years and forward seven years. A future NOL, if carried back, could eliminate the taxable income and thus the tax, and this can free up investment credits that had been earned and applied in that carryback year. This credit can, then, itself be carried back and then forward. For example, assume that in our prior example that the $4,000 tax for year 19xx−3 had been reduced to $1,000 by a $3,000 investment credit that had arisen in that year. The carryback and application of the NOL (in the amount of $10,000) would eliminate the taxable income, and the $3,000 investment credit would then be eligible for a carryback to 19xx−6. If it could be applied in that year, it would generate a $3,000 refund. If, however, the investment credit originally applied in 19xx−3 were from year 19xx−10, then it is in the last year of its carryforward and if not used it is lost. In this case an NOL carryback to 19xx−3 of $10,000 would only generate a $1,000 tax refund and the $3,000 tax credit would be lost forever.

Because NOLs retrigger tax credits or prevent their use in carryforward years, it is very common to see carryforwards of unused NOLs and unused tax credits appearing simultaneously in notes to financial statements. The data in Illustration 2–2 are from a certified annual report of a

Illustration 2–2

Year of Expiration	Operating Loss Carry-forwards ($000)	Investment Credit ($000)
19x4	–0–	$ 574
19x5	–0–	6,707
19x6	–0–	12,942
19x7	$ 33,600	16,350
19x8	73,700	14,285
19x9	41,000	13,440
19x0	—	27,640
	$148,300	$91,938

major corporation. At 12/31/x3 the amounts available to reduce future taxes were $148,300,000 of operating loss carryforwards and $91,938,000 of investment credits expiring in the years shown.

This disclosure, while representing common practice, is inadequate for most users because it does not tell them that *all* of the NOLs must be used before *any* of the investment tax credits can be applied. Thus, in the Illustration 2–2 all $148,300,000 of NOLs must be used before any of the investment credit can be applied.

Tax rates can be another reason to avoid a carryback of an NOL. If tax rates have just been increased, a carryforward may be more valuable than a carryback. If prior years tax rates are lower because of favorable rates on capital gains (28 percent), or if the taxable income were less than $100,000 thus taxed in $25,000 brackets at 17 percent, 20 percent, 30 percent, and 40 percent, a carryforward may be preferred. (There is also a complex situation involving the alternative tax on capital gain in which an NOL could be carried back and used in a prior year and not generate any tax refund; in this case a carryforward would be elected.[8]

Carryforwards of NOLs when There Are Deferred Tax Credits from Timing Differences

While this discussion is related to the NOL, it could involve any carryforward of a tax deduction or a tax credit (tax attributes). Because the accounting profession normally takes a conservative position, accountants generally recognize all expenses or losses as soon as possible but defer recognition of revenue or gain until realization is virtually

---

[8] The landmark case for this situation in *Foster Lumber Co., Inc.*, 38 AFTR 2d 76-6024; 97 S. Ct. 204, decided by the Supreme Court in 1976.

certain. Under this philosophy we recognize deferred tax credits (as liabilities) and the related tax provisions for timing differences even though we often know that under the going-concern concept this liability will never be paid. Also under this philosophy when there is an NOL carryforward, it is recognized as a receivable and taken into income *only* if its realization is "assured beyond any reasonable doubt." When both of these items (deferred credits and carryforwards) occur in the same period, we then recognize the inconsistency in our logic.

Under *APB Opinion No. 11* we are instructed to eliminate or draw down the deferred tax credits (debit the deferred tax credit accounts) by the *smaller* of (1) the potential tax effects of the NOL carryforward or (2) the amount of the *net* deferred tax credits (deferred tax credits less deferred tax charges) which would turn around (on an individual asset basis) in the carryforward period of the NOL.[9] This is necessary conceptually because if the timing differences really represented tax liabilities, these liabilities would have been eliminated by the NOL carryforward to the extent of this drawdown. *APB Opinion No. 11* goes on to state that if the NOL is realized (applied in measuring future taxable incomes), the deferred tax credits previously drawn down should be reinstated to the extent that they would not as yet have turned around.[10]

Returning to Illustration 2–1 and the unused NOL carryforward of $40,000 from year 19xx, assume that the corporation had previously recorded deferred tax credits net of deferred tax charges that would turnaround (reverse) in the 7-year carryforward period in the amount of $20,000. With the assumption of a 40 percent tax rate, the NOL could generate a $16,000 ($40,000 × 40%) tax savings. Thus, deferred tax credits would have to be reduced by the lower of the $20,000 or the $16,000 amount. This would be recorded by the corporation in 19xx as follows:

```
Deferred tax credit .......................................  16,000
    FIT provision (or benefit) ............................           16,000*
```
* Part of normal operations and not an extraordinary item.

It should be noted that the debit to the Deferred Tax Credit account results in an increase in reported earnings because the offsetting credit is taken against the Federal Income Tax Provision account.

Now assume that the corporation had a zero taxable income in year 19xx+1 but that the NOL is fully used in year 19xx+2 to reduce taxable income from $100,000 to $60,000. In this case the net deferred tax credits would have to be reinstated, but only to the extent that the timing differences that led to the $16,000 of net deferred tax credits had not as yet reversed. If $3,000 of these net deferred tax credits had reversed in

---

[9] *AICPA Professional Standards*, par. 4091.47; and the AICPA, *Accounting for Income Taxes an Interpretation of APB Opinion No. 11*, p. 25.

[10] Ibid.

19xx+1, and if the tax rate remained at 40 percent, the following entry would be necessary in 19xx+2 (no entry would have been made in 19xx+1) for the $3,000 reversal of deferred tax credits since they were part of the $16,000 reduction in deferred tax credits in year 19xx.

FIT provision ($100,000 × 40% − $3,000)	37,000	
FIT payable ($60,000 × 40%)		24,000
Deferred tax credit ($16,000 − $3,000)		13,000

This entry records (1) the tax applicable to the $100,000 of earnings but reduced for the turnaround of $3,000 of net deferred tax credits, (2) the liability on $60,000 of taxable income, and (3) the net deferred tax credits that had been removed (drawn down) in the NOL year but which have not as yet turned around.

It is also possible to have an NOL for both book and tax purposes and in differing amounts, due to timing differences, or to have a positive amount for one and a loss for the other. This can cause some additional reporting problems. For example, suppose that there is a $50,000 pretax book loss, no permanent differences, but timing differences of $15,000 resulting in an increase in deferred tax credits and $3,000 resulting in an increase in deferred tax charges. This results in an NOL for tax purposes of $62,000 (−$50,000 − $15,000 + $3,000). With an assumed 40 percent flat tax rate, the journal entry recording the tax effect would be as follows without the possibility of any carryback:

Certain of future use:

Anticipated future FIT benefit (asset) ($62,000 × 40%)	24,800	
Deferred tax charge ($3,000 × 40%)	1,200	
Deferred tax credit ($15,000 × 40%)		6,000
FIT provision ($50,000 × 40%)		20,000

Uncertain of future use and no net deferred tax credits which would reverse in the carryforward period:

Deferred tax charge ($3,000 × 40%)	1,200	
Deferred tax credit		1,200

But no entry would be made for the possible future tax benefit of the NOL ($24,800) and the federal income tax provision ($20,000), and no entry would be made for the excess deferred tax credits over deferred tax charges ($4,800 or $6,000 − $1,200). But if the entire NOL is applied in future years, it will result in an extraordinary gain of $15,200 ($20,000 − $4,800) from use of the NOL and $4,800 ($6,000 − $1,200) from the recording of the excess deferred tax credits.

Uncertain of future use but with older net deferred tax credits of $15,000 which would turn around in the carryforward period:

Deferred tax credit—old (reversal)	15,000	
Deferred tax charge	1,200	
FIT provision		15,000
Deferred tax credit—new		1,200

This entry leaves unrecorded new deferred tax credits of $4,800 ($6,000 − $1,200) and $5,000 ($20,000 − $15,000) of the tax effect of the book NOL. For tax purposes there is still a $62,000 NOL carryforward with a tax effect of $24,800 at a 40 percent tax rate.

Carryforwards of Investment Tax Credits When There Are Deferred Tax Credits from Timing Differences

It should be noted that if there is a carryforward of an investment tax credit (or any other tax credit), the drawdown of net deferred tax credits will be more difficult to measure because of the limitations on applications of the various tax credits.

Due to the general limitations on application of the investment credit and the presence of timing differences, it is possible to have a situation where the investment tax credit earned upon the purchase of an asset is recognized for book purposes before it is realized in a reduction of tax liabilities. The general limitations are that this credit can offset the first $25,000 of income tax liability plus the following percentages of the amounts of tax liability in excess of $25,000:

Year	%
1978	50%
1979	60
1980	70
1981	80
1982	90

For some industries there is currently a 100 percent offset.

To illustrate the application of an investment tax credit, assume a corporation has $500,000 of pretax book earnings, $100,000 of permanent differences where book exceeds tax income, and $300,000 of timing differences where book exceeds taxable income. Assume a 40 percent flat tax rate and $150,000 of investment tax credits.

For 1981 the computation would be as shown in Illustration 2–3. The journal entry to record the tax provision would then be,

FIT provision	27,000	
Deferred tax credit ($300,000 × 40%)		120,000
FIT payable		3,000

However, debits still have to equal credits, thus the deferred tax credit for timing differences will be reduced from $120,000 to $24,000 if the excess investment tax credit could not be carried back.[11]

FIT provision	27,000	
Deferred tax credit		24,000
FIT payable		3,000

---

[11] *AICPA Professional Standards,* pars. U4091.109 and U4091.114.

Illustration 2–3

Pretax book earnings	$500,000
Less permanent differences	100,000
Book equivalent of taxable income	400,000
Tax rate	×40%
Federal income tax provision before the investment credit	160,000
	−25,000
	135,000
Less $135,000 × 80%	−108,000
Income tax provision assuming flow-through recognition of the investment tax credit	$ 27,000
Book equivalent of taxable income	$400,000
Less timing differences	300,000
Taxable income	100,000
	×40%
	40,000
	−25,000
	15,000
Less $15,000 × 80%	−12,000
Tax liability	$ 3,000

If no investment tax credits can be carried back, for book purposes there is an unrecorded tax effect of timing differences of $96,000 ($120,000 − $24,000) and a book investment tax credit carryover of $17,000 ($150,000 − $25,000 − $108,000) for a total of $113,000. For tax purposes there is an investment tax credit carryover of $113,000 ($150,000 − $25,000 − $12,000).

These drawdowns of deferred tax credits due to timing differences can create some interesting results. The data in Illustration 2–4, including the quoted note at the end of the illustration, was taken directly from an actual earnings statement of a major corporation.

PART PERMANENT AND PART TIMING (MORE COMPLEXITY)

As noted in the discussion of intraperiod allocation, assets frequently have different bases for accounting purposes than they have for tax purposes. And while their sale will result in different amounts of gain and/or loss for book and tax purposes, the same type of problem can exist during the period of their use through different depreciation deductions. This basis problem frequently arises in corporate consolidations where cost in excess of book value (or book value in excess of cost) is allocated to the assets and liabilities acquired. If the book basis of an

Illustration 2-4

	Year Ended December 31			
	19x3	19x4	19x5	19x6
		($000)		
Loss before income taxes	$(39,071)	$(138,372)	$(58,730)	$ (13,088)
Deferred federal income tax credit	19,036*	54,363*	11,654*	4,016*
State and foreign income tax	(3,181)	(4,280)	(3,510)	(4,115)
Loss of consolidated companies	(23,216)	(88,289)	(50,586)	(13,187)
Equity in income of unconsolidated subsidiaries and associated companies	1,463	3,364	4,511	4,865
Loss before extraordinary items	(21,753)	(84,925)	(46,075)	(8,322)
Extraordinary items:				
Gain on debenture exchange				117,514†
Less income tax (expense)				(28,203)†
Tax effect of loss carry-forward				13,604‡
Net income (loss)	$(21,753)	$ (84,925)	$(46,075)	$ 94,593

* It should be noted that these are income items as deferred tax credits are being debited and the federal income tax provision is being credited.

† $117,514 × 24% = $28,203. The 24 percent equals the regular tax rate (48 percent) less a 50 percent reduction for investment tax credits.

‡ Use of about $56,000 of NOL carryforwards at a 24 percent effective tax rate equals a $13,604 extraordinary item.

"The deferred federal income tax credits for the years 19x2 [year 19x2 omitted] through 19x5 represent reversals of a portion of the deferred federal income taxes provided in prior years for the income taxes expected to be payable in later years as a result of timing differences in the recognition of certain expenses, principally depreciation, for financial reporting purposes as compared with income tax reporting purposes. Such federal income tax credits are used to reduce financial statement losses because it is appropriate to assume that tax loss carryforwards will be available to reduce taxes that would otherwise be payable as a result of the reversal of the timing differences. The utilization of federal income tax credits to reduce financial statement losses is limited to the lower of the tax effect of the loss or the tax effect of timing differences expected to reverse prior to the expiration of the seven-year period during which a tax loss carryforward is available. The 19x2 and 19x3 deferred federal income tax credits represent the statutory rate applied to the pretax income or loss of the companies included in the consolidated tax return utilizing state and foreign income taxes as deductions. The 19x4 and 19x5 deferred federal income tax credits were limited to the tax effect of timing differences expected to reverse in the carryforward periods.

"The deferred federal income tax credit for 19x6 results from the utilization of the loss before extraordinary items to offset the gain from the debenture exchange. The income tax expense related to the gain on the debenture exchange and the deferred federal income tax credit have been calculated at an effective federal income tax rate of 24 percent, which rate recognizes the full 50 percent allowable for investment tax credits, although such credits may not be claimed in income tax returns until future years.

"Approximately $56,000,000 of loss carryforwards were available as of December 31, 19x5, *for financial reporting purposes* for application against income reported subsequent to that date. This amount was fully utilized in 19x6; the tax effect of these loss carryforwards has been included as an extraordinary credit, also at an effective federal tax rate of 24 percent. (Emphasis added.)

"The company estimates that no federal income tax will actually be payable for 19x6 because of the availability of the tax loss carryforwards to offset taxable income."

asset exceeds the tax basis, some of the book depreciation will be a permanent difference without a tax effect.

> Amounts assigned to identifiable assets and liabilities should, for example, recognize that the fair value of an asset to an acquirer is less than its market value or appraisal value if all or a portion of the market or appraisal value is not deductible for income taxes.[12]

The problem is more complex if the tax basis is higher than the book basis, for in this case the permanent difference will generate a tax effect. Using the concept that tax deductibility is valuable, the excess tax deductibility could result in the recording of the related asset at an amount in excess of its fair market value (FMV) or the establishment of the excess tax deductibility as a separate asset.

Whenever there are both basis differences and timing differences involving the same asset, the complexity is increased.

The following example is taken from *An Appraisal of Interperiod Income Tax Allocation.*[13] This example assumes a $10,000 asset basis and a 5-year life for tax purposes, while for book purposes the basis is $6,000 and a 10-year life is used. For tax purposes DDB depreciation is used in year 1 and SYD in years 2 through 5 while straight-line is used for the full 10-year book depreciation life. A zero salvage value is assumed for both purposes (Illustration 2–5). If the book basis were increased (the

Illustration 2–5
COMBINED PERMANENT AND TIMING DIFFERENCES

Year	Tax Depreciation		Book Depreciation (3)	Permanent Difference (1 − 2)	Timing Difference (2 − 3)
	(1) Actual $10,000 Basis	(2) As If $6,000 Basis			
1............	$ 4,000	$2,400	$ 600	$1,600	$1,800
2............	2,400	1,440	600	960	840
3............	1,800	1,080	600	720	480
4............	1,200	720	600	480	120
5............	600	360	600	240	(240)
6............	–0–	–0–	600	–0–	(600)
7............	–0–	–0–	600	–0–	(600)
8............	–0–	–0–	600	–0–	(600)
9............	–0–	–0–	600	–0–	(600)
10............	–0–	–0–	600	–0–	(600)
Totals	$10,000	$6,000	$6,000	$4,000	–0–

---

[12] Ibid., par. 1091.89.

[13] James E. Wheeler and Willard H. Galliart, *An Appraisal of Interperiod Income Tax Allocation* (New York: Financial Executives Research Foundation, 1974), p. 103.

opposite of the situation in the previous quote) to reflect the tax advantage of the permanent difference, it would affect the amount of the timing difference. Tax effects from permanent differences are presumably not deferred—spread over the life of the asset.

Obviously, when there are basis differences, the accounting is complex and concurrent timing differences increase the complexity.

STOCK OPTION COMPLEXITY

The situation in which income tax can find its way into paid-in capital needs to be closely examined. Paragraphs 16 and 17 of *APB Opinion No. 25* state that:

> 16. *Accounting for Income Tax Benefits.* An employer corporation may obtain an income tax benefit related to stock issued to an employee through a stock option, purchase, or award plan. A corporation is usually entitled to a deduction for income tax purposes of the amount that an employee reports as ordinary income, and the deduction is allowable to the corporation in the year in which the amount is includable in the gross income of the employee. Thus, a deduction for income tax purposes may differ from the related compensation expense that the corporation recognizes,[*] and the deduction may be allowable in a period that differs from the one in which the corporation recognizes compensation expense in measuring net income.
>
> 17. An employer corporation should reduce income tax expense for a period by no more of a tax reduction under a stock option, purchase, or award plan than the proportion of the tax reduction that is related to the compensation expense for the period. Compensation expenses that are deductible in a tax return in a period different from the one in which they are reported as expenses in measuring net income are timing differences (section 4091.33–.36), and deferred taxes should be recorded. The remainder of the tax reduction, if any, is related to *an amount that is deductible for income tax purposes but does not affect net income. The remainder of the tax reduction should not be included in income but should be added to capital in addition to par or stated value of capital stock in the period of the tax reduction.* Conversely, a tax reduction may be less than if recorded compensation expenses were deductible for income tax purposes. If so, the corporation may deduct the difference from additional capital in the period of the tax reduction to the extent that tax reductions under the same or similar compensatory stock option, purchase, or award plans have been included in additional capital.[14] (Emphasis added.)

[*] A corporation may be entitled to a deduction for income tax purposes even though it recognizes no compensation expense in measuring net income.

---

[14] *AICPA Professional Standards,* par. 4062.16–17.

The following two examples will illustrate the rules of *APB Opinion No. 25*. First, assume stock options are issued to employees and that the option price is equal to the FMV of the stock at the date of grant. No compensation expense would be recorded for these options.[15] Suppose that through exercise and subsequent sale of the stock obtained, the employee recognizes $80,000 of ordinary income and that this amount becomes deductible to the corporation. With no compensation recorded at the date of grant (because the option price was equal to or in excess of the FMV at that date), the tax benefit of the deduction, according to *APB Opinion No. 25*, is to be recorded as paid-in capital instead of a reduction in federal income tax expense. A reduction of income tax expense seems much more logical than the credit to paid-in capital, especially when the "all financial resources" concept is required in the statement of changes in financial position.

The APB appears to have made a significant, conceptual error because under their method the amount of the federal income tax expense can forever exceed the amount paid to the federal government as taxes. This result apparently caused the APB to make a second error. The first example is obviously a permanent difference, as defined in *APB Opinion No. 11*, but the APB will allow its tax effect to be reversed by a second permanent difference with the opposite impact. Thus, for our second example assume that the option price is below the FMV by $100,000 at the date of grant but when the option is exercised, several years later, the option price is only $20,000 less than the FMV. If the compensation were recorded at $100,000 and a related and anticipated tax benefit were recorded, the amount recorded would be in excess of the tax benefit actually received if only a $20,000 tax deduction were allowed. In this case the excess anticipated (but never realized) tax benefit is written off against the paid-in capital recorded by the first example. If there is no tax benefit from prior stock options in paid-in capital, then the write-off of the excess anticipated tax benefit would be against income of the current year.

Offsetting the real tax effect of one permanent difference (first example) with an error in estimate on an entirely different permanent difference (second example) is not justified by accounting theory. And then to record the tax effects (which have been termed expenses) in paid-in capital must appear strange at best and totally inconsistent when one recalls the required use of the "all financial resources" concept.

FINANCIAL DISCLOSURE OF TAX ACCOUNTS

Before getting deeply into this discussion it should be noted that intraperiod tax allocation is essentially a disclosure problem whereas

---

[15] Ibid., par. 4062.10. Failure to recognize these options as compensation led the APB to exclude the tax benefit of these options from the earnings computation.

intercorporation tax allocation is primarily a measurement problem and interperiod tax allocation involves extensive measurement and disclosure problems. Thus, all three allocation concepts can be involved simultaneously in a single set of financial statements.

Our discussion involving financial disclosure has been concerned primarily with the earnings statement. We will now expand this to include the statement of financial position.

Another caveat is in order, it is impossible to due justice to any of the theoretical positions on accounting for income taxes in the confines of part of one chapter. The advocated positions are those favored by your author; others might argue strongly for different positions.

Net-of-Tax Concept

Deferred tax accounts due primarily to interperiod tax allocation could be recorded in the position statement under the net-of-tax, liability, or deferral concepts. Under the net-of-tax concept the tax effect of a timing difference is recorded as a direct offset to the related asset or liability. Thus, for a depreciable asset the tax effect of the timing difference, where straight-line depreciation is used for accounting purposes and accelerated depreciation for tax purposes, is recorded as an increase in depreciation expense and accumulated depreciation rather than as an increase in the tax provision and as a deferred credit. The theory is that tax deductibility is part of the value of an asset and as this value is exhausted it should be recorded as depreciation. Under this concept an asset is composed of two types of values, service potential and tax deductibility. Thus, ignoring the time value of money, if a firm buys a $10,000 machine and is in the 46 percent marginal corporate tax bracket, the tax deductibility value is $4,600 ($10,000 × 46%) and the service value is therefore $5,400 ($10,000 − $4,600). To make service value dependent on the marginal rate of a given taxpayer does not appear to be the correct answer. Should the service value be a full $10,000 for a corporation suffering losses? The net-of-tax method is not acceptable in accounting for income taxes under *APB Opinion No. 11*, and yet it is required under *APB Opinion No. 16* in recording the price paid for certain assets (see the quote under the prior heading "Part Permanent and Part Timing (More Complexity)").[16] Some accountants view the net-of-tax method as a naive approach to value determination.

> If the problem is depreciation and not tax allocation, the net of tax method does not solve it. The method is also without merit in situations other than depreciation.
>
> If the method [problem] is tax allocation rather than accounting for depreciation or some other item, it [the net-of-tax method] is the poorest

---

[16] Ibid., par. 4091.63.

of the three allocation methods. Its matching is sometimes unsatisfactory. Its presentation is always less informative than the other two methods and is potentially misleading.

The net of tax method is either a naive measurement of a high complex and unknown relationship between values and their causes or tax allocation in disguise. In neither form is it an acceptable accounting procedure.[17]

Many other accountants and academicians believe it is naive to handle tax effects in any way other than the net-of-tax concept.

Liability Concept

Under the liability approach, deferred tax credits are treated as liabilities (and deferred tax charges as assets) which require adjustment if tax rates change. The contra account to the deferred tax charge or credit is the tax provision. It should be noted that under this concept discounting should probably be required,[18] as it is for other liabilities. Thus, as to investment tax credit amounts there could be no deferral because there is no future liability even under an individual item reversal concept with or without discounting. This method would, therefore, preclude amortization of the investment tax credit over the life of the asset, and would recognize it as a reduction in income taxes (a selective rate reduction depending on the purchase of qualifying assets).

Deferral Concept

The deferral method is the one required by the APB. But the only real difference between it and the liability method is in terminology and in not adjusting tax deferral accounts for tax rate changes. The deferral method does, however, allow spreading the investment credit over future years as long as there is no discounting of the deferral, and this may have been the real reason for its selection by the APB as the required method for tax accounting.[19] The APB did not want the tax savings from

---

[17] Homer A. Black, *Accounting Research Study No. 9, "Interperiod Allocation of Corporate Income Taxes"* (New York: AICPA, 1966), p. 57.

[18] Discounting is not permitted under *APB Opinion No. 10*, "Deferred Taxes Should Not Be Accounted for on a Discounted Basis." *AICPA Professional Standards*, par. 4092.01.

[19] One very knowledgeable reviewer of these materials stated, "The real reason for the selection of the deferral method by the APB had absolutely nothing to do with the investment tax credit. The real reason was that the APB was not able to get sufficient votes for either the net-of-tax method or the liability method. While some of the 18 Board members at the time did favor the deferral method, probably more favored both the liability method and the net-of-tax method. The deferral method was adopted purely as a compromise. The liability people were reasonably happy because deferred credits ended up as liabilities and not as deductions from assets. The net-of-tax people could rationalize their view by arguing that the deferral method was simply the net-of-tax method grossed up. The in-

the investment credit to reduce the tax provision in the same year that it reduces the tax liability. This leads many accountants including the author to believe that deferral of investment tax credits overstates the tax provision and thus understates earnings.

Deferred Tax Accounts in the Statement of Financial Position

The SEC as well as the APB have stated that the deferred tax accounts are related to the asset or liability causing the timing difference. Thus, they require that the deferred tax account be reported in the same section (current or noncurrent) of the position statement as the item causing the timing difference. For example, assume a company uses the installment sales method for tax purposes when normal accrual accounting is required for financial reporting. This will result in a deferred credit for the timing difference; and since accounts receivable are current assets, the related deferred tax credit must be a current liability. Once the deferred tax accounts (charges and credits) have been established as current or noncurrent, they may be netted to show only one current and one noncurrent amount in the statement of financial position. In other words, current deferred charges and current deferred credits can be netted and noncurrent deferred charges and noncurrent deferred credits may be netted, but current charges and credits are not to be netted with noncurrent, and netting is optional in any event.

Thus, without netting, deferred tax accounts can appear in every major section of the position statement. Illustration 2–6 shows the various possible federal income tax accounts.

Required Disclosure in the Earnings Statement

In addition to the general accounting rules for intraperiod, intercompany, and interperiod tax allocation, the SEC in *Accounting Series Release 149* requires significant detail to be shown. These requirements are now contained in Rule 3-16(0) of Regulation S-X and apply to financial statements filed with the SEC.

> (0) *Income tax expense.* (1) Disclosure shall be made, in the income statement or a note thereto, of the components of income tax expense, including (i) taxes currently payable; (ii) the net tax effects, as applicable, of (a) timing differences (indicate separately the amount of the estimated tax effect of each of the various types of timing differences, such as deprecia-

---

vestment tax credit had no measurable effect on the deliberations of the Board in arriving at its conclusions on tax allocation." Your author simply does not believe that something as significant as the investment tax credit was, in reality, virtually ignored by the APB members in voting on accounting for income taxes. The result with no discounting is more than an accidental occurrence.

Illustration 2–6
POSITION STATEMENT

Current Assets	*Current Liabilities*
1. Deferred tax charges (due to timing differences involving current assets or liabilities).	1. Deferred tax credits (due to timing differences involving current assets or liabilities).
2. Tax refund receivable (due to NOL carryback or assured utilization of the carryforward).	2. Federal income tax payable (as measured on the tax return plus the pad for audit deficiency).
Noncurrent Assets	*Noncurrent Liabilities*
3. Deferred tax charges (due to timing differences involving noncurrent assets or liabilities).	3. Deferred tax credits (due to timing differences involving noncurrent assets or liabilities).
	4. Deferred investment tax credits (from amortization of the investment credit over the lives of the related assets).
	Owner's Equity
	5. Net tax benefits, from permanent differences in stock options, recorded as paid-in capital.

tion, warranty costs, etc., where the amount of each such tax effect exceeds five percent of the amount computed by multiplying the income before tax by the applicable statutory Federal income tax rate; other differences may be combined) and (b) operating losses; and (iii) the net deferred investment tax credits. Amounts applicable to United States Federal income taxes, to foreign income taxes and to other income taxes shall be stated separately for each major component. Amounts applicable to foreign or other income taxes each of which are less than five percent of the total of the major component need not be separately disclosed.

(2) If it is expected that the cash outlay for income taxes with respect to any of the succeeding three years will substantially exceed income tax expense for such year, that fact should be disclosed together with the approximate amount of the excess, the year (or years) of occurrence and the reasons therefor.

(3) Provide a reconciliation between the amount of reported total income tax expense (benefit) and the amount computed by multiplying the income (loss) before tax by the applicable statutory Federal income tax rate, showing the estimated dollar amount of each of the underlying causes for the difference. If no individual reconciling item amounts to more than five percent of the amount computed by multiplying the income before tax by the applicable statutory Federal income tax rate, and the total difference to be reconciled is less than five percent of such computed amount, no reconciliation need be provided unless it would be significant in appraising the trend of earnings. Reconciling items that are

individually less than five percent of the computed amount may be aggregated in the reconciliation. *The reconciliation may be presented in percentages rather than in dollar amounts.* Where the reporting person is a foreign entity, the income tax rate in that person's country of domicile should normally be used in making the above computation, but different rates should not be used for subsidiaries or other segments of a reporting entity. If the rate used by a reporting person is other than the United States Federal corporate income tax rate, the rate used and the basis for using such rate shall be disclosed.[20] (Emphasis added.)

It is unfortunate that the SEC permits the reconciliation in percentages rather than in dollars. Obviously the dollar amounts must be calculated in order to arrive at the percentages, and for most readers the dollar amounts would be much more informative. Some corporations in the interest of disclosure show both dollars and percentages, while others try to disclose as little as possible and thus show only the percentages. To aid in interpreting these requirements, an exhibit is contained in *Accounting Series Release No. 149.*

Rule 3-16(0)(2) requires the type of income tax disclosure given in Illustration 2-7. When timing differences are material (in excess of 5

Illustration 2-7

	Federal	Foreign	State and Local	Total
Currently payable	x	x	x	x
Deferred for timing differences (net)	x	x	x	x
Deferred investment tax credits	x	x	—	x
	x	x	x	x

percent of the hypothetical tax obtained by multiplying the statutory federal tax rate (now 46 percent) times the pretax accounting income), the net effect of each source of timing difference, such as depreciation, must be separately disclosed.

Rule 3-16(0)(2) requires disclosures if deferred tax credits for timing difference are expected to materially reverse within any of the next three years or if for some other reason cash outlay for taxes will exceed the provision for taxes.

Rule 3-16(0)(3) requires a reconciliation between (1) the tax provision that would have resulted if the statutory federal tax rate had applied to pretax accounting income and (2) the federal income tax provision re-

---

[20] Regulation S-X, Rule 3-16(0). The SEC is in the process of revising Rule 3-16(0) to increase disclosure.

ported in the earnings statement. While permanent differences often account for much of the difference between these amounts, other items such as differing tax rates, also are reflected. This reconciliation often appears as in Illustration 2–8. The example is from the 1976 10-K of Transamerica Corporation (their page 36).

Illustration 2–8

The difference between federal income tax amounts computed at statutory rates and the provision is as follows ($000):

	Year Ended December 31	
	1976	1975
Federal income taxes at statutory (48%) rate	$ 92,513	$ 57,547
Income not tax affected relating to:		
Taxation methods applicable to life insurance companies	(14,465)	(12,291)
Investment income of property and casualty insurance companies	(6,531)	(5,436)
Investment tax credits	(3,759)	(2,510)
State income taxes	4,795	3,247
Other	5,696	4,404
Consolidated provision for income taxes	$78,249	$ 44,961

It should be realized that the above disclosure requirements under Rule 3-16(0) apply to the annual 10-K registrations and not to annual reports to shareholders. Often the disclosure of tax data in annual reports is less adequate.

AN EVALUATION OF ACCOUNTING FOR INCOME TAXES

Economic Reality as a Guideline

To be of maximum usefulness to investors, creditors, and others, accounting must reflect economic reality. Unfortunately our present rules on accounting for income taxes fail this test; they are (1) overly complex, (2) designed for maximum income smoothing, and (3) often result in inadequate or irrelevant disclosure.

As an illustration of the failure to reflect economic reality, consider the effect on net earnings if a corporation uses straight-line depreciation and full economic life for financial reporting and uses for tax purposes either (1) short lives with accelerated depreciation or (2) full economic life with straight-line depreciation. In the first instance an enormous amount of taxes can often be saved, but because of our deferred tax accounting the tax savings is treated similarly to borrowing (at a zero interest rate) with the net earnings (after tax) being identical regardless of the depreciation method used for tax purposes. Is the rather permanent savings of huge amounts of taxes really worthless? Accountants are saying exactly that when these tax savings do not impact on net earnings.

In effect we record the tax provision as though we had used the book accounting methods for tax purposes. This normally overstates the tax provision (reducing earnings), and thus the taxes saved are reflected as liabilities (deferred tax credits) as though the cash saved arose from borrowing. Obviously those who advocate deferred tax accounting cannot favor discounting because most of these amounts will never be paid, and thus the present value of the net deferred credits is often zero.

To appreciate the enormous impact on cash flow from favorable tax depreciation, one need look no further than the financial statements of AT&T. This produces an excellent example because from 1954 (when accelerated depreciation was first permitted for tax purposes) until 1970 AT&T used straight line and full economic useful lines for both book and tax purposes. Then, in 1970 AT&T adopted accelerated depreciation. Therefore, deferred tax credits from use of accelerated depreciation first appeared in their 1970 position statement. Illustration 2–9 shows the AT&T results (excluding Western Electric).

Illustration 2–9
($ Millions)

Year	Net Earnings before Tax	Tax Provision	Current Portion	Deferred Portion ITC*	Deferred Portion Timing	Reduction in Income by Increasing Tax Expense
1969	$3,953	$1,979	$1,888	$ 91	$ 0	$ 91
1970	3,512	1,573	1,482	20	71	182
1971	3,377	1,433	989	53	391	626
1972	3,919	1,669	837	228	604	1,458
1973	4,641	1,963	932	225	806	2,489
1974	4,983	2,123	678	258	1,187	3,934
1975	5,215	2,174	129	742	1,303	5,979
1976	6,298	2,686	582	716	1,388	8,083
1977	7,052	2,997	617	820	1,560	10,463
1978†	8,230	3,482	1,296	706	1,480	12,649
1979	8,299	3,310	831	879	1,600	15,128
Accumulated deferrals (liabilities in the position statement)				$4,738	$10,390	$15,128

* Investment tax credit.
† The special adjustments for the Pacific Telephone and Telegraph case have not been reflected in order to keep all years on the same basis and somewhat in agreement with the tax return data.

How large will the tax savings (and the understatement of earnings) be by 1985? Will these amounts ($15 billion, $128 million) ever be paid to the government? What is the present value of these liabilities? What is the economic reality? Note that in 1975 through 1979 the tax provision was each year more than $2 billion larger than the tax paid.[21]

Almost the entire public ulility industry, their lobbists, and perhaps their accountants have fought to prevent the change to a real liability concept. They favor the deferral concept because this (in conjunction with some special provisions in the income tax law to hamstring state utility commissions in rate setting[22]) allows them to charge customers for taxes which they have not and probably never will pay.[23]

A Suggested Presentation

The tax effects of permanent and timing differences can be very significant, and therefore adequate presentation of these items should be required in such a way as to reflect as nearly as possible the real economic effect.

The financial statements are management's statements, and management is the best position to estimate the future tax effects of their decisions. Therefore, while the disclosure should be complete, it should emphasize Regulation S-X, Rule 3-16(0)(2) (quoted in the previous section of this chapter).

Reflection of economic reality would require that the tax provision exceed the tax currently payable only by an amount that can reasonably be anticipated will become payable in the next several years. This would, for many corporations, remove enormous "liabilities" from the position statement which today are largely secret reserves which in bad years help to smooth reported income. Certainly, building up huge deferred tax credits (liabilities) in the position statement for items which will never be paid is irrelevant information. The relevant part is that amount which will require future cash outflows in excess of an anticipated current tax provision.

In the interest of full disclosure, all of the timing differences could be shown in a note to the financial statements with only the relevant portion thereof recorded as added tax liabilities or assets. This could be accomplished with disclosure along the lines of Illustration 2–10.

---

[21] To appreciate the economics and politics involved, it should be mentioned that federal laws allow utilities to charge their customers for the tax provision. Thus AT&T, for example, has been reimbursed by its customers for billions of dollars of income tax it will never pay.

[22] *Internal Revenue Code*, secs. 46(f) and 167(1).

[23] A California rate commission is challenging the right to charge customers for taxes not paid; see *Pacific Telephone and Telegraph* case and *General Telephone Co.* v. *California Public Utilities Commission*.

Illustration 2-10

Sources of Timing Differences	Potential Tax Effect at Beginning of Year	Potential Current Year Increases or Decreases	Potential Tax Effect at End of Year
Potential deferred credits:			
Depreciation	$(100,000)	$(28,000)	$(128,000)
Potential deferred charges:			
Warranty accruals	20,000	5,000	25,000
Net potential deferrals	$ (80,000)	$(23,000)	$(103,000)

Any portion of the $103,000 net potential deferred tax credit that is expected to result in a cash outlay within the near-term planning horizon should be disclosed and recorded as a liability in the position statement. If it is anticipated that none of the $23,000 (or $103,000) will result in a near-term cash outflow, then none should be recorded as liabilities and the tax provision should equal the tax payable after adjusting both for any anticipated tax deficiency upon an IRS audit.

This would eliminate many of the position statement deferred tax accounts, it would make recording NOL carryforwards easier, it could be tested for reasonableness in an audit, and it would be tied much closer to economic reality. This should certainly increase the relevance of this information.

APPENDIX

Accounting for income taxes involves foreign and state and local income taxes as well as federal. In addition, there is a significant interplay between these taxes and the federal income tax.

Foreign Income Taxes

Earnings from foreign operations are subject to U.S. income taxation as well as foreign or host country taxes. If these earnings (or losses) are from branch operations, they are taxable under the U.S. rules in the year earned (assuming the use of the accrual rather than the cash basis for tax purposes); however, if the earnings are from the operations of a foreign subsidiary, they are taxed usually when remitted to the U.S. parent (in some cases, a distribution is imputed to the parent company so as to tax them when earned—Subpart F income of a controlled foreign corporation).

In many cases, foreign earnings of an investee or a subsidiary may never be remitted, even though they will be recorded for financial reporting (net of the foreign tax) under the equity method or through consolidation. In this case the *APB Opinion No. 23* "indefinite reversal criteria" applies.

In an effort to avoid dual taxation (by the host country and by the United States), the U.S. tax rules permit a dollar-for-dollar offset against the U.S. tax in the form of a foreign tax credit. The maximum amount of this credit that is permitted to be applied against U.S. taxes is determined by separating the taxable income (obviously requires translating foreign operations into U.S. dollar equivalents) into its foreign sources and U.S. sources. This is no easy task because there are many joint costs such as research and development to be allocated between the two sources. Once the determination of source has been completed and the gross U.S. income tax liability has been computed, the following formula is applied to determine the foreign tax credit limitation:

$$\frac{\text{Pretax foreign source income}}{\text{Total taxable income (U.S. and foreign source)}} \times \text{U.S. income tax liability} = \text{Limit on foreign tax credit}$$

If the foreign tax exceeds the limit (foreign tax rates may exceed U.S. tax rates), there will be excess foreign taxes over the amount of the credit. This excess can be carried back two years and forward five but subject to the same formula limitation in those years. Obviously, if the limit on the foreign tax credit exceeds the foreign tax, the credit is limited to the foreign tax (paid or accrued).

For purposes of illustration, assume that foreign source taxable income (from foreign branch operations or remitted foreign subsidiary earnings) is $40,000 (in U.S. dollars) and subject to a flat 25 percent foreign tax rate and that total taxable income (U.S. and foreign sources) is $100,000 and subject to a flat 30 percent U.S. tax rate. Also assume no timing or permanent differences. The tax provision would be recorded as follows:

Foreign income tax provision ($40,000 × 25%)	10,000	
U.S. FIT provision ($100,000 × 30% − 10,000)	20,000	
U.S. FIT payable		20,000
Foreign income tax payable		10,000

It should be noted that the U.S. federal income tax provision is $18,000 ($60,000 × 30%) on U.S. source income and $2,000 ($40,000 × (30% − 25%)) on foreign source income for a total of $20,000.

If the U.S. rate were 25 percent and the foreign rate were 30 percent, the limitation would apply. When the limitation applies there will be no U.S. tax on foreign source income.

$$\frac{\$40,000 \text{ (foreign source)}}{\$100,000 \text{ (total taxable income)}} \times \$25,000 \text{ (U.S. federal income tax liability)} = \$10,000$$

Thus, the maximum current year application of foreign taxes would be $10,000 when the foreign tax incurred was $12,000 ($40,000 × 30%). The $2,000 excess is eligible for carryback or carryforward. The journal entry would now be:

Foreign income tax provision ($40,000 × 30%)	12,000	
U.S. FIT provision	15,000*	
U.S. FIT payable ($25,000 − $10,000)		15,000
Foreign income tax payable		12,000

* $100,000 × 25% − $10,000 = $15,000, or $60,000 × 25% = $15,000.

Excess foreign tax credits, $2,000 in this case, are seldom disclosed in financial reporting.

Now let's go back to the first example and assume that none of the subsidiary net earnings of $30,000 ($40,000 − ($40,000 × 25%)) have been remitted. If there will be no remittance, the parent corporation will record this income for financial accounting as $40,000 less a $10,000 ($40,000 × 25%) foreign tax; but if remittance is anticipated, the 30 percent U.S. rate less the foreign tax credit at the 25 percent rate will have to be recorded, and this would appear as follows:

Foreign income tax provision ($40,000 × 25%)	10,000	
U.S. FIT provision (on foreign earnings)		
(($40,000 × 30%) − ($40,000 × 25%))	2,000	
U.S. FIT provision (on U.S. earnings) ($60,000 × 30%)	18,000	
Foreign income tax payable		10,000
Deferred tax credit (U.S. FIT payable when		
foreign earnings are remitted)		2,000
U.S. FIT payable		18,000

It should be noted that the foreign tax is not really a timing difference because it never effects *pretax* accounting income, but the effects of anticipated remittance produce similar results.

Just as the provisions for U.S. federal income taxes are affected by timing and permanent differences so is the foreign tax provision. If we assume that the foreign before-tax income were $40,000 and the foreign tax rate were 45 percent, the provision would be $18,000. Assume that this consists of $10,000 currently payable and $8,000 due to some timing difference resulting in a deferred credit.

	$40,000	Before-tax earnings
−	17,778	Timing difference
	$22,222	Foreign taxable income

The entry to record the foreign tax would be:

Foreign income tax provision ($40,000 × 45%)	18,000	
Foreign income tax payable ($22,222 × 45%)		10,000
Deferred tax credit—foreign tax ($17,778 × 45%)		8,000

Now, if remittance to the U.S. parent is anticipated, the U.S. tax must also be recorded. In order to avoid the limitation provision, assume a

U.S. federal income tax rate of 50 percent. In recording the U.S. federal income tax provision, should the actual foreign tax paid be used as the creditable foreign tax or should this amount be increased by the foreign deferred tax credit? If the earnings were remitted, only the foreign tax paid or accrued ($10,000) would be eligible for the credit. Considering only this year, the maximum remittance of before-tax income would be $40,000 for accounting purposes but only $22,222 for tax purposes. Thus, most firms would establish the entire provision of $18,000 as the credit for financial reporting because they would be recording the $40,000 as pretax income.

The tax on this would be recorded as follows:

Foreign income tax provision ($40,000 × 45%)	18,000	
U.S. FIT provision (on foreign source income) ($40,000 × 50% − $18,000)	2,000	
Foreign income tax payable		10,000
Deferred tax—foreign tax		8,000
U.S. FIT payable (currently) (($22,222 × 50%) − ($22,222 × 45%))		1,111
Deferred U.S. tax (payable when the timing difference reverses and is remitted) (($17,778 × 50%) − ($17,778 × 45%))		889

If one assumes that the foreign timing difference is not permitted for U.S. purposes, the U.S. taxable income from foreign sources will be $40,000 when remitted. Then, $10,000 in taxes (after the foreign tax credit) will be payable to the United States. This would be recorded as follows:

Foreign income tax provision ($40,000 × 45%)	18,000	
U.S. FIT provision (on foreign source income) (($40,000 × 50%) − ($40,000 × 45%))	2,000	
Deferred tax charge (prepaid U.S. tax on foreign source income) ($10,000 − $2,000 or excess of U.S. FIT payable over U.S. provision)	8,000	
Foreign income tax payable ($22,222 × 45%)		10,000
Deferred tax credit—foreign tax ($17,778 × 45%)		8,000
U.S. FIT payable ($40,000 × 50% − $10,000 foreign tax payable)		10,000

The $8,000 deferred tax charge is really a prepaid U.S. tax that would not have been incurred if we could have applied the deferred foreign tax credit of $8,000 against the U.S. tax. A foreign tax is not creditable until paid or accrued, and apparently a deferred tax credit is not considered as accrued for this purpose.

Obviously, accounting for the tax effect of foreign operations can become extremely complex.

State and Local Income Taxes

With most states and many cities having separate income taxes, businesses have a problem in determining how much of their income is taxable in each jurisdiction. Once the taxable income for a particular jurisdiction has been determined (often using a formula such as the three-factor formula consisting of sales, property, and payroll), the tax must be computed. Just as with the federal income tax (and foreign income taxes), there are often both timing and permanent differences between pretax accounting income and taxable income at the state or local level.

The presence of tax deferrals (charges or credits) for timing differences for a state income tax causes additional problems in measuring the provision for federal income taxes. State and local income taxes are deductible at the federal level but only to the extent paid or accrued. When a deferred tax credit exists in the recording of a state or local income tax provision, the increased state or local tax provision will not increase the amount currently deductible for federal income tax purposes. Thus, for every deferred tax charge (or deferred tax credit) for state or local income taxes there exists a deferred tax credit (or deferred tax charge) in recording the federal income tax provision.

To illustrate, assume that the Single Deferral Corporation has only one difference between the pretax book net earning of $85,000 and the taxable income for state income tax purposes. Assume that for state income taxes, accelerated depreciation of $65,000 was taken (the same amount that was taken for federal income tax purposes) while for book purposes only $30,000 was deducted. If this were the only difference and if the state income tax rate were a flat 10 percent, the journal entry to record the state income tax would be:

```
State income tax provision ($85,000 × 10%)....................  8,500
    State income tax payable
      (10% × ($85,000 − ($65,000 − $30,000)))................          5,000
    Deferred tax credit (state income tax) for
      depreciation (10% × ($65,000 − $30,000))...............          3,500
```

But then in recording the federal income tax provision, only $5,000 of state income tax would be deductible. Thus, the book provision of $8,500 exceeds the deduction by $3,500 or the amount of the deferred tax credit. This causes an "expense" for book purposes (state income tax provision) to be larger than the deduction on the federal income tax return, and this produces a deferred tax *charge* at the federal level. Thus, considering only this item, it would have the following effect in the recording of the federal income tax provision:

```
Deferred tax charge (state tax deferred credit)
    ($3,500 × 46%)...........................................  1,610
    FIT provision ...........................................          1,610
```

You should note that a deferred tax credit at the state level produces a deferred tax charge at the federal level and that a deferred tax charge at the state level would produce a deferred tax credit at the federal level.

Some states allow a deduction for federal incomes taxes paid or accrued. When this happens, we have a simultaneous equation problem to contend with. Often, however, this tax effect is not material enough to warrant consideration, and we do not carry the discussion further in this text.

REVIEW QUESTIONS

1. Why do the undistributed earnings of an investee cause both timing and permanent differences?
2. How can the undistributed earnings of a subsidiary result in only a permanent difference rather than both timing and permanent differences as with an investee?
3. What is the "indefinite reversal criteria," and when is it applicable?
4. How should a corporation record the potential tax benefit to be realized from a net operating loss carryforward?
5. Why are deferred tax credit accounts sometimes reduced when there are NOL carryforwards?
6. What are the carryback and carryforward periods for NOLs?
7. If a corporation has an NOL carryforward, why would it also often have investment tax credit carryforwards?
8. Assets sometimes have different bases for financial reporting than they have for tax purposes. What can cause these basis differences?
9. What effect can basis differences have on the fair value of an asset?
10. What can cause tax benefits to be recorded as an increase in paid-in capital?
11. What are the disclosure possibilities for all of the possible tax accounts that might appear in a balance sheet?
12. Evaluate the statement that "accounting for income taxes is an attempt to reflect economic reality."
13. Why is discounting not applied to deferred tax amounts?
14. Why is the identification of foreign source income significant, and why is it difficult to measure?
15. What is an excess foreign tax credit and of what value is it?
16. What are the carryback and carryforward periods for foreign tax credits?
17. Why do deferred tax charges or credits for state income taxes affect tax deferrals for federal taxes?

PROBLEMS

Problem 1: Anticipated Tax Company, Inc.

ANTICIPATED TAX COMPANY, INC
Earnings Statement
For the Year Ended 12/31/x5

Sales	$2,000,000
Cost of goods sold	1,000,000
Gross earnings	1,000,000
Operating expenses	400,000
Earnings from operations	600,000
Earnings from investees	100,000
Earnings before tax and extraordinary items	700,000
Federal income tax provision	280,000
Earnings before extraordinary items	420,000
Extraordinary gain (net of tax of $90,000)	210,000
Net earnings	$ 630,000

Additional information:

1. The federal income tax rate is assumed to be 40 percent on ordinary income and 30 percent on long-term capital gains.
2. The extraordinary gain is a capital gain.
3. Excess contributions of last year of $10,000 have been deducted this year for tax purposes only.
4. Tax depreciation exceeds book depreciation by $50,000.
5. The earnings from investees represent equity method earnings from 30 percent owned corporations. Of those earnings $40,000 have been remitted as dividends in the current year. It is anticipated that all of these earnings will eventually be paid as dividends.
6. The company earned only $1,000 in investment tax credits on assets purchased this year. For book purposes, investment credits are being amortized over the lives of the related assets; thus, $3,000 of current and prior year credits are amortized this year.
7. The company for financial accounting purposes provided $20,000 for anticipated warranty costs on current year sales and incurred $24,000 in actual costs on past and current year sales. For tax purposes, warranty costs are deductible only when incurred.

Required:

1. *Beginning with either the net earnings figure or with sales,* prepare in good form a schedule showing both taxable income and the book equivalent of taxable income.
2. Compute the federal income tax provision and the liability.
3. Prepare in detail form the journal entry(s) by which the total federal income tax provision was recorded.

Problem 2: Major and Minor Corporations

The earnings statement for Major Corporation as of 12/31/x5 appears as follows:

MAJOR CORPORATION
Earnings Statement
For the Year Ended 12/31/x5

Sales	$1,000,000
Cost of goods sold	450,000
Gross margin	550,000
Operating expenses	(200,000)
Other revenues and losses	80,000
Equity method earnings from Minor Corporation	70,000
Federal income tax provision	(200,000)
Extraordinary loss (net of a tax benefit of $32,000)	(48,000)
Net earnings	$ 252,000

Additional information:

1. The federal income tax rate is a flat 40 percent on ordinary income and 25 percent on capital gain.
2. Operating expenses include depreciation of $30,000, whereas $60,000 in depreciation was deducted for tax purposes. On some assets book depreciation exceeds tax depreciation by $10,000, and on other assets tax depreciation exceeds book depreciation by $40,000. The gross change method is used to account for the tax effects. In prior years the regular corporate tax rate was 50 percent.
3. Operating expenses also includes insurance expense of $12,000 for key officer life insurance. The corporation is the beneficiary, and thus this cost is not deductible for tax purposes.
4. Other revenue includes $5,000 of interest on City of Honolulu bonds which is not taxable.
5. Other revenue also includes $10,000 of dividends from several small percentage investments in domestic corporations. For tax purposes there is an 85 percent dividends received deduction.
6. Other revenues and losses include fines of $4,000 for overweight trucks on interstate highways. These fines are not deductible for tax purposes.
7. The Minor Corporation is 70 percent owned by Major Corporation and is accounted for under the equity method. During 19x5 Minor Corporation earned $100,000 and paid dividends of $40,000. Major Corporation is contemplating a sale of its interest in Minor which will produce capital gain income in 19x6. Current dividends from Minor are eligible for the 85 percent dividends received deduction.
8. Investments tax credits of $10,000 were earned and used this year for tax purposes. For book purposes the investment credit is amortized over the book life of the assets, and thus only $4,000 of investment credits were recorded as used this year.

Required:
1. Beginning with net earnings compute *both* the book equivalent of taxable income and the taxable income. (Label your calculations!)
2. From your computations in 1 above calculate *both* the federal income tax provision and the federal income tax liability. (Label your calculations!)
3. In journal entry form duplicate the entry that the bookkeeper made (or should have made) in recording the federal income tax provision. (Record all timing differences separately.)

Problem 3: Reality Corporation

Reality Corporation reported for financial accounting purposes $200,000 of before-tax net earnings and aftertax earnings of $130,000. Assume there is a flat 40 percent corporate income tax and a 28 percent capital gains tax. The $200,000 of before-tax earnings included the following items:

1. Depreciation for book of $30,000, while for tax purposes this was $45,000.
2. Equity method earnings from investments in domestic corporations, owned over 20 percent but not owned 80 percent or more, $80,000. These corporations paid dividends to Reality in the amount of $30,000. Dividend revenue is reported for tax purposes less an 85 percent dividend received deduction. It is anticipated that all undistributed earnings will eventually be realized as dividend revenue.
3. Reality sold a capital asset which resulted in a $10,000 capital gain. For tax purposes, due to the installment sales method, only $4,000 of the gain is recognized in the current year.
4. Reality provided for product warranty by crediting its Allowance for Product Warranty account for $10,000. During the year, however, actual costs of $14,000 were charged to this allowance account. Only the actual cost is deductible for tax purposes.
5. Reality earned $3,000 of investment tax credits this year but amortized only $2,000 of these and prior years' credits against the tax provision. For tax purposes all credits are taken in the year earned.
6. Reality received $5,000 of interest on State of Hawaii bonds. This interest is not subject to taxation.
7. Reality also paid insurance premiums on Mr. Reality's life. These payments resulted in $3,000 of key officer life insurance expense. For tax purposes, this amount is not deductible.

Required:
1. Beginning with the $200,000 before-tax net earning figure, compute *both* (*a*) the taxable income and (*b*) the book equivalent of taxable income.
2. From the amounts computed in 1 above, compute both the tax provision (before audit pad adjustment) and the tax liability.
3. Prepare the journal entry(s) by which the Reality Corporation recorded its $70,000 tax provision.

Problem 4: Foreign Tax Corporation (Requires use of the Appendix)

Foreign Tax Corporation had before-tax net earnings of $210,000 of which $80,000 were from foreign operations and $130,000 were from U.S. sources. The U.S. sources included $10,000 of tax-exempt state bond interest. The foreign tax rate is 50 percent, and the U.S. federal income tax rate is 45 percent.

Required:
1. Prepare the journal entry(s) to record the tax provisions.
2. Compute the amount, if any, of foreign tax credit carryovers.
3. If the tax depreciation had exceeded book depreciation by $20,000 on foreign operations and by $30,000 on U.S. operations, prepare the journal entries to record the tax provisions.
4. Compute the amount, if any, of foreign tax credit carryovers.
5. If the depreciation had been the same for both book and tax purposes (as under 1 above), prepare the journal entries to record the tax provisions assuming a 45 percent foreign tax rate and a 50 percent U.S. federal income tax rate.

Problem 5: State Corporation (Requires use of the Appendix)

State Corporation had before-tax (before state or federal tax) net earnings of $145,000 for financial reporting. For tax purposes tax depreciation exceeds financial accounting depreciation by $40,000, and there is $5,000 of tax-exempt state bond interest. The state income tax law is the same as the federal law except that the state does not allow a deduction for state income taxes. The state and federal tax rates are a flat 20 and 30 percent, respectively.

Required:

Prepare the journal entries to record the state and federal income tax provisions.

Problem 6: Shaky, Inc., Federal Income Tax Provision

Shaky began business on 1/1/x3 and has reported the following before-tax earnings each year. There are no timing and no permanent differences, and the effective federal income tax rate is a flat 30 percent.

Year	Before-Tax Earnings
19x3	$ 20,000
19x4	30,000
19x5	(70,000)
19x6	30,000
19x7	(40,000)

Required:

Prepare the journal entry(s) to record the federal income tax provision for each year.

Problem 7: I. M. Lost Corporation

Assume the I. M. Lost Corporation began business on 1/1/x1 and reported the following before-tax and aftertax results. Assume there were no timing differences, no permanent differences, and no pad for possible deficiency upon an IRS audit. Thus, pretax book earnings equaled taxable income. The effective tax rate is a flat 40 percent.

	Earnings before Tax	Tax	Earnings after Tax
19x1	$ 40,000	$16,000	$24,000
19x2	50,000	20,000	30,000
19x3	30,000	12,000	18,000
19x4	20,000	8,000	12,000
19x5	(150,000)		

Required:
1. Prepare the journal entry to record the tax effect of the net operating loss carryback.
2. Prepare the journal entry to record the tax effect, if any, from the net operating loss carryforward assuming the corporation elected to carryback and then forward and—
    a. It is certain to use the carryforward.
    b. It is uncertain if they will ever use the carryforward.

Problem 8: Red Ink Corporation

Assume Red Ink Corporation began business on 1/1/x1 and reported the following book equivalent of taxable incomes, timing differences, and taxable income:

Years	Book Equivalent of Taxable Income	Timing Differences Resulting in Deferred Credits	Taxable Income (before NOL carrybacks or carryforwards)
19x1	$ 100,000	$200,000	$(100,000)
19x2	40,000	20,000	20,000
19x3	10,000	20,000	(10,000)
19x4	(20,000)	30,000	(50,000)
19x5	40,000	20,000	20,000
19x6	(50,000)	10,000	(60,000)
19x7	60,000	30,000	30,000
19x8	10,000	(10,000)	20,000
Totals	$ 190,000	$320,000	$(130,000)

Required:

Prepare a schedule showing the cumulative total of each column by year and show how much, if any, of the $130,000 cumulative taxable income has no remaining potential for resulting in a tax benefit and the year each NOL will expire.

Problem 9: Federal Income Tax Provision and the NOL

Assume that for 19x8 both the book equivalent of taxable income and the taxable income are operating losses of $90,000 with no timing differences, and that the corporate tax rate is a flat 48 percent.

Required:
1. Prepare the journal entries to record the 19x8 provision (without an audit pad) assuming that—
   a. The NOL had been carried back and fully used against prior years' taxable income taxed at a 48 percent rate.
   b. The NOL could not be utilized on a carryback but that its use as a carryforward is assured beyond any reasonable doubt.
   c. The NOL could not be utilized as a carryback, its use as a carryforward is also doubtful, and there are no deferred tax credits.
   d. The NOL could not be utilized as a carryback, its use as a carryforward is also doubtful, but there are net deferred tax credits of $60,000 which will turn around in the next seven years.
   e. The NOL could not be utilized as a carryback, its use as a carryforward is also doubtful, but there are net deferred tax credits of $30,000 which will turn around in the next seven years.
2. Prepare the journal entries to record the 19x9 federal income tax provision (without an audit pad) assuming that the 19x8 NOL was fully utilized in year 19x9, that the pretax book income was $300,000, that there were no permanent differences, that tax depreciation exceeded book depreciation by $40,000 on a net change basis, that there was a flat 48 percent tax rate, and that the 19x8 tax provision had been recorded under—
   a. 1 (*b*) above.
   b. 1 (*c*) above.
   c. 1 (*d*) above and that $10,000 of deferred tax credits other than depreciation had turned around in 19x9. (Hint: The turnaround will increase taxable income.)
   d. 1 (*e*) above and that $10,000 of deferred tax credits other than depreciation had turned around in 19x9.
3. What additional tax problems might a carryback of an NOL as under 1 (*a*) above create?

Problem 10: Federal Income Tax Provision, Deferred Credits, and the NOL

Assume that for 19x8, pretax book income was $95,000 and that taxable income was a NOL of $90,000. The difference between these two amounts being a timing difference where tax depreciation exceeded book depreciation by $100,000 on a net change basis and a permanent difference of $85,000 due to the dividend received deduction. Assume the tax rate is a flat 48 percent.

Required:

1. Prepare the journal entries to record the 19x8 tax provision (without an audit pad) assuming that—
   a. The NOL had been carried back and fully used against prior years taxable income taxed at a 48 percent rate.
   b. The NOL could not be utilized on a carryback but that its use as a carryforward is assured beyond any reasonable doubt.
   c. The NOL could not be utilized as a carryback, its use as a carryforward is also doubtful, and there are no deferred tax credits which will turn around in the next seven years.
   d. The NOL could not be utilized as a carryback, its use as a carryforward is also doubtful, but there are net deferred tax credits of $60,000 which will turn around in the next seven years.
   e. The NOL could not be utilized as a carryback, its use as a carryforward is also doubtful, but there are net deferred tax credits of $30,000 which will turn around in the next seven years.
2. Prepare the journal entries to record the 19x9 tax provision (without an audit pad) assuming that the 19x8 NOL was fully utilized in year 19x9, that the pretax book income was $300,000, that there were no permanent differences, that tax depreciation exceeded book depreciation by $40,000 on a net change basis, that there was a flat 48 percent tax rate, and that the 19x8 federal income tax provision had been recorded under—
   a. 1 (*b*) above.
   b. 1 (*c*) above.
   c. 1 (*d*) above and that $10,000 of deferred tax credits (other than depreciation) had turned around in 19x9. (Hint: The turnaround will increase taxable income.)
   d. 1 (*e*) above and that $10,000 of deferred tax credits (other than depreciation) had turned around in 19x9.
3. What additional tax problems might a carryback of an NOL as under 1 (*a*) above create?

Problem 11: Basis Differences

P Corporation acquired the stock of S Corporation in exchange for P stock, and this resulted in a "tax-free" exchange for tax purposes, while for book purposes the acquisition failed the pooling of interests requirements. Therefore, the basis of one of S's assets for financial reporting was only $20,000 (its FMV adjusted for the tax effect) and $30,000 for tax purposes. The useful life was five years with straight-line depreciation being used for financial reporting, while for tax purposes the useful life was only three years with sum-of-the-years'-digits depreciation method being used.

Required:

1. Prepare a schedule showing separately by year the amounts of the permanent difference and the amounts of the timing difference.
2. If the $20,000 were the FMV of the asset, what effect, if any, should the tax basis difference have in recording the acquisition?
3. If the amounts for book and tax basis had been reversed and if this had been a taxable rather than a tax-free acquisition of stock—
    a. What effect would this have possibly had on the life of S Corporation and (this aspect is not covered in this chapter)?
    b. What effect would this have on financial reporting assuming the $30,000 represents the FMV of the asset?

Problem 12: Dual Basis Corporation (very tough problem)

Dual Basis Corporation reported for financial accounting purposes before-tax net earnings of $120,000 and aftertax earnings of $110,000 in 19x3. There is a flat 40 percent corporate tax rate, and the capital gains rate is 25 percent.

1. Depreciation was the same for book and tax purposes on all except one new asset. This asset had a tax basis of $40,000 and a book basis of $50,000; for book purposes, a 5-year life and straight-line depreciation is used, while tax depreciation is calculated on a 3-year life using SYD depreciation. The asset was acquired on 1/1/x3.
2. As reflected on last year's tax return for 19x2, Dual had a NOL carryforward in the amount of $50,000 (for both book and tax purposes). Because of deferred tax credits which would turn around in the 7-year carryforward period, $4,000 of the tax effect of the 19x2 NOL was reported for accounting purposes in 19x2. In the current year the entire NOL has been used and the deferred credits are restored as none has yet turned around.
3. Dual sold a nondepreciable capital asset for $100,000. Its book basis was $80,000, and its tax basis was only $60,000.
4. Dual received tax-free interest on Hawaii bonds in the amount of $10,000.
5. Dual established a warranty plan for its new products. Costs of $15,000 were accrued, but as of the end of the year only $2,000 in costs have been incurred. Only the actual costs are deductible for tax purposes.
6. Dual reported equity method earnings from investees of $40,000 and received $10,000 in dividends. Of the undistributed earnings, Dual expects to realize one third through future dividends and the other two thirds through the sale of the stock.
7. Investment credits amortized for book purposes were $4,000, while investment credits earned and taken for tax purposes were $7,000.
8. During the current year, Dual had favorably settled with the IRS several past years' tax-return problems. These years are now closed by the statute of limitations. There are no items of potential dispute in the current year's tax return.

Required:

1. Beginning with the before-tax earnings of $120,000, compute both (*a*) the book equivalent of taxable income and (*b*) the actual taxable income.
2. From the amounts computed in 1 above compute the federal income tax provision (before the audit pad adjustment) and the tax liability.
3. Prepare the journal entry or entries by which Dual recorded its $10,000 federal income tax provision.

3

Accounting for Equity Investments and Asset Acquisitions

Business Motivations for Equity Investments
Tax Motivations for Equity Investments
Categories of Equity Investments and Accounting Methods
    Cost Method
    Lower of Cost or Market
    Equity Method
    Consolidation Method
Acquisition of a Corporation
Accounting Concepts on Acquisition
    Pooling of Interests
    Purchase
Illustration of the Direct and Indirect Asset Acquisition by a Corporation Using the Purchase Concept
Allocation of the Purchase Price in a Multiple Asset Acquisition
    Fair Market Value (FMV) Allocation Method
    Modified FMV Allocation Method
    Residual Allocation Method
Appendix: A Summary of Accounting Requirements for Stock Investments and for the Timing Differences Created by Undistributed Earnings

BUSINESS MOTIVATIONS FOR EQUITY INVESTMENTS

It would be difficult to compile a list of all the nontax business reasons for corporate investments in stock equities of other corporations. The major motivations, however, would be related to operations; and these reasons might also dictate the size of the investment. A listing of major nontax business reasons would include a desire—

1. To obtain control and use of certain assets (including plant and equipment, patents, or even managerial talent).
2. To get an insider's look at a corporation that might be a target for a takeover or acquisition.
3. To enter a new market or geographic area.
4. To show an improved financial picture.
5. To obtain some control over sources of raw materials.
6. To obtain some control over certain customers so as to establish a more certain market outlet for goods and services.
7. To reduce competition.

The specific business reasons may also establish whether the investment should be in preferred or common stock or both. For example, a desire to obtain the use of certain assets might require a controlling voting interest of something in excess of 50 percent, whereas a 10 percent investment might be enough to elect a director and to get insider information.

It should also be realized that many subsidiaries have been created by their parent corporations rather than having been acquired from shareholders. Thus, there are also many business reasons for separate corporate (subsidiary) status rather than having branch or divisional operations.

For example, many of the operating Bell Telephone Companies have been created so as to facilitate the establishment of rates for service and to be subject to intrastate regulation rather than interstate. This can even affect the financial structure of a subsidiary. Bell Telephone subsidiaries are often financed largely by common stock with most of the debt equity being held in the parent, AT&T Company. In many states this allows the operating companies to have higher rates for service than if the debt were in the subsidiaries' capital structures. Rates of return allowed on common stock equity are usually higher than the aftertax interest cost of debt.

TAX MOTIVATIONS FOR EQUITY INVESTMENTS

While there are many valid business reasons for corporate investments in common and preferred shares of other corporations, there are also some tax motivations which further strengthen the desire for these investments. The ability to file a consolidated tax return may be the strongest of the tax motivations where ownership of 80 percent or more (of voting and nonvoting common and of voting preferred) is required for tax consolidation.[1] And for smaller investments the "dividends received deduction" may be the most significant tax factor. This latter item is a special tax deduction applicable to dividends received from a qualifying domestic corporation. In theory, at least, the reason behind this special treatment is the reduction or elimination of multiple taxation of corporate source income. If less than 80 percent of the stock of a domestic corporation is owned, the deduction is 85 percent of the dividends received. If 80 percent or more of the stock is owned, the deduction is 100 percent of the dividends received.[2] To show how this works, assume that a corporation has $1 million cash which will not be needed for business purposes for 16 days and that this amount can be invested in 8 percent notes at face value and maturing in 16 days, or stock can be purchased and sold 16 days later (both investments will ignore brokerage costs). By buying a common stock on which a dividend has already been declared but for which the date of record will be one of the days the stock is held, a corporation can significantly increase its yield on the $1 million. Assume an annual dividend yield of 6 percent but paid quarterly for a 1.5 percent payment (see Illustration 3–1).

Illustration 3–1

	Yield on the Notes	Yield on the Stock
8% × $1,000,000 × 16/365	$ 3,507	
1.5% × $1,000,000		$15,000
Less tax at a 46% marginal rate	(1,613)	
Less tax at 46% ($15,000 − ($15,000 × 85%))		(1,035)
Aftertax yield for 16 days*	$ 1,894	$13,965

* For a full quarter the aftertax yield on the stock would remain at $13,965, while the aftertax yield on the note would increase to $10,800 (8% × $1,000,000 × ¼) × 54%).

Now suppose that the note matures and that the stock is sold after the receipt of the dividend. The note would yield $1 million at maturity, but the stock price (if the market reflected only the dividend and the passage of time) might drop to about $985,000 because the dividend has been

---

[1] *Internal Revenue Code*, secs. 1501 and 1504.

[2] *Internal Revenue Code*, sec. 243. Once 80 percent or more is owned, the effect of the 100 percent dividend received deduction can be obtained through the dividend elimination feature of a consolidated tax return.

paid. If this were true, the sale would generate a $15,000 capital loss, which if there were other capital gains would generate a $4,200 tax benefit ($15,000 × 28% capital gains tax rate). These transactions would generate the aftertax yield and proceeds given in Illustration 3–2.

Illustration 3–2

	Note	Stock
Aftertax interest	$ 1,894	
Aftertax dividend		$ 13,965
Proceeds from maturity or sale of investments	1,000,000	985,000
Tax benefit on loss on stock ($15,000 × 28%)		4,200
Total aftertax yield and proceeds	$1,001,894	$1,003,165

Note that even assuming a loss on the sale of the stock equal to the dividend received, the aftertax results are better than on the interest-bearing investment for the 16-day period. Thus, even though the before-tax loss on sale of the stock wiped out the entire before-tax dividend, there was a gain of $3,165 ($4,200 − $1,035) attributable to a 28 percent effective tax rate on the loss and only a 6.9 percent effective tax rate on the dividend income. Note also that the marginal tax rate on the interest income is 46 percent. The tax was actually higher on the $3,507 of interest income than it was on the $15,000 of dividend income. The after tax yield on the note was 4.32 percent (4.32% × $1 million × 16/365 = $1,894) and on the stock, including the loss, it was 7.22 percent (7.22% × $1 million × 16/365 = $3,165).[3] While the aftertax yield on the note would remain at 4.32 percent over extended time periods, the aftertax yield on the stock could under the assumptions in this illustration gradually drop to about 5.67 percent if the stock were sold for $1 million immediately before the next quarterly dividend payment (5.67% × $1 million × 90/365 ≈ $13,965 or the aftertax dividend).

Once 80 percent or more of the stock is owned, then corporations filing separate returns receive a 100 percent dividend deduction or they can achieve the same effect by filing a consolidated tax return which may be even more beneficial especially if some subsidiaries are suffering losses when others are producing income. The ability to use the losses of

---

[3] The reason for the 16-day holding period in this example is because the *Internal Revenue Code* (sec. 246(c)) requires more than a 15-day holding period (more than 90 days for preferred stock) before the dividend received deduction is permitted. Apparently Congress does not want corporations to roll over this type of investment more than 22.8 (365 ÷ 16) times a year or to obtain this deduction for extremely short holding periods. If it were not for this provision (established in 1958), a 1-day holding period could generate about a 510 percent return on the stock investment versus a 4.32 percent return on the note (510% × $1 million × 1/365 ≈ $13,965).

one corporation to reduce or eliminate income tax on the gains of other corporations can be a significant tax advantage.[4]

CATEGORIES OF EQUITY INVESTMENTS AND ACCOUNTING METHODS

Regardless of whether the investment in corporate stock is motivated by sound business operating reasons, by tax reasons, or both, there is a significant amount of investment by corporations in equity securities of other corporations.

For financial accounting purposes, there are four possible accounting methods the use of which normally depends on the percentage of stock ownership. These methods are the (1) cost method, (2) lower-of-cost-or-market method for certain marketable securities, (3) equity method, or (4) consolidation. (For tax purposes there are only two methods—cost or consolidation.)

Cost Method

This method applies to most small and usually temporary investments in marketable securities, but this is only the starting point in the computation of the lower-of-cost-or-market method which is discussed in the next section. The essential element dictating the use of the cost method is lack of influence or control over the investee.

> In order to achieve a reasonable degree of uniformity in application, the Board concludes that an investment (direct or indirect) of 20% or more of the voting stock of an investee should lead to a presumption that in the absence of evidence to the contrary an investor has the ability to exercise significant influence over an investee. Conversely, an investment of less than 20% of the voting stock of an investee should lead to a presumption that an investor does not have the ability to exercise significant influence unless such ability can be demonstrated.[5]

Thus for financial reporting, ownership of less than 20 percent is initially accounted for using the cost method. For tax purposes the cost method is used whenever a consolidated tax return is not or cannot be filed. Thus, for tax purposes there is no designated ownership percentage under which this method must be used.

The cost method recognizes dividends received as income as long as

---

[4] There are many other advantages and disadvantages in filing consolidated tax returns, but since the 1969 Tax Reform Act the advantages have generally exceeded the disadvantages, and this has caused a significant increase in the number of consolidated tax returns.

[5] *AICPA Professional Standards, Accounting—Current Text* (New York, 1980), par. 5131.17. Copyright (1980) by the American Institute of CPAs.

these dividends represent a distribution of earnings. For financial accounting purposes the distribution must be out of earnings since the date the stock was acquired. For tax purposes, however, the date of the stock acquisition is ignored and the dividends will be taxable as income if out of "earnings and profits"[6] accumulated after March 1, 1913 (the effective date of our current income tax law). To illustrate the significance of the date of acquisition, assume Z Corporation was formed four years ago, in year 19x1, when its stock was sold for $500,000, and it has had earnings and paid dividends on the last day of the year as given in Illustration 3–3.

Illustration 3–3

Year	Earnings	Dividends Paid at Year End	Cumulative Undistributed Earnings	Change in Paid-In Capital by Year
19x1	$14,000	$6,000	$8,000	$500,000
19x2	1,000	3,000	6,000	–0–
19x3	(4,000)	3,000	–0–	(1,000)
19x4	10,000	2,000	8,000*	–0–

* Theoretically, undistributed earnings at 19x4 are $8,000 because the excess distribution of $1,000 in 19x3 must have been out of paid-in capital and thus subsequent earnings should not be used to restore the original paid-in capital amount unless such action is taken by the board of directors. The author prefers this treatment, although it is probably contrary to some if not most current practice which would permit a distribution to create a deficit in retained earnings rather than reducing paid-in capital. Technically, liquidating distributions do not create deficits in retained earnings (nor in earnings and profits for tax purposes), instead they reduce paid-in capital.

Assuming the earnings have been the same for financial reporting and for tax purposes and that 10 percent of the Z stock had been acquired by X Corporation for $50,000 when Z Corporation was formed, there would be $600 ($6,000 × 10%) of income reported by X Corporation in year 19x1 using the cost method. In year 19x2 the income would be $300 ($3,000 × 10%). In year 19x3 the income would be only $200 (($3,000 − $1,000) × 10%) and $100 ($1,000 × 10%) would be a return of invested capital because dividends would have exceeded earnings to date. In year 19x4 the income would be $200 ($2,000 × 10%).

Now let's assume X Corporation acquired the 10 percent interest on 1/1/x2 for $50,800. The extra $800 represents 10 percent of the $8,000 of undistributed 19x1 earnings. For an analysis of the 1/1/x2 investment of X in Z stock, it is assumed that any balance in the retained earnings of Z

---

[6] "Earnings and profits" is the tax term for the account on the tax set of books which determines the tax status of dividends paid.

had affected the purchase price of the stock and thus to X should be part of paid-in capital at this date. If this were the case, then Z's results for subsequent years as viewed by X would be as given in Illustration 3–4.

In year 19x2 the financial accounting income to X would be only $100 with $200 of the $300 dividend received treated as capital recovery, that

Illustration 3–4

Year	Earnings	Dividends Paid at year End	Cumulative Undistributed Earnings	Charged to Paid-In Capital by Year
19x2	$ 1,000	$3,000	–0–	$(2,000)
19x3	(4,000)	3,000	$(4,000)	(3,000)
19x4	10,000	2,000	4,000	–0–

is, as a partial return of the $800 extra investment for purchased prior year undistributed earnings. For 19x3 the entire $300 would be capital recovery, and for 19x4, $200 would be dividend revenue. The journal entries for X Corporation for these three years would be as follows:

19x2

Investment in Z stock.....	50,800	
Cash		50,800
Cash	300	
Dividend revenue		100
Investment in Z stock.....		200

19x3

Cash	300	
Investment in Z stock.....		300

19x4

Cash	200	
Dividend revenue		200

For tax purposes, however, under the cost method, the date of stock acquisition is ignored; thus each year's taxable dividend income would have been the same as if the stock had been purchased at the inception of the Z Corporation. Illustration 3–5 gives a comparison for years 19x2 through 19x4 of dividend income received by X Corporation.

Since the stock is a marketable security which will probably be sold at some future date, the extra $400 of taxable income represents a timing difference and would result in a prepaid or deferred tax charge. This amount will reverse on the sale of the stock because this difference has

Illustration 3–5

Year	Financial Dividend Revenue	Taxable Dividend Revenue	Timing Difference
19x2	$100	$300	$200
19x3	–0–	200	200
19x4	200	200	–0–
Total	$300	$700	$400

also affected the basis of the stock for financial reporting (see Illustration 3–6). Thus, a sale of the Z stock at the beginning of 19x5 for $51,000 would result in a $700 gain for financial reporting but only a $300 gain for tax purposes. This would be recorded as follows assuming that there had been a flat 40 percent tax rate for years 19x2 through 19x5:

Illustration 3–6

	X's Investment in Z Stock	
	For Financial Reporting	For Tax Purposes
At date of purchase	$50,800	$50,800
Capital recovery 19x2	(200)	–0–
Capital recovery 19x3	(300)	(100)
Capital recovery 19x4	–0–	–0–
Basis of investment in Z Stock	$50,300	$50,700

19x5 sale:

Cash	51,000	
Investment in Z Stock		50,300
Gain on sale of investment		700

Tax effect of the sale:

FIT provision ($700 × 40%)	280	
Deferred tax charge—dividends ($400 × 40%)		160
FIT payable ($300 × 40%)		120

The credit to the Deferred Tax Charge—Dividends represents the reversal of the timing difference.

If the Z stock had been sold for $50,400, it would have produced a $100 gain for financial reporting and a $300 loss for tax purposes. But the timing difference would still be turned around. This would be recorded as:

19x5 sale:

Cash	50,400	
Investment in Z Stock		50,300
Gain on sale of investment		100

Tax effect of the sale:

FIT provision ($100 × 40%)	40	
FIT payable ($300 × 40%)	120	
Deferred tax charge—dividends ($400 × 40%)		160

The debit to Federal Income Tax Payable recognizes the effect the $300 loss would have on this liability. Both of the prior examples ignore the fact that the real tax on capital gain is often less than the rate on ordinary income, and this last entry also assumes that the capital loss will be applied.

Tax: It should be noted that due to the layering concept employed in measuring earnings and profits (E&P), the cost method for tax purposes can produce different results from the cost method for financial reporting. For federal income tax purposes the E&P amount is divided into two layers (assuming the corporation began after 3/1/13, the starting date of the present *Internal Revenue Code*). These layers are current year E&P and undistributed prior years E&P (called accumulated E&P). In the event of a deficit in accumulated E&P and a positive current E&P, a distribution in the current year would be taxable to the extent of current E&P. To illustrate, assume that Z Corporation began business on 1/1/x1 and that there are no timing nor permanent differences and that E&P equals retained earnings until the distribution in year 19x2.

Z Corporation

Year	Pretax Earnings (Losses)	Year-End Distributions
19x1	$(10,000)	-0-
19x2	5,000	$1,000
19x3	8,000	7,000

If A Corporation owned 10 percent of Z, the dividend income would be as follows:

Year	Cost Method Financial	Cost Method Tax
19x1	-0-	-0-
19x2	-0-	$ 100
19x3	$ 300	700

> For financial reporting the 19x2 dividend is considered to be from paid-in capital because of the $5,000 (−$10,000 + $5,000) deficit in retained earnings. This leaves Z with a positive retained earnings of $3,000 (−$10,000 + $5,000 + $8,000) immediately before the 19x3 distribution of $3,000 from retained earnings and $4,000 from paid-in capital. For tax purposes, dividend income with 10 percent ownership is $100 and $700, respectively, out of current E&P. The differences in dividend incomes will result in a $500 lower basis for the stock investment for book than for tax purposes.
>
> If A acquired the 10 percent interest on 1/1/x2, the cost method dividends in this example would be the same for book and for tax purposes. This is due to the layering of E&P for tax purposes; thus a distribution out of a positive current E&P is a dividend for tax purposes even when the total of accumulated E&P and current E&P is negative. It should be remembered for tax purposes that there is only (1) the treasury's version of the cost method (with the dividend received deduction for dividends from domestic corporations) or (2) consolidation in taxing the earnings of a subsidiary.

Lower of Cost or Market

In a modification of the cost method, the Financial Accounting Standards Board in *Statement No. 12* adopted the lower of cost or market concept for financial reporting of marketable equity securities (other than redeemable preferred shares, convertible bonds, or treasury shares). Under this concept the portfolio of investments (in less than 20 percent owned corporations)[7] is subdivided into current and noncurrent classifications. If a classified statement of financial position is not prepared, these investments are all considered to be noncurrent.

The carrying amount for these portfolios is the lower of the aggregate cost or market value as of the date of the position statement. Therefore, where marketable securities have been written down, they may be written back up in subsequent periods, based on market recoveries, but not to exceed cost.

The change in the carrying amount of the current portfolio is included in net earnings for the period (as a realized loss or gain), while change in the carrying amount of the noncurrent portfolio is included in the stockholders' equity section of the position statement (as a valuation allowance). If, however, a write-down in the noncurrent group appears to be other than temporary, it is accounted for as a realized loss in net earn-

---

[7] Ownership of 20 percent or more usually requires the equity method of accounting.

ings with the new basis then considered to be the cost. A change in classification of an investment between the current and noncurrent sections is made at the lower of cost or market on the date of change with any loss recognized in the determination of net earnings of the period.

While this is but a cursory coverage of this topic, it is important to note that the write-downs will affect the financial statement basis of the investment causing differences between the book and tax basis as well as differences in reported incomes. The FASB went on to state that—

> Unrealized gains and losses on marketable securities, whether recognized in net income or included in the equity section of the balance sheet, shall be considered as timing differences, and the provisions of *APB Opinion No. 11*, "Accounting for Income Taxes," shall be applied in determining whether such net unrealized gain or loss shall be reduced by the applicable income tax effect. A tax effect shall be recognized on an unrealized capital loss only when there exists assurance beyond a reasonable doubt that the benefit will be realized by an offset of the loss against capital gains.[8]

This makes the differences between book and tax even more complex than that described under the cost method without consideration of the effect of market value.

Equity Method

For financial reporting, this method records as investor earnings the percentage of stock owned times the investee's earnings. The minimum ownership percentage to justify using this method is presumed to be 20 percent or more. In practice, use of the equity method with less than a 20 percent investment is not unusual. Use of the cost method for investments above 20 percent is more rare. The equity method is also used by some parent companies in accounting for 100 percent owned subsidiaries which for one reason or another are not consolidated in the financial statements.[9]

To illustrate this method, assume that X Corporation in Illustration 3–3 had acquired 30 percent of Z Corporation a domestic entity for $150,000 at the date of inception. It should be noted that under this method, dividends are always treated as a return of invested capital; thus, there is no problem, even with a later acquisition date, in the

---

[8] *FASB Statement No. 12*, "Accounting for Certain Marketable Securities," December 1975, par. 22.

[9] AT&T's 100 percent owned Western Electric Co., Inc. (the 17th largest manufacturing firm in the Fortune 500 list for 1978), is accounted for using the equity method even though it is 100 percent owned and is included in the consolidated AT&T tax return.

determination of liquidating dividends. The journal entries to record the income and receipt of dividends are as follows:

19x1

Investment in Z stock	150,000	
Cash		150,000
To record the acquisition.		
Investment in Z stock	4,200	
Earnings from investment in Z stock		4,200
To record earnings ($14,000 × 30%).		
Cash	1,800	
Investment in Z stock		1,800
To record dividends ($6,000 × 30%).		

19x2

Investment in Z stock	300	
Earnings from investment in Z stock		300
To record earnings ($1,000 × 30%).		
Cash	900	
Investment in Z stock		900
To record dividends ($3,000 × 30%).		

19x3

Loss from investment in Z stock	1,200	
Investment in Z stock		1,200
To record loss ($4,000 × 30%).		
Cash	900	
Investment in Z stock		900
To record dividends ($3,000 × 30%).		

19x4

Investment in Z stock	3,000	
Earnings from investment in Z stock		3,000
To record earnings ($10,000 × 30%).		
Cash	600	
Investment in Z stock		600
To record dividends ($2,000 × 30%).		

Because of the degree of ownership of 20 percent or more, X Corporation is deemed to have some influence over the operations of Z Corporation. With this influence, the accounting profession has dictated the use of the equity method for financial reporting. But for tax purposes, with a 30 percent ownership the cost method would be required.[10] The in-

---

[10] For tax purposes the cost method of accounting for this type of investment is used whenever separate tax returns are being filed. The equity method of accounting for the investment in a subsidiary is used for tax purposes (to determine the basis of the stock investment) only when a consolidated tax return is filed (this requires on 80 percent ownership interest).

comes under both the cost and equity methods are as given in Illustration 3–7.

For tax purposes, X Corporation will report and pay income tax on income under the cost method while using the equity method of reporting income for financial accounting purposes. The earnings under the

Illustration 3–7

	Equity Method for Financial Reporting			Cost Method for Tax Reporting		
	Percentage Share of Earnings (1)	Basis (2)	Distributions of Prior Year Earnings (3)	Dividend Income (4)	Basis (5)	Permanent or Timing Differences (6) = (1) − (4)
19x1 Acquisition		$150,000			$150,000	
19x1 Earnings	$ 4,200	4,200				
19x1 Dividends		(1,800)	−0−	$1,800		$ 2,400
19x2 Earnings	300	300				
19x2 Dividends		(900)	$600	900		(600)
19x3 Loss	(1,200)	(1,200)				
19x3 Dividends		(900)*	600*	600	(300)	(1,800)†
19x4 Earnings	3,000	3,000				
19x4 Dividends		(600)	−0−	600		2,400
Totals	$ 6,300	$152,100		$3,900	$149,700	$ 2,400

* There is also a distribution of $300 ($900 − $600) out of paid-in capital.
† $1,200 loss plus $600 in taxable dividends = $1,800.

equity method normally exceed the dividends received. When this happens, as in year 19x1, the investor corporation must determine at the end of that year whether the undistributed portion of the accumulated earnings of the equity method investee (20%–50% owned) will (1) be paid out as dividends (as was $600 ($2,000 × 30%) in year 19x2 and again in 19x3), or (2) be realized by the investor as a capital gain on a future sale of the investment.[11] If the investment is in a subsidiary (over 50% owned), another alternative is possible, (3), remain permanently with the investee.[12] Because of the basis difference a future sale will result in a different gain amount for financial and tax purposes. If Z were a subsidiary rather than an investee and if the assumption were (3) above, then X Corporation, in its own financial statements, would not

---

[11] *AICPA Professional Standards,* par. 4096.07.-08.
[12] Ibid., par. 4095.09-.12.

provide for any income tax on the undistributed earnings of Z Corporation. If the assumption were (1) above, X would then provide for income tax in year 19x1 on the basis that the timing difference (undistributed earnings) will reverse through future dividend distributions.[13] For 19x1 this amount would be $165.60 (46% × 15% ($4,200 − $1,800)) if it is assumed that all of the $2,400 of undistributed earnings will be received as dividends. This amount also reflects the fact that at a maximum only 15 percent of these earnings of the domestic corporation are taxed which shows the effects of the 85 percent dividends received deduction. If the assumption were (2) above, the tax, to provide for the undistributed 19x1 earnings, would assume that they will be realized in some future period as a capital gain. This would cause a tax of $672 ($2,400 × 28%)[14] to be provided.

It should be noted that the anticipated capital gains tax is more than four times larger than the tax provided for the anticipated dividends. (This fact often causes investors to force investees or subsidiaries to pay large dividends shortly before the sale of the stock. This act can save significant tax dollars unless the IRS determines the dividend to be part of the sales price.)

If management wishes to report smaller earnings or to have what could almost amount to a secret reserve, they would attempt to justify the use of the capital gain route. This would establish a "liability" for future taxes which might last many decades before being paid, if ever.

If the investment had qualified and if assumption (3) had been chosen, no additional tax would have been recorded in year 19x1. But an additional tax would have been incurred in years 19x2 and 19x3 because of the $600 distributions of 19x1 earnings. This tax increase would be recorded, but as part of the regular tax provision for the year and not as an extraordinary item. This would also raise questions about the continued propriety of assumption (3). The experience in this case indicates that indefinite retention of earnings is unlikely.

If assumption (1) had been selected, the tax on the $600 distributions of 19x1 earnings would have already been provided for, but this would result in the turnaround of a timing difference in 19x2 and 19x3 of $41.40 ($600 × 6.9%).[15] There also would have to be an adjustment in 19x3 to reflect the fact that the loss ($1,200) had removed some of the anticipated future dividend paying potential. This would be done by debiting the

---

[13] If Z were a domestic subsidiary and owned 80 percent or more, the dividend received deduction would be 100 percent.

[14] The current alternative capital gains rate is 28 percent for corporations. In addition, some of the capital gain income is a tax preference, and in certain cases this can result in a 15 percent additional tax.

[15] A 46 percent tax rate less an 85 percent dividend received deduction reduces that rate to only a 6.9 percent effective rate.

Deferred Tax Credit account and crediting the Federal Income Tax Provision account for $82.80 ($1,200 × 6.9%).

If assumption (2) had been selected for 19x1, the deferred tax liability would have to be reduced for the differing effective tax rates (ordinarily instead of capital gain) for the distributions in 19x2 and 19x3 out of 19x1 earnings. For each year the deferred tax account would have to be debited and the Federal Income Tax Provision account would be credited (reduced) by $126.60 ($600 × (28% − 6.9%)) plus the tax liability of $41.40 for the turnaround of the timing difference. In addition, the deferral for tax on the undistributed earnings eliminated by the $1,200 loss would have to be removed. This would be done by debiting the deferred tax "liability" for $336 ($1,200 × 28%) and in effect crediting income by crediting the Federal Income Tax Provision account.

This process is summarized in the tables and journal entries of Illustration 3–8.

Illustration 3–8

A. Undistributed earnings

Year	Equity Method Earnings from Z	Taxable Income from Z (before the dividends received deductions)	Undistributed Earnings (a timing difference)	Cumulative Undistributed Earnings
19x1	$ 4,200	$1,800	$ 2,400	$2,400
19x2	300	900	(600)*	1,800
19x3	(1,200)	−0−	(1,200)*	600
		600	(600)*	−0−
19x4	3,000	600	2,400	2,400

* Reversals of timing differences.

B. Tax on undistributed earnings

Year	Undistributed Earnings	Assumption 1: Dividend, 6.9% Rate	Assumption 2: Capital Gain, 28% Rate	Assumption 3: Indefinite Reversal*
19x1	$ 2,400	$165.60	$ 672	−0−
19x2	(600)	(41.40)	(168) = ($41.40 + $126.60)†	$41.40 ($600 × 6.9%)
19x3	(1,200)	(82.80)‡	(336)‡	−0−
	(600)	(41.40)	(168) = ($41.40 + $126.60)	41.40 ($600 × 6.9%)
Totals for years:				
19x1–x3	−0−	−0−	−0−	$82.80
19x4	2,400	165.60	672	−0−

* To use this method you need over 50 percent ownership. It is shown here only to illustrate possible effects.

† The $41.40 = $600 × 6.9%, while the $126.60 = $600 × (28% − 6.9%), or the excess of anticipated tax over the amount incurred.

‡ Excess of anticipated tax over actual due to the $1,200 loss.

The part of the journal entry for the income tax on the undistributed earnings for each assumption by years would be as shown in Illustration 3–9.

If Z Corporation had operated at a loss in year 19x1, there would be no effort by X to anticipate future tax benefits. The accounting position of anticipating losses but not gains or tax benefits would preclude X Corporation from recording a tax benefit from its share of the Z loss unless realization of the loss is assured beyond any reasonable doubt. The

Illustration 3–9

The part of the journal entries for the federal income tax on the undistributed earnings for assumption (1) (dividend income) would be:

	19x1		19x2		19x3		19x4	
	Dr.	(Cr.)	Dr.	(Cr.)	Dr.	(Cr.)	Dr.	(Cr.)
FIT provision	165.60						165.60	
Deferred tax credit ($2,400 × 6.9%)		(165.60)						(165.60)
Deferred tax credit			41.40		41.40			
FIT payable ($600 × 6.9%)				(41.40)		(41.40)		
Deferred tax credit					82.80			
FIT provision ($1,200 × 6.9%)						(82.80)		

The part of the journal entries for the federal income tax on the undistributed earnings for assumption (2) (capital gain rate) would be:

	19x1		19x2		19x3		19x4	
	Dr.	(Cr.)	Dr.	(Cr.)	Dr.	(Cr.)	Dr.	(Cr.)
FIT provision	672						672	
Deferred tax credit ($2,400 × 28%)		(672)						(672)
Deferred tax credit ($600 × 28%)			168.00		168.00			
FIT payable ($600 × 6.9%)				(41.40)		(41.40)		
FIT provision ($600 × (28% − 6.9%))				(126.60)		(126.60)		
Deferred tax credit					336.00			
FIT provision ($1,200 × 28%)						(336.00)		

The part of the journal entries for the federal income tax on the undistributed earnings for assumption (3) (indefinite reversal) would be:

	19x1	19x2	19x3	19x4
	Dr. (Cr.)	Dr. (Cr.)	Dr. (Cr.)	Dr. (Cr.)
FIT provision	–0–	41.40	41.40	–0–
FIT payable*	–0–	(41.40)	(41.40)	–0–

* 600 × 6.9% = $41.40, or the tax incurred when it was assumed that none would be paid.

Illustration 3–10

Assumptions Made in Recording the Tax on Undistributed Earnings	Undistributed Earnings—Actual Transaction			
	Received as a Dividend*	Received as Capital Gain	Never Received	Reduced by Future Losses
1. These earnings to be received as dividends (from an investee or a subsidiary).	Recorded tax correct†	Recorded tax too low‡	No tax should have been recorded§	Recorded tax too high‡
2. These earnings to be received as capital gain on sale of the stock (of an investee or a subsidiary).	Recorded tax too high‡	Recorded tax correct†	No tax should have been recorded§	Recorded tax too high‡
3. These earnings will never be received, that is, they will be permanently invested in the subsidiary (subsidiary only).	Tax should have been recorded‖	Tax should have been recorded‖	No tax recorded—correct†	No tax recorded—correct†

* Assumes that the 85 percent dividend deduction applies and that the 100 percent does not apply.
† This means that the tax recorded, if any, was recorded in the proper amount (ignoring the time value of money between the year recorded and the year paid).
‡ Adjustment in previously recorded tax liability required in the year the previously undistributed earnings are (1) received or (2) reduced or eliminated by current year losses.
§ The recorded tax results in a "permanent liability" unless removed and taken into earnings.
‖ The tax should be recorded when the assumption changes or when the previously undistributed earnings are received.

entire process of anticipating tax on undistributed earnings of domestic subsidiaries is summarized in Illustration 3–10.

Consolidation Method

In almost all cases, consolidation produces the same net earnings as the equity method. In fact, the equity method is often called a one-line consolidation. Thus, the only significant difference is the amount of disclosure.

For consolidation, the individual corporate entities are assumed to be all one entity. Thus, in the statement of financial position all assets (except the investment in subsidiary account) and liabilities are added (after offsetting of intercorporate accounts). The investment in the subsidiary account is in effect removed, and the subsidiary's assets and liabilities are substituted for it. In the earnings statement the "Equity in the Subsidiary's Earnings" account (assuming the equity method of accounting for this investment) is removed so as to leave only the subsidiary's various revenue and expense accounts.

Going back to Illustration 3–3, assume that Z Corporation's earnings consisted of the figures given in Illustration 3–11.

Illustration 3–11

	19x1	19x2	19x3	19x4
Sales	$100,000	$100,000	$110,000	$120,000
Cost of goods sold	(40,000)	(50,000)	(70,000)	(60,000)
Gross margin	60,000	50,000	40,000	60,000
Depreciation	(30,000)	(40,000)	(40,000)	(40,000)
Other operating expenses	(16,000)	(9,000)	(4,000)	(10,000)
Net earnings	$ 14,000	$ 1,000	$ (4,000)	$ 10,000

Now if X Corporation acquires 100 percent of Z and prepares consolidated financial statements, each component (sales, cost of goods sold, etc.) would be added to the same category for X in order to arrive at consolidated sales, cost of goods sold, and so forth. If X Corporation in its separate financial statements used the equity method, "equity in the earnings of subsidiary Z" would be shown in the separate (unconsolidated) earnings statement of X in the amount of $14,000 for year 19x1. Since this amount is the same as the revenues less expenses of Z, the only difference between consolidation and use of the equity method is the amount of disclosure.

The nondisclosure aspect of the equity method is usually much more significant in the statement of financial position. Here, under the equity method, the investment in subsidiary account is shown rather than the total assets and liabilities of the subsidiary which would be added to those of the parent company upon consolidation. The opportunity to keep large amounts of liabilities out of the consolidated statements by using the equity method, which only reflects net assets, may be attractive to some corporate managements.

The consolidation method ignores the legal reality of separate legal entities and combines the various accounts of two or more corporations as though they were really only one entity. This is an economic concept which is valid *only* to the shareholders and creditors of the parent corporation. Creditors of a subsidiary, unless the debts of that corporation have been guaranteed by another, can usually look only to the legal entity for payment.

It should be noted that the cost, lower of cost or market, and equity methods apply to the parent corporation's records while consolidation, in effect, creates a new entity. It is also important to realize that there are no formal books (journals, general ledger, etc.) for this consolidated entity. Thus, the various journal entries necessary to consolidate the various separate entities into the single economic entity are made on a work sheet only and normally are not recorded in any general ledger.

This has been just a mere introduction to the consolidation method. Later chapters will go into considerable detail showing how to consolidate entities that have intercorporate transactions, minority ownership, changing ownership interests, and so forth. The necessary work sheets will also be developed at that point.

ACQUISITION OF A CORPORATION

Before one of the four accounting methods for stock investments can be employed, a corporation must own stock of another corporation. But a corporation, in effect, can be acquired by acquiring all of its assets; however, this does not leave a stock investment to be accounted for.

An asset is normally acquired either by purchasing it from outsiders or by building it yourself. In building or constructing an asset, all the related costs are accumulated to form the recorded basis of the new asset. This basis, however, can be quite different from the fair market value (FMV) of the asset (e.g., a construction corporation's profit would not be included). A purchased asset, however, is recorded at the cost to the buyer, and this should normally equal its FMV. The seller's basis is normally thought to be irrelevant to the purchaser (this is not always true as will be seen later).

There are essentially two ways to purchase assets: (1) direct acquisition and (2) indirect acquisition by acquiring control of a corporation that owns the assets. Thus, assets can be purchased outright or acquired indirectly by acquiring control of a corporation owning the desired assets. In either form the compensation for the acquisition can be cash, other assets, and/or stock of the acquiring corporation.

Acquiring a corporation's assets can be diagramed as in Illustration 3–12.

Illustration 3–12

A. Direct acquisition

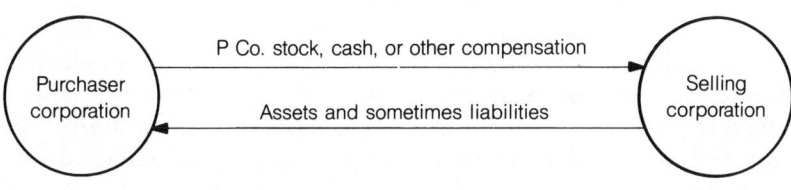

B. Indirect acquisition

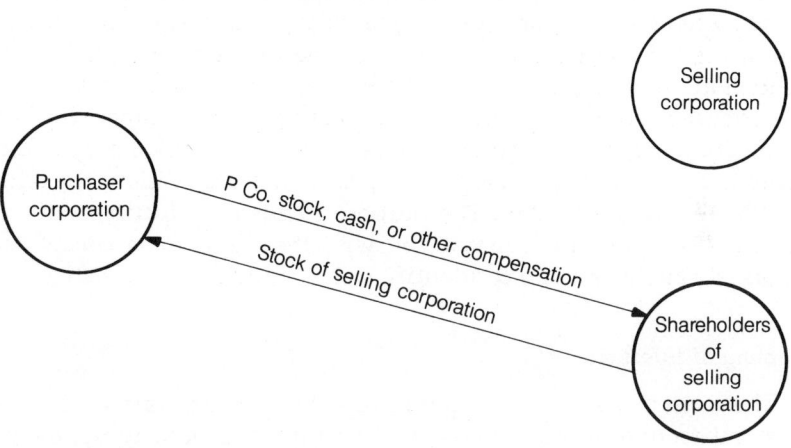

The stock of a corporation is, of course, acquired from the shareholders, whereas in a direct asset purchase, the assets are acquired from the corporation itself. In any acquisition, direct or indirect, the compensation paid can be cash, other assets, or stock or other securities of the acquiring corporation or some combination thereof. An exchange of stock of an acquiring corporation for stock of an acquired corporation is sometimes accounted for as if this were not a purchase (i.e., it is recorded as a pooling of interests). The direct acquisition of assets in exchange for stock of the acquiring corporation can also be accounted for, in certain cases, as a pooling. The concept of pooling (always an exchange of stock for assets or for stock) is discussed in more depth in the next major section of this chapter; it is sufficient to note, at this time, that a pooling is not a purchase.

It should be realized that when the compensation paid is the same, (1) the acquisition *of the assets* of a corporation followed by the liquidation of the selling corporation produces the same result (except for tax consequences) as (2) the acquisition *of the stock* of the corporation followed by a liquidation of that acquired corporation (a subsidiary). The first method is a direct asset acquisition, and the second is an indirect asset acquisition. In the second case the newly acquired subsidiary does not have to be liquidated; it could be accounted for in a consolidation and achieve the same result, a single entity.

ACCOUNTING CONCEPTS ON ACQUISITION

There are a lot of things to consider in the acquisition of another corporation, and among these are whether it is desirable to have the purchase or the pooling of interests concept applied. While it must be emphasized that these are not elective concepts, in many cases an acquisition can be constructed so as to use the desired concept. If certain criteria are met, the pooling of interests concept applies; and if any of the criteria is not met, the purchase concept applies. In other words, the acquisition can be framed so as to either pass or fail the established criteria. In a later chapter on planning corporate acquisitions the criteria will be reviewed in detail. The purpose of this introduction to the two concepts is merely to acquaint you with their impact on consolidated financial statements and to identify some of their characteristics.

Pooling of Interests

There are many ways to make payment in the acquisition of another corporation or of its assets; however, for this concept to apply, the payment must be in common stock of the so-called acquiring corporation. Technically, under this concept there is no acquiring or acquired corporation but instead it is assumed that the shareholders of each have pooled their interests (thus, the name of the concept, pooling of interests).

To illustrate a pooling, assume that A Corporation exchanges 2,000 shares of its previously unissued $50 par value A stock for all of the 1,000 outstanding shares of B stock with a par value of $100 (Illustration 3–13).

Illustration 3–13

A. Corporate structure before the exchange of shares

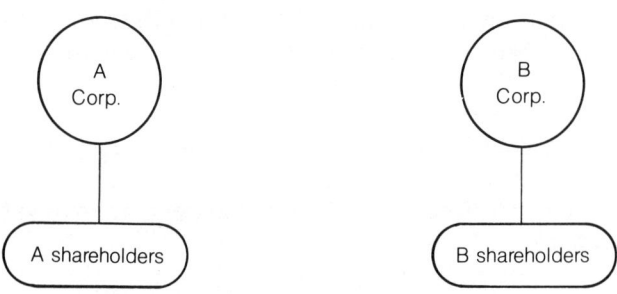

B. The exchange of shares

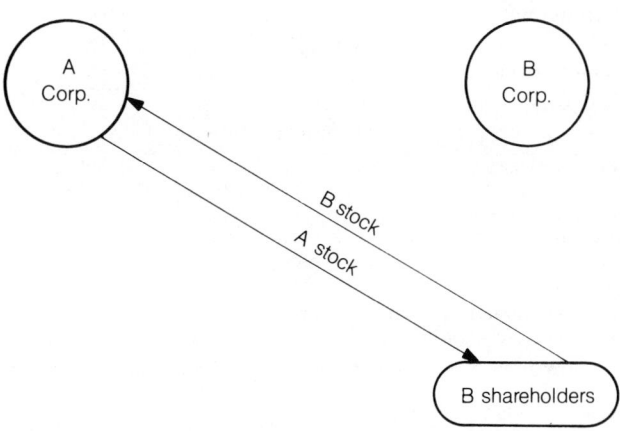

C. Corporate structure after the exchange of shares

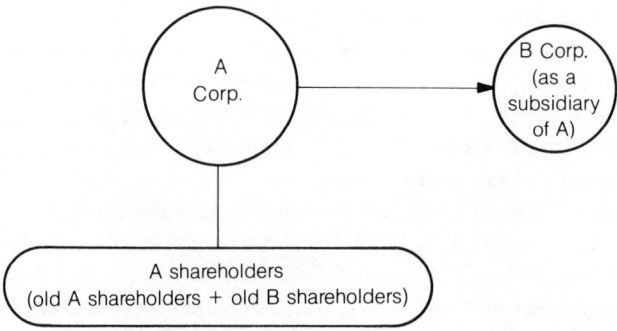

Under the pooling of interests concept it is assumed that B Corporation has always been a subsidiary of A and that the former B shareholders have always been shareholders of A Corporation. To achieve this, it is necessary to substitute the ownership equity represented by the newly issued A stock for the acquired B stock. The stock ownership equities immediately before the exchange of shares and the entry on A's books upon the issuance of the A stock are shown in Illustration 3–14. Note that no entry is needed on B's books (other than to note the change in shareholders).

Illustration 3–14

Stock ownership equities

	A Corporation	B Corporation
A Corporation stock, $50 par	$150,000	
B Corporation stock, $100 par		$100,000
Additional paid-in capital	200,000	225,000
Retained earnings	500,000	300,000
Total shareholders' equity	$850,000	$625,000

A's journal entry

Investment in B stock	625,000	
A stock		100,000
Additional paid-in capital		225,000
Retained earnings		300,000

To record on A's books the issuance of 2,000 shares of $50 par value A stock for the 1,000 shares of $100 par value B stock in a pooling of interests (no entry on B's books).

It should be noted that in Illustration 3–14 the newly issued A stock has, in effect, been substituted for the B stock, and the additional paid-in capital ($225,000) and retained earnings ($300,000) have been recorded on A's books as though A and B Corporations had always been together as one corporation.

It should also be noted that the account "Investment in B Stock" is recorded at the book value of the net assets of B Corporation, and thus later upon consolidation these assets and liabilities can be directly substituted for this investment account. There will be more elaboration on this in subsequent chapters.

In addition, it should be observed that if subsidiary B were liquidated into A, the result would be the same as if A had issued its stock for all of the assets and liabilities of B followed by a liquidation of B which would then put the A stock in the hands of the old B shareholders. This could be diagrammed as shown in Illustration 3–15.

Illustration 3–15

A. The exchange

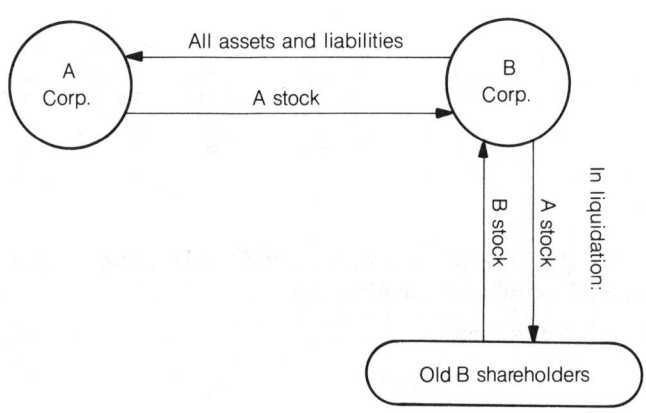

B. After the exchange

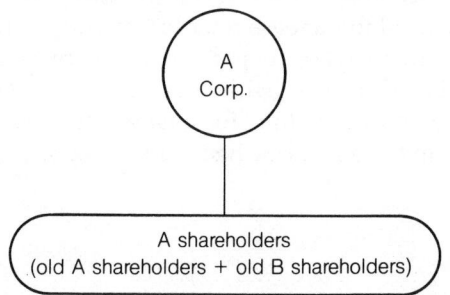

In every case under the pooling concept, when stock is exchanged for stock, the investment account will be recorded at an amount equal to the net assets underlying the book value of the acquired stock.[16] But the credit side of the entry can be affected by either the par values or the number of shares exchanged. In the previous example, the par value of the A stock issued in the exchange ($100,000) equaled the par value of the B stock acquired ($100,000). If the par value of the A stock were different from $50 per share, it would have affected the journal entry. The credit side of the journal entry would have been as given in Illustration 3–16 for the various par values as indicated.

---

[16] There is an exception to this rule when the transaction is a taxable exchange for tax purposes. The effects of "taxable poolings" are discussed in a later chapter.

Illustration 3–16

	Par Value of A Corporation Stock				
	$50	$1	$100	$200	$300
Common stock	$100,000	$ 2,000	$200,000	$400,000	$600,000
Additional paid-in capital ...	225,000	323,000	125,000	(75,000)	(200,000)
Retained earnings	300,000	300,000	300,000	300,000	225,000
Totals	$625,000	$625,000	$625,000	$625,000	$625,000

Note that the journal entry for $1 par value A stock would have appeared as follows on A's books:

Investment in B stock..................................	625,000	
A stock...		2,000
Additional paid-in capital............................		323,000
Retained earnings		300,000

The par value account, which appears as $100,000 on B's books but as only $2,000 on A's books, forces us to record the extra $98,000 as additional paid-in capital, bringing it to $323,000 ($225,000 × $98,000) on A's books.

While recording par value at a decreased amount can increase additional paid-in capital, it cannot be used to increase retained earnings. In the opposite direction, however, an increase in par value can reduce retained earnings but only after the additional paid-in capital has been exhausted in making up the increased par value. To illustrate this, the following journal entry assumes that the A stock had a $300 per share par value:

A's books:

Investment in B stock..................................	625,000	
Additional paid-in capital............................	200,000	
A stock...		600,000
Retained earnings		225,000

The $600,000 (2,000 shares × $300 par value) credit to A Stock is in effect composed of the $100,000 par value of the B stock on B's books plus the $225,000 additional paid-in capital associated with the B stock; and since this is still $275,000 short of the $600,000 amount, the Additional Paid-In Capital account on A's books is debited to make up the difference. But since this is only $200,000, $75,000 must be removed from retained earnings and capitalized as par value. This reduces the retained earnings increase on the pooling from $300,000 to $225,000.

Thus, the aggregate retained earnings ($800,000 in this example—$500,000, A, and $300,000, B) can never be increased in a pooling of interests but it will be decreased when the par value of the newly issued stock exceeds the par value of the acquired stock by more than the aggregate additional paid-in capital amount ($425,000 in this case).

A pooling combination is somewhat difficult to explain on a theoretical basis, but an understanding of the theory is almost essential for correct accounting. In theory, the two firms are treated as though they have always been one firm. Thus, when common stock is issued in exchange for shares of another company, it is treated as though the amount that was originally paid in (both in par value and in additional paid-in capital) for the shares being acquired is currently received for the shares now being issued. If the total paid-in capital originally received (by the other corporation) is less than the par value of the shares being issued, the difference should come from additional paid-in capital of the issuing corporation (as it might if there had only been one corporation). If this is still insufficient, retained earnings are then capitalized as par value to make up the difference. Obviously, if the corporation had always been together, their retained earnings should be reflected as one company. This is the theory underlying the above pooling entries. It is important to realize that no entries are made on the books of the corporation whose stock is being acquired, but that corporation's owners' equity accounts will, under the single entity concept, affect the entry on the records of the corporation issuing stock in the stock-for-stock exchange.

Purchase

Under this concept of acquisition, there is always an acquiring corporation, and it is buying either the stock (an indirect asset acquisition) or assets of the acquired corporation. Therefore, the recorded book values of the net assets of the acquired corporation are of little value for consolidated financial reporting because a purchase requires that market or fair values be recorded. In the stock-for-stock example given in Illustration 3–14 under the pooling concept), assume that the A shares were worth $350 per share and that the criteria for a pooling of interests were not met. In this case the acquisition would be recorded as a purchase on A's book as follows:

Investment in B stock....................................	700,000	
A stock ($50 par value).............................		100,000
Additional paid-in capital.............................		600,000

It should be noted that in a purchase the acquiring corporation's Retained Earnings account is never increased or decreased; it is not affected. It should also be noted that under the purchase method it would be a sheer coincidence if the fair value of the stock issued ever equaled the underlying book value of the acquired stock. Upon consolidation, the difference between the price paid and the book value of the net assets of the acquired corporation has to be properly allocated. Later chapters will go into this in great detail, stressing both the tax and financial reporting aspects. If assets had been acquired directly, the $700,000 purchase price plus any liabilities assumed would have to be allocated among the assets acquired as of the date of acquisition.

ILLUSTRATION OF THE DIRECT AND INDIRECT ASSET ACQUISITION BY A CORPORATION USING THE PURCHASE CONCEPT

We-Haul Trucking, Inc., has an opportunity to purchase from the Ace Trucking Corporation a tractor for $5,000 cash and the assumption of an equipment note payable with a 3-year life to maturity. The note has a current book value of $9,000 ($10,000 face value less $1,000 of unamortized discount) but with an $11,000 present value (due to changing interest rates). As an alternative, We-Haul can purchase all the assets of Fleet Trucking for $30,000 plus assumption of liabilities. These assets include, among other items, a tractor.

Purchasing the tractor from Ace Trucking for cash plus assumption of the liability would be recorded as follows:

Tractor	16,000	
Cash		5,000
Note payable		10,000
Premium on note payable		1,000
To record the acquisition of a tractor for cash plus the assumption of a related equipment note payable.		

It should be noted in the above purchaser's journal entry that the seller's book value of the tractor (original cost less accumulated depreciation) and of the equipment note ($9,000) are totally irrelevant pieces of information. In other words, the purchaser records the asset at its fair market value (FMV) at the date of acquisition, and this should normally equal the present value of the consideration given (cash in this case plus the liability assumed).[17]

The acquisition of all of Fleet's assets and liabilities presents many more difficulties than the single asset acquisition. First, all the assets of Fleet Trucking, both tangible and intangible, must be identified and valued, and all liabilities must be ascertained and valued. If the price the buyer is willing to pay plus the present value of the liabilities to be assumed equals FMV of the total identified assets, the buyer records the entry similar to that for the single asset acquisition. The only additional problem is in obtaining the FMV of *each* asset and liability, whereas

---

[17] An acquisition with a trade-in (the acquisition of a new truck by trading in an old truck and paying or receiving the difference in FMVs) presents special problems not covered here.

with a single asset acquisition the FMV could be assumed to equal the cash plus the present value of the liability assumed. In a group purchase, just the identification of *all* assets acquired (tangible and intangible) and all liabilities assumed can be a significant problem. Note that just as in the single asset case, the seller's book values of the various assets and liabilities are generally irrelevant to the purchaser. And only in the sheerest of coincidences would the FMV ever equal the book values of each item.

It sometimes happens that the total price that the buyer pays exceeds the FMV of all identifiable tangible and intangible assets. In this case accountants normally assume that the purchaser anticipates higher future earnings from this acquisition than the FMVs of all identifiable assets would indicate, and we call this excess "goodwill."

If the total price the buyer pays including liabilities assumed is less than the FMV of all identified assets, the carrying amounts of certain acquired assets are reduced below their FMVs. This aspect is covered in depth later; it is sufficient to note at this stage that this does not create a "bad-will" account.

Illustration 3–17 gives We-Haul's acquisition of all the assets, including goodwill, and liabilities of Fleet Trucking. At this point the shareholders of Fleet Trucking own a corporation whose only asset is $30,000 cash. The corporation could now liquidate or start a new business. The net $12,800 gain on the sale is composed of the $2,000 gain on trucking contracts and the agreement not to compete, the $3,000 gain on the repair equipment, the $150 loss on the office calculator, the $5,000 gain on the tractor, the $1,000 loss on the liabilities (due to changing interest rates it would cost $4,000 to buy and retire the $3,000 note payable), and the $3,950 gain on the sale of the goodwill.

> **Tax:** The detailed breakdown of gains and losses is necessary for tax purposes because different tax rates might apply to different items of gain or loss.

The journal entry on We-Haul's books to record the purchase would be as follows:

Trucking contracts and agreement not to compete	2,000	
Repair equipment	3,000	
Office equipment	50	
Tractor	15,000	
Other assets	10,000	
Goodwill	3,950	
Liabilities (at face value plus premium)		4,000
Cash		30,000

To record We-Haul's acquisition of the assets and assumption of the liabilities of Fleet Trucking for $30,000.

Illustration 3–17

Fleet's Assets and Liabilities	FMV (cost to buyer)	Seller's Book Value	Cost in Excess of Book Value
Trucking contracts and agreement not to compete	$ 2,000	–0–	$ 2,000
Fully depreciated repair equipment	3,000	–0–	3,000
Office calculator	50	$ 200	(150)
Tractor	15,000	14,000	5,000
Accumulated depreciation—tractor	—	(4,000)	
Other assets	10,000	10,000	–0–
Liabilities	(4,000)	(3,000)	(1,000)
Total identified net assets (tangible and intangible)	26,050	17,200	$ 8,850
Cost of net assets to buyer	30,000	30,000	
Total cost in excess of book value (seller's net gain or loss)		12,800	
Identified excess		8,850	
Unidentified excess—goodwill	$ 3,950	$ 3,950	

The journal entry for Fleet's *sale* of its assets would be:

Cash (received)	30,000	
Liabilities	3,000	
Accumulated depreciation—tractor	4,000	
Tractor		14,000
Office calculator		200
Other assets		10,000
Gain on sale of assets		12,800

To record Fleet Trucking's sale of all of its assets and transfer of all liabilities to We-Haul Trucking for $30,000.

In the purchase of a group of assets the fair value of each item should be separately determined. When there are many individual items involved (e.g., depreciable assets and inventories), this could be a time consuming and expensive process. Nevertheless it would be needed; and once a FMV has been established it should always represent both the buyer's cost and the seller's sales price.

> **Tax:** Sometimes a buyer and seller will allocate differently while agreeing on the total price—while this could be an honest disagreement, it is usually an effort at tax avoidance and may be unjustified. The seller receives what the buyer pays for an asset and vice versa.

Assume that instead of buying the assets directly from Fleet, We-Haul acquires 100 percent of the capital stock of Fleet Trucking from its shareholders for $30,000.[18] Now there is a parent (We-Haul) and a subsidiary (Fleet) relationship. This corporate structure (parent and subsidiary) can continue and be accounted for in consolidated financial statements, or Fleet can now be liquidated into the parent We-Haul Trucking.

The acquisition entry on We-Haul's Books would be as follows:

Investment in Fleet Trucking stock	30,000	
Cash		30,000

If Fleet were liquidated (into the parent We-Haul Trucking), the liquidation entries on each set of books would be as follows:

Fleet's books:

Accumulated depreciation—tractor	4,000	
Liabilities	3,000	
Stockholders' equity (equals net assets)	17,200	
Office calculator		200
Tractor		14,000
Other assets		10,000

To liquidate the subsidiary, Fleet Trucking, into its parent, We-Haul Trucking, immediately after the acquisition of 100 percent of Fleet stock.

We-Haul's books:

Trucking contracts and agreement not to compete	2,000	
Repair equipment	3,000	
Office calculator	50	
Tractor	15,000	
Other assets	10,000	
Goodwill	3,950	
Liabilities		4,000
Investment in Fleet Trucking stock		30,000

To eliminate the investment account and liquidate the Fleet Trucking subsidiary into the We-Haul parent corporation.

If, instead of liquidation, the parent corporation prefers to operate Fleet as a subsidiary, the $30,000 investment account on We-Haul books would be replaced in the consolidated statement of financial position by the assets and liabilities of Fleet. If this substitution entry were not made, the acquired corporation's book values would have an effect on the financial statements and this would be double counting. The effects of the *substitution* work sheet entry is shown on the work sheet of Illustration 3–18 and is presented in much greater depth in the chapters that follow.

---

[18] Because of tax consequences of corporate liquidation, and the possible creation of additional income tax liabilities (which will be discussed later), the price for buying the assets will usually differ from the price for buying the stock.

Illustration 3–18

A. Asset acquisition and assumption of liabilities

	We-Haul Trial Balance before Acquisition	We-Haul's Acquisition of Fleet's Assets and Liabilities	We-Haul Trial Balance after Direct Acquisition of Fleet's Assets and Liabilities
Cash	$ 50,000	$(30,000)	$ 20,000
Other assets	60,000	10,000	70,000
Liabilities	(20,000)	(4,000)	(24,000)
Stockholders' equity	(90,000)		(90,000)
Trucking contracts and agreement not to compete		2,000	2,000
Repair equipment		3,000	3,000
Office calculator		50	50
Tractor		15,000	15,000
Goodwill		3,950	3,950
Totals	–0–	–0–	–0–

B. Stock acquisition followed by liquidation of the subsidiary

	We-Haul Trial Balance before Acquisition	Acquisition of Fleet Stock	Liquidation of Fleet into We-Haul (substitution entry)	We-Haul Trial Balance after Liquidation of Fleet
Cash	$ 50,000	$(30,000)		$ 20,000
Other assets	60,000		$ 10,000	70,000
Liabilities	(20,000)		(4,000)	(24,000)
Stockholders' equity	(90,000)			(90,000)
Investment in Fleet stock		30,000	(30,000)	–0–
Trucking contracts and agreement not to compete			2,000	2,000
Repair equipment			3,000	3,000
Office calculator			50	50
Tractor			15,000	15,000
Goodwill			3,950	3,950
Totals	–0–	–0–	–0–	–0–

C. Stock acquisition followed by consolidation

	We-Haul Trial Balance after Buying Fleet Stock	Fleet Trucking Trial Balance	Substitution Book Value	Substitution Cost in Excess of Book	Consolidated Trial Balance
Cash	$ 20,000				$ 20,000
Investment in Fleet stock	30,000		$(17,200)	$(12,800)	–0–
Other assets	60,000	$ 10,000			70,000
Liabilities	(20,000)	(3,000)		(1,000)	(24,000)
Stockholders' equity	(90,000)	(17,200)	17,200		(90,000)
Trucking contract				2,000	2,000
Repair equipment				3,000	3,000
Office calculator		200		(150)	50
Tractor		14,000		1,000	15,000
Accumulated depreciation		(4,000)		4,000	
Goodwill				3,950	3,950
Totals	–0–	–0–	–0–	–0–	–0–

The value of the Fleet capital stock is directly related to the value of its net assets. Therefore, the end result of an asset acquisition or of a stock acquisition followed by liquidation or consolidation should be identical.[19] In theory, this means that (1) all acquisitions of corporations by buying 100 percent of the capital stock are equivalent to total asset acquisitions where all liabilities are assumed[20] and (2) after one corporation acquires all of the stock or assets and liabilities of another there is really only one *economic entity* not two or more. The end result of the acquisition process (the financial statements) should be identical regardless of whether the assets and liabilities were acquired directly or indirectly.

The symmetry of the acquisition routes ((A) total asset and liability acquisition, (B) 100 percent stock acquisition followed by liquidation or (C) 100 percent stock acquisition followed by consolidation) and the one corporation (one economic entity) concept are illustrated in the work sheets of Illustration 3–18 (note that the ending trial balance amounts are the same for every account).

ALLOCATION OF THE PURCHASE PRICE IN A MULTIPLE ASSET ACQUISITION

In either the direct or indirect acquisition routes, when the purchase concept is required, one of the major problems is determining the proper amounts by which to record or reflect the acquired assets.

Fair Market Value (FMV) Allocation Method

Suppose $48,000 is paid for five tractors. A quick allocation could produce a $9,600 ($48,000 ÷ 5) unit price, but this assumes that each truck is in every significant aspect identical. More often the trucks may be of different years, weights, types, and so on. In this case an independent appraisal may be necessary to determine the FMV of each tractor. An independent appraiser, however, may not know what is to be paid, and without this bias the total appraised value will probably be something other than $48,000. Suppose the appraisal tends to confirm a favorable purchase by giving the figures in Illustration 3–19.

---

[19] This again ignores the fact that the method of acquisition can affect income tax liabilities. This could, of course, impact differently on the price for the acquisition of assets as opposed to the price for the acquisition of stock.

[20] Frequently a corporation will acquire only certain assets or only the assets and not assume the liabilities. There are often practical reasons for favoring the asset acquisition over the stock acquisition route. Note, however, in the We-Haul illustration to buy all the assets and not acquire any liabilities would require a $34,000 initial cash outlay. In other situations, as we will see later, the stock acquisition may possess some advantages.

Illustration 3–19

Tractor	FMVs
1	$10,000
2	20,000
3	15,000
4	5,000
5	10,000
Total appraised value	$60,000

An *allocation* of the purchase price based on appraisal values would produce the basis for each tractor given in Illustration 3–20.

Illustration 3–20

Tractor	Basis*	
1	$ 8,000	= 10/60 × $48,000
2	16,000	= 20/60 × $48,000
3	12,000	= 15/60 × $48,000
4	4,000	= 5/60 × $48,000
5	8,000	= 10/60 × $48,000
Total basis	$48,000	

* The alternative would be to record each tractor at its appraisal value and to recognize a $12,000 ($60,000 − $48,000) gain on the purchase. Due to the nature of most appraisals this is not usually an acceptable alternative. If this transaction were between the corporation and a major shareholder (related parties), the $12,000 bargain might be credited to donated capital with the assets recorded at their appraisal values.

Suppose the appraisal results showed the figures given in Illustration 3–21.

Illustration 3–21

Tractor	FMVs
1	$ 7,000
2	17,000
3	12,000
4	2,000
5	7,000
Total appraised value	$45,000

We might question the wisdom of the buyer. Since we have purchased only five tractors and nothing else, the excess $3,000 ($48,000 − $45,000) cannot be designated as goodwill. In this case, if the appraisal is accurate, the $3,000 should be written off as a loss and the tractors recorded at their respective FMVs. Presumably this type of transaction should not occur because the appraisal should take place before the tractors are purchased.

Modified FMV Allocation Method

The FMV allocation method works reasonably well when similar assets are purchased; it, however, is sometimes criticized when dissimilar assets are acquired. Suppose that five assets are again acquired for $48,000 but they consist of $10,000 in cash, a $19,000 face value treasury note, inventory, a tractor, and an unidentified intangible item called goodwill.[21] An appraiser now provides the figures given in Illustration 3–22.

Illustration 3–22

Asset	FMVs
Cash	$10,000
Treasury note	20,000
Inventory	15,000
Tractor	5,000
Goodwill	10,000
Total appraised value	$60,000

Based on relative FMVs, the figures in Illustration 3–23 would be produced.

Illustration 3–23

Asset	Basis
Cash	$ 8,000
Treasury note	16,000
Inventory	12,000
Tractor	4,000
Goodwill	8,000
Total basis	$48,000

---

[21] In a real situation goodwill would probably not be appraised.

It is wrong, however, to assign cash a value less than its face value; therefore, a modification of the FMV method would assign full fair value to the cash, and in most cases to the Treasury note and allocate the rest. This would produce the figures in Illustration 3–24.

Illustration 3–24

Asset	Basis	
Cash	$10,000	
Treasury note	20,000	
Inventory	9,000	= 15/30* × $18,000†
Tractor	3,000	= 5/30 × $18,000
Goodwill	6,000	= 10/30 × $18,000
Total basis	$48,000	

* $60,000 − $10,000 − $20,000 = $30,000.
† $48,000 − $10,000 − $20,000 = $18,000.

In practice with an appraisal value of tangible assets in excess of the price paid, goodwill often disappears. This would produce the results given in Illustration 3–25.

Illustration 3–25

Assets	Basis	
Cash	$10,000	
Treasury note	20,000	
Inventory	13,500	= 15/20 × $18,000
Tractor	4,500	= 5/20 × $18,000
Goodwill	–0–	
Total basis	$48,000	

Suppose that instead of acquiring these five assets for $48,000 in cash, the buyer pays only $45,000 and assumes a $3,000 equipment note payable for which the tractor has been pledged as collateral. Some would allocate the note directly to the asset to which it is pledged. If consideration is given to goodwill, the allocation of basis shown in Illustration 3–26 would be produced.

Illustration 3–26

Asset	Net FMV	Basis
Cash	$10,000	$10,000
Treasury note	20,000	20,000
Inventory	15,000	8,333 = 15/27* × $15,000†
Tractor ($5,000 − $3,000)	2,000	4,111 = $3,000 + 2/27 × $15,000
Goodwill	10,000	5,556 = 10/27 × $15,000
Totals	$57,000	$48,000

* $60,000 − $10,000 − $20,000 − $3,000 = $27,000.
† $48,000 − $10,000 − $20,000 − $3,000 = $15,000.

Residual Allocation Method

The same argument for full FMV application that applies to the cash amount can be applied, but perhaps to a lesser extent to other assets. Thus, the residual method of allocation is favored by many. Based on the above appraisal, the residual method would assign full FMVs to each item in order of liquidity. This would produce the figures given in Illustration 3–27. In practice, inventory would seldom be stated at full FMV at retail. It would often be limited to replacement cost or perhaps to net realizable value less a normal profit margin as under the lower of cost or market inventory valuation method. To the extent that it is replacing drawn-down Lifo layers, it might even be assigned those particular values.

Illustration 3–27

Asset	Basis
Cash	$10,000
Treasury note	20,000
Inventory	15,000
Tractor	3,000 ($48,000 − $10,000 − $20,000 − $15,000)
Goodwill	−0−
Total basis	$48,000

Because of the problems in accounting for goodwill and for tax reasons, most accountants (including the author) would probably favor the residual method but adjusted to reflect inventory at replacement cost or some other amount below fair value. Note, however, that if the buyer paid more than the FMVs for the identifiable assets, the entire excess would normally be considered goodwill under either method, or stated another way, no asset may be assigned an amount in excess of its FMV, except perhaps for goodwill.

> **Tax:** The Internal Revenue Service (IRS) generally prefers (at least when the price paid is less than the total FMV of the identified assets) the modified FMV allocation method in that it would result in a basis for goodwill (if it exists) which is not depreciable for tax purposes.

Obviously, if the seller and the buyer are to have the same allocation, they must agree on the appraisal *and* on the allocation method. Frequently the seller will not have access to the buyer's appraisal and vice versa; they should nevertheless agree on the final allocation amounts regardless of the method employed. This makes economic sense; it does not smell of tax avoidance which sometimes borders on evasion; and it saves problems with later IRS audits. For financial reporting, however, there is no requirement that the seller and buyer use the same allocation.

> **Tax:** Due to favorable capital gains taxation and the speed with which an asset can be written off, the buyer and seller are in most cases in adversary roles. That is, on the assets that the buyer would normally want a high basis (e.g., inventory), the seller would want the smallest allocation of the sales price; and on the items that the seller would want a high allocation, the buyer would normally want the lowest possible allocation (e.g., goodwill).

APPENDIX: A SUMMARY OF ACCOUNTING REQUIREMENTS FOR STOCK INVESTMENTS AND FOR THE TIMING DIFFERENCES CREATED BY UNDISTRIBUTED EARNINGS

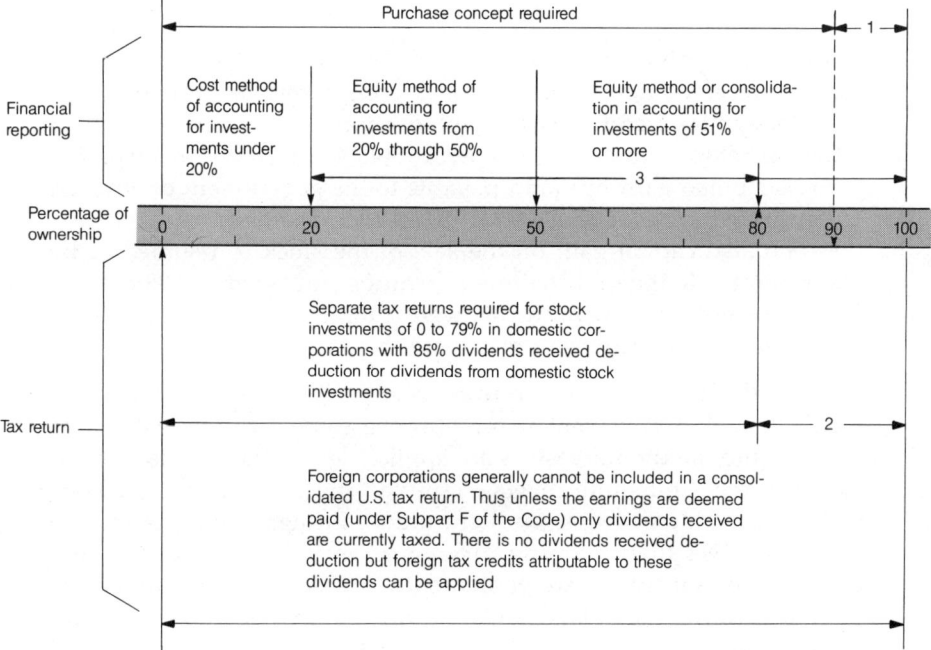

1. Pooling concept must be used if all requirements (12 items) are met; otherwise the purchase concept must be used.
2. Either separate tax returns with 100 percent dividends received deduction for domestic subsidiaries owned 80 percent or more *or* a consolidated return with 100 percent dividend elimination for domestic subsidiaries owned 80 percent or more must be filed (a foreign subsidiary generally cannot be included in the consolidated return with a domestic parent and domestic subsidiaries).
3. Because of the use of either the equity method or consolidation for financial reporting, with ownership between 20 percent and 100 percent, there is a potential second corporate income tax on undistributed earnings recorded as income from equity method investees (20 percent through 50 percent owned) and from subsidiaries (51 percent through 100 percent owned). Where a second corporate income tax is recorded, it is because the undistributed earnings are viewed as a timing difference. There is no potential second corporate income tax for cost method investees (corporations owned less than 20 percent) because this method does not record as income the undistributed earnings. There is also no potential second corporate income tax on domestic subsidiaries owned 80 percent or more because at this level of ownership there is a 100 percent dividends received deduction on separate tax returns and 100 percent dividend elimination on consolidated tax returns. There could be a potential second corporate income tax on undistributed earnings of a foreign subsidiary (51 percent to 100 percent owned) because there is no dividend received deduction for these earnings and these subsidiaries cannot be included in a consolidated U.S. tax return. The potential second or U.S. corporate income tax on the undistributed earnings of a foreign subsidiary might be reduced or eliminated entirely by the foreign tax credit.

For equity method investees (20 percent through 50 percent owned) the potential second corporate income tax, on the recorded but undistributed earnings of the investee, is recorded as either a tax on anticipated dividends or as a tax on anticipated capital gain or as a combination of both.

1. Anticipated dividends would be eligible for the 85 percent dividends received deduction (unless a foreign investee in which case the foreign tax credit would apply). For domestic investees the effective tax rate would be only 6.9 percent (46% − (85% × 46%)) on the undistributed earnings (and payable to the government only when distributed and not when anticipated and recorded).
2. Anticipated capital gain on the sale of the stock is assumed to be attributable to the undistributed earnings and taxed at a 28 percent effective tax rate. (Again if this were a foreign investee the foreign tax credit might reduce or eliminate this tax.)

For subsidiaries (50 percent up to 80 percent if domestic and from 50 percent through 100 percent if foreign) the same two alternatives as apply to equity method investees are applicable and there is also a third possibility, the "indefinite reversal criteria." Because of absolute control, the APB believed that undistributed earnings could result in a permanent rather than a timing difference. Thus, if the undistributed earnings of the subsidiary are permanently invested and the subsidiary is not sold or if the subsidiary can be liquidated tax-free into the parent, then the indefinite reversal criteria are met and no potential second corporate income tax need be recorded. (For corporate joint ventures the same rules apply as for subsidiaries.)

For example, assume P acquires 70 percent of S, a domestic corporation, on 1/1/x1 and that S earns $20,000 in 19x1 and distributes $8,000 in dividends. If P were to record the earnings and dividends from S in a single entry, it would appear as follows:

```
Cash ($8,000 × 70%) ..................................... 5,600
Investment in S stock ($12,000 × 70%) ................... 8,400
    Earnings from S stock ($20,000 × 70%) ...................    14,000
```

In recording the tax for P (or P and S consolidated financial statements) the $5,600 dividend would be included in the tax return while the $8,400 of undistributed, but currently recorded, earnings would not be currently taxed. But *if* a future tax on the $8,400 is anticipated, it must be currently recorded as follows:

Anticipated as future dividends:

```
FIT provision ............................................. 580
    Deferred tax credit (46% × ($8,400 − (85% × $8,400))
    or 6.9% × $8,400 ≈ $580) .............................    580
```

Anticipated as future capital gain:

FIT provision	2,352	
Deferred tax credit ($8,400 × 28% = $2,352)		2,352

The future tax could also be anticipated as zero under the "indefinite reversal criteria." Of course, in the future if any of these anticipations proved to be incorrect, they would have to be adjusted in that future period but not as extraordinary items. (It should be noted that this gives management a significant opportunity for manipulating net earnings from subsidiaries or corporate joint ventures.)

Another problem area not covered in depth in this chapter or text concerns what to do with tax accruals or lack thereof when an investee (20%–50% owned) becomes a subsidiary (51%–100% owned) or vice versa. This problem is discussed in *AICPA Profession Standards, Accounting—Current Text,* pars. 4095.13 and 4096.10.

There is also a problem of accounting for the potential tax benefit of losses of an investee or subsidiary which are recorded by the parent company before being recognized for tax purposes. The potential tax benefit of these losses is given the same treatment as net operating losses as discussed in Chapter 2, Accounting for Income Taxes—Special Considerations.

REVIEW QUESTIONS

1. There are various reasons for one corporation to acquire stock of another corporation.
    a. List three nontax business motivations for these investments.
    b. List two tax motivations for these investments.
2. a. How does the "dividend received deduction" work?
    b. How does it effect the tax rate on the dividend income of an investing corporation?
3. For financial accounting, what are the four methods for accounting for an investment in another stock?
4. a. Which two of the methods in (3) above normally produce the same net earnings figures?
    b. What would be required in order for the cost or lower-of-cost-or-market methods to produce the same amount of net earnings as the' equity method or consolidation?
    c. Which three methods result in journal entries which are posted to a corporation's general ledger?
5. a. What income tax filing methods are applicable to corporations that consolidate for financial reporting?
    b. When corporations (1) file separate tax returns or (2) when they file consolidated tax returns, what method(s) are used for tax purposes to account for an investment in the subsidiary corporation's stock?

6. *a.* What is a liquidating dividend for accounting purposes?
   b. What is a liquidating dividend for tax purposes?
7. *a.* Why is a 20 percent ownership percentage significant for financial reporting?
   b. What significance, if any, does the 20 percent have for tax purposes?
8. When using the equity method or consolidating for financial reporting, what problem does undistributed current earnings of a subsidiary present?
9. *a.* In recording the potential second corporate income tax on undistributed subsidiary (50%–80% owned) earnings, what are the three possible tax effects?
   b. In recording the potential second corporate income tax on undistributed earnings of any equity method investee (20%–50% owned), what are the two possible tax effects?
10. What basic concept distinguishes a pooling from a purchase?
11. *a.* In a pooling where shares of stock of a corporation are acquired, what amount is recorded for the asset—investment in subsidiary stock?
    b. In a purchase where shares of stock of a corporation are acquired, what amount is recorded for the asset—investment in subsidiary stock?
12. *a.* In what circumstances *involving a pooling* will the aggregate retained earnings be decreased upon exchange of stock?
    b. In what circumstances *involving a pooling* will the aggregate retained earnings be increased upon exchange of stock?
    c. In what circumstances *involving a purchase* will the retained earnings of the acquiring corporation be increased or decreased?
13. What is the one economic entity concept and how does it differ from the separate legal entity concept?
14. What are the distinguishing characteristics of a direct versus an indirect asset acquisition?
15. What are some of the practical problems in recording a direct or an indirect acquisition using the purchase concept?
16. In a multiple asset acquisition what allocation methods are used to prorate the lump-sum purchase price?

PROBLEMS

Problem 1: Cost and Equity Methods

Johnson Company, Inc., began business on 1/1/x1 and reported the following earnings (losses) and dividend payments (on the last day of the year) in its first three years of life!

Year	Earnings (Losses)	Dividends
19x1	$ 30,000	$ 8,000
19x2	(20,000)	5,000
19x3	50,000	35,000

Required:

1. Hartley, Inc., purchased 20 percent of the Johnson stock for $40,000 on 1/1/x1. Determine the following for Hartley, Inc.'s investment in Johnson stock at the end of each year:

	Cost Method		Equity Method		Tax Purposes	
Year	Income	Basis of Stock	Income	Basis of Stock	Income*	Basis of Stock
19x1						
19x2						
19x3						

* Before the dividend received deduction.

2. Galliart, Inc., purchased 20 percent of the Johnson Stock on 1/1/x2 for $44,000. Determine the following for the Galliart investment in Johnson stock at the end of each year:

	Cost Method		Equity Method		Tax Purposes	
Year	Income	Basis of Stock	Income	Basis of Stock	Income*	Basis of Stock
19x2						
19x3						

* Before the dividend received deduction.

Problem 2: Dividend, Income, and Basis

Assume Maher Corporation was formed four years ago, in 19x1, and had earnings and paid dividends in the following amounts on the last day of the year:

Year	Earnings	Dividends
19x1	$14,000	$6,000
19x2	1.000	3,000
19x3	(4,000)	3,000
19x4	10,000	2,000

Assume that 20 percent of the Maher Corporation stock had been acquired by Keller Corporation for $40,000 at the date that Maher Corporation was formed. Also assume that Danos Corporation acquired 20 percent of Maher Corporation on 1/1/x2 for $41,600 ($40,000 + ($8,000 × 20%)) of undistributed earnings).

Required:

1. For Keller Corporation, give the following for its investment in Maher Corporation:

Year	Cost Method Earnings	Cost Basis of Investment	Taxable Income (before the dividends received deduction)	Tax Basis of Investment	Equity Method Earnings	Equity Basis of Investment
19x1 ...						
19x2 ...						
19x3 ...						
19x4 ...						

2. For Danos Corporation, give the following for its investment in Maher Corporation:

Year	Cost Method Earnings	Cost Basis of Investment	Taxable Income (before the dividends received deduction)	Tax Basis of Investment	Equity Method Earnings	Equity Basis of Investment
19x2 ...						
19x3 ...						
19x4 ...						

Problem 3: Equity Method Corporation

Equity began business on 1/1/x1 and has incurred the following earnings and losses for both book and tax purposes:

Year	Net Earnings	Dividends Paid at Year-End
19x1	$(10,000)	–0–
19x2	4,000	$1,000
19x3	8,000	5,000

Funding Corporation has purchased 20 percent of Equity on 1/1/x1 for $50,000.

Required:

1. For Funding's investment in Equity determine the amounts under each of the following possibilities:

	For Financial Reporting				For Tax	
Year	Equity Method Earnings	Equity Basis of Stock	Cost Method Earnings	Cost Basis of Stock	Earnings	Basis of Stock
19x1						
19x2						
19x3						

2. Assume Funding's investment in Equity was made on 1/1/x2 for $48,000. Then determine the amounts under each of the following possibilities:

	For Financial Reporting				For Tax	
Year	Equity Method Earnings	Equity Basis of Stock	Cost Method Earnings	Cost Basis of Stock	Earnings	Basis of Stock
19x2						
19x3						

3. For 2 above record in journal entry format the tax effect of the timing differences (between the equity method earnings and the earnings for tax purposes) for years 19x2 and 19x3. Assume a flat 40 percent tax rate and only dividend revenue.

Problem 4: Wheels Corporation

Wheels Corporation was formed four years ago, in 19x1, and had earnings and paid dividends in the following amounts on the last day of the year:

Year	Earnings	Dividends
19x1	3,000	1,000
19x2	1,000	3,000
19x3	(5,000)	1,000
19x4	10,000	1,000

Boley Corporation acquired 30 percent of Wheels Corporation stock on 1/1/x2 for $40,000.

Required:

1. For Boley Corporation supply the following for its investment in Wheels:

	Equity Method Income	Equity Basis of Investment	Taxable Income*	Tax Basis of Investment
12/31/x2				
12/31/x3				
12/31/x4				

* Before the dividend received deduction.

2. For each year record Boley Corporation's income tax attributable to its investment in Wheels assuming a 40 percent flat tax rate, the anticipation of receiving all net earnings in the form of dividends but without assurance of being able to use all losses against future earnings.

Problem 5: The Minnow and Whale

	A Corporation	B Corporation
Assets	$400,000	$7,600,000
Liabilities	$ 20,000	$4,000,000
Capital stock (A, $100 par; B, $10 par)	100,000	1,000,000
Additional paid-in capital	—	200,000
Retained earnings	280,000	2,400,000
Total equities	$400,000	$7,600,000

A Corporation is going to issue 35,000 shares of its capital stock to B Corporation in exchange for all of B's assets and liabilities. B is then going to liquidate by distributing the A shares to B Corporation shareholders. Stock of A Corporation is currently selling for $115 per share. B Corporation liabilities are stated at fair value, and its assets are at historical cost less proper depreciation where applicable.

Required:

1. Record in general journal form the issuance of the 35,000 shares of stock by A Corporation; assume this is a pooling of interests.
2. Record the same thing as in (*a*) above but assuming a purchase which establishes $25,000 of goodwill. (Assume A is the acquiring corporation.)
3. What is the best estimate of the market value per share of B Corporation shares immediately preceding the acquisition of B by A. (Assume both corporations are publicly traded.)
4. The controller of B Corporation told you that B Corporation is really the acquiring corporation. How can you support this conclusion? (Recording this transaction under the purchase method with B Corporation being the acquiring corporation is covered in a later chapter.)

Problem 6: Purchase or Pooling Stock Acquisition

A CORPORATION

Assets	$5,000,000	
Liabilities		$2,000,000
Capital stock, $10 par		100,000
Additional paid-in capital		400,000
Retained earnings		2,500,000
Totals	$5,000,000	$5,000,000

B Corporation exchanges 40,000 of its previously unissued $10 par value stock for all the A Corporation outstanding stock. Market value of the B stock is

$100 per share and $400 per share for the A stock. Assume that the book values of A's assets and liabilities equals their fair values.

Required:
1. a. Record the acquisition on B's books as though it were a purchase.
    b. Same as (a) except as a pooling of interests.
2. The same as one above except the par value of the B stock is only $1.
    a. Record the acquisition on B's books as though it were a purchase.
    b. Same as (a) except as a pooling of interests.

Problem 7: Basket Purchase and Liquidating Corporations

Basket has just purchased all of the assets of Liquidating Corporation in exchange for 3,000 shares of Basket $10 par value common stock which has a fair value of $150 per share. Liquidating's assets were as follows:

	Book Value	Fair Value
Cash	$ 10,000	$ 10,000
Treasury note	20,000	20,000
Inventories	30,000	40,000
Building	80,000	70,000
Accumulated depreciation	(20,000)	
Land	40,000	100,000
Patent	-0-	200,000
Goodwill	50,000	10,000
	$210,000	$450,000

Liquidating did not have any liabilities and the owners' equity sections of both corporations appeared as follows immediately before this transaction:

	Liquidating	Basket
Capital stock, par values, $1 for Liquidating and $10 for Basket	$ 2,000	$ 950,000
Additional paid-in capital	10,000	50,000
Retained earnings	198,000	850,000
	$210,000	$1,850,000

Required:
1. Record this acquisition as a purchase on Basket's books.
2. Record this acquisition as a pooling on Basket's books.
3. Record this as a sale on Liquidating's books.
4. Record this as a pooling on Liquidating's books.
5. Record the liquidation of Liquidating Corporation assuming the above transaction had been a "tax-free" sale of its assets.

Problem 8: Big Oil and Power Companies

Big Oil has just purchased all the noncash assets of Power for $65,000,000; the assets are as follows:

	Book Value	Appraisal Value
Accounts receivable (net)	$ 100,000	$ 80,000
Inventories	400,000	100,000
Machinery (net)	500,000	400,000
Ships (net)	10,000,000	9,000,000
Pipeline (net) (underground)	20,000,000	10,000,000
Oil wells (net)	30,000,000	50,000,000
Buildings (net)	200,000	200,000
Land	100,000	220,000
	$61,300,000	$70,000,000

Required:
1. Allocate the cost to each asset using the residual method.
2. Allocate the cost to each asset using the FMV allocation method.
3. Show the value to be assigned to each asset if $73,000,000 had been paid for these assets.

4

Substitution of Assets and Liabilities for Capital Stock Investments in Preparing Consolidated Statements

Substitution under the Purchase Concept at the Date of Acquisition
    Investment at the Book Value of the Underlying Net Assets
    Investment at More than the Book Value of the Underlying Net Assets
    Investment at Less than the Underlying Book Value—100 Percent Acquisition
    Investment at Less than the Underlying Book Value—Majority Acquisition

Substitution under the Purchase Concept Subsequent to the Date of Acquisition
    Investment at the Underlying Book Value—100 Percent Acquisition
    Investment at More than the Underlying Book Value—100 Percent Acquisition
    Investment at More than the Underlying Book Value—Majority Acquisition
    Investment at Less than the Underlying Book Value—Majority Acquisition

Substitution under the Pooling of Interests Concept
    Substitution at Acquisition—with 90 Percent Minimum Ownership.
    Substitution Subsequent to Acquisition—with 90 Percent Minimum Ownership

Appendix: Possible Combinations of Book Value, Fair Value, and Cost

The prior chapter introduced the accounting concepts of pooling and purchase and also the cost and equity methods used in accounting for investments in capital stock of other companies. This chapter will describe how consolidated financial statements are prepared from records maintained on the cost or equity methods. For ease of illustration this chapter will assume that only the statement of financial position is being prepared. Subsequent chapters will illustrate the preparation of a consolidated earnings statement.

Generally, consolidated statements will not include a subsidiary unless it is more than 50 percent owned. It should be remembered that these statements are prepared from work sheets only; the underlying records of the individual entities are not changed. Normally, the equity method will be used in the investing corporation's books (parent corporation) to record transactions affecting the investment. In some cases, accountants might employ the cost method (even though this would violate the 20 percent or more ownership limit) instead of the equity method in accounting for an investment in a subsidiary.[1] Thus, the accounting method used by the parent corporation will impact on the substitution entry as will the accounting concept of pooling or purchase.

SUBSTITUTION UNDER THE PURCHASE CONCEPT AT THE DATE OF ACQUISITION

Investment at the Book Value of the Underlying Net Assets

Since consolidated statements bring together two or more separate legal entities as though they were one entity, the assets and liabilities of the subsidiary must replace the parent's "investment in subsidiary" account in forming the consolidated entity. To illustrate this, assume X acquires 100 percent of the capital stock of Z on 12/31/x1 for $100,000 and that the owner's equity section of Z's statement of financial position appears as in Illustration 4–1.

The combination of the work sheet and substitution entry allows us to add Z's assets and liabilities to those of X after removing both the investment in Z account and Z's owners' equity accounts. In journal entry format (but remember this is only made on a work sheet and is not

---

[1] It is also possible that a subsidiary might own less than 20 percent of another subsidiary which is directly owned over 50 percent by the parent corporation. In this case the investing subsidiary may be using the cost method on its separate financial statements to account for this investment. These multiple intercorporate investments will be covered in a later chapter.

Illustration 4–1

Z Corporation	Stock Equity (also net assets)
Capital stock	$ 40,000
Additional paid-in capital	10,000
Retained earnings	50,000
Total	$100,000

* Although under the purchase concept an acquisition at book value is highly unlikely, it is assumed here for ease in illustration. It is also assumed that the book value of each asset and liability of Z equals its fair value; thus, there are no offsetting differences.

recorded on the books for either X or Z) the substitution entry would appear as:

Capital stock	40,000	
Additional paid-in capital	10,000	
Retained earnings	50,000	
Investment in Z stock		100,000

This entry avoids double counting the net assets of Z, once when Z asssets and liabilities are added to those of X and within X itself in the Investment in Z Stock account. The work sheet would appear in abbreviated form as in Illustration 4–2.

Illustration 4–2

X AND Z CORPORATIONS
Consolidated Work Sheet
(Position Statement Only)

Statement of Financial Position	X Corporation	Z Corporation	Substitution Entry		X and Z Corporations Consolidated
			Dr.	Cr.	
Investment in Z stock	100,000	–0–		100,000	–0–
Other assets	800,000	160,000			960,000
Total assets	900,000	160,000			960,000
Liabilities	200,000	60,000			260,000
Capital stock	150,000	40,000	40,000		150,000
Additional paid-in capital	300,000	10,000	10,000		300,000
Retained earnings	250,000	50,000	50,000		250,000
Total equities	900,000	160,000	100,000	100,000	960,000

Another way to understand the consolidation (one entity) process is to visualize what the acquisition entry would have looked like if X had acquired the assets and liabilities of Z instead of acquiring the stock of Z. X actually recorded the acquisition of the stock as:

Investment in Z stock..................................	100,000	
Cash		100,000

If the assets and liabilities had been acquired, they would have been recorded in place of the Investment in Z Stock account, and then the consolidation (one company status) would have been achieved directly. Thus, it is necessary to convert the above stock acquisition entry into an acquisition of assets and liabilities via a consolidated work sheet. Therefore, the substitution entry removes the investment account and the subsidiary's owners' equity accounts, and the work sheet provides the vehicle by which the assets and liabilities of the two corporations are added together in forming one entity.

In many acquisitions, less than 100 percent ownership is acquired. In fact, one of the advantages of acquiring stock rather than assets is that *control* over the assets can be achieved at a lower cost by acquiring only a majority of the stock. Thus, X acquires 100 percent control over Z's assets by acquiring 60 percent of Z for $60,000. This leaves a minority interest of 40 percent. This can be diagramed and analyzed as shown in Illustration 4–3. The X shareholders own all of X which, through the Investment in Z Stock account, includes 60 percent of Z.

Illustration 4–3

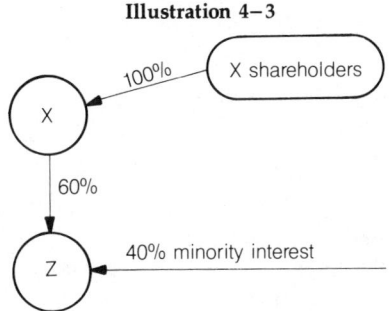

Z Corporation	Equal to Net Assets	60 Percent Majority	40 Percent Majority
Capital stock	$ 40,000	$24,000	$16,000
Additional paid-in capital	10,000	6,000	4,000
Retained earnings	50,000	30,000	20,000
	$100,000	$60,000	$40,000

Because all of Z's assets and liabilities and not just 60 percent of each are added to those of X, a minority interest amount will appear in the consolidated statement of financial position. Again, in journal entry form the work sheet substitution entry would appear as:

Capital stock	40,000	
Additional paid-in capital	10,000	
Retained earnings	50,000	
Investment in Z stock		60,000
Minority interest		40,000

While this work sheet *only* entry is removing the Investment in Z Stock account, it is establishing an amount for minority interest. Thus, there is no account entitled minority interest on the books of either X or Z. It comes into existence only when the consolidated (economic) entity is developed.

Investment at More than the Book Value of the Underlying Net Assets

Under the purchase concept, acquisition of the stock of a successful corporation is likely to cost more than the book value of the underlying net assets. Thus, assume that X acquires 100 percent of Z but pays $120,000 for the stock. It may be recalled from the prior chapter that the investment cost must be allocated to the identifiable tangible and intangible assets and liabilities, and if it exceeds the fair value of the net assets, a Goodwill account will be created. Assume in this illustration that the $20,000 excess over book value is allocated $15,000 to land and that all other assets and liabilities of Z have fair values equal to their book values. Thus, the remaining $5,000 is allocated to goodwill. This can be analyzed as in Illustration 4–4.

Illustration 4–4

Z Corporation	Net Assets
Capital stock	$ 40,000
Additional paid-in capital	10,000
Retained earnings	50,000
Book value	100,000
Increase in land	15,000
Establishment of goodwill	5,000
Price paid	$120,000

The work sheet substitution entry (in journal entry format) would appear as follows:

Capital stock	40,000
Additional paid-in capital	10,000
Retained earnings	50,000
Land	15,000
Goodwill	5,000
Investment in Z stock	120,000

Thus, the *increase* in land and goodwill will appear as such only on the *consolidated* statement of financial position and not on the books of either X or Z. The $15,000 and $5,000 amounts, however, are part of the $120,000 Investment in Z Stock account on the books of X.

Now suppose that X acquires only 60 percent of Z paying $72,000 for that interest. In this case the $72,000 is 60 percent of $120,000. The analysis leads to the three possibilities given in Illustration 4–5 for recording the $12,000 ($72,000 − ($100,000 × 60%)) excess of cost over underlying book value.

Illustration 4–5

Alternative 1: Fair value allocation for majority interest portion only

Z Corporation	Net Assets	60 Percent Majority	40 Percent Minority
Capital stock	$ 40,000	$24,000	$16,000
Additional paid-in capital	10,000	6,000	4,000
Retained earnings	50,000	30,000	20,000
	100,000	60,000	40,000
Land (15/20 × $12,000)	9,000*	9,000 ⎫	–0–
Goodwill (5/20 × $12,000)	3,000†	3,000 ⎬ $12,000	–0–
	$112,000	$72,000	$40,000

* Or 60% × $15,000 of FMV in excess of book value for land.
† Or 60% × $5,000 of FMV in excess of book value, which is zero, for goodwill.

Alternative 2: Total fair value allocation for land (and other assets and liabilities if any) but majority interest only on goodwill

Z Corporation	Net Assets	60 Percent Majority	40 Percent Minority
Capital stock	$ 40,000	$24,000	$16,000
Additional paid-in capital	10,000	6,000	4,000
Retained earnings	50,000	30,000	20,000
	100,000	60,000	40,000
Land	15,000	9,000 ⎫	6,000
Goodwill ($72,000 − $60,000 − $9,000)	3,000	3,000 ⎬ $12,000	–0–
	$118,000	$72,000	$46,000

Illustration 4–5 (continued)

Alternative 3: Total fair value allocation for all assets and liabilities—only land and goodwill in this case

Z Corporation	Net Assets	60 Percent Majority		40 Percent Minority
Capital stock	$ 40,000	$24,000		$16,000
Additional paid-in capital	10,000	6,000		4,000
Retained earnings	50,000	30,000		20,000
	100,000	60,000		40,000
Land	15,000	9,000	$12,000	6,000
Goodwill	5,000	3,000		2,000
	$120,000	$72,000		$48,000

It should be noted that all three alternatives have the same effect on the majority interest. The only difference is in the reporting of the assets and the minority interest.

Alternative 3 seems clearly preferable, at least in this case where we had established in the first example the fair value of both the land and goodwill by acquiring 100 percent and then, in the next example, basing the price of 60 percent on the amount established for 100 percent. In a real-world situation, however, things are seldom this clear-cut. In fact, the prices paid for different percentages may not be proportional. For example, there may well be a bonus paid for 80 percent as opposed to something less than 80 percent because at this level the subsidiary can be included in a consolidated tax return. There may also be a "bonus" paid for 90 percent in a stock-for-stock exchange, for this level of ownership is needed for the application of the pooling of interests concept. Tender offers to acquire a particular corporation's stock normally contain a provision which makes the offer good only if at least 80 percent (or some other percentage) of the stock is tendered.

Of these three possibilities, the FASB, while not specifically precluding alternative 3, appears to favor alternative 1 or possibly 2. Perhaps it did not choose to support alternative 3 because one cannot always presume that a price paid for 60 percent is equal to 60 percent of what 100 percent ownership would cost. In practice, alternative 1 is used almost exclusively even though it is not the best method conceptually.

> An acquiring corporation should allocate the cost of an acquired company to the assets acquired and liabilities assumed. . . .
>
> First, all *identifiable* assets acquired, either individually or by type, and liabilities assumed in a business combination whether or not shown in the

financial statements of the acquired company, *should be assigned a portion of the cost of the acquired company, normally equal to their fair values at the date of acquisition.*

Second, the excess of the cost of the acquired company over the sum of the amounts assigned to identifiable assets less liabilities assumed should be recorded as goodwill.[2] (Emphasis added.)

Note that the above quotation does *not* state that the unassignable excess ($3,000 in this case) should be divided by the percentage of ownership (60 percent in this case) in order to arrive at the full amount of the goodwill (or $5,000 in this case). In other words, only majority interest in this goodwill is reflected in the consolidated financial statements.

Alternatives 1 and 2 both tend to understate total assets of the consolidated entity with the understatement most extreme under alternative 1. Perhaps conservatism and a heavy reliance on the historical cost basis of accounting led the APB away from alternative 3 in the recording of goodwill and other assets and liabilities. If goodwill must be recorded, then your author tends to favor alternative 3 because of its logic and consistency with other consolidation accounting rules.[3] When measurable, it seems more logical to record all assets and liabilities at full fair values. It is also easier to analyze and account for the results of this alternative in subsequent years as is shown later (on pages 147 and 151). *It should be noted that only the assets and liabilities of the acquired corporation and of not the acquiring corporation are being restated.* This is the standard procedure in any purchase of assets.

The work sheet substitution entry for each alternative is as follows:

	Alternatives					
	(1)		(2)		(3)	
Capital stock	40,000		40,000		40,000	
Additional paid-in capital	10,000		10,000		10,000	
Retained earnings	50,000		50,000		50,000	
Land	9,000		15,000		15,000	
Goodwill	3,000		3,000		5,000	
Investment in A stock ...		72,000		72,000		72,000
Minority interest		40,000		46,000		48,000

---

[2] *AICPA Professional Standards, Accounting—Current Text* (New York, 1980), par. 1091.87. Copyright (1980) by the American Institute of CPAs. While the quotation is from an *APB Opinion,* it must be remembered that the FASB has endorsed those *Opinions.*

[3] In the elimination (deferral) of intercorporate gains and losses where the subsidiary is the selling entity, the accounting rules recommend 100 percent elimination and not just elimination of the majority interest (this will be fully explained later).

The theoretical support for alternative 1 is a parent corporation or majority interest only concept. Under this concept little interest is shown in perfecting a measurement of the minority interest (and its share of assets and liabilities); measurement efforts are concerned with reflecting the majority interest. For alternative 3, the entity theory is the theoretical concept employed. Under this theory the emphasis is on the entity as opposed to only the majority interest. Thus, a full-blown entity approach would require recording all assets (including goodwill) and liabilities at their fair values regardless of whether the net asset are attributable to majority or minority interests. The theoretical support for alternative 2 is a combination of the above—majority interest only for goodwill and the entity theory for all other assets and liabilities.

Whichever of the three alternatives is used, it should be realized that an increase in the recorded book values of any assets (land and goodwill in this case) does not increase their basis for tax purposes. This causes basis differences for book and tax purposes which when depreciated or otherwise written off or sold will result in permanent differences in accounting for income taxes. The following was partially quoted in the Chapter 2, Accounting for Income Taxes—Special Considerations, and it seems appropriate to quote the entire paragraph here because the nondeductibility for tax purposes can affect (reduce) the recorded book values.

> The market or appraisal values of specific assets and liabilities . . . may differ from the income tax bases of those items. Estimated future tax effects of differences between the tax bases and amounts otherwise appropriate to assign to an asset or a liability are one of the variables in estimating fair value. Amounts assigned to identifiable assets and liabilities should, for example, recognize that the fair value of an asset to an acquirer is less than its market or appraisal value if all or a portion of the market or appraisal value is not deductible for income taxes. The impact of tax effects on amounts assigned to individual assets and liabilities depends on numerous factors, including imminence or delay of realization of the asset value and the possible timing of tax consequences. Since differences between amounts assigned and tax bases are not timing differences . . . the acquiring corporation should not record deferred tax accounts at the date of acquisition.[4]

In recording the resulting changes in the book values of the assets and liabilities, there is a fourth possibility which should be given much more consideration but which is precluded by the previously quoted (on pages 132 and 133) APB pronouncement concerning goodwill. This alternative would not record any goodwill but would require that the

---

[4] *AICPA Professional Standards*, par. 1091.89. Chapter 9 of this text, Planning Corporate Acquisitions and Liquidations, will show how to bet the higher or "stepped-up basis" for both book and tax purposes.

cost in excess of the full *fair value* of *all* underlying net assets be recognized as a loss on acquisition. In other words, if cost exceeds the net fair values of *all* identifiable assets and liabilities, both tangible and intangible, then there should be a strong case for saying that perhaps the buyer paid too much. In this case, no amount could be attached to unidentifiable assets. Under today's rules, a buyer, anxious to acquire another corporation, can offer too much knowing that any excess cost (for unidentifiable or even nonexistent assets) will be capitalized as goodwill and spread over the next 40 years via amortization. Paying too much probably happens most often when stock rather than cash is used as compensation in an acquisition. A rule requiring loss recognition would cause buyers (management) to be more careful in their dilution of current shareholder interests. Only two groups readily overpay—fools and someone paying with some other person's money or equity.

Investment at Less than the Underlying Book Value—100 Percent Acquisition

If, in the previous illustration, X had acquired 100 percent of Z for only $80,000, in preparing consolidated statements the $20,000 excess of book value over cost must be subtracted from the book values of individual assets or added to the book values of the liabilities. This is accomplished by restating net assets to their fair values (normally reducing assets and/or increasing liabilities). Since the value of the stock should equal, at least theoretically, the value of the net assets, this restatement should account for the difference between the book value of the net assets and the cost of the stock. But in the real-world environment, things are seldom this precise and the fair value of net assets and of the stock may differ. The appraisal process itself may not be totally accurate, and income tax factors in buying stock rather than buying assets may cause some differences.

If the restatement to fair value reduces the carrying amount of the net assets below the price paid for the stock, goodwill would be established. The presence of goodwill with fair value of net assets below book value is perhaps unlikely.[5]

For whatever the reason, if restatement of net assets fails to account for all of the excess book value over cost, the remaining excess is arbitrarily *but proportionately* allocated against noncurrent assets other than investments in marketable securities. If the excess exceeds the amount of these assets, the remaining excess (after these noncurrent assets have been reduced to zero) is established as a deferred credit somewhat like

---

[5] The Appendix at the end of this chapter shows all possible combinations of book value, fair value, and cost of stock which can result in goodwill.

negative goodwill. (Some persons might be tempted to call this "bad-will.")

> The sum of the market or appraisal values of identifiable assets acquired less liabilities assumed may sometimes exceed the cost of the acquired company. If so, the values otherwise assignable to noncurrent assets acquired (except long-term investments in marketable securities) should be reduced by a proportionate part of the excess to determine the assigned values. A deferred credit for an excess of assigned value of identifiable assets over cost of an acquired company (sometimes called "negative goodwill") should not be recorded unless those assets are reduced to zero value.[6]

In other words, this deferred credit amount will not appear on the consolidated statements unless a corporation is acquired for an amount which is less than the sum of its current assets and marketable securities less liabilities.

Tax: Perhaps it should be noted that in cases where stock is acquired and where net asset book values exceed the cost of the stock to the acquiring corporation, the acquired corporation's book values may be very relevant to the acquiring corporation. By continuing to operate the acquired corporation and by filing a consolidated tax return, the high book values of the acquired corporation, through depreciation deductions and other write-offs, can reduce the consolidated tax liability. For tax purposes, there is no requirement to restate (reduce) the value of the net assets. There is a limiting factor in the consolidated return income tax regulations called built-in deductions, but it is usually ineffective in preventing these deductions.* This may be another reason for acquiring the stock rather than the assets of a corporation. It should also be noted that any restatement of assets for financial reporting will produce basis differences between book and tax. These differences between pretax book and taxable incomes will affect the recording of income taxes. In addition, the extra tax deductibility, because of the higher tax basis, can result in reporting assets in the consolidated statement of financial position at amounts in excess of their appraised or fair market values.† These aspects are covered in greater depth in Chapter 9, Planning Corporate Acquisitions and Liquidations.

   * *Income Tax Regulations,* sec. 1.1502-15.
   † *AICPA Professional Standards,* par. 1091.89.

---

[6] *AICPA Professional Standards,* par. 1091.87. As illustrated on pages 138–140 of this chapter the reduction of fixed assets to zero causes conceptual problems when less than 100 percent of the subsidiary's stock has been acquired.

If the $20,000 excess book value on X's acquisition of Z's stock could be attributable solely to land (i.e., for all other accounts the book values equal fair values except for land where the book value exceeds the fair value by $20,000), the investment analysis would appear as in Illustration 4–6.

Illustration 4–6

Z Corporation	Net Assets
Capital stock	$ 40,000
Additional paid-in capital	10,000
Retained earnings	50,000
	100,000
Land	(20,000)
Price paid	$ 80,000

The work sheet substitution entry in journal format would be:

Capital stock	40,000	
Additional paid-in capital	10,000	
Retained earnings	50,000	
Land		20,000
Investment in Z stock		80,000

If the $20,000 excess could not be attributable to any asset or liability (i.e., the book values of all assets and liabilities equal their fair values), it would have to be proportionately allocated to noncurrent assets other than marketable securities. If the only noncurrent assets were land and buildings with book values (and fair values) of $10,000 and $30,000, respectively, and no accumulated depreciation, the $20,000 would have to be apportioned one fourth to the land and three fourths to the building. In this case the work sheet substitution entry would be:

Capital stock	40,000	
Additional paid-in capital	10,000	
Retained earnings	50,000	
Land		5,000
Building		15,000
Investment in Z stock		80,000

If the book values of the land and building, the only noncurrent assets, were $7,000 and $8,000, respectively, the substitution entry would establish a deferred credit amount for $5,000. Assume the building cost $18,000 and that depreciation of $10,000 had been accumulated. Whenever noncurrent but depreciable assets are either partially or totally reduced, the accumulated depreciation accounts will usually require restatement.

The substitution entry would be:

Capital stock	40,000	
Additional paid-in capital	10,000	
Retained earnings	50,000	
Accumulated depreciation	10,000	
Land		7,000
Buildings		18,000
Unallocated book value in excess of cost (negative goodwill)		5,000
Investment in Z stock		80,000

These accounting *procedures are arbitrary at best, and proportional allocation does not improve on this.* It would be easier and not any less arbitrary to reduce or eliminate the nondepreciable, noncurrent assets other than marketable securities first rather than mandating proportional allocation among only these noncurrent assets. The alternatives to some form of allocation would be (1) recognize the bargain purchase and record the gain on the acquisition or (2) record the entire excess as a deferred credit (negative goodwill). In some rare cases your author would be inclined to recognize the gain on the acquisition;[7] however, where fair values are difficult to determine (the usual case), recording the entire excess of fair values over cost as a deferred credit seems rational. This, however, creates an almost impossible task of finding an *appropriate* amortization period. The recognition of gain on the purchase would seem most acceptable where a corporation is acquired with the intent of liquidating it through the sale of its assets.

Investment at Less than the Underlying Book Value— Majority Acquisition

The allocation of excess book values becomes even more difficult when less than 100 percent ownership is acquired. Assume that X acquires 80 percent of Z for $64,000 and that *the book values of Z's assets and liabilities equal their fair values.* An analysis would show the figures given in Illustration 4–7.
At this point the proportionate book value of the underlying net assets (also their fair value) exceeds the cost of the investment to the majority ownership by $16,000. Presumably the $16,000 amount would be the figure by which the noncurrent assets should be reduced. It should be noted that this is similar (except that it involves a reduction in book values) to the goodwill example in Illustration 4–5, alternative 1, where only the majority portion is considered. The substitution work sheet entry could be as follows assuming that the land and building are the only noncurrent assets, in the amounts of $7,000 and $8,000, respec-

---

[7] In business operations, purchasing can be as important as selling, although the point of sale is the usual time for revenue recognition.

Illustration 4-7

Z Corporation	Net Assets	80 Percent Majority	20 Percent Minority
Capital stock	$ 40,000	$32,000	$ 8,000
Additional paid-in capital	10,000	8,000	2,000
Retained earnings	50,000	40,000	10,000
Book value (and fair value) in	100,000	80,000	20,000
excess of cost	(16,000)	(16,000)	-0-
Price paid	$ 84,000	$64,000	$20,000

tively, where the $8,000 is the net of $18,000 original cost and $10,000 of accumulated depreciation:

Capital stock	40,000	
Additional paid-in capital	10,000	
Retained earnings	50,000	
Accumulated depreciation	10,000	
Land		7,000
Building		18,000
Investment in Z stock		64,000
Unallocated excess book value over cost		1,000
Minority interest		20,000

An alternative and perhaps somewhat more logical solution would be to limit the reduction of noncurrent assets to 80 percent, X's ownership interest. This would leave the minority interest amount in land and buildings intact but would increase the deferred credit. The following work sheet substitution entry would reflect this:

Capital stock	40,000	
Additional paid-in capital	10,000	
Retained earnings	50,000	
Accumulated depreciation (80% × $10,000)	8,000	
Land ($7,000 × 80%)		5,600
Building ($18,000 × 80%)		14,400
Investment in Z stock		64,000
Deferred tax credit—excess fair value over cost (($16,000 − $5,600 land) − ($14,400 − $8,000 buildings))		4,000
Minority interest		20,000

Another alternative would involve the full-blown entity concept. Under this concept the $16,000 of book value in excess of cost would be divided by 80 percent (its majority only source) producing a total book value of net assets in excess of the fair value of the entire owners' equity of $20,000. The minority interest share of the $20,000 would be 20 percent or a $4,000 reduction in the amount of the minority interest. If this were done, the arbitrary allocation scheme would produce the following substitution entry:

Capital stock	40,000
Additional paid-in capital	10,000
Retained earnings	50,000
Accumulated depreciation	10,000
Land	7,000
Buildings	18,000
Investment in Z stock	64,000
Deferred credit—excess of the fair value of net assets over the fair value of the entire owners' equity ($20,000 − $7,000 land) − ($18,000 − $10,000 buildings)	5,000
Minority interest ($20,000 − $4,000)	16,000

Theoretically the fair value of the total owners' equity stock should equal the fair value of the underlying net assets. When the fair value of the net assets exceeds the cost of the related stock equity, the required financial statement allocation method, which is arbitrary and void of theoretical support, can yield ridiculous values for plant assets and make accounting for income taxes more difficult.[8]

SUBSTITUTION UNDER THE PURCHASE CONCEPT SUBSEQUENT TO THE DATE OF ACQUISITION

The examples in this chapter continue to assume that only the statement of financial position is being prepared. The earnings statement substitution entry is shown only at the end of this chapter and in subsequent chapters.

Investment at the Underlying Book Value—100 Percent Acquisition

The substitution entry will be affected by the accounting method (cost or equity) used by the parent to account for its investment in the subsidiary. This work sheet entry will change to reflect changes in the retained earnings of the subsidiary in subsequent years.

Assume the same owner's equity section for Z with book values equal to fair values and 100 percent acquisition of Z stock by X on 1/1/x1 for $100,000. Also assume that the net earnings and dividends paid by Z have been as follows:

	19x1	19x2	19x3
Net earnings	$14,000	$(10,000)	$12,000
Dividends paid	(8,000)	(1,000)	(2,000)
Totals	$ 6,000	$(11,000)	$10,000

---

[8] Unfortunately there have been cases where plant assets have been reduced to zero value.

On X's books the Investment in Z Stock account would appear as in Illustration 4–8 under the cost or equity methods (with 100 percent ownership the equity method would often be used to account for this investment).

Illustration 4–8

Investment in Z Stock

	Under the Cost Method	Under the Equity Method
Original 1/1/x1 cost	$100,000	$100,000
Basis at 12/31:		
19x1	100,000	106,000 ($100,000 + $6,000)
19x2	99,000 ($100,000 − $1,000)	95,000 ($106,000 − $11,000)
19x3	99,000	105,000 ($95,000 + $10,000)

The analysis of Z would appear as:

Z Corporation		Net Assets
Capital stock		$ 40,000
Additional paid-in capital		10,000
Retained earnings, 1/1/x1		50,000
Net assets at 1/1/x1		100,000
Earnings, 19x1	$ 14,000	
Dividends, 19x1	(8,000)	6,000
Net assets at 12/31/x1		106,000
Earnings, 19x2	(10,000)	
Dividends, 19x2	(1,000)	(11,000)
Net assets at 12/31/x2		95,000
Earnings, 19x3	12,000	
Dividends, 19x3	(2,000)	10,000
Net assets at 12/31/x3		$105,000

If the parent corporation used the cost method consistently, the substitution entry at the end of each year would appear as follows:

SUBSTITUTION ENTRIES IN COLUMN FORMAT

	12/31/x1 Dr. (Cr.)	12/31/x2 Dr. (Cr.)	12/31/x3 Dr. (Cr.)
Capital stock	$ 40,000	$ 40,000	$ 40,000
Additional paid-in capital	10,000	10,000	10,000
Retained earnings	56,000	45,000	55,000
Investment in Z stock	(100,000)	(99,000)	(99,000)
Retained earnings of X (adjustment to change earnings from Z from the cost to the equity method)	(6,000)	4,000	(6,000)
	–0–	–0–	–0–

Again, because 20 percent or more of the stock is owned, the cost method should not be used by X in recording the income from its investment in Z. But if this were done, there would annually have to be an adjustment on X's books to, in effect, convert from the cost to the equity method. If this adjustment were not made, the net earnings of X would be in error. If this adjustment were made as part of the substitution entry, the work sheet only nature of this entry would be clearly reflected. Because consolidation work sheet entries are not posted on any corporation's books, each year's work sheet entry would have to remake the effects of the prior years' entries.[9]

The $6,000 19x1 adjustment (increase) in X's retained earnings reflects the undistributed earnings of Z which would have to be recorded as earnings by X under the equity method. The $4,000 19x2 adjustment (decrease) in the retained earnings of X is composed of the $6,000 increase from 19x1 less the $10,000 loss from 19x2. Note that the $1,000 19x2 distribution was correctly treated as a liquidating dividend. For 19x3 the retained earnings adjustment for X would be a $6,000 increase which is composed of the 19x1 $6,000 increase, the 19x2 $10,000 decrease, and the $10,000 19x3 increase.

At the end of each year the substitution entry, if the equity method were used by X to account for its investment in and income from Z, would be:

	12/31/x1 Dr. (Cr.)	12/31/x2 Dr. (Cr.)	12/31/x3 Dr. (Cr.)
Capital stock	$ 40,000	$ 40,000	$ 40,000
Additional paid-in capital	10,000	10,000	10,000
Retained earnings	56,000	45,000	55,000
Investment in Z stock	(106,000)	(95,000)	(105,000)
	–0–	–0–	–0–

Investment at More than the Underlying Book Value—100 Percent Acquisition

While the adjustment of asset and liability values for cost in excess of book value or for book value in excess of cost are made as of the date of acquisition, this is a work sheet entry only, and thus it must be "repeated" for each subsequent consolidation. The passage of time, however, will, due to depreciation, amortization, and so on, cause some changes in this substitution entry.

---

[9] It should be realized that this would still leave the separate entity financial statements of X in error.

Assume that the facts are the same as in the prior example except that on 1/1/x1 X paid $130,000 for 100 percent of the Z stock. Also assume in the allocation process that of the $30,000 cost in excess of book value, $4,000 is attributable to inventories, $11,000 to land, $8,000 to a building, and $7,000 to goodwill. Assume a Fifo inventory flow, a 10-year remaining life on the building with straight-line depreciation, and a 40-year amortization period for goodwill. Also assume that X uses the equity method to account for its investment in Z. This investment (and the net assets) could be analyzed as shown in Illustration 4–9.

Illustration 4–9

	Z Corporation	Net Assets	
	Capital stock	$ 40,000	
	Additional paid-in capital	10,000	
	Retained earnings, 1/1/x1	50,000	
	Book value	100,000	
To restate at fair value	Inventory	4,000	
	Land	11,000	
	Building	8,000	
	Subtotal	123,000	
To record	Goodwill	7,000	
	Price paid on 1/1/x1 and adjusted net assets	130,000	
	Z's 19x1 dividends	(8,000)	
	Z's 19x1 reported net earnings	14,000	
19x1	Inventory adjustment (cost of goods sold)	(4,000)	$9,025 adjusted net earnings
	Depreciation adjustment ($8,000 ÷ 10 years)	(800)	
	Goodwill amortization ($7,000 ÷ 40 years)	(175)	
	Investment account and adjusted net assets, 12/31/x1	131,025	
	Z's 19x2 dividends	(1,000)	
19x2	Z's 19x2 reported net loss	(10,000)	$(10,975) adjusted net loss
	Depreciation adjustment	(800)	
	Goodwill amortization	(175)	
	Investment account and adjusted net assets, 12/31/x2	119,050	
	Z's 19x3 dividends	(2,000)	
19x3	Z's 19x3 reported net earnings	12,000	$11,025 adjusted net earnings
	Depreciation adjustment	(800)	
	Goodwill amortization	(175)	
	Investment account and adjusted net assets, 12/31/x3	$128,075	

The substitution entry at acquisition and at the end of each year would be:

	1/1/x1	12/31/x1
Capital stock	40,000	40,000
Additional paid-in capital	10,000	10,000
Retained earnings	50,000	56,000*
Inventory	4,000	–0–
Land	11,000	11,000
Building	8,000	8,000
Goodwill	7,000	6,825
Investment in Z stock	130,000	131,025†
Accumulated depreciation	–0–	800

* $50,000 on 1/1/x1 + $14,000 reported net earnings − $8,000 dividends = $56,000.
† $130,000 on 1/1/x1 + $9,025 adjusted net earnings − $8,000 dividends = $131,025.

	12/31/x2	12/31/x3
Capital stock	40,000	40,000
Additional paid-in capital	10,000	10,000
Retained earnings	45,000*	55,000†
Land	11,000	11,000
Buildings	8,000	8,000
Goodwill	6,650	6,475
Investment in Z stock	119,050‡	128,075 §
Accumulated depreciation	1,600	2,400

* $56,000 − $10,000 reported net loss − $1,000 dividends = $45,000.
† $45,000 + $12,000 reported net earnings − $2,000 dividends = $55,000.
‡ $131,025 − $10,975 adjusted net loss − $1,000 dividends = $119,050.
§ $119,050 + $11,025 adjusted net earnings − $2,000 dividends = $128,075.

The work sheet only nature of these entries is demonstrated by the fact that the annual accumulated depreciation figure must include the amounts for prior years. Thus, by 19x3 this account must be credited for $2,400. In addition, the allocation of the cost in excess of book value to individual assets must be repeated annually in the substitution entry.

Also, on X's books the depreciation and amortization of these assets must be reflected in the equity method investment account for Z. *Thus, in the separate earnings statement for X, the account "Earnings from Investment in Z Stock" must reflect Z's reported earnings plus or minus any adjustments due to cost in excess of book value on acquisition of the Z stock.* These are, of course, real entries in the financial records of X. Without these entries the equity method would not produce the same net earnings result as reported on the consolidated statements and would be in error. The entries on X's books for both earnings and dividends from Z would be as follows for each year:

For dividends:

	19x1	19x2	19x3
Cash	8,000	1,000	2,000
Investment in Z stock	8,000	1,000	2,000

For income or loss:

	19x1	19x2	19x3
Investment in Z stock....	9,025		11,025
Earnings from investment in Z stock...........		9,025		11,025
Loss from investment in Z stock		10,975	
Investment in Z stock			10,975	

Under the equity method both the Earnings from Investment in Z Stock and the Investment in Z Stock accounts must reflect the write-off of the cost in excess of book value.

For example, if the accountant for X had recorded the reported Z earnings for 19x1 as $14,000, the separate earning statement for X would be in error; and this would require the following adjusting entry on X's books for 19x1.

Earnings from investment in Z stock 4,975
  Investment in Z stock..................................... 4,975
To reflect the $4,000 increase in the cost of goods sold,
the $800 increase in depreciation expense, and the $175
increase in goodwill amortization expense due to acquiring
the stock of Z at a cost in excess of book value.

Note that this produces the same result as if X had purchased the assets of Z rather than the stock. It should also be realized that if the underlying book value of the net assets of Z had been in excess of the cost of the stock, allocation of this excess and adjustments of reported earnings would be required for X under the equity method.

The work sheet in Illustration 4–10 shows the consolidation of X and Z as of 12/31/x1. It assumes that X has correctly recorded the adjusted net earnings from Z in the amount of $9,025 and dividends from Z of $8,000 and that Z has correctly recorded net earnings of $14,000 and dividends of $8,000 thus increasing its retained earnings from $50,000 to $56,000.

Investment at More than the Underlying Book Value—
Majority Acquisition

Continuing the same example, assume that on 1/1/x1 X purchased only 90 percent of the stock of Z for $130,000. (Note that this cannot be a pooling because cash was used to acquire the Z stock instead of using X stock in exchange for the Z stock.) Assume the trial balance for Z on 1/1/x1 given in Illustration 4–11.

Illustration 4–10

X AND Z CORPORATIONS
Consolidated Work Sheet (Position Statement Only)
(100 percent acquisition with cost in excess of underlying book values)

Statement of Financial Position	X Corporation 12/31/x1	Z Corporation 12/31/x1	Substitution Entry Dr.	Substitution Entry Cr.	X and Z Corporation Consolidated 12/31/x1
Cash	10,000	15,000			25,000
Accounts receivable	125,000	80,000			205,000
Inventories	100,000	90,000			190,000
Investment in Z stock	131,025	–0–		131,025	–0–
Land	40,000	20,000	11,000		71,000
Buildings	80,000	40,000	8,000		128,000
Accumulated depreciation	(25,000)	(16,000)		800	(41,800)
Machinery and equipment	100,000	50,000			150,000
Accumulated depreciation	(65,000)	(35,000)			(100,000)
Goodwill	–0–	–0–	6,825		6,825
Total assets	496,025	244,000			634,025
Accounts payable	5,000	20,000			25,000
Long-term debt	40,000	118,000			158,000
Capital stock	200,000	40,000	40,000		200,000
Additional paid-in capital	50,000	10,000	10,000		50,000
Retained earnings	201,025	56,000	56,000		201,025
Total equities	496,025	244,000	131,825	131,825	634,025

Illustration 4–11

Z CORPORATION
Trial Balance
(Position Statement Only)
1/1/x1

	Book Value	FMV
Cash	$ 8,000	$ 8,000
Accounts receivable	77,000	77,000
Inventory	85,000	89,000
Land	20,000	31,000
Buildings	40,000	48,000
Accumulated depreciation	(12,000)	(12,000)
Machinery and equipment	50,000	50,000
Accumulated depreciation	(30,000)	(30,000)
Total assets	$238,000	$261,000
Accounts payable	$ 20,000	$ 20,000
Long-term debt	118,000	118,000
Capital stock	40,000 ⎫	
Additional paid-in capital	10,000 ⎬	123,000
Retained earnings	50,000 ⎭	
Total equities	$238,000	$261,000

Note that X paid $130,000 for only 90 percent of the $123,000 (FMV of net assets) thus requiring the establishment of goodwill of at least $19,300 ($130,000 − ($123,000 × 90%)) under alternatives 1 or 2.

Illustration 4-12

Z Corporation	Net Assets	90 Percent Majority	10 Percent Minority
Capital stock	$ 40,000	$ 36,000	$ 4,000
Additional paid-in capital	10,000	9,000	1,000
Retained earnings, 1/1/x1	50,000	45,000	5,000
Recorded net assets, 1/1/x1	100,000	90,000	10,000
To restate Inventory	4,000	3,600	400
at fair Land	11,000	9,900	1,100
value Building	8,000	7,200	800
Subtotal	123,000	110,700	12,300
Goodwill ($130,000 − $110,700)	19,300	19,300	−0−§
Adjusted net assets, 1/1/x1	142,300	130,000	12,300
Z's 19x1 dividends	(8,000)	(7,200)	(800)
Z's 19x1 reported net earnings	14,000	12,600	1,400
Inventory adjustment*	(4,000)	(3,600)	(400)
Depreciation†	(800)	(720)	(80)
Goodwill amortization‡	(483)	(483)	−0−§
Adjusted net assets, 12/31/x1	$143,017	$130,597	$12,420

Middle annotations: $8,717 adjusted net earnings; $7,797 adjusted net earning for majority interest.

* Assumes a Fifo flow and thus part of the cost of goods sold.
† $8,000 ÷ 10-year life = $800.
‡ $19,300 ÷ 40 years = $483 rounded.
§ It should be noted that since only the majority interest in the goodwill was picked up in the analysis, 100 percent of the amortization must be charged to the 90 percent majority interest. Thus, the Investment in Z Stock account is not 90 percent of the adjusted net assets and the minority interest is not 10 percent. If in reporting adjusted net assets, alternative method 3 had been used, the 90 percent and 10 percent ratios would have remained constant. This would occur if the $21,444 ($19,300 ÷ 90%) total goodwill had been recorded ($19,300 for the majority and $2,144 for the minority) with amortization in 19x1 of $536 ($483 for the majority and $53 for the minority). The 12/31/x1 adjusted net assets would then total $145,108 with 90 percent or $130,597 for the majority and 10 percent or $14,511 for the minority.

Using the alternative 2 method (see Illustration 4–5),[10] the analysis of the investment as of 12/31/x1 would appear as in Illustration 4–12 assuming Z reported $14,000 in net earnings and paid $8,000 in dividends. The 12/31/x1 substitution entry in journal entry format would be:

Capital stock	40,000	
Additional paid-in capital	10,000	
Retained earnings	56,000	
Land	11,000	
Building	8,000	
Goodwill ($19,300 − $483)	18,817	
Accumulated depreciation		800
Investment in Z stock		130,597
Minority interest		12,420

[10] It should be recalled that in practice alternative 1 is used almost exclusively even though it is perhaps inferior to alternative 3 conceptually, and both alternatives 1 and 2 destroy the relationship between the ownership interests and the net assets.

Illustration 4-13

X AND Z CORPORATIONS
Consolidated Work Sheet (Position Statement Only)
(90 percent majority acquisition with cost in excess of underlying book values)

Statement of Financial Position	X Corporation 12/31/x1	Z Corporation 12/31/x1	Substitution Entry Dr.	Substitution Entry Cr.	X and Z Corporations Consolidated 12/31/x1
Cash	10,000	15,000			25,000
Accounts receivable	125,000	80,000			205,000
Inventories	100,000	90,000			190,000
Investment in Z stock	130,597*	–0–		130,597	–0–
Land	40,000	20,000	11,000		71,000
Buildings	80,000	40,000	8,000		128,000
Accumulated depreciation	(25,000)	(16,000)		800	(41,800)
Machinery and equipment	100,000	50,000			150,000
Accumulated depreciation	(65,000)	(35,000)			(100,000)
Goodwill	–0–	–0–	18,817		18,817
Total assets	495,597	244,000			646,017
Accounts payable	5,000	20,000			25,000
Long-term debt	40,000	118,000			158,000
Minority interest	–0–	–0–		12,420	12,420
Capital stock	200,000	40,000	40,000		200,000
Additional paid-in capital	50,000	10,000	10,000		50,000
Retained earnings	200,597	56,000†	56,000		200,597
Total equities	495,597	244,000	143,817	143,817	646,017

* $130,000 + $7,797 adjusted net earnings − $7,200 dividends received = $130,597 (see Illustration 4–12).
† $50,000 + $14,000 recorded net earnings − $8,000 dividends paid = $56,000.

This example is given in work sheet format in Illustration 4–13 with the net assets of Z increased by the $6,000 of undistributed 19x1 earnings.

There are several important things to note about the work sheet. First, the two trial balance columns (for X and for Z) are taken from the accounting records of these separate legal entities and the substitution entry columns convert these separate legal entities into a single, hypothetical, economic, consolidated entity. Thus, the substitution entries are not recorded on the books of either X or Z.

Next, the Investment in Z Stock account under the equity method is reflected on X's books after taking into account the adjustments to Z's reported earnings due to the acquisition price being different from the underlying book value of the acquired Z stock. In addition, Z will not have an Investment in Z Stock account unless it were to record treasury stock as an asset which is normally an unacceptable procedure.

Third, in the legal entity trial balance columns, in this example, there are no amounts shown for goodwill. If goodwill were on the books of either X or Z, it would show up in the real trial balance columns. Thus, the goodwill in the consolidation column in the amount of $18,817 ($19,300 − $483) is solely attributable to the consolidation process less the first year of amortization. In addition, this example reflects only the majority interest in goodwill which is the APB's recommended approach.

Finally, the minority interest does not and never will appear in the trial balance columns reflecting the real legal entities. It is always created in the process of converting to the single economic entity.

This can be diagramed as shown in Illustration 4–14. On a separate entity basis neither X nor Z has any minority interest shareholders. The minority interest develops in consolidation because X does not own all of the Z stock.

Illustration 4–14

A. Separately

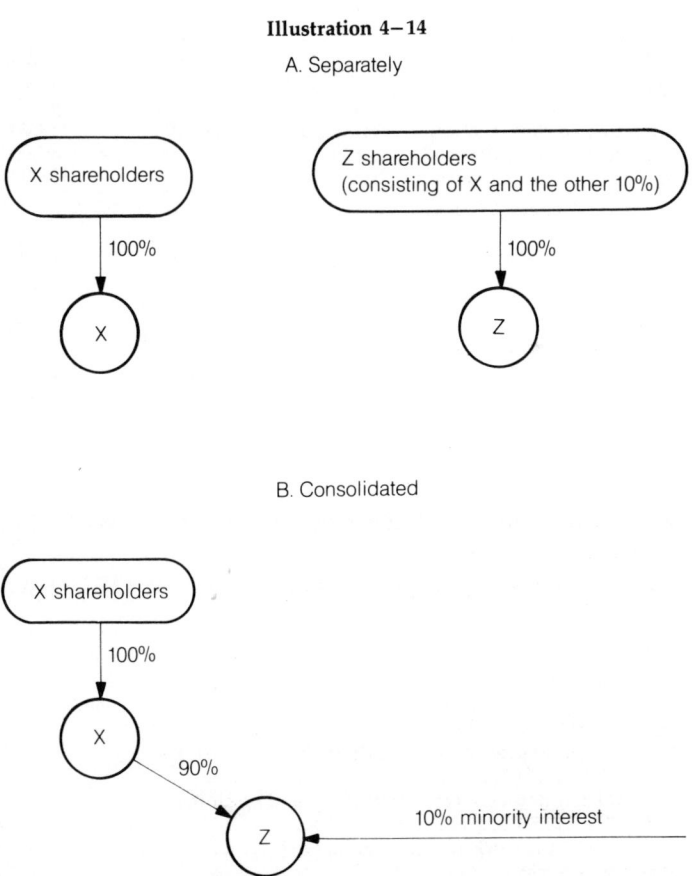

B. Consolidated

Investment at Less than the Underlying Book Value—Majority Acquisition

Continuing the same example but with different fair values, assume that on 1/1/x1 X purchases 70 percent of the Z stock for $60,000. Also assume a 10-year remaining life for both the building and the machinery and equipment with straight-line depreciation in both cases (see Illustration 4–15).

Illustration 4–15

Z CORPORATION
Trial Balance
(Position Statement Only)
1/1/x1

	Book Value	Fair Value
Cash	$ 8,000	$ 8,000
Accounts receivable	77,000	77,000
Inventory	85,000	89,000
Land	20,000	15,000
Buildings	40,000	40,000
Accumulated depreciation	(12,000)	(19,000)
Machinery and equipment	50,000	50,000
Accumulated depreciation	(30,000)	(30,000)
Total assets	$238,000	$230,000
Accounts payable	$ 20,000	$ 20,000
Long-term debt	118,000	118,000
Capital stock	40,000	
Additional paid-in capital	10,000	92,000
Retained earnings	50,000	
Total equities	$238,000	$230,000

The acquisition with net book value in excess of cost could be analyzed as in Illustration 4–16.

The substitution entry in journal entry format at 12/31/x1 would be:

Capital stock	40,000	
Additional paid-in capital	10,000	
Retained earnings	56,000*	
Land ($5,000 + $1,179)		6,179
Accumulated depreciation—buildings ($7,000 + $1,650 − $700 − $165)		7,785
Accumulated depreciation—machinery and equipment ($1,571 − $157)		1,414
Investment in Z stock		62,212
Minority interest		28,410

* $50,000 + $6,000 of undistributed 19x1 earnings.

Illustration 4-16

Z Corporation	Net Assets	70 Percent Majority	30 Percent Minority
Capital stock	$ 40,000	$28,000	$12,000
Additional paid-in capital	10,000	7,000	3,000
Retained earnings, 1/1/x1	50,000	35,000	15,000
Recorded net assets (book value), 1/1/x1	100,000	70,000	30,000
To restate at fair value — Inventory	4,000	2,800	1,200
To restate at fair value — Land	(5,000)	(3,500)	(1,500)
To restate at fair value — Accumulated depreciation—buildings	(7,000)	(4,900)	(2,100)
Net assets at fair value 1/1/x1	92,000	64,400	27,600
Fair value in excess of price paid = $4,400 ($64,400 − $60,000 price paid)			
Proportionate allocation:			
Land $\frac{\$15,000}{\$56,000} \times \$4,400^* =$	(1,179)	(1,179)	–0–†
Buildings net $\frac{\$21,000}{\$56,000} \times \$4,400 =$	(1,650)	(1,650)	–0–†
Machinery and equipment net $\frac{\$20,000}{\$56,000} \times \$4,400 =$	(1,571)	(1,571)	–0–†
Adjusted net assets, 1/1/x1	87,600	60,000	27,600
Z's 19x1 dividends	(8,000)	(5,600)	(2,400)
Z's 19x1 reported net earnings	14,000	9,800	4,200
Inventory adjustment	(4,000)	(2,800)	(1,200)
Adjustment for fair value depreciation: Building, $7,000 ÷ 10-year remaining life	700	490	210
Adjustments for fair value in excess of cost: Depreciation building, $1,650 ÷ 10 years	165	165	–0–†
Depreciation machinery and equipment, $1,571 ÷ 10 years	157	157	–0–†
Adjusted net assets, 12/31/x1	$ 90,622	$62,212	$28,410

$11,022 adjusted net earnings

$7,812 majority interest in adjusted net earnings

* Note that if the $4,400 amount were larger than the 70 percent majority interest in these fixed assets, then theoretically, at least, a negative goodwill should be established.

† Note that the proportionate allocation only considers the bargain element to the majority. Thus subsequent write-off of the $4,400 bargain or proportionate allocation amount is charged 100 percent to the 70 percent majority interest. Recording the $4,400 decrease in asset book values and the subsequent reduction in depreciation destroys the original 70% and 30% relationships of majority and minority interests in adjusted net assets.

To summarize, the procedures used above when the book value of the underlying net assets of the acquired stock exceeds the cost of the stock were:

1. The assets and liabilities (for consolidation purposes) were restated at fair values (normally established by appraisal).

2. The remaining excess of the majority portion of the fair value over cost was proportionally allocated to noncurrent assets (excluding marketable securities).
3. Changes including effects on net earning from recording fair values were prorated to the majority and minority interests.
4. Changes including effects on net earning from prorating the majority's excess of fair value over cost were charged 100 percent to the majority interest.

This process can be diagramed as in Illustration 4–17.

Illustration 4-17

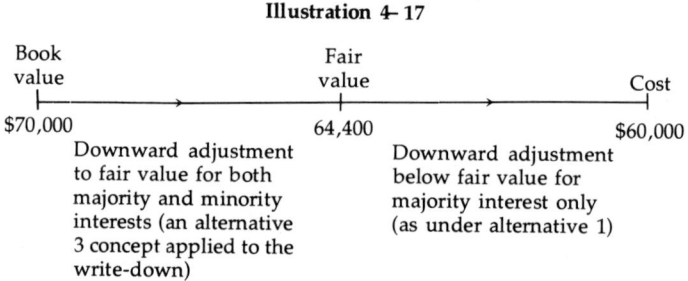

The work sheet format for the above would appear as in Illustration 4–18 after again reflecting the $6,000 of undistributed 19x1 earnings in the net assets of Z.

SUBSTITUTION UNDER THE POOLING OF INTERESTS CONCEPT

In preparing consolidated financial statements the substitution of the assets and liabilities of the subsidiary for the parent's investment account is much easier if the combination is treated as a pooling than if it is treated as purchase. This is because of the pooling requirement that the investment account equal the book value of the underlying net assets of the subsidiary when the stock is exchanged. Thus, there is neither cost in excess of book value nor book value in excess of cost, which would require allocation.[11] In addition, under pooling, the subsequent use of the equity method of accounting will retain the equivalency between the investment in the subsidiary account and the book value of the underlying net assets of the subsidiary.

---

[11] An exception to this rule can occur if this is a taxable acquisition (i.e., a taxable pooling). This is discussed in a later chapter on planning corporate acquisitions.

Illustration 4-18
X AND Z CORPORATIONS
Consolidated Work Sheet (Position Statement Only)
(70 percent majority acquisition at less than underlying book values)

Statement of Financial Position	X Corporation 12/31/x1	Z Corporation 12/31/x1	Substitution Entry Dr.	Substitution Entry Cr.	X and Z Corporations Consolidated 12/31/x1
Cash	10,000	15,000			25,000
Accounts receivable	125,000	80,000			205,000
Inventories	100,000	90,000			190,000
Investment in Z stock	62,212	-0-		62,212	-0-
Land	40,000	20,000		6,179	53,821
Buildings	80,000	40,000			120,000
Accumulated depreciation	(25,000)	(16,000)		7,785	(48,785)
Machinery and equipment	100,000	50,000			150,000
Accumulated depreciation	(65,000)	(35,000)		1,414	(101,414)
Total assets	427,212	244,000			593,622
Accounts payable	5,000	20,000			25,000
Long-term debt	40,000	118,000			158,000
Minority interest	-0-	-0-		28,410	28,410
Capital stock	200,000	40,000	40,000		200,000
Additional paid-in capital	50,000	10,000	10,000		50,000
Retained earnings	132,212	56,000	56,000		132,212
Total equities	427,212	244,000	106,000	106,000	593,622

Substitution at Acquisition—with 90 Percent Minimum Ownership

Continuing the X and Z example with total assets of $238,000 at 1/1/x1, assume that X, in exchange for 10,000 X shares, receives 90 percent ownership in Z or 3,600 of the 4,000 outstanding Z shares.[12] While irrelevant to a pooling, assume that the X stock is worth $12.60 per share and the Z stock $35 per share. The value paid in stock by X would equal $126,000 (10,000 shares × $12,60), and the value received in stock of Z would also equal $126,000 (3,600 shares × $35). The net assets of Z are $100,000 ($238,000 − $138,000 of liabilities); thus, under the purchase concept there would be a $36,000 ($126,000 − ($100,000 × 90%)) cost in excess of underlying book value. But under the pooling concept, the $36,000 is not considered because this is not an acquisition; it is a pooling of book values. Thus, the investment account is recorded on X's books at the $90,000 book value of 90 percent of Z's net assets.

---
[12] The 90 percent ownership is the minimum for pooling and thus all other requirements must be fully met. All 12 requirements for pooling are fully discussed in a later chapter.

The analysis of the acquisition entry for the 90 percent ownership interest (which would be recorded on X's books) and the substitution worksheet entry would appear as in Illustration 4–19 assuming that the 10,000 X shares have $4.10 par values.

Illustration 4–19
ANALYSIS

Z Corporation	Net Assets	90 Percent Majority	10 Percent Minority
Capital Stock	$ 40,000	$36,000	$ 4,000
Additional paid-in capital	10,000	9,000	1,000
Retain earning	50,000	45,000	5,000
Totals	$100,000	$90,000	$10,000

The acquisition entry (recorded on X's books) would be:

Investment in Z stock	90,000	
Capital stock of X (10,000 shares × $4.10)		41,000
Additional paid-in capital ($9,000 − ($41,000 − $36,000))		4,000
Retained earnings		45,000

The substitution entry in journal entry form would be:

Capital stock of Z	40,000	
Additional paid-in capital	10,000	
Retained earnings	50,000	
Investment in Z stock		90,000
Minority interest		10,000

Substitution Subsequent to Acquisition—with 90 Percent Minimum Ownership

In every case the parent company should be using the equity method of accounting. Thus, at 12/31/x1 the net assets will be $106,000 ($100,000 + $14,000 income − $8,000 dividends). Thus, under the equity method at 12/31/x1 the investment account will be $95,400 ($90,000 + ($14,000 × 90%) − ($8,000 × 90%)). The minority interest will be $10,600 ($106,000 × 10%). The substitution entry is simply:

Capital stock	40,000	
Additional paid-in capital	10,000	
Retained earnings	56,000	
Investment in Z stock		95,400
Minority interest		10,600

The fact that following a pooling, the investment account using the equity method always equals the percentage of ownership times the net assets makes the substitution entry easier than the substitution entry following a purchase.[13] But regardless of whether an acquisition of a majority of the stock of another corporation is accounted for as a pooling or as a purchase, a substitution entry is necessary on every consolidated work sheet.

It should be noted that throughout this chapter the substitution entries were made *after the closing of current year earnings to retained earnings*. In other words, the substitution entries only involved the statement of financial position. Obviously, consolidation also involves the earnings statement, and here the subsidiary's revenue and expense accounts are substituted for the "Equity in the Earning of the Subsidiary" account on the parent corporation's books. This substitution entry is as follows assuming the parent corporation properly recorded the subsidiary's $14,000 in earnings and the $8,000 dividend payment:

Equity in subsidiary income ($14,000 × 90%)	12,600	
Investment in subsidiary		12,600

This entry removes the parent corporation's current year share of the subsidiary income which prevents double counting when the two corporations are combined as one on the work sheet. In other words, this entry and the work sheet complete the substitution of the subsidiary revenue and expense accounts for the equity in subsidiary income account.

It should also be noted that the $12,600 would not have been closed to the parent corporation's retained earnings. Thus, the statement of financial position substitution entry before closing would be as follows:

Capital stock	40,000	
Additional paid-in capital	10,000	
Retained earnings	42,000*	
Investment in Z stock		82,800†
Minority interest		9,200‡

* 1/1/x1 retained earnings of $50,000 less an $8,000 dividend.
† 1/1/x1 investment of $90,000 less a $7,200 dividend.
‡ 1/1/x1 minority interest of $10,000 less an $800 dividend.

Trying to visualize the substitution entries before closing the income statement accounts is more difficult. This and the effects of intercorporate transactions are covered in depth in subsequent chapters.

APPENDIX: POSSIBLE COMBINATIONS OF BOOK VALUE, FAIR VALUE, AND COST

As has been discussed in this chapter, the official pronouncements on "cost in excess of book value" or on "book value in excess of cost" are

---

[13] Only in a "taxable pooling" will the investment account not equal the book value of the underlying net assets.

not always precise. In theory at least, this should not be so difficult. The theory of consolidation includes the idea that the purchase of stock is the equivalent of the purchase of assets. Thus, theoretically the book values of all assets and liabilities should always be restated to fair values. Then, if the cost exceeds the total fair value of the net assets, the excess is called goodwill. The official pronouncements prevent calling this excess cost over fair value a loss. But if the cost is less than the total fair value of the net assets, our official pronouncements state that this excess must proportionately reduce noncurrent assets other than investments; and if these assets are reduced to zero, any remaining excess is recorded as negative goodwill, a deferred credit. The official pronouncements prevent calling this excess of fair value over cost a gain.

Using the idea that the purchase of stock is equivalent to the purchase of assets, there are only six possible combinations of cost, fair value, and book value to consider where no two of these amounts are the same.

The six theoretical combinations where no two amounts are the same and the proper method of recording the facts are:

1.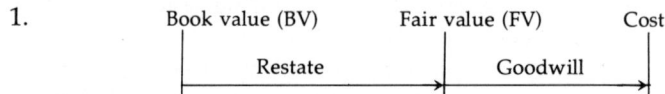

FV greater than BV and cost greater than FV.
(Restatement accounts for some of the excess of cost over BV with goodwill being reported as the remaining excess cost.)

2.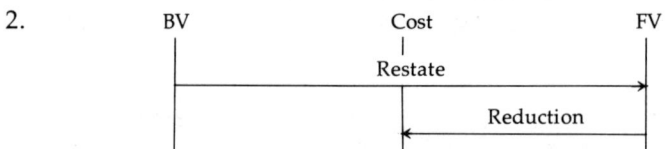

Cost greater than BV and FV greater than cost.
(The restatement here could increase any asset (or decrease liabilities) with the reduction from FV to cost then coming proportionately from the noncurrent assets other than investments.)

3.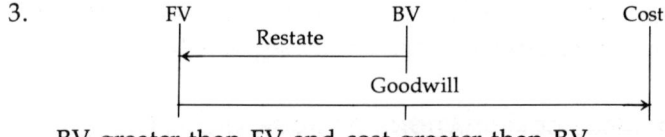

BV greater than FV and cost greater than BV.
(The restatement here would increase goodwill.)

4.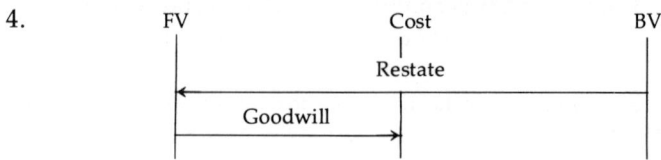

Cost greater than FV and BV greater than cost.
(Full restatement here would cause goodwill to be shown.)

5.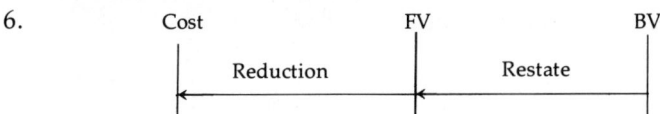

BV greater than cost and FV greater than BV.
(Just as in example 2 above, restatement here could increase assets or decrease liabilities with the reduction from FV to cost coming proportionately from noncurrent assets other than investments.)

6.

FV greater than cost and BV greater than FV.
(This combination is the one illustrated on page 151. Restatement accounts for only some of the excess of BV over cost with the remaining excess then reducing noncurrent assets other than investments.)

Other combinations where two or more amounts are the same are:

7.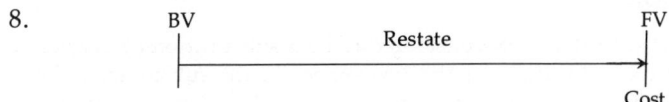

(Restatement would account for the entire excess of book value over cost. Theoretically FV and cost should be the same for each acquisition.)

8.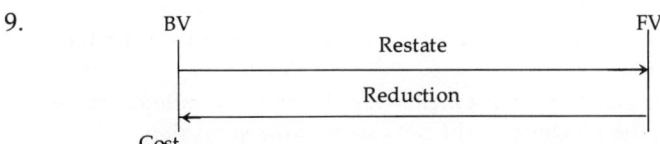

(Restatement would account for the entire excess of cost over book value.)

9.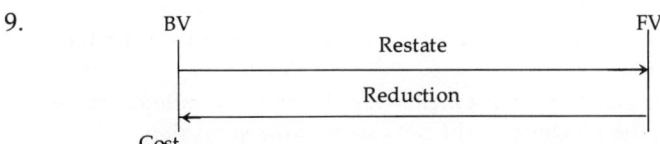

(The restatement followed by the reduction would in all likelihood effect different assets and liabilities especially noncurrent assets other than investments.)

10.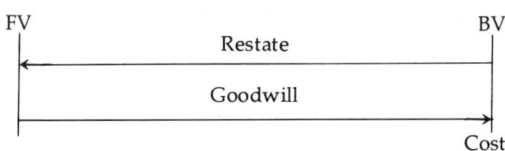

(Restatement here would result in reporting an equal amount of goodwill.)

11.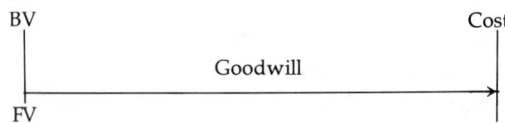

(Any restatement here, among the BVs and FVs of the assets and liabilities, would have to offset and goodwill would be reported for the cost in excess of FV.)

12.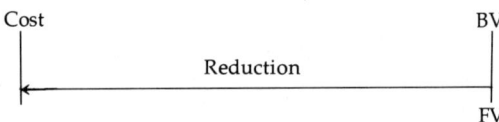

(Any restatement here (among BVs and FVs) would have to offset and the reduction would then be taken proportionately from the noncurrent assets other than investments.)

13.

(Even here there could be offsetting restatements of assets and liabilities. Note that such restatements could affect future earnings by affecting depreciation, etc.)

REVIEW QUESTIONS

1. Why is the substitution entry considered to be a substitution of assets and liabilities of the subsidiary for the investment in the subsidiary account when the debit side of the entry is to the owners' equity accounts of the subsidiary?
2. What causes goodwill to arise in the preparation of a consolidated statement of financial position?
3. Does the account minority interest appear on the parent's or on the subsidiary's books?
4. Why is a consolidation of a purchased subsidiary considered to be the equivalent of the purchase of the net assets of the subsidiary?
5. What procedures are used in a consolidation to account for the excess of cost of an investment in subsidiary stock over the book value of that stock when 100 percent of the subsidiary stock is acquired?

6. *a.* What are the three alternative methods for reporting cost in excess of book value and in excess of fair value where less than 100 percent ownership has been acquired?
   b. What effect does each method have on the majority interest?
   c. What effect does each method have on the minority interest?
7. What procedures are used to account for an investment in subsidiary stock where there is an excess of cost over book value and the subsidiary is not consolidated?
8. What procedures are used in a consolidation to account for an excess of book value over the cost of stock in a 100 percent owned subsidiary?
9. How is the excess book value over cost recorded if the parent only owns 80 percent of the subsidiary?
10. If a negative goodwill amount appears on a consolidated statement of financial position as a deferred credit, what can you say about the assets of the subsidiary which are included in the consolidation?
11. How does the allocation of cost in excess of book value or of book value in excess of cost impact on the federal income tax provision assuming a consolidated tax return is filed?
12. How does income taxation impact on the allocation of cost in excess of book value or of book value in excess of cost (*a*) at the date of acquisition and (*b*) in subsequent periods?
13. What group of investors is a consolidation really concerned with?
14. Why is the consolidation substitution entry under a pooling of interests concept so much easier than under a purchase concept?
15. If 100 percent of the stock of a subsidiary were acquired for $100,000 cash and if the book value (of each asset and liability) of the subsidiary is equal to its fair value for a total value of $100,000, how will this purchase acquisition differ from a pooling in (*a*) the consolidated statement of financial position and (*b*) the earnings statement?

PROBLEMS

Problem 1: Three Alternative Methods

On 1/1/x1 A Corporation acquired 70 percent of B Corporation's stock for $70,000. At the date of acquisition the B Corporation statement of financial position reflected the following:

	Book Value	Fair Value
Cash	$ 5,000	$ 5,000
Receivables	10,000	10,000
Inventory	74,000	80,000
Noncurrent assets (net)*	10,000	30,000
Total assets	$99,000	$125,000
Accounts payable	$ 5,000	$ 5,000
Long-term debt	20,000	25,000
Common Stock	30,000 ⎫	
Additional paid-in capital	10,000 ⎬	95,000
Retained earnings	34,000 ⎭	
Total equities	$99,000	$125,000

*Does not include any investments.

Required:

1. Prepare in journal entry format the *three* substitution entries, one for each alternative method.
2. Assume that the fair value of each asset and liabilities equaled its book value and that A Corporation acquired the 70 percent stock interest for $37,800. Employing the best acceptable theory prepare the substitution entry in journal entry format again reflecting the minority interest.

Problem 2: The M & N Acquisition and Work Sheet

Assume that the 12/31/x1 statements of financial position for M and for N are as follows.

	M	N
Cash	$ 245,000	$ 15,000
Accounts receivable	400,000	30,000
Inventories	700,000	10,000
Investment in N	?	-0-
Land	100,000	40,000
Buildings	300,000	100,000
Accumulated depreciation	(100,000)	(50,000)
Machinery and equipment	2,000,000	600,000
Accumulated depreciation	(600,000)	(125,000)
Goodwill	10,000	-0-
Total assets	?	$ 620,000
Accounts payable	$ 100,000	$ 10,000
Long-term debt	200,000	60,000
Minority interest	-0-	-0-
Capital stock	?	100,000
Additional paid-in capital	?	50,000
Retained earnings 12/31/x1	?	400,000
Total equities	?	$ 620,000

4 / Preparing Consolidated Statements

On 1/1/x1 M acquired 90 percent of the N outstanding stock by exchanging with the shareholders of N 5,500 shares of M $50 par value stock for 9,000 shares of N $10 par value stock. For N (but not true for M) the book values of the assets and liabilities equaled their fair values. The M stock was actively traded at $100 per share, and the N stock had been closely held and therefore did not have an established market value. On 1/1/x1 N's retained earnings were $350,000; during 19x1 N earned $70,000 and paid $20,000 in dividends. M's liabilities and owners' equity accounts were as follows immediately before the 1/1/x1 exchange of shares:

Accounts payable	$ 150,000
Long-term debt	150,000
Capital stock, $50 par	825,000
Additional paid-in capital	100,000
Retained earnings	1,675,000

During the year 19x1 M recorded earnings from its own operations of $177,000 and paid $40,000 in dividends. M also accounted for its investment in N under the equity method, and this is not included in the $177,000 earnings figure.

Required:

Assume the stock-for-stock exchange constitutes a purchase acquisition of N by M, then (1) prepare an investment analysis, then (2) supply the missing figures in M's trial balance, and then (3) enter the trial balances on a work sheet and prepare the consolidated statement of financial position.

Accounts in the Statement of Financial Position	M	N	Work Sheet Entries		M&N Consolidated
			Dr.	Cr.	
Cash					
Accounts receivable					
Inventories					
Investment in N					
Land					
Buildings					
Accumulated depreciation					
Machinery and equipment					
Accumulated depreciation					
Goodwill					
Total assets					
Accounts payable					
Long-term debt					
Minority interest					
Capital stock					
Additional paid-in					
Retained earnings					
Total equities					

Problem 3: Acquisition and Substitution under Pooling and Purchase

A acquired 90 percent or 9,000 shares of the capital stock of B in exchange for 6,000 shares of A. The A stock has a FMV of $90 per share, and the B stock a FMV of $60 per share. The owners' equity sections of A and B immediately before the exchange were as follows:

	A	B
Capital stock, $40 par	$400,000	
Capital stock, $10 par		$100,000
Additional paid-in capital	40,000	50,000
Retained earnings	500,000	300,000
	$940,000	$450,000

All of B's assets and liabilities have book values equal to their FMV except for land which is worth $20,000 more than its book value and inventory which is worth $40,000 more than its book value.

Required:

1. Record A's acquisition of B stock as a pooling of interests.
2. Prepare the substitution entry at the date of acquisition assuming a pooling of interests.
3. Record A's acquisition of B stock assuming a purchase.
4. Prepare the substitution entry at the date of acquisition assuming a purchase.

Problem 4: Consoli Corporation and Dated Corporation

Consoli purchased 100 percent of the Dated Corporation outstanding stock on 12/31/x1 for $800,000 in cash. The trial balances for both corporations as of 12/31/x1 are as follows:

	Trial Balances 12/31/x1	
	Consoli	Dated
Cash	$ 50,000	$130,000
Accounts receivable (net)	250,000	100,000
Inventory	300,000	400,000
Investment in dated stock	800,000	–0–
Machinery and equipment	700,000	100,000
Accumulated depreciation	(300,000)	(50,000)
Buildings	100,000	200,000
Accumulated depreciation	(60,000)	(50,000)
Land	10,000	40,000
Goodwill	40,000	–0–
Total assets	$1,890,000	$870,000
Accounts payable	60,000	20,000
Long-term debt	400,000	80,000
Capital stock	200,000	100,000
Additional paid-in capital	150,000	200,000
Retained earnings	1,080,000	470,000
Total equities	$1,890,000	$870,000

The book values of the assets and liabilities of Dated equal their fair values.

Required:
1. Prepare a consolidated statement of financial position as of 12/31/x1.
2. Assume that everything is the same except that Consoli only purchased 90 percent of Dated for the $800,000 price. Prepare a consolidated statement of financial position as of 12/31/x1.

Problem 5: Acquiror, Inc., and Acquiree, Inc.

The condensed statements of financial position for the Acquiror and Acquiree Corporations as of 1/1/x1 immediately before the stock-for-stock exchange, are as follows:

	Acquiror	Acquiree
Assets	$6,000,000	$2,000,000
Liabilities	$2,800,000	$ 700,000
Capital stock	500,000	100,000
Additional paid-in capital	100,000	400,000
Retained earnings	2,600,000	800,000
Total equities	$6,000,000	$2,000,000

On 1/1/x1 Acquiror exchanges with the shareholders of Acquiree 5,400 shares of Acquiror's previously unissued stock for 9,000 shares of Acquiree stock. The par value per share of the Acquiror stock was $50 and $10 for the Acquiree stock. The market value per share of Acquiror stock was $400, and since Acquiree is a family owned corporation, there is no active market in its stock.

Required:
1. Diagram this transaction.
2. Record the acquisition on Acquiror's books as though it were a purchase.
3. Record the "acquisition" on Acquiror's books as though it were a pooling of interests.
4. Assume that the book values of each of Acquiree's assets and liabilities equaled their fair values on 1/1/x1 except for land which was undervalued by $400,000. During 19x1 Acquiree earned $20,000 and paid $5,000 in dividends.
    a. Prepare the investment analysis through year 19x1 assuming the acquisition was a purchase and use alternative 3 as the reporting method.
    b. What entry(s) would Acquiror make on its books in 19x1 to account for the equity method income from Acquiree.
    c. Prepare the substitution entry at 12/31/x1.
5. Assume the same fair values as for 4 but that Acquiror had issued its 5,400 shares to Acquiree in exchange for *all* of Acquiree's assets and liabilities.
    a. Diagram this transaction.
    b. Record the exchange as a purchase acquisition.
    c. Record the exchange as a pooling of interests.

Problem 6: Direct and Indirect Corporations

Direct purchases 90 percent of the capital stock of Indirect for $837,000 on 1/1/x1 when Indirect's owners' equity accounts reflected the following:

INDIRECT CORPORATION

Capital stock, 10,000 shares at $10 par	$100,000
Additional paid-in capital	250,000
Retained earnings, 1/1/x1	450,000
Total	$800,000

An appraisal of Indirect's assets indicated that land and buildings were undervalued by $60,000 and $50,000, respectively, while inventory was overvalued by $10,000. Indirect Corporation estimates the building to have a 10-year remaining useful life, and the straight-line depreciation method is used on depreciable assets and a Fifo flow assumption is used on the inventory. Direct wishes Indirect to show the largest possible earnings. For the year ended 12/31/x1, Indirect reports earnings from its records of $80,000 and pays a $50,000 dividend on 12/15/x1. For the year ended 12/31/x2, Indirect reports a loss of $8,000 from its records and pays $10,000 in dividends. The corporate tax rate is a flat 40 percent, and separate returns are filed.

Required:
1. Prepare an investment analysis from the date of the stock purchase through 12/31/x2 using alternative method 2.
2. Assuming that Direct has correctly reported its share of the earnings of Indirect, prepare the substitution entry (in journal entry format) for the 12/31/x2 consolidated work sheet again assuming alternative method 2.

3. Assume that instead of paying $837,000 Direct issued 18,000 shares of its $10 par value common stock in a 2-for-1 exchange to acquire 9,000 shares of Indirect and records this combination as a pooling of interests. Now prepare the 12/31/x2 substitution entry.

Problem 7: P & S Treasury Substitution

P acquired 80 percent of S stock on 1/1/x1 for $43,200. At 1/1/x1 the book value of all of S's assets and liabilities equaled their FMVs. S's income for 19x1 was $30,000, its retained earning at 1/1/x1 was $14,000, and $10,000 in dividends were paid by S in 19x1.

	Trial Balances 12/31/x1	
	P	S
Cash	$ 10,000	$ 5,000
Receivables	30,000	10,000
Inventory	80,000	20,000
Investment in S stock	59,200	4,000
Fixed assets (net)	240,800	60,000
Total assets	$420,000	$99,000
Accounts payable	$ 8,000	$ 5,000
Long-term debt	50,000	20,000
Common stock	100,000	30,000
Additional paid-in capital	60,000	10,000
Retained earnings	202,000	34,000
Total equities	$420,000	$99,000

Required:
1. Prepare the 12/31/x1 substitution work sheet entry in journal entry format for the consolidation.
2. Prepare the 12/31/x1 substitution entry assuming that P and S desire to report the largest consolidated earnings and that P had paid $80,000 on 1/1/x1 for the 80 percent interest in S.

Problem 8: Lobo and Shields Corporations

Lobo Corporation had purchased on 1/1/x1 80 percent of the capital stock of Shields Corporation for $140,000. The stockholders' equity of Shields appeared as follows for 1/1/x1:

	Net Assets
Capital stock, $10 par	$ 40,000
Additional paid-in capital	30,000
Retained earnings	120,000
Total stockholders' equity	$190,000

For all the assets and liabilities of Shields, the fair value equals book value except for inventory which is overvalued by $20,000 and land which is overvalued by $6,000.

For year 19x1 Shields has reported earnings of $30,000 and has paid $16,000 in dividends. They use the Fifo inventory flow concept, and all depreciable or amortizable assets are written off over 20-year lives using appropriate methods.

Required:

Assume Lobo had used the cost method to account for its investment in Shields.

1. What effect does the Lobo investment have on the separately reported earnings of Shields (show calculations)?
2. What effect should the Lobo investment in Shields have on the separate entity earnings of Lobo (show calculations)?
3. If Lobo had earned $60,000 without considering any earnings from its investment in Shields, what would be the amount of the consolidated net earnings.
4. Prepare the substitution entry.

5

Accounting for Intercorporate Transactions Which Defer Gains or Loss Recognition

Effect of the Single Entity Concept
Accounting Periods and Methods
Offset, Deferral, and Restoration Entries
    Terminology
    Offsets
    Deferrals and Restorations
        Sale of Nondepreciable Fixed Assets
        Consideration of Ownership
        Tax Effects of Transactions where Intercorporate Gain or Loss Is Deferred
        Sale of Depreciable Fixed Assets
        Intercorporate Sales from the Subsidiary to the Parent
        Intercorporate Sales of Inventory
Subsidiary Sales to Parent
A Complete Illustration
Impact on Earnings under the Equity Method when the Parent Is the Selling Affiliate

EFFECT OF THE SINGLE ENTITY CONCEPT

Just as a corporation should not recognize gain or loss on transfer of goods or property between divisions or departments, there should be no gain or loss recognized in consolidated financial statements on transactions between any of the separate legal entities making up the consolidated group.[1] In other words, gain or loss should only be recognized in consolidated financial statements when a member of the consolidated entity has transactions with entities which are not members of the group. In its separate financial statements, however, each separate legal entity recognizes gain or loss on transactions with *all* other legal entities. Thus, in converting from separate to consolidated financial statements, whenever the other party to a transaction is a member of the same consolidated group, recognition of gain or loss *and* the related tax effect must be deferred. These deferred gains or losses and their tax effects must be restored to earnings when some outside entity becomes a purchasing party.

For financial reporting, the effects of intercorporate transactions must be removed from all consolidated financial statements. For consolidated tax returns, however, the emphasis is solely on the measurement of (1) taxable income and (2) dividend paying potential (in the measurement of undistributed "earnings and profits"). This concentration on income while generally ignoring the balance sheet accounts will cause some differences in accounting procedures between financial reporting and tax reporting of intercorporate transactions.

ACCOUNTING PERIODS AND METHODS

In consolidated financial reporting a subsidiary may have a different year-end than the parent corporation by as much as three months and still be included in the consolidation.[2] In filing a consolidated tax return, however, a subsidiary generally must have the same year-end as the parent. In fact, when a consolidated tax return is being filed and a subsidiary is acquired (by any member of the group), normally the subsidiary's current year ends and a new year begins. In addition, it must usually adopt the year-end of the common parent.[3]

As to the use of various acceptable accounting methods for the same type of transactions, the only requirement for financial reporting is one of disclosure.

---

[1] Since the equity method is a one-line consolidation, the rules on nonrecognition would also apply when this accounting method is used.

[2] *AICPA Professional Standards, Accounting—Current Text* (New York, 1980), par. 2051.05. Copyright (1980) by the American Institute of CPAs.

[3] *Federal Income Tax Regulations*, sec. 1.1502-76(a).

> A description of all significant accounting policies of a reporting entity should be included as an integral part of the financial statements.[4]

This does not preclude the use of more than one acceptable accounting method. For example, it is very common to see a percentage of the inventory which is under the Lifo method with the balance under Fifo or some other method. More than one method is also permitted for tax purposes. In fact, even the accounting bases can be different, for example, a cash basis entity can be included in a consolidated tax return with an accrual basis entity. Preasumably the same could not be done for financial reporting because the cash basis would have to be converted to the accrual basis to be in accordance with "generally accepted accounting principles."[5]

OFFSET, DEFERRAL, AND RESTORATION ENTRIES

Terminology

Most accounting literature including the official pronouncements group all adjustments necessary to produce consolidated statements under the title "eliminations."[6] In this text there are no work sheet elimination entries. Labeling all consolidation entries as elimination entries is very unfortunate in that it fails to convey an accurate description of the purpose of these work sheet entries. Thus, in the prior chapter we used the term *substitution entry* (in lieu of "elimination entry") in describing the work sheet adjustment for replacing the Investment in Subsidiary account with the assets and liabilities of the subsidiary. In this chapter we use the terms *offset, deferral,* and *restoration* in place of "elimination" to describe some of the additional work sheet entries necessary to produce consolidated financial statements. The next chapter will introduce *advanced recognition entries.*

Memorization of these five new items of terminology is not really important nor difficult, the terms almost describe themselves. The advantage of this terminology is that it provides classification of the heretofore elimination entries into their five major purposes. This permits a more easily organized approach to the study of consolidations; and for offset, deferral, and restoration entries, the terminology is similar to that used in the federal income tax law. Definitions of each of the

---

[4] *AICPA Professional Standards,* par. 2045. 08.
[5] Ibid., par. 1025.08.
[6] For example, see ibid., par. 2051.07.

five consolidation entries, which replace the so-called elimination entries in most texts on consolidation, are as follows:

Substitution entry—The entry which together with the work sheet substitutes the net assets of a subsidiary for the investment in the subsidiary account.

Offset entry—An entry which recognizes that a consolidated entity cannot have a receivable and a payable to itself nor revenue and expense from itself.

Deferral entry—The entry that prevents a consolidated entity from recognizing either gain or loss on sales to itself.

Restoration entry—The entry which recognizes the previously deferred gain or loss from a sale between affiliates when the buying member "resells" the item to an outside entity. Depreciation can also be a restoration event.

Advanced recognition entry—An entry which recognizes gain or loss for consolidated financial statements in a period prior to when the gain or loss would be recognized by the separate entities which compose the consolidated entity.

Offsets

An entity cannot have a payable to itself and a receivable from itself. Therefore, if a parent loans $1,000 to a subsidiary, a receivable would be on the parent's books as a separate legal entity, and the subsidiary's books would show a payable. Since a consolidation of these two separate legal entities treats them as though they were one entity, the receivable is in effect offset against the payable in the consolidation work sheet.

This work sheet offset entry in journal format would be:

Loans payable	1,000	
Loans receivable		1,000

Suppose that because of the loan the subsidiary had paid $100 interest to the parent. This would require offsetting interest revenue (to the parent) against interest expense (to the subsidiary).

The work sheet offset entry would simply be:

Interest revenue	100	
Interest expense		100

The work sheet only nature of consolidation entries has been repeatedly stressed and should be obvious in the above offset entries. For example, if the last entry were a real entry, recorded on the separate records of P and S, neither set of books would balance. Because the Interest Income and Interest Expense accounts are on different sets of books, there would be only one debit or credit for each company. This is characteristic of consolidation work sheet entries, and you may have noticed this from the substitution entries in the prior chapter.

There are many types of offset work sheet entries, but they usually involve some form of receivable and payable or revenue and expense; thus the above is only a simple example. This concept will come up again in more complete form in the next chapter when we discuss intercorporate-held bonds.

> **Tax:** It may be interesting to note that for a consolidated tax return offset entries such as the interest income and interest expense entry would not be made. This is because the net effect of the income and expense amount is zero and thus there is no net effect on taxable income. In other words, for consolidated tax return purposes, the amounts recorded for interest income and interest expense are overstated, but as long as there is no effect on taxable income, the "overstatements" are acceptable.* In addition, since the loans receivable and loans payable entry does not affect taxable income, it is also ignored for tax purposes.
>
> * *Federal Income Tax Regulations,* sec. 1.1502-13(b).

Deferrals and Restorations

These work sheet entries usually involve the sale of assets between members of a consolidating group.

Entries for transactions between an investor corporation and an investee (a corporation owned less than 50 percent) are not immediately discussed as these entities are not consolidated. In addition, the following discussion ignores, at first, implications due to the use of the equity method even between a parent and a subsidiary. The impact of the equity method is presented after first presenting some of the deferral and restoration entries necessary to convert the totally separate financial statements of a parent and subsidiary into consolidated financial statements.

Sale of Nondepreciable Fixed Assets. Perhaps the easiest example to illustrate the deferral and restoration concept is an intercorporate sale of land. If S sold land to P for $40,000 which originally cost S $25,000, the entries on each corporation's books would be as follows:

On S's books:

Cash	40,000	
Land		25,000
Gain on sale of land		15,000

On P's books:

Land	40,000	
Cash		40,000

Given these entries the deferral entry(s) would be:

Deferral entry for the gain in the year of the sale:

Gain on sale of land	15,000	
Land		15,000

The $15,000 debit to "Gain on Sale of Land" defers or prevents the current year recognition of this amount in the consolidated earnings statement, while the $15,000 credit to land reduces the separate corporation basis of this asset from $40,000 to its original $25,000 amount for the consolidated statement of financial position. If P and S filed separate tax returns, S would have paid tax on the $15,000 gain, and on S's books the tax would have been reported as part of the tax provision. For financial consolidation purposes, where the gain is being deferred, any tax paid (or recorded) on that gain would also have to be deferred. Assuming a 30 percent tax rate, the tax deferral work sheet entry would be:

Prepaid tax ($15,000 × 30%)	4,500	
FIT provision		4,500

There is also a possibility of having to make this tax entry even if a consolidated tax return were filed. There is a rather unusual provision in the tax rules which permits corporations to elect to recognize (with the consent of the Commissioner of the Internal Revenue Service) intercorporate gains and losses.[7] If this election were made requiring the tax to be paid on the $15,000 gain, for financial reporting the same tax deferral entry would be required.

In a normal consolidated tax return the gain would not be currently recognized. In this case S, *on its separate books,* would have recorded a deferred tax credit because the gain recognition would constitute a timing difference requiring interperiod tax allocation. While this would be only one part of the tax entry, its effects *on S's books* would be as follows:

FIT provision	4,500	
Deferred tax credit		4,500

---

[7] *Federal Income Tax Regulations,* sec. 1.1502-13(c)(3).

If this were the case and if consolidated financial statements were to be prepared, a work sheet entry, in addition to deferring the gain in the year of the intercorporate sale, would defer the tax on the gain by merely reversing the above entry.

Deferred tax credit	4,500	
FIT provision		4,500

A work sheet entry is also necessary to defer the gain for each year subsequent to the year of sale. This is required because the consolidation deferral entry in the year of sale is *not recorded* on the records of P and S as separate legal entities. In other words, these are deferral entries, and they are necessary in order to *continuously defer* the gain on this sale until P sells the land to an outside entity.

Deferral entry for the gain in each subsequent year:

Retain earnings (1/1/xx)	15,000	
Land		15,000

If income tax had been paid on the $15,000 gain, a work sheet deferral entry for the tax would also have to be made in each subsequent year; it would appear as follows at a 30 percent rate:

Prepaid tax	4,500	
Retained earnings (1/1/xx)		4,500

If the income tax on the gain had not been paid, S would have accrued it in the form of a deferred tax credit. In each subsequent year this would require the following work sheet entry:

Deferred tax credit	4,500	
Retained earnings (1/1/xx)		4,500

Now suppose P sells the land, which is on its separate records at $40,000, to an outsider for $52,000. The separate records of P will show a $12,000 gain, but for consolidation purposes the gain should be $27,000 ($52,000 − $25,000 original cost). Thus, in the year of sale to an outsider, the work sheet restoration entry would be:

Restoration entry on subsequent sale to outsider:

Retained earnings (1/1/xx)	15,000	
Gain on sale of land		15,000

This entry, in effect, restores to income the gain that has been deferred every year since the original sale by S to P. When this $15,000 is added to the $12,000 reported by P, the full $27,000 gain is reported in the same year that P sold the land to an outside party. The $15,000 debit to Retained Earnings removes the gain (which had been reported as income by S in the year S sold to P) from the beginning-of-the-year retained earnings of S.

The recognition of the heretofore deferred gain will require recognition of the related income tax. If the tax had already been paid (on a separate tax return or under the special recognition election on a consolidated tax return), the following work sheet entry for the tax effect would be required:

FIT provision	4,500	
Retained earnings (1/1/xx)		4,500

If the tax had not been paid, S would have accrued it as a deferred tax credit for the timing difference. The restoration of the gain would require the following work sheet entry:

FIT provision	4,500	
Retained earnings (1/1/xx)		4,500

As noted, the debit would be to the Federal Income Tax Provision account rather than to the Deferred Tax Credit account. The Deferred Tax Credit account would already have been debited on S's books because the federal income tax payable would exceed the tax provision. This is the effect of a timing difference which would have turned around (in the consolidated tax return).

To summarize, the effects of the work sheet entries would be as follows:

In the year of sale:

	Without Tax Being Paid until Sold to Outsider		With Tax Paid in Year of Intercorporate Sale	
Gain on sale of land	15,000		15,000	
Prepaid FIT	–0–		4,500	
Deferred tax credit	4,500		–0–	
Land		15,000		15,000
FIT provision		4,500		4,500

In each subsequent year:

Retained earnings (at 1/1/xx)	10,500*		10,500*	
Prepaid FIT	–0–		4,500	
Deferred tax credit	4,500		–0–	
Land		15,000		15,000

* $15,000 income less $4,500 tax.

In the year of resale:

Retained earnings (at 1/1/xx)	10,500		10,500	
Provision for income tax	4,500*		4,500	
Gain on sale of land		15,000		15,000

* The tax paid on the sale to an outsider would be on the entire $27,000 gain, and thus on S's separate books the Deferred Tax Credit account would have been debited because of the turnaround of the timing difference. It should be noted that this is an example of interperiod income tax allocation on the separate corporation records combined with intercorporate tax allocation because of the consolidated tax return.

Consideration of Ownership. The equity method should produce *in the parent corporation* the same net earnings as consolidation would reflect in almost every case (an exception will be discussed in a later chapter). Therefore, the effect on net earnings from any deferral, restoration, or advanced recognition consolidation entry should also be reflected as an adjustment of equity method earnings in measuring the parent's net earnings.

For example, assume that P had sold the land to S for a $15,000 before-tax gain. Now assume P reports separate earnings of $90,000 including the $10,500 of aftertax gain on the sale of land to S and that S reports separate earnings of $40,000. S is owned 80 percent by P. The equity method earnings of P would *not* be $122,000 ($90,000 + ($40,000 × 80%)). P would have to adjust its own separately reported earnings down to $79,500 ($90,000 − ($15,000 − $15,000 × 30%)), and then record its $32,000 ($40,000 × 80%) share of S earnings. Thus, both the equity method and consolidation would reflect net earnings of $111,500 ($79,500 + $32,000). It should be noted that P must adjust its own reported earnings when it is the seller (due to the ownership of S) and not the earnings of S. This entry must be made because the gain did not arise in a transaction with outsiders. On P's books the reduction of the $90,000 to $79,500 *would be recorded* as follows:

Prepaid FIT	4,500	
Gain on sale of land (to S)	15,000	
FIT provision		4,500
Unrecognized gain (a deferral)		15,000

Because this would be a recorded deferral type entry there would be no need to repeat it for intervening years. Then, in some future year when P sells the land to an outsider, P would *record* the following entry:

Unrecognized gain	15,000	
FIT provision	4,500	
Prepaid FIT		4,500
Gain on sale of land (to S)		15,000

Obviously, when P is the seller the recorded deferral type entry and the previously discussed and corresponding consolidation entries (similar to when S was the seller) would not both be made. Thus, if after recording the deferral entry P wishes to also prepare consolidated financial statements, the difference between the recorded entry and the consolidation entries must be adjusted for on the consolidation work sheet. In the year of the sale by P to S, this would be as follows:

Unrecognized gain	15,000	
Land		15,000

This same consolidation entry would be made in each intervening year until S (the buyer) resells the land to an outsider. In the year of the resale to an outside entity, no restoration consolidation entry will be needed because of the restoration recorded by P recognizing the previously deferred gain and the related tax effect.

If we reverse the buyer and seller by assuming that S sold the land to P and that P resells it later to an outsider, there would be no recorded deferral entries on the separate records of S because S does not own P. To any minority interest in S, P is an outside party because S does not own P. P's ownership of S, however, would force an adjustment of P's earnings from S. S's $40,000 of net earnings would have to be reduced to $29,500 ($40,000 − ($15,000 − $4,500)) in calculating P's 80 percent equity method income from S. P's equity in S's earnings would then be $23,600 ($29,500 × 80%). The equity method earnings from S, $23,600, would be removed in the substitution process in the preparation of consolidated statements. Thus, the previously discussed consolidation entries (deferral and restoration) for the intercorporate gain and tax effect on the sale of the land by S to P would have to be made because S would not be recording deferral entries as P would do if it were the seller.

The rest of this chapter and subsequent chapters will generally present the consolidation entries as though P has not recorded the proper deferral and restoration entries when it is the seller in an intercorporate transaction. While this would mean that P has the wrong equity method earnings when it is the seller, this (and the complete, majority and minority, deferral concept) will allow us to make the same analysis and consolidation entries regardless of whether the parent or the subsidiary is the selling corporation.

Tax Effects of Transactions where Intercorporate Gain or Loss Is Deferred. To obtain an understanding of the complexity in the income tax implications of deferring intercorporate gains or losses in the preparation of consolidated financial statements, it is necessary to realize that complete, separate financial statements are prepared first. In other words, separate financial statements are usually prepared including the recognition of the tax effect from including intercorporate gains or losses in net earnings. Separate financial statements are generally necessary for each separate legal entity even if consolidated financial statements are *also* prepared. It is these separate financial statements that report to the subsidiary's creditors and minority shareholders. It must be remembered that (1) consolidated financial statements are for a fictitious legal entity, and thus, in effect, represent pro forma statements, *as if* it were a single corporation; and (2) the separate corporation records are the beginning point in preparing consolidated statements and tax returns.

To provide an example, Illustration 5–1 reflects the effect on accounting for income taxes when there is a $10,000 intercorporate gain on a sale by a subsidiary (with a significant minority interest) to a parent and a 40 percent marginal tax rate. Accounting for the tax effects of this gain in

Illustration 5-1
POTENTIAL DEFERRALS OF INTERCORPORATE GAIN OR LOSS WHEN THE *SUBSIDIARY* IS THE SELLING CORPORATION

Four Possible Combinations of Financial and Tax Reporting	Financial Statements			Tax Returns		
	Separate		Consolidated	Separate		Consolidated
	Subsidiary	Parent		Subsidiary	Parent	
1. Separate financial only with separate tax returns.	R*	→ED	Potential timing difference	R	→N	
2. Separate financial only with a consolidated tax return.	→R† ← Removal of timing difference	ED§	Timing difference			→D
3. Separate financial and consolidated financial with separate tax returns.	R*	→ED	Potential timing difference → D‡ Timing difference	→R	→N	
4. Separate financial and consolidated financial with a consolidated tax return.	→R† ← Removal of timing difference	ED§	Timing difference D			→D

R = recognized gain or loss; D = deferral of gain or loss; ED = equity method deferral of gain or loss; N = gain or loss not recognized nor postponed on buying entity's tax return.

*With no postponement of intercorporate gain or loss (because the equity method would not impact on the subsidiary's earnings) no tax deferrals are needed because no timing differences exist.

†Requires a tax deferral on the subsidiary's books for the timing difference created by recognition for book and postponement for tax.

‡Requires a tax deferral only on the consolidated financial statements where the gain or loss is postponed while being recognized by S for separate financial and tax. The tax deferral may already have been recorded by the parent under the equity method.

§Since a tax deferral for a timing difference would have been recorded on the separate financial books of the subsidiary, its effect would have to be removed from the consolidated financial statements (or parents separate equity method statements) because for consolidated financial statement (or parents

the four possible combinations of financial statements and tax returns when the subsidiary is the seller would be as follows:

Combination 1—separate financial statements and separate tax returns:

To the subsidiary: The $10,000 gain would be recognized (in order to report it to the minority interest) for both book and tax purposes. Thus, there would not be a timing difference nor a tax deferral. The tax on the gain would be recognized and paid. (Chart symbols: R for both book tax.)

To the parent: The aftertax $6,000 gain on S's books would have to be subtracted from S's separate earnings before P's share of S's earnings under the equity method is computed. With separate tax returns there could be a timing difference as to P's share of S's undistributed earnings. But this would not be due to the intercorporate sale; dividend payments would determine if there is a timing difference. Any tax effect would then depend on factors such as the indefinite reversal criteria and the dividend received deduction. (Chart symbols: ED for book and N for tax.)

Combination 2—separate financial statements with a consolidated tax return:

To the subsidiary: With recognition for book and deferral for tax there would be a timing difference requiring a deferred credit for tax accounting. (Chart symbols: R for book and D for tax.)

To the parent: With deferral of intercorporate gain caused by the use of the equity method, there would be no difference between P's books and the consolidated tax return for this gain (except for the minority interest in S's earnings). Thus, the parent would have to remove the aftertax intercorporate gain, recognized by S, in calculating P's ownership share under the equity method. (Chart symbols: ED for book and D for tax.)

Combination 3—separate *and* consolidated financial statements with separate tax returns:

To the subsidiary: For the separate statements there would not be a timing difference as the gain would be recognized and the tax paid for both purposes. (Chart symbols: R for both book and tax.)

To the parent: The postponement under the equity method could create or eliminate a timing difference depending on the amount of dividends received. A tax deferral for undistributed earning of the subsidiary would depend on factors such as the indefinite reversal criteria. (Chart symbols: ED for book and N for tax.)

To the consolidated financial entity: The use of separate tax returns would result in recognition of the gain. The postponement for consolidated financial purposes would cause a timing difference. This would result in the tax paid by S on the gain to be reported as a prepaid tax (or deferred charge) by the consolidated entity. (Chart symbols: D for financial and R and N for tax.)

Combination 4—Separate *and* consolidated financial statements with a consolidated tax return:

To the subsidiary: A timing difference would exist with recognition of intercorporate gain for book and postponement for tax. This would require you to anticipate a tax and establish a deferred tax credit due to the recognized gain. (Chart symbols: R for book and D for tax.)

To the parent: With postponement both under the equity method and for tax, no timing difference would exist. But in order to postpone under the equity method, the effects of the subsidiary's recognition and the related tax would have to be removed in computing the parent's share of the subsidiary's earnings. (Chart symbols: ED for book and D for tax.)

To the consolidated financial entity: With postponement for both book and tax no timing difference would exist. But a consolidation entry would be necessary to remove the subsidiary's recognized gain and the related tax deferral. (Chart symbols: D for financial and tax.)

When the parent corporation has sold to the subsidiary the deferred tax effects are much easier to visualize. These effects are presented in the Illustration 5–2 and are not discussed further.

Sale of Depreciable Fixed Assets. The deferral process is used to postpone recognition of gain or loss until the item is sold outside the consolidated entity. But when the item is being depreciated there is, in effect, a partial sale to outsiders. This occurs because the intercorporate gain has resulted in a higher basis for the asset and therefore in increased depreciation. This increased depreciation will be part of the cost of goods sold or included in operating expenses of the purchasing corporation and, therefore, assumed to be a necessary expense being recovered through current revenues.[8]

To illustrate some of the problems encountered with intercorporate sales of depreciable assets, assume that P sells a machine to S for $24,000 on 12/31/x2. This machine had cost P $40,000 on 1/1/x1 and has a 5-year

---

[8] It is also possible to have some of the depreciation, through the overhead charged to the cost of goods manufactured, end up in the ending inventory. This can cause additional complexity when these goods are involved in intercorporate sales.

Illustration 5-2
POTENTIAL DEFERRALS OF INTERCORPORATE GAIN OR LOSS WHEN THE *PARENT* IS THE SELLING CORPORATION

Possible Combinations of Financial and Tax Reporting	Financial Statements			Tax Returns	
	Parent Separate		Consolidated	Separate	Consolidated
	Without recording the deferral*	With recording the deferral			
1. Separate financial only with separate tax returns.	R	→D‡ Timing difference	Timing difference	→R	
2. Separate financial only with consolidated tax return.	→R† ← Removal of the timing difference	D	Timing difference		→D
3. Separate financial *and* consolidated financial with separate tax return.	R	→D‡ Timing difference	Timing difference	→R	
4. Separate financial *and* consolidated financial with consolidated tax return.	→R† ← Removal of the timing difference	D	Timing difference D		→D

R = recognized; D = deferred.

Notes: 1. Separate financial statements without the use of the equity method adjustment when the parent sells to a subsidiary are not generally acceptable.
2. Separate financial statements with the use of the equity method when the parent sells to a subsidiary has the same result (deferral) as when consolidated financial statements are prepared.

* Not an acceptable method of accounting. See Note 1.

† Would require a tax deferral for the timing difference if this were an acceptable accounting method, but the deferral would then be reversed for equity method accounting or upon consolidation.

‡ Requires a tax deferral for the timing difference.

useful life with straight-line depreciation and no salvage value. With the sale at book value ($40,000 − $16,000 in depreciation), there would be no gain or loss to defer and thus no tax effect. As long as S uses the same remaining useful life, salvage value, and the straight-line depreciation method, there will not be any difference in the depreciation charged to expense. The only difference is that the intercorporate sale has reduced the "original" cost of the asset from $40,000 to $24,000 and has reduced accumulated depreciation by the same amount. Thus, a consolidation entry would reinstate the original cost and accumulated depreciation as follows:

Machinery	16,000	
Accumulated depreciation—machinery		16,000

If S decides to use the sum-of-the-years'-digits depreciation method for 19x3 and records $12,000 ($3/6 \times $24,000) as depreciation expense, it will cause a difference in the depreciation expense. P would have expensed only $8,000 ($40,000 ÷ 5 years) in 19x3 if the sale had not been made. Presumably P could have also recorded $12,000 if it had change its depreciation method. Using this logic, no work sheet entry for the depreciation difference would be required.

If a work sheet entry were made for the increased depreciation in 19x3, it would be:

Accumulated depreciation—machinery	4,000	
Depreciation expense		4,000

This would reduce the depreciation expense to the $8,000 amount that P would have recorded in absence of the sale or change in depreciation method.

Illustration 5–3 shows the depreciation deductions of P and S over the full 5-year life of the asset assuming S uses a 3-year SYD life and no salvage value. The depreciation increase in 19x3 reverses in 19x5. Thus, for consolidated financial statements there could be a deferral of depreciation in 19x3, a continuation of the deferral in 19x4, and a restoration of the deferral in 19x5. These work sheet entries would be as follows:

Deferral in 19x3*:

Accumulated depreciation	4,000	
Depreciation expense		4,000

Continuation of the deferral in 19x4*:

Accumulated depreciation	4,000	
Retained earnings (1/1/x4)		4,000

Restoration of the deferral in 19x5*:

Depreciation expense	4,000	
Retained earnings (1/1/x5)		4,000

* Not posted to either corporation's books. Note that there is no depreciation difference for year 19x4.

Illustration 5-3

On P's Books		On S's Books		On a Corporation (consolidated) Basis	
Cost on 1/1/x1	$40,000			Cost on 1/1/x1	$40,000
Depreciation, 19x1	8,000			Depreciation, 19x1	8,000
Depreciation, 19x2	8,000			Depreciation, 19x2	8,000
Gain or loss on sale	–0–	Cost on 12/31/x2	$24,000		
		Depreciation, 19x3	12,000	Depreciation, 19x3	8,000
		Depreciation, 19x4	8,000	Depreciation, 19x4	8,000
		Depreciation, 19x5	4,000	Depreciation, 19x5	8,000

In addition, there would be some tax impact to defer due to the financial consolidation. If separate tax returns were filed using the same depreciation methods as used for book purposes and assuming a 30 percent tax rate, the work sheet entries would be:

Deferral of tax in 19x3*:

FIT provision ($4,000 × 30%)	1,200	
Deferred tax credit		1,200

Continuation of the tax deferral in 19x4*:

Retained earnings (1/1/x4)	1,200	
Deferred tax credit		1,200

Restoration (reversal) of the tax deferral in 19x5*:

Retained earnings (1/1/x5)	1,200	
FIT provision		1,200

* Not posted to either corporation's books.

All students should be aware of the fact that different depreciation methods and useful lives for tax return calculations and for the separate entity financial reports are frequently encountered.

The previous intercorporate sale of a depreciable asset was made at book value. To illustrate the additional problems caused by having a gain on an intercorporate sale, assume that P and S prepare consolidated financial statements and file separate tax returns on a calendar-year basis with no timing or permanent differences between the separate entity books and the tax returns. Also assume that on 1/1/x1 P acquired a machine for $40,000 from an outside party, and that this machine had a 5-year useful life with a zero salvage value and with straight-line depreciation being used. Also assume that S, a 100 percent owned subsidiary, purchased this machine from P for $30,000 on 12/31/x2, continued to use the straight-line depreciation method over the same remaining life (three years), and sold the machine to an outside entity on 12/31/x4 for $6,000. Assume that the effective tax rate for every year is 30 percent (see Illustration 5–4).

In recording this 12/31/x2 sale P would have made the following entry on its books, including the tax effect:

Cash	30,000	
Accumulated depreciation	16,000	
FIT provision	1,800	
Machinery and equipment		40,000
Gain on sale of machinery		6,000
FIT payable		1,800

In recording the purchase of the machinery, S on its separate book would have made the following entry:

Machinery and equipment	30,000	
Cash		30,000

Illustration 5-4
AN ANALYSIS

On P's Books		On S's Books		On a 1-Corporation (consolidated) Basis	
Cost on 1/1/x1	$40,000			Cost on 1/1/x1	$40,000
Depreciation, 19x1	8,000			Depreciation, 19x1	8,000
Depreciation, 19x2	8,000			Depreciation, 19x2	8,000
Gain on 12/31/x2 sale to S ($30,000–$24,000)	6,000	Cost on 12/31/x2	$30,000	*Prepaid* tax ($6,000 × 30%) ...	1,800
Tax provision ($6,000 × 30%) ..	1,800	Depreciation, 19x3	10,000	Depreciation, 19x3	8,000
				Prepaid tax ($2,000 × 30%) ...	(600)
		Depreciation, 19x4	10,000	Depreciation, 19x4	8,000
				Prepaid tax, 19x4	(600)
		Loss on 12/31/x4 sale to outsider ($6,000 – $10,000)	4,000	Loss on 12/31/x4 sale to outsider ($6,000 – $8,000)	2,000
		Tax provision (benefit) ($4,000 × 30%)	(1,200)	Prepaid tax on 19x4 sale	(600)

The consolidation entry (assuming that P has not made the required equity method deferral adjustments) to defer the gain and the income tax on the 12/31/x2 intercorporate sale and to restate the asset at its original net amount would be:

(1)
Gain on sale of machinery	6,000	
Machinery and equipment	10,000	
Prepaid FIT	1,800	
Accumulated depreciation		16,000
FIT provision		1,800

This entry defers recognition of this intercorporate sale by restoring the Machinery and Equipment account to its $40,000 original cost and the Accumulated Depreciation account to its $16,000 amount and also defers current recognition of both the $6,000 gain and the related income tax recorded on P's books. The debit to Prepaid Federal Income Tax instead of to Federal Income Tax Payable recognizes that this liability will soon be paid if it has not already been paid by P (on the separate tax return).

Again, because this entry is not recorded except on the work sheet, it must be repeated on 12/31/x3 (assuming that P has not made the corresponding equity method adjustments) but after taking into consideration changes due to the passage of time. The work sheet entry(s), in journal entry format, to defer the gain as of 12/31/x3 would be:

Work sheet entry 1—Deferral for the prior year (12/31/x2) intercorporate sale:

Retained earnings (1/1/x3) (P)	4,200*	
Prepaid FIT	1,800	
Machinery and equipment	10,000	
Accumulated depreciation		16,000

* $6,000 gain − $1,800 tax = $4,200.

Work sheet entry 2—Restoration for 19x3 depreciation:

Accumulated depreciation	2,000	
FIT provision	600	
Depreciation expense		2,000
Prepaid FIT		600

The reduction of depreciation expense (technically on S's separate books) in effect prevents the $6,000 gain (included in the basis of the asset to S) from affecting consolidated earnings during the period of the deferral.

Because work sheet entry 1 adjusts everything as it would be at the beginning of 19x3 while work sheet entry 2 adjusts for changes during the year, the two entries can be combined into one entry as follows:

Work sheet entries 1 and 2 combined:

Retained earnings (1/1/x3)	4,200	
Prepaid FIT	1,200	
Machinery and equipment	10,000	
FIT provision	600	
Accumulated depreciation		14,000
Depreciation expense		2,000

The combined entry is more difficult to visualize because of subsequent events (depreciation in this case). The 19x2 original gain of $6,000 less a 30 percent tax of $1,800 leaves a $4,200 adjustment to 1/1/x3 retained earnings. By reducing depreciation expense, $2,000 of the initial $6,000 gain is being currently recognized leaving a balance of $4,000 with an accompanying $1,200 in prepaid tax deferred as of 12/31/x3.

The work sheet entry(s) in journal entry format at 12/31/x4 (again assuming that no corresponding equity method deferral or restoration adjustments have been made by P) would be:

Work sheet entry 1—Deferral for the 12/31/x2 intercorporate sale and for 19x3 depreciation restoration:

Retained earnings (1/1/x4) ($4,200 − $1,400)	2,800	
Prepaid FIT ($1,800 − $600)	1,200	
Machinery and equipment	10,000	
Accumulated depreciation ($16,000 − $2,000)		14,000

Work sheet entry 2—Restoration for 19x4 depreciation:

Accumulated depreciation	2,000	
FIT provision	600	
Depreciation expense		2,000
Prepaid FIT		600

The $2,800 debit to Retained Earnings as of 1/1/x4 reflects the 19x2 deferred gain net of tax of $4,200 less the 19x3 restoration due to depreciation net of tax of $1,400 because prior year deferral and restoration entries were not posted to the records of either corporation.

At the time of the sale to the outsider, S̲ would have recorded the following journal entry excluding the income tax effect (which would be part of the year's tax provision entry and would reflect the tax affect of both the loss and the depreciation).

On S's books:

Cash	6,000	
Accumulated depreciation	20,000	
Loss on sale of machinery	4,000	
Machinery and equipment		30,000

The last 12/31/x4 work sheet entry to adjust this on a consolidated basis, in journal entry format, would be:

Work Sheet entry 3—Restoration for sale to outsider:

Accumulated depreciation ($14,000 − $2,000)	12,000	
FIT provision	600	
Loss on sale of machinery		2,000
Machinery and equipment		10,000
Prepaid FIT		600

The $2,000 reduction in the reported loss of $4,000 reflects the net $2,000 loss that would have been incurred had the intercorporate sale never taken place ($6,000 sales price less net book value of $8,000 ($40,000 cost − $32,000 in depreciation)). The two debits to Accumulated Depreciation of $20,000 on S's books and $12,000 in the consolidation entry represent the removal of the $32,000 ($8,000 × 4 years) of accumulation which would have been on P's books at the date of sale if P had not sold to S.

All three of the 12/31/x4 work sheet entries could be combined into one entry as follows:

Work sheet entries 1, 2, and 3—Combined:

Retained earnings (1/1/x4)	2,800	
FIT provision	1,200	
Loss on sale of machinery		2,000
Depreciation expense		2,000

This may be a little more difficult to follow; however, since both P and S would have recorded the asset sale on their separate records (P on 12/31/x2 and S on 12/31/x4), the asset and accumulation depreciation accounts would already have been removed. Thus, the combined work sheet entry need only adjust for the current year's excess depreciation, reduce the loss on sale of machinery to its consolidated $2,000 amount, and recognize the tax effects on both of these amounts. The $2,800 debit to Retained Earnings as of 1/1/x4 is the unrecognized gain net of tax as of that date.

The combined journal entry may be easier to visualize if the three work sheet entries it replaces are listed side by side. In any event, there is nothing wrong with using three work sheet entries instead of one (see Illustration 5–5).

Illustration 5–5

19x4 Work Sheet Entries

	(1) Dr. (Cr.)	(2) Dr. (Cr.)	(3) Dr. (Cr.)	Combined Dr. (Cr.)
Retained earnings	$ 2,800			$ 2,800
Prepaid federal income tax	1,200	$ (600)	$ (600)	−0−
Machinery and equipment	10,000		(10,000)	−0−
Accumulated depreciation	(14,000)	2,000	12,000	−0−
Federal income tax provision		600	600	1,200
Depreciation expense		(2,000)		(2,000)
Loss on sale of machinery			(2,000)	(2,000)
Totals	−0−	−0−	−0−	−0−

Tax: In preparing a consolidated federal income tax return the deferral and restoration entries are quite different from those for financial reporting. In the prior example of a sale of a depreciable asset by P to S, the entries for consolidated tax return purposes at 12/31/x2 would be:

Gain on sale of asset (P)	6,000	
Deferred gain (P)		6,000

Then each year (19x3 and 19x4) that S depreciates the asset, the entry would be:

Deferred gain (P)	2,000	
Gain on sale of asset (P) ($10,000 ÷ $30,000 × $6,000 = $2,000)		2,000

Thus, as S depreciates this asset (one third each year), one third of the deferred gain is recognized because of the depreciation taken by S. The recognition of the deferred gain offsets the $2,000 yearly increase in depreciation because of the intercorporate sale. The sale to the outsider on 12/31/x4 would trigger the remaining deferred gain. Thus, in 19x4 $2,000 of the gain would be recognized because of the depreciation by S and $2,000 would be recognized on the sale to the outsider.* The $2,000 of deferred gain recognized because of the sale to the outsider, in effect, reduces the consolidated loss on that sale from $4,000 to $2,000.

The tax return entries are a lot easier than the financial accounting entries because they are on a before-tax basis. In addition, these entries do not have to adjust the individual balance sheet accounts and recognizing $2,000 of the deferred gain in years 19x3 and 19x4, due to depreciation, offsets the excess depreciation expense being reported on the return. Thus, being able to offset gains against expenses also makes the tax return entries easier. This also has the significant advantage of keeping the results for each separate legal entity intact. This is very important for tax purposes; it is necessary in determining each firm's dividend paying potential and for obtaining a basis upon which to apportion the consolidated tax liability among the entities filing the consolidated tax return.

* *Federal Income Tax Regulations,* sec. 1,1502-13(d)(1) and (f)(1).

Intercorporate Sales from the Subsidiary to the Parent. While the previous discussion concentrated on intercorporate sales from the parent to the subsidiary, the same rules (absent deferral and restoration adjustments by the parent) also apply when the subsidiary is the selling member. In this case, however, the deferrals and restorations (but not offsets) can affect the minority interest. It is important to realize that restoration of deferred gain or loss is always attributed to the selling corporation even though the buying corporation's depreciation amount is in effect being reduced or increased in order to reflect consolidated depreciation. A reduction in depreciation results in increased income, and this income is attributed to the selling corporation.

To illustrate this, assume that P corporation purchases on 1/1/x1 80 percent of S Corporation for $300,000. As of January 1, 19x1, the par value of S Corporation's outstanding common stock was $100,000, additional paid-in capital was $20,000, and retained earnings were $250,000. Assume that S reports $40,000 of net earnings each year and pays $20,000 in dividends. Also assume that any cost in excess of book value is attributable to machinery with a 10-year useful life with straight-line depreciation being used. On 12/31/x1 S sells a depreciable asset which originally cost $40,000 and which had a book value of $20,000 to P for $30,000 cash. Assume P depreciates the asset over the remaining 5-year useful life using the straight-line method. Separate tax returns are filed, and there is a flat 30 percent corporate tax rate.

The analysis of S Corporation would appear as shown in Illustration 5–6 using alternative methods 2 or 3.

If P had purchased this asset with a note payable, the interest expense of P would be offset against the interest income of S. But since this would not increase or decrease consolidated net earnings, the offset would not be reflected in the net asset analysis. At this point there is one corporation and no net effect on earnings.

Intercorporate Sales of Inventory. This is probably the most common of all intercorporate transactions, and it often involves both offset and deferral type consolidation entries. Just as with the sale of any other asset, the gain on these sales is not recognized until the items are sold outside the affiliated group. The determination of this fact depends on the inventory flow assumption (e.g., Fifo, Lifo) used by the buying affiliate.

For purposes of illustration, assume that all of P's sales are to S and at a markup of 25 percent on P's cost. Assume further that all of S's purchases are from P and that there are no ending and no beginning inventories. Assume that S uses a 30 percent markup on costs. This is summarized in Illustration 5–7.

Since consolidation is a one entity concept, the following offset entry in journal entry format is necessary for financial reporting:

Sales 750,000
    Cost of goods sold   750,000

The $750,000 sales to S are intercorporate and must be removed. The debit to Sales and the credit to Cost of Goods Sold offset, and this leaves only S's sales and P's cost of goods sold. It should be noted that

Illustration 5-6

S Corporation	Net Assets	80 Percent Majority	20 Percent Minority
Capital stock	$100,000	$ 80,000	$20,000
Additional paid-in capital	20,000	16,000	4,000
Retained earnings, 1/1/x1	250,000	200,000	50,000
	370,000	296,000	74,000
To increase machinery to fair value	5,000*	4,000	1,000
Adjusted net assets, 1/1/x1	375,000	300,000	75,000
Dividends, 19x1	(20,000)	(16,000)	(4,000)
Earnings, 19x1	40,000		
Depreciation of machinery	(500)*	26,000	6,500
Deferral of gain on sale to P	(10,000)		
Deferral of tax on deferred gain	3,000		
Adjusted net assets, 12/31/x1	387,500	310,000	77,500
Dividends, 19x2	(20,000)	(16,000)	(4,000)
Earnings, 19x2	40,000		
Depreciation of machinery	(500)*		
Restoration of gain (due to depreciation taken by P)	2,000†	32,720	8,180
Restoration of tax	(600)†		
Adjusted net assets, 12/31/x2	$408,400	$326,720	$81,680

(Consolidation adjustments bracket the rows from Dividends, 19x1 through Deferral of tax on deferred gain; $32,500 adjusted net earnings. Consolidation adjustments bracket the rows from Dividends, 19x2 through Restoration of tax; $40,900 adjusted net earnings.)

* There is no tax effect involved in depreciating the cost in excess of book value attributed to machinery as this is a permanent difference. Reporting this item at full value allows us to retain the 80% and 20% relationship between the majority and the minority interests. Again, actual practice almost always follows alternative 1 which would destroy the 80%–20% ownership relationship.

† This is the restoration of one fifth of the gain net of tax on the 19x1 sale to P and is recognized because depreciation expense, as reported by P, will be reduced by $2,000.

on a consolidated basis S's cost of goods sold is not a cost at all since it is really P's sales and that P's sales are not sales to outsiders. S's sales, $975,000, are to outsiders; and P's cost of goods sold, $600,000, represents the cost of these sales, thus the consolidated gross margin is $375,000 (S's sales of $975,000 − P's costs of goods sold of $600,000, or P's gross margin of $150,000 + S's gross margin of $225,000).

Illustration 5-7

	P	S
Sales	$750,000 →	$975,000
Cost of goods sold	600,000	→ 750,000
Gross margin	$150,000	$225,000
	25% markup on cost	30% markup on cost

> **Tax:** On a consolidated tax return the gross margin would also be $375,000, but there would be no adjustment for sales or cost of goods sold because they offset; thus, on the tax return sales would be $1,725,000 ($750,000 + $975,000) and the cost of goods sold would be $1,350,000 ($600,000 + $750,000).

If S in the prior example had a $50,000 ending inventory and no beginning inventory, the summary would be as shown in Illustration 5–8.

Illustration 5–8

	P	S	S's Ending Inventory
Sales	$750,000	$910,000	
Cost of goods sold	600,000	700,000	+ $50,000 (at P's sales price)
Gross margin	$150,000	$210,000	−10,000 (25% markup on P's cost*)
	25% markup on cost	30% markup on cost	$40,000 (at P's cost)

* Translates to a 20 percent markup or P's sales price.

The combination offset and deferral entry in journal entry format would be (again assuming that P has not made corresponding equity method adjustments):

```
Sales ............................................................. 750,000
    Inventory ....................................................         10,000
    Cost of goods sold ($700,000 + $40,000) ..............        740,000
```

The $750,000 debit to Sales offsets or removes all of P's sales to S including the portion that remains in S's inventory. The cost of that inventory was also recorded as a part of P's cost of goods sold, and on a consolidated basis this has not yet been sold to outsiders. Thus, the above entry defers the $10,000 gross margin (25 percent of P's cost or 20 percent of P's sales price) from S's ending inventory reducing it to cost on a consolidated basis. The entry also offsets or removes S's costs of goods sold ($700,000) and *reduces* P's costs of goods sold for the cost of S's ending inventory ($40,000) which on a consolidated basis is *unsold*. Therefore, the consolidated gross margin is $350,000 ($910,000 consolidated sales less $560,000 ($600,000 − $40,000) consolidated cost of goods sold) or (P's gross margin of $150,000 less the $10,000 deferral of gross profit in S's ending inventory plus S's gross margin of $210,000).

> **Tax:** If P and S were filing a consolidated tax return, the only consolidation entry would be:
>
> Cost of goods sold* 10,000
>   Deferred gross profit on inventory 10,000
>
> * This debt could be to either revenue or cost of goods sold.
>
> As affected by the above entry, the tax return would then show sales of $1,660,000 ($750,000 + $910,000) and cost of goods sold of $1,310,000 ($600,000 + $700,000 + $10,000) which would produce the same $350,000 gross margin as shown on the financial statements. Thus, the tax return would reflect only the deferral part of the entry and not the offset part.

If we assume for the following year that the same intercorporate sales and same markups exist but that S's ending inventory (on its separate books) is now $70,000, the summary (temporarily ignoring the beginning inventory) would be as given in Illustration 5–9.

Illustration 5–9

	P	S	S's Ending Inventory	
Sales...............	$750,000 ⟶	$884,000		
Cost of goods sold	600,000 =	680,000	+ $70,000	(at P's sales price)
Gross margin	$150,000	$204,000	− 14,000	(25% markup on P's cost at P's cost)
	25% markup on cost	30% markup on cost	$56,000	

The deferral entry assuming a Fifo flow would be:

Sales 750,000
    Inventory 14,000
    Cost of goods sold ($680,000 + $56,000) 736,000

While this deferral takes care of current year intercorporate sales and the ending inventory, it does not consider the impact of the beginning intercorporate inventory on S's costs of goods sold. It must be remembered that last year's consolidation entry was not recorded on S's books; thus, the beginning inventory was "overstated" by $10,000, which was P's gross margin in that inventory. In the analysis, the sale of the beginning inventory would have increased S's cost of goods sold and sales by $50,000 and $65,000, respectively. An analysis including the effects of the beginning inventory would be as shown in Illustration 5–10.

Illustration 5–10

	P	S	
			$ 50,000 Beginning inventory
			750,000 Purchases
			800,000 Available for sale
Sales................	$750,000	$949,000	70,000 Ending inventory
Cost of goods sold	600,000	730,000	→ $730,000 Cost of goods sold
Gross margin	$150,000	$219,000	
	25% markup on cost	30% markup on cost	

Or if you look only at the effects of the beginning inventory this would be:

	S		Beginning Inventory
			$40,000 (at P's cost)
Sales................	$65,000		10,000 (P's gross margin)
Cost of goods sold	50,000	→	$50,000 (at S's cost)
Gross margin	$15,000		
	30% markup on cost		

Another entry is necessary to restore the effects of last year's deferral of gross profit in S's beginning inventory of this year:

Retained earnings (1/1/xx)	10,000	
Cost of goods sold		10,000

Because last year's consolidation entry was not recorded, P's retain earnings is "overstated" (again assuming no prior equity method adjustments) as is S's cost of goods sold. The consolidated cost of goods sold would be the $40,000 cost of S's beginning inventory plus $600,000 cost of current year sales by P to S less $56,000 cost of S's ending inventory or $584,000. This can also be calculated as $600,000 P's cost of goods sold plus $730,000 S's cost of goods sold less the two work sheet credits to the cost of goods sold of $736,000 and $10,000 or $584,000.

Our analysis of the intercorporate inventory aspects of preparing consolidated financial statements has thus far ignored the income tax consequences. Since this cannot be ignored in the real world, it is not ignored in this accounting text. Thus, at this point we return to the illustration where there was an ending intercorporate inventory but no beginning inventory and look at the potential income tax problems involved in the process.

First, let's assume that separate federal income tax returns were filed by P and S in which case income tax would have been paid by P on the intercorporate gain which was included in S's ending inventory. Assuming a 30 percent tax rate, P as a separate entity would have recognized the $10,000 gain (again assuming no prior equity method adjustments) and would have paid a $3,000 tax on it. This would have resulted in the following tax effect on P's books.

FIT provision	3,000	
FIT payable (or cash)		3,000

For consolidated statements the tax would have to be deferred until the $10,000 gain is recognized. The *consolidation* entry would be:

Prepaid FIT (or deferred charge)	3,000	
FIT provision		3,000

In the example for the following year the gain in the ending inventory of S is $14,000. This will necessitate a $4,200 tax deferral, and under the Fifo flow assumption, recognition of last year's deferred gain and related tax. The recognition of the tax on the gain in the beginning inventory would merely reverse the above work sheet entry except that the credit would be to Retained Earnings because the tax provision would have been closed to Retained Earnings on P's books.

FIT provision	3,000	
Retained earnings (1/1)		3,000

The work sheet entry to defer the tax on the deferred gain in the ending inventory would be:

Prepaid FIT	4,200	
FIT provision ($14,000 × 30%)		4,200

If P and S have filed consolidated income tax returns rather than separate returns and if the intercorporate gains in inventory have been deferred for tax purposes, a timing difference would have been created. In this case on P's separate books the $10,000 gain (in S's ending inventory) would not be deferred. In addition, current recognition by P would require the recognition of the related income tax. Thus, on P's separate books for the first year the $10,000 gain would be recognized for book purposes (again assuming no equity method adjustment) but not for tax purposes. Now a timing difference has been created, and P would have to record the related tax. On P's books this would be:

FIT provision	3,000	
Deferred tax credit		3,000

For the next year under the Fifo flow assumption and the consolidated tax return, the $3,000 deferred tax credit would be paid. The effect of this on P's books would be:

Deferred tax credit	3,000	
FIT payable (or cash)		3,000

In addition, however, P would record deferred tax on the $14,000 gain in S's ending inventory. The effect of this would be:

FIT provision	4,200	
Deferred tax credit		4,200

Now that we have seen what would have been recorded on P's books (absent equity method adjustments), the income tax deferral for consolidated financial statements should be easier.

For the first year the work sheet deferral entry would be:

Deferred tax credit	3,000	
FIT provision		3,000

For the second year there would be a restoration and a deferral entry for the tax on the inventory profits. The restoration work sheet entry would be:

FIT provision	3,000	
Retained earnings		3,000

The deferral work sheet entry would be:

Deferred tax credit	4,200	
FIT provision		4,200

In summary, for the two years the consolidation intercorporate sales and related tax entries would be as shown in Illustration 5–11.

Illustration 5–11

	Financial Consolidation Work Sheet Entries	With Current Recognition of Gain on Separate Tax Returns		With Deferred Recognition of Gain on Consolidated Tax Returns	
	First year:				
Deferral entries	Sales	750,000		750,000	
	Inventory		10,000		10,000
	Cost of goods sold		740,000		740,000
	Prepaid FIT	3,000			
	FIT provision		3,000		
	Deferred tax credit			3,000	
	FIT provision				3,000
	Second year:				
Restoration entries	Retained earnings	10,000		10,000	
	Cost of goods sold		10,000		10,000
	FIT provision	3,000		3,000	
	Retained earnings		3,000		3,000
Deferral entries	Sales	750,000		750,000	
	Inventory		14,000		14,000
	Cost of goods sold		736,000		736,000
	Prepaid FIT	4,200			
	FIT provision		4,200		
	Deferred tax credit			4,200	
	FIT provision				4,200

It should be noted that even when corporations are preparing consolidated financial statements and are filing a consolidated tax return that on separate corporation records, intercorporate gain and its related tax are recognized (except for equity method deferrals when the parent is the selling corporation). Thus, work sheet tax deferral or offset entries are necessary even when filing a consolidated tax return.

SUBSIDIARY SALES TO PARENT

Thus far, except for a brief discussion after intercorporate sales of fixed assets, we have considered only those cases where the subsidiary is the purchasing entity in an intercorporate transaction. Theoretically, at least, the analysis of an intercorporate sale is more difficult when the subsidiary is the selling entity. This is because the deferral and restoration of the intercorporate gains or losses will also impact on the investment in the subsidiary account under the equity method and on the minority interest's share of the subsidiary's earnings under the recommended 100 percent deferral concept. To illustrate this, assume that X purchased 90 percent of the stock of Z on 1/1/x1 for $110,000 and that the book value of each asset and liability equaled its fair value. Also assume that the owner's equity accounts for Z were capital stock, $40,000; additional paid-in capital, $10,000; and retained earnings, $50,000; and that Z reported earnings of $15,000 for 19x1 and paid $6,000 in dividends. The analysis would appear as follows for alternative methods 1 or 2 (see Illustration 5–12). It should be noted that under these methods only the majority interest in goodwill is reported, and thus all of the subsequent amortization of goodwill is charged against the majority interest.

Illustration 5–12

Z Corporation	Net Assets	90% Majority	10% Minority
Capital stock	$ 40,000	$ 36,000	$ 4,000
Additional paid-in capital	10,000	9,000	1,000
Retained earnings, 1/1/x1	50,000	45,000	5,000
Net assets	100,000	90,000	10,000
Goodwill ($110,000 − $90,000)	20,000	20,000	–0–
Adjusted net assets, 1/1/x1	120,000	110,000	10,000
Dividends, 19x1	(6,000)	(5,400)	(600)
Earnings, 19x1	15,000	13,500	1,500
Goodwill amortization ($20,000 ÷ 40 years)	(500)	(500)	–0–
Adjusted net assets, 12/31/x1	$128,500	$117,600	$10,900

Now suppose X and Z have been filing separate tax returns with a 30 percent tax rate and that Z in 19x2 has $25,000 of earnings and pays $5,000 in dividends. Assume that Z had sold $20,000 of goods to X in 19x1 at a 50 percent markup on sales price and that $4,000 of these items were still on hand at 12/31/x1. Also assume the same intercorporate sales and markup in 19x2 and that $6,000 of the items were in the ending inventory of X on 12/31/x2. If the 100 percent deferral concept is followed, these intercorporate sales where the subsidiary is the selling corporation will affect the above analysis as shown in Illustration 5–13.

Illustration 5–13

Z Corporation	Net Assets	90% Majority	10% Minority	
Capital stock	$ 40,000	$ 36,000	$ 4,000	
Additional paid-in capital	10,000	9,000	1,000	
Retained earnings, 1/1/x1	50,000	45,000	5,000	
Net assets, 1/1/x1	100,000	90,000	$10,000	
Goodwill ($110,000 − $90,000)	20,000	20,000	−0−	
Adjusted net assets, 1/1/x1	120,000	110,000	$10,000	
Dividends, 19x1	(6,000)	(5,400)	(600)	
Earnings, 19x1	15,000	13,500	1,500	$1,360 minority share of adjusted earnings
Goodwill amortization ($20,000 ÷ 40)	(500)*	(500)	−0−	
Inventory—deferral of earnings	(2,000)	(1,800)	(200)	
Deferral of tax ($2,000 × 30%)	600 $13,100 adjusted earnings	540 $11,740 share of earnings	60	
Adjusted net assets, 12/31/x1	127,100	116,340	$10,760	
Dividends, 19x2	(5,000)	(4,500)	(500)	
Earnings, 19x2	25,000	22,500	2,500	$2,430 minority share of adjusted earnings
Goodwill amortization	(500)*	(500)	−0−	
Restoration of 19x1 deferral	2,000	1,800	200	
Restoration of the tax	(600)	(540)	(60)	
Inventory—deferral of earnings	(3,000) $23,800 adjusted earnings	(2,700) $21,370 share of adjusted earnings	(300)	
Deferral of tax	900	810	90	
Adjusted net assets, 12/31/x2	$145,900	$133,210	$12,690	

* Note that goodwill amortization is a permanent difference without a tax effect.

On a separate corporation basis Z would recognize the intercorporate gains in the year of the intercorporate sales in order to report them to the minority interest, and on a separate tax return these gains would be currently taxed. Thus, some accounting theorists argue that only the majority portion should be deferred in consolidation. In fact, this position would be consistent with the official position that only the majority portion of goodwill should be shown when cost exceeds fair value. Nevertheless the official position is for 100 percent deferral. This is based on the concept that consolidation is accounting for the interests of the shareholders of the parent corporation, and that minority shareholders should always look to the separate financial statements of the subsidiary to examine the accounting for their interests.

The previous analysis would appear as shown in Illustration 5–14 if majority only deferral had been followed instead of 100 percent deferral.

Illustration 5–14

Z Corporation	Net Assets	90% Majority	10% Minority	
Capital stock	$ 40,000	$ 36,000	$ 4,000	
Additional paid-in capital	10,000	9,000	1,000	
Retained earnings	50,000	45,000	5,000	
Net assets, 1/1/x1	100,000	90,000	10,000	
Goodwill ($110,000 − $90,000)	20,000	20,000	−0−	
Adjusted net assets, 1/1/x1	120,000	110,000	10,000	
Dividends, 19x1	(6,000)	(5,400)	(600)	Minority share of earnings
Earnings, 19x1	15,000	13,500	1,500	
Inventory—deferral (90% × $2,000)	(1,800)	(1,800)	−0−	
Deferral of tax ($1,800 × 30%)	540	540	−0−	
Goodwill amortization ($20,000 ÷ 40)	(500)	(500)	−0−	
Adjusted net assets, 12/31/x1	127,240	116,340	10,900	
Dividends, 19x2	(5,000)	(4,500)	(500)	Minority share of earnings
Earnings, 19x2	25,000	22,500	2,500	
Restoration	1,800	1,800	−0−	
Tax on the restored gain	(540)	(540)	−0−	
Deferral ($3,000 × 90%)	(2,700)	(2,700)	−0−	
Tax on the deferred gain	810	810	−0−	
Goodwill amortization	(500)	(500)	−0−	
Adjusted net assets, 12/31/x2	$146,110	$133,210	$12,900	

($13,240 adjusted earnings; $11,740 share of adjusted earnings; $23,870 adjusted earnings; $21,370 share of adjusted earnings)

It should be noted that there is no difference between 100 percent or majority only deferral as far as the majority interest is concerned. The only difference is in the size of the minority interest and in the consolidated net assets. By recognizing their share of the intercorporate gains (or losses), the minority interest and the adjusted net assets are increased (or decreased). Throughout the remainder of this text the 100 percent deferral concept is employed.

A COMPLETE ILLUSTRATION

The following facts will be used to illustrate the preparation of the analysis of the subsidiary, the consolidation entries, and the three-section work sheet:

Illustration 5–15

X AND Y CORPORATIONS
Trial Balance
12/31/x2

	X	Y
Cash	$ 171,067	$ 43,800
Accounts receivable (net)	141,200	60,000
Inventory, 12/31/x2	210,000	40,000
Prepaid tax	–0–	–0–
Plant assets	654,700	550,000
Accumulated depreciation	(336,900)	(129,000)
Investment in Y stock	324,400*	–0–
Accounts payable	(10,000)	(12,200)
Accrued liabilities (including taxes)	(105,000)	(46,000)
Bonds payable	–0–	(100,000)
Premium on bonds payable	–0–	(1,600)
Minority interest	–0–	–0–
Capital stock	(200,000)	(100,000)
Additional paid-in capital	(100,000)	(20,000)
Retained earnings, 1/1/x2	(600,000)	(270,000)
Dividends declared	10,000	5,000
Sales	(700,000)	(400,000)
Cost of goods sold	390,000	200,000
Selling expenses	90,000	80,000
Administrative and other expenses (including taxes)	78,933	100,000
Equity in Y earnings	(18,400)*	–0–
Totals	–0–	–0–
Inventory, 1/1/x2	$ 200,000	$ 80,000

* Agrees with the investment analysis in Illustration 5–6.

X Corporation purchased, on 1/1/x1, 80 percent of the outstanding shares of Y Corporation for $300,000. As of 1/1/x1, the par value of Y Corporation's outstanding common stock was $100,000, additional paid-in capital was $20,000, and retained earnings were $250,000. Y Corporation had net income of $40,000 during 19x1 and paid $20,000 in dividends. All depreciable assets are assumed to have 10-year useful lives, and the straight-line write-off method is used. Assume that any cost in excess of book value or book value in excess of cost is attributable to an office building.

1. On 12/31/x2 X Corporation records show an account payable to Y Corporation of $6,000 for purchases. In addition, Y Corporation records show that X owes Y $6,000.
2. X Corporation's inventory of $210,000 at 12/31/x2 includes $10,000 worth of goods which are part of the $100,000 worth purchased from Y this year at a 50 percent markup based on Y's sales price.
3. X Corporation's $200,000 inventory on 1/1/x2, included $20,000 of

goods purchased from Y in the previous year. Y's gross profit as a percentage of sales price for that year was 50 percent.
4. Y Corporation reported earnings and dividends of $40,000 and $20,000, respectively, for 19x1 and $20,000 and $5,000, respectively, for 19x2.
5. Assume a flat 30 percent corporate income tax rate with separate tax returns being filed.
6. X does not anticipate every disposing of the Y stock.

The trial balances of X and Y Corporations as of 12/31/x2 are given in Illustration 5–15. Illustration 5–16 gives an analysis of X's investment in Y Corporation. The work sheet of X and Y Corporation is shown in Illustration 5–17.

Illustration 5–16
ANALYSIS OF INVESTMENT IN Y CORPORATION USING ALTERNATIVE METHODS 2 OR 3

	Y Corporation	Net Assets		80% Majority Interest		20% Minority Interest	
	Capital stock	$100,000		$ 80,000		$20,000	
	Additional paid-in capital	20,000		16,000		4,000	
	Retained earnings, 1/1/x2	250,000		200,000		50,000	
	Net assets, 1/1/x1	370,000		296,000		74,000	
	To reflect depreciable building at fair value	5,000		4,000		1,000	
	Adjusted net assets, 1/1/x2	375,000		300,000		75,000	
	Recorded dividends, 19x1	(20,000)*		(16,000)		(4,000)	
Consolidation adjustments	Recorded earnings, 19x1	40,000	$32,500 adjusted earnings	32,000	$26,000 share of adjusted earnings	8,000	$6,500 share of adjusted earnings
	To reflect depreciation on asset increase	(500)†		(400)		(100)	
	Markup remaining in the ending inventory of X	(10,000)		(8,000)		(2,000)	
	Tax on inventory markup	3,000		2,400		600	
	Adjusted net assets, 12/31/x1	387,500		310,000		77,500	
	Recorded dividends, 19x2	(5,000)		(4,000)		(1,000)	
	Recorded earnings, 19x2	20,000	$23,000 adjusted earnings	16,000	$18,400 share of adjusted earnings	4,000	$4,600 share of adjusted earnings
Consolidation adjustments	To reflect depreciation	(500)		(400)		(100)	
	To restore beginning inventory markup	10,000		8,000		2,000	
	Tax effect	(3,000)		(2,400)		(600)	
	Markup in ending X's inventory	(5,000)		(4,000)		(1,000)	
	Tax effect	1,500		1,200		300	
	Adjusted net assets, 12/31/x2	$405,500		$324,400		$81,100	

* It should also be noted that X would not have to pay any federal income tax on the dividends received from Y because with 80 percent or more ownership there is a 100 percent dividends received deduction. In addition, this means that X will not have to provide any federal income tax on the unremitted earnings of Y unless they would anticipate recognizing this income through the sale of the Y stock.

† No tax effect on the depreciation since the write-up of the assets to fair value would not be made for tax purposes. The purchase of Y stock by X does not increase the tax basis of Y's assets.

Illustration 5–17
X AND Y CORPORATIONS CONSOLIDATED WORK SHEET

	Trial Balances, 12/31/19x2		Consolidation Entries		Con-solidated
	X Corp. Dr. (Cr.)	Y Corp. Dr. (Cr.)	Dr.	Cr.	Dr. (Cr.)
Earnings statement:					
Sales	(700,000)	(400,000)	(2) 100,000		(1,000,000)
Cost of goods sold	390,000	200,000		(2) 95,000	485,000
Selling expenses	90,000	80,000		(4) 10,000	170,000
Administrative expenses (including taxes)			(5) 3,000		
Equity in Y earnings	78,933	100,000	(8) 500	(3) 1,500	180,933
	(18,400)		(7) 18,400		–0–
Minority interest deduction	–0–	–0–	(6) 4,600		4,600
Earnings	(159,467)	(20,000)	126,500	106,500	(159,467)
Retained earnings statement:					
Retained earnings, 1/1/x2	(600,000)	(270,000)	(4) 10,000	(5) 3,000	(600,000)
Dividends declared	10,000	5,000	(9) 5,000	(9) 5,000	10,000
Earnings—brought forward	(159,467)	(20,000)	(10) 258,000		(159,467)
			126,500	106,500	

Retained earnings, 12/31/x2	(749,467)	(285,000)	399,500		114,500	(749,467)
Statement of financial position:						
Cash	171,067	43,800				214,867
Accounts receivable—net	141,200	60,000		(1)	6,000	195,200
Inventory, 12/31/x2	210,000	40,000		(2)	5,000	245,000
Prepaid tax	-0-	-0-	(3) 1,500			1,500
Plant assets	654,700	550,000	(10) 5,000			1,209,700
Accumulated depreciation	(336,900)	(129,000)		(8)	500	(466,900)
				(10)	500	
Investment in Y stock	324,400	-0-		(7)	18,400	-0-
Accounts payable	(10,000)	(12,200)	(1) 6,000	(10)	306,000	(16,200)
Accrued liabilities (including taxes)	(105,000)	(46,000)				(151,000)
Bonds payable	-0-	(100,000)				(100,000)
Premium on bonds payable	-0-	(1,600)				(1,600)
Minority interest equity	-0-	-0-		(6)	4,600	(81,100)
				(10)	76,500	
Capital stock	(200,000)	(100,000)	(10) 100,000			(200,000)
Additional paid-in capital	(100,000)	(20,000)	(10) 20,000			(100,000)
Retained earnings— brought forward	(749,467)	(285,000)	399,500		114,500	(749,467)
	-0-	-0-	532,000		532,000	-0-

The 19x2 consolidation entries in journal entry format would be as follows:

(1)

Accounts payable	6,000	
Accounts receivable		6,000

To offset intercorporate receivables and payables.

(2)

Sales	100,000	
Inventory ($10,000 × 50%)		5,000
Cost of goods sold ($90,000 + $5,000)		95,000

To offset intercorporate sales and cost of goods sold and to defer the markup in the ending inventory of X.

(3)

Prepaid tax ($5,000 × 30%)	1,500	
Administrative expenses—FIT provision		1,500

To defer the federal income tax on the deferred gain in inventory.

(4)

Retained earnings (1/1/x2)	10,000	
Cost of goods sold		10,000

To remove the effect of the gain in the beginning inventory from the cost of goods sold.

(5)

Administrative and other expenses	3,000	
Retained earnings (1/1/x2)		3,000

To reflect the tax on the gain in the beginning inventory.

(6)

Minority interest deduction	4,600	
Minority interest equity		4,600

To reflect minority share of Y earnings as a deduction in the earnings statement and as an increase in minority interest equity.

(7)

Equity in Y earnings	18,400	
Investment in Y stock		18,400

To remove equity method income.

(8)

Administrative expense—depreciation	500	
Accumulated depreciation		500

To reflect the 19x2 depreciation on restatement of the asset to fair value.

(9)
Retained earnings 5,000
    Dividends declared 5,000
To close the effect of dividends paid by Y.

(10)
Capital stock 100,000
Additional paid-in capital 20,000
Retained earnings (1/1/x2) 258,000*
Plant assets 5,000
    Accumulated depreciation (as of 1/1/x2) 500
    Investment in Y stock .... 306,000†
    Minority interest equity .... 76,500‡
To reflect the substitution entry.

* $270,000 at 1/1/x2 less 19x2 dividend of $5,000 and less the aftertax markup in 12/31/x1 inventories of $7,000 (entries 4 and 5) = $258,000.
† $310,000 at 1/1/x2 less share of 19x2 dividend of $4,000 = $306,000.
‡ $77,500 at 1/1/x2 less share of 19x2 dividend of $1,000 = $76,500. It should be noted that the credits to Investment in Y Stock total $324,400 ($18,400 + $306,000) and the credits to Minority Interest Equity total $81,100 ($4,600 + $76,500).

Many students find the three-section work sheet difficult primarily because it combines what would normally be the closing process with the consolidation entries. This forces some consolidation entries to be reflected as adjustments of beginning-of-the-year retained earnings (for example, see journal entry 10). The process of bringing the totals from the earnings statement section of the work sheet to the retained earnings section and from the retained earnings section to the statement of financial position section in effect closes the revenue and expense accounts to retained earnings for current year operations.

If one only needed a consolidated statement of financial position, the consolidation entries would be as follows:

(1)
Accounts payable 6,000
    Accounts receivable 6,000

(2)
Retained earnings 3,500
Prepaid FIT 1,500
    Inventory 5,000

(3)
Capital stock 100,000
Additional paid-in capital 20,000
Retained earnings 281,500*
Plant assets 5,000
    Accumulated depreciation 1,000
    Investment in Y stock .... 324,400†
    Minority ineterest equity .... 81,100†

* $285,000 per trial balance − $3,500 from entry number 2 = $281,500.
† Per the Y Corporation analysis.

IMPACT ON EARNINGS UNDER THE EQUITY METHOD WHEN THE PARENT IS THE SELLING AFFILIATE

If consolidated statements were not being prepared, use of the equity method would normally be required. It should be realized that use of the equity method is not appreciably easier than consolidating. Under the equity method, all of the intercorporate gains and losses, and deferrals and restorations, would have to be analyzed and then the parent's share of the subsidiary's reported earning would have to be adjusted. This would be necessary so that the equity method would reflect the same net earnings as would be reported under consolidation. In addition to adjusting the parent's share of earnings from the subsidiary for intercorporate gains or losses, the parent's own earnings would have to reflect deferrals and restorations whenever it sells items to the subsidiary. Without this the use of the equity method would produce different net earnings than would be shown under consolidation.

This chapter has introduced intercorporate transactions involving offsets, deferrals, and restorations as well as the three-section work sheet. The next chapter continues on this introduction but differs in that it examines intercorporate debt transactions which trigger gain or loss recognition.

REVIEW QUESTIONS

1. What concept causes us to defer intercorporate gains or losses?
2. Why do subsidiaries often have the same year end as the parent corporation?
3. What is meant by a deferral entry, a restoration entry, and an offset entry? Give an example of each.
4. Why do the income tax consolidation rules ignore offset entries?
5. Why do offset entries not impact on minority interest?
6. Why must the prior year's deferral entries either be restated or restored?
7. What two things frequently trigger restoration of gain or loss involving intercorporate sales of fixed assets?
8. Why are deferral and restoration entries net of the tax effect often necessary for separate financial reporting?
9. Why are tax deferral and tax restoration entries necessary when gain or loss is being deferred or restored regardless of whether separate or consolidated tax returns are being filed?
10. Why are there no tax deferral or restoration entries necessary for cost in excess of book amounts due to acquisition of a subsidiary?
11. Why do intercorporate sales of inventory often involve both offsets and deferrals?
12. Why are restorations of gain or loss on intercorporate sales always attributed to the selling affiliate?

13. Why on intercorporate sales of inventory items is it important to know whether the seller's percentage markup is based on cost or on sales price?
14. Why in restoring profit included in the beginning inventory is Retained Earnings debited and Cost of Goods Sold credited?
15. Why in deferring the income tax on an intercorporate gain is a Deferred Tax Credit account involved in one case and a Deferred Tax Charge (or Prepaid Tax) account involved in another case?
16. Why are intercorporate sales from the subsidiary to the parent corporation somewhat more complex than when the parent is the selling corporation?
17. In a three-section consolidation work sheet how are the closing entries made?
18. What are the three sections of a three-section work sheet?
19. In what sections will minority interest usually appear?
20. As to intercorporate sales of inventory is the consolidation entry the same regardless of whether the parent (assuming no equity method adjustments have been made) or the subsidiary is the seller? If not, why not?
21. What effect does the majority only deferral and restoration concepts have when the parent is the selling corporation?
22. What effect does the majority only deferral and restoration concepts have when the subsidiary is the selling corporation?
23. When the parent is the selling corporation, what effect does this have on minority interest?
24. In reporting income under the equity method what effect is there on the parent's earning when it sells to the subsidiary?

PROBLEMS

Problem 1: Equity Consolidation

P Corporation has owned 90 percent of S since its inception. On 1/1/x1 P sold land to S for $80,000; the land originally cost P $30,000. Including this transaction, P had $150,000 of 19x1 net earnings from its own operations (excluding any earnings from S). S had net earnings of $60,000 in 19x1. On 1/1/x3 S resells the land to an outsider for $100,000. Assume separate tax returns are filed and that there is a flat 30 percent corporate tax rate.

Required:
1. Calculate P's 19x1 net earnings including its equity in S's net earnings.
2. Prepare P's equity method adjusting (deferring) entries, if any, for the intercorporate land sale for years 19x1, 19x2, and 19x3.
3. Assuming P and S also prepare consolidated statements, prepare the consolidation entries, if any, for years 19x1, 19x2, and 19x3.
4. Assume the 19x1 net earnings figures did not change but that S was the original seller and sold the land to P for $80,000 on 1/1/x1. The land had cost S $30,000 years earlier. On 1/1/x3 P sells the land to an outsider for $100,000.

a. Calculate P's 19x1 net earnings including its equity in S's net earnings.
b. Prepare the equity method adjusting (deferring) entries, if any, for the intercorporate sale for years 19x1, 19x2, and 19x3.
c. Assuming P and S also prepare consolidated statements, prepare the consolidation entries, if any, attributable to the land sale for years 19x1, 19x2, and 19x3.

Problem 2: Service and Potential Corporations

Service has owned 90 percent of Potential for many years. On 1/1/x1 Potential sold machinery it had used in its business to Service for $30,000. Potential originally paid $70,000 for this machinery and had taken $56,000 in depreciation on the machine. Thus, depreciation was taken on eight years of a 10-year straight-line life at $7,000 per year. Service has assigned this machine a 5-year life and is using the straight-line method. The corporations file separate tax returns, and the corporate tax rate is a flat 40 percent.

Required:

Prepare any deferral, restoration, and offset entries for this item for consolidated financial statement purposes as of 12/31/x1.

Problem 3: Invest and Divest

Invest, Inc., owns 90 percent of Divest, Inc. On 1/1/x1 Divest purchased a machine for $45,000 and used SYD depreciation with a 5-year life and zero salvage value. On 7/1/x3 Divest sold this machine to Invest for $20,000. Invest uses a 4-year life and straight-line depreciation with a zero salvage value for this asset. The corporations file separate tax returns, and the corporate income tax rate is a flat 30 percent.

Required:

In regard to this machine, prepare any deferral, offset, or restoration work sheet entries (in journal entry format) necessary for the preparation of consolidated financial statements at 12/31/x3, x4, x5, x6, and x7.

Problem 4: Asset Sales (AS) Corporation

The AS Corporation sold, on 1/1/x3, to its 80 percent owned subsidiary a machine which cost AS $80,000 and had been depreciated for two years of its seven-year estimated useful life under the SYD depreciation method assuming a zero salvage value. The Subsidiary Sales (SS) Corporation paid AS $90,000 for this machine. SS uses SYD depreciation and estimates a 7-year remaining life for the machine and a zero salvage value.

Required:

1. Assuming the corporations prepare consolidated financial statements and file separate tax returns (assume a flat 40 percent tax rate), prepare the deferral and restoration entries for years 19x3 and 19x4 (ignore any investment tax credit implications).

2. Assuming the corporations had used straight-line depreciation for financial reporting and SYD for tax purposes and prepared consolidated financial statements and filed a consolidated tax return, prepare the deferral and restoration entries for 19x3 and 19x4. (This part is difficult.)

Problem 5: High and Low Corporations

Low Corporation has been a subsidiary of High for many years. In the current year Low developed a new product which High had previously purchased from outsiders.

In December of this year High purchases $100,000 of this item from Low. Low sells to High at its cost plus 50 percent. Due to the use of the Lifo inventory flow, all but $10,000 of these items are deemed to have been sold to outsiders by High. The corporate tax rate is a flat 40 percent, and separate tax returns are filed.

Required:

Prepare any offsetting, deferral, and restoration entries needed to correctly reflect this item in the consolidated financial statements of the current year.

Problem 6: Tidings, Inc., and Action, Inc.

Tidings, Inc., owns 80 percent of Action, Inc. Last year Action sold inventory items to Tidings at a markup of one third of cost. Tidings had $40,000 of these items in its year-end inventory. In the current year Tidings purchased $300,000 of these items from Action and had $20,000 left in its ending inventory. Action's markup in the current year remained the same as in the prior year. The corporations file separate tax returns; assume a flat 30 percent corporate tax rate.

Required:

Prepare in journal entry format all deferral, offset, and restoration work sheet entries which would be necessary for these items in the preparation of current year consolidated financial statements.

Problem 7: Invent Corporation

Invent Corporation is an 80 percent owned subsidiary of Tory Corporation after its acquisition on 1/1/x4. Because of the nature of Invent's business, it sells most of its product to Tory where it is further processed before being sold. Last year, 19x4, Invent's sales to Tory were $600,000. Of this sum $550,000 was entered into production. Of these items, $40,000 was in work in process and $30,000 was in finished goods as of 12/31/x4. During 19x5 Invent's sales to Tory were $800,000. Of this sum $720,000 was entered into production; Tory uses a Fifo flow. Of the $720,000, $20,000 was in work in process and $50,000 was in finished goods as of 12/31/x5. Invent uses a standard markup of one third of cost on all its sales.

Required:

Prepare in journal entry form all of the offset, deferral, and restoration entries for the consolidated financial statements for these inventory items for years 19x4 and 19x5. Assume the corporations file separate tax returns and that there is a flat 40 percent tax rate.

Problem 8: Five Corporations

X Corporation was formed by Parent Corporation on 1/1/x6 with a net investment—an investment of assets in excess of liabilities—of $87,000. X Corporation is 100 percent owned by Parent Corporation; in addition, Parent Corporation rents most of the plant and facilities which it uses in its operations from X Corporation for an annual rental fee of $60,000. An 80 percent interest in Y, a domestic operating corporation, was acquired by Parent Corporation on 1/1/x7 for $300,000. Parent Corporation also acquired a 70 percent interest in Z Corporation, a South American operating affiliate, on 1/1/x7, for $60,900 (Z Corporation's financial statements have been recast in dollars). On 1/1/x7, a 30 percent interest in W Corporation was purchased at a cost of $240,000 by Parent Corporation as an investment. W Corporation is a major supplier of raw materials used in Parent Corporation's manufacturing operations. It is also a widely held corporation. In addition, Parent Corporation owns 100 shares of General Motors which had been purchased several years ago at a cost of $64 per share. For all corporations, assume that *book values equal fair values.*

Trial Balances
12/31/x7

	Parent	W	X	Y	Z
Current assets (except securities)	$ 529,628	$ 200,000	$ 49,000	$ 110,000	$ 100,000
Marketable securities (W and GM)	246,400	–0–	–0–	–0–	–0–
Investment in X Stock	89,000	–0–	–0–	–0–	–0–
Investment in Y Stock	300,000	–0–	–0–	–0–	–0–
Investment in Z Stock	60,900	–0–	–0–	–0–	–0–
Fixed assets	140,000	600,000	400,000	300,000	150,000
Liabilities	(310,900)	(80,000)	(360,000)	(90,000)	(125,000)
Capital stock	(500,000)	(200,000)	(67,000)	(200,000)	(50,000)
Additional paid-in capital	(60,000)	(300,000)	(20,000)	(10,000)	(10,000)
Retained earnings, 1/1/x7	(286,400)	(146,000)	(1,000)	(80,000)	(27,000)
Dividends declared and paid	20,000	6,000	1,000	30,000	1,000
Sales	(1,000,000)	(700,000)	(60,000)	(500,000)	(200,000)
Operating costs and expenses	800,000	620,000	58,000	440,000	161,000
Dividend income, W	(1,800)				
Dividend income, Y	(24,000)				
Dividend income, Z	(700)				
Dividend income, GM	(128)				
Subsidiary income, X	(2,000)				
Debits in excess of credits	–0–	–0–	–0–	–0–	–0–

Required:

1. Diagram the ownership network.
2. Prepare an analysis of each investment in a subsidiary or investee.
3. Prepare a consolidated balance sheet and income statement for the Parent Corporation and its subsidiaries except that Z Corporation is not to be consolidated. The equity method is to be used in accounting for Z.

Hint: You may wish to prepare the statements directly without the time delay of first preparing a work sheet (but support your answers—this may be done in the statements themselves).

6

Accounting for Intercorporate Debt—Transactions Which May Advance Gain or Loss Recognition

Pathways for Debt Acquisition
Direct Acquisition from the Member Issuing the Debt
Disposal of Directly Acquired Debt
    Sale to an Outsider
    Sale to Debtor or to Another Member
Acquisition from an Outside Party
The Problem of Allocating Gains and Losses
Years Subsequent to Acquisition from an Outside Party
The Minority Interest Aspects
A Working Paper Analysis

The previous chapter dealt extensively with the concepts underlying deferral and restoration type entries and introduced the idea of offset entries. This chapter extends the discussion of offset and deferral entries and deals extensively with the concept of advanced recognition. Advanced or triggered recognition is the opposite of the deferral concept. Under the deferral concept, recognition of intercorporate gain or loss on separate corporation records is deferred because intercorporate gain or loss is not recognized in the consolidation concept of a single entity. In other words, intercorporate corporation gain or loss becomes intracorporate gain or loss under the single-entity concept, and thus it is not recognized until a restoration event takes place.

The same single-entity concept requires offsets of intercorporate investments and debts, and of intercorporate interest revenue and interest expense. It may also require advancing the date of recognition of gains or losses whenever one member's debt obligations are acquired by another member of the consolidated group. Accounting for debt acquisitions varies greatly depending on how the intercorporate debt is acquired.

PATHWAYS FOR DEBT ACQUISITION

A member of the consolidated group can acquire a debt issue of another member (1) from the debtor corporation, (2) from another investing member (who may have acquired this security either from the debtor, from another member, or from an outside party), or (3) from an outside party (who may have acquired the security from the debtor or from a member of the debtor's group or from another outside party). In a partial diagram this would appear as shown in Illustration 6–1.

The paths for disposal of this investment before maturity would simply be the reverse of these three paths. Gain or loss, however, is recognized on a consolidated basis *only on the acquisition* of the investment *from an outsider* and not on a subsequent sale of the investment before maturity. Thus, before any gain or loss is recognized on a consolidated basis, an outside party must have been a holder of the debt. This principle is discussed in depth in the following sections of this chapter.

Correctly reflecting intercorporate held bonds or notes in consolidated financial statements is often considered to be among the more difficult consolidation entries. In this regard, it is necessary to remember constantly that the prior year's consolidation entries were not recorded on the separate entity records and that amortization of premium or discount (on the separate entity records) is a continuous process over the life of the bond issue. This amortization eliminates the need for restoration entries in regard to these transactions.

Illustration 6–1
PATHS FOR ACQUISITION OF INTERCORPORATE DEBT

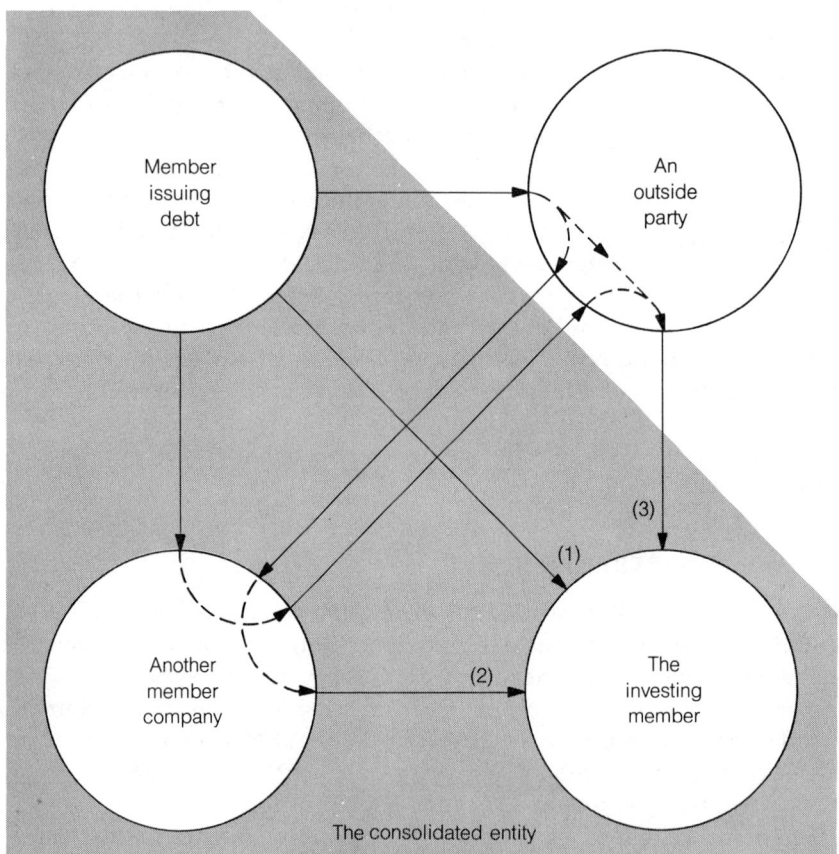

DIRECT ACQUISITION FROM THE MEMBER ISSUING THE DEBT

The least complex consolidation entries for intercorporate held debt arise when the investing member buys the entire bond issue of the issuing member at the date of the issue. In this case there are only offsetting entries to consider.

Assume that P on 1/1/x1 issues $100,000 of 5-year bonds with a 10 percent interest rate payable annually on 12/31. Assume that S, a 100 percent owned subsidiary, buys the entire issue for the $100,000 face value. The consolidation (offset) entries would be as follows for the first three years:

	19x1		19x2		19x3	
Bonds payable	100,000		100,000		100,000	
Bond investment		100,000		100,000		100,000
Interest revenue	10,000		10,000		10,000	
Interest expense		10,000		10,000		10,000

It should be noted here that the separate corporation tax effects from interest revenue and interest expense will offset perfectly in the consolidated work sheet without any consolidation entry being necessary (if the corporations are in the same marginal tax bracket). If they are in different tax brackets, the resulting difference in tax effect remains in the consolidated federal income tax provision.

If these bonds had been issued at 102 rather than at face value, and assuming straight-line amortization of the $2,000 premium or $400 per year, the consolidation entries would be only slightly more complex.

	19x1		19x2		19x3	
Bonds payable	100,000		100,000		100,000	
Premium on bonds payable	1,600		1,200		800	
Investment in bonds		101,600		101,200		100,800
Interest revenue	9,600		9,600		9,600	
Interest expense		9,600		9,600		9,600

It should be noted that these are all offset entries, and no gain or loss has been recognized. It should also be recalled that investors usually record their investment net of premium or discount while debtors normally record debt at face value with premium or discount recorded in separate accounts.

If P and S had filed consolidated tax returns, there would be no tax effect from this intercorporate held debt. If separate tax returns were filed and if both companies were in the same tax bracket, the tax paid on the interest income on S's return would be offset in consolidated financial statements against the tax benefit received by P because of the interest expense deduction.

Tax: It should be recalled that offset entries are not made on consolidated tax returns. Thus, interest revenue and interest expense would both be overstated on the return with no net effect on taxable income or on the tax due.*

* *Income Tax Regulations*, sec. 1.1502-13(b)(1).

DISPOSAL OF DIRECTLY ACQUIRED DEBT

Sale to an Outsider

Continuing the illustration where P issued bonds due in five years with $100,000 face value on 1/1/x1 and where S acquired all of the P bonds directly from P on 1/1/x1 at a premium of $2,000, assume that on 1/1/x4 S sells these bonds to an outside party for $100,000. This price reflects an increase in the market rate of interest on these bonds from an effective rate under 10 percent on 1/1/x1 to the coupon rate of 10 percent on 1/1/x4. S would record this on its separate books as follows:

Cash	100,000	
Loss on sale of P bonds	800	
Investment in P bonds		100,800

The work sheet consolidation entry at 12/31/x4 would defer and reclassify the "loss on sale of P bonds" as an interest element. Thus, the loss on the sale of the P bonds is treated as a discount on the issue of the P bonds. Indeed, the sale to an outsider can be viewed as an issue of these bonds (2-year life and issued at face value). This discount is then offset against the unamortized premium still reflected on P's records. This then reflects the issue of these bonds at face value. On 12/31/x4 P would record the interest expense as:

Interest expense	9,600	
Premium on bonds payable	400	
Cash		10,000

The 12/31/x4 consolidation entry would then appear as:

Premium on bonds payable	400	
Interest expense	400	
Loss on sale of P bonds		800
To remove the loss on "issuance" of bonds and the Premium on Bonds Payable account and to adjust the consolidated interest expense.		

It should be noted that the $400 debit to interest expense, in effect, offsets P's 19x4 amortization of the "Premium on Bonds Payable" account and thus leaves the interest expense at $10,000 or 10% of the $100,000 face value of the issue. This reflects its issuance at face value to the outsider.

> **Tax:** For consolidated tax return purposes the result generally would be the same as for financial reporting because the "loss on sale of P bonds" would have to be spread over the remaining life of the issue.* Separate tax returns would make this more complex. P would report $400 more of taxable income due to the amortization of bond premium reducing interest expense to $9,600, while S

> **Tax:** *(continued)*
> would report the entire $800 loss on the sale of the bonds. Consolidation for financial statement purposes would require postponing half the tax benefit from the $800 loss and offsetting the other half against the additional tax to P from amortizing the premium. This would be further complicated because the loss to S on the sale would result in a capital loss which might not be currently deductible (because capital losses can only offset capital gains on a corporate tax return), and in any event the capital loss tax benefit would be at a different tax rate than the ordinary income tax rate that P would have to pay on the increased taxable income (due to the bond premium amortization).
>
> * *Income Tax Regulations,* sec. 1.1502-14(d)(2).

Assuming separate tax returns and a 30 percent tax rate, S would have reported a tax benefit of $240 ($800 × 30%) on the $800 loss on the sale of P's bonds in 19x4. P through amortization of the premium, on the original issue to S, would be reporting a tax increase of only $120 ($400 × 30%) due to the reduction in interest expense. Thus, at 12/31/x4 a consolidation entry is necessary to defer the tax on the extra $400 of loss which will be offset in 19x5 by amortization of the final $400 of premium on P's books. The consolidation entry to defer the tax would be as follows at 12/31/x4:

FIT provision ($400 × 30%)	120	
Accrued or deferred tax liability		120

Sale to Debtor or to Another Member

If the bonds were acquired from the debtor and then sold to another member, no outside party would ever have been an owner of the bonds. Since the bonds would have always been held within the single consolidated entity, no gain or loss should be reflected in the consolidated financial statements. Any gain or loss on the sale from one member to another member would "wash out" in the process of preparing offsetting and deferral consolidation entries. (The only exception to this might be caused by filing separate tax returns where the tax benefits would not offset the tax costs due to differences between capital gain and ordinary income tax rates and where the gain or loss on the sale would be reflected in one year for tax purposes rather than being spread over the remaining life of the issue.)

To illustrate the internal sale, assume that S sells the P bonds to T, another member of the group, on 1/1/x4 for only $99,000. S would record this on its separate books as:

Cash	99,000	
Loss on sale	1,800	
Investment in P bonds		100,800

The tax effect of the loss on S's books assuming separate tax returns and a flat 30 percent tax rate would be:

FIT payable ($1,800 × 30%)	540	
FIT provision		540

T would record the bond purchase on its records as a bond investment but with a $1,000 discount on the investment. Thus, if a consolidation entry were made on 1/1/x4 immediately after the sale, it would appear as follows (it is entirely an offset entry except for the deferral of the loss on sale of P bonds by S):

Bonds payable (P)	100,000	
Premium on bonds payable (P)	800	
Bonds investment (T)		99,000
Loss of sale of P bonds (S)		1,800

The deferral of the loss of $1,800 would require deferral of the related tax benefit; thus, the consolidation entry on 1/1/x4 would be:

FIT provision ($1,800 × 30%)	540	
Deferred credit—tax effect on loss on bonds deferred		540
To defer the tax on the $1,800 loss recognized in the separate tax return.		

At 12/31/x4 this entry would be:

Bonds payable (P)	100,000	
Premium on bonds payable (P)	400	
Interest revenue (T)	10,500	
Bond investment (T)		99,500
Loss on sale of P bonds (S)		1,800
Interest expense (P)		9,600

The tax effect consolidation entry would be:

FIT provision (($1,800 − ($10,500 − $9,600)) × 30%)	270	
Deferred credit—tax effect on loss on bonds deferred		270

The tax on the $900 of excess interest income in excess of interest expense on the separate corporation books would have in effect reduced the deferred loss from $1,800 to only $900, and thus the tax deferral from $540 at 1/1/x4 to only $270 at 12/31/x4.

At 12/31/x5 the consolidation entries would be (assuming the bonds have been retired):

Interest revenue (T)	10,500	
Interest expense (P)		9,600
Retained earnings (1/1/x5) (S)		900*

* To reflect the $900 of deferred loss in the 1/1/x5 retained earnings.

Retained earnings (1/1x5) (S)	270	
FIT provision (($10,500 − $9,600) × 30%)		270*

* To remove the tax on the excess of interest revenue over interest expense in 19x5.

If S had acquired the P bonds from T, a member of the group, following T's acquisition of the bonds from P, the entries would be similar to those already presented. Thus, the discussion of intercorporate sales or purchases of another member's bonds is left at this point.

ACQUISITION FROM AN OUTSIDE PARTY

When a corporation acquires its own debt at or before maturity, gain or loss, if any, generally must be recognized on the debt retirement. This is true even if the debt issue is being refunded by issuing new debt.[1] This gain or loss net of tax effect is reported as an extraordinary item in the earnings statement unless it is an early extinguishment due to current or future sinking fund requirements. Gain or loss in the latter case will re reported as part of normal operations.[2]

In a consolidating group there is an early extinguishment of debt whenever one member of the group acquires prior to maturity its own debt or the debt of another member *from an outside party*. The acquisition of one member's debt from another member is not considered a retirement since this debt would not have been considered as outstanding on a consolidated basis. Thus, gain or loss on debt retirement occurs *only when* the debtor or another member of the group acquires the debt *from an outside party*.

For example, assume that for $100,000 P issued to an outside party on 1/1/x1 100 10-year bonds with a face value of $1,000 per bond and bearing interest at 8 percent payable annually on 12/31. Then assume that S buys all of these bonds on 1/1/x8 from the outside party at a cost of $98,500. On their separate corporation records P will continue to show bonds payable of $100,000 while S will now show an asset, "investment in P bonds," of $98,500 (or an investment of $100,000 less a $1,500 discount on bond investment) as of the acquisition date. In effect, on a single corporation consolidated basis there has been an early extinguishment of the $100,000 debt just as though P had purchased its own bonds for $98,500. The gain on this transaction is $1,500, and this will gradually show up on S's separate records as S amortizes the discount on the investment.

At 12/31/x8 the consolidation offset and gain triggering entry would be:

```
Bonds payable (P) ........................................   100,000
Interest revenue ($8,000 + $500) (S) ........................     8,500
    Investment in bonds ($98,500 + $500) (S) ...............            99,000
    Interest expense (P) .....................................             8,000
    Gain on bond retirement (S) ............................             1,500
```

[1] *AICPA Professional Standards, Accounting—Current Text* (New York, 1980), par. 5362.19. Copyright (1980) by the American Institute of CPAs.
[2] Ibid., par. 2013.08.

If this entry were broken into as many parts as possible, the following would be shown on 12/31/x8.

Offset entry:

Bonds payable	100,000	
Investment in bonds (at face value)		100,000

Offset entry:

Interest revenue (cash portion only)	8,000	
Interest expense		8,000

Gain advancement entry:

Investment in bonds (discount)	1,000	
Interest revenue	500	
Gain on bond retirement		1,500

Because the work sheet entry(s) would not be recorded on the separate records of P or S, this entry would have to be remade each year but reflecting the changes due to the passage of time. Thus, the 12/31/x9 consolidation entry would be:

Bonds payable (P)	100,000	
Interest revenue ($8,000 + $500) (S)	8,500	
Investment in bonds ($99,000 + $500) (S)		99,500
Interest expense (P)		8,000
Retained earnings (1/1/x9) ($1,500 − $500) (S)		1,000

The credit to the 1/1/x9 retained earnings of S reflects the fact that a $1,500 gain was recognized as of 1/1/x8 for consolidated statement purposes; while on S's separate books, due to the amortization of the discount on the acquisition of the bonds in 19x8, only $500 has been recognized as of 1/1/x9. Thus, $1,000 remained to be recognized on the separate books of S as of 1/1/x9. After closing the 19x9 earnings, S will have recognized $1,000 of the $1,500 gain. It should be noted that the adjustment for the "as yet unrecognized gain" must be to the beginning-of-the-year retained earnings because the revenue and expense accounts have not yet been closed for the current year.

Thus, the consolidation entry at 12/31/x10, after the bonds had been retired, would appear as follows:

Interest revenue ($8,000 + $500) (S)	8,500	
Interest expense (P)		8,000
Retained earnings (1/1/x10) (S)		500

The $500 credit to the 1/1/x10 retained earnings reflects the fact that as of that date the gain on retirement had not been fully recognized on a separate corporation basis. Upon closing the year 10 earnings statement accounts, the entire $1,500 will then have been fully recognized on the consolidated worksheet *and* in the separate records of S.

Thus far this illustration has ignored the tax implications, and since such an approach is unacceptable, this transaction will be revisited assuming separate tax returns and a flat 30 percent tax rate. With consolidation advancing the gain (or loss) on debt retirement, the tax effects must be anticipated and reflected by the consolidated (single) entity.

When S purchased on 1/1/x8 for $98,500 bonds of P with a face value of $100,000 maturing on 12/31/x10, an immediate gain was recognized just as if these bonds had been retired on 1/1/x8. The $1,500 gain at a 30 percent tax rate requires a $450 tax provision. But it must be remembered that these bonds have not been retired and that S records the 8 percent interest as follows on 12/31/x8:

Cash	8,000	
Investment in P bonds	500	
Interest revenue		8,500

The discount amortization which takes place on the separate entity records of S results in recognition of $500 of the $1,500 consolidated gain on debt "retirement," and thus S incures $150 of tax on this $500 of increased taxable income.

Thus, the consolidation entry on 1/1/x8 would have been:

FIT provision ($1,500 × 30%) (S)	450	
Bonds payable (P)	100,000	
Investment in bonds (S)		98,500
Gain on bond retirement (S)		1,500
Deferred tax credit—bond discount (S)		450

But because consolidation entries are not posted, the 12/31/x8 consolidation entry would be:

FIT provision (($1,500 − $500) × 30%)	300	
Bonds payable (P)	100,000	
Interest revenue (S)	8,500	
Investment in bonds (S)		99,000
Interest expense (P)		8,000
Gain on bond retirement (S)		1,500
Deferred tax credit—bond discount (S)		300

Because interest revenue exceeds interest expense by $500 on the separate entity records, S would have recorded, on its separate records, $150 of federal income tax provision and federal income taxes payable. This leaves only $300 more to be reflected on the consolidated statements on the as yet unrecognized gain of $1,000 (discount) × 30 percent tax rate.

The consolidation entries at 12/31/x9 would reflect the following:

Bonds payable (P)	100,000	
Interest revenue (S)	8,500	
Interest expense (P)		8,000
Investment in bonds (S)		99,500
Retained earnings (1/1/x9) ($1,500 − $500) (S)		1,000
Retained earnings (1/1/x9) (S)	300	
Deferred tax credit—bond discount (S)		150
FIT provision (S)		150

Since by 12/31/x9 $1,000 of the original $1,500 in gain on debt "retirement" has been recognized, the income tax deferral is only on the $500 not yet recognized on the separate corporation's books at the 30 percent tax rate. In addition, since S recorded a tax provision in year 9 on the $500 recognized on its separate books in that year (but in year 8 for consolidation), this provision must be removed. The combination of reflecting the tax deferral and the as yet unrecognized gain of $500 and of removing the tax provision on the $500 gain (due to amortization) recognized by S in year 9 is balanced by the $300 debit to the 1/1/x9 retained earnings for the tax effects on the $1,000 of unrecognized gain at that date.

For another slightly more complex example, assume that P issued to an outside party at 102 on 1/1/x1 100 5-year bonds with a face value of $1,000 each and with interest at 10 percent payable annually at 12/31. Then assume that subsidiary S buys these bonds for $99,000 on 1/1/x4. On their separate legal entity records, P will continue to show these bonds as an outstanding liability and S will show them as an investment. For the single consolidated entity these bonds must be treated as retired on 1/1/x4 with the resulting gain or loss being recognized as an extraordinary item. (To have this treated as an normal operating gain or loss, the debtor corporation would have had to acquire its own bonds and under a sinking fund requirement.) At 1/1/x4 P and S separate financial records would show:

P		S	
Bonds payable	$100,000	Bond investment	$99,000
Premium on bonds payable	800		

At 12/31/x4 these same financial records would show:

P		S	
Bonds payable	$100,000	Bond investment	$99,500
Premium on bonds payable	400	Interest revenue	10,500
Interest expense	9,600		

On a consolidated basis, however, none of these accounts would remain because these bonds would have been treated as retired on 1/1/x4. Thus, if there were only one entity and if it had acquired its own bonds for $99,000 which on 1/1/x4 were being carried at $100,800 (including premium), there would have been an $1,800 gain before tax to record on the retirement.

It should be noted that on the separate books of P and S the $1,800 gain *will gradually be recognized* due to the amortization of the premium of P's books (which decreases interest expense thus increasing earnings) and due to the amortization of the discount on S's books which increases interest revenue. Thus, P over the next two years, year 4 and year 5, will recognize $800 as additional earnings while S will recognize $1,000 of increased earnings on a before-tax basis.

The consolidation entry at 12/31/x4 assuming separate tax returns and a flat 30 percent income tax rate would be as follows:

FIT provision ($500 × 30%) (S)	150*	
FIT provision ($400 × 30%) (P)	120*	
Bonds payable (P)	100,000	
Premium on bonds payable (P)	400	
Interest revenue (S)	10,500	
Interest expense (P)		9,600
Investment in bonds (S)		99,500
Gain on bond retirement (S)		1,000
Gain on bond retirement (P)		800
Deferred tax credit—bond premium and discount amortization (($500 + 400) × 30%)		270
	111,170	111,170

* Tax on the as yet unrecognized gain on separate books.

Since half the 1/1/x4 gain attributable to each corporation has been recognized by 12/31/x4, the deferred credit for the timing difference is only necessary on the as yet unrecognized half on the separate corporation records. It is important especially when a less than 100 percent owned subsidiary is involved to show the gain (or loss) and the related tax provision for each corporation separately so that the minority interest can be correctly computed (under the complete deferral or recognition concept).

The consolidation entry triggers or advances the recognition of gain or loss on intercorporate debt when acquired from an outside party by a member other than the debtor. Not only is the recognition sooner than on separate corporation statements, it also changes its character from ordinary interest expense and interest revenue to extraordinary gain or loss on debt retirement.

Because premium or discount amortization gradually returns the carrying amount of the bond payable or investment to its face value over the life of the issue, the net gain or loss is shared between the debtor and the investing member according to the premium or discount on each company's books at the date of acquisition from the outsider.

Thus, if S had purchased this bond issue from the outsider on 1/1/x4 for $102,000, the net loss would have been $1,200 ($100,800 liability or sales price less $102,000 investment or purchase price). The $1,200 net loss would be recognized immediately for consolidated financial statements. Of this $1,200 net loss, a $2,000 loss would be attributed to S and a gain of $800 would be attributed to P for these are precisely the loss and gain amounts which would be recognized by each through future amortization of the premiums.

It should be noted that in the case of separate federal income tax returns the tax effects of a loss attributable to S would result in a deferred tax charge (for a deduction not yet taken for tax purposes) while the gain attributable to P would result in a deferred tax credit (for income not yet recognized for tax purposes). Again, this would make it important to keep the earnings statement amounts separate for each corporation so that the adjusted net earnings of each can be properly computed.

THE PROBLEM OF ALLOCATING GAINS AND LOSSES

Some profit manipulation is possible due to the allocation process used in this text for assigning gains and losses. If the acquisition of the bonds will result in a gain on the consolidated statements, either the parent or a 100 percent owned subsidiary could be the investing corporation. If, however, the acquisition will result in a loss on the consolidated statements, a subsidiary with a large minority interest could be the investment corporation. In this event the loss will be attributed in part to the minority interest rather than being considered as 100 percent attributable to the consolidating majority interests.

It should be realized that this is not a disservice or injury to a minority interest as long as the price paid to acquire the issue results in a fair market or arm's-length yield on the investment. In other words, if the current market rate of interest has fallen below the coupon rate on the bonds, the acquisition will involve a premium and thus a loss on consolidation, but this does not alter the fact that it is still yielding a current market rate of interest.

Some accounting theorists argue against allocation of gains or losses based on premiums or discounts. They dislike the possibility of any "management" of earnings through selection of the investing corporation. Thus, they normally argue for allocation of all gains or loss on early debt retirement to the parent corporation because this corporation controls the actions of all the subsidiaries. Others might assign all the gain or loss to the debtor corporation. It should be recognized, however, that allocation between the debtor and the investor corporations based on the existence of premiums and discounts is in complete agreement with the separate legal entity results, now and in the future. Any allocation different from this is somewhat arbitrary and once made will for the life of the consolidated entity result in disagreement between the separate entity records and the results achieved through any arbitrary allocation system. An arbitrary allocation system, such as allocating all gains and losses to the parent, will necessitate continuous annual adjustments. In addition, the income tax aspects will be much more complex, and the investment account analysis, as used in this text, will not equal the majority's percentage of the adjusted net assets.

Because of the agreement with the separate legal entity results at maturity and in absence of a firm theory for proper or correct allocation, your author prefers allocation of gain or loss on premature debt retirement based on premiums and discounts. The opportunity for "managed" earnings is normally small, and as long as a fair market price is paid to acquire an investment, minority interests are not being cheated.

YEARS SUBSEQUENT TO ACQUISITION FROM AN OUTSIDE PARTY

For this example assume that S, a 100 percent owned subsidiary of P issued to outside parties on 1/1/x1, 10-year, 8 percent interest-bearing bonds with a total face value of $200,000 for $210,000 with interest payable semiannually on 6/30 and 12/31. Also assume that bond issue costs were $6,000. On 9/1/x8 P acquires $100,000 face value of these bonds for $98,000 plus accrued interest. This is recorded as follows on P's books on 9/1/x8:

Investment in S bonds....................................	98,000	
Accrued interest receivable ($100,000 × 8% × 2/12)...........	1,333	
Cash		99,333

At 12/31/x8 P records the following:

Cash	4,000	
Investment in S bonds ($2,000 × 4/28 months)	286	
Interest revenue ($8,000 × 4/12 + $286).................		2,953
Accrued interest receivable		1,333

At 12/31/x8 S records the following:

Interest expense	7,500	
Premium on bonds payable ($10,000 × 6/120)	500	
Cash ($200,000 × 8% × 1/2)		8,000
To record interest for 6 months.		
Bond issue expense ($6,000 ÷ 10)	600	
Unamortized bond issue cost		600
To record amortization of bond issue cost for the year.		

For consolidation purposes, however, half the bond issue would be treated as retired on 9/1/x8. The consolidated net gain or loss is calculated by subtracting the cost of the bond acquisition, $98,000, from the carrying amount of the retired bonds including the appropriate part of the unamortized issue costs. This adjusted carrying amount using straight-line amortization of bond premium is determined as shown in Illustration 6–2.

Thus, the net gain is $100,467 less $98,000 or $2,467 of which $2,000 is attributable to P the investing corporation and $467 to S the debtor corporation.

If a consolidation entry were prepared immediately after the acquisi-

Illustration 6-2

Face value			$100,000
Plus: Premium at 1/1/x1	$5,000		
Amortization from 1/1/x1 to 9/1/x8			
($5,000 × 92 ÷ 120)	−3,833		1,167
			101,167
Less: Bond issue cost at 1/1/x1		3,000	
Amortization from 1/1/x1 to 9/1/x8			
($3,000 × 92 ÷ 120)		−2,300	700
Carrying amount of bonds adjusted for unamortized bond issue cost at the date of the intercorporate acquisition, 9/1/x8			$100,467

tion, it would be as follows assuming separate tax returns and a flat 30 percent income tax rate:

Bonds payable (S)	100,000	
Premium on bonds payable (S)	1,167	
Unamortized bond issue cost (S)		700
Investment in S bonds (P)		98,000
Gain on bond retirement (P)		2,000
Gain on bond retirement (S)		467

The tax effects would be reflected as follows:

FIT provision ($2,000 × 30%) (P)	600	
FIT provision ($467 × 30%) (S)	140	
Deferred tax credit—bond retirement		740

For year-end consolidation purposes, the gain recognition is advanced from future periods (where it will be recognized through amortization) to the acquisition date of 9/1/x8. This requires the following consolidation entry at 12/31/x8:

Bonds payable (S)	100,000	
Premium on bonds payable ($1,167 − ($1,167 × 4/28)) or ($1,167 − $167) (S)	1,000	
Interest revenue (($8,000 × 4/12) + ($2,000 × 4/28)) or ($2,667 + $286) (P)	2,953	
Bond issue expense ($700 × 4/28) (S)		100
Unamortized bond issue cost ($700 − $100) (S)		600
Interest expense ($2,667 − $167) (S)		2,500
Investment in S bonds ($98,000 + $286) (P)		98,286
Gain on bond retirement (P)		2,000
Gain on bond retirement (S)		467
	103,953	103,953

The tax entry at 12/31/x8 would be:

FIT provision (($2,000 − $286) × 30%) (P)	514	
FIT provision (($467 − $167 + 100*) × 30%) (S)	120	
Deferred tax credit—bond retirement		634

* Amortization of bond issue costs.

This entry reflects the effects of separate corporation amortization from 9/1/x8 to 12/31/x8 or 4 of the 28 months of life to maturity.

The preceding nontax entry is quite complex, and it may assist understanding if it is broken into parts. The following reflects this multiple entry approach:

An offset entry:

Bonds payable (S)	100,000	
Investment in S bonds (at face value) (P)		100,000

An offset entry:

Interest revenue (cash portion only) (P)....................	2,667	
Interest expense ($8,000 × 4 ÷ 12) (S)		2,667
To reflect one-third year's interest.		

Gain advancing entry to S:

Premium on bonds payable ($1,167 − $167) (S)	1,000	
Interest expense (S)	167	
Bond issue expense (S)................................		100
Unamortized bond issue cost ($700 − $100) (S)		600
Gain on bond retirement ($1,167 − $700) (S)		467

Gain advancing entry to P:

Investment in S bonds ($2,000 − $286) (P)	1,714	
Interest revenue (P).......................................	286	
Gain on bond retirement (P)		2,000

The complex consolidation entry combines the offset and advance recognition aspects. Like all consolidation entries, however, it is not recorded on any corporation records. Thus, on 12/31/x9 the entry must be remade but reflecting the passage of time and thus the gradual recognition of the gain by amortization of bond premium, and bond issue cost by S and by amortization of the discount on bond investment by P. Thus the 12/31/x9 consolidation entries would be as follows:

Bonds payable (S)	100,000	
Premium on bonds payable ($1,000 − $500) (S)	500	
Interest revenue ($8,000 + $857) (P)	8,857	
Bond issue expense ($600 ÷ 2) (S).....................		300
Unamortized bond issue cost ($600 − $300) (S)		300
Interest expense ($8,000 − $500) (S)		7,500
Investment in S bonds ($98,286 + $857) (P)		99,143
Retained earnings (1/1/x9) ($2,000 − $286) (P)		1,714
Retained earnings (1/1/x9) ($467 − $167 + $100) (S)		400
	109,357	109,357

Because the 12/31/x8 entries were not posted to any corporation's records, the gain on bond retirement is still *partially* unrecognized and should now be part of the retained earnings. Thus, retained earnings must be credited for the as yet unrecognized portion. As of 1/1/x9 for P this was $2,000 less the $286 of discount amortized after acquisition in year 8 or $1,714. At 1/1/x9 for S this was $400 or $467 ($1,167 premium less $700 bond issue cost) less $67 which is the net of the $167 premiums amortization less the $100 of bond issue cost amortization after acquisition in year 8.

The tax entry at 12/31/x9 would be:

Retained earnings (1/1/x9) (($2,000 − $286) × 30%) (P)	514	
Retained earnings (1/1/x9) (($467 − $167 + $100) × 30%) (S)	120	
Deferred tax credit—bond retirement		317
FIT provision ($857 × 30%) (P)		257
FIT provision 30% (−$500 + $300) (S)		60

This entry reflects the income tax effect on the as yet unrecognized gain at 1/1/x9 of $1,714 for P and $400 for S and removes the tax provision on the year 9 amortization of $857 by P and $200 by S.

The 12/31/x10 consolidation entries after the bonds have been retired would be:

(1)

Interest revenue ($8,000 + $857) (P)	8,857	
Bond issue expense (S)		300
Interest expense ($8,000 − $500) (S)		7,500
Retained earnings (1/1/x10) ($1,714 − $857) (P)		857
Retained earnings (1/1/x10) ($400 − $200) (S)		200

(2)

Retained earnings (1/1/x10)	257	
Retained earnings (1/1/x10)	60	
FIT provision ($857 × 30%) (P)		257
FIT provision ($200 × 30%) (S)		60

To remove the tax effects of the year 10 amortization on separate corporation records.

Thus, when the separate corporation earnings statement accounts are closed to retained earnings at the end of year 10, P will have recognized the $2,000 gain on its separate records (by discount amortization) and S will have recognized $467 (by premium amortization of $1,167 less $700 of amortization of bond issue costs) occurring after the date of intercorporate bond acquisition. The separate books now agree with the consolidated result which was recognized, in effect, as of 9/1/x8.

Tax: Gain on Early Extinguishment of Debt Can Be Excluded from Taxable Income The income tax law permits a corporation to exclude from taxation the gain from discharge of indebtedness, but if the exclusion is elected, the taxpayer must consent to the regulations which require a reduction in the basis of some assets.* Without the filing of this consent the gain would be currently taxable. Thus, if a calendar-year corporation retired on 9/1/x1 $100,000 face value of its debt which had a $2,000 unamortized premium at-

Tax: (*continued*)

tached as of 1/1/x1 for $90,000, the gain would be $12,000 ($10,000 + $2,000). The amortization of the premium from the first of the year to the date of the debt extinguishment is not included in taxable income. If there had been an unamortized discount of $2,000 on 1/1/x1, the excluded gain attributable to the 9/1/x1 debt retirement would have only been $8,000 ($10,000 − $2,000) for tax purposes.

In the latter case if the "exclusion" has been elected, the $8,000 would be applied in a specific sequence to reduce the basis of some assets held by the corporation.† Thus, the gain is not really excluded; it is, in effect, postponed because the basis reduction will mean less depreciation or higher gains when the assets with reduced bases are sold. In the meantime, however, this gain would be recognized for financial reporting creating a difficult timing difference situation for deferred income tax accounting. Thus, the gain on debt retirement for financial reporting would then reverse as the assets with reduced bases are depreciated or sold.

As to the treatment of gain or loss on intercorporate debt transactions in consolidated tax returns, the tax law appears to be less than complete. It does state that when a member has gain or loss on the sale (or other disposition) of another member's debt, the gain or loss is deferred; and if the gain or loss arose on a sale to an outsider, the deferred gain or loss is then recognized "ratably over the remaining term of the obligation."‡ The law, however, has been silent on the treatment of another member's debt acquired from an outsider. Thus, whether this triggers gain or loss on debt retirement in a consolidated return is questionable, and if it does, whether the investing member would be allowed to elect to exclude the gain (under *Code* section 108) and reduce the basis of its assets, are questions left unanswered in today's tax law. Because nonrecognition of gain on the purchase of another member's debt followed by amortization of premium or discount would spread the gain over the remaining life of the issue, the gain is probably not recognized at acquisition in a consolidated tax return. This would generally result in the same tax on this transaction as though separate tax returns were filed. For losses, however, this would not be the optimal tax result.

* *Internal Revenue Code,* sec. 108.
† *Internal Revenue Code,* sec. 1017.
‡ *Income Tax Regulations,* sec. 1.1502-14(d). Presumably gain on intercompany bond retirement is to become taxable in 1981 but these regulations have not as yet been issued.

THE MINORITY INTEREST ASPECTS

Under the concept of complete advanced recognition, more gain or loss may be recognized than under the majority interest only recognition concept. When a transaction involves a deferral of gain or loss, the amount has already been recognized on a separate corporation basis; however, when recognition of gain or loss is being advanced, it has not yet been recognized on a separate corporation basis. Thus, when gain is involved, the minority interest shown on the consolidated statement of financial position can be a larger amount than that represented by their percentage ownership of the stockholders' equity of the subsidiary before the earnings are adjusted for this gain.

A WORKING PAPER ANALYSIS

Assume that P acquired 80 percent of S Corporation on 1/1/x1 for $200,000 when S's owners' equity appeared as follows:

Capital stock	$100,000
Additional paid-in capital	80,000
Retained earnings, 1/1/x1	60,000
	$240,000

Also assume that all of the S assets except land were stated at fair values and that the book value of the land was $10,000 less than its fair value. The earnings for S were $20,000 per year, and $8,000 were paid in dividends. In addition, on 7/1/x1 S purchased $50,000 face value of P bonds from an outsider for $48,000. These bonds pay interest on 6/30 and 12/31 at 8 percent annual rate and have exactly five years to maturity. These were 10-year bonds when issued by P for $53,000. Assume a flat 30 percent corporate tax rate and the filing of separate tax returns. An investment account analysis would appear as shown in Illustration 6–3 using alternative method 3 and the 100 percent recognition concept (or alternative method 2 due to the absence of goodwill).

It should be noticed from the analysis in Illustration 6–3 that the $2,000 gain attributable to S on debt retirement is realized for consolidated financial reporting, but only the recognition caused by amortiziation of this discount would be reported for tax purposes (unless the changing tax law would require full recognition). Recognition of income for consolidation purposes prior to its recognition for tax purposes causes a deferred tax credit account to be established in accounting for income taxes. In this case the amount of the deferred tax credit account was initially $600 ($2,000 × 30%) less $60 ($200 × 30%) for 19x1 amortization or $540. In 19x2 $120 of the $540 deferred tax reverses due to the $400 turnaround of the timing difference in that year.

Illustration 6-3

S Corporation	Net Assets	80% Majority	20% Minority
Capital stock	$100,000	$ 80,000	$20,000
Additional paid-in capital	80,000	64,000	16,000
Retained earnings, 1/1/x1	60,000	48,000	12,000
Book value	240,000	192,000	48,000
Land adjustment	10,000	8,000	2,000
Fair value = price paid	250,000	200,000	50,000
Dividends, 19x1	(8,000)	(6,400)	(1,600)
Earnings, 19x1	20,000	16,000	4,000
Gain on intercorporate debt retirement	2,000	1,600	400
Less portion of this gain recognized in the $20,000 of 19x1 earnings as amortization of discount $2,000 ÷ 5 × ½ yr.	(200)	(160)	(40)
Less 30% tax on $1,800 or ($2,000 − $200) deferred credit timing difference	(540)	(432)	(108)
Adjusted net assets, 12/31/x1	263,260	210,608	52,652
Dividends, 19x2	(8,000)	(6,400)	(1,600)
Earnings, 19x2	20,000	16,000	4,000
Less portion of gain on debt reported in 19x1 and included in the $20,000 of 19x2 earnings ($2,000 ÷ 5)	(400)	(320)	(80)
Tax $400 × 30% timing difference reversal	120	96	24
Adjusted net asset, 12/31/x2	$274,980	$219,984	$54,996

($21,260 adjusted net earnings; $19,720 adjusted net earnings; $17,008; $15,776; $4,252; $3,944)

After going through the complexity of advanced recognition of gain or loss on intercorporate debt (acquired from an outsider), you may wonder if this is not reason enough to avoid such debt acquisitions. In practice, such acquisitions happen frequently.

REVIEW QUESTIONS

1. What are the three principal pathways for a member to acquire bonds of another member?
2. When is gain or loss recognized on the sale of bonds of another member?
3. When, if ever, is gain or loss recognized on the purchase of bonds of another member?
4. How is the recognized gain or loss on intercorporate debt transactions allocated between the debtor and the investing member?
5. a. How is the gain or loss on this debt reported in the consolidated earnings statement?
   b. How is the gain or loss on this debt reported in the separate entity earnings statements?

6. How is intercorporate interest revenue and interest expense reflected in a consolidated tax return?
7. How do advanced or triggered gain or loss recognition entries differ from deferral entries?
8. Do restoration entries have the same relationship to advanced recognition entries as they do to deferral entries?
9. What is the purpose of the offset entries?
10. Why is it necessary to adjust retained earnings in advance recognition entries in years subsequent to the gain or loss recognition on the acquisition of the debt of another member?
11. When an investing member sells to a second investing member an investment in bonds of another member, how is the resulting gains or gain or loss treated in consolidated financial statements?
12. Why can difficult timing differences be created for financial reporting (in either separate or consolidated financial statements) by the operation of sections 108 and 1017 of the *Internal Revenue Code*?
13. What effect can the advanced recognition concept have on the minority interest amount as shown on a consolidated financial statement?
14. What effect does filing separate tax returns have when gain or loss is subject to advanced recognition in consolidated financial statements?
15. What effect does filing separate tax returns have on consolidated financial statements when an investing member sells bonds of another member to an outside party?
16. What effect does filing separate tax returns have on consolidated financial statements when an investing member sells bonds of a member to another investing member?
17. How can a consolidated group achieve higher consolidated net earnings when intercorporate debt will be acquired and result in a loss?

PROBLEMS

Problem 1: Investor, Inc., and Debenture, Inc.

Debenture, Inc., is an 80 percent owned subsidiary of Investor, Inc. On 1/1/x1 Debenture, Inc., issued $100,000 of 10 percent bonds for $110,000. These bonds mature on 12/31/x10. On 1/1/x1 Investor purchased directly from Debenture $50,000 of these bonds for $55,000. On 1/1/x6 Investor purchased for $45,000 the remaining $50,000 of these bonds from outsiders. Assume that the corporations file separate tax returns and that the corporate income tax rate is a flat 30 percent.

Required:

Prepare in journal entry format all deferral, offset, restoration, and advance recognition work sheet entries which would be necessary for these bonds in the preparation of consolidated financial statements for years 19x6 and 19x7. Make separate entries for each block of bonds purchased by Investor and for each year. (Don't forget the tax effects.)

Problem 2: Intercorporate Debt Issues

Parent issued $100,000 face value of 8 percent 5-year bonds on 1/1/x1 for $105,000. Subsidiary A purchased $50,000 of these bonds from Parent for $52,500 on 1/1/x1. On 1/1/x3 Subsidiary A sold these bonds to Subsidiary B for $49,000. The tax rate is a flat 30 percent.

Required:
1. Prepare the consolidation work sheet entries for these bonds without the tax effect for each year that they are outstanding. Assume they are retired at maturity on 12/31/x5.
2. Prepare the tax effect work sheet entries for each year assuming separate returns are filed.
3. Prepare the tax effect work sheet entries for each year assuming a consolidated tax return is filed annually.

Problem 3: Wheeler, Inc., and Dealer, Inc.

Wheeler, Inc., owns 90 percent of Dealer, Inc. On 1/1/x1 Wheeler issued to outsiders $100,000 of 10-year 8 percent bonds for $103,000 with interest payable annually on 12/31. On 1/1/x5 Dealer purchased the entire $100,000 issue for $98,000. Wheeler and Dealer file separate tax returns, and there is a flat 40 percent tax rate.

Required:
1. Prepare the advance recognition and offset entry(s) for these bonds as of 12/31/x5.
2. Prepare the advance recognition and offset entries as of 12/31/x6.

Problem 4: Smith and Jones Corporations

The Smith Corporation has owned 90 percent of the Jones Corporation since its inception. On 1/1/x1 Jones sold its 8 percent, 10-year bonds with a face value of $100,000 for $98,000.

On 1/1/x4 Smith acquires $50,000 face value of Jones bonds for $48,000. The corporate tax rate is a flat 40 percent and separate tax returns are filed.

Required:
1. Prepare the 12/31/x4 consolidation entry(s) for these bonds.
2. Prepare the 12/31/x5 consolidation entry(s) for these bonds.

Problem 5: Bonded

Parent Corporation acquired from outsiders on 1/1/x5 for $58,000 bonds of subsidiary S which have a face value of $60,000 and pay 8 percent interest annually on 12/31. The bonds were issued by S for $63,000 and will be retired at maturity on 12/31/x7. The bonds had a 10-year life when issued. The corporations file separate tax returns, and there is a flat 30 percent tax rate.

Required:

Prepare the advance recognition and offset entries for the consolidated financial statements for each year of remaining life of these bonds.

Problem 6:   Elimination Corporation

Elimination Corporation's condensed statement of financial position as of 12/31/x7 is presented below:

Assets	$400,700
Liabilities (bonds, 4%, $60,000 face)	$ 53,700
Common stock, $10 par	200,000
Additional paid-in capital	30,000
Retained earnings	117,000
Total equities	$400,700

Investment Corporation for $240,000 acquired 80 percent of the Elimination Corporation common stock on 1/1/x6 when the retained earnings were $60,000. Assume any difference is due to machinery with a 10-year remaining life. The Investment Corporation used the equity method in accounting for this investment.

Investment Corporation acquired from an outside party for $34,900 on 7/1/x6 $40,000 face value of Elimination Corporation bonds. Bonds were originally issued for $51,000 on 1/1/x5, had a face value of $60,000, a 4 percent coupon rate, and a 10-year life to maturity. Interest is paid on 6/30 and 12/31.

All bond amortization has been correctly reported using the straight-line method. Separate tax returns are filed and the corporate tax rate is a flat 40 percent.

Required:
1. Prepare the investment account analysis schedule.
2. Prepare the consolidation work sheet entries at 12/31/x7.

Problem 7:   X and Y Intercorporate Transactions

X Corporation purchased, on 1/1/x1, 80 percent of the outstanding shares of Y Corporation for $300,000. As of 1/1/x1, the par value of Y Corporation's outstanding common stock was $100,000, paid-in capital was $20,000, and retained earnings were $250,000. Y Corporation had net income of $40,000 during 19x1 and paid $20,000 in dividends. All depreciable and/or intangible assets are assumed to have 10-year useful lives, and the straight-line write-off method is used. Assume any cost in excess of book value or vice versa is attributable to depreciable assets used in manufacturing.

Y Corporation, on 1/1/x2, purchased 10 percent of Z Corporation for $200,000. Z lost $4,000, and paid no dividends in 19x2.

The trial balances of X and Y Corporations as of 12/31/x2 are as follows:

X AND Y CORPORATIONS
Trial Balance
12/31/x2

	X	Y
Cash	$ 26,000	$ 8,800
Accounts receivable (net)	86,240	54,000
Accrued interest receivable	3,600	–0–
Inventory, 12/31/x2	210,000	40,000
Plant assets	654,700	350,000
Accumulated depreciation	(336,900)	(129,000)
Investment in Z stock	–0–	200,000
Investment in Y stock	323,018	–0–
Investment in Y bonds	61,067	–0–
Accounts payable	(10,000)	(12,200)
Accrued liabilities (including taxes)	(5,000)	(6,000)
Bonds payable	–0–	(100,000)
Premium on bonds payable	–0–	(1,600)
Common stock	(200,000)	(100,000)
Additional paid-in capital	(100,000)	(20,000)
Retained earnings, 1/1/x2	(600,000)	(270,000)
Sales	(700,000)	(400,000)
Cost of goods sold	390,000	200,000
Selling expenses	90,000	80,000
Administrative and other expenses	82,400	100,000
Interest revenue	(5,867)	–0–
Equity in Y earnings	(13,018)	–0–
Tax provision	43,760	6,000
	–0–	–0–
Inventory, 1/1/x2	$ 200,000	$ 80,000

1. X Corporation records show an account payable to Y Corporation of $2,000 for purchases. In addition, Y Corporation records show that X owes $6,000; the $4,000 difference being a 12/31/x2 inventory shipment from Y to X (FOB shipping point) which has not yet been received or recorded in any way by X.
2. X Corporation's $200,000 inventory on 1/1/x2 included $20,000 of goods purchased from Y in the previous year. Y's gross profit percentage for that year was 50 percent.
3. X Corporation's inventory of $210,000 includes $10,000 worth of goods which are part of the $100,000 worth purchased from Y this year. The $100,000 is included in the computation of the $390,000 cost of goods sold.
4. X Corporation, for $61,200, purchased from outsiders $60,000 face value of Y Corporation bonds on 1/1/x2. (Assume straight-line amortization of premium or discount.)
5. The Y Corporation bonds were originally issued on 1/1/x1 at 102. These are 10 percent, 10-year debenture bonds with interest payable annually on December 31. Interest expense of Y Corporation was paid on 12/31/x2 and has been included in administrative and other expenses. (Assume straight-line amortization of premium or discount.)

6. Assume that there is a flat 30 percent corporate tax rate and that separate tax returns are filed.
7. No dividends were paid by either X or Y in 19x2.

Required:
1. Prepare an analysis of Y Corporation using the headings as shown below:

Net Assets	Majority	Minority

2. Prepare in general journal form any adjusting and/or eliminating entries which would be necessary *if* a consolidated balance sheet and income statement were to be presented. (Do not prepare the statements themselves—support all figures and round all amounts to the nearest dollar.)
3. Using the journal entries prepare a three-section work sheet.

7

Accounting for Complex and Changing Capital Structures within a Subsidiary

Complex Structures
    The Problem of Distinguishing between Debt and Owners' Equity
    The Tax Incentive
    The Analysis of Investments with Both Common and Preferred Stock
        Preferred Stock as a Second Class of Owners' Equity
        Preferred Stock as Debt
        Preferred Stock as a Common Stock Equivalent
        Bonds as Common Stock Equivalents
Changing Ownership Interests
    Change in Ownership through Conversion of Securities
        Conversions Which Decrease Ownership Percentages
        Conversions Which Increase Ownership Percentages
    Change in Ownership through the Issuance of Shares by the Subsidiary
    Change through Options
    Change through New Share Issues
        None of the New Issue Purchased by the Parent
        All of the New Issue Purchased by the Parent
        Half of the New Issue Purchased by the Parent
    Change through Treasury Stock Transactions
        Purchase of Treasury Shares from the Minority Interest
        Purchase of Treasury Shares from the Parent Corporation
    Change through Sale of a Part or of All of the Ownership Interest

The previous chapter discussed intercorporate held bonds which in certain cases within a consolidation can result in triggering gain or loss recognition before it would be recognized on separate entity records. With the exception of the bond chapter, our discussion of intercorporate investments has centered on common stock. This chapter emphasizes a theoretical approach to (1) accounting for preferred stock (convertible and nonconvertible) and convertible bonds within a subsidiary and (2) accounting for changes in a subsidiary's capital structure.

It should also be noted that some of the discussion in this chapter is based on theoretical concepts even beyond that which the FASB has considered in its public releases. The material presented in this chapter is perhaps the most theoretically complex of all consolidation topics. Thus, you will have to give this material your undivided attention. You will find that for some of the situations presented there are several possible solutions and no established rules to guide selection. Actual practice in this area frequently leaves something to be desired. It is the goal of this chapter to present a theoretical approach as well as to show how these items are treated in practice.

COMPLEX STRUCTURES

The Problem of Distinguishing between Debt and Owners' Equity

Preferred stock is normally considered to be a form of owners' equity whereas bonds are normally debt equities. But the line, if any, distinguishing bonds from stock is not always distinctly visible. For example, is a bond issue, which is convertible into common stock and with interest payable only if earned, debt equity or is it owners' equity or is it some of each? Most often it is the latter. On the other hand, preferred stock which is cumulative, nonparticipating, nonvoting, nonconvertible, and callable at the option of the holder (in effect a put) has most of the characteristics of a debt issue.[1] In some cases only the name—bond or stock—seems to identify the type of equity. But names are often deliberately misleading.

Unfortunately current practice generally looks no further than the name of the security in determining whether it is a debt or stock issue for purposes of determining the percentage ownership of a subsidiary. Only in measuring earnings per share (EPS) does practice even recognize that the name might not indicate the true nature of a security. Therefore, in the EPS computation we sometimes designate convertible

---

[1] The SEC now requires certain preferred issues such as those callable at the option of the holder or where redemption is mandatory or is outside the control of the issuer to be reclassified, in a new section of the statement of financial position, between debt and owners' equity, see *Accounting Series Release No. 268.*

bond and convertible preferred stock issues as "common stock equivalents." The test for such status for EPS purposes is based on yield at the date of issue, and once established the status as a "common stock equivalent" never changes.[2] When this produces unrealistic results, the fully diluted EPS computation becomes more relevant than the primary EPS computation. In determining consolidated net earnings there is no second computation, such as fully diluted earnings, in order to produce more realistic results. In the measurement of consolidated net earnings the test for common stock equivalency status must permit change in order to determine the proper amount of subsidiary earnings belonging to the consolidated entity.

The Tax Incentive

Because interest is deductible for tax purposes whereas preferred (and common) dividends usually are not, there is often thought to be a significant bias in favor of debt issues.[3] And this is true from the point of view of the issuing corporation. When the investor is considered, however, some if not all of this advantage may be eliminated, especially if the investor is a corporation. To an investing corporation, interest income is fully taxable and at ordinary income rates which are often the highest rates. Dividend income, on the other hand, is often eligible for an 85 percent and sometimes a 100 percent dividends received deduction. The 85 percent deduction reduces the highest currently effective U.S. corporate federal income tax rate from 46 percent to 6.9 percent on dividends from other domestic corporations. Thus, corporate investors would usually prefer dividend income to interest income while the issuing domestic corporation prefers the interest deduction to nondeductible dividends. Perhaps utopia would be a security which would be designed so as to be debt to the issuer and stock equity to the corporate investor. Such a security has not yet been developed.

> **Tax:** The debt versus stock problem has long plagued the IRS. In the Tax Reform Act of 1969, Congress sought to make the distinction easier; in this act, Congress gave the Secretary of the Treasury authority to prescribe regulations which would separate debt and equity.
>
> The Secretary is authorized to prescribe such regulations as may be necessary or appropriate to determine whether an interest in a cor-

---

[2] *AICPA Professional Standards, Accounting—Current Text* (New York, 1980), pars. 2011.28 and 2011.33. Copyright (1980) by the American Institute of CPAs.

[3] There is an exception to nondeductibility of dividends. For certain public utility preferred shares generally issued prior to October 1, 1942, there is a deduction for dividends paid. *Internal Revenue Code,* sec. 247.

> **Tax:** (*continued*)
> poration is to be treated for purposes of this title as stock or indebtedness.*
>
> If this were an easy task Congress could have prescribed the rules. But, this is a difficult task and one that could result in a significant tax revenue loss to the federal government. Once the debt versus equity line is drawn there will be even less difference between debt and equity. Many debt issues will march right up to that line and stop there, and some stock issues might be replaced with debt issues. Thus, the authority, granted in 1969, to prescribe the identifying characteristics of debt and equity was not exercised in the decade of the 1970s. The IRS waited until 1980 to release *proposed* regulations in this area and these have just been finalized but are still subject to extensive criticism.
>
> * *Internal Revenue Code*, sec. 385.

The Analysis of Investments with Both Common and Preferred Stock

The question of whether preferred stock is really (1) debt, or (2) the equivalent of common stock, or (3) a second class of stock has significance beyond the income tax question of deductibility and the EPS computation. The designation can also, at least theoretically, affect financial reporting through the investment account analysis.

Preferred Stock as a Second Class of Owners' Equity. Assume P Corporation purchases on 1/1/x1 60 percent of the common stock and 40 percent of the $6 preferred stock of S Corporation for $200,000 and $50,000, respectively.

This situation is analyzed in Illustration 7–1. Here the preferred stock is deemed to be a second class of owners' equity.

Illustration 7–1

		Majority		Minority	
S Corporation	Net Assets	60 Percent Common	40 Percent Preferred	40 Percent Common	60 Percent Preferred
Preferred stock, 1,000 shares ...	$100,000		$40,000		$60,000
Common stock, 1,000 shares ...	100,000	$ 60,000		$ 40,000	
Additional paid-in capital	20,000	12,000		8,000	
Retained earnings, 1/1/x1	200,000	120,000	–0–	80,000	–0–
Totals	$420,000	192,000	40,000	$128,000	$60,000
Cost in excess of book value....		8,000	10,000		
Price paid		$200,000	$50,000		

Before proceeding with the analysis, however, the identity of the preferred stock as equivalent to debt, as equivalent to common equity, or as a second class of owners' equity needs to be established.[4] This can impact on the allocation of retained earnings. For example, if the preferred stock were considered as owners' equity (but not the equivalent of common stock) and if it were cumulative but nonparticipating with one year's dividend in arrears, of the $200,000 in retained earnings $6,000 would be allocable to the preferred and $194,000 to the common. This or any other allocation would affect the difference between the underlying book value of the net assets and the cost of both the common and the preferred stock. If the preferred shares were noncumulative but fully participating, $100,000 ($200,000 × $100,000 ÷ $200,000) of the retained earnings might be allocated to the preferred and $100,000 to the common with the additional paid-in capital normally attributable entirely to the common stock.[5]

The allocation of the owners' equity accounts to the various ownership interests affects the difference between the underlying book value of the net assets and the cost of the stock (supposedly equal to the fair value of the net assets). Thus, the subsequent allocation of cost in excess of book value or of book value in excess of cost to the assets and liabilities can impact on the reported earnings of the consolidated entity or of a subsidiary accounted for under the equity method.

Preferred stock can have many characteristics. Sometimes it is voting stock; if it is voting stock can it be classified as debt?[6] The answer is probably no. Preferred stock can also be convertible, but depending on the terms, the conversion privilege may be almost worthless; in this case it is not a common stock equivalent. Thus, a particular preferred issue might be considered to be the equivalent of debt, the equivalent of common stock, or a second form of owners' equity, and it might have characteristics of all three of these possibilities. If it is classified as a second class of owners' equity, any cost in excess of book value on the date of acquisition would be attributable at least theoretically to (1) its claim on underlying net assets or (2) its established dividend yield. Where a premium is paid because of a high yield (assuming the amount attributable to this factor can be separately measured), a strong, theoret-

---

[4] Some accountants object to this use of common stock equivalency status (for convertible preferred stock or debt) and term it "as if" accounting, but these same accountants do not object to "as if" accounting for leases. Thus, there is some precedent for recognizing substance over form.

[5] Additional paid-in capital received upon the issue of preferred stock is often associated with the preferred especially if it is to be returned to the preferred shareholders in the event of liquidation.

[6] In one of the largest acquisitions ever made, ITT acquired the stock of Hartford Fire Insurance Company in exchange for ITT voting, convertible, preferred stock.

ical case can be made for amortization of that premium. Without a maturity date an arbitrary period would have to be selected for amortization (a precedent for this has been established in the amortization of goodwill). When a preferred issue is not participating and there are no dividends in arrears (if cumulative) none of the retained earnings are attributable to this stock. Or in other words, its value would be attributable to its yield and to the present value, if any, of its claim on net assets in the event of liquidation.

A diagram of the possibilities for categorizing preferred stock appears in Illustration 7–2.

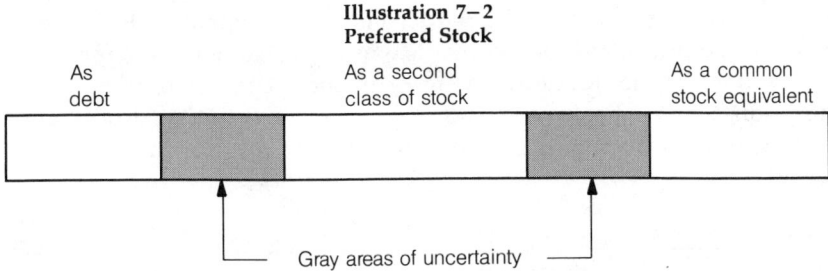

Preferred Stock as Debt. If we assume that the initial allocation of net assets to owners' equity groups was correct but that the preferred is the equivalent of debt, then its $10,000 cost in excess of underlying net assets might be considered to be an adjustment of the dividend rate on the preferred, similar in effect to a premium paid on an investment in bonds. The accounting alternatives then are to reflect this $10,000 in current earnings as a loss, or to defer and amortize it against earnings over some future period as an adjustment of the dividend yields. In this case, of the two choices an adjustment of the stock yield seems clearly preferable. If, however, the preferred stock is similar to debt and has been acquired by another member from an outsider at a premium, recognition of loss (or gain), inside the consolidated financial statements, as though it were debt retirement seems consistent.

In practice, if preferred stock has a maturity date, any premium or discount would be amortized over the period from date of issue to maturity. Such amortization is reflected through stockholders equity accounts and does not affect the earnings statement. This amortization does, however, affect the earnings per share calculation through adjustment of the preferred dividends.

Preferred Stock as a Common Stock Equivalent. If the preferred were fully participating, convertible into common on a 1-to-1 basis (thus perhaps a "common stock equivalent"), and callable, the value of the shares of both common and preferred might be deriving most if not all their value from the underlying net assets. In this case, if a proper allocation of the amounts of additional paid-in capital and retained earnings can be made, the difference between the book values of the underlying net assets and the cost of the shares should be reflected in the asset or liability values in the consolidated statement of financial position.

The presence of the fixed "minimum" dividend rate for the preferred shares obviously complicates the allocation of book values to the shares. If this corporation had established a precedent of paying at least 6 percent to the common shareholders, the effect of the yield on the fair value of the preferred stock might be reduced or even eliminated. If this were the case, the price paid for the shares would probably be different than we assumed in the debt equivalent or in the second class of stock assumption for the preferred. The investment account analyses, with changes in the prices paid for the shares, might now appear as in Illustration 7–3.

Illustration 7–3

S Corporation	Net Assets	Majority		Minority	
		60 Percent Common	40 Percent Preferred	40 Percent Common	60 Percent Preferred
Preferred stock, 1,000 shares	$100,000		$ 40,000		$ 60,000
Common stock, 1,000 shares	100,000	$ 60,000		$40,000	
Additional paid-in capital	20,000	6,000	4,000	4,000	6,000
Retained earnings, 1/1/x1	200,000	60,000	40,000	40,000	60,000
Totals	$420,000	126,000	84,000	$84,000	$126,000
Cost in excess of book value		24,000	16,000		
Price paid		$150,000	$100,000		

If the "minority" held stock is worth the same price as the "majority" held stock, the fair value of the net assets should be $500,000 or (2 × ($150,000 + $100,000)). It should also be obvious that the assumption as to the nature of the preferred stock in this example has serious consequences for consolidation. If the preferred were considered to be equivalent to common stock, the ownership percentage would fall to 50–50, and therefore consolidation of this "subsidiary" could be questionable.

As a common stock equivalent the percentage ownership of the "majority" interest would be 30 percent (600 ÷ 2,000 shares) on the common and 20 percent (400 ÷ 2,000 shares) on the preferred. The excess of the fair value of the net assets over book value would be $80,000 ($24,000 ÷

30%, or $16,000 ÷ 20%, or $500,000 − $420,000). If the preferred is a true common stock equivalent, the proportionate price difference (the difference between the price of the stock and the underlying net assets divided by the ownership percentage) should be proportionally the same for both the common and the preferred stock as it is in this example ($80,000). This assumes that the investments in common and preferred were made at the same date. It should be noted from the example that in order to obtain the $80,000 total excess of fair value over book value from both the common and preferred investments that the price per share of the common and of the preferred (with the 1-to-1 conversion) would have to be identical (i.e., $150,000 divided by 6,000 shares equals $25 per share price on the common and $100,000 divided by 4,000 shares equals $25 per share price on the preferred). Thus, for true common stock equivalents the total fair value of the convertible issue must equal the total fair value of the total number of shares of common stock into which it is convertible. Using total values rather than per share values allows one to test for common stock equivalency status when conversions ratios are at other than 1-to-1 rates.

Convertible preferred, however, may often have a slightly higher price because of less risk and a stated yield, especially if this yield exceeds that historically paid on the common. In such a case the fair value of the preferred will exceed that of the common into which it is convertible. The price will reflect some of the characteristics of both classes of stock, and conversion will not take place (unless callable and called) until the dividend yield on the common exceeds that of the preferred. At such a time there should no longer be a significant difference in the price of the convertible preferred and of the common into which it is convertible.

If the preferred and common stocks are purchased at different dates, the test for common stock equivalency must be made at the date of whichever one was purchased last, and the fair value of the other must be the test amount and not the carrying amount of the prior investment. This common stock equivalency test would also have to be made at the end of each year using the fair values of each type of security as test amounts.[7] When purchased at different dates, the preferred and the common could be treated as different blocks of stock even though the preferred might be classified as a common stock equivalent. The problem of second or multiple blocks of stock is discussed later in this chapter.

---

[7] In *APB Opinion No. 9* for EPS purposes, before it was superseded by *Opinion No. 15*, the common stock equivalency status of an issue could change with changes in price. Such reflection of economic reality would seem essential for showing percentage ownership of subsidiaries for determining consolidated or equity method earnings.

> **Other Tax Factors:** In addition to issuing preferred stock because of its favorable tax treatment to the corporate investor, it is also possible to use the "preferred gets theirs first" concept in tax planning. If a corporation has a fairly constant "current earnings and profits" figure (from which taxability of dividends is determined), there may be some potential for paying "tax-free" dividends. A preferred issue owned by corporate investors would allow them to receive the "current earnings and profits" as taxable dividends and thus eligible for the dividend received deduction; then the common dividends could be "tax free" which would favor and thus be attractive to high-bracket individual shareholders. This type of tax planning appears to be used by some public utility companies. Thus, in certain cases, the tax law encourages the use of preferred stock.

Bonds as Common Stock Equivalents. The following will illustrate possible price changes of convertible debt (or convertible preferred stock) in relation to price changes in the common stock. Assume that $100,000 of 10 percent, 10-year convertible bonds are issued at face value when the bank prime interest rate is 10 percent. Each $1,000 bond is convertible into five shares of common stock which is currently selling at $20 per share. Assume no change in general market interest rates over the life of the bonds so that the value of the bonds will change only in relationship to the fortunes of the corporation. With each $1,000 bond convertible into only $100 worth of stock at the date of the bond issue, the stock will have to increase in value more than tenfold within ten years to make this convertible feature worth anything immediately prior to debt maturity. At the date of the bond issue, the conversion feature may have been almost worthless, but as the stock value advances the conversion feature may gain value. If the market value of the stock increases from $20 to over $200 per share (five shares then worth $1,000), the market value of the bonds will track the stock price with any market value difference then being due to yield and risk differences. The market premium for risk difference will decrease as the price of the stock advances.

If the dividend on the stock exceeds $20 per share so that the total yield on five shares exceeds the $100 interest yield on a $1,000 bond, conversion will probably take place (as depicted at the end of year 9). If the bondholders were corporations, the dividend yield could be as low as $12 per share and still exceed the aftertax yield on the bonds. With the bonds yielding only $54 after tax ($100 − ($100 × 46%)) to a corporate shareholder, a dividend of $12 per share on five shares would yield $55.86 if converted ($12 × 5 shares − 46% ($60 − ($60 × 85%))).

In Illustration 7–4 between years 2 and 3, the conversion feature begins to grow in value, and by the end of year 5 the bonds were tracking the price of the common stock. Only the higher yield on the bonds and the lower risks associated with the bonds keeps the two values from merging. By the end of year 9, the dividend yield on the stock must equal or exceed the yield on the bonds causing conversion or

Illustration 7–4

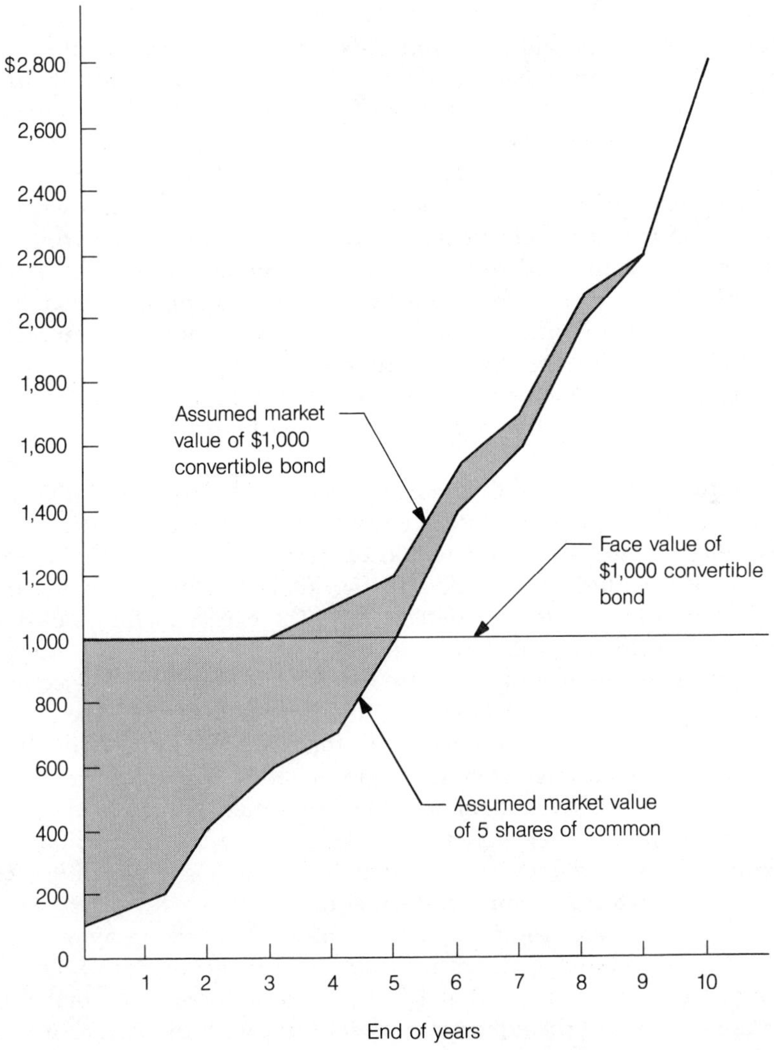

at least the two value lines to merge. In this case the bonds would be converted prior to maturity.

Under these assumptions, when should this issue be considered to be the equivalent of common stock for measuring ownership? For measuring primary EPS only, conversion would create common stock because the issue failed the common stock equivalency test at the date of issue. But in measuring percentage ownership of a subsidiary for consolidation or for use of the equity method, a test at the date of issue is not relevant for subsequent years. In this example, by the end of year 5, when the value of the common equals the face value of the bonds, only the differences in yields (and perhaps to some extent risk) keeps the value of the bonds above the value of the stock. Once the value of the stock into which a bond is convertible exceeds the face value of the debt (or carrying amount when issued at a premium or discount), then, absent changes in market interest rates, the debt issue could be considered the equivalent of common stock for purposes of measuring ownership percentages and thus consolidated or equity method earnings. In current practice, however, this would not be recognized as an ownership interest, and thus the effects on earnings would not be shown.

It should be realized that if a parent corporation buys convertible debt of a subsidiary, there might be debt retirement or instead an increased ownership interest. In addition, actual yield differences between dividends on the stock and interest on the common stock equivalents can cause problems in the analysis of the parent's investments in these securities. The difference in yields will be presented later in this chapter.

It is quite possible and theoretically correct to have a convertible bond issue treated as a "common stock equivalent in the net asset analysis." If this were the case, the bonds would be deemed to be a form of owners' equity and should be included in the analysis along with the other owners' equity accounts in determining the excess of the book value over the cost (or vice versa) of an investment. This would also affect the percentage ownership. Again, if the convertible bonds are true common stock equivalents, the total excess of the fair value of the issue over the book value of the underlying net assets for the corporation should be the same whether computed from the common stock investment or from the convertible bond investment if these investments were made on the same date. Or in other words, the total value of the convertible issue would equal the total value of the common shares into which it is convertible if it is a true common stock equivalent.

To illustrate this, assume that S has $100,000 carrying amount (and face value) of bonds outstanding which are convertible into 1,000 common shares. Also assume that 1,000 preferred shares are outstanding and are considered the equivalent of debt but with dividends at $6 per share one year in arrears. Assume that P acquires 80 percent or 800 shares of S common stock for $200,000, 40 percent of S bonds for $100,000, and 20 percent of S preferred stock for $22,000. An investment analysis with the designated amounts for common stock, paid-in capital (entirely attributable to common and equivalent shares), and retained earnings might appear as shown in Illustration 7–5.

With the bonds originally issued at par, and assuming they paid a going interest rate, they were not common stock equivalents when issued. In fact, little value would apparently have been placed on the convertibility feature at that date. Subsequently, however, the convertibility aspect grew in value. The increase in the market value of the bonds would not be reflected in the price paid if the majority interest acquired these bonds at the date of issue. It is apparent, in this example, that the majority did not invest in these bonds at the date of issue, but apparently acquired them at the same time that the common stock was acquired.

The bonds are true common stock equivalents in that they produce the same total excess of fair value of net assets over book value as does the common stock investment, or $86,000 ($34,000 ÷ 40%, or $17,200 ÷ 20% with the percentages reflecting ownership assuming conversion). Or looking at total values, the entire bond issue was worth $250,000 ($100,000 ÷ 40%) and the stock into which it is convertible is worth $250,000 ($200,000 ÷ 800 shares × 1,000 shares). Again, current practice would probably consider these bonds to be debt and not equivalents to common stock.

The timing of the common stock equivalency test for consolidation purposes should be different from the one currently employed in EPS calculations. The *initial* determination of this status for consolidation purposes should be made at the latter of (1) the date the convertible investment is acquired or (2) at the date the convertible bonds (or convertible preferred shares) were issued if no bonds (or preferred shares) were acquired but common stock were owned. It would also be essential that this determination be made anew annually for consolidated financial statement preparation.

In the example, the acquired preferred shares were assumed to be the equivalent of debt and purchased for $22,000 when they had a par value (face value for debt) of $20,000 and a $1,200 claim for dividends in arrears leaving an $800 premium. If this issue is essentially debt, a case could be made for amortization of the $800 as an adjustment of the dividend (interest) rate and for immediate recognition in consolidation as loss on debt retirement.

To illustrate the effect a difference in dividend and interest yields can have, assume the owners' equity of the Yield Corporation is as shown in Illustration 7–6 and that the book value of each asset and liability, ex-

Illustration 7–5

S Corporation	Net Assets	Majority			Minority		
		80 Percent Common	40 Percent Bonds	20 Percent Preferred	20 Percent Common	60 Percent Bonds	80 Percent Preferred
Preferred stock, 1,000 shares	$100,000			$ 20,000			$ 80,000
Common stock, 1,000 shares	100,000	$ 80,000			$20,000		
Debt common stock equivalent, 1,000 shares	100,000		$ 40,000			$ 60,000	
Additional paid-in capital	20,000	8,000	4,000		2,000	6,000	
Retained earnings	200,000	77,600[a]	38,800[b]	1,200[e]	19,400[d]	58,200[d]	4,800[f]
Totals	520,000	165,600	82,800	21,200	41,400	124,200	84,800
Less preferred stock as debt	106,000			(21,200)			(84,800)
Totals	$414,000	165,600	82,800	–0–	$41,400	$124,200	–0–
Cost in excess of book value or (book value in excess of cost)		34,400	17,200				
Price paid		$200,000	$100,000				

[a] ($200,000 − $6,000) × $80,000 ÷ $200,000 = $ 77,600
[b] $194,000 × $40,000 ÷ $200,000 = 38,800
[c] $194,000 × $20,000 ÷ $200,000 = 19,400
[d] $194,000 × $60,000 ÷ $200,000 = 58,200
[e] $6,000 × 20% = 1,200
[f] $6,000 × 80% = 4,800
Retained earnings $200,000

Illustration 7-6
YIELD CORPORATION

Common stock, $10 par value	$100,000
Additional paid-in capital	30,000
Retained earnings, 1/1/x1	150,000
Book value, 1/1/x1	$280,000

cept for convertible bonds, equals its fair value. Assume Diff Corporation acquires 9,000 shares of Yield common on 1/1/x1 for $35 per share, or $315,000, but none of the $50,000 face value (and carrying amount) of Yield's convertible bonds are acquired by Diff. Each $1,000 bond is convertible into 40 common shares. The fair value of a $1,000 bond on 1/1/x1 was in excess of $1,400 (40 shares at $35) due to the yield and risk differences. The conversion privilege was considered worthless when the 20-year, 10 percent bonds were first issued, on January 1, 18 years prior to 19x1, and now this privilege is quite valuable. Yield earns $45,000 in 19x1 and pays $20,000 in dividends.

The investment analysis as of 12/31/x1 for Diff's investment in Yield is shown in Illustration 7–7. It should be noted that the totals for the majority and minority interest columns are not in line with their percentages (75 percent, 8⅓ percent, and 16⅔ percent), and this is due to the differences in yields ($2 per share on the stock and the equivalent of $2.50 per share on the bonds). In addition, the $70,000 adjusted book value of the bonds on 1/1/x1 would be less than their fair values because of the yield difference (and risk premium if any). Without this difference the $70,000 (2,000 shares × $35 price per share) would be accurate. The columns can be kept in line with their percentages if the difference in yield is ignored in the analysis (see Illustration 7–8).

This method may be the best approach even though it ignores the real dividend yield; or the same result could have been achieved in the first analysis by shifting investment dollars as shown in Illustration 7–9.

If practice followed theory as to ownership determination, enormous accounting complexities would exist in complex capital structures. This would create at least some motivation to retain simple capital structures within the subsidiaries. On the other hand, perhaps a complex structure would make a corporation targeted for acquisition somewhat less attractive. At this point even though the discussion has been less than complete, we drop some of the theoretical problems involving convertible issues. Needless to say, there are many theoretical issues left for future accounting theorists to ponder. The complexity involved in convertible issues makes it easier to see why practice looks at the name of the security rather than at the substance, but practice might change in future years.

Illustration 7–7
INVESTMENT ACCOUNT ANALYSIS

Yield Corporation	Net Assets	Majority Stock $\frac{9,000}{12,000^*} = 75\%$	Minority Stock $\frac{1,000}{12,000} = 8\frac{1}{3}\%$	Minority Bonds $\frac{2,000}{12,000} = 16\frac{2}{3}\%$
Convertible bonds, 2,000 shares	$ 50,000	$ 37,500	$ 4,167	$ 8,333
Common stock, $10 par value	100,000	75,000	8,333	16,667
Additional paid-in capital	30,000	22,500	2,500	5,000
Retained earnings, 1/1/x1	150,000	112,500	12,500	25,000
Book value, 1/1/x1	330,000	247,500	27,500	55,000
Goodwill	90,000†	67,500	7,500	15,000
Adjusted book value, 1/1/x1	420,000	315,000	35,000	70,000
Dividends ($2 per share), 19x1	(20,000)	(18,000)	(2,000)	–0–
Interest on common stock equivalents (CSE), 19x1	(5,000)	–0–	–0–	(5,000)
Earnings, 19x1	45,000 ⎫			
Add back equivalent interest on CSE	5,000 ⎬ $47,750	35,813	3,979	7,958
Amortization goodwill (90,000 ÷ 40 years)	(2,250) ⎭			
Adjusted net assets, 12/31/x1	$442,750	$332,813	$36,979	$72,958

* 10,000 shares originally issued + 2,000 to be issued upon conversion.
† Alternative method 3.

Illustration 7–8

Yield Corporation	Net Assets	Majority Stock 75 Percent	Minority Stock $8\frac{1}{3}$ Percent	Minority Bond (CSE) $16\frac{2}{3}$ Percent
Adjusted book value, 1/1/x1	$420,000	$315,000	$35,000	$70,000
Dividends ($2 per share), 19x1	(20,000)	(18,000)	(2,000)	–0–
Equivalent yield on CSE (2,000 × $2), 19x1	(4,000)	–0–	–0–	(4,000)
Earnings, 19x1	45,000 ⎫			
Add back equivalent interest on CSE	4,000 ⎬ $46,750	35,062	3,896	7,792
Goodwill amortization	(2,250) ⎭			
Adjusted net assets, 12/31/x1	$442,750	$332,062	$36,896	$73,792

Illustration 7–9

Yield Corporation	Net Assets	Majority 75 Percent	Minority 8⅓ Percent	Minority 16⅔ Percent
Adjusted net assets, 12/31/x1	$442,750	$332,813	36,979	72,958
Yield adjustment	–0–	(751)†	(83)†	834*
Adjusted net assets, 12/31/x1	$442,750	$332,062	36,896	73,792

* $73,792 − $72,958 = $834, or 16⅔% × $442,750 = $73,792.
† $834 × 90% = $751; $834 × 10% = $83.

CHANGING OWNERSHIP INTERESTS

The percentage ownership of a corporate entity can change in many ways, and these include the conversion of convertible preferred stock or convertible bonds, exercise of options, issuance of new stock, purchase or reissue of treasury stock, as well as either the acquisition or sale of some subsidiary stock by the parent corporation. These changes in ownership interest where the ownership percentage is *decreased* will often result in gains or losses for financial reporting. Unfortunately, existing practice fails to reflect these gains or losses, and in this case there is no overwhelming complexity.

The recognition of gain or loss on changes in ownership interest where the percentage ownership decreases and nonrecognition of gain or loss where the percentage ownership increases is consistent with the single entity concept and the recognition that the minority interest is indeed a form of owners' equity. Some accountants argue that the minority interest should be treated as a liability rather than as a form of stock ownership. Your author rejects the liability notion.

Therefore, when the majority's *percentage* interest falls, this is treated as a sale with recognition of gain or loss if any. When the majority's *percentage* interest increases, this is treated as a purchase of additional interest without recognition of gain or loss. This is shown in Illustration 7–10.

Once again actual practice falls far short of acceptable accounting theory and without the support of excessive complexity. Practice today fails to recognize gain or loss on these transactions, but instead these gains or losses are taken to paid-in capital of the parent corporation. The total inferiority of this position over recognition will be demonstrated later in this chapter. It should be mentioned at this point that present practice in this area has been greatly influenced by the SEC which supports and requires this nonrecognition treatment.

Illustration 7–10

Majority	Ownership Percentage Decreased (sale)	Ownership Percentage Increased (purchase)
Share of underlying net assets increased	Recognition of gain	Nonrecognition of gain
Share of underlying net assets decreased	Recognition of loss	Nonrecognition of loss

Change in Ownership through Conversion of Securities

Conversions which Decrease Ownership Percentages. If outstanding convertible securities, which were not previously considered as a part of owners' equity, are converted into common stock, perhaps after a sharp rise in the market price of the common, the parent's percentage ownership of the net assets of the subsidiary will decrease. This, of course, assumes that others are doing the exercising or converting rather than the parent. To illustrate this, assume that on 1/1/x1 P Corporation helped form S Corporation and received 80 percent of the S Corporation stock. Also assume that S subsequently issued some convertible bonds at $100,000 face value with the coupon interest rate approximately equal to the market interest rate on nonconvertible issues. With this interest rate, even though the bonds were convertible into 200 shares, the conversion privilege is almost worthless at the date of issue. Now five years later, after a rapid rise in market values, these bonds are converted. The investment account analysis immediately prior to the conversion and after the conversion would appear as in Illustration 7–11 if the convertible debt were treated as debt rather than equity. The $100,000 of former debt is represented by 200 more shares of common stock outstanding, a $20,000 increase in total par value of common, and an $80,000 increase in additional paid-in capital. Thus, the conversion produces $100,000 increase in net assets from $580,000 to $680,000.

One should note that the conversion normally is recorded using the book value or carrying amount of the prior debt and not its fair market value (FMV). If FMV were used in a conversion, the assets and liabilities would have to be revalued just as they are when a parent corporation acquires a major interest in a subsidiary.

It should be noticed, however, that the conversion is equivalent to P selling some of its investment in S. In effect P made this result possible by allowing S to issue convertible debt and by not acquiring at least 80 percent of the debt issue. P has, in effect, sold or reduced its ownership

Illustration 7–11

A. Prior to conversion

S Corporation	Net Assets	800 Shares or 80 Percent Majority	200 Shares or 20 Percent Minority
Common stock, 1,000 shares	$100,000	$ 80,000	$ 20,000
Additional paid-in capital	80,000	64,000	16,000
Retained earnings	400,000	320,000	80,000
Totals	$580,000	$464,000	$116,000

B. After conversion

S Corporation	Net Assets	800 Shares or 66⅔ Percent Majority	400 Shares or 33⅓ Percent Minority
Common stock, 1,200 shares	$120,000	$ 80,000	$ 40,000
Additional paid-in capital	160,000	106,667	53,333
Retained earnings	400,000	266,667	133,333
Totals	$680,000	453,334	$226,666
Basis of investment account prior to conversion		464,000	
Loss—decrease in underlying net assets		$ (10,666)	

from 80 percent to 66⅔ percent for a 13⅓ percentage *point* decrease (80% − 66⅔%). This decrease represents 16⅔ percent (13⅓% ÷ 80%) of the prior holding. Thus P gained $66,667 or 66⅔ of the $100,000 debt which is now part of owners' equity but gave up $77,333 or 13⅓ percent of the $580,000 owners' equity before the conversion for a $10,666 loss ($66,667 − $77,333). The amount given up can also be computed as a sale of 16⅔ percent times the basis of the investment of $464,000 or $77,333. This would require the following entry on P's books:

Loss on S stock 10,666
    Investment in S stock (+$66,667 − $77,333) 10,666*

    * It should be noted for tax purposes that unless some shares are actually sold by P that any of these recognized gains or losses for book purposes will not be recognized for tax purposes. This will result in a permanent difference which will be reflected in a difference between the book and tax basis for the investment in S.

In practice, even though the percentage ownership has fallen, the loss amount would not be recognized (unless P actually sold some S stock). Instead, the loss amount would be debited to P's additional paid-in capital and the investment account credited.

Now assume the same transaction except that the converted debt had a face value and a carrying amount of $150,000 instead of $100,000. This increases net assets by $150,000 from $580,000 to $730,000. The account analysis immediately after the transaction would now be as given in Illustration 7–12.

Illustration 7–12

S Corporation	Net Assets	800 Shares or 66⅔ Percent Majority	400 Shares or 33⅓ Percent Minority
Common stock, 1,200 shares	$120,000	$ 80,000	$ 40,000
Additional paid-in capital	210,000	140,000	70,000
Retained earnings	400,000	266,667	133,333
Totals	$730,000	486,667	$243,333
Basis of investment account prior to conversion		464,000	
Gain increase in underlying net assets		$ 22,667	

In effect P has again "sold" some of its investment in S. On the "sale" P received $100,000 or 66⅔ percent of the $150,000 of converted debt which is now part of owners' equity ($20,000 increase in par value of S stock and $130,000 increase in additional paid-in capital) and gave up $77,333[8] or 13⅓ percent of $580,000 (owners' equity before conversion) for a gain of $22,667 ($100,000 − $77,333). P would thus record the effect of the conversion of S bonds on P's books as follows:

Investment in S stock (+$100,000 − $77,333) 22,667
    Gain on S stock* 22,667

* An SEC registrant would have to record this gain as an increase in additional paid-in capital.

The transaction to record the "sale" (conversion of S bonds) appears unusual in that the asset "sold" increases in amount.[9] This is, of course, caused by the fact that the carrying amount per share of the new stock before conversion, $750 ($150,000 ÷ 200 shares), is greater than the book value of the old stock, $580 ($580,000 ÷ 1,000 shares). Thus, the book value per share rises from $580 to about $608 ($730,000 ÷ 1,200 shares) after conversion.

It should also be noted that if the convertible debt had been issued when S was formed and had it been considered a "common stock equiv-

---

[8] This can also be computed as $464,000 × 16⅔ percent or the prior investment times the percentage decrease in ownership.

[9] Of course in a normal sale at a gain net assets increase, but the gain does not show up as an increase in the remaining asset (part of which had been sold).

alent" during each year, there would not have been any gain or loss on conversion. In this case P would always have been considered to be a 66⅔ percent owner and the debt would have been considered as part of the owners' equity attributable to the minority interest.

In practice, not only would the convertible security be ignored upon issue for purposes of determining ownership percentage, the gain on the conversion would not be recognized. This gain would instead be credited to P's paid-in capital to offset the increase in the investment account.

The theory behind present practice is incorrectly applied. If P has owned all 10,000 shares of S since inception and has an investment in S of $1,000,000 as adjusted for the equity method, the ownership could be diagramed as shown in Illustration 7–13.

Illustration 7–13

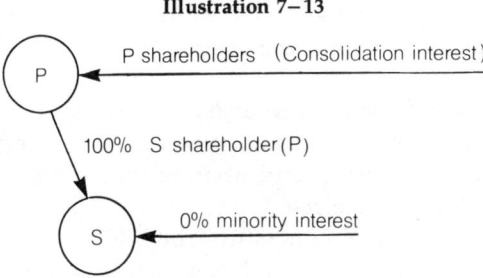

If half of the S stock were sold for $800,000, P would report a gain of $300,000 ($800,000 − $500,000). If P desires to avoid reporting a gain (or a loss under other price assumptions), P could have S issue 10,000 additional shares for $1,600,000 to outside parties. Current practice would analyze and have P record this as follows:

S's owner's equity before the issue	$1,000,000
Issue of 10,000 new shares	1,600,000
Total owners' equity	$2,600,000
P's 50% interest	$1,800,000
P's old 100% interest	1,000,000
Gain to P	$ 800,000
Investment in S stock	800,000
Additional paid-in capital	800,000

This entry prevents gain recognition even though P's interest in S has decreased from 100 percent to only 50 percent. By crediting additional paid-in capital, practice is, in effect, saying that gain (or loss) should not be recognized on stock transactions between the consolidated entity and its shareholders, and this is correct. But this theory is incorrectly applied in practice because *minority shareholders are not shareholders in the consolidated entity;* they are outsiders. Only shareholders of the parent corporation are shareholders in the consolidated entity. It is fundamentally wrong to treat an outside or minority interest as a shareholder in the consolidated entity. In addition, the emphasis should not be on shareholders but instead on ownership of net assets. It should be remembered that consolidation is a single economic entity concept. Thus, when its ownership interest in a subsidiary is reduced, this single economic entity has, in effect, sold some of its assets (that subsidiary's assets), and gain or loss on this sale should be recognized. When its ownership interest in a subsidiary has increased, the parent has, in effect, made a purchase of assets. But because there is no actual payment in some of these types of purchases, an adjustment is made to the parent's additional paid-in capital. The purchase situation will be discussed in greater depth in the following section of this chapter. In the remainder of the chapter only the theoretically correct concept will be discussed.

Conversions Which Increase Ownership Percentages. Now return to the assumption that the debt was not a common stock equivalent in the years prior to the conversion and assume that P owned the $100,000 convertible bond issue and elected to convert it. The 200 shares received on conversion increase the ownership from 80 percent to 83⅓ percent (1,000 shares ÷ 1,200 shares). And the aggregate basis of the investment account would go to $564,000 ($464,000 + $100,000). After conversion, however, the investment account analysis would be as given in Illustration 7–14.

Illustration 7–14

S Corporation	Net Assets	1,000 Shares or 83⅓ Percent Majority	200 Shares or 16⅔ Percent Minority
Common stock, 1,200 shares	$120,000	$100,000	$ 20,000
Additional paid-in capital	160,000	133,333	26,667
Retained earnings	400,000	333,333	66,667
Totals	$680,000	566,666	$113,334
Investment account after conversion ($464,000 + $100,000)		564,000	
Increase in underlying net assets		$ 2,666	

Because gain or loss is normally recognized only on "sales" (conversions which decrease the percentage ownership) and not on "purchases" (conversions which increase the percentage ownership), P would record this as follows:

```
Investment in S stock ($100,000 + $2,666) ................   102,666
    Investment in S bonds ...............................             100,000
    Other contributed capital ...........................               2,666
```

If the bonds had been carried at $150,000, the conversion would have had the effect given in Illustration 7–15.

Illustration 7–15

S Corporation	Net Assets	83⅓ Percent Majority	16⅔ Percent Minority
Common stock, 1,200 shares	$120,000	$100,000	$ 20,000
Additional paid-in capital	210,000	175,000	35,000
Retained earnings	400,000	333,333	66,667
Totals	$730,000	608,333	$121,667
Investment account after conversion ($464,000 + $150,000)		614,000	
Decrease in underlying net assets		$ (5,667)	

Just as gains are not recognized on "purchases" (an increase in ownership percentage) neither are losses. Thus, P would record this on its books as:

```
Investment in S stock ($150,000 − $5,667) ................   144,333
Additional paid-in capital ..............................     5,667
    Investment in S bonds ...............................             150,000
```

Again, if the bonds had always been considered to be "common stock equivalents," the conversion would not have had any effect because the carrying amount ($150,000 in this case) would have been considered to be part of the shareholders' equity. In this case, however, the issuance of the debt as a "common stock equivalent" would trigger at the date of issue these types of analyses and entries depending on what party(s) purchased the bonds. In addition, the bond issue could obviously have been purchased partly by the majority and partly by the minority.

These examples have been somewhat oversimplified in that a part of the carrying amount of the debt, even where it is convertible, might be due to its debt characteristics and not entirely to its convertibility. This additional complexity has been deliberately ignored herein.

It should be recalled from the chapter on intercorporate debt that a debt issue (classified as debt and) owned since inception by a member of the group is not treated as outstanding debt for consolidation. Thus, for consolidation the group will not recognize gain or loss even if P sells this bond investment. The debt issue would only become outstanding at the date of the sale. If, however, the debt issue had been recognized and classified as an equivalent to common stock, a sale of the convertible debt issue by P would be treated as a sale of a stock investment in a subsidiary with gain or loss recognized even on a consolidated basis. The gain or loss in this case however would be measured from the change in control over underlying net assets rather than from the original cost of the debt issue after allowing for amortization of premium or discount.

> **In theory:** When convertible issues have been consistently considered as owners' equity, the conversion should be based on carrying amounts for historical cost analysis. When the convertible issue previously has been considered as debt, perhaps a case can be made for use of FMV in the conversion or in the realization of common stock equivalency status with recognition of gain or loss. The use of fair values at these dates would, however, complicate an already difficult process, and it would amount to a form of current value accounting whereby the assets would be revalued based upon the price of the common stock as of a particular date. Then, arguments would be made that if this were the correct approach at the date of conversion it should be used at the end of each fiscal or calendar year. While the fair value of the net assets may equal the value of the stock when 100 percent control or a large percentage of a corporation is being acquired, it is doubtful that this would be true based on day-to-day changes in stock prices especially when the stock is being sold in small lots. Thus, while your author presently favors the continued use of historical carrying amounts to measure gain or loss on conversion or on realization and recognition of common stock equivalency status, he acknowledges that the use of current values (if they could be properly measured) would produce more relevant and therefore more useful information. Your author would favor current value measurements if he were more confident in the reliability of these measurements. A strong case could be made for use of fair value when a conversion will result in a significant block of shares being issued. Theoretically, current value is the correct approach, and if it could be measured, it would be superior to historical cost in almost every aspect. And, theoretically, the value of the stock should equal the value of all of the net assets in a going concern except for possible income tax factors. For example, a later sale of the stock would produce favorably taxed capital gains whereas a sale of the assets would likely produce a combination of heavily taxed ordinary income and favorably taxed capital gain.

Change in Ownership through the Issuance of Shares by the Subsidiary

The assumption for this section is that the parent corporation will not acquire any of the new issue (nor will other members acquire any of the issue). Purchases and sales by the parent of stock of a subsidiary are discussed in a later section. Thus, under this assumption the issuance of new shares will reduce the parent's percentage ownership of the subsidiary. This reduction will be similar to a sale of some of the shares held by the parent.

Change through Options

First assume that a subsidiary issues new shares as the result of an exercise of stock options. Since options are always considered "common stock equivalents" for purposes of computing EPS, they might be considered as owners' equity in determining the share percentage owned by the parent. Most likely, however, they will be ignored until exercised.

When exercised, additional cash in the amount of the exercise price will flow into the subsidiary. This amount per share may be more, less, or equal to the book value per share of previously outstanding stock, and it may also be more, less, or equal to the per share basis to the parent Corporation for its investment in the subsidiary. But, in any event, it will reduce the parent's percentage ownership when exercised (or when the option was granted if it were considered to be owners' equity).

Assuming the dilution of ownership interest is to take place when exercised, if ever, and that the owners' equity section of the subsidiary is as follows on 1/1/x1 when the parent first acquired its 80 percent interest for $280,000. Assume that on 1/1/x1 the book values of the assets and liabilities equaled their fair values except for land which was understated by $50,000 (see Illustration 7–16).

Illustration 7–16

S Corporation	Net Assets	80 Percent Majority	20 Percent Minority
Common stock, 10,000 shares	$100,000	$ 80,000	$20,000
Additional paid-in capital	60,000	48,000	12,000
Retained earnings, 1/1/x1	140,000	112,000	28,000
Book value	300,000	240,000	60,000
Excess of fair value over book value of land	50,000	40,000	10,000
Price paid by parent		$280,000	

If stock options for 2,000 shares with an exercise price of $50 per share were issued to key employees on 1/1/x2, after the subsidiary had $40,000 of undistributed net earnings in 19x1 the option price would exceed book value by $16 ($50 − $34)[10] per share and would exceed the basis of the parent's investment by $11 ($50 − $39)[11] per share on the date the options were granted. If S continued to have $40,000 of undistributed earnings per year and if the options were exercised on 1/1/x5, the analysis both immediately before and after the exercise of the options would appear as in Illustration 7–17.

Illustration 7–17

A. Before exercise of stock option

S Corporation	Net Assets	80 Percent Majority	20 Percent Minority
Common stock, 10,000 shares	$100,000	$ 80,000	$20,000
Additional paid-in capital	60,000	48,000	12,000
Retained earnings, 1/1/x5	300,000*	240,000	60,000
Book value	460,000	368,000	92,000
Unrecorded land value at 1/1/x1	50,000	40,000	10,000
Equity method investment ($280,000 + ($160,000 × 80%))		$408,000	

B. After the exercise of stock option

S Corporation	Net Assets	66 2/3 Percent Majority	33 1/3 Percent Minority
Common stock, 12,000 shares	$120,000†	$ 80,000	$ 40,000
Additional paid-in capital	140,000†	93,333	46,667
Retained earnings, 1/1/x5	300,000	200,000	100,000
Book value	560,000	373,333	186,667
Unrecorded land value at 1/1/x1	50,000	33,334	16,666
Totals	$610,000	$406,667	$203,333

* ($140,000 + $160,000 undistributed earnings since 1/1/x1) = $300,000.
† 2,000 shares × $50 = $100,000 received on exercise which is reflected as $20,000 of par value and $80,000 of additional paid-in capital.

In this case the exercise price exceeded the book value per share at the date of exercise by $4 per share ($50 − $46), and it was $1 ($50 − $51)[12] less per share than the basis of the parent's investment in the subsidiary. The exercise of the options thus resulted in a loss of $1,333

---

[10] ($300,000 + $40,000 undistributed 19x1 earnings) ÷ 10,000 shares = $34 per share.
[11] ($280,000 + ($40,000 × 80%) undistributed 19x1 earnings) ÷ 8,000 shares = $39 per share.
[12] $408,000 ÷ 8,000 shares = $51 per share (equity method) before exercise of options.

($406,667 − $408,000) to the parent on the assumed sale. The parent received $66,667 (66⅔ percent of the $100,000 total option price) and gave up $68,000 (13⅓ × $510,000 *or* the percentage decrease in ownership of 16⅔ (13⅓ ÷ 80) times the $408,000 basis of the investment) for a loss of $1,333. Since the exercise resulted in a decrease in ownership percentage, the loss would be recognized as follows:

Loss on S stock* 1,333
    Investment in S stock (+$66,667 − $68,000) 1,333
    * Again, current practice would debit additional paid-in capital.

Change through New Share Issues

When the parent does not exercise its preemptive right or otherwise acquire a proportionate interest in a new issue, it has elected to "sell" some of its ownership. When the subsidiary is controlled by the parent, this is obviously an intended decrease in ownership interest. If the purchase price per share of the new issue differs from the underlying *adjusted* book value per share, the parent should realize a gain or a loss. Through the analysis of owners' equity the gain or loss, if any, can be measured and recognized.

None of the New Issue Purchased by the Parent. To illustrate the effects of a new stock issue by the subsidiary, assume that on 1/1/x5, S Corporation issues 2,000 new shares identical to those currently outstanding for $130,000 or $65 per share to minority interest shareholders. Assume 80 percent of S had been acquired by P on 1/1/x1 for $400,000, that S had undistributed earnings from 1/1/x1 until 1/1/x5 of $80,000, and that the analysis of the investment account before the new stock issue appeared as in Illustration 7–18.

Due to S issuing new shares P has in effect sold 13⅓ (80% − 66⅔%) percentage points of its interest in S or 16⅔ percent (13⅓% ÷ 80%) of its holdings. P, in effect, received 66⅔ percent of the $130,000 issue price, or approximately $86,666, and gave up 16⅔ percent of its basis before the new issue of $464,000, or $77,333. This produced a net gain of $9,333 ($86,667 − $77,333) or ($473,333 − $464,000) to P. This $9,333 also must be the net asset reduction to the minority interest (or $116,000 + $130,000 − $236,667 = $9,333). This should result in the following entry on P's books:

Investment in S stock (+$86,667 − $77,333) 9,333
    Gain on S stock* 9,333
    * Current practice would credit additional paid-in capital.

All of the New Issue Purchased by the Parent. If the parent purchases any of the new issue, the cost will probably differ from the basis of

Illustration 7–18

A. Before the new stock issue

S Corporation	Net Assets	80 Percent Majority	20 Percent Minority
Common stock, 10,000 shares	$100,000	$ 80,000	$ 20,000
Additional paid-in capital	60,000	48,000	12,000
Retained earnings, 1/1/x1	290,000	232,000	58,000
Book value, 1/1/x1	450,000	360,000	90,000
Unrecorded land value at 1/1/x1	50,000	40,000	10,000
Adjusted book value, 1/1/x1	500,000	400,000*	100,000
Undistributed earnings from 1/1/x1 to 1/1/x5	80,000	64,000	16,000
Adjusted book value, 1/1/x5	$580,000†	$464,000	$116,000

B. After the new stock issue (none purchased by P)

S Corporation	Net Assets	66⅔ Percent Majority	33⅓ Percent Minority
Common stock, 12,000 shares	$120,000	$ 80,000	$ 40,000
Additional paid-in capital	170,000	113,333	56,667
Retained earnings, 1/1/x5	370,000	246,667	123,333
Book value, 1/1/x5	660,000	440,000	220,000
Unrecorded land value at 1/1/x1	50,000	33,333	16,667
Adjusted book value, 1/1/x5	$710,000	$473,333	$236,667

* Price paid on 1/1/x1 for 80 percent interest.
† Adjusted book value per share on 1/1/x5 under alternatives 2 or 3 is $58 ($580,000 ÷ 10,000 shares). In determining adjusted book values per share under alternative 1, there would be a different amount per share for the minority interest shares; in this case it would be $53 (($116,000 − $10,000 of unrecorded land value) ÷ 2,000 shares) or the unadjusted book value per share (($450,000 + $80,000) ÷ 10,000 shares).

existing ownership. This will create a second block of stock at a different price per share.

Since the determination of cost in excess of book value or vice versa is initially calculated as of the date of acquisition of the shares, each block of stock purchased may produce different per share values for its portion of the underlying net assets.

It is also possible to view a small or insignificant second block of stock as a continuation of the first block of stock. This, in effect, considers the cost of both blocks as one amount in order to find the average cost, while ignoring the cost in excess of adjusted book value or of adjusted book value in excess of cost for the second block. In this case the book values are adjusted only for the cost difference for the first block. This might be acceptable but only when the second block is very small in relationship to the prior purchase. For example, this might be used where the parent corporation has acquired 95 percent of the stock of a subsidiary and over subsequent years is gradually acquiring the remaining amounts as the shareholders of this stock are located.

Assuming each block purchased is a material amount, the question arises as to which alternative allocation method to use. Alternative 3 described in the substitution chapter would require each prior purchase as well as any remaining minority interest to be reflected at the FMV per share of the last block purchased. On the other hand, alternative 1 would keep each block separate. It must be remembered, however, that investments in stock where control exists is not the purchase of shares but rather it is theoretically, at least, an indirect purchase of net assets. Where two blocks of stock, 60 percent and 30 percent, have been purchased at different dates, would it be reasonable to have 60 percent of an asset reported at one price and 30 percent of the same asset reported at a different price and the remaining 10 percent owned by minority interest reported at book value? This is what alternative 1 (and current practice) would produce. Alternative 2 would follow alternative 3 on valuing everything except goodwill where it would then be like alternative 1.

Under alternative 3 if another member purchased the second block of stock, the purchase by a second investing member could affect the allocation of the first block previously acquired by a different member.

If P had purchased some or all of the new issue, a second block of stock would have been created. Assume that P on 1/1/x5 purchased all of the new issue for $130,000 and that immediately before the new issue the analysis of the original 1/1/x5 acquisition appeared as in Illustration 7–19. Because the minority interest share of net assets increased by $2,334 ($118,334 − $116,000), there would be a "loss"; however, since P's total interest in S increased to 83⅓ percent from 80 percent, this is a purchase, and thus a loss would not be recognized. Of the $11,667 cost in excess of book value for the new stock, $9,333 ($473,333 − $464,000) was "recovered" by the first block of stock and $2,334 is "received" by the minority. This could be recorded on P's books as follows, but this ignores the idea that the excess cost over book value or vice versa is attributable to the underlying net assets:

Investment in S stock—block 2 (new)	118,333	
Investment in S stock—block 1 (old)	9,333	
Paid-in capital	2,334	
Cash		130,000

In practice, the purchase of the 2,000 shares would simply be recorded as:

Investment in S Stock—block 2	130,000	
Cash		130,000

Upon consolidation, the cost in excess of the underlying book value of $20,000 ($130,000 − $110,000) would then be allocated to the assets (of

Illustration 7–19

A. Before the new stock issue

S Corporation	New Assets	8,000 Shares Majority	2,000 Shares Minority
Common stock, 10,000 shares	$100,000	$ 80,000	$ 20,000
Additional paid-in capital	60,000	48,000	12,000
Retained earnings, 1/1/x5	370,000	296,000	74,000
Book value	530,000	424,000	106,000
Unrecorded land value	50,000	40,000	10,000
Adjusted book value	$580,000	$464,000	$116,000

B. After the new stock Issue (all purchased by P)

S Corporation	Net Assets	Majority Block 1 8,000 Shares 66⅔ Percent	Majority Block 2 2,000 Shares 16⅔ Percent	Minority 2,000 Shares 16⅔ Percent
Common stock, 12,000 shares	$120,000	$ 80,000	$ 20,000	$ 20,000
Additional paid-in capital	170,000	113,334	28,333	28,333
Retained earnings, 1/1/x5	370,000	246,666	61,667	61,667
Book value, 1/1/x5	660,000	440,000	110,000	110,000
Unrecorded land value of 1/1/x1	50,000	33,333	8,333	8,334
	710,000	473,333	118,333	118,334
Balance before new issue plus amount paid	710,000	464,000	130,000	116,000
Increase (decrease)	–0–	$ 9,333	$(11,667)	$ 2,334

the subsidiary) or reported as goodwill. This would cause some assets to be reflected in the consolidated position statement based on three different prices (1) book value for minority interest, (2) fair value for block 1 ownership at the date it was purchased (adjusted for depreciation, etc.), and (3) fair value when block 2 was purchased. In addition, practice generally ignores the effect on block 1 when its ownership decreased from 80 percent to 66⅔ percent due to the block 2 purchase. This is theoretically improper in that the $20,000 cost in excess of book value for block 2 has been partially recognized because of the block 1 cost in excess of book value (which is reflected in the $8,333 figure in the analysis or $40,000 increase in land value under alternative 1 × 16⅔% = $6,667).

Another way to analyze the purchase of block 2 from a theoretical perspective would be to view the $130,000 or $65 per share as a payment for only 3⅓ percent or the increase in ownership (3⅓% × 12,000 shares = 400 shares). This would require shifting enough shares, 1,600 of the 2,000 acquired, and enough investment, $104,000 (1,600 shares × $65), to the first block to retain its 80 percent ownership (80% × 12,000 shares = 9,600 shares). In other words, because of the 80 percent ownership, only 400 shares were really purchased (2,000 shares − (2,000 shares × 80%), and of the $130,000 paid, $104,000 ($130,000 × 80%) was, in effect, paid to the buyer. Thus, the real cost of the 400 shares or 3⅓ percentage points of interest was $26,000. This could be analyzed as shown in Illustration 7–20. Unrecorded land value retains the 1/1/x1

Illustration 7−20

		Majority		Minority
S Corporation	Net Assets	9,600 Shares 80 Percent	400 Shares 3⅓ Percent	2,000 Shares 16⅔ Percent
Common stock, 12,000 shares	$120,000	$ 96,000	$ 4,000	$ 20,000
Additional paid-in capital	170,000	136,000	5,667	28,333
Retained earnings, 1/1/x5	370,000	296,000	12,333	61,667
	660,000	528,000 ⎱ $568,000†	22,000	110,000
Unrecorded land value at 1/1/x1	50,000	40,000 ⎰	1,667	8,333
Increase in unrecorded land value to 1/1/x5	70,000	56,000	2,333	11,667
	$780,000	$624,000	$26,000*	$130,000

* (2,000 share purchase − 1,600 shares to block 1 to retain 80%) × $65 = $26,000.
† $464,000 investment before the new issue plus $104,000 (1,600 shares × $65) equals $568,000.

$40,000 increase attributable to block 1 and reduces block 2's share from $8,333 to $1,667 ($8,333 − $6,667 attributable to block 1).

Under this analysis with recognition of the *increase* in the unrecorded land value of $70,000 ($2,333.33 ÷ .03⅓), the purchase could be recorded on P's books as:[13]

Investment in S stock—block 1	160,000*	
Investment in S stock—block 2	26,000	
Cash		130,000
Appraisal capital increase in land value owned by the subsidiary		56,000

* $624,000 − $464,000 = $160,000 or $104,000 + $56,000 increase in land value. Under alternative 1 this could have been $104,000 ($568,000 − $464,000) (or $65 × 1,600 shares = $104,000) without the appraisal increase.

---

[13] This fair value approach obviously violates the historical cost concept adhered to in practice. Accounting simply has not progressed to the point where it would recognize the $56,000 as an additional asset.

The substitution entry would be:

Common stock	120,000	
Additional paid-in capital	170,000	
Retained earnings	370,000	
Land	120,000	
Investment in S stock—block 1		624,000
Investment in S stock—block 2		26,000
Minority interest		130,000

Since the purchase by P does decrease the minority interest ownership (from 20 to 16⅔ percent) and increase the total majority ownership (to 83⅓ percent from 80 percent), the blocks of stock could be viewed as separate purchases. As separate blocks, the first block's percentage falls from 80 percent to 66⅔ percent and the second block has 16⅔ percent ownership. This would then require the $11,667 cost in excess of book value on the acquisition of the 2,000 shares of new stock to be recognized as an increase in land value since the 1/1/x1 first-block acquisition (see Illustration 7–21).

Illustration 7–21

		Majority		Minority
S Corporation	Net Assets	66⅔ Percent	16⅔ Percent	16⅔ Percent
Book value at 1/1/x5	$660,000	$440,000	$110,000	$110,000
Unrecorded land value at 1/1/x1	50,000	33,333	8,333	8,334
Increase in unrecorded land value to 1/1/x5	70,000	46,667	11,667	11,666
	$780,000	$520,000	$130,000*	$130,000

* Amount paid.

Under alternatives 2 and 3 the increase in land value would be $120,000 or $50,000 as of 1/1/x1 with an increase of $70,000 between 1/1/x1 and 1/1/x5. The acquisition of the second block could be recorded on P's books as:

Investment in S stock—block 2	130,000	
Cash		130,000

This could also result in an adjustment to block 1 to bring it up to $520,000 from its $464,000 basis before the new issue.[14] This could be:

Investment in S stock—block 1	56,000*	
Appraisal capital for increase in subsidiary's land value to 1/1/x5		56,000

* $520,000 − $464,000 = $56,000.

---

[14] Adjusting block 1 value based on the block 2 purchase would be unacceptable in practice because of the adherence to alternative 1.

If this entry were not made, under alternatives 2 or 3 it would become part of the substitution entry. The substitution entry assuming the above entry had been made would be:

Common stock	120,000	
Additional paid-in capital	170,000	
Retained earnings	370,000	
Land	120,000	
Investment in S stock—block 1		520,000*
Investment in S stock—block 2		130,000
Minority interest		130,000

* $464,000 + $56,000 = $520,000.

Half the New Issue Purchased by the Parent. Assume that P purchased half the new issue or 1,000 shares for $65,000, and that the cost in excess of book value is attributable solely to land with the other 1,000 shares purchased by the minority interest for $65,000. In this situation there is both a purchase and a "sale" by P. The *net* effect is a sale of 5 percentage points of ownership because the minority interest increases from 20 percent before to 25 percent after the new issue while the majority interest falls from 80 percent to 75 percent (66⅔% + 8⅓%). Continuing the prior example but before the new issue, the investment analysis would have been as given in Illustration 7–22.

The entry to record the purchase of the second block of stock on P's books and, in effect, the sale of some of the first block would be as follows for alternative 2 or 3 (result is the same for both alternatives due to the absence of goodwill):

Investment in S stock—block 1	56,000*	
Investment in S stock—block 2	65,000	
Cash		65,000
Gain on S stock		3,500†
Appraisal capital—valuation increase in S land		52,500‡

* $520,000 − $464,000 = $56,000.
† Decrease in minority interest before the increase since 1/1/x1 in the value of land $116,000 + $65,000 − $177,500 = $3,500; or increase in the basis of block 1 (before adjustment for increase in land value since 1/1/x1), thus $532,500 ($473,333 for block 1 + $59,167 for block 2) less $529,000 ($464,000 for block 1 + $65,000 for block 2) or $3,500 gain.
‡ That portion of the increase in land value owned indirectly by P, $46,667 + $5,833 = $52,500.

Under alternative 1 with each block of stock separately valued, the analysis becomes more difficult due to recording only a part (majority portion) of the undervalued land. When the 8,000 shares making up the first block are reduced from 80 percent to 66⅔ percent, it impacts on the unrecorded land value. (If this $40,000 had been a depreciable asset during the period from 19x1 to 19x5, there would have been further adjustments.) (See Illustration 7–23.)

Presumably, under alternative 1, once the $40,000 of unrecorded land value were recognized on prior consolidated financial statements, it could not be suddenly reduced to $33,333. The difference due to the reduction in percentage ownership for the block should then be as-

Illustration 7−22

A. Before the new issue (under alternatives 2 or 3)

S Corporation	Net Assets	80 Percent Majority	20 Percent Minority
Common stock, 10,000 shares	100,000	80,000	20,000
Additional paid-in capital	60,000	48,000	12,000
Retained earnings, 1/1/x5	370,000	296,000	74,000
Book value	530,000	424,000	106,000
Unrecorded land value at 1/1/x1	50,000	40,000	10,000
Adjusted book value, 1/1/x5	580,000	464,000*	116,000

* Price paid for the 80 percent on 1/1/x1 plus equity method adjustments since acquisition.

B. After issuing 2,000 new shares for $130,000 (under alternatives 2 and 3)

		Majority		Minority
S Corporation	Net Assets	8,000 Shares 66 2/3 Percent	1,000 Shares 8 1/3 Percent	3,000 Shares 25 Percent
Common stock, 12,000 shares	$120,000	$ 80,000	$10,000	$ 30,000
Additional paid-in capital	170,000	113,333	14,167	42,500
Retained earnings, 1/1/x5	370,000	246,667	30,833	92,500
Book value	660,000	440,000	55,000	165,000
Unrecorded land value at 1/1/x1	50,000	33,333	4,167	12,500
Adjusted book value, 1/1/x5	710,000	473,333	59,167	177,500
Increase in unrecorded land value from 1/1/x1 until 1/1/x5	70,000	46,667	5,833	17,500
Fair value, 1/1/x5	$780,000	$520,000	$65,000	$195,000

signed to the new shares. Thus, block 2 and the minority interest each pick up half of the $6,667 ($40,000 − $33,333) reduction or approximately $3,333 each.

The entry to record on P's books the purchase of the second block under alternative 1 would be:

Investment in S stock—block 1 ($473,333 − $464,000)	9,333	
Investment in S stock—block 2	65,000	
Cash		65,000
Gain on S stock		6,000*
Appraisal capital—valuation increase in S land		3,333†

* Minority interest decrease in *book value* ($106,000 + $65,000 − $132,500 − $32,500 = $6,000) is gain to majority ($171,000 − ($168,334 − $3,334)).

† That portion of the increase in land value owned indirectly by P ($33,333 + $3,333 + $6,667 − $40,000 = $3,333).

Illustration 7–23

A. Before the new issue (under alternative 1)

S Corporation	Net Assets	80 Percent Majority	20 Percent Minority
Book value, 1/1/x5	$530,000	$424,000	$106,000
Unrecorded $50,000 land value at 1/1/x1	40,000	40,000	—0—
	$570,000	$464,000	$106,000

B. After issuing 2,000 new shares for $130,000 (under alternative 1)

		75 Percent Majority		Minority
S Corporation	Net Assets	8,000 Shares 66⅔ Percent	1,000 Shares 8⅓ Percent	3,000 Shares 25 Percent
Book value, 1/1/x5	$530,000	$353,333	$44,167	$132,500
Issue of new stock	130,000	86,667	10,833	32,500
Unrecorded land value $50,000 at 1/1/x1	40,000	33,333	3,333	3,334
			58,333	
Unrecorded land value at 1/1/x5 ($120,000 − $40,000 = $80,000)	6,667	—0—	6,667*	—0—
	$706,667	$473,333	$65,000	$168,334

* 8⅓ percent × $80,000 = $6,667.

While this shows how alternative 1 should be recorded, current practice would simply record the second block as follows and not change the first block:

Investment in S stock—block 2	65,000	
Cash		65,000

In addition, the $40,000 increase in land value on 1/1/x1 attributable to block 1 would not be changed. Also, the $10,000 ($65,000 − $44,167 − $10,833) cost in excess of book value for block 2 would probably be allocated to land. If $50,000 costs in excess of book values are allocated to land, this will be overstated by $6,667 ($50,000 − $33,333 block 1 − ($3,333 + $6,667 block 2)).

The substitution entries at 1/1/x5 for each alternative would be as follows:

For alternatives 2 or 3 (from the analysis in Illus. 7–22):

Common stock	120,000
Additional paid-in capital	170,000
Retained earnings	370,000

Land	120,000	
Investment in S stock—block 1		520,000
Investment in S stock—block 2		65,000
Minority interest		195,000

For alternative 1 (from the analysis in Illus. 7–23):

Common stock	120,000	
Additional paid-in capital	170,000	
Retained earnings	370,000	
Land	46,667	
Investment in S stock—block 1		473,333
Investment in S stock—block 2		65,000
Minority interest		168,334

> **Tax:** For tax purposes each block will have an initial basis of the price paid for that block. No amounts may be assigned from one block to another block. It is also important, for all investments in other corporations, to keep good records for each block of stock purchased so that they may be separately identified. When some shares are sold without separate identification they will be deemed to be from the first block(s) first, a Fifo flow. With separate identification, however, you can select the shares sold. For example, if two separate 500 share blocks of XYZ had been purchased, one in 1930 for $5,000 and the other in 1975 for $100,000, and if 250 shares were sold in the current year for $40,000, Fifo would produce a gain of $37,500 ($40,000 − $2,500 cost) while identification of those shares as from block 2 would produce a $10,000 loss ($40,000 − $50,000 basis). While this assumes no adjustment to the basis of the shares since acquisition (cost method for tax purposes), it does show the desirability of being able to select the block from which the sale is to be made.

Change through Treasury Stock Transactions

The reissuance of treasury shares will have the same effect as the issuance of shares not previously outstanding. The effect of acquisition of treasury shares depends on whether they are acquired from the parent or from the minority interest. When acquired from the parent, there will be a decrease in the parent's ownership percentage unless the subsidiary is 100 percent owned and an increase in the minority ownership percentage. This decrease in the parent's ownership can result in recognized gain or loss for financial reporting.[15]

---

[15] In practice, as explained before, gain or loss is often taken to the parent's additional paid-in capital account.

Purchase of Treasury Shares from the Minority Interest. When treasury shares are acquired from a minority interest, it is the equivalent of an acquisition by the parent of additional shares because the parent's ownership will increase. But in this event there will not be a separate block of stock actually created, although percentagewise it could be accounted for as a second purchase. The acquisition of treasury shares are reflected in Illustration 7–24 where the parent initially acquired its interest at book value. With the book value per share of $30 assume that S acquires 1,000 shares from the minority for $40 per share and accounts for the treasury stock under the cost method (as opposed to the par value method). This would be analyzed in (B) of Illustration 7–24.

Illustration 7–24

A. Before the acquisition

S Corporation	Net Assets	80 Percent Majority	20 Percent Minority
Common stock, 10,000 shares	$100,000	$ 80,000	$20,000
Additional paid-in capital	60,000	48,000	12,000
Retained earnings	140,000	112,000	28,000
	$300,000	$240,000	$60,000

B. After the acquisition
(using the cost method for treasury stock acquisitions)

S Corporation	Net Assets	88.8$\bar{3}$ Percent Majority	11.1$\bar{1}$ Percent Minority
Common stock, 10,000 shares	$100,000	$ 88,889	$11,111
Additional paid-in capital	60,000	53,333	6,667
Retained earnings	140,000	124,444	15,556
Treasury stock 1,000 shares	(40,000)	(35,556)	(4,444)
	$260,000	$231,110	$28,890

While the percentage ownership has gone up, the amount of underlying net assets has gone down. This was caused by the purchase of the treasury stock at a price in excess of book value. With the per share purchase price $10 higher than the book value per share and with 1,000 shares purchased, the net assets underlying the majority interest decreased by approximately $8,890 ($10,000 × 88.88% or $240,000 − $231,110). But since this is the equivalent of a purchase of shares by P, no gain or loss is recognized. P makes the following entry in its records:

			8,890	
Additional paid-in capital				
Investment in S stock				8,890

In current practice the above entry would not be made, and the Investment in S stock account would remain at $240,000. Thus, in the substitution entry $8,890 would emerge as goodwill. This is an interesting result, considering the insistence of practice on the use of alternative method 1, because the $8,890 of goodwill is associated with the minority and not the majority interest. The minority interest of $60,000 before the acquisition less the $40,000 acquisition price plus the $8,890 goodwill equals the $28,890 minority interest in underlying net assets after the treasury stock acquisition. In practice, the substitution entry would be:

Common stock	100,000	
Additional paid-in capital	60,000	
Retained earnings	140,000	
Goodwill	8,890	
Treasury stock		40,000
Investment in S stock		240,000
Minority interest		28,890

If P recorded the increase in percentage ownership as if it were a second block of stock, the analysis would appear as in Illustration 7–25.

Illustration 7–25

		Majority		11.11 Percent Minority (or 1,000 shares)
S Corporation	Net Assets	80 Percent (or 7,200 shares)	8.8$\bar{8}$ Percent (or 800 shares)	
Common stock, 10,000 shares	$100,000	$ 80,000	$ 8,889	$11,111
Additional paid-in capital	60,000	48,000	5,333	6,667
Retained earnings	140,000	112,000	12,444	15,556
Treasury stock, 1,000 shares	(40,000)	(32,000)	(3,556)	(4,444)
	$260,000	$208,000	$23,110	$28,890

As a second block of stock, a transfer of 800 shares ($9,000 × .0888) from block 1 to block 2 would be required with recognition of the $8,890 decrease in the book value of the underlying net assets. This would be recorded as:

Additional paid-in capital	8,890	
Investment in S stock—block 2	23,110	
Investment in S stock—block 1		32,000*

* $240,000 − $208,000 = $32,000.

Another way to analyze this transaction would be to assume that the purchase of the treasury stock by S was mandated by P. And since the purchase was from outsiders, an arm's-length transaction has taken place which would "justify" establishing the $40 price paid per share for the treasury stock as the value per share of the 9,000 shares of outstanding stock (similar in effect to alternative 3). This would be analyzed as in Illustration 7–26.

Illustration 7–26

S Corporation	Net Assets	$88.8\overline{8}$ Percent Majority	$11.1\overline{1}$ Percent Minority
Common stock, 10,000 shares	$100,000	$ 88,889	$11,111
Additional paid-in capital	60,000	53,333	6,667
Retained earnings	140,000	124,444	15,556
Treasury stock	(40,000)	(35,556)	(4,444)
Book value of 9,000 shares	260,000	231,110	28,890
Unrecorded asset value	100,000	88,889	11,111
Fair value of 9,000 shares at $40 each	$360,000	$319,999	$40,001

Since P acquired its original interest at book value, the following entry would be required on P's books:[16]

Investment in S stock ($319,999 − $240,000)	79,999*	
Appraisal capital		79,999

* $231,000 + $88,889 − $240,000 = $79,999.

Had S purchased the treasury shares from the minority interest for $15 per share, the analysis after the acquisition would have been as given in Illustration 7–27. Both the percentage ownership and the amount of underlying net assets have increased. But again, no gain or loss would be recognized under this concept because this is essentially equivalent to a purchase of more shares by P. This would be recorded on P's books as:

Investment in S stock	13,333	
Paid-in capital ($253,333 − $240,000 = $13,333)		13,333

Again, in current practice the above entry would not be recorded, and in the substitution process the $13,333 would result in negative

---

[16] Practice, in adhering to historical cost, would not record this entry. Increasing the remaining assets and capital by $79,999 because of the purchase price above book value seems much more logical than decreasing the investment in the subsidiary and additional paid-in capital by $8,890 (if this was an arm's-length price).

Illustration 7–27

S Corporation	Net Assets	88.8̄ Percent Majority	11.1̄ Percent Minority
Common stock, 10,000 shares	$100,000	$ 88,889	$11,111
Additional paid-in capital	60,000	53,333	6,667
Retained earnings	140,000	124,444	15,556
Treasury stock, 1,000 shares	(15,000)	(13,333)	(1,667)
	$285,000	$253,333	$31,667

goodwill (assuming other assets were not written down). This substitution entry would appear as follows:

Common stock	100,000	
Additional paid-in capital	60,000	
Retained earnings	140,000	
Negative goodwill		13,333
Treasury stock		15,000
Investment in S stock		240,000
Minority interest		31,667

The alternatives of viewing this as a second block of stock or as a transaction justifying revaluation are also possible. Under the revaluation assumption the investment analysis would appear as in Illustration 7–28.

Illustration 7–28

S Corporation	Net Assets	88.8̄ Percent Majority	11.1̄ Percent Minority
Common stock, 10,000 shares	$100,000	$ 88,889	$ 11,111
Additional paid-in capital	60,000	53,333	6,667
Retained earnings	140,000	124,444	15,556
Treasury stock, 1,000 shares	(15,000)	(13,333)	(1,667)
Book value of 9,000 shares	285,000	253,333	31,667
Overstated net assets	(150,000)	(133,333)	(16,667)
Fair value of 9,000 shares at $15 each	$135,000	$ 120,000	$ 15,000

This would require the following entry on P's books:

Additional paid-in capital	120,000	
Investment in S stock		120,000*

    * $240,000 − $120,000 = $120,000 or the increase in book value of $13,333 ($253,000 − $240,000) less the overstated net assets of $133,333.

If the overstated net assets on S's books are written down, the loss would flow through S's earnings, and under the equity method, this would result in a reduction of the investment account and in the earnings of the P company without going through the prior entry. With the book value ($285,000) being in excess of the "fair value" ($135,000) of the underlying net assets, the normal write-down procedure for book value in excess of cost would be employed in the substitution entry, and this would force the recognition of this loss on a consolidated basis. Where there has been such a large loss in the stock value, this latter method (loss recognition) seems clearly justified.

Purchase of Treasury Shares from the Parent Corporation. If the purchases of 1,000 treasury shares at $40 per share had been made from the parent, gain would have been recognized on P's separate books. The investment account analysis would appear as in Illustration 7–29. The

Illustration 7–29

S Corporation	Net Assets	77.77 Percent Majority	22.22 Percent Minority
Common stock, 10,000 shares	$100,000	$ 77,778	$22,222
Additional paid-in capital	60,000	46,667	13,333
Retained earnings	140,000	108,889	31,111
Treasury stock, 1,000 shares	(40,000)	(31,111)	(8,889)
	$260,000	$202,223	$57,777

following entry would now be recorded on P's separate records to record the sale which decreased P's ownership of S from 80 percent to 77.77 percent:

Cash	40,000	
Investment in S stock ($240,000 − $202,223)		37,777
Gain on sale of S stock		2,223*

*Current practice would not record this gain. Instead, the investment account would be credited for $40,000, and negative goodwill of $2,223 would arise through the substitution entry.

There is also an unrecognized gain of $15,561 ($2,223 × 7) on the 7,000 shares of S still in P's possession. Normally anticipated gains are not recorded.

If the purchase had been made from P at $15 per share, a loss would have been recognized (see Illustration 7–30). P would record this on its separate records as follows:

Cash	15,000	
Loss on the sale of S stock	3,333*	
Investment in S stock ($240,000 − $221,667)		18,333

*If current practice did not recognize this loss, goodwill of $3,333 would arise through the substitution entry.

Illustration 7–30

S Corporation	Net Assets	77.7̄7 Percent Majority	22.2̄2 Percent Minority
Common stock, 10,000 shares	$100,000	$ 77,778	$22,222
Additional paid-in capital	60,000	46,667	13,333
Retained earnings	140,000	108,889	31,111
Treasury stock, 1,000 shares	(15,000)	(11,667)	(3,333)
	$285,000	$221,667	$63,333

There is also a potential loss of $23,331 ($3,333 × 7) on the remaining 7,000 shares. Conservatism might cause some accountants to record this anticipated loss. Note that the investment in S stock is not classified as a marketable security, thus the "lower-of-cost-or-market" rule would not apply.

Tax: If P and S were filing separate tax returns, a gain or loss on the sale of S shares by P to S would be recognized on P's separate tax return as capital gain or loss measured, of course, from the tax basis of the shares. The purchase of treasury shares by S from either P or from the minority interest does not create taxable income to S nor will taxable income be created if these treasury shares are reissued. Corporations may deal in their own stock without recognition of gain or loss for tax purposes.*

If P and S were filing consolidated tax returns, any gain or loss on the sale by P to S of the S stock would be recognized but deferred until S is no longer a member of the group.† The rules would be different if this were a liquidation ("partial" or complete) of S. In our example, however, the ownership of S fell below the 80 percent needed to continue to file a consolidated tax return, thus the gain or loss would be recognized. The failure to qualify for a consolidated tax return would also cause any and all prior deferrals of gain or loss between P and S for tax purposes to be recognized.

Any time a transaction is contemplated which might cause a subsidiary to become a nonmember of the group (e.g., ownership of less than 80 percent), expert tax advice should be obtained *before* the transaction is entered into. Failure to do so can result in some severe and often otherwise avoidable tax consequences.

* *Internal Revenue Code*, sec. 1032.
† *Income Tax Regulations*, sec. 1.502-14(b)(2) + (3).

Change through Sale of a Part or All of the Ownership Interest

The sale of shares of a subsidiary can have effects far beyond the gain or loss on that particular transaction. When consolidated financial statements have been prepared and a subsidiary becomes an outside party, all previously deferred gains or losses involving that subsidiary are suddenly brought into recognition immediately prior to the subsidiary's becoming an outside party.

In addition to measuring the gain or loss on the sale of the shares, the basis of the shares must be adjusted for activity up to the date of their disposition. Thus, for a sale of subsidiary stock midway through a year there will have to be a measurement of gain or loss from operations up to the date of sale so that the basis of the shares can be properly determined under the equity method concept. Also if the subsidiary being sold owns shares in another subsidiary, the sale of one subsidiary may cause other subsidiaries to fail to quality for consolidation.

Suppose that P owns 80 percent of both S and T. The basis of the investment in S stock is as indicated in the account analysis given in Illustration 7–31. This analysis assumes that P paid $320,000 for the 80

Illustration 7–31

S Corporation	Net Assets	80 Percent Majority	20 Percent Minority
Common stock, 10,000 shares	$100,000	$ 80,000	$ 20,000
Additional paid-in capital	80,000	64,000	16,000
Retained earnings, 1/1/x1	120,000	96,000	24,000
Book value (also fair value of recorded net assets), 1/1/x1	300,000	240,000	60,000
Goodwill	100,000	80,000	20,000
Adjusted book value (total fair value), 1/1/x1	400,000	320,000	80,000
Reported earnings from 1/1/x1 to 1/1/x5	195,000	156,000	39,000
Amortization of goodwill (over 40 years)	(10,000)	(8,000)	(2,000)
Deferral of gain on sale of land to P	(40,000)	(32,000)	(8,000)
Adjusted book value, 1/1/x5	$545,000	$436,000	$109,000

percent investment on 1/1/x1 and that all assets and liabilities were recorded at their fair values. The resulting goodwill is being amortized over 40 years, and the earnings since 1/1/x1 of $195,000 had not been adjusted for the $10,000 ($100,000 ÷ 40 × 4 years) of amortization of goodwill. In addition, the $195,000 of reported earnings of S had not been decreased for a $40,000 gain on sale of land to P in year 19x2.

Now if the entire block of S stock is sold on 7/1/x5, it will be necessary to adjust the basis in the S stock for operations to the date of the sale. If S reports $30,000 of net earnings (after tax) as of 6/30/x5 and has paid no dividends, the analysis would be as shown in Illustration 7–32.

For P to have a gain on the 7/1/x5 sale, P will have to sell the shares for more than $491,000 and anything less than $491,000 will produce a loss.

Illustration 7–32

S Corporation	Net Assets	80 Percent Majority	20 Percent Minority
Adjusted book value, 1/1/x5	$545,000	$436,000	$109,000
Earnings to date of the sale	30,000	24,000	6,000
Amortization of goodwill (2,500 × 1/2)	(1,250)	(1,000)	(250)
Subtotal	573,750	459,000	114,750
Recognition of 19x2 deferred gain on sale of land to P	40,000	32,000	8,000
Adjusted book value 7/1/x5 date of sale	$613,750	$491,000	$122,750

If P is going to sell only 1,000 of the 8,000 shares it owns of S, one eighth of the $491,000, or $61,375, is apportioned to the 1,000 shares to be sold (assuming that there are not separate blocks of stock making up the 80 percent), and $429,625 would be applicable to the 7,000 shares still held less 70 percent of the $40,000 gain on the sale of land to P, or $28,000.

Illustration 7–33

S Corporation	Net Assets	70 Percent Majority	30 Percent Minority
Common stock, 10,000 shares	$100,000	$ 70,000	$ 30,000
Additional paid-in capital	80,000	56,000	24,000
Retained earnings, 1/1/x1	120,000	84,000	36,000
Book value, 1/1/x1	300,000	210,000	90,000
Goodwill	100,000	70,000	30,000
Undistributed reported earnings 1/1/x1 until 7/1/x5($195,000 + $30,000)	225,000	157,500	67,500
Amortization of goodwill ($10,000 + $1,250)	(11,250)	(7,875)	(3,375)
Deferral of gain on sale of land to P	(40,000)	(28,000)	(12,000)
Adjusted book value at 7/1/x5	$573,750	$401,625	$172,125

This would produce an adjusted book value of these 7,000 shares as of 7/1/x5 or $401,625. The analysis would be as shown in Illustration 7–33.

On the sale of the 1,000 shares for $75,000, P would record a gain and would reduce the basis of its investment to $401,625. But P would first record its share of S earnings to the date of the sale.

To record 80 percent share of S earnings to the date of sale, under the equity method:

Investment in S stock	27,000	
Income from S stock		27,000*

* ($30,000 − $1,250 + (⅛ × $40,000)) × 80% = $27,000.

The adjustment of the investment in S to the date of the sale represents 80 percent of the sum of the $30,000 of net earnings less 1,250 of goodwill amortization plus $5,000 or ⅛ of the previously deferred gain on the sale of land by S to P.

To record the sale of 1,000 S shares:

Cash	75,000	
Investment in S stock		61,375*
Gain on sale of S stock		13,625

* $436,000 + $27,000 − $401,625 or ⅛ × $491,000 = $61,375.

The determination of the gain up to the date of sale is difficult if for no other reason than it is normally reported on an aftertax basis. The tax for the year will not be fully determined until after the year-end, and the gain or loss on the sale of S stock could impact on the total tax to be paid.

Tax: For federal income tax purposes the above transaction could be disastrous in that it would trigger the entire deferred gain on the 19x2 sale of land by S to P. This would happen because S can no longer be included in the consolidated return since it is owned less than 80 percent. In addition, for tax purposes the basis of the remaining shares would be determined as if the cost method had been used. Thus ⅞ × $320,000 (the original price paid for the 80 percent interest), or $280,000, would become the tax basis of the remaining 7,000 shares. With a book basis of $401,625 and a tax basis of $280,000, another sale of stock would produce more tax than would be anticipated from the $401,625 book basis.

In addition, if all of the S stock were sold to A Corporation and if S had any unused tax attributes such as net operating losses, investment tax credits, foreign tax credits, contribution carryovers, net capital losses, and so on, these items could impact on the purchase price and would not be eligible to be used in future consolidated tax returns of P and T. They could, however, be used in the 19x5 consolidated tax return of P, S, and T which will be filed in 19x6.

Therefore, A Corporation, which is buying on 7/1/x5 the 80 percent of S stock owned by P, has a problem in that the unused tax attributes (which might be available for use on the A consolidated return which would include S) cannot be determined at the date of

> **Tax:** *(continued)*
> the sale. These tax attributes can only be determined after the consolidated P, S, and T return for 19x5 has been filed. This return would include P and T operations for the entire year and S for only the first half of 19x5.
>
> For example, assume S had a large capital loss carryforward which A would like to use (there are some substantial limitations on the use of tax attributes where a corporation is acquired). If A paid more for the S stock because of this, they may be disappointed. The capital loss could disappear because P might deliberately recognize some capital gain before the year-end and after the sale of the S stock. This gain could consume the entire capital loss otherwise attributable to S.

REVIEW QUESTIONS

1. How is debt capital distinguished from equity capital and vice versa?
2. Why is the EPS concept of a common stock equivalent significant for consolidations?
3. For consolidation how might preferred stock be treated in analysis of investment accounts?
4. What test can be made for common stock equivalency in ascertaining percentage ownership for consolidation?
5. What would the test for common stock equivalency show if the security were a "true" common stock equivalent?
6. What effect does convertibility of bonds or preferred stock have on the percentage ownership of the subsidiary?
7. What can cause a parent's ownership of a subsidiary to change without changing the number of shares owned by the parent corporation?
8. If P's ownership percentage increases without a change in the number of shares held by P, will gain or loss be recognized and why?
9. If P's ownership percentage decreases without a change in the number of shares held by P, will gain or loss be recognized and why?
10. What impact will the issuance of more shares by a subsidiary have on the parent's investment in subsidiary account if the parent does not acquire a proportionate number of shares?
11. If a subsidiary issues more shares and the parent does acquire a proportionate amount, what impact will this have on the investment in subsidiary account(s)?
12. What problems are encountered when a parent acquires several blocks of stock of a subsidiary but at different dates and different prices?
13. If a significant second block of stock purchased by the parent from minority interests is treated as a continuation of the first block, how is a cost in excess of book value for the second block accounted for?

14. If a significant second block of stock is treated as independent of the first block of stock, how is a cost in excess of book value for the second block accounted for?
15. What impact will a subsidiary's purchase of treasury stock from the minority interest have on the parent company accounting records?
16. What impact will a subsidiary's purchase of treasury shares from the parent have on the parent company accounting records if the subsidiary is not 100 percent owned?
17. What impact will a subsidiary's purchase of treasury shares from the parent have on the parent company accounting records if the subsidiary is owned 100 percent?
18. What adjustments are necessary to the basis of an investment in a subsidiary when that investment is being sold?
19. What are some of the problems encountered in selling some shares of a subsidiary which remains as a subsidiary?
20. What is one thing you should always do before selling any shares of a subsidiary?
21. If a subsidiary that your parent company wishes to acquire is included in a consolidated tax return of another group, can this affect the price you might pay for that stock and if so why?

PROBLEMS

Problem 1: Preferred Corporation

The owners' equity section for Preferred Corporation follows. Assume book value of all assets and liabilities equals their fair values.

PREFERRED CORPORATION

Preferred stock, 10%, $100 par	$ 300,000
Premium on preferred	100,000
Common stock, $10 par	200,000
Additional paid-in capital	400,000
Retained earnings, 1/1/x5	600,000
	$1,600,000

On 1/1/x5 Pierpont, Inc., purchased 90 percent of Preferred Corporation's common stock for $70 per share or $1,260,000. During 19x5 Preferred Corporation earned $200,000 and paid the preferred dividends and $20,000 to the common shareholders.

Required (using the theoretical approach):

1. Prepare the investment analysis at 12/31/x5 for Pierpont's investment in Preferred Corporation assuming the preferred shares are the equivalent of debt and will be called in ten years for $300,000 and were issued on 12/31/x4.
2. Record the entry(s) on the books of Pierpont, Inc., to reflect the earnings and dividends of Preferred Corporation.
3. Prepare the work sheet substitution entry.

Problem 2: Preferred Revisited

Required:

Using the data from problem 1—
1. a. Prepare the investment analysis at 12/31/x5 assuming the noncumulative preferred stock is a second class of stock and entitled to $400,000 in event of liquidation.
    b. Record the earnings and dividends of Preferred Corporation on the books of Pierpont, Inc.
    c. Prepare the work sheet substitution entry.
2. a. Prepare the investment analysis at 12/31/x5 assuming the preferred stock is convertible into common (at 4 common to 1 preferred) and is the equivalent of the common.
    b. Record the earnings and dividends of Preferred Corporation on the books of Pierpont, Inc.
    c. Prepare the work sheet substitution entry.

Problem 3: Con Corporation and Vertible Corporation

Con Corporation has owned for many years 80 percent of Vertible Corporation. As of 12/31/x7 the investment account for this interest has a $480,000 balance before conversion of some Vertible Corporation bonds. The owners' equity accounts at 12/31/x7—immediately before the conversion of an issue of convertible bonds—are as follows:

Common stock, $10 par value	100,000
Additional paid-in capital	200,000
Retained earnings	300,000

The outsider owned bonds have a carrying value of $90,000 on 12/31/x7 which is equal to their face value less $10,000 of unamortized discount. The bonds were not considered to be common stock equivalents during any previous year. The common stock is currently selling at $100 per share, after a rapid rise in price due to the sudden discovery, in October of 19x7, of oil on some Vertible Corporation owned land. The bonds are converted into 2,000 common shares at 12/31/x7.

Required:

1. Using historical cost prepare—
    a. The 12/31/x7 conversion entry as recorded on Vertible's books.
    b. An investment analysis immediately prior to the conversion.
    c. An investment analysis immediately following the conversion.
    d. The theoretical journal entry, if any, that Con Corporation would record on its records because of the conversion of Vertible bonds by outside parties.
    e. The work sheet substitution entry in journal entry format at 12/31/x7 after the conversion.
2. Prepare the journal entries necessary if Vertible records the appraisal value of the oil deposit (assumed equal to the excess of the fair value of the stock over its book value after conversion).

3. Prepare the 12/31/x7 substitution entry after the appraisal increase and conversions have been recorded.

Problem 4: Dilution Corporation

On 1/1/x1 Skadden, Inc., acquired 90 percent of the outstanding stock of Dilution for $630,000 and one half or $50,000 face value of the convertible bonds of Dilution for $70,000. The owners' equity at 1/1/x1 was as follows:

DILUTION CORPORATION

Common stock, $10 par value	$200,000
Additional paid-in capital	100,000
Retained earnings, 1/1/x1	300,000
Book value, 1/1/x1	$600,000

The convertible bonds are common stock equivalents for EPS purposes due to their low 4 percent yield when the bank prime interest rate was 8 percent; however, they were issued at par. Each $1,000 bond is convertible into 40 shares of common stock and has three more years to maturity. On 1/1/x1, for all assets and liabilities (other than for the convertible bonds), fair value equals book value. During 19x1 Dilution reported earnings of $70,000 and paid $10,000 in dividends.

Required (using the theoretical approach):

1. Prepare the 12/31/x1 investment analysis for Skadden's investment in Dilution (be sure that the column totals retain their percentages).
2. Prepare the entries on Skadden's books for the investments in Dilution.
3. Prepare the work sheet substitution entry.

Problem 5: Equivalent Corporation

A Corporation acquired 90 percent of the outstanding stock of Equivalent for $540,000 on 1/1/x1. The owners' equity at 12/31/x1 is as follows:

EQUIVALENT CORPORATION

Common stock, $10 par	$100,000
Additional paid-in capital	150,000
Retained earnings, 12/31/x1	300,000
Book value, 12/31/x1	$550,000

During year 19x1 Equivalent reported earnings of $80,000 and paid $30,000 in dividends. All assets on 1/1/x1 were reported at fair value except for machinery which has a 10-year remaining life; the straight-line depreciation method is being used. The fair value of the machinery exceeds the book value by $30,000. All liabilities on 1/1/x1 except for the convertible bonds were also reported at fair values. When the Equivalent Corporation was formed, $60,000 face value convertible bonds were issued at face value with interest a 8 percent. The convertibility feature at that date was considered almost worthless. The bank prime rate then was 6 percent and has not changed materially since then. Due to the subsequent success of the corporation, these bonds are worth $140,000 at 12/31/x1 and are about to mature. They are convertible into 2,000 common shares currently selling for $70 per share. On 1/1/x1 these bonds were worth $120,000 and the stock was selling at $60 per share.

Required:

1. Prepare an analysis of the investment account as of 12/31/x1 treating the convertible bonds as debt.
2. Prepare an analysis of the investment account as of 12/31/x1 treating the bonds as though they were common stock equivalents on 1/1/x1.
3. Assume on 1/1/x1 that A Corporation also acquired $30,000 face value of the convertible bonds of Equivalent Corporation for $60,000. Prepare an analysis of the investment accounts as though these bonds were common stock equivalents.
4. How would the convertible bonds be classified for EPS purposes for the separate financial statements of the Equivalent Corporation as of 12/31/x1?

Problem 6: Treasury Stock Acquisitions

P acquires 9,000 shares of S for $450,000 on 1/1/x1. The owners' equity of S was as follows as of 1/1/x1:

Common stock, $10 par value	$100,000
Additional paid-in capital	150,000
Retained earnings, 1/1/x1	200,000
Book value, 1/1/x1	$450,000

The book value of each asset and liability equaled its fair value. S's reported earnings for year ended 12/31/x1 of $40,000, or $3,333 per month, and no dividends were paid. On 7/1/x1, S acquired 500 shares of treasury stock from outside parties at $55 per share. S uses the cost method to account for treasury stock.

Required (using the theoretical approach):

1. Prepare—
   a. The investment analysis at 6/30/x1.
   b. The investment analysis at 12/31/x1.
   c. Any entries affecting P's investment in S and the year-end work sheet substitution entry.
2. Assume the treasury stock only cost $30 per share. Prepare—
   a. The investment analysis as of 12/31/x1.
   b. Any entries affecting P's investment in S.
   c. The year-end substitution entry.
3. Same as 1 above except the treasury stock was purchased from P.
4. Same as 2 above except the treasury stock was purchased from P.
5. If under 2 above the parent thought that the $30 price represented a permanent reduction in the value of S's assets, prepare—
   a. The investment analysis at 12/31/x1.
   b. The resulting journal entries on the books of S and P.
   c. The substitution entry.

Problem 7: Second Block Open Market

P acquires 60 percent of S on 1/1/x1 for $400,000 and acquires another 30 percent on 1/1/x7 for $400,000. S's owners' equity accounts on 1/1/x1 and on 1/1/x7 appeared as follows:

S's Owners' Equity	1/1/x1	1/1/x7
Capital stock, $10 par	100,000	100,000
Additional paid-in capital	200,000	200,000
Retained earnings	300,000	700,000
Totals	600,000	1,000,000

All assets and liabilities are recorded at their fair values except for buildings which are undervalued by $30,000 on 1/1/x1 and by $100,000 on 1/1/x7. Assume a 10-year remaining life at 1/1/x1 and also at 1/1/x7. Earnings in 19x7 are $80,000, and dividends paid are $50,000.

Required:
1. Prepare the 12/31/x7 investment analysis and substitution entries using alternative method 1. Keep each block of stock separate.
2. Prepare the 12/31/x7 investment analysis and substitution entries using alternative method 2. Keep each block of stock separate except where the alternative 2 method forces a change in the first block (for net assets other than goodwill).

8

Accounting for Tiered Operations

Development of Tiered Structures
Acquisition with Parent Corporation Stock
Acquisition of a Chain of Corporations
    Under the Pooling Concept
    Under the Purchase Concept
Indirect Acquisition of Marketable Securities under the Purchase Concept
Reporting the Operations of a Tiered Chain of Corporations
    Reporting for Tiered Operations where the Subsidiaries Were "Acquired" under Pooling
        Without Intercorporate Transactions under Pooling
        With Intercorporate Transactions under Pooling
    Reporting for Tiered Operations where the Subsidiaries Were Acquired by Purchase
Reciprocal Interests
    Recognition of Reciprocal Interests
    Treasury Stock Treatment of Reciprocal Interests

An increasing number of tiered corporate structures is a logical outcome of the growth of conglomerate operations. A tiered corporate structure is a group of corporations with several parent corporations within the group but with only one top or common parent corporation. Subsidiaries which own or control other subsidiaries are parent corporations; there is, however, only one common parent in each group. Consolidated financial statements usually are prepared for shareholders and other parties interested in the financial affairs of the top or common parent corporation which in many cases is a holding company only. A pure holding company has no operations of its own other than its investments in subsidiaries.

Tiered structures can have many configurations; they can be a single chain of subsidiaries or multiple chains, so interwoven as to form almost a pyramid. Illustration 8–1 is an illustration of a tiered structure.

Illustration 8–1

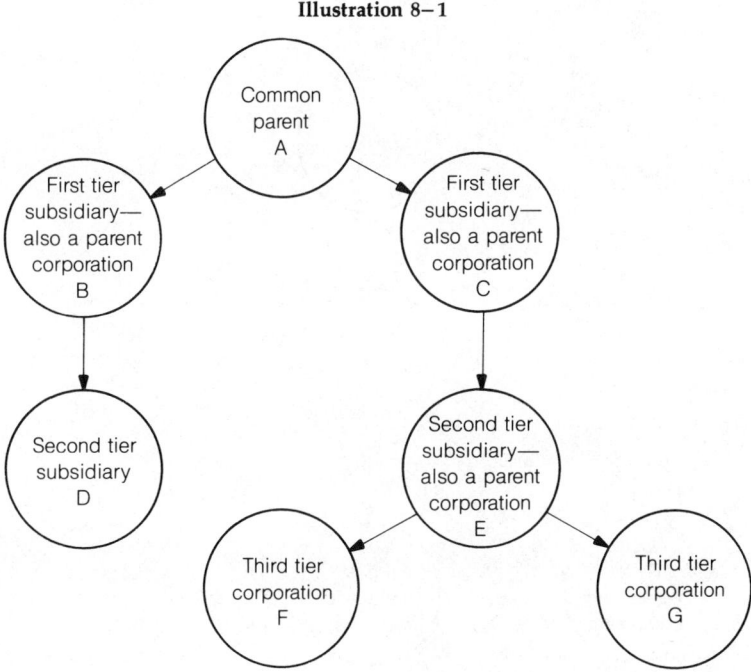

DEVELOPMENT OF TIERED STRUCTURES

Tiered structures may be developed, for example, in order to have all segments of a particular product line organized within one chain of corporations. Thus, all manufacturing, transportation, finance, insurance, and so on, operations could be grouped in separate chains of corporations under one common parent. Separate chains by product line may allow a corporation to utilize better its management talent.

In addition, the creation of multiple separate legal entities can reduce risk of loss. Thus, if a lowest tier subsidiary goes into bankruptcy, the maximum loss is the investment in that subsidiary as long as none of its liabilities have been guaranteed by another affiliate or by the parent corporation or the parent's shareholders. It is therefore important to keep risky operations in separate corporations which do not own other corporations. If a higher tier subsidiary goes into bankruptcy, all of its assets including its investments in lower tier subsidiaries may be seized by its creditors. If the common parent goes bankrupt, the assets of the entire chain will be subject to various creditors claims. This is one reason for having the common parent be only a holding company.

If an individual were to start a new manufacturing business, it might be formed to reduce risk of loss as diagramed in Illustration 8–2. Here P

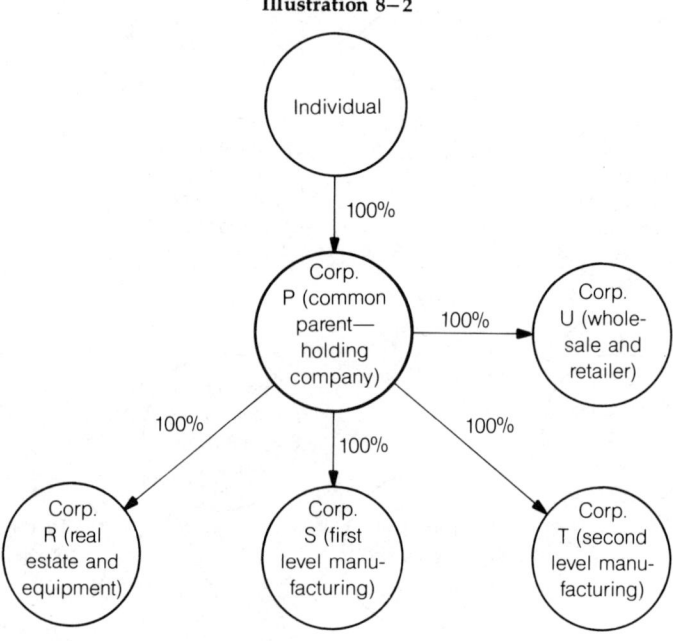

Illustration 8–2

Corporation is the common parent holding company whose only assets are the investments in the subsidiary corporations. R Corporation owns the real estate and equipment and rents these assets to the more risky S, T, and U Corporations. S could be producing raw materials which in turn are sold to T (and perhaps to outsiders) for further processing. T after additional processing sells its finished product to U which in turn sells to outside customers. With the operating assets distributed through four subsidiaries, the risk of total loss due to negligence or uninsured product liability judgments or to operating losses have been greatly reduced.

Multiple corporations connected through an ownership chain, often serve other very useful purposes. They may make it less of a task to comply with state income tax laws and state regulatory requirements for industries such as power and telephone companies. For example, one corporation doing business in many states might find it quite difficult to allocate its earnings to the proper states. In addition, the state taxing authorities will be interested in the allocation results. There is an allocation formula (based on factors such as sales, payroll and property) that some states have agreed to use which prevents the same earnings from being taxed by more than one of these states. California has developed a unitary concept which in effect allows that state to tax its share of the consolidated earnings including earnings of foreign operations based on an allocation formula. In many cases U.S. corporations may be tempted to shift their earnings to states with low or no income tax or to foreign operations. The U.S. federal income tax law makes separate corporations virtually a certainty at least for profitable foreign operations.

> **Tax:** Under the U.S. federal income tax law, income or losses from branch or divisional operations generally are taxed currently (when earned) even when these operations are in a foreign country. Foreign operations in subsidiary form generally are not taxed until the dividends from "earnings and profits" are remitted to a U.S. corporation (or to other U.S. taxpayers). When foreign earnings are subject to the U.S. tax, a foreign tax credit is allowed as an offset against the U.S. tax on the remitted foreign earnings on a dollar-for-dollar basis, but not in excess of the U.S. tax on those earnings. By contrast, a New York corporation with a California subsidiary would be taxed currently by the U.S. on both operations (either through separate tax returns or through a consolidated tax return), and the New York and California state income taxes would only be deductible and not creditable against the U.S. income tax.

While chains of corporate organizations may be desirable, an established structure may not be easy to maintain. Tiered structures may be acquired rather than developed. Frequently common parent corporations are acquired, and in that process their particular tiered structures are also acquired. It may be difficult and costly to shift ownership of subsidiaries in order to maintain the desired structure. In an acquisition of a parent corporation (or any corporation) it is not uncommon to acquire control of some unwanted operations. Thus, frequently, acquisitions will be followed by pruning operations to rid the organization of duplicate facilities or unwanted corporations (or divisions).

ACQUISITION WITH PARENT CORPORATION STOCK

Often the shareholders of a corporation to be acquired will want stock of the parent corporation rather than shares of the particular subsidiary under which the acquired corporation would normally be organized. This is usually desired by the shareholders of the acquired corporation because the parent corporation's stock may be more widely traded.[1] One way to achieve this is for a subsidiary to exchange shares of its parent corporation for the shares (or net assets) of the acquired corporation. This form of acquisition is sometimes called a triangular merger or acquisition. In this situation (illustrated below) the parent increases its investment in the first tier subsidiary and increases its own owners' equity accounts for the newly issued stock. The subsidiary, in turn, records the receipt of the parent's stock as additional paid-in capital in a purchase or as additional paid-in capital and retained earnings in a pooling and debits its investment in the acquired second tier subsidiary stock. These entries are at fair market value (FMV) if this acquisition is a purchase, and at the book value of the proportionate part of the acquired corporation's underlying net assets if the acquisition is accounted for as a pooling of interests.

To illustrate this assume that P owns 100 percent of S and that S exchanges 1,000 previously unissued P shares for 90 percent or 1,800 T shares with fair values of $108 and $60 per share, respectively. The book value of the T shares is $40 per share, and the par value of both P and T shares is $10 per share. T's owners' equity section appears as in Illustration 8–3.

Illustration 8–3

T's Owners' Equity	Net Assets	90 percent Majority	10 percent Minority
Common stock (2,000 × $10)	$20,000	$18,000	$2,000
Additional paid-in capital	24,000	21,600	2,400
Retained earnings	36,000	32,400	3,600
Book value	$80,000	$72,000	$8,000

---

[1] The parent corporation may also prefer this so that it does not have to decrease its percentage ownership of the acquiring subsidiary.

If the exchange of P stock for T stock were a pooling of interests, it would be recorded as:

On P's books:

Investment in S stock	72,000	
Common stock (1,000 shares × $10)		10,000
Additional paid-in capital ($21,600 +		
$18,000 − $10,000)		29,600*
Retained earnings		32,400

    * In practice, the Additional Paid-In Capital account would often be credited for $62,000, and then in the consolidation process $32,400 would be removed from additional paid-in capital and credited to consolidated Retained Earnings. Due to the theory of pooling, your author prefers the method shown above.

This entry records the issuance of the P stock in an amount equal to the underlying book value of the T stock and treats this as an additional investment in S.

On S's books:

Investment in T stock	72,000	
Additional paid-in capital (of S)		39,600*
Retained earnings		32,400

    * Again, current practice would often record additional paid-in capital at $72,000, but in the consolidation process this would be removed in a substitution entry. Your author prefers recording the retained earnings change because of the theory underlying the pooling on interests concept.

This entry records the investment in T stock and the additional capital contribution of P in S with the increase in retained earnings at the underlying book value of the T stock. The credit of $32,400 to the Retained Earnings of S and also to the Retained Earnings of P reflects the pooling concept that the companies had always been together. Thus, if S had always owned 90 percent of T, S's retained earnings would have been $32,400 ($36,000 × 90%) larger. And since P owns S 100 percent, P's retained earnings would also have been $32,400 larger. This does not double count the retained earnings in the consolidated financial statements because all of the owners' equity accounts of both S and T (including the retained earnings) are removed in the substitution entries.

On T's books:

    Since this was a stock-for-stock (rather than a stock for assets) acquisition, there would not be an entry on T's books.

If the exchange were a purchase rather than a pooling, it would be recorded as follows:

On P's books:

Investment in S stock (1,000 shares × $108)	108,000	
Common stock		10,000
Additional paid-in capital		98,000
To record the contribution of the P stock to S		
at its market value.		

On S's books:

Investment in T stock	108,000	
Additional paid-in capital		108,000
To record the purchase of the T stock, in exchange for P stock received by S, as a capital contribution from P.		

On T's books:

    Again, because this was a stock-for-stock exchange, there is no entry on T's books.

Had this been a direct asset acquisition, an exchange of the P stock for all of the assets and liabilities of T, it would have been recorded as follows on T's books:

P stock	108,000	
Liabilities	xx	
Assets		xxx
Gain on sale of assets		28,000

This would usually then be followed by a distribution of the P stock to the shareholders of T in a liquidating distribution. T would then go out of existence.

Tax: The triangular acquisition in a closely held family corporation setting offers an opportunity to shift wealth among family members possibly without the impact of a gift tax. To illustrate, assume that the A Corporation has been owned by one person (Mr. Dealer) for many years; now in year 19x1 the A Corporation and Mr. Dealer's three children form B Corporation with A corporation owning 55 percent and each of the young Dealers owning 15 percent. Sometime later, say in 19x2, B Corporation acquires C Corporation in a stock-for-stock exchange but using A stock as compensation in a triangular acquisition. Suppose 100 percent of the C stock is acquired in exchange for 10,000 shares of A nonvoting $10 par value preferred stock worth $100 per share.

    Because the $1,000,000 worth of A preferred stock has purchased 100 percent of the C stock (also presumably worth $1,000,000), B Corporation has been increased in value by the $1,000,000 of which 45 percent (3 × 15%), or $450,000, is now owned by Mr. Dealer's children.

    Perhaps A should be forced to recognize, for financial reporting, the value of the gift rather than record a $1,000,000 increase in its investment in B. In the preceding situation the issuance of the preferred stock would then be recorded as follows:

> **Tax:** (*continued*)
>
> | | | |
> |---|---:|---:|
> | Investment in B Corporation ($1,000,000 × 55%) ..... | 550,000 | |
> | Gift (or loss) on triangular acquisition* | | |
> | ($1,000,000 × 45%) .... | 450,000 | |
> | Preferred stock (10,000 shares × $10) .... | | 100,000 |
> | Additional paid-in capital .... | | 900,000 |
>
> * Gift to minority shareholders of B.
>
> In a normal situation involving a triangular acquisition, the acquiring subsidiary is owned 100 percent by the parent corporation whose stock is used as compensation. If there is a minority interest present in the acquiring subsidiary, their interest after a triangular acquisition would become more valuable without any effort or contribution on their part.

ACQUISITION OF A CHAIN OF CORPORATIONS

Under the Pooling Concept

In the example of the acquisition of the T stock, if T were the parent corporation of X and Y, both owned 80 percent, additional problems are presented other than the fact that the acquisition has resulted in three tiers of subsidiary corporations. The new tiered structure could be as in Illustration 8–4. As long as the acquisition of T met the pooling requirements the fact that less than 90 percent of X and Y were owned has no significance for pooling.

Illustration 8–4

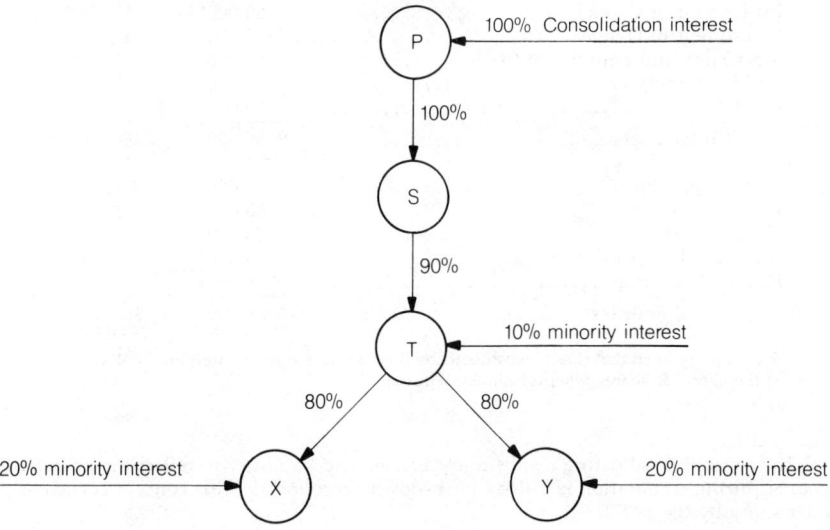

Under the Purchase Concept

As is normally true with the purchase concept, the problems are in the valuation of the acquired assets. It must be remembered that the acquisition of the T stock is, in effect, the indirect acquisition of T's assets which includes T's investments in X and Y stock (which is an investment in X and Y net assets). In the example where the market value ($108,000) exceeded the book value ($72,000) of the acquired shares, the cost in excess of book value of $36,000 must be allocated to the proper assets in the preparation of the consolidated financial statements. The $36,000 difference may be due to assets or liabilities within T, X, or Y Corporations or within some combination of all three.

The easiest way to handle this problem might be to simply adjust the assets and liabilities on the actual records of the appropriate subsidiary(s).[2] This would require an appraisal capital amount, on the books of the subsidiary, which will be removed via the substitution entry in the process of preparing consolidated financial statements. In the usual situation where the book values of the subsidiary's assets or liabilities are not changed, the adjustments for changes in assets and liabilities and the related adjustments such as depreciation must be made each year.

Illustration 8–5
B CORPORATION
Position Statement
As on 1/1/x1

	Book Value	Fair Value
Cash	$ 8,000	$ 8,000
Receivables	20,000	20,000
Inventory	60,000	56,000
Investment in C stock	80,000*	120,000
Investment in D stock	100,000*	150,000
Machinery and equipment (net)	50,000	50,000
Buildings (net)	70,000	70,000
Land	20,000	30,000
Total assets	$408,000	$504,000
Current liabilities	$ 10,000	$ 10,000
Long-term debt	80,000	80,000
Capital stock	100,000	
Additional paid-in capital	80,000	414,000
Retained earnings	138,000	
Total equities	$408,000	$504,000

* It is assumed that these investments by B were made at the underlying book value of the C and D shares when originally acquired.

---

[2] The concept of adjusting a subsidiary's assets and liabilities to reflect the price paid by an acquiring corporation is called "push-down" accounting. This concept is currently under study by the FASB.

In framing a new example to illustrate this point, assume that B owns 80 percent of both C and D and that on 1/1/x1 the position statement of B appears as in Illustration 8–5.

Now assume that P acquires 90 percent of the B stock for $372,600 ($414,000 × 90%) on 1/1/19x1.[3]

This affiliation would now appear as in Illustration 8–6.

Illustration 8–6

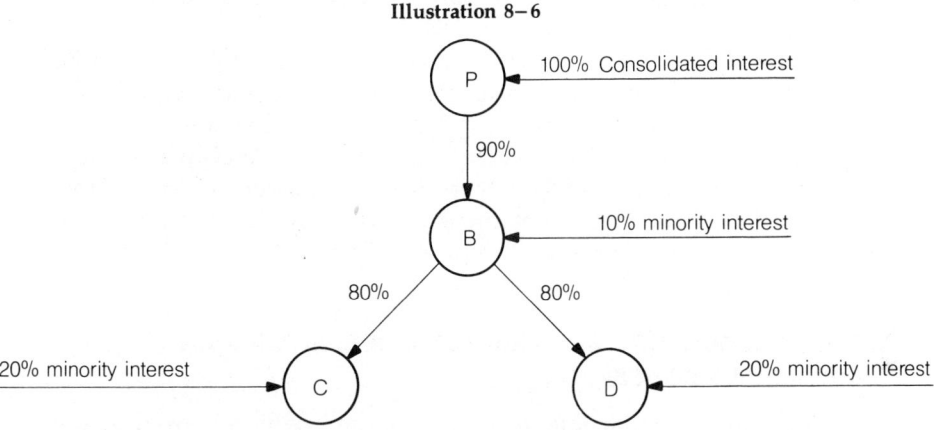

The analysis of the P's investment in B on 1/1/x1 would appear as given in Illustration 8–7 under alternatives 2 and 3 (these are the same due to the absence of goodwill):

Illustration 8–7

B Corporation	Net Assets	90 percent Majority	10 percent Minority
Common stock	$100,000	$ 90,000	$10,000
Additional paid-in capital	80,000	72,000	8,000
Retained earnings, 1/1/x1	138,000	124,200	13,800
Book value	318,000	286,200	31,800
To adjust net assets to their fair values (from Illustration 8–5):			
Inventory	(4,000)	(3,600)	(400)
Investment in C stock	40,000	36,000	4,000
Investment in D stock	50,000	45,000	5,000
Land	10,000	9,000	1,000
Adjusted book value, 1/1/x1	$414,000	$372,600*	$41,400

* Equals price paid thus no goodwill nor excess fair value over price paid.

---

[3] In a real-world situation an acquisition of a 90 percent block of a corporation's stock would usually cost much more than 90 times what 1 percent would cost. There are often synergistic effects between the acquired and the acquiring corporations which makes the acquisition more valuable.

Of the cost in excess of book value of $86,400 ($372,600 − $286,200), $81,000 ($36,000 + $45,000) is caused by B's investments in C and D. Thus, in a consolidation the $81,000 must be allocated to assets which are on the books of second tier subsidiaries C and D. The remaining $5,400 is attributable to the majority interest share of the increase in land, or $9,000, and the majority interest in the decrease in inventory, or $3,600. The adjustment of the inventory book value will affect the cost of goods sold in the subsequent year under Fifo.

Theoretically, adjustments which affect earnings would have to be considered even if P did not consolidate B but instead accounted for it under the equity method. About the only time that the equity method earnings theoretically can be different from what the consolidated earnings would have been is when there are investments in marketable securities (less than 20 percent owned and accounted for under the lower-of-cost-or-market method) by a subsidiary. This is discussed in the next section.

INDIRECT ACQUISITION OF MARKETABLE SECURITIES UNDER THE PURCHASE CONCEPT

Accounting for marketable securities will be briefly reviewed before the problems of consolidation are presented. Marketable securities are those accounted for under the cost method (actually lower of cost or market for less than 20 percent owned corporations). These securities are separated between those classified as current and as noncurrent.

For financial statements, marketable securities are reported at the lower of cost or market with the current and noncurrent portfolios being reported separately. When the market value is less than cost, a valuation allowance (credit balance account) is created. The contra to a change in the valuation account for current marketable securities is to a recognized gain or loss account, while the contra to a change in the valuation allowance for noncurrent marketable securities is to a shareholders' equity account.[4]

To illustrate these rules assume that Z Corporation invests $25,000 in marketable securities on 1/1/x1 and that subsequent market values are as follows:

Z CORPORATION INVESTMENTS IN MARKETABLE SECURITIES

	Cost 1/1/x1	Market Value 12/31/x1	Market Value 12/31/x2
Current	$10,000	$ 9,000	$12,000
Noncurrent	15,000	10,000	8,000

---

[4] For a more complete review of accounting for marketable securities, see *FASB Statement No. 12*.

The journal entries to record the lower-of-cost-or-market results would be as follows:

At 12/31/x1:

Loss on marketable securities (recognized)....................	1,000	
Valuation allowance for current marketable securities		1,000
Owners' equity account (for unrecognized loss on noncurrent marketable securities)..	5,000	
Valuation allowance for noncurrent marketable securities ...		5,000

At 12/31/x2:

Valuation allowance for current marketable securities	1,000	
Gain on marketable securities (recognized)		1,000
Owners' equity account (for unrecognized loss on noncurrent marketable securities)..	2,000	
Valuation allowance for noncurrent marketable securities ...		2,000

Thus, the carrying amount of the current marketable securities portfolio has been returned to its cost of $10,000 while the carrying amount of the noncurrent marketable securities portfolio has been reduced to $8,000 ($15,000 cost less a $7,000 valuation allowance).

It should be noted that the cost figure is an important measuring point in applying the lower-of-cost-or-market rules. It should also be realized that a second cost figure for these securities may be created when this company is acquired by another in a purchase acquisition. The second cost figure relates only to the acquiring corporation in a purchase acquisition and is not relevant to the direct owner of the stock (the acquired corporation).

If Z had been acquired in a purchase acquisition by A Corporation on 1/1/x2, the second cost basis of the current marketable securities would have been $9,000 and not $10,000 and the second cost basis for the noncurrent marketable securities portfolio would have been $10,000 and not $15,000. These new cost bases can obviously affect future consolidated earnings. For consolidated financial statements the current and noncurrent marketable security portfolios of all the affiliated entities are grouped to make the lower-of-cost-or-market measurements. Even on an equity method basis the new cost figures should be $9,000 and $10,000, respectively. But for equity method measurement, the lower-of-cost-or-market calculation is made separately for each entity.

Continuing the prior example of B, C, and D to illustrate the problem marketable securities can cause, assume for both C and D that the book value of each asset and liability equals its fair value except for investments in marketable securities (less than a 20 percent ownership interest) classified as current assets (see Illustration 8–8). Present accounting rules require certain lower-of-cost-or-market adjustments to these assets for changes in market values on an aggregate (portfolio) basis. In this

Illustration 8–8
B CORPORATION
Position Statement
As of 1/1/x1

	Book Value	Fair Value
Cash	$ 8,000	$ 8,000
Receivables	20,000	20,000
Inventory	60,000	56,000
Investment in C stock (80% owned)	80,000*	120,000
Investment in D stock (80% owned)	100,000*	150,000
Machinery and equipment (net)	50,000	50,000
Buildings (net)	70,000	70,000
Land	20,000	30,000
Total assets	$408,000	$504,000
Current liabilities	$ 10,000	$ 10,000
Long-term debt	80,000	80,000
Capital stock	100,000	
Additional paid-in capital	80,000	414,000
Retained earnings	138,000	
Total equities	$408,000	$504,000

* It is assumed that these investments by B were made at the underlying book value of the C and D shares when originally acquired.

case it would be easier to adjust the individual corporation records for B, C, and D, as of the date P acquires B, than to readjust for changes in market values of these marketable securities on a consolidated basis each year. In other words, where marketable securities have been indirectly acquired, there has been established for consolidation purposes a new or second cost basis to be used in the measurement of the lower-of-cost-or-market valuation. Thus, on the books of a subsidiary corporation, changing the "cost basis" by removing the original cost basis and recording the second cost basis might make subsequent adjustments easier. Adjusting the acquired corporations' books at the date of acquisition is the application of the "push-down" accounting concept. This, however, might not be permitted by the FASB, at least where there is a substantial minority interest, because this would increase or decrease the "cost basis" on the individual subsidiary's records and thus impact on its separate financial statements.

To illustrate this, the position statements of C and D (aggregating most assets and liabilities) appear on 1/1/x1 as shown in Illustration 8–9.

On a consolidated basis, the $90,000 and the $92,500 are established as the "cost basis" (instead of the $40,000 and $30,000) from which to measure the "lower of cost or market." And on a consolidated basis the portfolios of P, B, C, and D would have to be treated as one current and one noncurrent portfolio in measuring the lower of cost or market.

Illustration 8–9
C AND D CORPORATIONS
Position Statements
As of 1/1/x1

	Corporation C		Corporation D	
	Book Value	Fair Value	Book Value	Fair Value
Marketable securities (current):				
Cost	$ 40,000 }	$ 90,000	$ 30,000 }	$ 92,500
Valuation allowance	–0–		–0–	
Other assets	120,000	120,000	145,000	145,000
Total assets	160,000	210,000	175,000	237,500
Less liabilities	60,000	60,000	50,000	50,000
Owners' equity	$100,000	$150,000	$125,000	$187,500
B's 80% of owners' equity	$ 80,000*	$120,000	$100,000*	$150,000
B's 80% indirect ownership of fair value over book value of marketable securities	(80% × $50,000) = $40,000		(80% × $62,500) = $50,000	

* It should be noted that B's previous investment in both C and D was in proportion to the book value of owners' equity, thus there was no cost in excess of book value nor book value in excess of cost (at the date B acquired these investments) to allocate.

The substitution entries at the date P acquires B would appear as follows assuming the records of C and D have not been changed at the date P acquires B.

For B's investment in C stock:

Owners' equity accounts of C	100,000	
B's investment in C stock		80,000
Minority interest in C stock		20,000

For B's investment in D stock:

Owners' equity accounts of D	125,000	
B's investment in D stock		100,000
Minority interest in D stock		25,000

For P's investment in B (under alternative 1):*

Capital stock of B	100,000	
Additional paid-in capital of B	80,000	
Retained earnings of B	138,000	
Marketable securities of C ($40,000 × 90%)	36,000	
Marketable securities of D ($50,000 × 90%)	45,000	
Land of B ($10,000 × 90%)	9,000	
Inventory of B ($4,000 × 90%)		3,600
P's investment in B stock		372,600
Minority interest in B stock		31,800
	408,000	408,000

* See the analysis in Illustration 8–7.

For P's investment in B (under alternatives 2 or 3 due to the absence of goodwill):*

Capital stock	100,000	
Additional paid-in capital of B	80,000	
Retained earnings of B	138,000	
Marketable securities of C	40,000	
Marketable securities of D	50,000	
Land of B	10,000	
Inventory of B		4,000
P's investment in B stock		372,600
Minority interest in B stock		41,400
	418,000	418,000

* See the analysis in Illustration 8-7.

There are many and more difficult situations which could be illustrated involving marketable securities and consolidation, but the aspect of marketable securities is left at this point. It should be stated, however, that in measuring the lower-of-cost-or-market value the stock portfolios of all the consolidated corporations are treated as one group in measuring the aggregate change in market values. On an equity basis, however, the measurement of aggregate change in market values is made on a corporation by corporation basis. Thus, this is one situation in which equity method reported earnings might differ from consolidated earnings.[5]

REPORTING THE OPERATIONS OF A TIERED CHAIN OF CORPORATIONS

The more tiers of subsidiaries in a consolidation the more difficult it usually is to prepare proper consolidated statements. The acquisition of some subsidiaries under pooling and some under purchase adds to the complexity. Good working papers, however, can make the accounting task less difficult.

Reporting for Tiered Operations where the Subsidiaries Were Acquired under Pooling

The same situation, no change in recorded assets, would exist if the stock were acquired under the purchase method but only if the cost equaled the underlying book value of each asset and liability. In practice this seldom happens.

Without Intercorporate Transactions under Pooling. Assume that P owns 100 percent of S and 10 percent of T and 10 percent of U. The 10

---
[5] *AICPA Professional Standards, Accounting—Current Text* (New York, 1980), par. 5132.09. Copyright (1980) by the American Institute of CPAs.

percent of T and U had been transferred from S to P. S owns 80 percent of T, and 85 percent of U. This affiliation would be diagramed as shown in Illustration 8–10.

Illustration 8–10

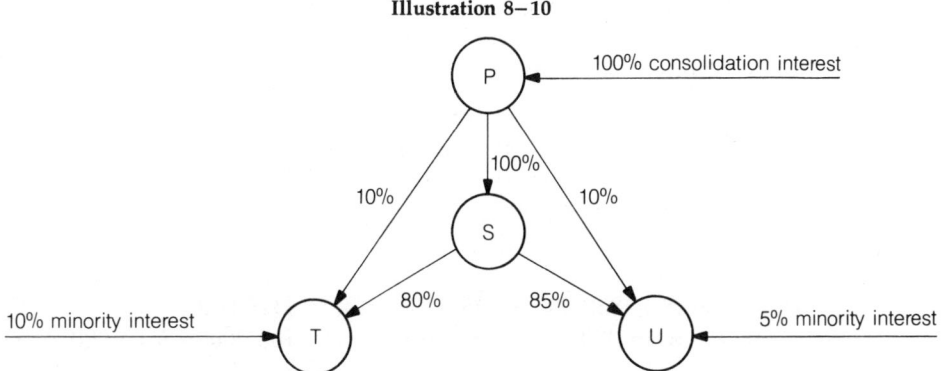

Assume in this affiliation that the earnings of each corporation excluding any earnings from investments in other members under either the cost or equity methods were:

P	$ 80,000
S	40,000
T	30,000
U	60,000
Total earnings	$210,000

Consolidated earnings are calculated always beginning with the lowest tier subsidiary(s) first. In this example, ignoring the possible difference created by marketable securities, the equity method earnings of P would equal the consolidated earnings (and P's retained earnings would equal the consolidated retained earnings) of the group. Thus, the working paper in Illustration 8–11 converts the separate entity results

Illustration 8–11

	U	T	S		P		Minority	
U's earnings	$60,000	–0–	(85%)	$ 51,000	(10%)	$ 6,000	(5%)	$3,000
T's earnings	–0–	$30,000	(80%)	24,000	(10%)	3,000	(10%)	3,000
S's earnings	–0–	–0–		40,000				
S's equity method earnings				$115,000	(100%)	115,000		–0–
P's earnings	–0–	–0–		–0–		80,000		–0–
Equity method earnings	$60,000	$30,000		$115,000		$204,000		$6,000*

* Deduction in the consolidated earnings statement.

into equity method results beginning with the lowest tier subsidiary. The $204,000 equity method earnings of P are equal to the consolidated earnings of the group. The consolidated earnings of $204,000 plus the minority interest in subsidiary earnings of $6,000 equals the total earnings of $210,000. The consolidated earnings could also be calculated with the use of linear algebra:

$$P = \$80{,}000 + S + .1T + .1U$$
$$S = \$40{,}000 + .8T + .85U$$
$$T = \$30{,}000$$
$$U = \$60{,}000$$

Thus:

$$S = \$40{,}000 + .8 \times \$30{,}000 + .85 \times \$60{,}000 = \$115{,}000$$
$$P = \$80{,}000 + \$115{,}000 + .1 \times \$30{,}000 + .1 \times \$60{,}000 = \$204{,}000$$

If the separate earnings figures had been equity method amounts, then P's $80,000 would equal consolidated net earnings and P's retained earnings would equal consolidated retained earnings. If, however, the separate earnings figures had been net earnings calculated under the cost method, adjustments must be made to obtain consolidated net earnings. If we assume that each corporation paid $30,000 in dividends, the effects of dividend revenue must be removed and equity method earnings from lower tier subsidiaries must be included to arrive at consolidated net earnings (see Illustration 8–12).

The consolidated net earnings could also be calculated by picking up the undistributed earnings without backing out the dividend revenue. Then, to P's $80,000 cost method earnings we would add 10 percent of U's $30,000 of undistributed earnings and 100 percent of S's $35,500 of undistributed earnings and obtain the $118,500 ($80,000 + $3,000 + $35,500) consolidated net earnings figure.

Using the linear algebra route and starting with separate earnings we would have:

$$P = \$44{,}000 + S + .1T + .1U$$
$$S = -\$9{,}500 + .8T + .85U$$
$$T = \$30{,}000$$
$$U = \$60{,}000$$

Thus:

$$S = -\$9{,}500 + .8 \times \$30{,}000 + .85 \times \$60{,}000 = \$65{,}500$$
$$P = \$44{,}000 + \$65{,}500 + .1 \times \$30{,}000 + .1 \times \$60{,}000 = \$118{,}500$$

Many persons might believe that the cost method would never be used in the accounts of the parent. But when the complexity of the equity method is considered, the cost method with adjustment at year-end, to produce either the equity method or consolidated results, may be vir-

Illustration 8–12

	U	T	S	P
Reported cost method earnings	$60,000	$30,000	$40,000	$80,000
To remove U's dividend from S and P earnings	(30,000)	–0–	(25,500)	(3,000)
To remove T's dividend from S and P earnings	–0–	(30,000)	(24,000)	(3,000)
Undistributed earnings of U and T	$30,000	$ –0–		
S's loss from own operations			(9,500)	
To remove S's dividend from P earnings			(30,000)	(30,000)
P's earnings from its own operations				44,000
Share of U's $60,000 earnings			(85%) 51,000	(10%) 6,000
Share of T's $30,000 earnings			(80%) 24,000	(10%) 3,000
Undistributed S earnings			$35,500	
Share of S's $65,500 ($30,000 + $35,500 or $51,000 + $24,000 – $9,500) earnings				(100%) 65,500
Consolidated and equity method earnings of P				$118,500

tually as easy or easier than use of the equity method in the accounts of the parent especially where intercorporate transactions are involved. Generally accepted accounting principles require financial statement presentation on the equity method or by consolidation, but do not prescribe the bookkeeping approach to be followed by the parent or equity investor.

With Intercorporate Transactions under Pooling. Whenever intercorporate deferrals, restorations, or advanced recognition transactions are involved, the equity method is not simply the applicable percentage times the reported income of the subsidiary. The applicable percentage instead must be applied to the net earnings figure after adjustment for the effects of intercorporate transactions. *And the effect of any intercorporate sales from the common parent to any subsidiary must also be deferred and subsequently reinstated to arrive at the parent corporation's equity method net earnings.*

For example, assume the same P, S, T, and U stock relationships and separate earnings ($80,000, $40,000, $30,000, and $60,000, respectively). In addition, assume P sold in the current year unimproved land, with a basis of $25,000, to S for $37,000. S, in the current year, sold to T for $50,000 a building and reported a $10,000 gain on that sale. T has taken $5,000 of depreciation on that building this year. P purchased on 1/1 of the current year $100,000 of U's bonds for $90,000. These bonds had ten

Illustration 8–13
CONVERSION TO EQUITY METHOD WITHOUT TAX EFFECTS

	U	T	S		P		Minority
Separate entity earnings	$60,000	$30,000	$40,000		$80,000		–0–
U's gain on P's bond purchase, 1/1/x1	2,000^n						
U's 19x1 amortization of bond premium included in the $60,000 earnings figure (4,000 ÷ 20 years)	(200)^n						
U's adjusted (equity method) net earnings	$61,800			(85%)	52,530	(10%)	6,180 (5%) $3,090
T's adjusted net earnings		$30,000		(80%)	24,000	(10%)	3,000 (10%) 3,000
To defer $10,000 gain on sale to T			(10,000)				
To restore $5,000/$50,000 × $10,000 gain			1,000†				
S's adjusted (equity method) net earnings			$107,530	(100%)	107,530		
To defer P's $12,000 gain on the sale of land to S					(12,000)*		
P's gain on purchase of U's bonds					10,000*^{n}		
P's 19x1 amortization of the $10,000 discount on U bonds included in $80,000 earnings figure ($10,000 ÷ 10 years)					(1,000)*^{n}		
P's adjusted (equity method) net earnings also consolidated net earnings					$193,710		
Minority interest							$6,090

* These items are adjustments of the $80,000 separate entity earning amount from P's book and must be reflected whether the income of U, T, and S is consolidated with P or reported under the equity method.

† It should be noted that *consolidated* depreciation (and not T's depreciation) is overstated and that the reduction in consolidated depreciation will increase earnings and this increase is attributable to S the selling corporation. Gains and losses always belong to the seller.

^{n} All four of these adjustments are due to P's purchase of U's bonds from an outside entity.

Illustration 8–14
CONVERSION TO EQUITY METHOD WITH TAX EFFECTS

	U	T	S		P		Minority
Separate entity earnings	$60,000	$30,000	$40,000		$80,000		—0—
U's gain on P's bond purchase less 30% tax, 1/1/x1	1,400						
U's 19x1 amortization of bond premium included in the $60,000 earnings figure (4,000 ÷ 20 years) − (30% tax)	(140)						
U's adjusted (equity method) net earnings	$61,260			(85%)	52,071	(10%)	6,126[a]	(5%) $3,063
T's adjusted net earnings		$30,000		(80%)	24,000	(10%)	3,000[a]	(10%) 3,000
To defer $10,000 gain on sale to T less 30% tax			(7,000)				
To restore 5,000/50,000 × 10,000 gain less 30% tax			700				
S's adjusted (equity method) net earnings			$109,771	(100%)	109,771[a]		
To defer P's $12,000 gain on the sale of land to S less 30% tax					(8,400)*		
P's gain on purchase of U's bonds less 30% tax					7,000*		
P's 19x1 amortization of the 10,000 discount on U bonds included in 80,000 earnings figure (10,000 ÷ 10 years) less 30% tax					(700)*		
P's adjusted (equity method) net earnings also consolidated net earnings					$196,797		
Minority interest							$6,063

* These items are adjustments of the $80,000 separate entity earning amount from P's book and must be reflected whether the income of U, T, and S is consolidated with P or reported under the equity method.

[a] This assumes that the "indefinite reversal criterion" have been met thus there is no second tax on the undistributed earnings of the subsidiaries; at this level of ownership (80 percent or more) there would be a 100 percent dividend received deduction in any event.

years until maturity and bear interest at 6 percent. U issued these 20-year, 6 percent bonds 10 years before this purchase for $104,000. Converting from separate earning to the equity method now requires consideration of these intercorporate transactions.

It should be noted (in Illustration 8–13) that only the deferral, restoration, and advance recognition entries affect consolidated net earnings and only these entries can affect minority interest. Offset entries affect neither consolidated net earnings nor minority interest. For example, the cash portion of the interest revenue and interest expense ($100,000 × 6%) on the books of P and U, respectively, does not impact on the computation of equity method or consolidated net earnings. In other words, the $6,000 of cash paid by U as interest on the $100,000 face value of the bonds has reduced U's separate entity earnings by $6,000 and has increased P's separate entity earnings by $6,000. These amounts of revenue and expense are offset so as not to overstate interest revenue and interest expense in the consolidated earnings statement; however, these amounts are recognized (not offset) in separate financial statements and in the computation of minority interest. Thus, U's $60,000 of separate earnings is not increased by offsetting U's interest expense against P's interest revenue in the calculation of the minority interest.

The only entries which can impact on minority interest are those entries which can increase or decrease the total earnings of the group. And even then these entries must affect a subsidiary in which there is also a minority interest (with the possible exception of reciprocal interests).

The first solution to the P, S, T, and U problem ignores the income tax effects. Illustration 8–14 shows the tax effects assuming separate returns were filed with a flat 30 percent effective tax rate.

Reporting for Tiered Operations where the Subsidiaries Were Acquired by Purchase

The analysis process for purchased subsidiaries is the same as that just shown for poolings except that the separately reported earnings of the subsidiaries must be adjusted for any expensing of cost in excess of book value (or vice versa) at acquisition. In addition, if any of the assets affected by the cost in excess of book value (or vice versa) are sold, there will be a reversal of the permanent basis difference between tax and books. This can affect the tax provision.

RECIPROCAL INTERESTS

A reciprocal interest is a situation in which a lower tier subsidiary has an investment in a higher tier subsidiary or in the common parent corporation. Returning to the P, S, T, and U affiliation, assume ownership interests as shown in Illustration 8–15.

If in Illustration 8–15 the *separate* earnings of P, S, T, and U with no intercorporate transactions are $80,000, $40,000, $30,000, and $60,000,

Illustration 8–15

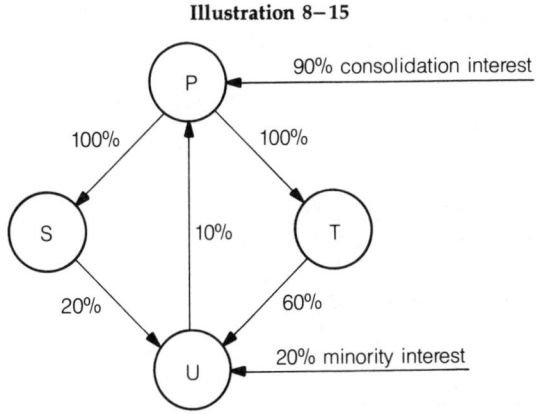

respectively, the consolidated earnings will change because of the different ownership percentages and because of the 10 percent reciprocal interest of U in P. Two recognized methods of accounting exist for a reciprocal interest. The first method is simply to recognize it in the computation of consolidated net earnings, and the second method is to treat the reciprocal interest of the subsidiary in the parent (in this case) as treasury stock.

Recognition of Reciprocal Interests

The computation under method 1, in this case would be made as shown in Illustration 8–16.

More minority interests make the problem only slightly more complex, as shown in Illustration 8–17 which assumes the same separate earnings as were used in Illustration 8–16.

The rationale underlying the recognition method is recognition of the fact that the minority interest owns, albeit indirectly, part of the parent corporation.

Treasury Stock Treatment of Reciprocal Interests

When a subsidiary owns shares of the parent, the authoritative position is nonrecognition of this ownership of the parent.

Illustration 8–16

$$P = \$80{,}000 + S + T$$
$$S = \$40{,}000 + .2U$$
$$T = \$30{,}000 + .6U$$
$$U = \$60{,}000 + .1P$$
$$S = \$40{,}000 + .2(\$60{,}000 + .1P)$$
$$S = \$52{,}000 + .02P$$
$$T = \$30{,}000 + .6(\$60{,}000 + .1P)$$
$$T = \$66{,}000 + .06P$$

$$P = \$80{,}000 + \$52{,}000 + .02P + \$66{,}000 + .06P$$
$$P = \$198{,}000 + .08P$$
$$.92P = \$198{,}000$$
$$P = \$215{,}217$$

$$U = \$60{,}000 + .1(\$215{,}217)$$
$$U = \$81{,}522$$

Thus:

Consolidation interest, .9($215,217)	= $193,695
Minority interest, .2($81,522)	= 16,305
Total separate earnings ($80,000 + $40,000 + $30,000 + $60,000)	= $210,000

Shares of *the* parent held by *a* subsidiary should not be treated as outstanding stock in the consolidated balance sheet (emphasis added).[6]

It should be noted that this method is consistent with the single entity concept of consolidation. If this were a single legal entity, shares of the parent held by a subsidiary (the subsidiary would have to be a branch in a single legal entity) would be classified as treasury stock. But, however, if this were a single entity there would not be a minority interest.

Treating the subsidiary's investment in P as though it were treasury stock (not outstanding stock) can impact on the consolidated earnings computation when there is a minority interest. Thus, in the last P, S, T, and U example, U's 10 percent interest in P could be treated as treasury stock to the consolidated entity. With the separate earnings of $80,000, $40,000, $30,000 and $60,000, respectively, the consolidated earnings would be as given in Illustration 8–18.

The consolidation interest under the treasury stock method is $179,600, whereas under the recognition method it was $173,062. But as noted above, the difference is compensated for through changes in the various minority interest amounts.

These two methods produce the same results when there are no minority interests (every subsidiary is owned 100 percent directly or

---

[6] *AICPA Professional Standards,* par. 2051.12. Apparently an investment by a lower tier subsidiary in a higher tier subsidiary should be recognized as they are not considered to be treasury shares within the above quote.

Illustration 8–17

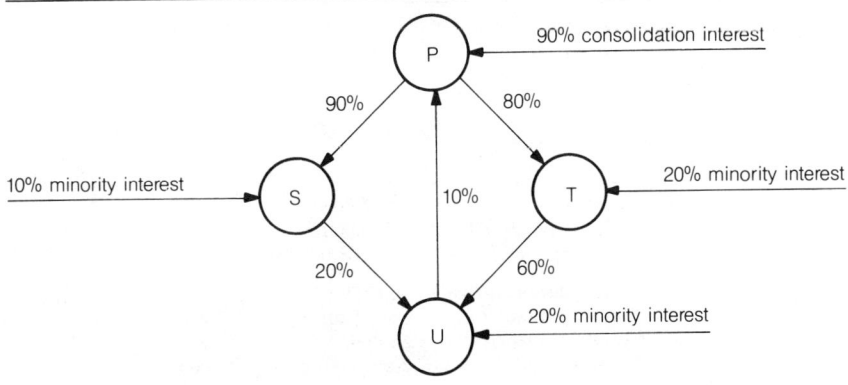

P = $80,000 + .9S + .8T
S = $40,000 + .2U
T = $30,000 + .6U
U = $60,000 + .1P

S = $40,000 + .2($60,000 + .1P)
S = $52,000 + .02P

T = $30,000 + .6($60,000 + .1P)
T = $66,000 + .06P

P = $80,000 + .9($52,000 + .02P) + .8($66,000 + .06P)
P = $80,000 + $46,800 + .018P + $52,800 + .048P
P = $179,600 + .066P
.934P = $179,600
P = $192,291

U = $60,000 + .1($192,291)
U = $79,229

S = $52,000 + .02($192,291)
S = $55,846

T = $66,000 + .06($192,291)
T = $77,537

Thus:

Consolidation interest, .9($192,291)	=	$173,062
Minority interest in S, .1($55,846)	=	5,585
Minority interest in T, .2($77,537)	=	15,507
Minority interest in U, .2($79,229)	=	15,846
Total *separate* earnings		$210,000

Illustration 8–18

P = $80,000 + .9S + .8T
S = $40,000 + .2U
T = $30,000 + .6U
U = $60,000

Thus:

U = $60,000
S = $40,000 + .2($60,000) = $52,000
T = $30,000 + .6($60,000) = $66,000
P = $80,000 + .9($52,000) + .8($66,000) = $179,600

Consolidation interest, 1.0($179,600)	=	$179,600
Minority interest in S, .1($52,000)	=	5,200
Minority interest in T, .2($66,000)	=	13,200
Minority interest in U, .2($60,000)	=	12,000
Total *separate* earnings		$210,000

indirectly). In addition, a minority interest in a subsidiary outside the subsidiary chain with a reciprocal interest will not cause different results; both methods would then produce the same result.

Tax: The income tax law is totally silent on reciprocal interests, but since there is no minority interest deduction on the consolidated tax return, there should be no effect on the actual income tax liability.

The idea of tiered structures is recognized, however, in consolidations and in the computation of the foreign tax credit.

REVIEW QUESTIONS

1. What is a tiered corporate structure?
2. What is a common parent corporation?
3. What are some of the reasons for tiered corporate structures?
4. What is a triangular acquisition?
5. Why do the shareholders of the subsidiary being acquired often desire shares of the common parent rather than of the higher tier subsidiary their corporation will be organized under?
6. Why would a parent corporation want to use its own stock rather than stock of the subsidiary as compensation when a subsidiary is an acquiring corporation?

7. How does a common parent record the acquisition of a lower tier subsidiary by a higher tier subsidiary using stock of the common parent as compensation in the acquisition—
   a. Assuming a purchase.
   b. Assuming a pooling of interests.
8. How does the acquiring subsidiary record the transaction in 7 above assuming (a) a purchase and (b) a pooling of interests?
9. What additional problems are encountered in the acquisition of a parent company in a purchase acquisition?
10. Why can the presence of marketable securities cause a difference between equity method earnings and consolidated earnings?
11. Where is the starting point in preparing consolidated financial statements where there are several tiers of subsidiaries?
12. How are intercorporate transactions treated in calculating the consolidated earnings of a multiple tiered corporate structure?
13. How do offset entries impact on minority interests?
14. What are reciprocal interests?
15. What are the two methods of accounting for reciprocal interests?
16. Which method of accounting for reciprocal interests is in accordance with GAAP?
17. When will the two methods of accounting for reciprocal interest produce the same results?
18. Assuming both a reciprocal and a minority interest and that all subsidiaries and the common parent have positive earnings from their separate operations, which method produces the highest consolidated earnings and why?

PROBLEMS

Problem 1: Triangular Acquisition

W owns 100 percent of X. X is going to acquire 90 percent of the Z stock in exchange for 3,000 shares of W stock. The owners' equity sections of W, X, and Z are as follows just prior to the acquisition:

	W	X	Z
Common stock	$400,000	$100,000	$ 10,000
Additional paid-in capital	200,000	50,000	40,000
Retained earnings	300,000	100,000	200,000
Total owners' equities	$900,000	$250,000	$250,000

The par values of the W, X, and Z shares are $10, $100, and $1, respectively, and their fair market values at the date of acquisition were $100, $200, and $33⅓, respectively. Assume the only differences between book values and fair values are attributable to land.

Required:

1. Record this "acquisition" on the books of each corporation assuming it qualifies for a pooling of interests.
2. Record this acquisition on the books of each corporation assuming it is accounted for as a purchase.

Problem 2: Triangular Asset

P owns R and S 100 percent and 90 percent, respectively. R is going to acquire on 1/1/x4 the assets and liabilities of Z in an exchange for P stock. The owners' equity accounts of Z appear as follows:

	Owners' Equity
Capital stock, $10 par	$100,000
Additional paid-in capital	200,000
Retained earnings, 1/1/x4	400,000
Total	$700,000

Assume that all of the assets and the only liability (notes payable, $100,000) are stated at fair value except for land which is undervalued by $50,000. Assume the Z stock is currently selling at $80 per share and the P stock at $100 per share. Assume 8,000 shares of P ($15 par value stock) are issued in exchange for all of Z's assets and liabilities.

Required:

1. Record this acquisition on the books of P, R, S, and Z as a pooling of interests.
2. Record this acquisition on the books of P, R, S, and Z as a purchase.

Problem 3: ZY Merger

Assume Y and Z are discussing merger possibilities. It is decided that rather than have either Y or Z be the acquiring corporation, a new corporation, ZY, be formed and acquire the stock of both Y and Z in a stock-for-stock exchange. Following are the balance sheets of both Y and Z on 1/1/x1 before the exchange:

	Y		Z	
	Book Value	Fair Value	Book Value	Fair Value
Cash	$ 10,000	$ 10,000	$ 19,000	$ 19,000
Marketable securities (current)	15,000	40,000	5,000	10,000
Receivables	30,000	30,000	10,000	10,000
Inventory (Fifo)	12,000	14,000	6,000	6,000
Plant assets	100,000	120,000	60,000	60,000
Accumulated depreciation	(30,000)		(20,000)	
Land	13,000	30,000	10,000	30,000
Goodwill	-0-	41,000	-0-	25,000
Total assets	$150,000	$285,000	$ 90,000	$160,000
Liabilities	$ 40,000	$ 40,000	$ 30,000	30,000
Capital stock $10 par both Y and Z	10,000		20,000	
Additional paid-in capital	30,000	245,000	80,000	130,000
Retained earnings	70,000		(40,000)	
Total equities	$150,000	$285,000	$ 90,000	$160,000

The plant assets have 10-year remaining lives. Straight-line depreciation is used.

In the 1/1/x1 exchange, 80 percent of the Y shares were acquired in exchange for 196 ZY shares. The Y stock was worth $245 per share, and the ZY stock was worth $1,000 per share. In addition, 90 percent of the Z shares were acquired in exchange for 117 ZY shares. The Z shares were worth $65 per share.

During year 19x1, Y reported earnings of $30,000 and Z of $20,000. They each paid $10,000 in dividends (cash distributions). The 12/31/x1 market values of the portfolios of marketable securities were $12,000 for Y and $6,000 for Z. Any "losses" were properly recognized by each corporation in reporting its earnings.

Due to the nature of these acquisitions Y is accounted for as a purchase and Z is accounted for as a pooling of interests. Use alternative 3 wherever appropriate.

Required:
1. Prepare an investment analysis for ZY's investment in Y as of 12/31/x1.
2. Prepare an investment analysis for ZY's investment in Z as of 12/31/x1.

Problem 4: Tiered Easy

G, H, I, and J Corporations are affiliates. G owns 80 percent of H, 20 percent of I, and 10 percent of J. H owns 60 percent of I and 30 percent of J. I owns 50 percent of J. All ownerships were acquired on 1/1/x4 at a price equal to the underlying book value of the assets less the liabilities except for G's investment in H. When the 80 percent of H was acquired, G paid $40,000 more than the underlying book value due to an understatement of inventory of $20,000 and of land of $10,000 and goodwill of $20,000 on H's books. All acquisitions were accounted for as purchases.

The separate net earnings of each corporation in the current year, 19x4, is as follows and these figures do not include either equity method nor cost method earnings from lower tier subsidiaries:

	19x4 Separate Earnings
G	$150,000
H	160,000
I	30,000
J	(60,000)
Total	$280,000

In addition, J sold on 7/1/x4 land to G for $50,000 that cost J $20,000. This gain is included in J's separate earnings. The companies file separate tax returns, and there is a flat 30 percent tax rate.

Required:

1. Prepare a diagram showing *all* the various ownership interests.
2. Prepare a schedule (using the following headings) which culminates in consolidated net earning and in the total minority interest share of current earning.

J	I	H	G	Minority

3. Prepare a reconciliation of consolidated earnings and minority interest to the $280,000 total separate earnings.

Problem 5: A, B, C, and D Tiered Ownership

As of 1/1/x1 A corporation owns 80 percent of B, 60 percent of C, and 10 percent of D. B Corporation owns 30 percent of C and 80 percent of D. C Corporation owns 10 percent of D. Their reported 19x1 earnings not including dividend revenue nor earning from investments in affiliated corporations were as follows:

Corporation	Reported Earnings	Dividends Paid
A	$ 40,000	$ (5,000)
B	(10,000)	(4,000)
C	18,000	(3,000)
D	90,000	(40,000)

The above earnings do include the following intercorporate transactions:

1. On 1/1/x1 A sold a machine to D for $60,000; this machine had originally cost A $80,000 and $48,000 in depreciation had been taken on it. D is depreciating this asset using the straight-line method over a four-year remaining life. This is the same depreciation method and remaining useful life used by A.
2. B sold land to C for $40,000; B had originally paid $55,000 for this land.

3. On 1/1/x1 A acquired B for $40,000 in excess of the underlying book value. This was attributable to machinery with a 10-year life, with straight-line depreciation being used. All other intercorporate stock investments were made at book value.
4. The indefinite reversal criteria has been met on all intercorporate earnings.

The corporations file separate income tax returns and there is a flat 30 percent tax rate.

Required:

1. Prepare a diagram showing all ownership interests.
2. Using either the following headings or linear equations compute *both* the consolidated net earnings and the minority interest deduction for the earnings statement.

D	C	B	A	Minority

Problem 6: Market Value (MV), Inc.

On 1/1/x5 MV, Inc., acquired 90 percent of the stock of Busy, Inc., in a stock-for-stock exchange. MV exchanged 5,000 shares of its previously unissued stock, with a $25 par value per share, for the Busy stock. The fair value of MV stock was $81 per share while the fair value of the Busy stock was $45 per share. The owners' equity section of Busy appeared as follows immediately before the exchange:

Busy, Inc.	Net Assets
Common stock, $10 par	$100,000
Additional paid-in capital	80,000
Retained earnings	220,000
Total owners' equity, 1/1/x5	$400,000

As of 1/1/x5 all of Busy's recorded assets and liabilities were carried at fair values except for marketable securities, classified as current assets, which were carried at $30,000 and had a $45,000 fair value. MV does not have any marketable securities. Busy reported $30,000 in earnings in 19x5 and paid $10,000 in dividends. Included in the earnings of $30,000 was an aftertax loss of $1,400 due to a decrease in the fair value of the marketable securities portfolio from $45,000 on 1/1/x5 to $28,000 on 12/31/x5. The effective tax rate is a flat 30 percent. The aftertax loss on marketable securities was $1,400 ($2,000 less the $600 anticipated tax benefit from the loss).

Required:

1. Prepare the investment analysis assuming that the highest net earnings are desired and that the acquisition is accounted for as a purchase.
2. Assume that all recorded assets and liabilities were carried at fair value on 1/1/x5 and that the portfolio of marketable securities had a fair value of

$28,000 (instead of $45,000). Busy, Inc., had established a valuation account for the current marketable securities portfolio of $2,000 in order to reduce the $30,000 cost to a $28,000 carrying value. Assume that the fair value of these securities had risen to $40,000 by 12/31/x5. The reported 19x5 earnings were $30,000, including the adjustment for the increased value of the marketable securities portfolio, and dividends of $10,000 were paid in 19x5. Prepare the investment analysis assuming the same owners' equity as before on 1/1/x5.
3. If this acquisition of Busy by MV had been accounted for as a pooling of interests, under 1 and 2 above what would have been the consolidation adjustments for the Busy portfolio of marketable securities?

Problem 7: B, C, and D Marketable Securities

On 1/1/x1 C and D, two unrelated corporations each purchased marketable securities for $10,000 and $20,000, respectively. Each portfolio is classified as a current asset. On 12/31/x1 the fair market values of these portfolios are $8,000 for C's investment and $30,000 for D's investments. This forced C to recognize a $2,000 loss, to establish a valuation account (a contra current asset) in the amount of $2,000, and to establish a deferred tax charge for the timing difference in the amount of $600 ($2,000 × 30% assumed tax rate).

On 1/1/x2 B acquired all of the stock of C and D in separate transactions accounted for as purchase acquisitions. The value of the C and D portfolio had not changed in the one day since 12/13/x1. B had previously acquired marketable securities, classified as current assets, for $20,000. The fair value of this portfolio on 1/1/x2 was $25,000.

For the year ended 12/31/x2, B, C, and D file consolidated financial statements. The fair values of their portfolios of current marketable securities are $15,000, $9,000, and $28,000, respectively. The corporate tax rate is a flat 30 percent, and separate tax returns are filed.

Required:

1. Prepare the 12/31/x2 journal entries to record the lower-of-cost-or-market results for each corporation on its separate financial statements.
2. Prepare the consolidation entry necessary to adjust these separate results to the consolidated result.
3. Assume A Corporation acquires B in a purchase acquisition on 1/1/x3. What is the second (or third) cost basis for marketable securities portfolios for B, C, and D.

Problem 8: Second Cost Basis for Marketable Securities

A Corporation acquires 90 percent of B Corporation stock on 1/1/x4 for $580,000. B has owned 100 percent of C and 90 percent of D since their inception. The owners' equity section of the financial position statement for B appeared as follows on 1/1/x4:

B CORPORATION

Capital stock, $10 par	$100,000
Additional paid-in capital	200,000
Retained earnings	300,000

The book value of B's assets and liabilities equaled their fair values except for B's investments in C and D which were worth $10,000 and $18,000, respectively, more than their book values.

Each corporation had the following portfolios of marketable securities (all less than 10 percent owned) and considered to be current assets:

Corporation	Original Portfolio Cost	Market Value 1/1/x4	Market Value 12/31/x4
A	$10,000	$ 8,000	$ 6,000
B	20,000	20,000	14,000
C	40,000	50,000	51,000
D	50,000	70,000	60,000

Assume separate tax returns are filed with a flat 30 percent corporate tax rate, and that their separate earnings (excludes either cost or equity method earnings from subsidiaries) and dividends paid were as follows in 19x4. Their separate earnings figures include their separate corporation adjustments for changes in market values of their portfolios of marketable securities.

Corporation	Separate Earnings	Dividends Paid
A	$10,000	$5,000
B	20,000	4,000
C	10,000	3,000
D	30,000	6,000

Required:

1. Prepare in journal format the entries on each corporation's separate books for their marketable securities portfolio at 12/31/x4.
2. Prepare the consolidation entry(s) for marketable securities at 12/31/x4 in journal entry format.
3. Prepare an investment analysis for A's investment in B from 1/1/x4 through 12/31/x4 (use alternative method 3).

Problem 9: Tiered Affiliation Without Intercorporate Transactions

W, X, Y, and Z Corporations are affiliates. W owns 90 percent of X, 80 percent of Y, and 10 percent of Z. X owns 5 percent of Y and 60 percent of Z. Y owns 20 percent of Z.

The separate net incomes of each corporation (not including any income or loss from investments in affiliated corporations) were as stated below. There were no intercorporate transactions, and all stocks were acquired at book values. The requirements for the "indefinite reversal criterion" have also been met.

Corporation	Separate Net Incomes	Dividends Paid
W	$ 80,000	$10,000
X	60,000	5,000
Y	40,000	5,000
Z	(20,000)	2,000
Total	$160,000	

Required:

1. Prepare a diagram showing *all* of the various ownership interests.
2. Using either a schedule with the following headings or linear equations compute the consolidated net income.

Z	Y	X	W	Minority

3. Compute consolidated net income but assume that all corporations in computing their separate incomes had recognized income from affiliates under the cost method. Assume that there were no liquidating dividends.
4. Calculate consolidated net income assuming that all corporations in computing their incomes had recognized income from affiliates under the equity method.

Problem 10: Tiered Affiliation with Intercorporate Transactions
(difficult problem)

A Corporation acquired 90 percent of the stock of B on 1/1/x1 in exchange for 7,000 shares of A stock. The fair market price of the A shares was $81 per share and $63 per share for the B shares. B's owners' equity immediately prior to this acquisition was $10 par value common stock $100,000; additional paid in capital $200,000, and retained earnings $300,000. The book value of all of B's assets and liabilities equaled their fair values except that machinery (with a 10-year remaining life and with straight-line depreciation being used for both book and tax purposes) was worth $20,000 more than its $50,000 book value.

Included in A's marketable securities is a 10 percent ownership of C with a cost and fair value of $24,000 acquired on 7/1/x1. C owns 100 percent of D which had been formed by C several years ago. C's investment in D at 7/1/x1 was $80,000. On 7/1/x1 B acquires 70 percent, or 28,000 shares, of C stock in exchange for 2,100 shares of newly issued A stock then valued at $80 per share. The C stock was valued at $6 per share.

The owners' equity portion of the statement of financial position for C and D as of 7/1/x1 were as follows:

	C	D
Common stock, $1 par	$ 40,000	$10,000
Additional paid-in capital	30,000	20,000
Retained earnings	120,000	50,000
	$190,000	$80,000

The book value of all of C's assets and liabilities equaled their fair values except for the investment in D which was worth $50,000 more than its $80,000 book value. For D the book value of all of its assets and liabilities equaled their fair values except for land which was worth $70,000 but had a book value of only $20,000.

The *separate* earnings of A and B were $100,000 and $60,000 for the year 19x1. The *separate* earnings for C and D for the period 7/1/x1 through 12/31/x1 were $20,000 and $10,000, respectively. On 12/15/x1 A, B, C, and D paid dividends of $40,000, $20,000, $10,000, and $5,000, respectively. Separate tax returns are filed, and the effective tax rate is 30 percent. While the separate earnings figures do not include either equity method earnings nor divided income from affiliates, these amounts do reflect gain or loss on intercorporate transactions. On 12/1/x1 D sold half its land to B for $40,000 cash.

On 10/1/x1 B sold for $72,000 to C all its machinery which had a depreciated basis of $46,250 ($50,000 − $3,750 depreciation 1/1/x1 to 10/1/x1) on B's books. C continued the depreciation method and useful life used by B. C paid $12,000 down and signed six $10,000 notes due one each year for the next 6 years on 10/1 with interest at 10 percent. B accrued $1,500 of interest income and C accrued $1,500 ($60,000 × 10% × ¼ year) of interest expense as of 12/31/x1.

Required:

1. Prepare a diagram showing *all* of the various ownership interests.
2. Assuming the acquisitions of B and C were purchases, use the following headings to prepare a schedule which culminates in consolidated net earnings and in total minority interests in current earnings.

	D	C	B	A	Minority
Separate earnings					

3. Prepare an investment analysis as of 12/31/x1 for every ownership interest in B, C, and D (this will, in effect, complete requirement 2 above).

Problem 11: Reciprocal Interest

A Corporation owns 80 percent of B, 10 percent of C, and 10 percent of D. B owns 70 percent of C and 70 percent of D. C owns 10 percent of D. D owns 20 percent of A. The *separately* reported net earnings (loss) of each corporation were $80,000, $70,000, $60,000, and ($50,000), respectively. No dividends were declared or paid by any corporation. There were no intercorporate transactions, and all stocks, except for A's investment in B, were acquired at book values. B's assets and liabilities were reported at fair values five years ago when the B stock was acquired by A but A paid $32,000 more than this for its 80 percent interest. Goodwill is spread over a 20-year life.

Required:

1. Prepare a diagram showing *all* the various ownership interests.
2. With linear equations calculate the consolidated net earnings and each

minority interest using the recognition method for the reciprocal interest (use alternative method 3 for valuation of goodwill). Assume no second corporate tax on undistributed earnings of any subsidiary.
3. With linear equations calculate the consolidated net earning and each minority interest using the treasury stock method (use alternative method 3 for valuation of goodwill). Assume no second corporate tax on undistributed earnings of any subsidiary.

9
Planning Corporate Acquisitions and Liquidations

Parties to an Acquisition or Combination
Reasons for Corporate Acquisitions
Types of Acquisitions or Combinations with Stock as Compensation
    The Accounting Concept for Taxable and Purchase Acquisitions
    The Accounting Concept for Tax-Free and Pooling Combinations
Some of the Basic Requirements for a Tax-Free Exchange
Some Theoretical Aspects of Pooling
    Pooling and Prior Years
    Origin of Pooling
    Perfect Case for Pooling
    Other Theoretical Questions for Pooling
    Part-Pooling and Part-Purchase
The 12 Requirements for Pooling of Interests Accounting
    Attributes of Combining Corporations
    Manner of Combining Interests
    Absence of Planned Transactions
Planning the Recorded Value of Corporate Assets
    For Financial Reporting
    For Tax Purposes
Other Planning Aspects
The ITT Acquisition of Hartford Fire Insurance Company
    The Acquisition
    The Tax Treatment
    The Pooling of Interests Effects
Pooling in Theoretical Perspective

The previous chapters have introduced, but only superficially, many of the items presented in more depth in this chapter. The rationale for asset or stock acquisitions is examined more closely along with the related and sometimes overriding tax aspects. The 12 pooling requirements are also examined, and an actual pooling combination is reviewed.

PARTIES TO AN ACQUISITION OR COMBINATION

In describing corporate acquisitions and combinations it is sometimes difficult to separately identify the various parties to a transaction. The identification problem is easier in a purchase acquisition than in a pooling combination. Usually in a purchase the buying and the selling corporations or shareholders are easily identified (except perhaps in a reverse acquisition).[1] Terminology thus becomes quite important especially if one is attempting to read the professional literature.

Basic combinations and acquisitions where stock is used as compensation can be identified as (1) stock-for-stock or (2) stock-for-asset transactions. In a stock-for-stock combination (the term combination is normally used when the transaction is accounted for as a pooling of interests), all corporations involved are called combining corporations but one is also called the issuing corporation. In Illustration 9–1 both A and B would be combining corporations, although only A can also be identified as the corporation issuing stock. In a stock-for-assets acquisition or combination there is also usually only one issuing corporation.

If Illustration 9–1 had been accounted for as a purchase, A would normally be the purchasing or acquiring corporation with the shareholders of B the sellers in a stock-for-stock acquisition and B Corporation the seller in a stock-for-assets acquisition. In either case B would be the acquired corporation.

For federal income tax purposes the designation "combining corporation" has no fixed meaning. Both taxable and tax-free—stock-for-stock or stock-for-assets—transactions are called acquisitions.

REASONS FOR CORPORATE ACQUISITIONS

Some motivations for equity investments and asset acquisitions were presented in Chapter 3. But additional motivations, both tax related and nontax related, exist when the objective is to acquire an entire corporation or substantially all of its assets.

---

[1] In reverse acquisitions a larger corporation is acquired by a smaller one and the larger corporation's shareholders end up controlling the new combined entity.

Illustration 9–1

A. Stock for stock

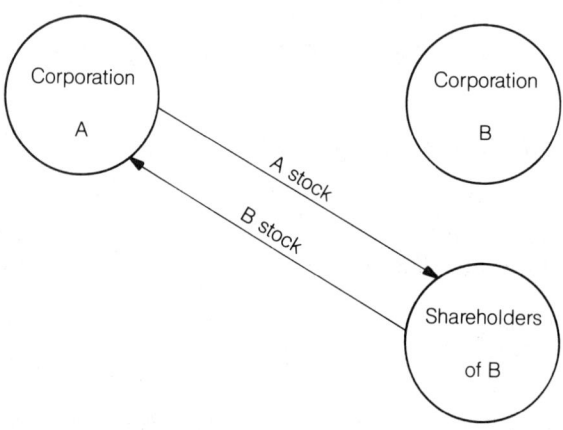

B. Stock for assets

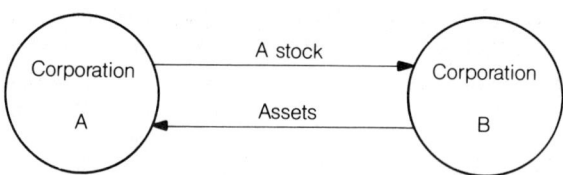

Some nontax reasons would include:

1. A desire for growth.
2. A desire for diversification.
3. A desire for vertical or for horizontal integration (whether or not within the antitrust framework).

Some tax reasons would include:

1. A desire to avoid the accumulated earnings tax (especially acute for profitable, privately held corporations with large amounts of working capital).[2]

---

[2] This is a penalty tax for unnecessary accumulations of earnings. It is not assessed very often, but when it has to be paid it is in addition to the regular corporate income tax. The penalty tax is supposed to encourage dividend payments.

2. The desire to obtain the tax attributes of the acquired corporation (recent tax changes have decreased or may soon decrease the availability of these tax attributes such as net operating losses (NOLs)).
3. The desire to use tax attributes may also be present from the viewpoint of a large corporation with excess tax attributes such as NOLs, investment tax credits, and foreign tax credits. In this case the corporation with unused attributes is often trying to acquire a business which, through operations, will produce taxable income such that when combined with the acquiring corporation (often in a consolidated tax return) will permit the application of these tax saving attributes.
4. The desire to obtain large future tax deductions (losses which have not as yet been realized by the corporation being acquired) resulting from a basis for assets in excess of their fair values.
5. The desire on the part of the owners of a usually small, often family-owned, businesses to, in effect "sell out" without the payment of any income tax. When the "sale" is made (often by an exchange of stock with a large conglomerate corporation), the highly profitable, high-risk small business investment will have been converted into an investment in a large diversified corporation and without a tax payment. This may be very desirable when the last family member interested in the family business is near retirement.

TYPES OF ACQUISITIONS OR COMBINATIONS WITH STOCK AS COMPENSATION

By now you should be familiar with the two basic types of acquisitions or combinations where stock is issued as compensation (1) in exchange for the outstanding stock of the corporation being "acquired" (an indirect asset acquisition) or (2) in exchange for the assets of a corporation (a direct asset acquisition). There are possible mutations from these two basic types such as where a subsidiary issues the parent's stock to acquire voting control of the stock of another corporation or of its assets (a triangular acquisition) or where a new corporation is formed and exchanges its stock with the shareholders of what would otherwise have been the acquiring and acquired corporations. This merely creates a new entity and may result in a name change rather than continuing either of the combining entities. For example, to illustrate the latter situation, (1) Bad-Luck Corporation might issue stock in exchange for either the assets or the stock of Worse-Luck Corporation, or (2) Worse-Luck could issue stock for either the assets or stock of Bad-Luck, or (3) a new corporation, Good-Luck, might be established and its stock could then be exchanged for either the assets or the stock of both Bad-Luck and Worse-Luck.

Nevertheless, sticking for now with the two basic types—stock for stock or stock for assets—there are in addition for both financial reporting and tax purposes two types of accounting for these acquisitions or combinations. For tax purposes these transactions are accounted for as either taxable or tax-free events, and for financial reporting the transactions are accounted for as either purchases or poolings of interests. The requirements for classification of an acquisition as tax free differ in many respects from the requirements for designating the combination a pooling. Thus, for example, an "acquisition" might be tax free for tax purposes but accounted for as a purchase for financial reporting or if it met the designated financial requirements it would have to be accounted for as a pooling.

For tax purposes, if the requirements for a tax-free transaction are met, then that treatment is required. Thus, taxable or tax-free status is not directly elective. The desired status must be achieved by either meeting or failing the established requirements for tax-free status. The same is true for a pooling as opposed to a purchase, but the requirements are different (see Illustration 9–2).

Illustration 9–2
THE RANGE OF POSSIBLE ACCOUNTING METHODS

Basic Type of Exchange	Financial Reporting	Tax Reporting	Financial and Tax Accounting Concept Applied and Results
Stock for stock	Purchase	Taxable	Same in concept and often different in results
	or	or tax-free	Different in concept and results
	Pooling	Taxable	Different in concept and results
		or tax-free	Same in concept but often different in results
Stock for assets	Purchase	Taxable	Same in concept and results
	or	or tax-free	Different in concept and results
	Pooling	Taxable	Different in concept and results
		or tax-free	Same in concept and often different in results

The Accounting Concept for Taxable and Purchase Acquisitions

In both cases, stock for stock or stock for assets, the accounting concept applied to the acquisition would be the same for tax and for financial reporting if it were a taxable acquisition and accounted for as a purchase. The concept is that assets have been bought. The acquiring corporation would record the item(s) acquired (either stock or assets) at the price paid (the fair value of the stock issued).

When assets are acquired, the price paid must be allocated among the acquired assets. In a truly arm's-length transaction the fair value of the assets received less the fair value of liabilities assumed, if any, should equal the fair value of the stock issued to achieve the acquisition. In this case, after the acquisition the tax basis and the book basis should usually be identical. Operating results will then differ only when different accounting methods are used for book and tax purposes.

In the indirect asset acquisition, stock for stock, the allocation of the price paid to the assets and liabilities acquired for financial accounting purposes takes place in the consolidation entries (the substitution entry and subsequent adjustments) necessary to produce consolidated financial statements. For tax purposes, however, even in a consolidated tax return, there is no adjustment of the recorded assets of the acquired subsidiary to reflect the price paid for the stock. Thus, any cost in excess of book value (or vice versa) never impacts on taxable income (unless the stock investment is sold or if the subsidiary is liquidated into the parent). This is an important distinction and one that frequently enters into the planning of acquisitions or combinations. For example, assume that B Corporation has assets (all depreciable) with a book value and tax basis of $500,000 and a fair value of only $300,000 (no liabilities). Then, in an acquisition of the B stock by A Corporation for $300,000 (of stock, cash, or other compensation), the book value in excess of cost would be $200,000. For financial reporting in consolidated statements the assets would be reported at $300,000 less any depreciation on this $300,000 value since the acquisition. For tax purposes the price paid for the stock is ignored and the depreciation would be calculated from the $500,000 basis amount. This will result in $200,000 more depreciation for tax purposes than for book purposes, and at a 46 percent corporate income tax rate this would save $92,000 in income taxes. (This is an example of the previously listed fourth tax reason for corporate acquisitions.)

If, on the other hand, $700,000 were paid to acquire the stock of a corporation with assets carried at only $500,000, consolidated financial statements would allocate the $200,000 of cost in excess of book value to the assets and liabilities of the acquired corporation. Depreciation, and so forth, would then be measured from the newly allocated $700,000 cost. For tax purposes, however, only the $500,000 basis would generate deductions such as depreciation on either separate tax returns or in a consolidated tax return. In this case the newly acquired subsidiary, *if acquired in a taxable exchange,* could be liquidated into its parent corporation, and the $700,000 cost of the stock would be allocated to the assets received. This liquidation must be made within two years of the acquisition of the stock of the acquired corporation. If the liquidation occurs after the two-year period, the basis of the assets carries over from the liquidated corporation to the acquiring corporation, and the cost in excess of the underlying book value of the stock disappears without producing a tax deduction.

Obviously, in a taxable acquisition with a large cost in excess of book value there is a strong tax motive to liquidate the acquired corporation within two years. If, on the other hand, this liquidation has not taken place within two years, there is a strong tax motive not to liquidate the subsidiary but instead, if disposition is desired, to sell the stock of the subsidiary because of its higher basis.

The Accounting Concept for Tax-Free and Pooling Combinations

Again, in both cases, tax free (for tax purposes) and pooling (for book purposes), the concept applied is the same whether this is a stock-for-stock or a stock-for-assets exchange. The concept is that no sale has taken place; thus there is no gain or loss recognized to either party and no reason to change the carrying amount of the assets and liabilities of either corporation. The basis of the assets, therefore, remains the same.

There is, however, a difference between a tax-free exchange and a pooling to the corporation issuing stock. Under a pooling the investment account for a stock-for-stock exchange is reported at the book value of the underlying net assets. For tax-free exchange purposes, however, the basis of the stock carries over; or in other words, the investment account equals the combined bases that the former shareholders had in the stock (of the nonissuing combining company) which has been exchanged in the transaction.[3]

Even though the investment in subsidiary stock account may differ in a pooling and tax-free exchange, the bases of the assets used in measuring earnings would be the same *if* the asset bases were identical for book and tax purposes before the combination. In reality, at least for major corporations, this is seldom the case; different accounting methods such as used in depreciation measurements and useful lives create basis differences between the book and tax records. These bases differences then result in major differences between pretax financial earnings and the taxable income computation.

If this were a stock-for-assets and liabilities combination, the carryover of the bases of the net assets to the corporation issuing the stock would also result in the same amount being recorded on the books of the corporation formerly owning the assets, as an investment in stock of

---

[3] *Internal Revenue Code*, sec. 362(b).

the acquiring corporation. (In this case the corporation formerly owning the net assets is usually liquidated by distributing the acquiring corporation's stock.) The recorded asset and liability bases would be the same for both book and tax purposes only if the tax and financial reporting bases of the net assets were identical before the tax-free exchange and pooling combination.

To illustrate these rules assume the data in Illustration 9–3 reflect the situation in which A Corporation issues its stock in a combination with B Corporation.

Illustration 9–3

	B Corporation
Fair value of B's net assets	$800,000
Book value of B's net assets	500,000
Tax basis of B's net assets	400,000
Tax and book bases of B shareholders' investments in B stock	100,000
Fair value of the A stock issued in the combination	800,000

Illustration 9–4
IF STOCK-FOR-STOCK-EXCHANGE AND IF THE COMBINATION IS TAX-FREE AND A POOLING

Basis of B's assets in the consolidated financial statements	$500,000
Basis of B's assets in a consolidated tax return (or separate return)	400,000
Basis of A's investment in B stock for separate financial statements	500,000
Basis of A's investment in B stock for tax purposes	100,000
Basis of the A stock now in the hands of the former B shareholders for tax purposes	100,000

Illustration 9–4 then reflects the situation where A Corporation acquires 100 percent of the B stock by issuing A stock in a stock-for-stock exchange with the B shareholders. If B were then liquidated into A (for tax purposes), the tax basis of the assets ($400,000) would replace the basis of the investment account ($100,000) and the $300,000 difference disappears without a tax impact.[4] For book purposes, in a liquidation of the subsidiary, the assets would retain their total $500,000 value which equals the investment account.

---
[4] *Internal Revenue Code,* sec. 334(b)(1).

Illustration 9–5
IF STOCK-FOR-STOCK EXCHANGE AND IF THE ACQUISITION IS TAXABLE AND A PURCHASE

Basis of B's assets and consolidated financial statements	$800,000
Basis of B's assets in a consolidated tax return	400,000*
Basis of A's investment in B stock for separate financial statements	800,000
Basis of A's investment in B stock for tax purposes	800,000*
Basis of the A stock now in the hands of the former B shareholders for tax purposes (This represents the $100,000 old basis plus the $700,000 of taxable gain reported on the exchange.)	800,000

* There is now a strong tax incentive to liquidate B into A within two years in order to step up the tax basis of the net assets of B from $400,000 to $800,000. *Internal Revenue Code,* sec. 334(b)(2).

Illustration 9–6
IF STOCK-FOR-STOCK EXCHANGE AND IF THE ACQUISITION IS TAXABLE AND A POOLING*

Basis of B's assets in consolidated financial statements	$500,000
Basis of B's assets in a consolidated tax return (or separate return)	400,000†
Basis of A's investment in B stock for separate financial statements	500,000
Basis of A's investment in B stock for tax purposes	800,000†
Basis of the A stock now in the hands of the former B shareholders for tax purposes	800,000

* Accounting literature sometimes refers to this as a "taxable pooling."
† There would be pressure to liquidate in order to increase the tax basis of the assets from $400,000 to $800,000. Without liquidation there are permanent differences to B Corporation of $100,000 ($500,000 − $400,000) with the aggregate book basis being higher than the aggregate tax basis. If liquidation takes place, the permanent difference will be $300,000 ($800,000 − $500,000) with the aggregate tax basis being the higher. These permanent differences would make accounting for income taxes quite complex.

Illustration 9–7
IF STOCK-FOR-STOCK EXCHANGE AND IF THE ACQUISITION IS TAX-FREE AND A PURCHASE

Basis of B's assets in consolidated financial statements	$800,000
Basis of B's assets in a consolidated tax return (or separate return)	400,000
Basis of A's investment in B stock for separate financial statements	800,000
Basis of A's investment in B stock for tax purposes	100,000*
Basis of the A stock now in the hands of the former B shareholders for tax purposes	100,000

* In a liquidation the tax basis of the assets, $400,000, would carryover and replace the $100,000 Investment in B Stock account, but the tax basis of the assets could not be increased to their $800,000 fair value.

Illustrations 9–5, 9–6, and 9–7 reflect the same stock-for-stock exchange as shown in Illustration 9–4 except that the accounting concepts (pooling and purchase) and the tax concepts (tax free and taxable) are changed to show the four possible results. Illustration 9–8 then brings together the prior four illustrations.

Illustration 9–8
IN SUMMARY—STOCK-FOR-STOCK EXCHANGE

		Illustrations		
For Tax Purposes—	9–4 Tax-Free	9–5 Taxable	9–6 Taxable	9–7 Tax-Free
For Book Purposes—	Pooling	Purchase	Pooling	Purchase
1. Basis of B's assets in consolidated financial statements	$500,000	$800,000	$500,000	$800,000
2. Basis of B's assets in a consolidated tax return (as in separate returns)	400,000†	400,000*	400,000*	400,000†
3. Basis of A's investment in B stock for separate financial statements	500,000	800,000	500,000	800,000
4. Basis of A's investment in B stock for tax purposes	100,000†	800,000*	800,000*	100,000†
5. Basis of the A stock now in the hands of the former B shareholders for tax purposes ...	100,000	800,000	800,000	100,000

* Liquidation within two years would be desirable for tax purposes as the basis of B's assets would then increase by $400,000.
† Liquidation at any time would carryover the basis of B's assets ($400,000) and replace A's investment in B stock ($100,000), but it would not increase the basis of the assets to their $800,000 fair value.

SOME OF THE BASIC REQUIREMENTS FOR A TAX-FREE EXCHANGE

In any attempt to arrange a tax-free exchange, tax experts (in the Subchapter C area of the *Internal Revenue Code*) should be consulted. This is not an area for a novice, and the general rules discussed in this text are far too superficial to be used as a guideline for structuring a corporate reorganization.

Basically a corporate reorganization can be tax free if it is

1. A stock for stock (type B)[5] exchange where—
    a. "Solely" voting stock (preferred or common) is issued in the exchange,

---
[5] A type B exchange (or an A or C) get their names from the particular *Internal Revenue Code* section number; in this case it is sec. 368(a)(1)(B).

b. At least 80 percent of the stock of the nonissuing corporation is acquired[6] or
2. A stock for assets (type C) exchange where—
   a. "Substantially all" of the assets are acquired (90 percent of net assets or 70 percent of gross assets), and
   b. Voting stock is issued in the exchange (and in some cases cash up to 20 percent of the assets acquired may be used).[7]

There are many refinements on the tax-free stock-for-stock and stock-for-asset exchanges identified above, and there are also other ways to make an acquisition a tax-free reorganization. In addition to the many statutory requirements (many of which have not been listed), there are also judicial requirements, such as continuity of interests, and business purposes (established in landmark court cases), to be met if the transaction is to remain tax free after examination. Even the tax experts do not trust themselves in this area; they will usually (except perhaps in a clear-cut stock-for-stock case) ask the Internal Revenue Service for a private letter ruling on how a proposed transaction will be taxed if it is undertaken. Normally a transaction will not be entered into until a favorable ruling has been received.

There is also danger in a taxable acquisition when stock is issued. If the requirements of a tax-free reorganization are met, that treatment is required. This might force a "seller" to forgo a tax loss that had been contemplated. Obviously the area of corporate acquisitions and reorganizations is one requiring the advice of extremely knowledgeable tax experts.

It should be realized that the "selling" shareholders in a stock-for-stock exchange will normally ask a higher price in a taxable exchange of stock when a gain will result from the exchange than they would if the exchange can be structured as a tax-free exchange. The ability to "sell out" and postpone the income tax on any gain arising from the transaction is a strong tax inducement for owners of small corporations to enter into tax-free stock-for-stock exchanges with large conglomerates.

When the aggregate tax basis of the assets is far below the total fair value of the assets, the acquiring corporation will normally want a taxable acquisition in a stock-for-stock exchange. It must be a taxable acquisition in order to liquidate within two years to get the stepped-up basis for the assets. In a liquidation of the newly acquired subsidiary there is almost always some tax cost (such as depreciation recapture) which must then be borne by the parent corporation.

It should be apparent that the tax desires of the acquiring corporation and the acquired corporation's shareholders are frequently conflicting.

---
[6] Ibid., sec. 368(a)(1)(B).
[7] Ibid., sec. 368(a)(1)(C).

Thus, knowledge of the tax consequences is essential in the bargaining process.

The accounting requirements for financial reporting may also affect how the acquiring corporation wishes to structure the acquisition.

SOME THEORETICAL ASPECTS OF POOLING

Pooling and Prior Years

Because the pooling of interests accounting concept is theoretically based on the idea that the combination of two or more previously separate corporations should be treated as though they had always been together, intercorporate transactions prior to the combination should receive the same consolidation treatment as those occurring after the combination. Thus, if A sold land at a gain to B in 19x1 and if B still owned that land when A and B were combined in a pooling in 19x8, for consolidation purposes B's land is overstated and A's retained earnings is overstated by the aftertax effect of the gain and A's prepaid tax is understated by the tax on that gain. If instead of land, this had been a depreciable asset, the consolidation entries must consider the effects of B's increased depreciation in measuring the remaining deferral. If B had sold the asset in 19x7 before the pooling, no consolidation adjustments would be necessary.

In practice, entries for periods prior to a pooling are sometimes ignored. Perhaps in most cases they are either nonexistent or not material. Theoretically, however, intercorporate transactions occurring prior to a pooling of interests should be treated the same as those occurring after the pooling. The effects on the new subsidiary's retained earnings, if it were the selling corporation, should be reflected as an adjustment of retained earnings before the exchange of shares and will impact on consolidated retained earnings.

Origin of Pooling

The concept of pooling has some of its history in the "tax-free" exchange rules of the *Internal Revenue Code*.[8] Tax-free exchanges predate pooling of interests accounting for financial reporting by about a decade.[9] There is, however, no restatement of prior earnings for transactions prior to the exchange for tax purposes (except for the so-called initial inventory adjustment if a consolidated tax return is filed, but this is due to consolidation and not to the stock acquisition).

---

[8] Russell D. Langer, *Accounting as a Variable In Mergers* (New York: Arno Press, 1978), pp. 123–25.

[9] Ibid., p. 126. Because of the carryover of asset bases, the tax-free exchange concept caused problems in determining the rate base in early public utility hearings.

Perfect Case for Pooling

For those persons drafting the rules which comprise "generally accepted accounting principles" (GAAP), the decision is often one of determining where to draw the limits. This is certainly true for pooling.

The most conservative position while still permitting pooling would perhaps allow pooling only where brother and sister corporations exist. Illustration 9–9 shows a perfect brother-sister situation.[10] B and C Cor-

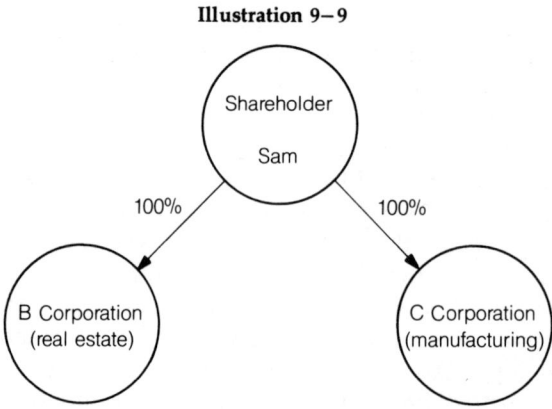

Illustration 9–9

porations are brother-sister because they have an identical shareholder. Similar shareholder groups create this form of controlled corporations.

In Illustration 9–9 the same shareholder(s) own identical interests in each corporation and have owned them since the inception of both corporations. The only real reason for two separate corporations was perhaps to protect the real estate from creditor claims in the event that the manufacturing operation proved to be unsuccessful. If after success is assured, the shareholder(s) desire to combine the two corporations, they could do so through a pooling (stock-for-stock exchange). They could also do this by liquidating one corporation and contributing its assets to the other to achieve the same effect. This is about as perfect a case for pooling as can be made.

Other Theoretical Questions for Pooling

If two corporations have different shareholders but still want to combine their corporations by pooling their shareholders' interests, should

---

[10] The terminology *brother-sister corporations* comes from the tax law. A brother-sister group is as much of a controlled group of corporations as are parent and subsidiary corporations.

this be allowed as a pooling? The GAAP's answer is yes, but this presents another problem. Should the shareholders of two radically different size corporations be allowed to pool their interests? The GAAP answer is again yes even when the shareholders who own 100 percent of A Corporation (the smaller corporation) end up with less than say .001 percent of B Corporation. Thus, relative size makes no difference. According to GAAP the A shareholders would not have sold; they would have merely pooled their 100 percent control of A for a .001 percent control of B.

If there are many shareholders, seldom will all agree with the idea of combining. How many shareholders as represented by voting interest may opt out without destroying the pooling concept? Here GAAP has established a rule that 90 percent of the voting interest must agree to exchange their interest for voting interest in the acquiror.

If less than 90 percent agree, how much manipulation should be permitted to obtain 90 percent? If the dissident shareholders will not sell to shareholders who favor the exchange, the GAAP rules permit no manipulation through redemption or new issues.

Part-Pooling and Part-Purchase

In discussing the possibilities in accounting for business combinations the Accounting Principles Board said,

> The Board also concludes that the two methods [purchase or pooling of interests] are not alternatives in accounting for the same business combination. A single method should be applied to an entire combination; the practice now known as part-purchase, part-pooling is not acceptable.[11]

Historically the part-purchase, part-pooling method was sometimes applied when both cash (or other assets) and stock was used to acquire control of another corporation. In an acquisition of either the assets or stock of another corporation, the cash portion of the price paid represented the purchase part and the stock issued by the acquiror represented the pooling part. This greatly complicates the allocation of any cost in excess of book value and fortunately is now "prohibited."

But in some ways the part-purchase, part-pooling method still exists. This can be illustrated with two examples. First, assume A acquires 100 percent of the stock of D on 1/1/x1 in exchange for both cash and stock of A. If the A stock were worth $900,000 and if $100,000 of cash were used to buy the stock of dissenting shareholders (10 percent interest), the $1 million "acquisition" could be a pooling! But the cash payment would have to be treated as a purchase.

---

[11] *APB Opinion No. 16*, "Business Combinations," par. 43.

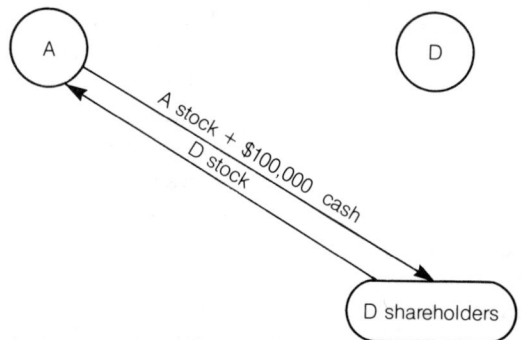

Second, if A had only acquired 90 percent of the D stock on 1/1/x1 and solely in exchange for A stock the acquisition would be a pooling (assuming all 12 requirements are met). Now, if at a subsequent date A acquires the remaining 10 percent for stock (or for cash), this 10 percent portion must be accounted for as a purchase.[12] This permits 90 percent to be accounted for as a pooling with the subsequently acquired 10 percent to be accounted for as a purchase.[13]

Going back to the $1,000,000 "acquisition" of D by A Corporation, the investment analysis might appear as in Illustration 9–10.

Illustration 9–10

	Net Assets	90 Percent Stock for Stock	10 Percent for Cash
Capital stock	$100,000	$ 90,000	$ 10,000
Additional paid-in capital	40,000	36,000	4,000
Retained earnings	260,000	234,000	26,000
Book value	$400,000	$360,000	40,000
Cost in excess of book value			60,000
Price paid			$100,000

If the two portions of the investment in D were kept separate, the substitution entries would appear as follows:

Substitution for the pooling portion:

Capital stock	90,000	
Additional paid-in capital	36,000	
Retained earnings	234,000	
Investment in D stock		360,000

---

[12] APB, *Accounting for Business Combinations: Accounting Interpretations of Section 1091,* par. 25.090.

[13] Ibid., par. 26.100.

Substitution for the purchase portion:

Capital stock	10,000	
Additional paid-in capital	4,000	
Retained earnings	26,000	
Cost in excess of book value	60,000	
Investment in D stock		100,000

The cost in excess of book value theoretically must be assigned to the related assets and liabilities based on fair values with any excess designated as goodwill. It must also be realized that the $60,000 excess is only 10 percent of the total excess. In earlier chapters the three alternative methods of allocation were discussed, but in those cases a minority interest owned the other stock and in this case A owns 100 percent of D. For ease of illustration assume that all assets and liabilities of D equaled their fair value except for one building where the fair value exceeded book value by $500,000. The substitution entries for the three alternative methods would be as follows (assuming one Investment in D Stock account of $460,000):

	Alternative Methods					
	(3)		(2)		(1)	
Capital stock	100,000		100,000		100,000	
Additional paid-in capital	40,000		40,000		40,000	
Retained earnings	260,000		260,000		260,000	
Building	500,000		500,000		50,000‡	
Goodwill	100,000		10,000		10,000‡	
Investment in D		460,000		460,000		460,000
Appraisal capital		540,000*		450,000†		–0–
	1,000,000	1,000,000				

* 90% × ($500,000 + $100,000) = ·$540,000.
† 90% × $500,000 = $450,000.
‡ 10% × $500,000 and 10% × $100,000.

Reflecting the net assets at fair values under alternative 3 (and except for goodwill under alternative 2) in effect converts the position statement to a purchase rather than a pooling basis. This would also affect consolidated earnings unless the extra depreciation and amortization were charged against appraisal capital instead of impacting on earnings. In practice, alternative 1 would generally be used, and it would have 10 percent of the building reported at fair value (the historical cost to A Corporation) and 90 percent at the older historical cost to D Corporation.

It is perhaps interesting to note that the same *APB Opinion* that makes part-purchase and part-pooling "not acceptable" theoretically, at least, requires its use. In practice, the cost in excess of book value on the purchased portion is frequently charged to goodwill without any effort at allocation. This treatment is rationalized based on a materiality concept.

There are many other problems in establishing rules permitting pooling. Some of these problems are readily apparent from the 12 pooling requirements which follow.

THE 12 REQUIREMENTS FOR POOLING OF INTERESTS ACCOUNTING

It should be noted that while the pooling concept and the tax-free exchange concept are similar, the requirements for a pooling are much more stringent, in most cases, than the requirements for a tax-free exchange. Thus, many acquisitions may qualify as tax-free exchanges but fail the pooling requirements, and for this reason they are accounted for as a purchase for financial reporting. When this happens, even the concept applied is different and only the Cash account will be the same on both sets of books (tax and financial). Permanent differences will exist for almost every account.

Once again the accounting method known as a pooling of interests is required if all 12 conditions are met. Thus, in many situations an "acquisition" can be framed to either meet or fail these requirements, depending on the accounting treatment desired. If only one of the 12 requirements is failed, the purchase method of accounting is required.

The 12 requirements are classified under the three categories of (1) attributes of the combining corporations, (2) manner of combining interests, and (3) absence of planned transactions. These requirements first became applicable to business combinations *initiated after* October 31, 1970.

Attributes of Combining Corporations

Only 2 of the 12 conditions fall under attributes of combining companies. The first of these is:

> (1) Each of the combining companies is autonomous and has not been a subsidiary or division of another corporation within two years before the plan of combination is initiated.[14]

"Combining" with separate units or pieces of one economic entity cannot be accounted for under a pooling of interests concept. In addition, if a corporation had been a subsidiary but is now a separate corporation, it cannot enter into a pooling combination until two years after becoming a separate independent company.

---

[14] *AICPA Professional Standards, Accounting—Current Text* (New York, 1980), par. 1091.46-a. Copyright (1980) by the American Institute of CPAs.

There are exceptions to this first requirement such as where divestiture of assets has been ordered by a governmental or judiciary body and where a subsidiary in a triangular combination uses its parents' stock as its part of the exchange. In the latter case, however, the parent and the other combining corporation must meet the above test.

The second requirement in this category is:

(2) Each of the combining companies is independent of the other combining companies.[15]

The definition of independent means that not more than 10 percent of the outstanding *voting common stock* of any combining corporation is owned at the date of the plan of combination by the combining corporation or corporations. It should be noted that 10 percent is a sizable holding in a large public company.

How voting preferred stock or common stock equivalents are to be treated is not covered in the above requirement.

Manner of Combining Interests

There are seven requirements in the category "manner of combining interests" (numbers 3 through 9); the first of these is:

(3) The combination is effected in a single transaction or is completed in accordance with a specific plan within one year after the plan is initiated.[16]

This prevents the so-called creeping acquisition from being accounted for as a pooling of interests. If the acquisition takes more than one year to complete due to litigation or proceedings of governmental authorities, the 1-year limit is extended.

The fourth requirement is perhaps the most difficult one to describe or comply with.

(4) A corporation offers and issues only common stock with rights identical to those of the majority of its outstanding voting common stock in exchange for substantially all of the voting stock interest of another company at the date the plan of combination is consummated.[17]

This requirement covers situations in which there is more than one class of voting common stock by designating the class with voting control as the majority. But the use of the words "substantially all" requires further definition, and obviously this requirement also needs modification for stock-for-asset combinations.

The "substantially all" test is satisfied if the issuing corporation is-

---

[15] Ibid., par. 1091.46-b.
[16] Ibid., par. 1091.47-a.
[17] Ibid., par. 1091.47-b.

sues voting stock and receives in exchange at least 90 percent of the voting common stock of the combining corporation outstanding at the date the combination is consummated. The remaining 10 percent could be acquired at this date for cash, and the acquisition could still qualify as a pooling as long as some shareholders did not take partly cash and partly stock in the exchange.

In meeting the 90 percent test any shares of the nonissuing combining corporation held by the issuing corporation or its subsidiaries at the date the combination is initiated are excluded. Also excluded are any shares subsequently acquired other than by issuing voting common stock. There are additional adjustments required for the 90 percent test such as when the nonissuing, combining corporation has an investment in the voting stock of the issuing corporation. This investment reduces the number of shares issued by the issuing corporation in attempting to meet the 90 percent test. To illustrate these rules assume A Corporation is going to acquire B Corporation by issuing 2 shares of A for each share of B. B has 40,000 shares outstanding of which A or its subsidiaries already own (1) 2,000 shares of B acquired (for any form of compensation) before the date the plan of combination is initiated and (2) 100 shares acquired in exchange for assets other than stock of A after the date the plan of combination is initiated, and (3) 800 shares of B are still owned by minority interests after the exchange. In addition, at the date of exchange B owns 2,000 shares of A. The computation for the 90 percent test would be as in Illustration 9–11.

Illustration 9–11

Outstanding B shares	40,000
Less shares owned by A:	
Through its subsidiaries	(2,000)
Shares acquired after the date the plan of	
combination is initiated	(100)
Less shares owned by minority	(800)
B shares exchanged for A shares	37,100
Less A shares held by B adjusted to	
equivalent B shares (2,000 ÷ 2 = 1,000)	(1,000)
Adjusted B shares exchanged for A	36,100*

* Meets the 90% × 40,000 shares test because 36,100 > 36,000.

Debt or other securities can be replaced with identical securities or the debt can be assumed. If, however, the debt or other securities were issued within two years of the date of initiation of the combination plan for voting stock of the combining corporation, they must be exchanged for voting stock of the issuing corporation.

When the net assets of the combining corporation are being exchanged for stock of the issuing corporation, all the net assets of the combining corporation must be exchanged at the date the plan is consummated. Again, an investment by the combining corporation in the voting stock of the issuing corporation will for purposes of the test be assumed to reduce the number of shares issued in the exchange. The 90 percent test for an asset exchange is then made by comparing the reduced number of voting shares issued to the applicable voting common stock interest in the combining corporation.

As can be seen, the fourth requirement is generally the most difficult to comply with, and to give it more strength, requirements 5 through 9 attempt to prevent erosion.

> (5) None of the combining companies changes the equity interest of the voting common stock in contemplation of effecting the combination either within two years before the plan of combination is initiated or between the dates the plan is initiated and consummated; changes in contemplation of effecting the combination may include distributions to stockholders and additional issuances, exchanges, and retirements of securities.[18]

This does not prevent normal dividends in relationship to the earnings of the period.

> (6) Each of the combining companies reacquires shares of voting common stock only for purposes other than business combinations, and no company reacquires more than a normal number of shares between the dates the plan of combination is initiated and consummated.[19]

Thus, normal treasury stock acquisitions, as established by past acquisitions, for stock option and compensation purposes are permitted.

> (7) The ratio of the interest of an individual common shareholder to those of other common shareholders in a combining company remains the same as a result of the exchange of stock to effect the combination.[20]

Thus, for example, if the shareholders of B Corporation were exchanging their stock for stock of A Corporation and if B were owned equally by two shareholders, they would each have to own the same percentage of A Corporation after the exchange no matter if this were 40 percent or .0004 percent.

> (8) The voting rights to which the common stock ownership interests in the resulting combined corporation are entitled are exercisable by the stockholders; the stockholders are neither deprived of nor restricted in exercising those rights for a period.[21]

This prevents restrictions on voting rights such as voting trusts.

---

[18] Ibid., par. 1091.47-c.
[19] Ibid., par. 1091.47-d.
[20] Ibid., par. 1091.47-e.
[21] Ibid., par. 1091.47-f.

(9) The combination is resolved at the date the plan is consummated and no provisions of the plan relating to the issue of securities or other consideration are pending.[22]

This prevents contingency compensation based, for example, on future operating results. It does, however, permit a revision of the exchange to compensate for changes in recorded (and presumably unrecorded) contingencies at the date of consumation. The loss of a major lawsuit might be such that the exchange is altered based on a contingency agreement. Normally the shares involving a contingency are held in escrow to await further developments.

Absence of Planned Transactions

To ensure the integrity of the fourth requirement, events following the consummation must also be considered. Thus requirements 10 through 12 are:

(10) The combined corporation does not agree directly or indirectly to retire or reacquire all or part of the common stock issued to effect the combination.

(11) The combined corporation does not enter into other financial arrangements for the benefit of the former stockholders of a combining company, such as a guaranty of loans secured by stock issued in the combination, which in effect negates the exchange of equity securities.

(12) The combined corporation does not intend or plan to dispose of a significant part of the assets of the combining companies within two years after the combination other than disposals in the ordinary course of business of the formerly separate companies and to eliminate duplicate facilities or excess capacity."[23]

Having listed and reviewed the 12 requirements for pooling you may suddenly realize that these rules sound almost like the type of rules that a federal income tax law might produce. And like a federal income tax law, there will be loopholes in this set of rules or at least ways to avoid the full intent if you so desire. With 12 requirements all of which must be met in order for pooling to apply, it is obviously easier to achieve a purchase acquisition than a pooling combination. One should also have noticed some basic differences between the tax-free exchange requirements (such as 80 percent control) and the pooling requirements (such as 90 percent control of the voting common stock). It may frequently happen that an exchange will be "tax free" for tax purposes but for financial accounting purposes accounted for as a purchase (or as a tax-

---

[22] Ibid., par. 1091.47-g.
[23] Ibid., par. 1091.48-a-c.

able exchange but accounted for as a pooling). This would result in different concepts being applied to determine the bases of the assets. Thus, there may be a carryover basis for tax purposes and a fair value basis for financial reporting (or vice versa). This would cause numerous and very difficult permanent differences to account for in the reporting of interperiod income tax allocation.

For purposes of illustration assume that A Corporation acquires all of B Corporation's assets *but assumes no liabilities* in exchange for 10,000 A shares valued at $100 per share with a $1 par value. Illustration 9–12

Illustration 9–12

	B Corporation		
	Basis for Financial Books	Basis for Tax Books	Fair Value
Cash	$ 14,000	$ 14,000	$ 14,000
Accounts receivable (net)	20,000	18,000	19,000
Inventory	40,000	40,000	47,000
Machinery and equipment	180,000	180,000	160,000
Accumulated depreciation	(70,000)	(120,000)	n.a.
Buildings	100,000	100,000	120,000
Accumulated depreciation	(30,000)	(60,000)	n.a.
Land	400,000	400,000	600,000
Goodwill	80,000	100,000	40,000
Total assets	$734,000	$ 672,000	$1,000,000
Notes payable	$ 40,000	$ 40,000	$ 35,000
Capital stock	100,000	100,000	
Additional paid-in capital	80,000	80,000	965,000
Retained earnings	514,000	452,000*	
Total equities	$734,000	$ 672,000	$1,000,000

n.a. = not applicable.

* For tax purposes this account is termed earnings and profits (E&P) and not retained earnings. In addition, the E&P amount is sometimes affected by one-sided journal entries, thus the tax set of books may not balance using the true or adjusted E&P figure.

gives B's statement of financial position immediately prior to the acquisition. The acquired assets without assumption of liabilities would be recorded on A's books as follows:

Financial books—If a purchase:

Assets (recorded individually;	1,000,000	
Capital stock		10,000
Additional paid-in capital		990,000

Financial books—If a pooling:

Assets (recorded individually)........................	734,000	
Capital stock		10,000
Additional paid-in capital		210,000*
Retained earnings		514,000

* ($80,000 additional paid-in + ($100,000 − $10,000) par value + $40,000 additional investment to replace liabilities) = $210,000.

Tax books—If a taxable transaction:

Assets (recorded individually)........................	1,000,000	
Capital stock		10,000
Additional paid-in capital		990,000

Tax books—If a tax-free exchange:

Assets (recorded individually)........................	672,000	
Capital stock		10,000
Additional paid-in capital		210,000
Retained earnings (earnings and profits)		452,000

Since any combination of one financial and one tax method of recording the transaction would be possible, the transaction could produce the results shown in Illustration 9–13 assuming it is a purchase for financial purposes and a tax-free exchange for tax purposes.

Illustration 9–13

	Financial Book Value	Tax Basis	Permanent Differences Financial Exceeds Tax Basis
Cash	$ 14,000	$ 14,000	–0–
Accounts receivable (net)	19,000	18,000	$ 1,000
Inventory	47,000	40,000	7,000
Machinery and equipment	160,000	180,000	
Accumulated depreciation..............	–0–	(120,000)	100,000
Buildings	120,000	100,000	
Accumulated depreciation..............	–0–	(60,000)	80,000
Land	600,000	400,000	200,000
Goodwill	40,000	100,000	(60,000)
Totals	$1,000,000	$ 672,000	$328,000

The permanent differences shown in Illustration 9–13 will destroy the commonly assumed relationship between the federal income tax provision and the before-tax earnings. In addition, the use of different depreciation methods and useful lives for book and tax purposes will further complicate the process of interperiod income tax allocation. This result is another reason for the use of two sets of books, one for financial reporting and one for tax purposes.

PLANNING THE RECORDED VALUE OF CORPORATE ASSETS

Planning corporate acquisitions most certainly must consider both financial reporting and tax results. Each of these can impact on the nature of the acquisition. The result desired for financial reporting, however, does not preclude obtaining a different result for tax purposes nor vice versa.

For Financial Reporting

In a purchase acquisition, it should be noted that only the assets of the acquired entity are restated to fair value and then adjusted for any remaining difference between the cost of the stock and fair value of the assets. Since it often makes little difference to the shareholders which corporation is the acquiring or acquiror, the decision in a stock-for-stock acquisition or stock-for-assets (purchase type) acquisition may hinge on which corporation's assets should be reflected at fair value (assuming cost equals fair value). This is reflected in Illustration 9–14.

Illustration 9–14

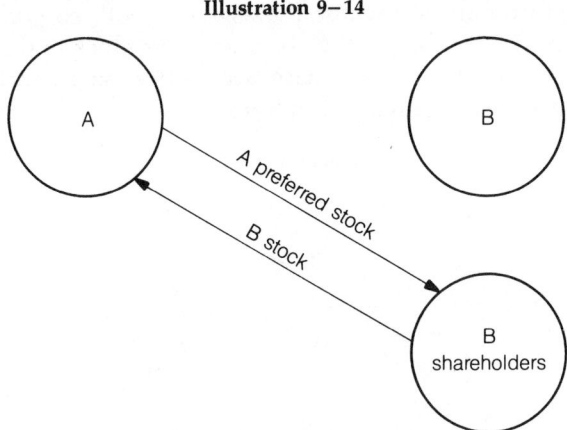

In a financial consolidation, as a one corporation concept following a purchase acquisition, A and B would appear as follows if this is not a reverse acquisition:

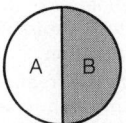

Darkened area equals revaluation. Light area equals historical cost.

If it is deemed that A's assets should be revalued, then B (even if it is a smaller corporation) should issue new B stock (possibly some nonvoting shares to the A shareholders) so as to become the parent corporation of A. To avoid a reverse acquisition the old B shareholders must have voting control after the acquisition.[24] In consolidation A and B would now appear as:

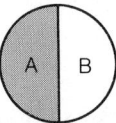

Darkened area equals revaluation. Light area equals historical cost.

It should be noted that if A were the larger corporation as measured by the fair value of shareholder interest and if voting stock (equal in voting power per share to the old B stock) were issued, this would be a reverse acquisition. In the reverse acquisition A would be the acquiring corporation, and B's assets and liabilities would be revalued.

It is almost impossible under historical cost to increase the assets and liabilities of both corporations to their fair values. If our desires for financial reporting are to revalue the assets of both corporations, then we could form C Corporation.[25] C then issues its stock to the shareholders of both A and B in a purchase acquisition so as to achieve the configuration shown in Illustration 9–15.

Illustration 9–15

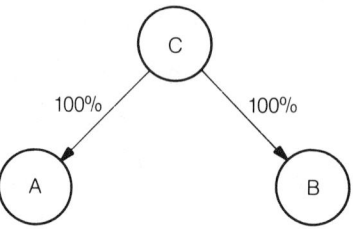

C is a holding corporation whose only assets are its investments in A and B. Since these investments are removed by substitution in the consolidation process, the consolidated entity would then appear as follows, but only if there is a dual acquisition. Thus, the old A and old B

---

[24] In a reverse acquisition the shareholders of the nonissuing corporation end up owning over 50 percent of the voting stock of the issuing corporation. Thus, the nonissuing corporation is really the acquiring corporation.

[25] The older terminology in the literature frequently would refer to the situation where either A or B would be the acquiring corporation as a "merger" and where C is created to be the acquiring corporation as a "consolidation." Such terminology is not employed in this text as these terms are unnecessary, confusing, and without meaningful significance.

shareholders must end up with equal voting power in C. If either A or B shareholders end up controlling C, then it will be an acquisition of one company by the other.[26]

Darkened area equals revaluation. Light area equals historical cost.

Note that if the voting power is split evenly and if the pooling of interests tests are failed, then there is a dual acquisition and all of the assets should then be restated to fair value. This will seldom happen; in practice there is almost always a clear acquiror in a purchase acquisition.

In the case where the A shareholders are bought out in a taxable acquisition, they will, of course, have to pay income tax on the gain (if any); and if the B shareholders are bought out, they will be taxed on the gain (if any). Thus, the basis of the various shareholders' interests may also affect the transaction.

Of course, if it is desired that no assets of either corporation be restated to fair value, then the transaction must meet the constraints of a pooling of interests.

	A Corporation	B Corporation
Assets	$800,000	$600,000
Liabilities	$200,000	$100,000
Capital stock (A = $10 par B = $20 par)	100,000	100,000
Additional paid-in capital	200,000	150,000
Retained earnings	300,000	250,000
Total equities	$800,000	$600,000

Assume A issues 12,000 shares to B in exchange for all of B's assets and liabilities. B then distributes its A stock to the B shareholders in liquidation. Assume that the A stock is worth $50 per share and that the assets and liabilities of B are reported at fair value. Assume that A's assets are reported at $50,000 less than fair value and that its liabilities are understated by $150,000.

Recording this as if A is the acquiror (this might be achieved if the stock issued to B were nonvoting stock):

Assets	600,000	
Goodwill	100,000	
Liabilities		100,000
Capital stock (12,000 × $10)		120,000
Additional paid-in capital		480,000

[26] Theoretically, this could be achieved without forming C (e.g., A could give up 50 percent of its voting stock in acquiring B).

Recording this as if B were the acquiror in a reverse acquisition (note that with equal voting stock the old B shareholders would then own 54.5 percent of A Corporation's stock) is more difficult. Because the old B is being liquidated a new entity (a new A Corporation actually old B) is being formed. This requires the following entry in a new ledger (or in the old A ledger), to replace the B stock with the new A stock. This is similar to a pooling in that the $100,000 of goodwill is not recorded because B is the acquiring corporation.

Assets	600,000	
Liabilities		100,000
Capital stock (12,000 × $10)		120,000*
Additional paid-in capital		130,000†
Retained earnings		250,000

Note. It should be noted that it is B's retained earnings and not A's that is being carried forward as the acquiring corporation.
* Because the B stock has been replaced by the A stock, the par value capital has been increased from $100,000 to $120,000.
† $150,000 − $20,000 (capitalized as par value) = $130,000.

In addition, the A Corporation net assets must be recorded at their fair values as if purchased by B Corporation which is now the new A Corporation. In a new ledger this would be recorded as follows:

Assets ($800,000 + $50,000)	850,000	
Liabilities ($200,000 + $150,000)		350,000
Capital stock		100,000
Additional paid-in capital		400,000*

* 10,000 shares × $50 − $100,000 par value = $400,000.

If the old A ledger were to be retained as the ledger for the new A Corporation, then this entry would be required for the acquisition of the old A Corporation:

Assets	50,000	
Retained earnings	300,000*	
Liabilities		150,000
Additional paid-in capital		200,000†

* To remove the retained earnings to reflect a purchase.
† $400,000 as in the prior entry less $200,000 already on A's books.

For Tax Purposes

Again a caveat is in order; this is only a bare-bones approach to illustrate what is often a very treacherous process. In practice, the assistance of a tax expert is essential.

To increase the assets of a corporation to the price paid, the acquisition must constitute a taxable transaction as opposed to a tax-free exchange. In a taxable acquisition of assets (a direct asset acquisition), restatement is automatically assured in the recording process. In a taxable acquisition of stock, the acquired subsidiary must be liquidated within two years of the acquisition in order to allocate the price paid for the stock (adjusted as under the equity method for the passage of time between the acquisition and liquidation) to the assets received. This permits the seller(s) of the stock to report only capital gain (assuming the purchased corporation was not a subchapter S corporation) and the buyer to step up the bases of the assets to the price paid, presumably fair value. As with financial reporting either corporation can be the acquiring corporation. Thus, reverse acquisitions are frequently desirable.

For tax purposes, to get an increased basis for the assets, a corporation must either acquire the assets directly or if the stock has been acquired the subsidiary must be liquidated into the parent corporation; in either event the original acquisition must be taxable.

To prevent a step up (or down) in the basis of the assets, the transaction can constitute a tax-free exchange in which either assets or shares of the corporation owning the assets are acquired. In the stock-for-stock and tax-free case, liquidation will carry over the basis from the subsidiary to the parent and replace the investment account. Of course a taxable stock-for-stock acquisition without liquidation within two years also retains the bases of the underlying net assets.

OTHER PLANNING ASPECTS

Frequently a corporate acquisition will take the form of an asset acquisition in order to select only the assets desired and to avoid taking the liabilities. In a taxable acquisition, buying the assets also prevents the need for and the cost of liquidation for the buyer. In an asset sale the selling corporation's shareholders normally liquidate the selling corporation and then some liquidation cost must be borne by them. In any liquidation one of the costs is usually taxes. The tax rules on depreciation recapture override the tax-free exchange rules on liquidation causing some of the gain to be taxed and at ordinary income tax rates.

Buying the stock rather than the assets is usually beneficial to the seller. These shareholders will receive the favorable capital gain taxation treatment. But in acquiring stock the buyer is acquiring indirectly the liabilities. These might include hidden liabilities which surface later such as income tax deficiencies due to an IRS audit. A carefully worded agreement will usually make the seller responsible for such liabilities. The buyer will want to acquire the stock if the book basis of the assets is greater than the fair value. In this case the sellers of the stock are indirectly selling the assets which include a larger than normal future tax write-off which they might be able to benefit from if the assets were sold rather than the stock.

Since the buyer and seller are usually in adversary positions, full knowledge of the potential tax costs and benefits are essential if both the seller(s) and buyer are to reach a mutually satisfactory price.

THE ITT ACQUISITION OF HARTFORD FIRE INSURANCE COMPANY

After having examined some of the requirements for tax-free acquisitions and pooling combinations and some of the potential results from both meeting and failing to meet these requirements, an actual stock-for-stock exchange will be examined. The acquisition of Hartford by ITT was chosen for this purpose because (1) it was one of the last major acquisitions before the adoption of *APB Opinion No. 16* which established the 12 requirements for poolings of interests, (2) it was accounted for as a pooling, (3) the tax treatment for this exchange may eventually have to be settled by the Spureme Court, and (4) the SEC conducted an extensive investigation of this transaction. Thus, more than a normal amount of information is available in the public literature on this acquisition.

The Acquisition

Hartford and ITT had agreed to a merger in 1969, but this merger (stock for assets) was not approved by the Insurance Commissioner for the State of Connecticut;[27] thus, a stock-for-stock exchange was arranged and completed in June 1970.[28] In this transaction 21,735,702 shares of convertible, voting, cumulative, $2.25 preferred series N shares were issued by ITT in a one-for-one exchange for about 99.8 percent of the approximately 21,777,336[29] outstanding shares of Hartford common stock. In May 1970 the asking price of the Hartford stock (an unlisted over-the-counter stock) was $38 per share and the ITT series N shares sold for about $42 per share during the first week after the exchange.

Thus, the market value of 99.8 percent of the *net* assets of Hartford as determined by the stock price may have been about $913 million ($42 × 21,735,702 shares ≃ $913,000,000) in June 1970. The price in a taxable transaction would have been higher (because the Hartford shareholders would have had to pay tax on the gain assuming they all had gains). The net book value of the net assets of Hartford are presented in Illustration 9–16 at December 31, 1969, and 1970. The book value of the net assets in

---

[27] *1969 Annual Report of International Telephone and Telegraph Corporation and Subsidiaries Consolidated*, p. 38.

[28] *1970 Annual Report of International Telephone and Telegraph Corporation and Subsidiaries Consolidated*, p. 32.

[29] Twenty-two million shares issued less treasury shares of which there were 222,664 at 12/31/70 and 222,894 at 12/31/69 (22 million − 222,664 = 21,777,336).

Illustration 9–16
HARTFORD FIRE INSURANCE COMPANY AND SUBSIDIARIES CONSOLIDATED
CONSOLIDATED BALANCE SHEETS
(DECEMBER 31, 1970, AND 1969)
($000)

	1970	1969
Assets		
Bonds, at amortized cost (market value $902,027 and $661,764)	$1,000,080	$ 848,854
Stocks, at cost (market value $733,236 and $720,674)	494,687	437,816
Investments in life insurance subsidiaries, at equity	41,198	38,634
Real estate and mortgage loans	73,766	61,376
Cash	22,007	21,774
Deposits/equities in underwriting associations	26,264	38,465
Accounts and notes receivable	271,403	213,891
Prepaid acquisition costs applicable to unearned premiums	163,807	142,343
Other assets	23,593	18,730
	$2,116,805	$1,821,883
Liabilities		
Unpaid claims and claim expenses	$ 806,894	$ 696,214
Unearned premiums	606,786	518,580
Accounts payable, accrued expenses, etc.	97,585	62,856
Deferred income taxes	70,688	57,856
	1,581,953	1,335,506
Stockholders' Equity		
Common stock:		
Authorized 40,000,000 shares $2.50 par value Issued 22,000,000 shares	55,000	55,000
Capital surplus	22,514	22,674
Retained earnings	464,141	415,526
Treasury stock, at cost (222,664 and 222,894 shares)	(6,803)	(6,823)
	534,852	486,377
	$2,116,805	$1,821,883

Source: *1970 Annual Report of International Telephone and Telegraph Corporation and Subsidiaries. Consolidated,* p. 37.

June 1970 may have approximated $511 million (($534,852,000 + $486,377,000) ÷ 2 ≃ $511 million).

Had the acquisition of Hartford been accounted for as a purchase (which it would have been if the 12 pooling requirements had been in effect then), the cost in excess of book value would have approximated $402,000,000 ($913 million − $511 million book value of net assets).[30] The above consolidated balance sheet indicates that about $238,549,000 ($733,236,000 − $494,687,000) of the $402 million would have been allo-

---

[30] It is very probable that if the 12 requirements had been in existence ITT would have structured the exchange to meet these criteria in order to still achieve a pooling of interests.

cated to stock investments. A question to be answered later in this chapter is: Why did ITT go along with a tax-free exchange and lose the opportunity to step up the bases of the Hartford assets by $402 million?

The Tax Treatment

Normally the taxability of an acquisition is settled before the transaction is undertaken. ITT had applied for and received in 1969 a favorable private letter ruling on its proposed tax-free stock-for-stock acquisition of Hartford, but this ruling was retroactively revoked in 1974. The stock-for-stock exchange had taken place in 1970. This resulted in former Hartford shareholders filing a suit against ITT because ITT advertised the exchange on the basis that it would be tax-free to the Hartford shareholders. (ITT has stated that it will reimburse the Hartford shareholders for any federal income tax paid on the exchange if the courts hold the transaction to be a taxable acquisition. This could cost ITT about $100 million if it loses the tax case.)

The entire tax case hinges on the interpretation of the word "solely" as used in the tax law in tax-free acquisitions. Prior to the exchange and in contemplation of the merger, ITT had acquired 1,741,348 shares of Hartford for cash at a cost of about $51 per share.[31] In its request for a favorable ruling, ITT pledged to sell this stock (about 8 percent of the outstanding Hartford stock) before the exchange; this ITT did not do. Having purchased so much for cash ITT believed that a *sale* of the 8 percent stock holding prior to the exchange would allow it to meet the "solely" for voting stock requirement and the IRS so ruled.[32] ITT, however, merely deposited the shares with Mediobanca (an Italian bank) and paid a fee of $1,332,131 by allowing the bank to select a purchase price for the shares equal to the price Mediobanca would receive on a later sale of the shares with the purchase price adjusted downward by the amount of the fee.[33] With no assumption of risk, a purchase price determined by the amount of its subsequent sales price, ITT had retained ownership of the Hartford shares acquired in cash purchases.

With 99.8 percent of the Hartford shares acquired in the exchange, ITT then claimed that it acquired more than the 80 percent required solely for voting stock (99.8% − 8% acquired for cash exceeds 80 percent). The Tax Court recently agreed with some ITT shareholders and ruled the acquisition "tax-free" in a badly split decision.[34] With the tax

---

[31] *SEC Docket,* October 31, 1977, p. 317; and *SEC Release No. 14049,* October 13, 1977.

[32] In a private letter ruling to ITT and in a public ruling, *Revenue Ruling* 72-354.

[33] SEC Docket, p. 318.

[34] C. E. *Graham Reeves and Joan M. Reeves et al., 71 United States Tax Court Reports* 727. The District Court for Delaware in a similar case, *Pierson* v. *U.S.,* agreed with the tax court findings.

court split, the government took the case to the Third Circuit Court of Appeals which reversed the tax court (and the District Court of Delaware case).[35] The government's position is that any consideration other than voting stock violates the solely for voting stock requirement. This case will probably end up in the Supreme Court.

If nothing else, this should point out the tax hazards in corporate acquisitions, reorganizations, and liquidations.

The Pooling of Interests Effects

Of the current requirements for a pooling, the ITT acquisition of Hartford would have failed many of them but it must be remembered that when Hartford was acquired there were no rigid requirements. At that time almost any acquisition with stock could be accounted for as a pooling.

It is interesting to examine the financial accounting ramifications of this acquisition. As an insurance company, Hartford had a large portfolio of investments in shares of other corporations. Under historical cost this portfolio contained a large amount of paper profit (approximately $238 million or $733,236,000 market value less $494,687,000 cost at December 31, 1970). By selectively selling off the appreciated securities (even if they were purchased right back) ITT consolidated could in effect report the appreciation as gain just as though the gain occurred during ITT's ownership period. If ITT (through Hartford or any other subsidiary) had purchased back the same type and quantity of securities sold, it would have effectively converted from a pooling to a purchase method of recording the value of the securities with the resulting difference being reported as earnings.[36] It should be noted that Hartford could also have done this to increase its own reported earnings.

The sale of stock investments by Hartford would probably have resulted in significant income tax payments. After being acquired by ITT and included in its consolidated tax return, the gain on the sale may have been tax-free, in effect, if the appreciated stocks were sold in a foreign country which did not have a capital gains tax and if the ITT group had excess foreign tax credits (a likely situation considering the size of their international operations). The excess foreign tax credits, if any, otherwise being wasted could offset the U.S. income tax on the sales of Hartford's investments.

---

[35] A similar case *Chapman et al.* was reversed by the First Circuit Court of Appeals.

[36] See "The Bottom Line: New Disclosures Explain ITT's Steady Profit Rise," *The Wall Street Journal,* January 10, 1974, where a $7.3 million sale of IBM stock by Hartford resulted in a $7.2 million profit and where after two months Hartford repurchased $7.4 million of IBM stock.

Illustration 9–17
HARTFORD FIRE INSURANCE COMPANY
SALES OF HARTFORD'S STOCK INVESTMENTS AND
ITS REPORTED EARNINGS

	1969	1970	1971	1972	1973
Realized investment gains	$11,465	$47,576	$ 51,388	$ 60,874	$ 58,040
Less applicable income taxes	3,450	13,765	15,343	19,073	20,341
Net realized investment gains	$ 8,015	$33,811	$ 36,045	$ 41,801	$ 37,699
Hartford net income	$50,174	$87,860	$105,490	$126,392	$124,809
Equity in Hartford's net earnings reported by ITT	$50,074*	$87,684	$105,385	$126,266	$124,684
Percentage	99.8%	99.8%	99.9%	99.9%	99.9%

* Retroactively restated under the pooling concept.
Source: ITT annual reports.

The desire for increased earnings may have been caused in part by the following:

> In connection with the affiliation with ITT in 1970, the Certificate of Incorporation of Hartford was amended to provide that, for a period of ten years, Hartford will not in any year transmit funds to ITT in excess of earnings of Hartford for the year as reported on the basis of generally accepted accounting principles.[37]

The intercorporate allocation of income taxes through which Hartford may have been reimbursing ITT for use of foreign tax credits is explained in the following:

> Hartford is included in ITT's consolidated U.S. Federal income tax return and remits to ITT the income taxes currently payable.[38]

By 1972 the over 400 percent increase in realized investment gains annually after the exchange as compared to the last year (1969) before the exchange, apparently brought forth the following note:

> (b) Hartford invests in common and preferred stocks to produce earnings from a combination of dividends and appreciation. Hartford feels that stockholders [ITT owned over 99%] are entitled to participate currently in the earnings generated by appreciation. However, present accounting rules require the sale of securities in order to record such earnings. Hartford, therefore, sells securities (on a specific cost identification basis)

---

[37] *1970 Annual Report of International Telephone and Telegraph Corporation and Subsidiaries Consolidated*, p. 38.

[38] *1971 Annual Report of International Telephone and Telegraph Corporation and Subsidiaries Consolidated*, p. 30.

to realize investment gains each year which are equivalent to the appropriate historical rate of return on its portfolio of stocks.[39]

While the above note to Hartford's financial statements, does not state that the sold shares are repurchased, it clearly leaves that possibility open.[40]

The end result is that the securities could be sold and the appreciation could be reflected in earnings and without any tax being paid. Under intercorporate allocation, Hartford, a subsidiary, could be charged with a tax effect and other subsidiaries or the parent corporation could be allocated the offsetting credit representing use of excess foreign tax credits. This would be a strong motive for a tax-free acquisition in addition to the lower purchase price. The pooling of interests accounting method made the acquisition favorable from a financial accounting point of view.

A sale without a tax payment (to the United States or any government) is a result which Hartford probably could not have accomplished on its own. Thus, the U.S. tax system with a foreign tax credits may have been one of the factors favoring the Hartford acquisition. A nontax factor may have been the large cash flows usually generated by an insurance company.

It is also interesting to note that even though Hartford was owned over 99 percent after the "acquisition," Hartford was not consolidated but was instead accounted for under the equity method. ITT's version of the equity method allowed the reporting of nonoperating earnings as earnings from operations. Thus, the gain on the sale of appreciated securities which was reported after income from operations on Hartford's separate earning statement was picked up by ITT as its equity in Hartford's net earnings. The 99.9 percent amount (including realized investment gains) was reported on one line as operating earnings in the consolidated earnings statement of ITT and subsidiaries (excluding Hartford). It could be argued that gains on stock investments belong in the operating earnings of an insurance company.

The reporting of nonoperating earnings as earnings from operations through the use of the equity method should not be permitted. The correct procedure under the equity method is to bring over the equity in each major section of the earnings statement of a subsidiary and report it in the same section of the parents' or consolidated earnings statement. In retrospect with segmental reporting there is no theoretical reason not to consolidate a domestic corporation almost 100 percent owned.

---

[39] *1972 Annual Report of International Telephone and Telegraph Corporation and Subsidiaries Consolidated,* p. 34.

[40] It should be noted that under historical cost accounting this type of transaction (sale and repurchase) to recognize a gain occurs often and by many companies in addition to ITT.

In reviewing the "combination" against the 12 pooling requirements it appears that at least requirements 3, 4, 9, 11, and 12 would have caused this to be accounted for as a purchase if they had been effective when the Hartford acquisition took place. The use of preferred stock even though voting and convertible would have caused the acquisition to fail the most significant fourth requirement. Considering the benefits of pooling and the obviously knowledgeable management of ITT, had the current pooling requirements been in effect the exchange probably would have been modified to meet them.

POOLING IN THEORETICAL PERSPECTIVE

Of the 18 members of the Accounting Principles Board, 6 dissented to *Opinion No. 16;* thus it barely passed by the two thirds required. Three members dissented to the absence of a relative size test, and the remaining three dissenting members (including both academic members) dissented to pooling itself. They visualize an entity growing through acquisition as a transaction which is almost always a purchase.

The perfect case for pooling was presented earlier in this chapter, and it is perhaps only in that case that pooling is theoretically justified. This justification then would require identical shareholder interests, and this ownership of each corporation would have to be from inception. This would preclude any corporation whose stock has been sold by the original owner(s) from ever being eligible for a pooling.

The identical interest concept for pooling would require identical ownership percentages in each corporation by each shareholder. Thus, X and Y Corporations could theoretically justify a pooling of interests if their four original shareholders' interests were as given in Illustration

Illustration 9–18

Shareholders	Corporations	
	X	Y
1	40%	40%
2	30	30
3	20	20
4	10	10
	100%	100%

9–18 and did not change. In this case each shareholder's interest in X is identical to that shareholder's interest in Y.

Assume X and Y are identical in net asset amounts and in shares outstanding and are owned by the same shareholders but not in identical

Illustration 9–19

Shareholders	Corporations	
	X	Y
1	40%	10%
2	30	20
3	20	30
4	10	40
	100%	100%

percentages as in Illustration 9–19. Because stock ownership is the indirect ownership of the underlying assets of a corporation, a merger of X and Y would, in effect be an indirect sale and purchase of assets. For example, shareholder 1 after the merger would own 25 percent of X and Y which means he or she would have, in effect, sold 15 percent of X's assets and purchased 15 percent of Y's assets. Shareholder 2 would have sold 5 percent of X's assets and purchased 5 percent of Y's assets. Pooling frequently allows major shifts of ownership without any recognition being given to the underlying purchases and sales of net assets.

Our present pooling concept allows far too much selling and buying of shareholder interest without recognition. For example, assume X and Y Corporations are pooled with Z Corporation, an entity many times larger than X and Y. The four shareholders could end up as distinct minority interests. Thus, they could be relinquishing their 100 percent control of X and Y and be receiving say .01 percent of Z, and this could constitute a pooling.

A pooling would treat the three corporations as though they had always been together even though the shareholders of X and Y had never owned any Z stock before the merger. Under pooling the bases of the assets would not change and the retained earnings accounts would be carried forward. The net earnings amounts for the corporations would also be aggregated regardless of the date of the pooling.

Certainly the 12 requirements established to justify a pooling of interests fall far short of the theoretical justification (established in this chapter) and thus permit many of the abuses inherent in the pooling concept. Many accounting theoreticians would totally eliminate pooling. Of all the abuses of pooling,

> The fundamental one is that pooling ignores the asset values on which parties have traded, and substitutes a wholly irrelevant figure—the amount on the seller's books. Such nonaccounting for bargained acquisition values permits the reporting of profits upon subsequent disposition of such assets when there really may be less profit or perhaps a loss. Had

the assets been acquired from the seller for cash, the buyer's cost would be the amount of the cash. Acquisition for stock should make no difference.[41]

The truth in the above quote can be seen in the ITT–Hartford pooling where ITT liquidates the Hartford portfolio in order to generate earnings. In addition, since the real cost of that portfolio was not recorded, the subsequent fall in market values of most stock (in the 1974 recession) saved ITT from having to recognize extensive losses in valuing marketable securities at the lower of cost or market.

Above all, the elimination of pooling would remove an aberration in historical-cost accounting that permits an acquisition to be accounted for on the basis of the seller's cost rather than the buyer's cost of the assets obtained in a bargained exchange.[42]

Since pooling as a concept appeared first in the tax-free exchange rules of the *Internal Revenue Code,* this is one more example of where income tax rules may have impacted adversely on the development of accounting.

REVIEW QUESTIONS

1. What is the difference between a corporate "acquisition" and a "combination" for financial reporting and for tax reporting?
2. Why might a closely held family corporation be involved in a tax-free exchange?
3. What four combinations of acquisitions or combinations are possible for financial and tax purposes?
4. What is the underlying concept of a taxable acquisition?
5. What can cause the tax basis of an asset to be different than its book basis?
6. If A acquires B stock in a taxable acquisition, why might B be liquidated into A or why might A prefer to operate B as a subsidiary?
7. Why should some intercorporate transactions prior to the date of a pooling have any effect on subsequent earnings?
8. What are the principal statutory requirements for a type B (stock-for-stock) tax-free exchange?
9. What are brother-sister corporations?
10. What effect will greatly decreased voting power to a shareholder due to a stock-for-stock exchange have on a pooling?
11. How many requirements must be met before pooling accounting is required, and what major categories are they classified under?

---

[41] In the dissents to A.P.B. *Opinion No. 16,* pp. 325–26.
[42] Ibid., p. 326.

12. In the fourth requirement for a pooling what does substantially all refer to and mean?
13. If A acquired stock of B Corporation in a taxable acquisition accounted for as a purchase, at what amount will the assets be reflected for financial reporting and for tax purposes?
14. If A is going to acquire B, how can the acquisition be recast so as to revalue only the assets of A for consolidated financial reporting?
15. If A is going to acquire B, how can the acquisition be recast so as to revalue the assets of both A and B for consolidated financial reporting?
16. For income tax purposes how can A acquire B and not have to change the tax bases of B's assets?
17. Why might a buying corporation want to acquire the assets of another corporation rather than its stock?
18. Why might a buying corporation want to acquire the stock of another corporation rather than its assets?
19. For consolidated financial reporting purposes what differences occur in the measurement of earnings if stock is purchased rather than assets?

PROBLEMS

Problem 1: Planning Basis Differences

P Corporation acquired the stock of S Corporation in exchange for P stock. This resulted in a "tax-free" exchange for tax purposes, while for book purposes the acquisition failed the pooling of interests requirements. Therefore, the basis of one of S's assets for consolidated financial statement purposes using the purchase concept was its FMV or only $20,000, and its basis for tax purposes was its book value of $30,000. The useful life was 10 years with straight-line depreciation being used for financial reporting, while for tax purposes the useful life was only five years with sum-of-the-years' digits depreciation method being used. (You may wish to review Chapter 2 for the tax effects of basis differences.)

Required:
1. Prepare a schedule showing separately by year the amounts of the permanent difference and the amounts of the timing difference.
2. With $20,000 as the FMV of the asset, what effect if any, should the permanent portion of the basis difference have in recording the acquisition?
3. If the amounts for book and tax basis had been reversed and had this been a taxable rather than a "tax-free" acquisition—
    a. What effect would this have possibly had on the life of S Corporation?
    b. What effect would this have on financial reporting assuming the $30,000 represents the FMV of the asset and $20,000 is its book value and tax basis?

Problem 2: Pool and Purchase Corporations

Pool Corporation acquired all of the stock of Purchase Corporation in exchange for 10,000 shares of Pool stock. The Pool stock had a fair value of $38 per share. The position statement of Purchase Corporation at the date of the stock-for-stock exchange appeared as follows:

	Book Value	Tax Basis	Fair Value
Cash	$ 10,000	$ 10,000	$ 10,000
Accounts receivable (net)	10,000	10,000	12,000
Inventory (Lifo)	20,000	20,000	48,000
Machinery (net)	80,000	40,000	100,000
Buildings (net)	60,000	30,000	120,000
Land	20,000	20,000	80,000
Goodwill	–0–	–0–	30,000
Total assets	$200,000	$130,000	$400,000
Accounts payable	$ 20,000	$ 20,000	$ 20,000
Capital stock, $10 par	50,000	50,000	
Additional paid-in capital	40,000	40,000	380,000
Retained earnings	90,000	20,000	
Total equities	$200,000	$130,000	$400,000

At the date of the exchange the shareholders of Purchase had an aggregate basis for their shares of $270,000.

Required:

1. Determine the tax basis of the Purchase stock to Pool Corporation if this were a taxable acquisition.
2. Determine the tax basis of the Purchase stock to Pool Corporation if this were a tax-free exchange.
3. Determine the book basis of the Purchase stock to Pool Corporation if this were a pooling of interests.
4. Determine the book basis of the Purchase stock to Pool Corporation if this were a purchase acquisition.
5. Determine the tax basis and the book basis of the total assets of Purchase if it is liquidated into Pool Corporation immediately after

For Tax Purposes	For Book Purposes
a. Tax-free exchange	Pooling
b. Tax-free exchange	Purchase
c. Taxable acquisition	Purchase
d. Taxable acquisition	Pooling

Problem 3: Arnett and Boley Corporation

The Arnett and Boley Corporation position statements appear as follows immediately before a stock-for-stock exchange on 1/1/x1.

Position Statements

	Arnett			Boley		
	Book Value	Tax Basis	Fair Value	Book Value	Tax Basis	Fair Value
Cash	$ 10,000	$ 10,000	$ 10,000	$ 30,000	$ 30,000	$ 30,000
Receivables (net)	20,000	20,000	20,000	10,000	10,000	10,000
Inventories	30,000	30,000	35,000	20,000	20,000	20,000
Machinery (net)	60,000	20,000	85,000	50,000	10,000	60,000
Buildings (net)	50,000	30,000	100,000	70,000	40,000	90,000
Land	20,000	20,000	50,000	30,000	30,000	60,000
Goodwill (net)	210,000	15,000	30,000	–0–	–0–	10,000
Total assets	$400,000	$145,000	$330,000	$210,000	$140,000	$280,000
Payables	$ 10,000	$ 10,000	$ 10,000	$ 10,000	$ 10,000	$ 10,000
Long-term debt	20,000	20,000	20,000	30,000	30,000	30,000
Capital stock, $10 par	50,000	50,000		30,000	30,000	
Additional paid-in capital	30,000	30,000	300,000	40,000	40,000	240,000
Retained earnings	290,000	35,000		100,000	30,000	
Total equity	$400,000	$145,000	$330,000	$210,000	$140,000	$280,000

The Arnett stock has a fair value of $60 per share, and the Boley stock has a fair value of $80 per share.

Required:

(Note: To reduce time, requirements 1, 2, and 3 can be done in three columns under separate headings.)

1. Prepare a consolidated position statement assuming Arnett issues 4,000 new shares to acquire 100 percent of the Boley stock and that this is accounted for as a purchase for financial reporting and as a tax-free exchange for tax purposes.
2. Prepare a consolidated position statement assuming Boley issues 3,750 nonvoting new shares to acquire 100 percent of the Arnett stock and that this is accounted for as a purchase for financial reporting and as a tax-free exchange for tax purposes.
3. Prepare a consolidated position statement assuming that a new Corporation, the Skadden Corporation, is formed and issues 13,500 shares of its $10 par value stock with a fair value of $40 per share to acquire 100 percent of Arnett (in exchange for 7,500 Skadden shares of which 1,500 are nonvoting) and 100 percent of Boley (in exchange for 6,000 Skadden shares). Assume this is accounted for as purchase acquisition for financial reporting and as tax-free exchange for tax purposes.
4. Prepare the consolidated position statements for 1, 2, and 3 above assuming pooling of interests accounting rather than purchase.
5. Prepare for financial reporting the consolidated position statement results under 2 and 3 above if all shares had identical voting power.
6. Prepare the journal entries to record the stock issue in 5 above.

Problem 4: Arnett and Boley Corporation Revisited

Assuming the same information as shown in the Arnett and Boley problem and that the shareholders immediately before the exchange have an aggregate basis of $150,000 in the Arnett stock and $400,000 in the Boley stock.

Required:

1. Assuming a tax-free exchange of 4,000 new shares of Arnett for 100 percent of the Boley stock—
    a. The basis of the investment in Boley stock is _____.
    b. The aggregate bases of the total assets of Boley in a separate tax return immediately after the stock for stock exchange is _____.
    c. The aggregate bases of the total assets of Arnett and Boley in a consolidated tax return immediately after the stock-for-stock exchange and ignoring the investment in Boley account is _____.
2. Assuming a tax-free exchange of 3,750 new nonvoting shares of Boley for 100 percent of the Arnett stock—
    a. The basis of the investment in Arnett stock is _____.
    b. The aggregate bases of the total assets of Arnett in a separate tax return immediately after the stock-for-stock exchange is _____.
    c. The aggregate bases of the total assets of Boley and Arnett in a consolidated tax return immediately after the stock-for-stock exchange and ignoring the investment in Arnett account is _____.
3. Return to 1 above and answer parts (a), (b), and (c) as if this had been a taxable rather than tax-free acquisition. In addition, would you advise liquidation of Boley and if so why?
4. Return to 2 above and answer parts (a), (b), and (c) as if this had been a taxable rather than tax-free acquisition. In addition would you advise liquidation of Arnett and if so why?

Problem 5: Danos and Duke Corporation

On 1/1/x6 the Danos Corporation issues 7,200 shares of its $20 par value stock with a fair value of $70 per share for 90 percent of the outstanding stock of the Duke Corporation and also acquires the remaining 10 percent for $56,000 in cash. Of the Duke shareholders, dissenters to the exchange owned 10 percent and wanted cash rather than stock of Danos Corporation. Immediately before this exchange the position statement for the Duke Corporation appeared as follows.

DUKE CORPORATION
POSITION STATEMENT
AS OF 1/1/x6

	Book Value	Fair Value
Cash	$ 20,000	$ 20,000
Receivables (net)	40,000	40,000
Inventories	80,000	100,000
Machinery (net)	120,000	160,000
Buildings (net)	80,000	140,000
Land	40,000	90,000
Patents (net)	60,000	80,000
Goodwill	–0–	30,000
Total assets	$440,000	$660,000
Accounts payable	$ 10,000	$ 10,000
Long-term debt	100,000	90,000
Capital stock, $10 par	80,000	
Additional paid-in capital	25,000	560,000
Retained earnings	225,000	
Total equities	$440,000	$660,000

Separate tax returns are filed, and there has been a flat 30 percent corporate income tax for many years.

Required:

1. Record this "acquisition" on the books of Danos Corporation assuming it qualifies as a pooling of interests. Danos has additional paid-in capital of $30,000 on its books before this transaction.
2. Record this acquisition on the books of Danos Corporation assuming it qualifies as a purchase.
3. Prepare the substitution entry as if the acquisition qualified as a pooling.
4. Compute the consolidated retained earnings at 1/1/x6 assuming the acquisition of Duke was a pooling of interests. The Danos retained earnings were $200,000 at 1/1/x6.

Problem 6: Hi and Ho Corporations

Hi Corporation has 200,000 shares outstanding and Ho Corporation has 50,000 shares outstanding. Hi and Ho initiate a plan on 7/1/x1 for a stock-for-stock exchange on 12/31/x1 whereby Hi will exchange 2 Hi shares for each Ho share. Hi already owns 2,000 shares of Ho; and between 7/1/x1 and 12/31/x1, the date for consummation of the exchange, Hi acquires 1,000 shares for cash. At 12/31/x1 Ho owns 6,000 Hi shares.

Required:

1. Prepare a computation showing whether the Hi "acquisition" of Ho meets the "substantially all test" for a pooling of interests assuming all Ho shareholders agree to the exchange.
2. What would the result be if Ho had sold all of its Hi shares prior to 12/31/x1.

10

Accounting for International Transactions, Investments, and Operations

Need for Translation
Effects of Translation
    Selling and Buying in a Foreign Market
    Speculation in a Foreign Currency
    Operations Located in a Foreign Country
Summary of Current Translation Rules*
    Translation of Financial Position Accounts
    Marketable Securities and Investments
    Inventories
    Deferred Income Taxes
    Translation of Earnings Statement Accounts
Example of the Effects of Rate Changes
Some Critics
Hedging Foreign Currency Commitments or Exposed Net Asset or Exposed Net Liability Positions
Some Additional Aspects of Translation and Investments in Subsidiaries
    Translation Following a Purchase Acquisition
    Translation Following a Pooling of Interests

10 / Accounting for International Transactions, Investments, and Operations

> *** Note to users:** As this book is going to press there is significant discussion as to possible changes in translation of foreign entity financial statements. Therefore, parts of this chapter could soon become outdated. The FASB reportedly will opt for use of a current rate method to translate foreign subsidiary balance sheets. This may result in some gains and loss being deferred while others are currently recognized. In addition, some gains and losses may be taken to the stockholders' equity while others affect earnings.

With the growth of various national, multinational (European Economic Community), and bloc (Organization of Petroleum Exporting Countries) economies it is unusual to find a substantial business (except perhaps for public utilities) without foreign involvement at least to the extent of sales or purchases. In addition, the low labor cost in many foreign countries encourages foreign manufacturing locations even when the manufactured goods are eventually sold in the United States. And on balance, the U.S. federal income tax law may also favor foreign investments over U.S. investments, further encouraging international operations.[1] Today many large corporations are so multinational in scope that they are truly international corporations without allegiance to any single country.

> There has occurred a substantial expansion in foreign operations and frequently such operations are conducted by corporate joint ventures or less than wholly-owned companies to permit local national interest ownership participation. In some countries, a local participation in ownership is required as a matter of law.[2]

The revelation of significant numbers and substantial dollar amounts of illegal and unethical corporate practices (including unrecorded funds, tax fraud, bribery of governmental officials, and bribery of members of royal families) caused the U.S. Congress to enact the Foreign Corrupt Practices Act of 1977. In this process the SEC has also added requirements to strengthen internal control and add to the reliability of audited foreign financial data. Thus, while this chapter deals almost exclusively with translation of foreign transactions and operations, management must consider the reporting requirements of the SEC, the provisions of the Foreign Corrupt Practices Act,[3] and the income taxation aspects of

---

[1] Deferral of U.S. taxation until the earning of foreign subsidiaries are transferred to the United States while earnings of U.S. subsidiaries are taxed when earned can have the effect of encouraging foreign over U.S. investment.

[2] George Watt, Richard Hammer and Marianne Burge, *Accounting for the Multinational Corporation* (New York: Financial Executives Research Foundation, 1977), p. 38.

[3] The foreign Corrupt Practices Act is really a misnomer in that it covers many items which are entirely domestic; thus all management, foreign and domestic, must be concerned with its provisions.

foreign source income in addition to the basic accounting and reporting problems.

NEED FOR TRANSLATION

Translation is the process of restating recorded financial data from one currency to another; this effort is necessary in several different situations. First, a U.S. entity may be either a borrower or lender of foreign currency. When this happens, the resulting payable or receivable if denominated (payment required in) in foreign currency and foreign currency holdings, if any, must be restated in U.S. currency at the date of the transaction and again at the date of subsequent financial statements.[4] Second, a U.S. entity may either be selling to or buying from a foreign entity. The currency of settlement if other than U.S. dollars will, until paid, result in a receivable or payable which will require conversion to U.S. currency at the date of the initial transaction and again at the date of any financial statements for the U.S. entity. Third, whenever a domestic entity (U.S. entity in this textbook) is doing business in a foreign country through a branch, division, investee, or subsidiary, the financial records of the foreign operation are normally kept in terms of the local currency. The resulting financial and operating results will have to be recast in terms of U.S. dollars before they can be combined with those from U.S. corporations.

> To incorporate foreign currency transactions and foreign currency financial statements in its financial statements, an enterprise must translate—that is, express in its reporting currency—all assets, liabilities, revenue or expenses that are *measured in foreign currency or denominated in foreign currency* and that arise in either of two ways:
> *Foreign currency transactions*—an enterprise (a) buys or sells on credit goods or services whose prices are stated in foreign currency, (b) borrows or lends funds and the amounts payable or receivable are denominated in foreign currency, (c) is a party to an unperformed forward exchange contract, or (d) for other reasons acquires assets or incurs liabilities denominated in foreign currency.
> *Foreign operations*—an enterprise conducts activities through a foreign operation whose assets, liabilities, revenue and expenses are measured in foreign currency.[5]

Translation of the results of foreign operations and of foreign located assets and liabilities will result in recognized exchange gains or losses if

---

[4] In order to simplify this material, especially in the subsequent discussion on hedging, your author deliberately chose to ignore the effects of differences between spot and future rates.

[5] *FASB Statement No. 8,* par. 3.

an exchange rate other than the rate by which these assets, liabilities, revenues, and expenses were originally recorded is used.

Because the required "temporal method" produces the same result as the more commonly understood monetary and nonmonetary classifications, the latter terms will be used throughout the discussion in this chapter.[6] Monetary assets and liabilities are money items or are contracts which will be settled, normally at maturity, at the contractually based amount of the nominal currency. Nonmonetary items are those, such as long-lived assets, revenue, and most expenses, which are reported at historical cost. The use of current exchange rates to report net monetary assets or net monetary liabilities denominated in foreign currencies will result in recognition of translation gains or losses.

But even before translation, reporting of foreign operations must be made to conform to GAAP (generally accepted accounting practice in the United States) if it does not already conform.

Whenever translation is required for financial statement purposes there will often be some gain or loss due to change in the exchange rate for the U.S. dollar and the particular foreign currency occurring since the initial transaction or since the last translation. *When* and *how* these exchange gains and losses are recognized is often very significant. In addition, some of the translation gains and losses will be realized currently for federal income tax purposes and others will not be currently recognized. This can further complicate accounting for federal income taxes.

EFFECTS OF TRANSLATION

Translation will impact a U.S. entity whenever a transaction is denominated in terms of a foreign currency (and whenever there is an investment in assets located in a foreign country). Thus, it is possible to view a purchase and subsequent payment for an imported or exported item as either one transaction or as two separate transactions.[7] The latter and generally required concept forces current recognition of gain or loss due to currency exchange fluctuations rather than adjusting the original dollar cost of the item purchased or the gain on the items sold.[8] Some accountants favor the single transaction concept (subsequent adjustment of the item purchased) especially for inventory items. This concept, by adjusting the basis of the purchased item, postpones recognition of exchange gains or losses until the purchased item is sold or is

---

[6] The particular classification scheme will lose importance if the FASB goes to the current rate method for all assets and liabilities.

[7] The two transaction approach (purchase and settlement) is in accordance with GAAP.

[8] The one transaction approach is used, however, on forward exchange contracts used to hedge certain foreign currency commitments. This is included in the discussion of hedging later in this chapter.

depreciated. These accountants believe that this is a better matching concept, especially when the sales price of the inventory is adjusted to reflect the fluctuation in currency values. In Illustration 10–1, whenever the foreign party is a subsidiary of a U.S. parent there will be an invest-

Illustration 10–1

Some of the types of transactions can be visualized as follows and

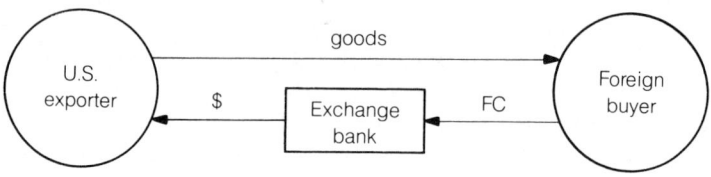

sometimes the foreign buyer or seller may be a foreign subsidiary of a U.S. parent

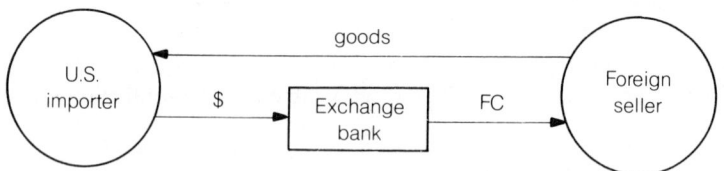

ment in assets, often of many different categories, located in the foreign country. Where there is a foreign subsidiary the U.S. parent will be investing resources in the subsidiary and receiving dividends and/or interest on this investment in addition to buying from or selling goods to the subsidiary (as well as to and from other foreign entities).

A foreign subsidiary, branch, or division of a U.S. parent corporation exposes the investment in the foreign operation to some risks of exchange gain or loss. The extent of the exposure depends on the nature of these assets and liabilities. The exposed net monetary asset or net monetary liability position is defined and illustrated later in this chapter.[9]

Selling and Buying in a Foreign Market

When a U.S. business sells its products to a foreign buyer, the transaction will be paid for either in a foreign currency or in U.S. dollars. If

---
[9] An exposed net monetary asset or net monetary liability position refers to those assets and liabilities translated at the current exchange rate for financial statement purposes.

the transaction is to be settled in U.S. dollars, the U.S. business will not incur any gain or loss on currency exchange. In this case any change in the exchange ratio between the U.S. dollar and the foreign currency between the date of sale and date of payment will result in an exchange gain or loss to the foreign buyer. If, on the other hand, the transaction is to be paid for in units of the foreign currency, the U.S. business will incur any exchange gain or loss.[10] To illustrate these possibilities, assume that the original sales/purchase transaction was recorded as follows when the exchange ratio was 2 units of foreign currency (FC) to 1 U.S. dollar with payment to be made in dollars:

U.S. Seller (dollar units)		Foreign Purchaser (foreign currency units)	
Accounts receivable...	10,000	Purchases............	20,000
Sales	10,000	Accounts payable ..	20,000

To record the sale and purchase on 6/1/x1.

Suppose this transaction is paid for 30 days later when the exchange ratio has changed to 1.9 FC units to 1 U.S. dollar.

U.S. seller (dollars)		Foreign buyer (FC units)	
Cash	10,000	Account payable	20,000
Accounts receivable ...	10,000	Cash	19,000
		Gain on currency exchange	1,000

To record the payment on 6/30/x1.

The foreign buyer has a gain because the required 10,000 U.S. dollars can be bought and delivered with fewer than the anticipated 20,000 foreign currency units at the date of the purchase. At 1.9 foreign currency units for each dollar, 10,000 U.S. dollars cost 19,000 in units of the foreign currency.

If payment of the above transaction were to be made in units of the foreign currency, (i.e., for 20,000 FC units) the sale/purchase and payment would have been recorded as follows:

U.S. seller's books (dollars)		Foreign buyer's books (FC units)	
Accounts receivable	10,000	Purchases ....,	20,000
Sales	10,000	Accounts payable	20,000

To record the sale and purchase.

Cash	10,526	Accounts payable	20,000
Accounts receivable ...	10,000	Cash	20,000
Gain on currency exchange	526		

To record payment.

---

[10] It is also possible to have a transaction denominated in terms of a third-country currency (this is usually done when the buyer and seller country currencies fluctuate widely). In this case both the buyer and seller could have gains and/or losses.

The U.S. seller will now report an exchange gain because the 20,000 units of foreign currency received will now buy more than the anticipated 10,000 U.S. dollars. At a 1.9-to-1 ratio 20,000 foreign currency units will buy 10,526 (20,000 ÷ 1.9) U.S. dollars.

If the U.S. dollar were growing stronger in relation to the foreign currency instead of weaker, as depicted in the prior example, on the settlement or payment date it might take 2.3 units of this foreign currency to acquire 1 U.S. dollar. Thus, if the sale had been denominated in (payment required in) U.S. dollars, the payment would be recorded as follows:

U.S. seller's books (dollars)		Foreign buyer's books (FC units)	
Cash 10,000		Accounts payable 20,000	
Accounts receivable ...	10,000	Loss on currency exchange.. 3,000	
		Cash	23,000

In this case the foreign buyer in order to obtain 10,000 U.S. dollars at a 2.3-to-1 exchange ratio would have to pay 23,000 in foreign currency units.

If the sale had been denominated in (payment to be made in) units of foreign currency, the payment would be recorded as:

U.S. seller's books (dollars)		Foreign buyer's books (FC units)	
Cash 8,696		Accounts payable 20,000	
Loss on currency exchange .. 1,304		Cash	20,000
Accounts receivable	10,000		

In this case the U.S. seller received 20,000 units of foreign currency which at 2.3-to-1 exchange ratio would only buy approximately 8,696 U.S. dollars (20,000 ÷ 2.3 = 8,696 rounded).

It is interesting to note that *in this case* as the dollar weakens vis-a-vis this particular foreign currency, the U.S. seller gains dollars *when the transaction is denominated in the foreign currency* and loses dollars if the dollar grows stronger vis-a-vis the foreign currency. If the transaction is denominated in U.S. dollars, the U.S. seller neither gains nor loses on exchange fluctuations; any exchange gain or loss would belong to the foreign buyer. When the transaction is denominated in units of a foreign currency, a U.S. party (buyer or seller) may wish to hedge against the possibility of gain or loss on currency fluctuations. Hedging exposed foreign currency commitments will be discussed later in this chapter.

In the prior illustrations if the U.S. business had been the purchaser rather than the seller, the same rules on recognition of gain or loss apply. For example, if the U.S. entity purchased a machine from a foreign manufacturer for 20,000 foreign currency units when the exchange ratio was 2 FC to $1, the purchase would have been recorded as follows:

U.S. entity		Foreign entity	
Machinery 10,000		Accounts receivable 20,000	
Accounts payable	10,000	Sales	20,000

If the transaction were to be settled in units of the foreign currency and if the exchange ratio changed to 1.9 FC to 1 by the settlement date, it would take approximately 10,526 dollars to acquire 20,000 units of FC. The payment would then be recorded as follows:

U.S. entity			Foreign entity	
Accounts payable	10,000		Cash	20,000
Loss on currency fluctuations	526		Accounts receivable	20,000
Cash		10,526		

It should be noted that under the two-transaction method the payment of more dollars at a later date results in a loss and not in an adjustment to the cost of the item originally purchased. That is, the machine still has a $10,000 basis and not a basis of $10,526 with no loss being recognized on the exchange.[11]

The timing of recognition of exchange gains or losses and whether they are reported as part of normal operating earnings is a significant problem. To the extent recognized, they are part of normal operating earnings. However, as will be discussed later, not all currency fluctuations result in immediate recognition of gain or loss on all assets and liabilities unless these assets and liabilities are monetary-type items.

Speculation in a Foreign Currency

It should be obvious that a speculator, one who buys, holds, and sells foreign currency, also incurs exchange gains and losses. A U.S. speculator who buys 20,000 units of foreign currency when the exchange ratio is 2 FC to 1 dollar is betting on a decrease in the value of the dollar or an increase in the value of the foreign currency or both. Thus, if the speculator pays 10,000 U.S. dollars to acquire the 20,000 FC units and if the exchange ratio falls to 1.9 to 1, he or she will be able to obtain $10,526.32 for 20,000 FC units; thus gaining about $526 in U.S. currency. On the other hand, if the ratio increases to 2.2 to 1, the speculator will only be able to obtain 9,090.91 U.S. dollars for an exchange loss of about $909 ($10,000 − $9,091).

Operations Located in a Foreign Country

Translation gains and losses are also incurred when a U.S. business has investments in foreign countries. These investments might be in branches (divisions) of the parent corporation, in partnerships or joint ventures, or in subsidiary or investee stock and bonds. Where there is a separate foreign entity, the financial records are normally kept in terms of the local (foreign currency). In these cases before a U.S. corporation

---

[11] The two-transaction method is also used for federal income tax purposes.

can record its equity method income or consolidate a foreign subsidiary, it must first measure the earnings of the foreign entity in terms of the local currency but adjusted for GAAP (generally accepted accounting principles) as the rules would apply if this were a U.S. entity. After reporting foreign earnings according to GAAP, the foreign currency financial statements are then translated to U.S. dollars.

Buying and selling, lending or borrowing, or speculating in a foreign market or currency will produce what some would call transaction exchange gains or loss in foreign currency. Where there are foreign operations (branch or subsidiary), there will be what some would call translation gains or loss.

> Since translation cannot transform the results obtained under dissimilar foreign accounting principles into acceptable measurements under U.S. accounting principles . . . before translation, foreign statements that are to be included by consolidation, combination, or the equity method in an enterprise's financial statements shall be prepared in conformity with U.S. generally accepted accounting principles. Those financial statements shall then be translated into dollars following the standards of this Statement.[12](*FASB Statement No. 8*)

While GAAP requires the aggregating of different "size" dollars, those of different value due to changes in purchasing power, it requires that all amounts included in a financial statement be specified in only one currency. Thus, when foreign operations have resulted in foreign currency financial statements, these statements must be translated into U.S. dollars for U.S. accounting purposes. A U.S. parent of a foreign subsidiary must translate the foreign currency financial statements of the subsidiary into U.S. dollars before preparing either consolidated or equity method financial statements. Since the parent's investment in the subsidiary will be carried in dollars, the subsidiary's financial statements must be recast in dollars before the substitution entry or any deferral, restoration, offset, or advanced recognition entries are made.

The translation must, however, retain the same historical cost concept as used by the U.S. parent. Therefore, various exchange rates will be necessary. For some assets with long useful lives such as machinery, equipment, buildings, and land, the exchange rate at the date of the original acquisition is retained for purposes of preparing current year financial statements. This affects the statement of financial position in reporting the assets and affects the earnings statement in the measurement of depreciation. It should be realized that use of the historical rate will prevent current recognition of gain or loss on these items through change in the exchange rates. For assets which do not possess service or use value and which are monetary items or represent direct claims on

---

[12] *AICPA Professional Standards, Accounting—Current Text* (New York, 1980), pars. 1083.009 and 1083.010. Copyright (1980) by the American Institute of CPAs.

10 / Accounting for International Transactions, Investments, and Operations

monetary assets, the current exchange rate is usually used.[13] Use of the current rate will result in recognition of exchange gains or losses.

SUMMARY OF CURRENT TRANSLATION RULES

Translation of Financial Position Accounts

The distinction between monetary and nonmonetary items is quite important because the use of the current exchange rate in converting monetary amounts to U.S. dollars will usually result in a gain or loss being recognized. The current recognition of exchange gains or losses may affect both book earnings and taxable income. These rules are applicable whether the assets or liabilities are those acquired directly by a U.S. corporation (through import or export activities or in foreign currency speculation or in operations through foreign branches or divisions) or indirectly through an investment in a foreign corporation, partnership, or joint venture. A listing of monetary items which require the use of the current translation rate according to *FASB Statement No. 8* include:[14]

1. Cash (non–U.S. dollar) on hand, in banks and bank overdrafts.
2. Accounts and notes receivable including any allowance for bad debts and accounts and notes payable (regardless of classification in a position statement as current or noncurrent).
3. Refundable deposits.
4. Bonds payable including any unamortized premium or discount,[15] other debts and accrued obligations *except* for unearned revenue, deferred income taxes (charges and credits), and unamortized investment tax credits.
5. Cash surrender value of life insurance.

These items comprise the monetary classification of assets and liabilities, and they are netted to arrive at the *net monetary asset* or *net monetary liability* position.

A listing of items to be translated at their historical rate(s) (the exchange rate at the date of the acquisition or transaction) according to *FASB Statement No. 8* would include:

1. Intangible assets such as goodwill, patents, trademarks, licenses, and formulas.

---

[13] Many accountants believe that the current rate should be used on all foreign assets regardless of their classification as monetary or as nonmonetary items.

[14] It should be emphasized that *FASB Statement No. 8* has caused substantial controversy and is in the process of being revised.

[15] Convertible bonds (which might be classified as common stock equivalents) are also translated at the current rate per *FASB Statement No. 8*.

2. Property, plant, and equipment including accumulated depreciation.
3. Prepaid expenses such as insurance, rent, or advertising.
4. Unearned revenue from sources such as rent or subscriptions.

Use of historical rates on these assets prevents recognition of exchange gain or loss on these items. Suppose a machine is purchased on account, translation of the payable using current rates would result in recognition of the exchange gain or loss, and this gain or loss would not be offset by an exchange loss or gain on translation of the machine because of use of the historical rate. Thus, some accountants favor the use of the current rate on all foreign currency denominated assets and liabilities.

Items which might be translated at either the current or at historical rates, per *FASB Statement No. 8,* depending on the accounting methods employed include:

1. Investments in marketable securities, investees, and subsidiaries.
2. Inventories.
3. Deferred income taxes.

Marketable Securities and Investments. Investments in debt securities essentially equivalent to notes receivable and intended to be held to maturity and carried at the present value (based on the effective rate of interest at the date of purchase) of future interest and principal payments to be received are to be translated at the current rate. All other debt and equity securities other than when the equity method is used or in certain cases where the investment is in preferred stock are translated at historical rates if they are carried at cost and at current rates if they are carried at market (as under the lower-of-cost-or-market concept).

When the equity method is employed in accounting for a foreign investee or subsidiary, the foreign corporation's accounts are translated as determined under *FASB Statement No. 8.* Then, the applicable ownership percentage of the translated net assets is assigned as the parent's or investor's equity investment in the subsidiary or investee.

While this seems easy enough, at least at a cursory glance, there are significant problems. If the subsidiary had been created by the parent or acquired in a "pooling of interests" combination, the exchange rate at the date of acquisition by the subsidiary of each asset and each liability requiring translation is the proper rate (a historical rate) to be applied.

In a pooling, complete translation of the financial position statement of the foreign subsidiary at the date of the combination, using the established historical rates, would be necessary in order to develop the related dollar amount to be recorded as the "investment in the subsidiary account" on the parent's books. For example, if a foreign corporation had only two identical nonmonetary assets, A and B, each costing

100,000 in foreign currency units, and no liabilities and if 100 percent of this corporation's stock were exchanged in a pooling transaction, the exchange rates on the dates assets A and B were purchased would determine the dollar amount of the investment in the foreign subsidiary. Thus, if the exchange rates were two FC units to $1 when A was purchased and four FC units to $1 when B was purchased, the investment account would be $75,000 (100,000 FC ÷ 2 + 100,000 FC ÷ 4) at the date of the pooling of interests.

Where the foreign subsidiary was acquired in a "purchase" acquisition, the exchange rate at the date of the acquisition of the subsidiary stock establishes the historical rate for existing subsidiary assets and liabilities requiring a historical rate for translation. Returning to the example above, if the exchange rate were five FC units to $1 when the foreign corporation's stock was acquired in a purchase, the investment account would be $40,000 (200,000 FC ÷ 5) at the date of the acquisition of the subsidiary.

An essentially permanent investment in preferred stock (which is not a common stock equivalent)[16] is translated at historical cost. When the historical rate is used, the preferred stock must be stated at less than the liquidation or redemption value, or the current rate must be used if it would result in a lower dollar amount. If a foreign investee or subsidiary has a preferred stock issue which is not owned by the investor or parent corporation and is being carried at liquidation or redemption value by the foreign corporation and if liquidation or redemption is imminent, the issue shall be translated at the current rate.

Inventories. If inventories are carried at cost, the historical rate(s) are used in translation. If inventories are carried at replacement price, current selling price, net realizable value, or contract price (under fixed price contracts), the current rate is used for translation.

For Lifo inventories the historical rate(s) would be applied to each year's Lifo layer (for each item or pool). For Fifo inventories when the lower of cost or "market" is used, translation may cause additional write-downs or cause the reinstatement of a write-down which had been made at the foreign subsidiary level as measured in local currency.[17]

Deferred Income Taxes. Deferred income tax charges or credits which relate to assets or liabilities translated at the current rate will likewise be translated at the current rate. Thus, most deferred charges except those

---

[16] How the carrying amount of a preferred stock which is a common stock equivalent is to be translated is not covered in *FASB Statement No. 8*. If it is a true common stock equivalent, translation is not really necessary as it will be removed in the substitution entry to produce consolidated statements. Theoretically it should be translated at a historical rate.

[17] For examples, see par. 48 and 49 of *FASB Statement No. 8*.

associated with unearned revenue shall be translated at current rates because most liabilities are translated at current rates. When the "gross change" method of measuring a timing difference is used *and* when the related asset or liability causing the timing difference is not translated at the current rate, the deferred tax account is translated at the historical rate.[18] When the "net change" method of measuring a timing difference is used *and* when the related asset or liability is not translated at the current rate, an increase in the timing difference is translated at an average exchange rate for the domestic and foreign currency in the current year. If the timing difference results in a decrease, the weighted average of the past exchange rates used in recording the timing difference should be used to translate the decrease or turnaround portion of the timing difference.

> **Accounting Theory:** It is interesting to note the difference in the treatment of deferred tax accounts between general price level accounting and foreign currency translation. For purposes of general price level (constant dollar) accounting, deferred charges and deferred credits are always considered to be nonmonetary items;* thus, they are never involved in recognition of price level gains or losses by being adjusted to the current dollar weighting. There is some significant disagreement with this position. Obviously, regulated corporations (especially public utilities) do not under these rules have to show the large price level gains that would result from the huge net deferred tax credits that are recorded on their books.
>
> * *AICPA Professional Standards,* par. 1071B.013.

Translation of Earnings Statement Accounts

Translation of revenue and expense accounts should use the rate in existence when the transaction was consummated. Most cost and expenses used in measuring net earnings are translated at an average exchange rate or weighted average exchange rate for the year. But to the extent an expense consists of costs reflected on the prior year balance sheet at other than the then current rate (from nonmonetary assets such as inventories, prepaid expenses, and deferred charges), it should be translated at historical rates. In addition, depreciation, depletion, and amortization expenses should be translated at the historical rates used to record the original acquisitions of the related assets.

---

[18] See Chapter 1 for a discussion of the "gross change" and the "net change" methods.

EXAMPLE OF THE EFFECTS OF RATE CHANGES

The following is an very simplified series of illustrations to reflect the effects of currency exchange fluctuations on the statement of financial position from the first two years of operations of Fore Corporation, a wholly owned foreign subsidiary. Fore was incorporated on 1/1/x1 when 140,000 FC units or 63,637 (rounded up) U.S. dollars were invested by the U.S. parent in exchange for all 5,000 shares of Fore common stock. The par value of these shares was 20 in FC units. The exchange rate was then 2.2 FC units to one U.S. dollar. Immediately after formation, Fore borrowed 200,000 in FC units and used this, the stock proceeds and proceeds from FC short-term notes to acquire land, buildings, and machinery and equipment and to begin business. The exchange rate remained constant until 12/31/x1 when it changed from 2.2 FC units to 1 U.S. dollar to 2.0 to 1. With exposed net liabilities of 180,000 (20,000 + 200,000 − 10,000 − 30,000) in FC units, as shown in Illustration 10–2, the result of the single rate change at year-end was a loss of $8,182 or 180,000 ÷ 2.2 less 180,000 ÷ 2.0 or ($81,818 − $90,000) on the exposed net liability position. Thus, without a rate change during the year, operating earnings (exclusive of the loss on foreign currency exchange) were 35,000 in FC units and 15,909 (35,000 ÷ 2.2) in U.S. dollars. When the exchange loss of $8,182 on the exposed net liability position is subtracted from the $15,909, we are left with $7,727 of retained earnings in U.S. dollars as shown in Illustration 10–2.

The earnings statement in Illustration 10–3 also reflects the net earnings of $7,727. Obviously, rate changes seldom behave so perfectly (changing at year-end only) so as not to affect the earnings statement directly during the year. This example, however, shows that once the foreign earnings statement has been translated to U.S. dollars (35,000 ÷ 2.2 in this case), the gain or loss on the exposed net asset or exposed net liability position can be added or substracted to arrive at the increase (or decrease) in retained earnings assuming no dividend payments or other events that might affect retained earnings.

Continuing the assumption of no dividends or transactions other than normal operations which might affect retained earnings, we further assume in Illustration 10–4 that the 2.0-to-1 exchange rate remains constant until 12/31/x2 when it again suddenly changes to 1.9 to 1.

With retained earnings at 12/31/x2 of 166,000 in units of the foreign currency, earnings during the year in terms of this currency must have been 131,000 (166,000 − 35,000). Now, however, the 131,000 includes costs and expenses at both the 2.2 and the 2.0 exchange rates. Because there were no unearned revenues, all the revenues would be at the 2.0-to-1 exchange rate. Thus, with different rates for costs and expenses we cannot merely divide the 131,000 by 2.0 to get the equivalent U.S. dol-

Illustration 10–2
FORE CORPORATION
Statement of Financial Position
As of 12/31/x1

	Foreign Currency Units	C = current h = historical	Dollars
Cash	10,000	C-2.0 to 1	$ 5,000
Accounts receivable	30,000	C-2.0 to 1	15,000
Inventory (cost with Fifo)	60,000	h-2.2 to 1	27,273
Prepaid expenses (not over 1 year in length)	5,000	h-2.2 to 1	2,273
Machinery and equipment	200,000	h-2.2 to 1	90,909
Accumulated depreciation	(40,000)	h-2.2 to 1	(18,182)
Buildings	100,000	h-2.2 to 1	45,455
Accumulated depreciation	(20,000)	h-2.2 to 1	(9,091)
Land	50,000	h-2.2 to 1	22,727
Total assets	395,000		$181,364
Accounts payable	20,000	C-2.0 to 1	$ 10,000
Notes payable (due in 10 years)	200,000	C-2.0 to 1	100,000
Capital stock (5,000 shares)	100,000	h-2.2 to 1	45,455
Additional paid-in capital	40,000	h-2.2 to 1	18,182
Retained earnings	35,000	*	7,727
Total liabilities and capital	395,000		$181,364

C = current rate, 2.0 to 1.
h = historical rate, 2.2 to 1 U.S. dollar.
* = forced or calculated.

Illustration 10–3
FORE CORPORATION
Earnings Statement
For the Year Ended 12/31/x1

	Foreign Currency Units Dr. (Cr.)	h = historical	Dollars
Sales	(435,000)	h-2.2 to 1	$(197,727)
Cost of goods sold:			
Material	100,000	h-2.2 to 1	45,454
Labor	110,000	h-2.2 to 1	50,000
Overhead—depreciation	60,000	h-2.2 to 1	27,273
Overhead—other	40,000	h-2.2 to 1	18,182
Administrative expense	50,000	h-2.2 to 1	22,727
Selling expense	40,000	h-2.2 to 1	18,182
Operating earnings	(35,000)	h-2.2 to 1	$ (15,909)
Loss on exposed net liability position of 180,000 FC			8,182
Net (earnings) loss			$ (7,727)

Illustration 10–4
FORE CORPORATION
Statement of Financial Position
As of 12/31/x2

	Foreign Currency Units		Dollars
Cash	25,000	C-1.9	$ 13,158
Accounts receivable	55,000	C-1.9	28,947
Inventory (cost with Fifo)	85,000	h-2.0	42,500
Prepaid expenses	4,000	h-2.0	2,000
Cash surrender value of life insurance	1,000	C-1.9	526
Machinery and equipment	200,000	h-2.2	90,909
Accumulated depreciation	(60,000)	h-2.2	(27,273)
Buildings	100,000	h-2.2	45,455
Accumulated depreciation	(24,000)	h-2.2	(10,909)
Land	150,000	{h-50,000 at 2.2 to 1} {h-100,000 at 2.0 to 1}	72,727
Total assets	536,000		$258,040
Accounts payable	30,000	C-1.9	$ 15,789
Notes payable (due in 9 years)	200,000	C-1.9	105,263
Capital stock	100,000	h-2.2	45,455
Additional paid-in capital	40,000	h-2.2	18,182
Retained earnings	166,000	*	73,351
Total equities	536,000		$258,040

C = current rate 1.9 to 1.
h = historical rates, 2.2 to 1 U.S. dollar and 2.0 to 1.
* Forced or calculated.

lars. This can be done, however, for all revenues and most expenses, but the expenses at the 2.2 rate must be translated at that rate or the 131,000 divided by 2.0 rate must be adjusted for the difference.

In analyzing last year's and the current year's statements of financial position we see the following, in foreign currency units, entering net earnings in 19x2 at the historical 2.2-to-1 rate.

	FC Units
Beginning inventory	60,000
Prepaid expenses	5,000
Depreciation on machinery and equipment (60,000 − 40,000)	20,000
Depreciation on buildings (24,000 − 20,000)	4,000
Total FC units at 2.2-to-1 rate	89,000

89,000 ÷ 2.2 =	$40,455
89,000 ÷ 2.0 =	44,500
Difference (over stated costs and expenses if translated at 2.0-to-1 rate)	$ 4,045

Thus, the operating net earnings in U.S. dollars exclusive of the exchange gain or loss on the net liability position is:

$$
\begin{array}{ll}
131{,}000 \div 2.0 = & \$65{,}500 \\
\text{plus adjustment for} & \\
\text{2.2-to-1 rate} & \underline{4{,}045} \\
\text{Total} & \underline{\underline{\$69{,}545}}
\end{array}
$$

The exchange gain or loss on the exposed net liability position of 149,000 (30,000 + 200,000 − 25,000 − 55,000 − 1,000) in foreign currency units is a loss of $3,921 which recognizes the year end change from 2.0 to 1.9 to 1 and is computed as follows:

$$
\begin{array}{ll}
149{,}000 \div 2.0 = & \$74{,}500[19] \\
149{,}000 \div 1.9 = & \underline{78{,}421} \\
& \underline{\$(3{,}921)}
\end{array}
$$

Thus, the 12/31/x2 net earnings of the subsidiary in U.S. dollars was $69,545 − $3,921 (exchange loss on net monetary items) or $65,624. And the 12/31/x2 retained earnings of the subsidiary in U.S. dollars is $7,727 at 12/31/x1 plus $65,624 of 19x2 earnings, or $73,351. Once all the assets, liabilities, and owners' equity accounts other than retained earnings have been translated, the translated increase in retained earnings can be forced, can be calculated as shown, or it can be obtained from the earnings statement as shown in Illustration 10–5.

In a real world situation exchange rates may change many times during the course of the year. Monthly or weighted average rates may be used for most revenues and expenses, and the use of average rates will produce rounding differences in the translation of retained earnings to U.S. dollars.

It should be noted that the translation of land involved two historical rates because of the 50,000 FC acquisition cost in 19x1 and the 100,000 FC acquisition cost in 19x2. Had this been a depreciable asset the depreciation taken would have been separated by year of asset acquisition in order to adjust using the proper historical cost rate.

In addition, the parent's investment in the Fore Corporation should be $71,364 ($63,637 + $7,727) at 12/31/x1 and $136,988 ($71,364 + $65,624) at 12/31/x2. This equals the entire translated owner's equity in the absence of a minority interest, and with this equality the substitution entry to produce consolidated financial statements is straightforward.

---

[19] If exchange rates change frequently during the year, the gain or loss on an exposed net asset or net liability position would have to be computed separately for each asset or liability in an exposed position. In addition, settlements of receivables and payable (if denominated in another currency) would have caused exchange gains or losses to be recognized.

Illustration 10–5
FORE CORPORATION
Earnings Statement
For the Year Ended 12/31/x2

	Foreign Currency Units		Dollars
Sales	(570,000)	h-2.0 to 1	$(285,000)
Cost of goods sold:			
Material—beginning inventory	60,000	h-2.2 to 1	27,273
Material—purchased	60,000	h-2.0 to 1	30,000
Labor	130,000	h-2.0 to 1	65,000
Overhead—depreciation	24,000	h-2.2 to 1	10,909
Overhead—prepaid	5,000	h-2.2 to 1	2,273
Overhead—other	35,000	h-2.0 to 1	17,500
Administrative expense	60,000	h-2.0 to 1	30,000
Selling expense	65,000	h-2.0 to 1	32,500
Operating earnings	(131,000)		$ (69,545)
Loss on exposed net liability position of 149,000			3,921
Net (earnings) loss			$ (65,624)

SOME CRITICS

Many accountants do not like the monetary nonmonetary classification in which gains and losses are recognized on the monetary items and postponed on the nonmonetary until these items are sold or enter into the production of revenue. For inventory they argue that its purchase from within the country of location created the FC accounts payable and its sale within the country of location will provide the FC units with which to meet the FC accounts payable. They suggest use of the current rate for all inventory items or even for all items in the position statement.

Mr. Mays in his dissent to *FASB Statement No. 8* stated that,

> assets acquired for local currency by a foreign subsidiary have no historical dollar cost; their historical cost exists only in local currency, and translation at the current rate does not change that basis.
>
> . . . the nature of foreign operations of U.S. companies is sufficiently diverse and complex that no single accounting treatment for foreign currency translation, whatever its conceptual merits, can be universally applied without producing irrational results in many instances.[20]

HEDGING FOREIGN CURRENCY COMMITMENTS OR EXPOSED NET ASSET OR EXPOSED NET LIABILITY POSITIONS

The use of forward exchange contracts for hedging presents a very complex financial accounting and reporting problem. This complexity is

---
[20] *FASB Statement No. 8*, pp. 17–18.

increased because the parent (or any other member of the consolidated entity) often hedges its own exposure and that of its subsidiaries as well. In addition, there are often both foreign income taxes and U.S. income taxes to be considered.

Exposure to possible recognition of gain or loss on translation comes from those assets and liabilities which are translated at the current rate (primarily monetary assets and liabilities). This exposure of course can be eliminated either by having equal amounts of monetary assets and liabilities or by hedging through acquiring a foreign exchange contract.

> A forward exchange contract (forward contract) is an agreement to exchange at a specified future date currencies of different countries at a specified rate (the forward rate). The purpose of a forward contract may be to hedge either a foreign currency commitment or a foreign currency exposed net asset position or exposed net liability position or to speculate in anticipation of a gain.[21]

If the forward contract is (1) an imperfect (see below) hedge of a foreign currency commitment[22] or (2) a hedge of an exposed net asset or net liability position or (3) held for speculation, gain or loss on translation of the forward contract is recognized in the net earnings for the period in which the exchange rate changes. Other gains and losses on forward contracts are deferred until the contract is closed by being included in the dollar basis of the related foreign currency transaction.

If the following conditions are met, the forward contract will be deemed a hedge of an identifiable foreign currency commitment and the gain or loss will be deferred; if they are not met, the forward contract is deemed an imperfect hedge and the gain or loss will be recognized currently.

> a) The life of the forward contract extends from the foreign currency commitment date to the anticipated transaction date or a later date.
> b) The forward contract is denominated in the same currency as the foreign currency commitment and for an amount that is the same or less than the amount of the foreign currency commitment on an after tax basis.
> c) The foreign currency commitment is firm and uncancelable.[23]

The following example has been taken from *FASB Statement No. 20*, "Accounting for Forward Exchange Contracts," which added the "aftertax basis" to the amount that may be covered by a forward contract.

---

[21] Ibid., par. 22.

[22] A commitment is an unrecorded or future entry. Thus, a commitment is a transaction that has not as yet been recognized but one that has been agreed upon for some specified future date.

[23] Ibid., par. 27.

Assumptions used in the example:

1. B Corporation is a wholly owned foreign subsidiary of A Corporation, a U.S. entity, and the accounting year for both corporations ends with the calendar year.
2. On 11/1/x1 B enters into a *commitment to sell to an outsider on 3/1/x2* for 2,120,000 FC units an asset which has a historical cost basis of 1,720,000 FC units. The exchange rate is $1 = 1FC unit on 11/1/x1.
3. The foreign income tax rate is 10 percent on B's taxable income.
4. The U.S. income tax rate is an assumed 48 percent.
5. There are no U.S. income taxes on B's earnings because no dividends will be paid and the other "indefinite reversal criteria" have been met.
6. There is no premium or discount on the forward exchange contract, thus the forward rate is FC1 = $1.
7. A has a 1 million FC receivable due to export sales to an outside party also due on 3/1/x2.
8. A enters into a forward exchange contract on 11/1/x1 in an amount to exactly hedge its FC exposed net asset position and B's commitment due to the sale; this hedge is a contract to sell 5 million FC units for delivery on 3/1/x2. It should be noted that A and not B will have a gain or loss on translation of B's accounts, thus A hedges the B commitment.
9. On 12/31/x1 the exchange rate changes to FC1 = $0.90 and then remains unchanged through 3/1/x2.

Thus:

The anticipated after foreign tax gain on the 11/1/x1 commitment to sell (on 3/1/x2) by B would be as follows:

FC sales price =	2,120,000
FC basis of asset =	1,720,000
	400,000
Less 10% foreign income tax	40,000
FC aftertax gain	360,000

The foreign commitment exposure equals the FC 2,120,000 sales price less the FC 40,000 income tax or 2,080,000 FC units. If this were all lost due to the FC becoming worthless, how much would A have to realize on the forward contract to break even? Because gain on the forward contract would be taxable to A, it would have to realize, with a 1-to-1 exchange rate on 11/1/x1, $2,080,000 after U.S. taxes or $4 million before U.S. taxes ($4,000,000 − 48% × $4,000,000 = $2,080,000). With A having a FC 1 million receivable on its books, any gain or loss on an exact hedge of this item with a forward contract would exactly offset the loss or gain on the receivable; and there would be a zero net U.S. income tax affect. Thus, a 5 million forward contract exactly hedges the FC risk. The effect of the 12/31/x1 exchange rate change would be calculated as follows:

Forward contract covering B's exposed net asset position = ...	FC 2,080,000
Change in exchange rate	× ($1 − $0.90)
Gain *deferrable* as hedge on sales commitment	$208,000
Forward contract covering A's U.S. income tax to have $2,080,000 after tax (4,000,000 × 48%)	FC 1,920,000
Change in exchange rate	× ($1 − $0.90)
Gain *deferrable* as a hedge of related U.S. tax effects	$192,000
Forward contract covering A's foreign currency asset position	FC 1,000,000
Change in exchange rate	× ($1 − $0.90)
Gain recognized in 19x1	$100,000

The recognition of the $100,000 gain will exactly offset the $100,000 loss on A's foreign currency receivable as of 12/31/x1. The deferral of the $208,000 gain will allow the anticipated aftertax dollar gain on B's sale of the asset to be realized on 3/1/x2, or in other words, it will replace the loss on B's exposed commitment of $208,000 (FC 2,080,000 × ($1 − $0.90). The deferral of the $192,000 gain will offset A's U.S. income tax to be paid on the hedge of B's exposed commitment; thus FC 4,000,000 × ($1 − $0.90) = $400,000 and $400,000 × 48% = $192,000 of income tax to be paid on this part of the forward contract. If the deferrals were not made, these gains ($208,000 + $192,000) would be recognized in 19x1 and the related loss (or reduced gain) and income tax effect would be reflected in 19x2.

It should be realized that commitments such as for B's sale of an asset in the following year are not usually recorded at the date of commitment, 11/1/x1 in this case. B would normally record the sale on 3/1/x2; thus the exposed net asset position is not really recorded until 3/1/x2. The hedge or forward contract entered into by A may also be unrecorded but certainly disclosed (via a footnote) at 2/31/x1. Because A has a recorded receivable, denominated in the same foreign currency, loss or gain on its translation should be reduced by the gain or loss on the related portion of the forward contract.

Hedging foreign operations and foreign currency commitments is obviously a difficult process, and this difficulty is reflecting in the related accounting rules.

SOME ADDITIONAL ASPECTS OF TRANSLATION AND INVESTMENTS IN SUBSIDIARIES

Whether consolidated or accounted for under the equity method, investments in foreign subsidiaries can present some rather complex problems. Accounting for the acquisition or combination as a purchase or as a pooling can also further complicate the problem.

Translation Following a Purchase Acquisition

Suppose A Corporation, a U.S. parent, acquires 900 shares or 90 percent of B Corporation, a foreign entity, for $200,000 on 1/1/x1 when the exchange rate was $1 = 2.5 FC. Immediately before the acquisition, the owner's equity section of B and the investment account analysis using alternative method 3 appear as in Illustration 10–6.

Illustration 10–6

	In Foreign Currency Units
Capital stock, par value 10 FC....	10,000
Additional paid-in capital	80,000
Retained earnings...............	410,000
	500,000

The investment account analysis would be as follows using alternative method 3:

B Corporation	FC Net Assets	Dollar Net Assets	90 Per-cent	10 Per-cent
Capital stock	10,000	$ 4,000	3,600	400
Additional paid-in capital	80,000	32,000	28,800	3,200
Retained earnings	410,000	164,000	147,600	16,400
	500,000	$200,000	180,000	20,000
Cost in excess of book value	55,555	22,222	20,000	2,222
	555,555	$222,222	200,000*	22,222

* Price paid for 90 percent.

Under alternative method 3 the $22,222 of excess fair value over book value would have to be allocated to the appropriate assets and liabilities based on their fair values after translation. If the fair value of the net assets exceeded book value (in dollars) by only $18,000, goodwill of $4,222 ($22,222 − $18,000) would arise. From 1/1/x1 on all of the nonmonetary assets and liabilities would (1) be assigned their fair values at 1/1/x1 as their cost basis and (2) future translation including depreciation would be at 2.5 FC = $1 ratio for these assets and liabilities. Thus, the goodwill of $4,222 would be reflected in foreign currency units as 10,555, and if written off over 40 years, each year's amortization would be about 264 FC units or $106 (264 ÷ 2.5).

Translation Following a Pooling of Interests

Continuing the prior example of A and B Corporations, assume that A exchanged 5,000 of its $1 par value shares for 900 shares of B stock. Assume the B stock was worth $222.22 per share and the A stock was worth only $40 per share and that the exchange constituted a pooling of interests.

Under the pooling concept, the two entities have always been together: thus, translation at the current 2.5 FC to $1 ratio would be in error. Therefore translation of the capital stock par value amount and additional paid-in capital amount would be at whatever rates of exchange existed when this stock was originally issued. But direct translation of retained earnings would be impossible because it is a composite of many prior exchange rates. To get a weighted average exchange rate (1) all assets and all liabilities would have to be identified and classified as monetary and nonmonetary, then (2) the nonmonetary items (including allowance for depreciation and any other such valuation accounts) would have to be translated at whatever the exchange rates were on the dates these assets or liabilities were acquired or incurred, then (3) the monetary items would be translated at the current 2.5 FC = $1 rate, then (4) the translated value of the total net assets could be determined, and then (5) the translated amounts for capital stock and additional paid-in capital would be subtracted leaving the translated value of retained earnings which if divided by 410,000 FC units would produce a type of weighted average exchange rate.

The investment in the subsidiary account should be recorded by A at 90 percent of the total translated value for the net assets. The credit entries by A for its stock issued in the exchange would depend on the translated values of the capital stock and additional paid-in capital of B.

While pooling is a fairly easy concept when domestic entities are involved, it becomes very complex when a U.S. and a foreign entity are combined. Theoretically, at least even before the translation process begins, the foreign entities retained earnings amount may need to be remeasured (in foreign currency units) using U.S. generally accepted accounting principles. This may be a significant problem due to the use of unacceptable accounting methods and to the rather frequent use of secret reserves by many foreign corporations.

REVIEW QUESTIONS

1. What is foreign currency translation?
2. What three common types of activity can cause foreign currency translation problems?
3. What does it mean to have a transaction denominated in a particular currency?

10 / Accounting for International Transactions, Investments, and Operations

4. In an import or export transaction between a U.S. and a foreign entity, which party incurrs translation gain or loss when that transaction is denominated in—
   a. U.S. dollars?
   b. The currency of the foreign party?
   c. The currency of a third country?
5. Does a U.S. entity incur a gain or loss or is there no effect when the U.S. dollar is growing stronger in relationship to the foreign currency in which a particular import or export transaction is denominated?
6. In measuring gain or loss on currency fluctuations, describe the "time of transaction basis" which is the two-transaction method?
7. In measuring gain or loss on currency fluctuations, describe the "time of settlement basis" which is the one-transaction method?
8. In regard to questions 6 and 7 above, which basis is generally required and are there any required exceptions?
9. What is a forward exchange contract and what is its purpose?
10. Why is the classification of an asset or liability as a monetary item significant if it is denominated in a foreign currency?
11. Why does translation of an asset or liability denominated in a foreign currency and classified as a nonmonetary item result in no recognition of exchange gain or loss?
12. Why are there some problems in determining which rate, current or historical, to apply to inventories of foreign operations?
13. Why do these same problems, in determining which rate, current or historical, to apply to investments in corporate stocks (common and preferred) recorded in foreign currencies, exist?
14. Why do these problems, in determining which rate, current or historical, to apply to deferred income tax accounts (charges or credits) recorded in foreign currencies, exist?
15. How are exchange rates affected when a foreign subsidiary is "acquired" in a pooling of interests?
16. How are exchange rates affected when a foreign subsidiary is acquired in a purchase?
17. How are exchange rates affected when an investment in a subsidiary is accounted for under the equity method?
18. What exchange rates are used to translate revenue and expense accounts for a foreign operation?

PROBLEMS

Problem-1: Export Corporation

Export Corporation, a U.S. entity, sells its products in many foreign countries. In December 19x1 the following sales were made:

Buying Firm	Location	Amount of Sales in Dollars	Currency of Denomination	Exchange Rate of Date of Sale	Exchange Rate at 12/31/x1 or When Paid If Before
A	Britain	$100,000	Pound	$1 = .4350 (pound)	$1 = .4320 (pound)
B	France	200,000	Franc	$1 = 4.0760 (franc)	$1 = 4.0800 (franc)
C	Italy	200,000	Lira	$1 = 806.50 (lira)	$1 = 806.15 (lira)
D	W. Germany	300,000	Mark	$1 = 1.7400 (mark)	$1 = 1.7450 (mark)
E	W. Germany	300,000	Dollar	$1 = 1.7380 (mark)	$1 = 1.7450 (mark)

Required:
1. Record these transactions on the books of the buyer and of the seller.
2. Assuming firms B and D paid before 12/31/x1, record the payment on both the buyer's and seller's books.
3. Compute the gain or loss to the Export Corporation on the outstanding receivables at 12/31/x1 and to the buyers on the outstanding payables.

Problem-2: Historical Corporation

In the past four years Historical, a foreign corporation, has purchased the following depreciable assets:

Machine	Date Acquired	Cost in FC Units	Estimated Useful Life	Depreciation Method	Fair Value on 1/1/x5 in FC Units
A	1/1/x1	100,000	10 years	SL	50,000
B	1/1/x2	200,000	15	SL	180,000
C	1/1/x3	300,000	20	DDB	260,000
D	1/1/x4	400,000	5	SYD	320,000

SL = straight line.
SYD = sum-of-the-years' digits.
DDB = double-declining balance.

The salvage value was estimated as zero in every case, and the estimated useful lives are accurate. A full year's depreciation is taken in the year of asset acquisition. On 1/1/x5 all of Historical stock was acquired by Hysterical Corporation, a U.S. entity. The foreign currency exchange ratios have been as follows:

FC 2.0 to $1 on 1/1/x1
FC 2.1 to $1 on 1/1/x2
FC 2.4 to $1 on 1/1/x3
FC 2.5 to $1 on 1/1/x4
FC 2.2 to $1 on 1/1/x5
FC 2.0 to $1 on 12/31/x5

Required:
1. Assuming the acquisition of Historical was accounted for as a purchase, calculate (a) the depreciation expense and (b) the book value of these assets as they would appear in the 12/31/x5 consolidated U.S. financial statement

10 / Accounting for International Transactions, Investments, and Operations 391

(assume the acquisition result in goodwill upon consolidation and that the same depreciation methods were continued).
2. Assuming a pooling of interests combination, calculate (a) the depreciation expense and (b) the book value of these assets as they would appear in the 12/31/x5 consolidated U.S. financial statements.

Problem-3: Revenue Corporation

Revenue Corporation, a foreign retail sales subsidiary, has been owned 90 percent since 1/1/x1 by the Cost Corporation, a U.S. entity. The earnings statement for Revenue, in foreign currency (FC) units, appeared as follows for the year ended 12/31/x3. All transactions for Revenue have been denominated in its own currency and thus there is no gain or loss on conversion in its earnings statement.

		FC Units
Sales		4,000,000
Cost of goods sold		1,800,000
Gross margin		2,200,000
Administration	800,000	
Selling expenses	900,000	1,700,000
Before tax net earnings		500,000
Income tax provision		100,000
Net earnings		400,000

1. The beginning inventory had been 200,000, and the ending inventory was 300,000 of which 200,000 was acquired on 12/1/x3 and 100,000 on 12/31/x3. The Fifo inventory flow was used.
2. Depreciation of 100,000 was included in administrative expenses and 200,000 was included in selling expenses. The 200,000 was from straight-line depreciation on a 10-year life for items costing 2,000,000.
3. Revenue's monetary assets exceeded its monetary liabilities by 80,000 at 12/31/x3, and to Cost Corporation this is an exposed position. The 80,000 arose on 12/1/x3.
4. The federal income tax provision contains the following parts.

    40,000—total paid on a monthly basis over the course of the year.
    10,000—which is to be paid on 1/1/x4
    50,000—which represents a deferred credit because tax depreciation on the store fixtures and delivery equipment exceeded the book depreciation of 200,000 (using the net change method)
    _____
    100,000 Total

5. The exchange rates were as follows:

    2.0 FC to $1 on 12/15/x2 and when the beginning inventory was purchased
    1.8 FC to $1 on 12/1/x3
    1.5 FC to $1 on 12/31/x3
    2.2 FC to $1· was the average exchange rate during the year
    3.0 FC to $1 was the rate on 6/1/x0 when the office equipment
        was originally acquired.

2.5 FC to $1 was the rate on 7/1/x1 when the store fixtures and delivery equipment were originally acquired.
2.6 FC to $1 was the rate on 1/1/x1 when Cost Corporation acquired its 90 percent ownership of Revenue.

Required:
1. Convert the foreign currency statement of Revenue to U.S. dollars assuming the "acquisition" of Revenue constituted a pooling of interests.
2. Convert the foreign currency statement of Revenue to U.S. dollars assuming the acquisition of Revenue constituted a purchase acquisition at book value where the book value adjusted to U.S. dollars equaled fair value.

Problem-4: R and S Corporations

On 1/1/x1 R Corporation, a U.S. entity, acquired 80 percent of the stock of S Corporation, a foreign entity, for $320,000. The owners' equity section of the S Corporation appeared as follows on 1/1/x1 in foreign currency (FC) units. The exchange rate on 1/1/x1 was 2 FC = $1, and all assets and liabilities were recorded at their fair values.

	Owners' Equity on 1/1/x1 in FC Units
Capital stock, 10 FC par	100,000
Additional paid-in capital	200,000
Retained earnings	400,000
Book value at 1/1/x1	700,000

The net earnings of S in FC units was 70,000 and converted into 33,000 U.S. dollars using proper exchange rates (including the exchange gain or loss on the net monetary asset and liability position of S).

On 11/1/x1 S paid dividends of 20,000 in FC units. Also on 11/1/x1 S sold to R for 10,000 FC units some inventory which cost S 4,000 in FC units on 8/1/x1. This transaction was denominated in FC units. R has not yet paid S but has resold half of those items to outsiders. The exchange rates were 2.1 FC = $1 on 8/1/x1, 2.2 FC = $1 on 11/1/x1, and 2.3 FC = $1 on 12/31/x1. The foreign income tax rate is 40 percent.

Required:
1. Based on the above prepare an investment analysis schedule for R's investment in S.
2. Prepare the equity method entries by which R records its share of the S earnings and dividends.
3. Prepare the work sheet substitution entry for R's investment in S.
4. Prepare the entires by R associated with the intercorporate inventory item.
5. Prepare the work sheet offset and deferral entries for intercorporate transactions associated with the inventory items.

Problem-5: Hedge and Row Corporations

Hedge Corporation owns 100 percent of Row Corporation which is a British corporation doing business entirely within Great Britain where the corporate income tax rate is 52 percent. Both corporations have year ends on December 31. The U.S. corporate income tax rate is 46 percent.

Row made on 11/15/x1 a noncancellable *commitment* to sell a certain parcel of land for 1,000,000 pounds on 2/1/x2. Hedge Corporation has an account receivable for 400,000 pounds due also on 2/1/x2. This receivable was incurred on a 11/15/x1 sale, and the transaction is denominated in pounds. The exchange rate on 11/15/x1 was $1 = .4310 pounds.

Hedge Corporation wants to eliminate the possibility of gain or loss on changes in exchange rates, on Row's unrecorded commitment, and on the Hedge receivable, on an aftertax basis. Row's basis in the land is 200,000 pounds.

Required:

1. Compute the amount of the forward exchange contract that Hedge must enter into on 11/15/x1 to hedge its exposure.
2. If the exchange rate for pounds is $1 = .4290 on 12/31/x1, calculate any recognized gains or losses and deferred gains or losses on the commitment, the receivable, and on the forward contract.

11

Accounting for Partnerships— Formation and Operation

Partnership Form of Business Entity
    Partnership Concept
    General Income Tax Aspects of Partnerships
    Partnerships as Compared to Proprietorships
    Partnerships as Compared to Corporations
    Partnerships as Compared to Joint Ownerships
    Types of Partners
        General Partners
        Limited Partners
    Some Types of Partnerships
        Family Partnerships
        Partnerships as Tax Shelters
        Professional Partnerships
        Corporate Partnerships
Large CPA Firms
Creating a Partnership
    Partnership Agreement
    Earnings and Loss Ratios
    Recording Contributed Assets and Liabilities
Partnership Operations
    General Aspects
    Corporate Partners

Admitting New Partners
    Routes to Becoming a Partner
    Premium Paid by a New Partner
    Premium Paid by Old Partners
    Admitting New Partners—Additional Examples
    Purchasing an Existing Partner's Interest
    Purchasing a Part of Each Partner's Interest
        Equal to Unequal Partnership

PARTNERSHIP FORM OF BUSINESS ENTITY

A partnership can be defined as the joining of two or more persons in a business venture usually with a profit motive. Persons as used here does not designate individuals; it could include corporations, other partnerships, government agencies, and so forth, as well as individuals. In addition, the profit motive is not a requirement; there may be substantial numbers of not-for-profit partnerships.

Partnership Concept

Theoretically a partnership can be viewed either as (1) a separate entity distinct from its partners or (2) as an aggregation of the partners' interests and thus not as a separate entity at all. Unfortunately neither of these competing concepts is clearly dominant. With both concepts (usually depending on the transaction) being actively employed in accounting for daily partnership operations, and also in the computation of income taxes, one must be aware of the possible application of either concept. The results can be strikingly different.

General Income Tax Aspects of Partnerships

While both the separate entity and the aggregation concepts are employed in measurement of income for taxation, the partnership is not a taxable entity. The federal income tax law provides for the conduit or aggregation principle whereby the earnings of the partnership are measured at the partnership level but (with an informational partnership tax return required) are taxed to the individual partners whether these earnings are withdrawn or not. Thus, a partner's withdrawals of earnings in excess of his or her share of the current year's earnings are "tax free" in that the tax, if any, would have been previously paid on those amounts. Partnership losses also pass through and thus are deductible by the partners on their separate returns.

There are many items of revenue or expense which receive either favorable or unfavorable treatment under the tax law. Most of these items retain their favorable or unfavorable tax consequences as they pass through the partnership informational tax return[1] and into the partners' tax returns. Thus, tax-exempt state and local bond interest will remain tax exempt in the hands of the partners, and capital gains will remain as capital gains when taxed at the partner level. Also, items such as nondeductible political contributions by a partnership will not become deductible in the partners' tax returns.

Partnerships as Compared to Proprietorships

There are a great many similarities between a general partnership and a proprietorship. The most common characteristic might be the unlimited legal liability of a general partner and a proprietor. In addition, proprietors and partners are both taxed on the earnings of their business whether withdrawn or reinvested.

The obvious difference in these business entities is in the number of owners. A partnership can have an almost unlimited number of partners, whereas a proprietorship has a single owner.

Partnerships as Compared to Corporations

While a corporation and a partnership may have multiple owners, a corporate shareholder's liability is generally limited to that shareholder's investment. In a partnership, limited liability is only extended to "limited partners." In addition, ownership of corporate shares generally makes changing ownership simpler and provides for continuity of the entity. A change in partnership interest through admitting new partners or retirement or death of old partners often causes the old partnership to terminate (legally and usually economically as to that partner) and a new one to begin. One of the significant differences between corporations and partnerships is the taxation of earnings. Contrary to the popular belief that corporate earnings have been doubly taxed (once when earned and once when distributed), they are often only taxed once.[2] And that tax is often at a much lower rate than if the corporate owners had been taxed as partners in a partnership.

---

[1] The required partnership tax return (for information purposes) is filed on Form 1065 which together with supporting schedules shows the earnings, losses, and deductions allocable to each partner.

[2] For a more complete discussion of the lack of double taxation, see Dennis Gaffney and James E. Wheeler, "The Double Taxation of Corporate Source Income: Reality or Illusion?" *The Tax Adviser*, September 1977, pp. 516–31. For example, if income tax is a cost which increases the price of the product, its cost is borne by the consumer (charging the customer for income tax is required for rate regulate public utilities) and not by the shareholder, and indeed the shareholder may be a tax-exempt pension plan, church, or other exempt entity. In addition, many very profitable corporations pay very low and sometimes no income tax.

Today the corporation, at least where there are profitable operations, is perhaps the greatest tax sheltering device. Even the tax it does pay may often be passed on to the customers and thus not borne by the shareholders.

There is a special form of corporation that is taxed similar to the way it would be taxed if it were a partnership. This is the so-called Subchapter S Corporation. While this special corporate tax provision is important, it should be noted that most corporations which do or could easily qualify do not elect this treatment (unless they are operating at a loss).[3] These owners usually elect to pay the corporate tax because in total it is usually lower than the individual income tax they would have to pay if they made a Subchapter S election.

Partnerships as Compared to Joint Ownerships

There are many different forms of joint ownership. They do not, however, automatically make the joint owners partners. This is true even if the property owned is income producing. In these cases the income is merely divided and each owner is treated as a sole proprietor. Joint ownership through unincorporated joint ventures is very common in the oil and gas industry as are partnerships.

Types of Partners

Partners are classified as either general or limited partners, but every partnership must have at least one general partner.

General Partners. In most nontax-shelter partnerships, the partners are all general partners. This means that they share (to various extents) the management and operations of the business and that they have unlimited liability. Of course if a corporation is a general partner, its liability and that of its shareholders is limited to the shareholders' equity in the corporation. In addition, new partners cannot be held personally liable for partnership losses arising prior to the date they became partners. In other words, their liability for these losses is limited to their investment in the partnership.

Limited Partners. In some partnerships, especially tax shelter ventures, there are limited partners. Similar to a corporate shareholder, a limited partner is not personally liable for partnership losses; the loss is limited to that partner's investment in the partnership.

Limited partners, while sharing in the profits or losses of the business, do not have a voice in the management or operations. If they let themselves be represented as general partners, they may forfeit their limited liability status. It should be noted that the partnership entity,

---

[3] Ibid.

which allows gains *and losses* to flow through to the partners, is a particularly attractive form of business where losses for tax purposes are incurred.

Some Types of Partnerships

This brief discussion may help to categorize some of the many different partnership entities.

Family Partnerships. There are family partnerships where each new born family member is given a partnership interest. This is often done for tax purposes in order to have the income taxed in lower brackets and to reduce future estate tax problems. These family partnerships might be in almost any profitable business.

Tax: Shifting income and wealth to lower income and younger family members is often a goal of wealthier families. In a prior chapter a triangular acquisition was illustrated as a way to shift wealth and thus income possibly without a gift tax effect. Partnerships also present income shifting possibilities while retaining the capital which earned the income. Suppose Mr. and Mrs. Dealer and their three children were all partners in the D partnership with equal earnings and loss-sharing ratios. By not withdrawing their earnings Mr. and Mrs. Dealer's capital accounts could exceed those of the three children. Suppose the capital accounts of the D partnership appeared as follows:

Mr. Dealer	$ 350,000
Mrs. Dealer	350,000
Child 1	100,000
Child 2	100,000
Child 3	100,000
	$1,000,000

The $250,000 of earning not withdrawn by Mr. and by Mrs. Dealer allows the partnership to have $500,000 more capital to invest. This will generate earnings 60 percent, which will be shifted to the children via the earnings ratio. The IRS has extensive regulations (Regulations Section 1.704-1(e)) governing earnings allocations in family partnerships. If these appear to be a threat, the use of interest-free loans from the parents to the children can accomplish the desired taxable income shifting result. Such loan arrangements have been upheld in several recent tax cases involving millions of dollars.

Partnerships as Tax Shelters. To the investor, tax shelter partnerships are ideally those designed to result in losses for tax purposes while generating real economic gains. These partnerships are often quite large with some requiring registration with the SEC in order to sell ownership interests. Tax shelter partnerships are often involved in coal, oil and gas, cattle, real estate, and movie ventures, among others. The conduit or aggregation concept which allows partnership losses to be deducted on the partners' individual tax returns (rather than treating the partnership as a separate entity) is particularly attractive when coupled with the limited partnership interests. The tax benefits of losses in a tax shelter can be magnified through leveraging, and in some cases (involving real estate) the debt can even be in nonrecourse form. These exaggerated early year losses are usually offset in future years through gain recognition.

> **Tax—Aspects of a Partner's Interest:** Since a partner's interest in a partnership is an asset, it has a tax basis (always either a positive or a zero amount). Like other assets this interest can be bought or sold. Because a partner is usually liable for the debts of a partnership, the tax basis of a partner's partnership interest includes that partner's share of partnership liabilities. Thus, the tax basis of a partner's interest on a particular date is equal to the original investment plus any earnings left in the partnership (not withdrawn) or less withdrawals in excess of earnings and plus the partner's share of any liabilities. Liabilities are shared according to each partners' loss ratio.
>
> Sometimes a partnership can borrow on a nonrecourse basis. In other words, a bank or financial institution will sometimes lend money to a partnership and have as security only a particular asset, such as a building, and not have a claim on the partners if the partnership fails and the pledged asset is sold for less than the loan. The combination of nonrecourse loans (which increase the basis of a partner's interest even where he is not liable) and a limited partnership position can offer an almost unlimited deduction for tax losses (the limit is the basis of the partner's interest) with a minimum of risk (the risk is only the investment). This combination allows tax sheltered real estate partners to often deduct in the first year more than the amount of their cash investment (more than four times the investment in some cases).* Thus, if the tax shelter throws off a large enough tax loss (primarily from depreciation, interest, and real estate taxes), a partner investing $20,000 may be able to take a tax deduction of $80,000 or more. This is obviously inequitable and can be rationalized only by

> **Tax:** (*continued*)
> realizing that the tax law is a product of Congress. Congress has recently limited loss deductions of partners to the amount they have at risk except for real estate where the limit is still the partner's basis including the "partner's share" of nonrecourse debt. Of course, in real terms the "partner's share" is zero, but the tax law allows, for example, a 20 percent limited partner to increase the basis of his or her investment by 20 percent of the nonrecourse debt. This loophole remains for wealthy limited partners interested in real estate tax shelters.
>
> * Staff of the Joint Committee on Internal Revenue Taxation, *Tax Shelter Investments: Analysis of 37 Individual Income Tax Returns, 24 Partnership and 3 Small Business Corporation Returns* (Washington, D.C.: U.S. Government Printing Office, September 3, 1975).

Professional Partnerships. There are partnerships of professional persons that range in size from 2 partners to more than 1,000. One of the requirements to be a partner in a professional partnership is that you must have passed the examination for that profession and have met any additional requirements such as years of experience. For a CPA this means passing all four parts of the CPA examination plus fulfilling other licensing requirements and being admitted as a partner. While most professional partnerships are probably small, there are some very large ones such as the major CPA firms. Most of the largest CPA firms have from 300 to 1,500 partners. In such a large firm it is likely that one would not even recognize all of one's partners or know all of their names.

Corporate Partnerships. Often very large corporations will form partnerships (or sometimes unincorporated joint ventures) to spread the risk involved in a new venture. This is very common in the oil and gas industry when exploring for and developing new fields.

LARGE CPA FIRMS

With over 1,000 partners in some of the largest firms, the idea of equal partners (or owners) should be immediately squelched; no business could operate with that number of equal, chief executives. Thus, there are partners and there are PARTNERS.

There are often various categories of partners. Some firms have local office partners, regional partners, and national partners.

Often one of the shortest-lived joyful occasions is becoming a partner in one of the large CPA firms. The junior partner (lowest tier) status is often quickly felt. As a partner in one of these firms said, he "knew after being with the firm only a few years that he would become a *successful* partner." The adjective *successful* was properly used, as he believed he would rise in the partnership's partner ranks.

With unlimited personal liability for partnership debts and losses, a professional partnership cannot afford incompetent partners (nor professional staff). Thus, while tremendous sums are spent on professional training, every professional partnership should provide for the possible removal (or early forced retirement) of partners. In fact, in most large firms partners can, in effect, be fired.

This should not deter students interested in becoming partners in large firms. But students should be aware of the possible gradations of partners, and they should aim at becoming successful partners. This may mean being the partner in charge of significant clients, being the managing partner of a large office or of a principal segment of the business, or becoming a member of the executive committee of the firm which in some firms is the governing body in addition to the managing partner of the firm. With average partners of large firms often earning around $100,000, the successful ones are truly well paid financially and in prestige.

CREATING A PARTNERSHIP

The actual creation of a partnership may depend on the type of partnership desired. Here we will discuss creating partnerships in general without emphasis on any particular type.

Partnerships are often formed when an additional person (often a relative) is to join an existing proprietorship as a partial owner in exchange for an investment of time, money, or other assets. With more than one owner the business is no longer a proprietorship.

Partnership Agreement

With two or more owners it is essential that all the rights and duties of the partners be expressed in writing even though an oral agreement is legally acceptable. This written document is called the partnership agreement. In addition to all the rights and duties of the partners, the agreement should cover the type of business to be undertaken, the life of the venture, and procedures for retiring old or admitting new partners, and any important matters effecting operations or taxes. Many states have adopted the Uniform Partnership Act which provides guidelines for partnership operation and for the rights and liabilities of the partners. The partnership agreement, however, may often modify or change the rules as provided by the Uniform Partnership Act. The act was designed to provide this flexibility.

One of the most important rights of a partner is to share in the earnings of the business. Thus, the partnership agreement should always list the earnings and the loss-sharing ratios of the partners. When losses are shared in the same ratio as earnings, the ratio is referred to as the earnings and loss ratio (or profit and loss ratio). If the agreement is silent on the sharing of earnings and losses, they are shared equally among all the partners regardless of the investment of money or time.

Restrictions on withdrawals of capital should also be included in the partnership agreement. In addition, this document should provide for events such as a sale or other transfer of partnership interests and retirement of partners.

Earnings and Loss Ratios

An equal earnings and loss-sharing ratio is undesirable except when the partners' responsibilities are identical, their capital investment is the same, they work the same hours, and their efforts are of equal value to the business. Such is seldom the case. To compensate for differences, interest is sometimes paid on average capital balances and guaranteed salaries are sometimes paid to compensate for the hours worked or the value of the services rendered, with any remaining earnings or loss divided in some established ratio.

Another way to provide proper compensation for value received is to create sharing units of equal value and then award varying numbers of these units to the partners depending on their status in the firm. These units may be assigned values such as $100 per unit. The number of units to be awarded is then determined by the earnings; thus, $5 million in earnings would require a distribution of 50,000 units of $100 each. The managing partner may be awarded 4,500 units or a $450,000 share of earnings whereas the most junior partner may be awarded only 800 units or an $80,000 share of earnings. The awarding of units is usually done by a compensation committee. Variations of this procedure often involving salaries plus units are used by most of the large CPA firms.

To illustrate the use of interest and salary, assume that A and B form a partnership and that A supplies all of the management and labor and that B supplies the $500,000 of necessary capital. The partnership agreement provides for a 50–50 earnings and loss-sharing ratio to be applied after payment to B of 10 percent interest on the $500,000 investment and after payment of a $20,000 salary to A. If the firm earns $120,000 before interest and salary payments to partners, the earnings would be divided as in Illustration 11–1. If the earnings before salary and interest were only $50,000, it would be divided as in Illustration 11–2. Under these types of sharing arrangements it is possible for one partner to suffer a net loss while another has a net gain. This would be the case if the before-salary-and-interest earnings were only $20,000 as shown in Illustration 11–3.

As noted in the tax discussion under family partnerships, distortions can develop when the balances in the partners' capital accounts are not

Illustration 11–1

	A	B	Total
Salary	$20,000	–0–	$20,000
Interest	–0–	$50,000	50,000
Remainder 50–50	25,000	25,000	50,000
Earnings distribution	$45,000	$75,000	$120,000

Illustration 11–2

	A	B	Total
Salary	$20,000	–0–	$20,000
Interest	–0–	$50,000	50,000
Remainder 50–50	(10,000)	(10,000)	(20,000)
Earnings distribution	$10,000	$40,000	$50,000

Illustration 11–3

	A	B	Total
Salary	$20,000	–0–	$20,000
Interest	–0–	$50,000	50,000
Remainder 50–50	(25,000)	(25,000)	(50,000)
Earnings distribution	$(5,000)	$25,000	$20,000

in the same ratio as the earnings and loss ratio. Capital invested by the partnership is producing earnings for the partnership and thus for the partners to share. Therefore, a larger capital balance, in relationship to the other partners' capital investments, than that partner's earnings ratio may result in an unintended gift or excess compensation to the other partners. When special interest or salary arrangements are not established nor intended, it is desirable to keep the capital balances in the same ratio as the earnings ratio especially when capital is a significant earnings-producing factor (e.g., in an investment partnership).

The reported earnings can also be affected by the basis to the partnership of the assets contributed to form the partnership. Basis differences and their tax effects can impact on the desired earnings and loss-sharing ratio. This is discussed in the following section.

Recording Contributed Assets and Liabilities

Assets and sometimes related liabilities are often transferred to a partnership during the formation of the venture or at later dates as additional capital contributions. When a partnership is being formed, it should, at least theoretically, be viewed as a new entity. Thus, assets and liabilities transferred to it should be recorded at fair values on that date. The transfer of assets to an ongoing partnership should also be made at fair values because the transferring partner is giving up some control over their use. In addition, the success of the partnership should be measured from the change in the values of the net assets (adjusted for withdrawals and additional capital contributions) beginning with the date these assets come under partnership control. Gains or losses economically occurring before the partnership was formed or before assets were transferred to it should not be recognized as earnings or losses of the partnership through subsequent sale or use of the contributed property.[4]

For income tax purposes, however, the aggregation concept is usually controlling for transfers to a partnership. Thus, for tax purposes the partner's basis of an asset (or carrying amount of liability) carries over to the partnership. The tax basis of the asset to the partnership is the same as it was in the hands of the partner.

Assume that A and B decide to form a partnership wherein B contributes cash of $95,000 and A contributes assets and liabilities as shown in

Illustration 11–4

	A		B	
	Basis	FMV	Basis	FMV
Cash	$ 3,000	$ 3,000	$95,000	$95,000
Accounts receivable (net)	10,000	8,000		
Inventory	4,000	9,000		
Building (net)	40,000	60,000		
Land	10,000	35,000		
Mortgage liability	(10,000)	(20,000)		
	$ 57,000	$ 95,000	$95,000	$95,000

Illustration 11–4. For financial reporting and for tax purposes the transfers should be recorded as in Illustration 11–5.

The different bases for the assets (other than cash) and for the liability will result in different earnings measurements for financial reporting and for tax purposes. Thus, for tax purposes, net gain of $38,000 ($95,000

---

[4] Failure to recognize the existence of a new entity produces results similar to those achieved through a pooling of interests at the corporate level. In both partnership and corporate accounting this often produces illogical results.

Illustration 11-5

	Financial Reporting		Tax Purposes	
Cash	98,000		98,000	
Accounts receivable (net)	8,000		10,000	
Inventory	9,000		4,000	
Building (net)	60,000		40,000	
Land	35,000		10,000	
Mortgage liability		20,000		10,000
A. Capital		95,000		57,000
B. Capital		95,000		95,000
	210,000	210,000	162,000	162,000

− $57,000) economically earned by A in A's proprietorship will be recognized by the partnership as it collects the receivables, depreciates or sells the assets, and pays off the liability.

> **Tax:** If A and B had agreed to share earnings and losses 50–50 without providing for special allocations to assign the $38,000 of gain to A when recognized, B would receive half the gain when it becomes recognized and would have to pay tax on this amount. Note that if B were A's son this might be a way to shift income to a lower tax bracket family member; the IRS, on the other hand, may want A to pay a gift tax on the transfer of A's property to B.
>
> Not only does the basis of the assets and liabilities carry over to the partnership, the net asset basis adjusted for proportional share of liabilities becomes the basis of the partner's investment in the partnership. Thus, A would have a tax basis for A's interest of $62,000 ($57,000 plus $5,000 which is one-half of the liabilities) while B's basis would be $100,000 ($95,000 plus $5,000); therefore, if C offers $100,000 for either A's or B's interest and if A sells, A would have to report the $38,000 gain in A's taxable income. This can create further basis problems for the purchaser of A's interest; these problems are discussed in the next chapter.
>
> There are also some potentially significant tax aspects when substantial liabilities are transferred to a partnership (or to a controlled corporation). When this appears likely, expert tax advice should be sought to avoid unanticipated taxable income to the transfering partner. When the carrying amount of the liabilities *exceeds* the basis of the assets transferred, the excess can become taxable income.

PARTNERSHIP OPERATIONS

General Aspects

Partnerships measure their earnings or losses using the same accounting methods that are available to corporate entities. There are, however, several significant differences.

First, partnerships often report their earnings before any remuneration to the partners, whereas a corporation records the compensation of its officers as an expense, a reduction of earnings. Neither entity, however, records the imputed interest or opportunity cost of having capital invested. Both, however, record the interest cost of borrowed capital usually as an expense.

Second, partnerships are not taxable entities as are corporations. Partnership earnings are, in effect, on a pretax basis even though the partners themselves are taxed. Partnerships do, however, report taxable income; thus, they have timing and permanent differences (differences between pretax accounting earnings and taxable income). Even though there is no accounting for income taxes at the partnership level, such accounting may be necessary at the partner level at least for corporate partners.

Corporate Partners

Since corporate partners often report their share of financial pretax earnings as a different amount from their share of partnership taxable income, they will have some accounting for income tax problems in regard to these earnings. Because of the conduit principle, tax-exempt partnership earnings would constitute permanent differences when flowed through to a corporate partner. The partnership might even have some investments in other corporate stocks, the dividend yield of which would be eligible for the 85 percent dividends received deduction when the conduit principle is applied to the corporate partner. This could become complex if a partnership owned some of the outstanding shares of a corporate partner and had received dividends on these shares. Timing differences can, of course, result from the use of different accounting methods for book and for tax purposes (e.g., different depreciation methods).

As stated before, corporate partners are common in the oil and gas industry where partnerships are formed to spread the risk in exploration and development. Even though the equity method of accounting, for certain corporate investments in shares of other corporations, does not apply to partnerships, many of the equity method rules would apply to a significant partnership interest. This includes deferral and restoration of intercompany gains or losses between the corporate partner and the partnership.[5] Theoretically, the form of the business entity should not be a major factor in accounting for an investment in it; if a subsidiary should be consolidated or accounted for on the equity method, so should a significant partnership interest.

It is also possible to have a partnership involved in a pooling of interests. Exchanging stock for a partnership interest or for partnership assets can meet the requirements for a pooling of interests combination.[6] The form of the investee, business entity, is therefore not controlling.

ADMITTING NEW PARTNERS

Often the admittance of a new partner causes the termination of the old partnership and the formation of a new one. The legal fate of the old partnership upon the admission of a new partner or upon the death or retirement of old partners should be part of the original partnership agreement.

Routes to Becoming a Partner

Partners may become partners through several different routes. For example, a contribution may be made by the new partner to a partnership for a specified partnership share, or the existing partners might each sell a fraction of their partnership interest to a new partner, or one partner may leave the partnership by selling his or her entire interest. In the latter case the purchaser is not automatically a partner even though he or she would have rights to partnership earnings. The same would be true if a partner dies and someone inherits the partnership interest or receives it as a gift.

The admission of a new partner and the price paid may depend on many factors, one of which is the type of partnership. In a tax sheltered limited partnership, a new limited partner is merely buying, albeit indirectly, the future cash flows of the partnership entity plus whatever cash flow effect the "tax losses" will have on his or her own income tax situation. To someone in the top 70 percent bracket the tax losses may be worth more than to someone in a lower bracket. Some tax shelter limited partnerships are advertised as only for investors in at least the 50 percent bracket. (Tax losses are often offset later by taxable gains; thus it is desirable to have the losses in high-bracket years and the gains in low-bracket years.)

---

[5] *AICPA Professional Standards, Accounting—Current Text* (New York, 1980), pars. U5131.009–.012. Copy (1980) by the American Institute of CPAs.

[6] Ibid., pars. U1091.103–.111.

Theoretically, at least, whenever a new partner is admitted to a partnership, either through a contribution to the partnership entity or through a purchase of some or all of an existing partner's interest, a new entity is created. The admission of a new partner should thus result in a restatement of all partnership assets and liabilities at fair value.

If the partnership is a professional one such as a CPA firm, the new partner must be a CPA. In this case, in addition to any cash investment, the new partner is also contributing future earning potential. As a member of the firm this potential may be greater than the partner's earning power as a sole practitioner, and as a member of the firm the partner's share of the partnership earnings may also be greater than his or her separate earnings would have been.

The routes by which a partner might be admitted can be described based on Illustration 11–6.

Illustration 11–6

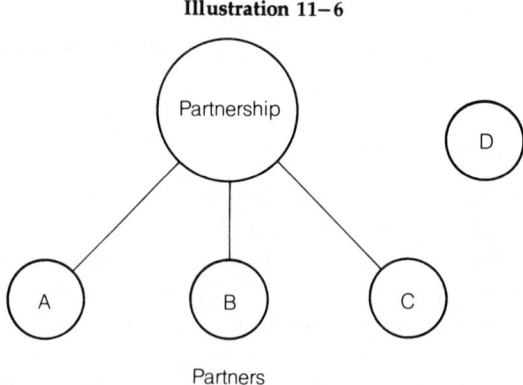

Partners

If A, B, and C are equal partners with $100,000 capital accounts and if the recorded values of the assets and liabilities were the same for both tax and financial reporting purposes and *if* the recorded values equaled their fair values, D might be willing to pay (1) $100,000 to the partnership for a 25 percent interest—with a reduction to 25 percent for A, B, and C,[7] or (2) $100,000 to either A, B,[7] or C for their one-third share, or (3) $25,000 each to A, B, and C for 8⅓ percentage points of each of their interests. The latter would mean that all partners would then have a 25 percent interest (33⅓ − 8⅓ percent for A, B, and C and 3 × 8⅓ percent for D). The partnership assets after admission of D would be $400,000 in the first case and only $300,000 in the latter two situations. These three cases are summarized in Illustration 11–7.

---

[7] Theoretically, this is an indirect sale by A, B, and C of some of their interest. It is similar to a subsidiary issuing stock to outside parties.

Illustration 11-7

	A	B	C	D	Partnership Total
Case 1:					
Capital	$100,000	$100,000	$100,000	$100,000	$400,000
Interest	25%	25%	25%	25%	100%
Case 2 (if A sold):					
Capital	–0–	$100,000	$100,000	$100,000	$300,000
Interest	–0–	33⅓%	33⅓%	33⅓%	100%
Case 3:					
Capital	$ 75,000	$ 75,000	$ 75,000	$ 75,000	$300,000
Interest	25%	25%	25%	25%	100%

Premium Paid by a New Partner

When a new partner is willing to pay a premium to the partnership to be a partner, the admittance is often recorded as either goodwill or as a bonus to the old partners. For example, assume that the R and S Partnership has net assets of $100,000 represented by R capital of $50,000 and S capital of $50,000. Assume that these two partners are going to admit T, as a new partner with a one-third interest with an equal (16⅔ percentage points) reduction in their own interest percentages, upon T's contribution of $80,000 to the partnership. This will increase the net assets of the firm to $180,000. But if one third of the firm is worth $80,000, the firm must be worth $240,000 (3 × $80,000) rather than $180,000. Recorded as goodwill to the old partners this would be:

```
Cash ..................................................... 80,000
Goodwill ($240,000 – $180,000) ........................... 60,000
    R, capital ...........................................          30,000
    S, capital ...........................................          30,000
    T, capital ...........................................          80,000
```

If $180,000 ($100,000 + $80,000) is deemed to be the correct net asset value, the new partner is paying a bonus to join the partnership. Recorded as bonus to the old partners would mean that some of the purchase price of $80,000 paid by T will be credited to R and S.

```
Cash ..................................................... 80,000
    R, capital ...........................................          10,000
    S, capital ...........................................          10,000
    T, capital (⅓ × $180,000) ............................          60,000
```

Illustration 11–8 shows the effects of the goodwill and the bonus concepts on the partners' interests.

Neither of these rather standard entries emphasizes the real nature of the transaction. When a new partner is admitted with a significant interest, a new partnership is being formed and therefore the assets and

Illustration 11–8

Partner	Profit and Loss Ratio		Capital Accounts	
	Old	New	Old	New
As goodwill:				
R	50%	33⅓%	$ 50,000	$80,000
S	50	33⅓	50,000	80,000
T	-0-	33⅓	-0-	80,000
Totals	100%	100%	$100,000	$240,000
As bonus to old:				
R	50%	33⅓%	$ 50,000	$ 60,000
S	50	33⅓	50,000	60,000
T	-0-	33⅓	-0-	60,000
Totals	100%	100%	$100,000	$180,000

liabilities should be restated at fair value. *The automatic recording of goodwill is no more justified in a partnership setting than in a corporate situation.* Thus, if the accounts receivable were understated by $45,000 and land by $15,000, the admittance of a significant new partner (the formation of a new partnership) should recognize this situation and record the assets at their fair values. The entry to admit T would be:

```
Accounts receivable ..................................... 45,000
Land ....................................................  15,000
    R, capital ...........................................          30,000
    S, capital ...........................................          30,000

Cash ....................................................  80,000
    T, capital ...........................................          80,000
```

The admission of T to the partnership in exchange for an $80,000 contribution can be analyzed as though T were a corporation buying one third of the R and S Corporation's stock by acquiring a new stock issue. The form of the business entity (corporation or partnership) should not affect the amount of goodwill to be recorded (see Illustration 11–9).

The standard bonus entry may also be defective because the assets may be understated. If T, after the assets and liabilities have been restated at their fair values, is still paying a premium and if goodwill (superior future earning potential of the firm) does not exist, then T is in effect paying the premium (bonus) for T's one-third interest. There should be no bonus to the old partners unless T believes that R and S will economically be earning more than T for the partnership. In this case T would be paying the premium in order to receive one-third share

Illustration 11-9

	Net Assets	Partners		
		R—1/3	S—1/3	T—1/3
Before admission of T.....	$100,000			
Contribution of T	80,000			
	180,000	$60,000	$60,000	$60,000
Revaluation of assets and liabilities:				
Accounts receivable	45,000	15,000	15,000	15,000
Land	15,000	5,000	5,000	5,000
	$240,000	$80,000	$80,000	$80,000*

* Price paid equals share of net assets at fair value this no goodwill exists.

of the extra earnings generated by R and S. The alternative would be to take less than a one-third share in the future earnings. If only the land were understated and if goodwill did not exist, then the bonus could be recorded as follows:

```
Land ........................................................ 15,000
    R, capital ..............................................          7,500
    S, capital ..............................................          7,500

Cash ........................................................ 80,000
    R, capital ..............................................          7,500†
    S, capital ..............................................          7,500†
    T, capital ..............................................         65,000*
```
* 1/3 ($100,000 + $15,000 + $80,000) = $65,000 for T.
† 1/2 ($80,000 − $65,000) = $7,500 for R and S.

Premium Paid by Old Partners

If the existing partners, R and S, decide to admit T to a one-third interest for only $40,000, the old firm's assets and liabilities should be revalued. If the new firm is worth only $120,000 (3 × $40,000), the net assets of the old firm must be overstated by $20,000 ($100,000 + $40,000 − $120,000). If this is the case, the assets of the old partnership should be written down to their $80,000 ($100,000 − $20,000) fair value before T is admitted. This and the admission of T would require the following entries:

```
R, capital ................................................. 10,000
S, capital ................................................. 10,000
    Assets ................................................         20,000

Cash ....................................................... 40,000
    T, capital ............................................         40,000
```

It is also possible that R and S may believe that T's contribution to the future earnings of the partnership may be greater than their own. In this case R and S might admit T to a one-third interest for only $40,000 even if the book value of the net assets of the firm, before T, equaled their $100,000 fair value. Partners R and S would then be paying a bonus to T for their one-third shares of the extra earnings to be generated by T. This could be recorded as:

```
Cash ............................................................ 40,000
R, capital (($46,667 − $40,000) × ½) ......................  3,333
S, capital ....................................................   3,334
    T, capital (⅓ × $140,000) ..............................          46,667
```

Since partners seldom like to have their capital accounts reduced, some would record T's extra future earning power over that of R and S as goodwill by making T's capital equal to that recorded for R and for S.

```
Cash ............................................................ 40,000
Goodwill ....................................................... 10,000
    T, capital .................................................          50,000
```

At least theoretically, it is better to avoid recording goodwill when it is nothing but the extra future earning power of one partner over other partners in the same firm. Goodwill, if recorded, should designate superior future earning power of the firm over other firms in that industry.

Normally in admitting a new partner the old partnership is dissolved and a new one created. In the creation of the new partnership, the assets and liabilities, theoretically at least, should be recorded at their fair values on that date.

Admitting New Partners—Additional Examples

The problem of identifying a bonus or goodwill entry is more of a textbook problem than a real-world problem. In an actual situation the accounts to be adjusted will be identified by the parties to the transaction. In any event for financial reporting before admission of a new partner, the assets and liabilities of the partnership should always be stated (or carried) at fair value including goodwill. Goodwill recorded before admission of the new partner is goodwill to the old partners. If new partners bring goodwill with them (as part of their contribution), this is goodwill to the new partner.

If bonus is to be recorded instead of goodwill,[8] in place of goodwill to the old partners some of the capital contribution of the new partner is credited to the capital accounts of the old partners. And if bonus to the

---

[8] Theoretically, if goodwill exists, recording it as "bonus" is wrong; and if a "bonus" situation exists (excess share of earnings), recording it as goodwill is wrong.

new partner is to be recorded rather than goodwill to the new partner, some of the capital of the old partners is credited to the capital account of the new partner.

Assume that there are three partnerships, with equal earnings and loss ratios (⅓ to each partner) and equal fair values but with different capital amounts, and that U is going to join each and receive a 25 percent capital interest for a contribution of $70,000 to each partnership. The capital portions of the statement of financial position for each partnership immediately prior to the admission of U are shown in Illustration 11–10. In each case, Illustration 11–10 assumes all assets (other than goodwill, if any) and liabilities are recorded at fair value.

Illustration 11–10

Partnerships					
ABC		MNO		RST	
Partner	Capital	Partner	Capital	Partner	Capital
A	$ 40,000	M	$ 70,000	R	$ 80,000
B	50,000	N	70,000	S	90,000
C	60,000	O	70,000	T	100,000
	$150,000		$210,000		$270,000

If there is no bonus situation, goodwill should be recorded if it exists. For the ABC partnership (with unequal capital accounts and with a one-third share of earnings for each partner before admission of U and one-fourth after admission of U) there is apparently an unrecorded goodwill amount of $60,000 (4 × $70,000 − ($150,000 + $70,000)) based on U's contribution. This should be recorded as:

Goodwill	60,000	
A, capital		20,000
B, capital		20,000
C, capital		20,000

Then:

Cash	70,000	
U, capital		70,000

For the MNO partnership (equal partners with equal capital accounts) no goodwill exists based on U's contribution (4 × $70,000 = $210,000 + $70,000). Thus:

Cash	70,000	
U, capital		70,000

For the RST partnership (again equal partners even though the capital accounts are unequal) based on U's contribution there would be negative goodwill (4 × $70,000 ≠ 270,000 + $70,000) and with assets and liabilities carried at fair value this cannot be correct. But if the goodwill (attributable to U) is measured from the old partners capital accounts (which average $90,000), there is $20,000 ($270,000 ÷ 75% − ($270,000 + $70,000)) of goodwill *attributable to U's admission* which is recorded as:

Cash	70,000	
Goodwill	20,000	
U, capital		90,000

Returning to the ABC partnership, assume a bonus is to be recorded (instead of goodwill) due to U's higher than otherwise justified earnings ratio.[9] This is then measured from the old partners capital accounts (after recording all assets and liabilities at fair value) plus U's contribution and amounts to $15,000 ($150,000 + $70,000) ÷ 4 = $55,000. $70,000 − $55,000 = $15,000). U's admission is then recorded as:

Cash	70,000	
A, capital (⅓ × $15,000)		5,000
B, capital		5,000
C, capital		5,000
U, capital		55,000

For the RST partnership the admission of U results in a bonus to U if goodwill does not exist. With assets totaling $340,000 ($270,000 + $70,000) after U's admission, U receives a $15,000 bonus ($340,000 × 25% − $70,000 = $15,000) presumably to compensate for U's lower than otherwise justified earnings ratio. This is recorded as follows:

Cash	70,000	
R, capital		5,000
S, capital		5,000
T, capital		5,000
U, capital		85,000

A 25 percent partner's capital account now averages $85,000 ($340,000 ÷ 4 = $85,000).

Some partnership agreements provide for continuity of existence upon the admittance of new partners and upon the retirement or death of old partners. This is the case for the large CPA firms. In these firms revaluation of assets and liabilities may not be necessary. New partners may total less than 10 percent of total partners, and their share of profits and losses will be even less. (One advantage of using a unit share rather than percentage share system to allocate earnings is that it is easier to change the number of units than to adjust percentages.) For

---

[9] U is paying the bonus because U's one-fourth share of earnings is greater than U's earnings contribution to the entity.

many if not most CPA firms their established clients may constitute their most valuable asset, and this asset is usually not recorded.

Purchasing an Existing Partner's Interest

If admitted to partnership by the remaining partner(s), it is possible to become a partner by buying out an existing partner's interest. Thus, again assuming an R and S partnership with equal partners and $50,000 capital accounts for each, T could become a partner by buying either R's or S's partnership interest if the remaining partner agrees to making T a partner. Note that this saves the cost of a formal dissolution of the R and S partnership and the cost of creating the new S and T partnership (assumes T purchased R's interest). If the R and S partnership had been formally liquidated and if T then acquired R's partnership assets, received by R in the liquidation, T and S could then contribute these assets to the new S and T partnership. If, however, T paid R $80,000 for R's share of the net assets, R would report a $30,000 gain and the basis to T for the acquired net assets would be $80,000. Therefore, when the S and T partnership was formed, T's contribution (a one-half interest in the same assets owned one half by S) would have an $80,000 basis and S's contribution would still have only a $50,000 basis at least for tax purposes. Theoretically, both the T and S interests should be recorded at fair value for financial reporting as this is a new entity. Again, theoretically, the liquidation of the R and S partnership (termination of an entity) should have caused S to recognize the $30,000 as gain. For tax purposes, however, a partnership's net assets distributed to a partner retain their basis (in a full liquidation this replaces the partner's capital interest).[10] This basis retention concept is also applied when these same assets are recontributed to a new partnership. Through formal liquidation (of the R and S partnership), with the purchase of the assets received by one partner (T's purchase of R's assets from liquidation) and recontribution of the identical assets involved in the liquidation, T's contributed assets have a $30,000 increase in basis for tax purposes. If T buys R's capital interest and the old partnership is not liquidated, the tax law provides an election whereby the basis of the assets now indirectly owned by T can be increased to the price T paid R for that interest.[11] Thus, an asset which has appreciated in value will have one basis as to T and a lower basis as to S for income tax purposes. But fair value should be used for financial reporting; for S this basis difference

---

[10] A partner's capital interest may have to be prorated over the assets received; this is discussed further in the next chapter.

[11] *Internal Revenue Code*, secs. 754 and 743(b). An interesting tax case might develop if S were to buy T's interest and T were to buy S's interest. At the cost of a capital gains tax (perhaps) they could get a step up in the basis of the assets.

should be a permanent difference but one that will reverse as depreciation is taken or when the asset is sold.[12]

> **Tax:** If the election to increase the bases of the assets held in the partnership and indirectly purchased by T is not made, and if there is a distribution of partnership assets to T within two years of the acquisition of T's interest, T can elect to increase the basis of these assets (except for cash, unrealized receivables, and appreciated inventory) to reflect the price T paid.* This provision applies only to partners who have purchased or inherited their interest and not to partners who have acquired their interest through a capital contribution. Thus, a prospective partner who may be willing to pay a premium for admittance might be better advised to consider purchasing this interest from existing partners rather than making a capital contribution.
>
> One should also note that there is no mandatory basis reduction for partnership assets. If T buys R's investment for only $20,000, the basis for the assets on the partnership's tax books remains unchanged. The taxation of partnerships is a very complex area and made even more complex when there are changes in partnership interests. Expert tax advice should always be sought in these cases and before the transaction is consummated. Tax advice should always enter at the planning stage.
>
> * *International Revenue Code*, sec. 732(d).

Purchasing a Part of Each Partner's Interest

Buying part of each partner's interest is not unlike buying out one partner's interest. The only difference is that now there will be one more partner and a change in every partner's capital interest and earnings and loss-sharing ratio. In addition, the purchase of a partnership interest from existing partners (or buying a partner's entire interest) is quite similar to purchasing a stock interest in a corporation from existing shareholders. Thus, the same type of investment analysis can be employed. Perhaps the easiest way to illustrate this is through a problem and solution. For purposes of this illustration we will be concerned only with the financial accounting rules and not the federal income tax rules.

---

[12] Note that this is not the reversal of a timing difference; the possibility of reversal of a permanent difference was discussed in Chapter 1 and in Chapter 2 where the tax basis of an asset is greater than the book basis.

Equal to Unequal Partnership. The Equal Partnership was composed of three equal partners (A, B, and C) with capital accounts of $60,000 each. The 1/1/x1 statement of financial position before the sale of capital interests to D is shown in Illustration 11–11.

Illustration 11–11

	Book Value	Fair Value
Cash	$ 2,000	$ 2,000
Accounts receivable	3,000	3,000
Oil deposits	190,000	306,000
Land	5,000	6,000
Total	$200,000	$317,000
Liabilities	$ 20,000	$ 20,000
A, capital	60,000	99,000
B, capital	60,000	99,000
C, capital	60,000	99,000
Total	$200,000	$317,000

1. On the partnerships books, journalize every possibility for recording the purchase on 1/1/x1 of two thirds of each partner's interest by D for $210,000, $70,000 to each old partner.
2. On the partnership books, journalize every possibility for recording the purchase on 1/1/x1 of two thirds of each partner's interest by D for $30,000, $10,000 to each old partner. The 1/1/x1 statement of financial position for this part shows the following before the sale of a capital interest to D:

	Book Value	Fair Value
Cash	$ 2,000	$ 2,000
Accounts receivable	3,000	3,000
Oil deposits	190,000	120,000
Land	5,000	15,000
Total	$200,000	$140,000
Liabilities	$ 20,000	$ 20,000
A, capital	60,000	40,000
B, capital	60,000	40,000
C, capital	60,000	40,000
Total	$200,000	$140,000

Solution to Equal to Unequal Partnership:

1. Possibilities:
    a. No entry (other than transfer of ownership) on the partnership's books because the partnership entity was not a party to the transaction. (This is an application of the separate entity con-

cept similar to when someone acquires some of the outstanding stock of a corporate entity.) However, it is necessary to establish a capital account for the new partner.

A, capital (⅔ × $60,000).............................	40,000	
B, capital...	40,000	
C, capital	40,000	
D, capital		120,000

This is a transfer of ownership at book value much like a transfer agent's problem of identifying new shareholders as corporate stock is bought and sold.

b. Under the aggregation of interests concept, the change in interests would have to be recognized. It would therefore be possible to recognize that a new business entity had been started. If the old records are to be retained and adjusted for the new entity, the following three possibilities could be recorded:

Oil deposits (⅔ × ($306,000 − $190,000))	77,333	
Land (⅔ × ($6,000 − $5,000)).....................	667	
A, capital	40,000	
B, capital...	40,000	
C, capital	40,000	
D, capital		198,000

In addition, the partnership entity could also recognize that D paid $210,000 for D's interest which would require goodwill to be recorded.

Goodwill...	12,000	
D, capital ($210,000 − $198,000)		12,000

Note the above two entries combined are similar to alternative 1 for corporate acquisitions. Thus, recording as alternatives 2 or 3 would also be possible.

Oil deposits	116,000	
Land	1,000	
Goodwill...	12,000	
A, capital ($40,000 − ⅑ ($116,000 + $1,000))	27,000	
B, capital...	27,000	
C, capital	27,000	
D, capital		210,000

This is similar to alternative 2 for corporate acquisitions.

Oil deposits	116,000	
Land	1,000	
Goodwill...	18,000	
A, capital (40,000 − ⅑ × $135,000)	25,000	
B, capital...	25,000	
C, capital	25,000	
D, capital		210,000

This is similar to alternative 3 for corporate acquisitions.

Since the similarity between this and a corporate acquisition has been established, we can examine it in the familiar investment account analysis format given in Illustration 11–12.

Illustration 11–12

	Net Assets	D—2/3	A—1/9	B—1/9	C—1/9
Capital accounts 1/1/x1	$180,000	$120,000	$20,000	$20,000	$20,000
Oil deposits	116,000	77,333	12,889	12,889	12,889
Land	1,000	667	111	111	111
Subtotal	297,000	198,000	33,000	33,000	33,000
Goodwill	18,000	12,000	2,000	2,000	2,000
	$315,000	$210,000	$35,000	$35,000	$35,000

Thus, A's, B's or C's capital (minority interests to D) would be $20,000 ($60,000 − $40,000) under alternative 1, $33,000 ($60,000 − $27,000) under alternative 2, and $35,000 ($60,000 − $25,000) under alternative 3. The $35,000 can also be computed as the $99,000 (⅓ × $297,000) fair value of recorded net assets plus $6,000 (⅓ × $18,000) of goodwill less $70,000 received from D on the sale of part of their interests.

Possibilities for the solution to part 2 of this problem would appear as follows:

2. a. Again the separate entity theory could be applied and record only the switch in ownership.

A, capital (⅔ × 60,000)	40,000	
B, capital	40,000	
C, capital	40,000	
D, capital		120,000

But, certainly this is unrealistic without first recognizing the decrease in asset value.

b. Again, the aggregate interests concept could be applied which is the same as recognizing a new separate entity. The investment analysis would then be as in Illustration 11–13.

The recording possibilities now appear to be:

A, capital ($40,000 basis sold + 1/9 × $60,000 net write-down)	46,667	
B, capital	46,667	
C, capital	46,666	
Land	10,000	
Oil deposits		70,000
D, capital		80,000

Illustration 11–13

	Net Assets	D—2/3	A—1/9	B—1/9	C—1/9
Capital accounts, 1/1/x1	$180,000	$120,000	$20,000	$20,000	$20,000
Oil deposit	(70,000)	(46,667)	(7,778)	(7,778)	(7,777)
Land	10,000	6,667	1,111	1,111	1,111
Subtotals	120,000	80,000	13,333	13,333	13,334
Proportionate reductions:*					
Oil deposits:					
$\frac{\$120,000}{\$135,000} \times \$50,000$†	(44,444)	(44,444)	–0–	–0–	–0–
Land:					
$\frac{\$15,000}{\$135,000} \times \$50,000$	(5,556)	(5,556)	–0–	–0–	–0–
Totals	$ 70,000	$ 30,000‡	$13,333	$13,333	$13,334

* It should be noted that this is in agreement with the proportionate allocation scheme (from noncurrent assets other than investments) devised by the Accounting Principles Board in *Opinion No. 16*.
† $80,000 − $30,000 = $50,000.
‡ Price paid for interest.

Proportionate reduction:

D, capital	50,000	
Land		5,556
Oil deposits...		44,444

Some may not want to follow the APB and *Opinion No. 16*. In order to retain the 2/3, 1/9, 1/9, 1/9 capital account relationship, they would either (1) not record the above proportionate allocation entry or (2) increase the write-down to $75,000 ($50,000 ÷ 2/3) so that it could be spread proportionately against all capital accounts. Your author would favor not recording the proportionate reduction entry which has the effect of leaving D's capital account at $80,000, or a full two thirds of the $120,000 fair value of the underlying net assets. Then, all capital accounts would be stated at fair value just as though records were established for a new entity.

It should now be obvious to all students that accounting for partnerships is a complex process and one in which substantial disagreement exists. From the tax point of view accounting for partnerships is equally, if not more, complex.

REVIEW QUESTIONS

1. How is a partnership defined?
2. What two mutually exclusive concepts are used in reporting partnership transactions?

3. Is a partnership taxed using individual or corporate tax rates?
4. How do partnerships differ from proprietorships?
5. How do partnerships differ from corporations?
6. How do partnerships differ from joint ownerships?
7. What are the two common types of partners?
8. Which type of partner is most often associated with tax shelters?
9. What are some of the common types of partnerships?
10. What is the limit on the deduction of losses to partners for tax purposes?
11. What characteristic is peculiar to partnerships of professional persons?
12. By what process do the large CPA firms usually allocate their earnings?
13. How is it possible to be an unsuccessful partner in a successful partnership?
14. What is the partnership agreement and what should it contain?
15. What are the earnings and loss ratios?
16. Do all partnerships have earnings and loss ratios? Explain.
17. What are some of the ways a partnership can compensate a partner for the value of his services as compared to the value of the services of other partners?
18. How is it possible for one partner to suffer losses while another partner receives gain on his or her capital investment?
19. What is the basis of assets and liabilities transferred to a partnership by a partner for tax and for financial reporting purposes?
20. Does a partnership have timing and permanent differences between pretax book income and taxable income? Explain.
21. How is accounting for income tax effects of timing differences, and so forth, handled?
22. Can a partnership be included in consolidated financial statements? Explain.
23. How can an individual become a partner?
24. Why might a premium be paid to become a partner?
25. Why might the old partners "pay a premium" to admit a new partner (the equivalent of admitting the new partner at a discount)?
26. What should goodwill represent when recorded on a partnership's records?
27. What basis problems are encountered when a new partner buys an interest from an existing partner or partners?

PROBLEMS

Problem 1: Sharing of Gains and Losses

The ABC partnership had three partners with capital accounts as shown below as of 1/1/x1. During 19x1 each partner withdrew $20,000. In the sharing of earnings and losses, partners A and B are awarded annual salaries of $30,000 and $10,000, respectively, and only partner C is awarded interest at 8 percent on his beginning capital balance in excess of $50,000. Remaining earnings after salaries and interest are divided equally, whereas losses are born only by partners A and B at 60 percent and 40 percent, respectively.

Capital	1/1/x1
A	$ 40,000
B	20,000
C	550,000
Total	$610,000

Required:
1. Compute the 12/31/x1 capital balance for each partner assuming earnings from operations were $150,000.
2. Compute the 12/31/x1 capital balance for each partner assuming that earnings from operations were only $50,000. Any deficit balances are offset by additional capital contributions on 12/31/x1.
3. Compute the 12/31/x1 capital balance for each partner assuming the partnership lost $20,000 from operations. Any deficit balances are offset by additional capital contributions on 12/31/x1.
4. If there were no additional capital contributions and no withdrawals and if the financial and tax records were in agreement, how much income or loss would each partner report from the partnership in each of the above situations?

Problem 2: Admitting a New Partner

The M, N, and O partnership shares earnings and losses, one third for each partner. Their capital accounts are as follows on 1/1/x1 before admitting T to the partnership:

Partner	Capital Balance
M	$100,000
N	120,000
O	130,000

These partners have agreed to admit T to a 10 percent partnership interest (with a 3⅓ percent reduction in each old partner's earnings and loss ratio) as of 1/1/x1 for a partnership capital contribution of $20,000.

Required:
1. Assuming that the book value of the net assets equals fair value, prepare the journal entry to admit T using the so-called goodwill method.
2. Prepare the journal entry to admit T using the so-called bonus method (assume fair value equals book value and an equal bonus from each of the old partners).

Problem 3: MAD to MADE Partnership

Assume the MAD Partnership is composed of three equal partners (M, A, and D) each with capital accounts of $50,000.

a. Assume they decide to admit E as a 25 percent partner for a capital contribution of $68,000.
b. Assume they decide to admit E as a 25 percent partner for a capital contribution of $41,000.

Required:

1. Record (a) and (b) above on the partnership books first using the standard goodwill approach.
2. Record (a) and (b) above using the standard bonus approach.
3. If under (a) above land were undervalued by $50,000, record the admission of E using the modified goodwill approach.
4. If under (a) above land were undervalued by $50,000, record the admission of E using the modified bonus (to the old partners) approach.
5. If under (b) above land were overvalued by $24,000, record the admission of E using the modified goodwill approach.
6. If under (b) above land were overvalued by $24,000, record the admission of E using the modified bonus approach.

Problem 4: H&W Forming a Partnership

Helen and Wilbur decide to form a partnership after having competed for many years. Helen owns a pharmacy but also sells some grocery items (mostly bread and milk) at prices below cost to attract Wilbur's customers. Wilbur owns a grocery store and also sells some nonprescription items (mostly cold remedies and dental products) at prices below cost to attract Helen's customers.

Helen and Wilbur had also contemplated marriage, but upon discussing their plans (merger and marriage) with their CPA they learn of the heavy penalty tax on married couples where both have income. Therefore, they decide to form the business partnership and live together without marriage to save income taxes.

	Pharmacy		Grocery	
	Book	FMV	Book	FMV
Cash	$ 5,000	$ 5,000	$ 10,000	$ 10,000
Inventory	140,000	130,000	350,000	365,000
Fixtures (net)	40,000	20,000	30,000	20,000
Buildings (net)	50,000	75,000	–0–	–0–
Land	15,000	60,000	–0–	–0–
Totals	$250,000	$290,000	$390,000	$395,000
Mortgage	$ 30,000	$ 30,000	–0–	–0–
Trade payables	10,000	10,000	$ 20,000	$ 20,000
Owners' equity	210,000	250,000	370,000	375,000
Totals	$250,000	$290,000	$390,000	$395,000

In forming the partnership Wilbur is to receive a 60 percent interest and Helen a 40 percent interest. Because Wilbur rents the building in which he operates his grocery business, he has no money invested in fixed assets.

Required:
1. Record the creation of the partnership by opening its books with a journal entry recording the transfer of all assets and liabilities to the partnership for financial accounting purposes.
2. Show the tax basis to the partnership of all its assets (individually). Assume the book and tax bases were the same amounts before the transfer.
3. What is the tax basis for Helen's partnership interest?
4. What is the tax basis for Wilbur's partnership interest?
5. If they move the pharmacy assets, cash, inventory, and fixtures into the grocery store building and sell the pharmacy building and land at fair market value, how much gain will be recognized for book and for tax purposes and how will this gain be split between Helen and Wilbur?

Problem 5: Partnership Interperiod Income Tax Allocation

Assume that the Major Partnership had three partners, A an individual, B another partnership, and C a corporation. The partners share earnings and losses equally and have equal capital accounts. The following reflects the results of the first year of operations:

	Financial Earnings	Taxable Income	Difference
Gross margin	$200,000	$160,000	Due to installment sales
Depreciation	(50,000)	(80,000)	Due to accelerated depreciation and short lives
Warranties	(10,000)	(5,000)	Deductible only when paid for tax purposes
Other deductions	(80,000)	(80,000)	
Dividends received	50,000	50,000	Or less if 85% dividend received deduction applies
Interest revenue	10,000	6,000	$4,000 state bond interest which is nontaxable
Totals	$120,000	$ 51,000	

The partnership also earn $2,100 of investment tax credits due to purchases of qualifying assets on January 1 of this year. This credit is available to the partners based on their partnership interests. These assets have 10-year lives for tax depreciation purposes. There were no withdrawals of earnings during the year by any partner.

Required:
1. Compute and record C Corporation's share of the partnership earnings for financial statement purposes.

2. Compute and record the federal income tax on these earnings assuming a flat 30 percent corporate tax rate and the deferral method of recording the investment tax credit. Assume the partnership earnings are the only earnings of C Corporation and no audit pad is necessary.

Problem 6: DEF Partnership

The DEF partnership of bicycle retailers was formed on 1/1/x1 by contributions of assets from each partner as follows:

	D		E		F	
	Basis	Fair Value	Basis	Fair Value	Basis	Fair Value
Cash	$10,000	$ 10,000	$ 8,000	$ 8,000	$ 5,000	$ 5,000
Inventory	5,000	20,000			10,000	15,000
Buildings (net)	20,000	40,000	9,000	50,000		
Land	20,000	30,000	20,000	42,000	50,000	80,000
Totals	$55,000	$100,000	$37,000	$100,000	$65,000	$100,000

Thus, the partnership of three equal partners began without any liabilities.

Required:
1. Determine the book and tax basis of each partner's interest.
2. If all the land and buildings are sold for their fair values shortly after forming the partnership, determine the gain to each partner for book and for tax purposes (with no special allocations made).
3. Under 2 above what would be the tax basis of each partner's interest after the sale and assuming no withdrawals?
4. If the partners had made for tax purposes a special agreement to allocate to the contributing partner(s), all gain arising prior to partnership formation upon subsequent sales of contributed assets determine how much gain each partner would recognize from the sale of the land and buildings at fair value and from operations. Assume normal operations produced earnings of $86,000. Also determine the tax basis of each partner's interest assuming each withdrew $20,000.

12

Accounting for Partner to Partnership Transactions and Terminations

Partner to Partnership Transactions and Vice Versa
    Sales at Gains
        Partner to Partnership
        Partnership to Partner
    Potential for Tax-Free Diversification
    Sales at Losses
        Partner to Partnership
        Partnership to Partner
    Impact of Contributed, Appreciated, or Depreciated Assets on Earnings and Loss Ratios
Liabilities and Loans
    Liabilities of a Partnership
    Loans from a Partner
    Loans to a Partner
Termination of a Partner's Interest
    Termination in General
    Sale of a Partnership Interest
        Sale to an Outside Party
        Sale to the Partnership
        Death of a Partner
        Retirement of a Partner
Termination of a Partnership
    Partnership Split-offs and Mergers
    Partnership Liquidations
Tiered Partnerships
Tax-Free Incorporation of Partnerships

12 / Accounting for Partner to Partnership Transactions and Termination

Partnership formation and operations (division of earnings or losses and admission of new partners) were briefly discussed in the prior chapter but without coverage of transactions between a partner and the partnership except for partnership formation and admission of a new partner. Other transactions between a partnership and its partners are discussed in this chapter including partnership liquidation.

But even here the discussion is somewhat oversimplified in that it usually ignores the problems created when one form of income, that is, capital gain, is treated more favorably than normal business earnings. To prevent artificial conversion of a large amount of partnership earnings to capital gain classification, the federal income tax law contains a multitude of special rules which are beyond the scope of this text. Thus, transactions of the type discussed in this chapter normally should be reviewed by a tax expert before being undertaken.

In most of these transactions (sales, purchases, and loans) between the partner and the partnership, the parties are treated as separate entities. Thus, in many of these transactions gain or loss is recognized even though partners, under the aggregate concept, may be dealing partly with themselves.

Unfortunately, many partnerships use the income tax rules for financial reporting purposes, and therefore the basic aspects of these rules must be covered in some depth. Financial reporting should, in theory, reflect the separate entity concept which requires that all transfers of property between separate entities (e.g., a partner and a partnership) be recorded at fair value. Unfortunately, accounting pronouncements are generally silent in the area of transactions between related parties.

PARTNER TO PARTNERSHIP TRANSACTIONS AND VICE VERSA

With transfers (contributions) of property by a partner to a partnership being treated for tax purposes the same as transfers in partnership formation (carryover of basis for tax purposes) but differently from sales to the partnership, there may be tax reasons to choose one means over the other of moving property. Because of this difference, the conflict between the competing aggregate and separate entity theories can be clearly demonstrated.

Sales at Gains

Partner to Partnership. Suppose partner A, who has a 50 percent interest in capital and earnings, sells an asset with a basis of only $20,000 to the AB partnership for $80,000. For tax purposes, if A had contributed the asset to the partnership, the gain would not be recognized.[1] The partnership would record the $20,000 as its basis, and A would increase the basis of A's interest in the partnership by $20,000.[2] With a sale, however, the gain of $60,000 is recognized and taxed to A. The sale would not immediately or directly affect A's basis for A's interest in the partnership; in fact, A is treated as an outsider. As a result of the sale, the basis of the asset to the partnership becomes $80,000, the price paid. With a $60,000 increased basis in the asset, due to the sale, future depreciation or a subsequent resale of the asset will produce smaller partnership earnings, by $60,000, than if the asset had been contributed to the partnership. These reduced future earnings will be shared by A (if A remains as a partner), and in effect gradually reduce A's $60,000 gain to $30,000.

The full gain on the sale was recognized because of the separate entity concept, that is, the partnership is a separate entity from its partners (owners). By comparison, use of the aggregate concept, which recognizes partners *and their share* of the partnership as one entity, would have required recognition of the fact that A through A's partnership interest still owns half the asset after the sale. Under this concept then, because of A's 50 percent partnership interest, only half the gain or $30,000 would be recognized (on the half, in effect, sold to B). Application of this concept would cause an extension of bookkeeping problems, for if this were a depreciable asset, future depreciation would have to be taken on a $10,000 basis for A ($\frac{1}{2} \times \$20,000$) and on a $40,000 basis for B ($\frac{1}{2} \times \$80,000$). Any gain or loss on a later sale of the asset should also in this case affect the allocation to the partners. This can be illustrated as follows assuming a 5-year useful life and straight-line depreciation for an asset, with a $50,000 ($10,000 as to A + $40,000 as to B) initial basis, and a sale at the end of year 3 for $35,000:

Basis	$50,000
Depreciation for 3 years	30,000
Adjusted basis	$20,000

A's share of depreciation for 3 years
  = $30,000 \times \$10,000 \div \$50,000 = \$6,000$
B's share of depreciation for 3 years
  = $30,000 \times \$40,000 \div \$50,000 = \$24,000$

A's share of the gain on the resale
  = $\frac{1}{5} \times \$15,000 = \$3,000$
B's share of the gain on the resale
  = $\frac{4}{5} \times \$15,000 = \$12,000$

Thus, the distribution of the depreciation and the gain on resale would not reflect the 50 percent earnings and loss ratio.

---

[1] *Internal Revenue Code,* sec. 721; and *Income Tax Regulations,* sec. 1.721-1(a).

[2] *Internal Revenue Code,* sec. 722.

For financial reporting purposes the separate entity concept should be consistently applied. Even when the asset is contributed to the partnership, the transfer should be recognized based on the fair value of the asset. Only in this way does each entity, partner and partnership, receive immediate credit for appreciation or reduction in value during the period in which they held the asset. But because the separate entity concept would force recognition of gain in cases where no asset with tax-paying ability (e.g., cash) was received, Congress has chosen to limit situations in which gain is recognized. Thus, Congress tries to allow transfers (contributions) of assets so as to permit change in the form of a business (from a proprietorship to a partnership, or from a partnership or proprietorship to a corporation)[3] without a tax penalty. Unfortunately, in many cases, accounting practice follows the carryover tax basis rules which were not designed for proper income measurement.

Tax Planning: The position taken by Congress allows partners to contribute assets to a partnership if they want to avoid the recognition of gain (or loss) or to sell appreciated assets to the partnership if they want to recognize gain, for example, to offset losses on other operations. If the assets have decreased in value, the partner normally wants to sell them to the partnership, rather than contribute them, so as to recognize immediately the loss for tax purposes. As will be discussed later there are some limitations on this.

Partnership to Partner. In general, the same rules on gain recognition apply for tax purposes when the partnership becomes the seller and the partner becomes the buyer. If partner A buys an asset for $80,000 from the AB partnership which had a basis to the partnership of $20,000, the gain is recognized to the selling entity. It should be noted that the separate entity concept and the conduit principle will cause A, because of A's 50 percent earnings ratio, to be taxed on half of the gain, or on $30,000 on the sale to A. Thus, the gain on the sale results in a higher basis to A which will be recovered through future depreciation or sale of the asset.

If the partnership transfers the asset to partner A as a withdrawal or distribution (as opposed to selling it to A), the basis of the asset to A becomes the $20,000 basis of the asset to the partnership; A then has a corresponding reduction in the basis of A's partnership interest.[4] If A's

---

[3] A reverse direction or downward change in form is also possible, but in many of these cases there will be some tax effect.

[4] B might object to this transfer unless similarily treated or unless a gift to A is intended.

partnership interest is less than $20,000, say $15,000, the asset has a basis of only $15,000, and A's partnership interest is reduced to a zero basis.

For financial reporting this transfer should be made at fair value in order to reflect properly the appreciation to the partnership for the period of time it held the asset.

Illustration 12–1 is a summary of the tax rules on sales and contributions of appreciated assets.

Illustration 12–1

A. Sale at gain (illustration of tax rules)

Seller	Buyer	Seller's Basis	Sale Price and Buyer's Basis	Gain	Gain Recognized to Partnership	Gain Recognized to Partner A with a 50 Percent Interest
Partner A	Partnership	$20,000	$80,000	$60,000	–0–	$60,000
Partnership	Partner A	20,000	80,000	60,000	$60,000	30,000

B. Contribution or distribution of appreciated property (illustration of tax rules)

Contributor or Distributor	Adjusted Basis of Asset	Fair Value of Asset	Gain Recognized	Basis to Recipient of the Assets	Effect on Partner's Interest
Partner (contributor)	$20,000	$100,000	–0–	$20,000 to partnership	$20,000 increase
Partnership (distributor)	20,000	100,000	–0–	$20,000 to partner	$20,000 decrease*

* This assumes the partner's basis for his or her interest is at least $20,000 before the distribution. If the basis of a partner's interest is less than the adjusted basis of the asset distributed, the basis of the asset is limited to the basis of a partner's interest. In the latter case there would be an allocation problem if two noncash assets were distributed with an aggregate basis to the partnership in excess of the partner's interest. If one asset were a capital asset and the other an ordinary income-producing asset, there are additional allocation problems beyond the scope of this text. Cash distributions (withdrawals) reduce the partner's basis dollar for dollar and before allocation of basis to other assets simultaneously distributed. A cash distribution in excess of basis will result in gain recognition (but it might constitute ordinary income).

Potential for Tax-Free Diversification

The nonrecognition of gain upon partnership formation (or on a later transfer of properties) may often permit individuals to diversify investments without paying taxes. For example, assume A is the proprietor of a very successful small business with appreciated assets and B is the owner of some highly appreciated real estate. If they each wished to sell one half of their assets and buy one half of the other's assets, there would be an extensive tax due for both individuals. They could, however, achieve the desired diversification without any tax payment by forming a partnership and contributing the assets to it. Through their partnership interests, they would each own half of the total partnership assets. Or if they were already partners in a partnership, they could each contribute appreciated assets to that partnership and achieve the desired diversification without a tax impact.

> **Tax:** The transfer of assets such as securities to a partnership to form an "investment company" is done at fair values so as to tax the contributors on the exchange of their stock. But if the partnership were not an "investment company," the loophole remains open.

Sales at Losses

Partner to Partnership. For financial reporting, the consistent use of the separate entity concept would require recognition of a loss to the partner assuming, of course, that the transaction were consummated at fair value. Knowing the difficulty of determining fair value for some assets, and the apparently sometimes irresistible urge to reduce one's taxes, the Internal Revenue Service has convinced Congress that different rules need be applied to losses in some cases.

The tax law disallows a deduction for losses on sales to "related" parties while allowing losses on sales to "nonrelated" parties. As one might imagine, the definition of what constitutes a related party is a very complex undertaking.[5]

Generally, the rules on disallowance of losses on partner to partnership sales or vice versa require a *more* than 50 percent partnership interest (capital interest or profits interest) by the selling (or buying) partner.[6] There are very extensive and highly complex rules on ownership attribution which are used to test for the 50 percent limit. Thus, partner A in the prior example could recognize a loss if A were not "related" to B in any way. But if B were, for example, a corporation (a corporate partner) in which A owned stock, or a trust in which A was a fiduciary and a beneficiary or a family member (within the range designated by the Internal Revenue Code), some or all of the partnership interest of B would then be attributable to A, and A would then be considered to

---

[5] In addition, the degree of control is different for different types of transaction (e.g., it may be more than 50 percent for one tax purpose but more than 80 percent for other tax purposes).

[6] *Income Tax Regulations,* sec. 1.707-1(b)(1).

own more than a 50 percent partnership interest.[7] In that case, none of the loss on a sale from partner A to the AB partnership would be deductible because partner A and the partnership would be related parties. Thus, if A sold to the partnership for $5,000 land which had a $20,000 basis, the $15,000 loss would not be deductible to A.

A could, instead, transfer the land to the partnership which would then assume A's $20,000 basis. A's basis in the partnership would then increase by $20,000, but this would not produce a $15,000 currently deductible loss to A. If the partnership later distributed to A $5,000 in cash, the distribution would merely reduce the basis of A's partnership interest as long as the IRS would not treat the whole thing as a sale at a loss and nondeductible. If it were treated as a sale at a loss (nondeductible), the partnership's basis in the asset would be only $5,000.

Partnership to Partner. The same nonrecognition rules for income tax treatment apply when the partnership is the seller. But in either case a sale at a loss reduces the basis of the asset in the hands of the buyer (whether partner or partnership). A subsequent sale (second sale) by the buyer to an unrelated party could trigger loss recognition but measured from the basis of the related buyer. On a second sale at a gain, however, the seller can use the loss on the related party sale to reduce the recognized gain. For example, assume that the partnership sold to A, a "related" party partner, land for $10,000 which had a basis to the partnership of $15,000. The $5,000 loss to the partnership would be disallowed due to the presumed related party status. If partner A later sold this same asset for $8,000, A would report a loss of only $2,000 ($10,000 − $8,000). If, however, A sold this land for $30,000, A would report a gain of $15,000 ($30,000 − $10,000 basis − $5,000 loss previously disallowed to the partnership).[8]

The rationale for this treatment is confusing. Apparently Congress believed that it might be difficult to ascertain fair value on sales between related parties on some assets. Thus, on the subsequent resale to an unrelated party, presumably at arms' length, Congress wished to provide a possibility to deduct previously nondeductible losses on the prior sale of this item between related parties. But the law, in effect, allows the deduction to the first transaction buyer rather than to the first transaction seller. Presumably this is to prevent the need for an amended tax return. (Related party sales present a possibility for shifting taxable income (appreciation) on resales of the property to lower tax bracket family members, and the rules on disallowance of losses merely prevent

---

[7] *Income Tax Regulations,* sec. 1.707-1(b)(3); and *Internal Revenue Code,* sec. 267(c)(1), (2), (4), and (5).

[8] *Income Tax Regulations,* sec. 1.707-1(b)(1)(ii).

artificial creation of appreciation by first creating a loss deduction in the higher tax bracket members return.)

Impact of Contributed, Appreciated, or Depreciated Assets on Earnings and Loss Ratios

If a partnership disposes of property received from a partner as a contribution and that property had appreciated (or depreciated) in value as of the date of the contribution, precontribution gain (or loss) will be recognized. The allocation of this gain in the established earnings and loss ratio will usually produce an unintended benefit to one or more partners at the expense of other partners (normally the contributor if appreciated property). Thus, the tax law allows the partners to provide, in the partnership agreement, a special allocation of any or all of the appreciation (or depreciation in value) that arose prior to the contribution.[9] If the appreciated, contributed property were depreciable, the annual partnership depreciation deduction will be affected by the lower carryover basis. In this case the partners can provide for a special allocation (in the partnership agreement) to compensate for this effect.

> If the partners so provide in the partnership agreement, depreciation, depletion or gain or loss with respect to contributed property may be allocated among the partners in a manner which takes into account all or any portion of the difference between the adjusted basis and the fair market value of contributed property at the time of contribution. The allocation may apply to all contributed property or to specific items.[10]

Failure to provide for a special allocation will result in allocation according to the earnings ratios. (This also presents another possibility of shifting earnings to lower taxed family members in a family partnership.)

LIABILITIES AND LOANS

Liabilities of a Partnership

Because partners (except limited partners) are individually liable for the debts of their partnership, the bases of their partnership interests for tax purposes includes their share of partnership liabilities. The allocation of partnership liabilities to the tax basis of a partner's interest is made according to the loss-sharing ratio.[11] A partner's share of partner-

---

[9] *Internal Revenue Code,* sec. 704(c).
[10] *Income Tax Regulations,* sec. 1.704-1(c)(2)(i).
[11] *Internal Revenue Code,* sec. 704(c).

ship losses, if any, is then deductible but not to exceed the basis for the partner's partnership interest. The tax basis of a partner's interest is the limiting factor in deducting losses incurred by the partnership. Excess losses are carried forward by the partner and become deductible on the partner's tax return in the year the tax basis of the partner's interest before the loss deduction becomes positive through either contributions or earnings.

Except in certain cases involving real estate, limited partners, who have contributed the amount agreed upon, do not increase their basis for liabilities because their loss potential is limited to the amount of the agreed-upon contribution. Limited partners in real estate ventures may increase the tax basis of their partnership interest (and thus take larger tax deductions on tax shelter losses) even for nonrecourse debt, though they are not personally liable for these liabilities.

The tax basis effects of debt and the limit on the deductions are shown in Illustration 12–2 for A, B, and C—all general partners who share losses 50, 30, and 20 percent, respectively, and gains one third each.

Illustration 12–2

	A	B	C
Basis of partnership interest, 1/1/x1	$ 30,000	$ 40,000	$ 60,000
Partnership liabilities, 12/31/x1, $100,000	50,000	30,000	20,000
Basis of partnership interest before losses	80,000	70,000	80,000
Loss for tax purposes in 19x1, $200,000	(100,000)	(60,000)	(40,000)
Basis of partnership interest, 12/31/x1	–0–*	10,000	40,000
Increase in partnership liabilities in 19x2, $10,000 ($110,000 − $100,000)	5,000	3,000	2,000
Additional capital contributions	18,000	–0–	–0–
Gain for tax purposes in 19x2, $30,000	10,000	10,000	10,000
Withdrawals in 19x2	(12,000)	(12,000)	(12,000)
Use of tax loss carryforward	(20,000)	–0–	–0–
Basis of partnership interest, 12/31/x2	$ 1,000	$ 11,000	$ 40,000

* Tax loss carryforward = ($20,000).

Loans from a Partner

When a partner loans money (or property) to a partnership, the partner is treated as an outsider in that a loan rather than a capital contribution amount is recognized. Any loan should be established so as to earn interest for the partner. For purposes of limiting the amount of partnership losses which a partner may deduct, the loan is considered to be the equivalent of a capital interest (an increase in the basis of that partner's partnership interest). Thus, these loans are not apportioned for tax purposes according to the loss ratio.

Loans to a Partner

When a partnership loans money (or other property) to a partner, it is treated as a loan to an outsider and not as a reduction or withdrawal of invested capital. In the event of liquidation, however, the right of offsetting the loan against the capital account would exist.

TERMINATION OF A PARTNER'S INTEREST

In this section, both termination of a partner's interest, with the partnership continuing, and termination of a partnership as an entity are discussed.

Termination in General

Partners may terminate their relationship with a particular partnership through a sale of their interest, death, retirement, or through liquidation of the partnership entity.

In professional partnerships, such as CPA firms, the sale of a partnership interest may be restricted so as to permit a sale only to the partnership. In these situations if a partner wishes to leave the partnership before retirement, the partner's claim to partnership assets is usually restricted to capital interest plus claim to any accrued net earnings from operations which have not as yet been recorded. In some cases, there may also be some vested pension benefits. Sometimes a partner in a CPA firm will leave the firm before retirement in order to take a management position with a client.

Sale of a Partnership Interest

The previous chapter described some of the problems encountered in a transfer of a partner's interest but primarily from the buyer's point of view. In this chapter we examine this transaction from the seller's side.

Sale to an Outside Party. Whether the remaining partners accept the buyer as a new partner does not prevent a partner from selling an interest. This may, however, depending on the partnership agreement, cause a termination of the partnership; and the buyer would then receive a liquidating distribution. A new partnership might then be formed. Partnership agreements often force a selling partner to first offer the interest to the partnership or to other partners before selling to outsiders.

A partner's interest is in reality an undivided interest in each asset. Thus, in the normal situation, a 20 percent partner could have an undivided one fifth interest in each asset. Because of potential personal liability, the partner would also be responsible for one fifth of all partnership debts.

> **Tax:** Here the aggregation concept controls; by looking through the partnership entity to the partners, the liabilities are, in effect, allocated to each partner. Thus, the partnership as an entity would not have any debts. These debts would instead be apportioned to each partner according to the partner's loss-sharing ratio and treated as individual debts with a corresponding increase in the basis of the partner's interest. Thus if partners sell their interest, they are selling their undivided share of each asset and are being relieved of their personal liability on any of the partnership debts.
>
> While a partner's interest is a capital asset the sale of which can produce favorable capital gains taxation, the tax law forces the selling partner, in most cases, to recognize as ordinary gain that gain attributable to unrecognized receivables, depreciation recapture, and appreciated inventories. If a partner uses the installment sales method to report the taxable gain, the partner must report the ordinary income before reporting any of the capital gain. In addition, the sale of a partnership interest may result in some investment tax credit recapture as an additional tax liability.

If R, S, and T had a partnership with equal capital accounts and equal earnings and loss ratios and if the partnership had the following assets and liabilities and if R sold his or her one-third interest, the gain would be computed as though the individual assets were sold (see Illustration 12–3).

Illustration 12–3

	Carrying Amount	Fair Value
Cash	$ 27,000	$ 27,000
Accounts receivable	–0–*	30,000
Inventory	9,000	18,000
Building	18,000	36,000
Accumulated depreciation	(9,000)	
Land	30,000	45,000
Liabilities	(21,000)	(18,000)
Partners' capital accounts	$ 54,000	$138,000

* Assumes cash basis.

If C buys R's interest for $46,000 ($138,000 ÷ 3), R will report a gain of $28,000 ($46,000 − ($54,000 ÷ 3)).[12] This gain is composed of the figures given in Illustration 12–4.

---
[12] The $28,000 gain could also be measured as $46,000 + $7,000 of relief from liabilities less ($18,000 + $7,000 or R's capital plus share of liabilities) or $53,000 received less $25,000 basis of R's partnership interest.

Illustration 12–4

Accounts receivable	$10,000	(($30,000 − 0) ÷ 3)
Inventory	3,000	(($18,000 − $9,000) ÷ 3)
Building	9,000	(($36,000 − $9,000) ÷ 3)
Land	5,000	(($45,000 − $30,000) ÷ 3)
Liabilities	1,000	(($21,000 − $18,000) ÷ 3)
Gain ⅓ ($138,000 − $54,000)	$28,000	

Thus, for tax purposes R would report $13,000 of ordinary gain (for the accounts receivable and the inventory) and $15,000 of capital gain, and this assumes there is no depreciation recapture on the depreciation of the building. Note that if the partnership could not adjust the basis of these assets upward in respect to the buyer, the same gain would be taxed twice. (This upward adjustment was briefly discussed in the previous chapter.)

Thus, after the sale of R's interest to C, assuming the partnership continued, C's partnership interest would be $46,000 excluding liabilities and S's and T's interest would still be $18,000 each excluding liabilities or $53,000 and $25,000, respectively, considering the impact of the liabilities. If the partnership sells all the assets for their fair values and retires the liabilities at fair value, there will be a gain of $84,000 ($138,000 − $54,000), one third of which, $28,000 ($84,000 ÷ 3), would be taxable to C (and one third also to S and T) even though the gain of $28,000 on the sale (indirect) of these assets by R to C has already been taxed to R. There is a recovery of this second reporting of $28,000 gain (by C) if and when the partnership is liquidated. In liquidation, each partner S, T, and C would receive $46,000 ($138,000 ÷ 3). S's and T's basis would be $46,000 ($18,000 + $28,000 gain), and they would have no gain or loss. But C's basis would be $74,000 ($46,000 + $28,000), and this would produce a $28,000 loss ($74,000 − $46,000) deduction, in. the year of partnership liquidation, to offset C's $28,000 share of partnership gain.

There may be many years between the second reporting of gain and the offsetting loss deduction. The tax law allows for an election to adjust the basis of the partnership assets and liabilities but only with respect to partner C. Having different bases for the assets for a particular partner can cause extensive bookkeeping complications.

Sale to the Partnership. Just as buy-out agreements are common for closely held corporations, they also exist for partnerships. If the RST partnership buys out R's interest at book value (perhaps at R's death or at retirement), the effects are the same as though the remaining partners have proportionately purchased R's interest. Thus, S and T become 50 percent partners through the partnership buying R's interest, but the basis of the S and T partnership interests would not change. If the buy-out price exceeded the book value of R's interest, the remaining book value of S's and T's interests would decrease and vice versa. (This is very similar to a subsidiary's acquisition of treasury stock from minority interests at more or less than book value.)

Death of a Partner. At death, the partner's estate has a claim at least equal to the deceased partner's capital account. Therefore, in the preceding example if the partnership does not terminate at R's death, the estate would lose all of the $28,000 potential gain if there is a buy-out agreement at book value. Most continuing partnerships have provisions within the partnership agreement to acquire a deceased partner's interest and how to compensate for unrecognized gains or losses. These provisions should be part of every partnership agreement for continuing partnerships.

Retirement of a Partner. At retirement, often established by an age limitation within the partnership agreement, a partner's capital interest becomes a partnership liability. Most major CPA firms, for example, immediately return to the retired partner the partner's capital investment; smaller firms often establish a liability for this amount and then pay it off over an established number of years.

In addition to returning a partner's capital investment, many partnership agreements provide for pension or retirement benefits to be paid to retired partners. For many firms this pension plan liability may be unfunded or only partially funded. Unfunded liabilities sometimes supply incentive for merger. If several key partners are about to retire and are entitled to substantial unfunded future pension benefits, they may try to ensure the future receipt of these funds by merging their firm with a larger CPA firm.

TERMINATION OF A PARTNERSHIP

Termination may be caused by the death of a partner (this is often followed by creation of a new partnership). It may also be caused by a merger of existing partnerships or by liquidation of the entity.

Small, two- or three-partner firms, may terminate upon the death of a partner. Large professional firms have continuity of life with provisions for buying out deceased partner's interests from the estate or heirs.

Professional partnerships are often terminated through merger into larger firms. This trend has been particularly strong among CPA firms in recent years. The large CPA firms often have a partner designated as in charge of mergers. Thus, smaller firms often become targets for merger or acquisition.

Partnership Split-offs and Mergers

Professional partnerships such as CPA firms and law firms seldom liquidate, but they are often involved in mergers or in split-ups. When partners decide that they can no longer remain in a particular partnership, they sometimes break off, taking as many clients with them as they can, and start new firms. The firm of Touche Ross & Company began many years ago as a split-off from Ernst & Whinney (then Ernst and Ernst). Often when a firm is being swallowed up in a merger, some of its partners may not be satisfied with the arrangement and may decide not to go along but instead to split off. In almost every merger there are some dissatisfied partners. There are few real liquidations because the most important asset is normally the client list. When a firm is sold or merged, the acquiring firm is normally interested in obtaining the clients of the former firm.

The acquisition of additional professional talent may be a second motive for a merger. On the other hand, if either firm's partners do not have strong professional reputations, the fact that they will have partnership status may be a negative factor in a merger. In addition, there will be a very real problem in that one firm's partners are going to have to learn the new way of conducting their affairs and of processing the paperwork.

The "acquisition" of one firm by another should be visualized similar to one corporation acquiring another. If most of the partners (with 90 percent or more of the partnership interest) of the smaller firm remain as partners in the "newly" merged firm, the merger might be considered a pooling of interests. If on the other hand there are significant losses of partners due to split-offs over opposition to the merger or substantial rearrangements of partnership interests, the acquisition should be treated as a purchase rather than a pooling. As nearly as possible, the rules that apply to corporate acquisitions should be applied to partnership acquisitions in determining whether the merger is a pooling or a purchase.[13]

Tax: For tax purposes the partnership with the largest dollar value of assets is deemed to be the surviving partnership in a merger even when the merger includes many partnerships.* In a merger of two partnerships the partnership whose partners have more than a 50 percent aggregate interest is the continuing partnership. The other partnership is terminated and must file a final return. If the partners of each merged firm receive 50 percent, both firms terminate and a new partnership is created.

* Revenue Ruling 77-458 discusses the merger of ten partnerships; see Rev. Rul. 77-458, 1977-2 CB 220.

---

[13] *AICPA Professional Standards, Accounting—Current Text* (New York, 1980), pars. 1091.05 and U1091.103-111.

Partnership Liquidations

Partnership liquidations are much easier for financial accounting purposes than for tax purposes. First, we will examine the financial accounting rules which theoretically require distributions of noncash assets to partners (or other parties) to be made at fair values rather than book values. This forces gain or loss recognition to the partnership.

The easiest way to liquidate a partnership is simply to convert all assets to cash and pay off all liabilities before making any distributions of cash to the partners. This prevents the overpayment to one partner to the detriment of others by having all gains and losses determined (and capital accounts properly adjusted) before any distributions are made to partners. In practice, this approach would seldom be followed (unless it were a small partnership with few assets) because as assets are sold partners will want their share of the cash (due to the time value of money). In addition, conversion of all assets to cash may, in many cases where there is appreciated property, maximize rather than minimize the tax liabilities of the partners.

In any event, it is possible to prepare a schedule reflecting a safe order for cash payment, if any, to partners in the event of an installment liquidation assuming all partnership assets are to be converted to cash before distribution to partners. For example, suppose the M, N, and O partnership shared earnings and losses 30, 30, and 40 percent, respectively, and that their statement of financial position appeared as in Illustration 12–5 just prior to the beginning of a forced liquidation.

Illustration 12–5

Notes receivable from partner M	$ 30,000
Other assets	770,000
Total assets	$800,000
Liabilities to outside creditors	$100,000
Notes payable to partner N	120,000
Notes payable to partner O	90,000
M, capital	210,000
N, capital	120,000
O, capital	160,000
Total liabilities and capital	$800,000

Loans from a partner, as in Illustration 12–5, are treated, for liquidation purposes, as additional capital investment, and loans to a partner are treated as reductions in the capital investment of that partner. Therefore, the first $100,000 available should be paid to or set aside for the outside creditors before anything is made available to any partner. After the creditors have been paid or provided for, it is then necessary to determine how additional funds, if any, will be distributed and to which of the individual partners. A so-called safe payment schedule can be prepared to answer this question (see Illustration 12–6).

Illustration 12–6

	M—30%		N—30%		O—40%	
	Notes Receivable	Capital	Notes Payable	Capital	Notes Payable	Capital
	$30,000	$ 210,000	$120,000	$ 120,000	$90,000	$ 160,000
		(30,000)		120,000		90,000
Total investment........		180,000		240,000		250,000
Loss to wipe out M ($180,000 ÷ 30% = $600,000)						
Loss to wipe out N ($240,000 ÷ 30% = $800,000)						
Loss to wipe out O ($250,000 ÷ 40% = $625,000)						
Smallest loss, $600,000		(180,000)		(180,000)		(240,000)
Remaining investment ..		–0–		60,000		10,000
Loss to wipe out N ($60,000 ÷ 3/7 = $140,000)						
Loss to wipe out O ($10,000 ÷ 4/7 = $17,500)						
Smallest loss $17,500				(7,500)		(10,000)
Remaining investment.....		–0–		$ 52,500		–0–

By dividing each partner's interest by the partner's loss ratio, it is possible to determine which partner's interest would be consumed first by potential losses. Then, once one partner has been removed, that partner is assumed to be personally bankrupt. Thus, the new loss ratio includes only the remaining partners. After M is eliminated, by an assumed $600,000 loss, the ratio for N and O becomes 3/7 and 4/7, respectively. A further loss of $17,500 would eliminate O and leave N with a $52,500 balance.

Therefore, the order of payments would be the first $100,000 to outside creditors, the next $52,500 to N (as a payment on the $120,000 note), the next $17,500 would be divided 3/7 and 4/7, respectively, between N and O, and the remaining amounts, if any, would be distributed in the original 30, 30, and 40 percent ratio.

If at least $70,000 ($52,500 + $7,500 to N and $10,000 to O) is not distributed, then N and O will have a claim on M's personal assets, if any. For example, if only $30,000 were distributed (to N), then losses would have totaled $640,000 and M's share at 30 percent should have been $192,000 ($640,000 × 30%). With only $180,000 in M's adjusted capital account before the loss, M would owe the partnership another $12,000, or $5,143 ($12,000 × 3/7) to N and $6,857 ($12,000 × 4/7) to O. If at least $52,500 is not distributed, then N will have a claim on both M's and O's personal assets. Where the loss-sharing ratio differs from the gain ratio, a new schedule will need to be prepared whenever the partnership realizes any gains during the process of liquidating the assets as this will change the partners' capital balances.

A variation of the safe payment schedule approach can be employed in making payments to partners as the assets are converted into cash. By using the prior MNO partnership example, except for a change in the earnings and loss ratio to 50, 30, and 20 percent for M, N, and O respectively, we can demonstrate the realization and liquidation approach as well as the very common noncash distribution of assets.

The beginning balances are as listed in the schedule in Illustration 12–7, and the right of offsetting loans from and to partners is the first change in balances reflected in the schedule. Then, the following transactions are reflected:

Transactions:

1. Assets with book values of $250,000 are sold for $100,000.
2. Recorded liabilities of $100,000 are settled in full for only $80,000.
3. Cash of $100,000 is distributed to the partners (at this point a safe payment schedule is necessary).
4. Assets with book values of $300,000 are sold for $100,000.
5. A noncash asset with a book value of $70,000 and a fair value of $50,000 is distributed to O, and cash is then distributed to other partners to maintain their capital balances in the proper ratios.
6. The remaining noncash assets are sold for $10,000.
7. M is declared hopelessly bankrupt, and nothing can be obtained from M's personal estate.
8. Previously unrecorded attorney fees in the amount of $20,000 are paid.
9. Cash is distributed in complete liquidation.

Illustration 12–7
SOLUTION FOR MNO PARTNERSHIP

	Cash	+	Noncash Assets	=	Total Liabilities	+	M—50 Percent Capital	+	N—30 Percent Capital	+	O—20 Percent Capital
Balances	$ 100,000		$ 700,000		$ 310,000		$ 210,000		$120,000		$160,000
Loans from partners					(210,000)				120,000		90,000
Loans to partners			(30,000)				(30,000)				
Trans. 1	100,000		670,000		100,000		180,000		240,000		250,000
	100,000		(250,000)				(75,000)		(45,000)		(30,000)
Trans. 2	200,000		420,000		100,000		105,000		195,000		220,000
	(80,000)				(100,000)		10,000		6,000		4,000
	120,000		420,000		–0–		115,000		201,000		224,000
Trans. 3 See Schedule A	(100,000)						–0–		(6,000)		(94,000)
	20,000		420,000				115,000		195,000		130,000
Trans. 4	100,000		(300,000)				(100,000)		(60,000)		(40,000)
Trans. 5 † $50,000 + 20% ×	120,000		120,000				15,000		135,000		90,000
$20,000 = $54,000			(70,000)				(10,000)		(6,000)		(54,000)†
Trans. 5 ‡ $129,000 – 150% ×	120,000		50,000				5,000		129,000		36,000
$36,000 = $75,000	(75,000)								(75,000)‡		
Trans. 6	45,000		50,000				5,000		54,000		36,000
	10,000		(50,000)				(20,000)		(12,000)		(8,000)
	55,000		–0–				(15,000)		42,000		28,000
Trans. 7	–0–						15,000		(9,000)		(6,000)
	55,000						–0–		33,000		22,000
Trans. 8	(20,000)								(12,000)		(8,000)
	35,000								21,000		14,000
Trans. 9	(35,000)								(21,000)		(14,000)
	–0–								–0–		–0–

(*continued*)

Illustration 12–7 *(continued)*

Schedule A:

	M—50 Percent Capital	N—30 Percent Capital	O—20 Percent Capital
Loss to wipe out M = $230,000	$ 115,000	$ 201,000	$224,000
	(115,000)	(69,000)	(46,000)
	–0–	132,000	178,000
Loss to wipe out N = $220,000			
$220,000 times ³/₅ and ²/₅ respectively		(132,000)	(88,000)
		–0–	$ 90,000
Distribution of $100,000:			
First	$ 90,000	–0–	$ 90,000
Next	10,000	$ 6,000	4,000
Totals	$100,000	$ 6,000	$ 94,000

Note that after this distribution N's capital will be 150 percent of O's capital which reflects the 30 percent to 20 percent earnings and loss-sharing ratios.

12 / Accounting for Partner to Partnership Transactions and Termination

Tax: The so-called tax shelter partnerships are frequently involved in liquidations, especially when they were originally sold by less than reputable persons and often to people more interested in tax avoidance than in sound investment.

Liquidations of tax shelter partnerships may require partners to report gain even when no assets are received through the liquidation process. This happens when partners have deducted losses in excess of their contributions to the partnership. It should be remembered that for tax purposes their basis for their partnership interests includes their share of liabilities, and losses can be deducted up to the amount of their partnership interest (for general partners and limited partners in real estate ventures). Thus, when the liabilities of a partnership are paid and had previously been deducted as part of partnership losses, the payment of the liability constitutes income to the partner (relief from a liability) to the extent the partner had received a tax deduction.

For example, if a partner's capital interest is $1,000 and share of the liabilities is $4,000, then the partner's partnership interest is $5,000. If the tax shelter partnership throws off large losses so that this partner's share is $5,500, the partner could only deduct $5,000 (up to the amount of the original partnership interest; the remaining $500 might be deductible in the future). Thus, at this point the partner has invested only $1,000 but has deducted $5,000. If the partnership produces economic as well as tax losses, it will probably be liquidated. In this event, if the sale of partnership assets generates only enough cash to pay off the creditors (the general partners would not have to invest more), the payment of the liabilities becomes a taxable event to this partner in the amount of $4,000 or the partner's share of the liabilities. Thus, when the $4,000 income (in the year of liquidation and without receiving any assets) is subtracted from the previously deducted $5,000, the partner is left with a $1,000 net deduction which is equal to the investment which has been lost.

TIERED PARTNERSHIPS

It is possible, for example, to have partners which are themselves partnerships. In fact, in some operations there are often partnership partners and corporate partners. When a partnership becomes the dominant partner in a second partnership, that second partnership is in effect, a lower tier partnership. Just as consolidation rules are used in reporting the financial results from operations of a chain of corporations, these same rules may be applied to a chain of partnerships. Consolidation would seem to be a logical way to report the operations of partnership chains whenever the partnership's partnership interest exceeds 50 percent of the capital or profits.

It is also quite common, especially in the oil and gas industry and in some tax sheltering partnerships, to find a mixture of corporate and partnership entities. While partnerships may often be subsidiary entities to corporations, there are probably many situations were partnerships may own a controlling interest in a corporation. The concept of consolidation is sufficiently broad to cover any aggregation of business interests regardless of the form the various entities take.

TAX-FREE INCORPORATION OF PARTNERSHIPS

Since there is usually no gain or loss recognized for tax purposes in forming a corporation, a tax-free incorporation of a partnership presents problems primarily in the liquidation of the partnership. Generally, property transferred to a controlled corporation results in a carryover basis to the corporation and no gain or loss to the transferor(s). The basis the transferor had in the transferred assets becomes the basis of the stock received in the transfer.

Incorporation of a partnership could be achieved in two ways. First, the partnership could transfer its assets and liabilities to a corporation which it then would control. Then, the partnership could be liquidated by distributing the stock received, for its net assets, to its partners. The partners' bases for their partnership interest then becomes the bases for the stock received in the partnership liquidation.

Alternatively, the partnership could be liquidated by distributing its assets. In this case the partners' bases in their partnership interests is apportioned to the assets received. In some cases (involving unrealized receivables or substantially appreciated inventory or depreciation recapture, etc.), there may be gain recognized in this process. Then, the apportioned bases of the assets transferred to the controlled corporation becomes the bases of the stock received by the transferring partners. The "advantages" of liquidating the partnership first are (1) not all partners would have to transfer their assets to the corporation and (2) not all of the property received in the liquidation of the partnership would have to be transferred to the corporation. Of course, this latter advantage could also be achieved under the first method by the partnership transferring only part of its assets to the corporation. The other advantage could also then be achieved by the first method (incorporation) by distributing in liquidation of the partnership the corporate stock to some partners and the withheld assets to other partners.

A third possibility for incorporating a partnership could be achieved if the partners transferred their partnership interests to a controlled corporation in exchange for stock. The corporation could then liquidate the partnership.

To qualify as a controlled corporation for tax purposes the transferor(s) must own 80 percent or more of the voting stock or value of the corporation immediately after the transfer. Of course, if a new corporation were formed for this purpose, the control would be 100 percent.

In liquidating a partnership for tax purposes the allocation of partnership interest to the assets received must follow some very strict rules to prevent conversion of ordinary income to capital gain. These highly technical allocation rules can result in recognition of taxable income in some cases and are clearly beyond the scope of this text. In the liquidation of any corporate or partnership entity the services of a tax expert(s) should be obtained.

Once again for financial reporting, at least theoretically, all transfers of assets, whether or not in liquidation or in creation of a new entity, should be made at fair value. This results in assigning gain or loss to the entity that held the appreciated (or depreciated) property during the time the value changed.

REVIEW QUESTIONS

1. Why does your author recommend the use of the separate entity concept for all transfers of property between a partner and the partnership for financial reporting purposes?
2. How does the tax law (which uses a carryover basis rule for most property transfers from a partner to the partnership) allocate gain to the individual partners when gain has arisen largely from the sale of appreciated property which had been contributed to the partnership by a particular partner?
3. If a partner with a 40 percent share in partnership earnings and losses sells for $100,000 to the partnership an asset with a $40,000 adjusted basis, (a) how much gain is recognized by that partner and (b) what is the effect on the basis of the partner's partnership interest?
4. If in question 3 above the partner had contributed the property to the partnership, (a) how much gain would be recognized by the partner for tax purposes and (b) what would be the effect on the basis of the partner's partnership interest?
5. If in question 3 above the partner had contributed the property to the partnership and if the separate entity concept were being used, (a) how much gain would be recognized for financial reporting and (b) what would be the effect on the partner's capital investment in the partnership?
6. If a partnership sold for $100,000 an asset with a $40,000 basis to a partner with a 40 percent share in earnings and profits, (a) how much gain would the partnership report, (b) how much gain would be allocated to the buy-

ing partner, and (c) what effect would this have on the basis of the partner's partnership interest?

7. If in question 6 above, the partnership had distributed, as opposed to selling the asset, to the partner, (a) for tax purposes how much gain would the partnership report, (b) what would be the effect on the basis of the receiving partner's partnership interest, and (c) what amount would be the basis of the asset to the partner?

8. How can persons with appreciated assets achieve diversification of their investments without triggering a tax payment on the sale of some of their appreciated assets?

9. If a partner with a 60-percent interest in partnership earnings and losses sells for $40,000 to the partnership an asset with a $90,000 adjusted basis, (a) for tax purposes how much loss would this partner recognize and (b) what effect would this have on the basis of the partner's partnership interest?

10. If the partnership later sells the asset acquired in question 9 above for (a) $100,000, (b) $75,000, or (c) $30,000, how much gain or loss would the partnership recognize for tax purposes under each of the three sales prices?

11. If the partner in question 9 above had contributed, instead of selling, the asset to the partnership, (a) for tax purposes how much loss would the partner recognize, (b) what would be the basis of the asset to the partnership, and (c) what effect, if any, would this have on the basis of the partner's partnership interest?

12. If the partner in question 9 above had 50 percent interest in the partnership earnings and losses and in its capital and if the partner were totally "unrelated" to the remaining partners, (a) for tax purposes how much loss would this partner recognize and (b) what effect would this have on the basis of the partner's partnership interest?

13. When a partnership in its normal operations incurs some liabilities, what effect, if any, does this have on the tax basis of the partners' interests in the partnership?

14. When a partner sells his or her appreciated interest in a partnership to an individual who is to be admitted as a new partner, (a) what tax problems does the selling partner have and (b) what tax problems does this create for the buying partner?

15. In question 14 above, if the partner under a buy-out agreement sells his or her partnership interest back to the partnership, (a) what tax problems does the selling partner have and (b) what tax problems does this create for the remaining partners?

16. In question 14 above, if the partner sells his or her partnership interest to an existing partner, (a) what tax problems does the selling partner have and (b) what tax problems does the buying partner have?

17. Why are professional partnerships such as CPA firms seldom liquidated?

18. In what ways might the concepts of pooling of interest or purchase be applied to partnership acquisitions?

19. What is meant by a tiered partnership?
20. When, if ever, does consolidation apply to partnership activities?
21. When might a partner have to report additional taxable income without receiving any assets or an increase in partnership interest.
22. When in partnership liquidation is a safe payment schedule beneficial and how is it constructed?
23. What effect do loans from partners have when determining the allocation of distributions in partnership liquidations?

PROBLEMS

Problem 1: Big Sail Partnership

Big Sail is owned by partners A and B who share earnings and losses 60 percent and 40 percent, respectively. Their capital accounts are also kept in 60 percent and 40 percent ratios. The partnership operates sailboat excursions in the Hawaiian Islands. Partner A sells a 38-foot sloop to the partnership for $80,000, its fair value. The basis to A for the boat was $100,000.

Required:

1. Compute A's recognized gain or loss for financial reporting and for tax purposes.
2. If B had been the seller of the single mast sailboat with the same basis and fair value, compute B's gain or loss for both financial reporting and for tax purposes.
3. If under 1 above the partnership keeps the boat one year and then sells it for $90,000 after taking $5,000 in depreciation, compute the financial and tax gain or loss to the partnership.
4. If in 1 above A had contributed the boat to the partnership, compute how much gain or loss the partnership would realize for both financial and tax purposes on a later sale for $85,000 after taking 10 percent in depreciation.

Problem 2: XAT Partnerships

Partners X and A are individuals while T is a corporation. Earnings and losses are shared 30 percent, 20 percent, and 50 percent, respectively. The contributions to form the partnership on 1/1/x1 were as follows:

	X	A	T
Cash	$ 50,000	$60,000	$ 100,000
Other assets—basis to partner	60,000	70,000	100,000
Other assets—fair value	150,000	40,000	300,000
Mortgages attached to other assets	(50,000)	–0–	(150,000)

PARTNERSHIP EARNINGS OR (LOSSES)

Year	Financial Reporting	Tax Reporting
19x1	$10,000	$(200,000)
19x2	50,000	(90,000)
19x3	80,000	(80,000)
19x4	70,000	(60,000)
19x5	90,000	50,000

There was no change (increase or decrease) in any liability during this 5-year period, and no withdrawals were made.

Required:

Compute as of 12/31 for each year both (a) the financial and (b) the tax basis of each partner's partnership interest.

Problem 3: KEY Partnership

The partners K, E, and Y formed the KEY partnership many years ago when they each contributed cash for their partnership interests. K, E, and Y share earnings and losses on an equal basis, respectively. The statement of financial position on 1/1/x5 reflects the following:

KEY PARTNERSHIP
Statement of Financial Position
As of 1/1/x5

	Book Value	Fair Value
Cash	$ 30,000	$ 30,000
Accounts receivable (net)	25,000	25,000
Inventories (Lifo)	15,000	45,000
Machinery (net)	100,000	140,000
Buildings (net)	80,000	120,000
Land	50,000	100,000
Goodwill	–0–	40,000
Total assets	$300,000	$500,000
Accounts payable	$ 10,000	$ 10,000
Long-term debt	50,000	40,000
K, capital	80,000	
E, capital	80,000	450,000
Y, capital	80,000	
Total equities	$300,000	$500,000

S wishes to join the partnership, and Y is considering early retirement. On 1/1/x5, S offers to (a) buy Y's partnership interest for $150,000 or (b) to contribute the $150,000 to the partnership for a 25 percent interest in earnings and net assets or (c) to pay $37,500 each to K, E, and Y for 8⅓ percentage points of each of their 33⅓ percent interests. The book value and the tax basis are the same for the KEY partnership assets and liabilities before the admission of S; all depreciable assets and goodwill have 10-year remaining lives; straight-line depreciation is used; and inventory amounts have increased.

Assume the partnership earns a 20 percent return based on the book value of its total assets after the admission of S on 1/1/x5.

Required:

1. Compute S's share of the earnings under each of the above (*a*), (*b*), and (*c*) possibilities for admission to partnership for both book and tax purposes without special election adjustments for tax purposes.
2. Compute S's share and the shares for each of the other partners under each of the above (*a*), (*b*), and (*c*) possibilities for admission of S for both book and tax purposes assuming a special election adjustment for tax purposes where possible such that S is to receive an allocation based on the price paid for this interest.

Problem 4: ACE Partnership

A, C, and E share earnings and losses 60 percent, 30 percent, and 10 percent, respectively. Earnings for the year 19x3 excluding the effects of the depreciable asset contributed by E on 1/1/x1 for his partnership interest were $80,000. The basis of the contributed asset to E was $30,000, and its fair value was $75,000 when contributed on 1/1/x1. The partnership uses a 5-year life and SYD depreciation for both book and tax purposes. The partnership sold this asset on 12/30/x3 for $40,000. The gain or loss is not included in the $80,000 earnings figure.

Required:

1. Assuming no special allocations compute A's, C's, and E's share of the 19x3 $80,000 earnings but after adjustment for the depreciable asset for both (*a*) financial reporting and (*b*) tax purposes.
2. Assuming special allocations of depreciation and gain or loss on disposition of contributed assets, such that the contributing partner is to receive the benefits, and effects of the appreciation or depreciation that existed on the date of contribution, compute A's, C's, and E's share of the $80,000 earnings for both (*a*) financial reporting and (*b*) tax purposes for each year (19x1, 19x2, and 19x3) assuming $80,000 had been earned each year before adjustment for the effects of the contributed asset.

Problem 5: RED Ink Partnership

The partners R, E, and D share earnings and losses 60 percent, 30 percent, and 10 percent, respectively. The partnership has suffered losses consistently in recent years; in addition, partner R is bankrupt and his personal creditors are looking at his share of the partnership assets for their only source of funds. The partners decide to cease business on 12/31/x4 and to liquidate immediately. The statement of financial position is as follows:

RED INK PARTNERSHIP
Statement of Financial Position
As of 12/31/x4

Cash	$ 26,000
Loans to partner R	14,000
Other assets	660,000
Total assets	$700,000
Loans from partner E	$ 49,000
Liabilities to outside parties	451,000
R, capital	110,000
E, capital	50,000
D, capital	40,000
Total equities	$700,000

You have been appointed receiver for the liquidation of the partnership and may charge a $10,000 fee for your service. R has requested an additional capital withdrawal of $20,000 in order to pay off his loan to the partnership and allow $6,000 for personal use.

Required:

1. Prepare a safe payment schedule for the liquidation.
2. Compute the results that must be achieved before you can safely pay $20,000 as a withdrawal of capital to R.

Problem 6: A Partnership Tier

As of 1/1/x5 Corporation G was an 80 percent owner of H Corporation, a 60 percent partner in the I Partnership, and a 10 percent owner of the J Corporation; H Corporation was a 30 percent partner in the I Partnership and a 10 percent owner of the J Corporation; I Partnership was an 80 percent owner of the J Corporation.

The 19x5 separate earnings of each entity (not including dividend revenue nor earnings from investments in affiliated entities) were as follows:

	Separate Earnings	Dividend or or Distributions Made*
Corporation G	$800,000	$(200,000)
Corporation H	140,000	(100,000)
Partnership I	5,000	–0–
Corporation J	100,000	(60,000)

* Assume these dividends are eligible for the 100 percent dividends received deduction for affiliated corporations.

1. In 19x4 when the ownership percentages were the same as in 19x5, G sold a building to I for $100,000. The building had originally cost G $80,000, and $40,000 in depreciation had been taken under the straight-line method. I adopted the straight-line method and the same 10-year remaining useful life as G had when the asset was sold to I.

12 / Accounting for Partner to Partnership Transactions and Termination   **453**

2. G acquired its investment in H for $30,000 in excess of the underlying net assets of H at that 1/1/x4 date. This excess was attributable to machinery with a 10-year life; straight-line depreciation is used.
3. J sold land to G on 7/1/x5 for $100,000. J's basis in this land was only $60,000.
4. The indefinite reversal criteria have been met on all undistributed corporate earnings.
5. The corporations file separate tax returns, and there is a flat 30 percent tax rate.

Required:

1. Prepare a diagram showing all ownership interests.
2. Using the following headings compute both the consolidated earnings and the minority interest deduction for the consolidated earnings statement.

Description	J	I	H	G	Minority

13

An Introduction to Accounting for Governmental Operations and Certain Aspects of Other Nonbusiness Operations

Function of Government
Funds Concept
Standard Governmental Accounting System for a Municipality
    Governmental Group of Funds
        General Fund
        Special Revenue Fund(s)
        Capital Project Fund(s)
        Debt Service Fund(s)
        Special Assessment Fund(s)
    Proprietary Group of Funds
        Enterprise Funds
        Intragovernmental Service Funds
    Fiduciary Group of Funds
    Self-balancing Noncurrent Groups of Accounts
        General Fixed Asset Group
        General Long-Term Debt Group
Concept of Stewardship
Users of Governmental Reports
Development of a Fund Accounting System
Various Audit Concepts

A System for Control
   Use of Agencies
   Budgeting Process
   Encumbrance Accounting
   Accounting Bases
Future of Governmental Accounting
A Glance at the Federal Government
   Federal Revenues
   Federal Expenditures
A Glance at State and Local Governments
   State and Local Revenues
   State and Local Expenditures
Tax Aspects of Financing Governmental Operations
   Taxation of Investors' Earnings
   Use of Industrial Development and Mortgage Bonds
Other Nonbusiness Units Requiring Accounting and Auditing Services

This chapter can be but an introduction to accounting for governmental and other nonbusiness operations which together constitute a very important segment of the gross national product of the United States. The growth, complexity, and size of the entire "nonbusiness" sector fully justify a complete course on accounting for these entities. In addition, to all governmental units this sector would include most universities, hospitals, health and welfare organizations, charities, pension plans, and professional and trade associations.

The majority of this chapter is devoted to governmental accounting with very limited discussion of other nonbusiness operations (as opposed to the more common profit-oriented enterprises). The funds system described later in this chapter, is appropriate, however, for most nonbusiness entities.

Much of the material for this chapter is derived from *Governmental Accounting, Auditing and Financial Reporting* (*GAAFR*). This 1968 publication of the National Committee (now Council) on Governmental Accounting (NCGA) is a revision of earlier works, and now *GAAFR*, itself, has been partially revised. This most authoritative source is sometimes referred to as the "blue book" on governmental accounting. In the AICPA audit guide, *Audits of State and Local Governmental Units* (*ASLGU*) issued in 1974, *GAAFR* was accepted as constituting generally accepted accounting principles. These two publications, *ASLGU* and *GAAFR*, plus *Statement No. 1, Governmental Accounting and Financial*

Reporting Principles (the revision or restatement of *GAAFR*) by the NCGA, issued in 1979, constitute most of the authoritative literature on governmental accounting.

FUNCTION OF GOVERNMENT

Because governments can provide valuable services, the extent to which services are deemed public and thus a responsibility of government varies greatly from country to country, city to city, and from one economic system to another. But even in a capitalistic society, many of the services which are not directly within the public domain are subject to some form of governmental regulation or influence. In addition, the classification of a given area as either public or private is by no means static, and even for areas clearly within the public domain (e.g., welfare) amounts spent per capita will vary greatly from state to state.

Perhaps the most striking difference between the governmental or nonbusiness and business categories, except for enterprise fund accounting, is the accuracy, or lack thereof, in the measurement of accomplishment (revenue or benefit). The measurement of accomplishment (social benefit) in many governmental functions is very difficult and much different from the measurement of revenue in a profit-oriented business. The measurement of effort (expenses and expenditures) is, however, roughly comparable between the entire nonbusiness and business sectors of our economy. In governmental accounting, more than one basis of accounting, such as cash and accrual, might be used and depreciation is often ignored.

> Although governments are usually described as not-for-profit institutions, their operations should be conducted so that there is net gain for society. A governmental operation which does not produce a clear profit in terms of an excess of social benefits over costs has no rationale for existence. It is the task of governmental accounting to measure costs and where possible, to provide some measure of benefits.[1]

FUNDS CONCEPT

A governmental unit has many objectives to which resources are applied. Each primary objective is often accounted for on a separate basis as a fund, and each fund is completely independent of other funds. Thus, each fund is treated as if it were a separate entity. For one fund, the general fund, the major revenue comes from legislative ap-

---

[1] Ernest Enke, "Municipal Accounting," in *Management Policies in Local Government Finance*, ed. J. Richard Aronson and Eli Schwartz (New York: International City Management Association, 1975), pp. 287–88.

propriations of tax revenues. Other funds receive some specified tax revenue or other revenue directly, but often one of their primary sources of money will be transfers from the general fund.

> Governmental accounting systems should be organized and operated on a fund basis. A fund is defined as an independent fiscal and accounting entity with a self-balancing set of accounts recording cash and/or other resources together with all related liabilities, obligations, reserves, and equities which are segregated for the purpose of carrying on specific activities or obtaining certain objectives in accordance with special regulations, restrictions or limitations.[2]

Since funds are separate entities, transactions between funds in the same governmental unit are treated as though each fund were an outsider. This leaves interfund receivables and payables (between funds) reflected in the separate fund balance sheets. Thus, the total assets of a governmental unit, such as a city, may be overstated and so may its liabilities. This may also be true for its revenues and expenditures.

STANDARD GOVERNMENTAL ACCOUNTING SYSTEM FOR A MUNICIPALITY

Many governmental units use a funds system. While the number of funds will increase with the size of the governmental unit, they should be kept to a minimum. The eight common types of funds and two groups of accounts in a governmental accounting system can be classified into one of four classifications: governmental funds, proprietary funds, fiduciary funds, and self-balancing noncurrent groups of accounts.[3]

Governmental Group of Funds

This group may contain many funds, but the following five types of funds are often present: general fund, special revenue fund(s), capital projects fund(s), debt service fund(s), and special assessment fund(s).

General Fund. GAAFR describes the general fund as follows:

> The General Fund accounts for all revenues and expenditures of a governmental unit which are not accounted for in other funds, and it is usually the largest and most important accounting activity for state and local governments. It normally receives a greater variety and number of taxes

---

[2] National Committee on Governmental Accounting, *Governmental Accounting, Auditing, and Financial Reporting* [hereafter cited as *GAAFR*] (Chicago, 1968), pp. 6–7.

[3] This classification is the one presented in National Council on Governmental Accounting, *Statement No. 1, Governmental Accounting and Financial Reporting Principles* [hereafter cited as *Statement No. 1*] (Chicago, 1979), pp. 7–8.

and other general revenues than any other fund. In many large cities, for example, this fund might have flowing into it such revenues as general property taxes, sales taxes, income taxes, licenses and permits, business gross receipts taxes, fines and penalties, rents, charges for current services, state-shared [and federal-shared] taxes and interest earnings. The funds resources also finance a wider range of activities than any other fund. In fact, most of the current operations of government will be financed from this fund.[4]

While the adoption of the annual budget affects virtually every fund, its principal impact is on the general fund. The budget, and thus the accounting basis for the general fund, should be on a modified accrual basis.[5] This requires accrual of some taxes, such as property taxes, while other revenues such as sales taxes, fines, and so forth, are normally accounted for on the cash basis.

Special Revenue Fund(s). A special revenue fund is normally established to account for specific taxes or earmarked revenues to be used only for a particular purpose usually designated by law. This revenue might be from special taxes (e.g., a motor fuel tax), or from special additions to property taxes for operation of schools, parks, and so forth.

> A special revenue fund may be required for financing either current operating expenditures or capital outlays or both. It may have a definite, limited life or it may remain in effect until discontinued or revised by appropriate legislative action. It may be used for a very limited purpose, such as maintenance of a historic landmark, or it may finance an entire function of government, such as public education or highways. In some cases, a Special Revenue Fund may be created to account for a particular activity within a single function, with the remainder of the activities under the function being accounted for in the General Fund. In any event, the uses and limitations of each Special Revenue Fund are specified by the legal authority creating it, and generally the revenues of a given fund cannot be diverted to other areas.[6]

Enactment of too many special revenue provisions by a legislature will hinder the management of a city's resources and make the accounting system more complex. In addition, if revenue exceeds need in a special revenue fund, there is pressure to spend excessively because the money cannot be used for any other purpose.

Capital Project Fund(s). This fund provides accounting for revenues and expenditures in the acquisition of a capital asset, normally one requiring an extended time period for completion such as the creation of a bridge, road, or building. Acquisition of assets such as equipment

---

[4] *GAAFR,* p. 15.

[5] This is discussed in greater depth later in this chapter.

[6] *GAAFR,* p. 28.

and vehicles are normally made through expenditures of general fund receipts and do not require separate accounting for their acquisition. A capital project fund is generally created in the capital budget of the particular governmental unit, and an appropriation for it will not lapse until the project is completed.

Frequently a separate capital project fund is established for each major project. This is particularly useful when a bond issue is floated for a particular project. The use of the revenues are usually restricted to that project. Many if not most major city projects today contain some federal government financing as well as bond or other revenue.

When the project is completed, the constructed or acquired asset will be transferred to the "general fixed asset group" (to be discussed later). When bonds have been issued to obtain revenue for a project, the bond yield goes into the capital projects fund and the long-term liability for interest and repayment of the principal goes to the "long-term debt group" (to be discussed later). Current interest requirements and current installments for bond retirements require expenditures from the "debt service fund" (discussed next). If the bonds are revenue bonds,[7] they will usually be recorded as liabilities of the particular enterprise fund (to be discussed later) for which the asset is being constructed rather than being recorded in the long-term debt group. The enterprise fund will also be required to provide for their retirement rather than having this done through debt service fund.

Debt Service Fund(s). The main purpose of a debt service fund is to accumulate money with which to pay both the interest and principal of a particular debt issue. All debt issues are not serviced by this fund. Bonds issued by a proprietary operation (fund) are often recorded as liabilities of that fund and are serviced out of the revenues from operating that enterprise. In addition, depending on the law establishing a special revenue fund, a special revenue fund may have to provide for retirement and interest payments on bonds issued for its specific purpose. Most debt is serviced, however, from the debt service fund.

The nature of the fund varies significantly with the type of debt to be serviced. Term debt, where the principal matures in one lump sum at the end of an extended time period, usually requires building up resources for retirement. In this case, the debt service fund usually receives periodic payments from the general fund for payment of interest and eventual retirement of the principal. This builds up an investment pool for future bond retirement. Differences between actuarial assumptions and the actual earnings from these investments will impact on

---

[7] Revenue bonds are those which generally must be retired from the revenue generated by the item they financed. For example, city parking structures are sometimes financed with revenue bonds to be retired from parking fees.

future receipts from the general fund. It is also possible that a city may pass a special tax or provide other revenues, the proceeds of which are to be used to retire the debt. In these cases the collections may vary and this can also impact on the actuarial assumptions.

With installment debt, where the principal matures periodically, the amount received from the general fund will meet the annual interest and principal requirements. Thus, for these bonds, there is no accumulation of resources in the debt service fund to meet future debt retirement needs. As the name implies, the debt service fund carries as liabilities only the current portion of the bonded debt, with the long-term portion carried in the general long-term debt group of accounts which are discussed later.

Special Assessment Fund(s). This fund represents construction which has a disproportional benefit to adjacent property owners, and thus the costs are often borne entirely or at least partially by these owners.

> Special Assessment Funds are employed to . . . account for the construction and financing of certain public improvements such as residential streets, sidewalks or storm sewers or the provision of services which are to be paid for wholly or in part from special assessments levied against beneficial property. . . . A special fund must be created for each special assessment project, because each has a legal identity and financial obligations which are separate and distinguishable from every other special assessment fund.[8]

Because of the impact on adjacent property owners, special assessments are generally spread over a period of years. In this case bonds are usually floated to obtain money for construction costs. The special assessments must then pay both the interest and principal on the bonds.

Bonds issued to finance special assessment projects remain as liabilities of the special assessment fund (they are not transferred to a long-term debt group or financed from the debt service fund). Thus, a special revenue fund remains active until the bonds are retired or the asset is completed, whichever is later. When the project (asset) is completed, it is transferred to the general fixed asset group (presented later in this chapter).

It is important for the governmental unit to identify separately the principal and interest charge. To the property owner the assessment for principal payments is capitalized, but the assessments for interest are currently deductible for income tax purposes if separately identified.

Proprietary Group of Funds

Two major types of activities fall within the concept of a commercially oriented or proprietary group of funds. First, there are commercial ven-

---

[8] *GAAFR*, p. 86.

tures such as a city owned and operated electric power generation and distribution. The second major type is a city (or governmental unit) operated service center or function which replaces commercial services: an example could be a city garage and repair shop for all city owned automobiles and buses or a city owned printing shop for all forms, stationery, and printing.

Enterprise Funds. These operations are those that could be performed by profit-making enterprises but are instead owned and operated by the governmental unit and are self-supporting, that is, customers are charged at rates that cover all costs plus usually a reasonable amount of earnings. Because of efforts at generating earnings, a full accrual system and the normal GAAP rules that apply to profit-making enterprises are employed in measuring these revenues and expenses including depreciation. These funds also have their own long-term debt with retirement either serially or at maturity from assets provided through accumulated earnings.

> Enterprise funds are established to account for the financing of self-supporting activities of governmental units which render services on a user charge basis to the general public. The most universal type of government enterprise is the public utility engaged in the provision of such basic services as water, electricity, and natural gas. Sanitary sewer systems financed by user charges have also assumed the status of public utility operations in many urban areas, and many cities have combined water and sewer systems under the same management. In addition, numerous other activities of a commercial nature are being performed by governments in response to public demand and the inability or unwillingness of private organizations to provide them. Examples of the latter are hospitals, airports, transportation systems, dock and wharf facilities, off-street parking lots and garages, public housing, and recreational facilities, such as amusement parks, swimming pools, and golf courses.[9]

Some of these services may be financed by a combination of user charges and special revenues. As such, questions frequently arise as to whether the particular activity should be accounted for in a special revenue fund or in an enterprise fund; the decision is usually made based on the degree of support from each revenue source.

The financial statements of an enterprise fund usually include (1) an earnings statement, (2) a statement of financial position, (3) a statement of changes in financial position, and (4) statement of changes in retained earnings. In addition, uncommitted assets (cash) are often reduced in order to establish a sinking fund for items such as bond retirements.

Intragovernmental Service Funds. These funds are described in *GAAFR* as follows:

> Intragovernmental Service Funds . . . are established to finance and account for services and commodities furnished by a designated agency of a

---

[9] Ibid., p. 50.

governmental unit to other departments of the same governmental unit. Since the services and commodities are supplied exclusively to other departments of a governmental jurisdiction, they are distinguishable from those public services which are rendered to the public in general and which are accounted for in General, Special Revenue, or Enterprise Funds. Typical examples of Intragovernmental Service Funds are those established for central garages and motor pools, central printing and duplicating services, and central purchasing and stores departments.[10]

An intragovernmental service fund services only other governmental funds. Expenditures from the other funds for these services are restricted by appropriations, thus the aggregate appropriations for these services acts as a ceiling on the estimated revenue for any particular service fund. Therefore, the budget for one of these funds should concentrate on the expenditure side.

Often an intragovernmental service fund will bill for its services on a monthly basis. A normal billing usually covers all direct material and labor costs plus a flat charge for overhead. Overhead in service funds often includes depreciation expense. At the end of the year any difference between actual overhead and that billed results in an adjustment billing to the funds receiving the services, or if the difference is small it may be absorbed in the retained earnings of the service fund. Because the billings do not usually include a profit margin, the retained earnings amount may be small or nonexistent.

The initial establishment of a service fund is usually made by a contribution from the general fund. Additional resources are sometimes received from the general and other funds in the form of advances.

The financial presentation for an intragovernmental service fund includes (1) a balance sheet, (2) an earnings statement, and (3) a statement of changes in retained earnings.

Fiduciary Group of Funds

Funds in this group are used to account for assets held in a trust or agency capacity. These include expendable and nonexpendable trust funds (i.e., where the corpus may or may not be spent), pension trust funds, and agency funds.

Trust and agency funds can be of many different types and for many different purposes. But the common characteristic is that the principal of the fund and sometimes the income does not belong to the governmental unit. Thus, there is a fiduciary responsibility to operate the fund according to the agreement with the contributor of the principal or corpus. In many instances only the income from the corpus can be spent for

---

[10] Ibid., p. 70.

the designated purpose, and in other cases the governmental unit may be given the right to invade the corpus.

Trust funds are frequently established to perpetuate a family name. Thus, a wealthy family may be willing to create a trust fund for a city fountain, park, or building if the project will carry the family name. Often these trusts provide only for the construction and are conditional upon the city being willing to provide annual funds for maintenance. In other cases the trust may provide so much for acquisition with the remaining corpus to be held to produce income which can be used for maintenance. In the latter case where corpus and income are to be separated, it is quite important that the trust document spell out precisely what is to be considered income and what is capital. For example, the treatment of depreciation and gains or losses on sale of fund investments need to be specified as either part of corpus or part of income.

Perhaps the largest trust or agency funds for governmental units involve employee retirement plans. Like all pension plans the accounting is greatly affected by the actuarial requirements for items such as funding, vesting, and benefit payments.

The accounting statements for trust and agency funds other than retirement funds include (1) a balance sheet, (2) a statement of cash receipts and disbursements, and (3) a statement of changes in fund balances. It is often necessary to identify separately the corpus and unspent income portion of the fund assets.

Self-balancing Noncurrent Groups of Accounts

The two self-balancing groups of accounts are not funds—general fixed asset group and general long-term debt group.

General Fixed Asset Group. This is not a fund but is merely an accounting listing for control purposes. The assets of this group are generally not depreciated.

> General Fixed Assets are those fixed assets of a governmental jurisdiction which are not accounted for in an Enterprise, Working Capital or Trust Fund. To be classified as a fixed asset in this category, a specific piece of property must possess three attributes: (1) tangible nature, (2) a life longer than the current fiscal year; and (3) a significant value.[11]

Items of small unit value do not justify the expense of record keeping, whereas recorded items (land, buildings, machine, etc.) may exceed all other assets of the governmental unit. Many of the largest items in the group will be transfers from the capital projects fund or the special assessments fund. Other assets, usually of lower cost, will result from

---
[11] Ibid., p. 93.

expenditures of the general fund or special revenue fund. Gifts of property are also an important source of assets.

Each asset in the group should have a separate record and serial number. The record should disclose the source of the asset, its location, maintenance costs (which usually reflects expenditures from the general fund), capital additions (betterments), and other aspects such as estimated useful life. Funds received upon disposal of these assets often go back to the fund from which the asset arose (e.g., general fund).

General Long-Term Debt Group. This group of accounts is used to account for all forms of long-term debt (bonds and notes with more than one year to maturity) where the full faith and credit of the governmental unit are used to back the debt. This is the case regardless of which fund(s) consumed the bond revenues. Thus, while most long-term debt would be reflected in this group, special assessment bonds or revenue bonds of a governmental enterprise fund would not be included if this debt were not also backed by the full faith and credit of the governmental unit.

> The purpose of the General Long-Term Debt Group of Accounts is to record and fairly present a governmental unit's liability for long-term debt at any time from date of issuance until the debt is finally retired. Under generally recognized accounting principles, the proper valuation of this liability at any date is the sum of (1) the present discounted value of the principal payable at some stipulated maturity date in the future and (2) the present discounted value of the periodic interest payments to this maturity date.[12]

At the date of the debt (bond) issue the entry in the long-term debt group would be:

Amount to be provided (for payment of bonds)	xx	
Bonds payable		xx

As the debt service fund builds up resources for debt retirement the entry in long-term debt group would be:

Amount available for debt retirement	x	
Amount to be provided		x

When a bond is retired from resources accumulated in the debt service fund, the entry in the long-term debt group would be:

Bonds payable	xx	
Amount available for debt retirement		xx

If serial bonds are retired without prior accumulation of resources (e.g., from general fund expenditures), the entry in the long-term debt group would be:

Bonds payable	xx	
Amount to be provided		xx

---

[12] Ibid., p. 101.

Separate records should be maintained for each debt issue and should indicate whether they are term or serial bonds and when they mature.

CONCEPT OF STEWARDSHIP

Stewardship in governmental accounting is much more than control and security of assets; it also covers proper employment of the resources and reporting on the use of "public" moneys and other assets. Accounting for this stewardship must show whether or not legal restrictions have been met.

USERS OF GOVERNMENTAL REPORTS

Primary among the users of governmental reports has to be management. The managerial group needs reliable and relevant data in order to manage the governmental unit well and to report on its operation. The accounting system must permit management to report on its functions (police, fire protection, schools, etc.) separately. This is of particular importance to the various interest groups comprising the general public.

The legislature must also rely on financial data in order to provide new laws and direction and to be reasonably certain that existing legislative mandates have been followed. Thus, an accounting system *must be designed to produce data needed for legal compliance.*

The general public has a direct interest in the government as the public is both the primary beneficiary and, as taxpayers, the primary resource from which revenues are obtained. Within the general public are subgroups or special interest groups which, through their influence on both the legislative and executive branches of government (federal, state, and local), attempt to obtain special benefits in the form of extra services or tax reductions or both. Usually special interest groups are very active politically and thus are users of governmental accounting data.

An investor lending money to a governmental unit is interested in both the aftertax yield and the security of the principal. It is perhaps the "tax-free" nature of the yield that has often led this group to invest without adequate accounting information. While separate reporting for different functions by funds serves many parties well, investors are more interested in the total picture. The particular source of government revenue is not as important as the total available to meet their claims for interest and principal payments.

In addition, there are research groups and compilers of statistical data who need accounting data for research and reporting purposes. Research groups may be interested in individual sources of revenues and types of expenditures. But whatever their particular interest they are usually concerned most with consistency of the accounting measurements over extended time periods. The needs of each group of users should be taken into account in designing the accounting system.

DEVELOPMENT OF A FUND ACCOUNTING SYSTEM

A governmental accounting system usually permits an evaluation of lines of responsibility by the use of separate funds, appropriations, and budget lines. This provides management with useful data, and it also usually permits compliance with both legal constraints and generally accepted accounting principles (GAAP). Whenever legislated requirements conflict with GAAP, the GAAP principles take precedence. But in every event the legislated requirements should also be met even if this requires separate schedules or notes to the financial statements.[13]

Thus, the audit guide, *Audits of State and Local Governmental Units* (*ASLGU*), states that,

> In financial reporting, in the event of a conflict between legal provisions and generally accepted accounting principles, the latter should take precedence. . . .
>
> A governmental accounting system should incorporate such accounting information in its records as necessary to make it possible to both (*a*) show compliance with all applicable legal provisions and (*b*) present fairly the financial position and results of operations of the respective funds and financial position of the self-balancing account groups of the governmental unit in conformity with generally accepted accounting principles. Where these two objectives are in conflict, generally accepted accounting principles take precedence *in financial reporting*.[14] (Emphasis added.)

VARIOUS AUDIT CONCEPTS

Because most governmental operations are not on a profit measurement basis, the effectiveness of management cannot be inferred by the size of the earnings. But management can be judged on how well it has performed in comparison to the budget (the expectation) and on whether it has met all of the legal requirements established by the legislature and on their control of the assets of each fund. The ability to meet future bond interest and principal payments can also be evaluated.

Thus, the financial position of each fund and of the governmental unit as a whole can be evaluated. Measuring the performance of each fund will depend on its nature and purpose. In addition, the basis for recording the transactions (accrual, modified accrual, or cash basis all of which are described later) will have to be considered. Some attention will also

---

[13] *Statement No. 1*, p. 5.
[14] *ASLGU*, pp. 12–13.

have to be given to the nonfund group of accounts for fixed assets and long-term debt.

Some governmental units, usually the larger ones, will have internal audit agencies that usually report to the legislature. Today some governmental units are not audited by either internal auditors or by independent certified public accountants. There is also some concern that some of these units offer bonds for sale to the public without proper disclosure of financial data and that they do not follow GAAP for governmental units. In some jurisdictions (states and municipalities), the legislative requirements may be far short of the GAAP requirements.

A SYSTEM FOR CONTROL

Without the discipline of an earnings measurement, control over expenditures is difficult. For most governmental functions, the matching concept cannot be used because of the absence of revenue generation from the expenditure of resources. Therefore, a governmental accounting system must rely on separate accounting for expenditures, along functional lines and budgets, to provide some limits to spending.

In this regard management of the sources and uses of resources is most important; thus, the statement of changes in financial position often becomes the basic operating statement, as an income statement cannot be produced for nonprofit oriented governmental operations.

Use of Agencies

As in any organization, large governmental units such as the states or the federal government are organized through an aggregation of smaller units. Thus, divisions, departments, commissions, districts, bureaus, and agencies are some of the terms which indicate the establishment of functional organizations within a larger governmental unit. Some subdivisions are responsible for their own fund accounting system with revenue appropriations normally made through the general treasury.

These subdivisions normally represent continuing functions of the governmental unit, and they are sometimes established as "independent" agencies. The establishment of independent agencies frees that particular function from the full pressure of the political process and domination by the executive branch of the governmental unit.

Budgeting Process

GAAFR states:

An annual budget should be adopted by every governmental unit, whether required by law or not, and the accounting system should provide budgetary control over general governmental revenues and expenditures.

Defined in its most general sense, a budget is a plan of financial operation embodying an estimate of proposed expenditures for a given period of time and the proposed means of financing them.[15]

For control purposes the budget details the expected revenues by source and the anticipated expenditures often by type (e.g., wages) and usually by program (e.g., education) and always by fund. The separation of revenues, including interfund transfers and expenditures, by fund is necessary for control purposes and because each fund is treated as a separate entity. Some governmental units will have master budgets and separate, or subbudgets, for each fund. This is a natural result as most complex budgets are prepared from the bottom up. That is, with some guidance from the top, a budget is prepared for each fund, and then the master budget evolves from these separate budget efforts.

The master budget request is normally prepared by the executive branch. At the federal level, the Office of Management and Budget is responsible for its development. Once completed, the budget is sent by the chief executive to the legislative branch for review, modification, and adoption. In this process, it is the legislature's responsibility either to ensure that resources are available to meet the proposed expenditures or to reduce the proposed expenditures if a deficit is to be avoided. Whether provided in separate acts or as part of the budget approval, appropriations serve as authorization for expenditures and as maximum limits on such expenditures. Normally each separate fund or function receives its own appropriation. The appropriation is sometimes allotted, perhaps quarterly, by the chief executive to the separate agencies to prevent premature expenditure of the total appropriation for any given year.

Unspent appropriations at the end of the fiscal year may either lapse or continue into the future. For better control, unspent appropriations should lapse. This, however, encourages governmental units to spend any unused appropriations prior to year-end. But this spending philosophy is also present when the unit believes that next year's budget will be adversely affected if all of this year's appropriation is not used (even if it does not lapse).

Budgets must be prepared on the same accounting basis, full accrual, modified accrual, or cash basis, as employed in the accounting system. For most general operating funds the modified accrual accounting basis is recommended.

> On this basis, general revenues capable of accrued accounting treatment should, to the extent permitted by law, be recorded in the budget accord-

---
[15] *GAAFR,* p. 5.

ing to the period in which they are earned or for which they are levied. With the exception of accrued interest on general obligation debt, general expenditures should be budgeted on the basis of liabilities expected to be incurred during the fiscal year. This method of budgeting allocates the expenditures of a governmental unit to the time period in which the benefits from such outlays were received and thus provides the most practical and logical method of calculating and analyzing the value of resources consumed by a government in providing the services required of it during a fiscal period.[16]

For some cities such as New York, use and abuse of the cash basis of accounting failed to disclose soon enough enormous financial difficulties. It and many other cities failed to accrue liabilities such as pension fund obligations.

Encumbrance Accounting

Once adopted, the budget best serves as a control device if it is recorded in the fund accounts. Thus, the following entries serve as a short illustration for a general fund. The first entry records the budget when estimated revenue is $100,000 and budgeted appropriations are $98,000:

Estimated revenues	100,000	
Appropriations		98,000
Fund balance (for excess estimated revenues)		2,000

As orders are placed, their *estimated* cost, say $90,000, is recorded as follows:

Encumbrances	90,000	
Reserve for encumbrances (estimated liability)		90,000

When goods are received which were anticipated to cost only $80,000 but which actually cost $84,000, the following entries are made:

Reserve for encumbrances	80,000	
Encumbrances		80,000
To reverse the order placing entry.		
Expenditures	84,000	
Accounts payable		84,000
To record the expenditure at its actual cost.		

Not all expenditures are previously encumbered. Some items are bought without placing orders, and some items such as payrolls are often recorded as expenditures without first recording them as encum-

---

[16] Ibid., p. 6.

brances. If goods costing $3,000 were purchased on account without previously placing an order, it would be recorded simply as:

Expenditures	3,000	
Accounts payable		3,000

At the end of the year the Expenditures account and any remaining encumbrances are closed against the appropriations amount (from recording the budget) with any unspent or uncommitted amounts increasing the fund balance as shown below:

Appropriations	98,000	
Encumbrances (unfilled orders at estimated cost)		10,000
Expenditures (at actual cost)		87,000
Fund balances		1,000

A debit to the fund balance in closing indicates that someone has illegally overspent their authority and may be liable for such action.[17] It should be noted that for orders placed which have not yet been received, $10,000 in this case, the reserve for encumbrances account (similar in effect to a liability) would still be present in the balance sheet at the estimated cost.

Revenues for the general fund are usually from various taxes, licenses, fines, rents, and so forth. Revenues for certain other funds are received as transfers of funds from the general fund (where it will be recorded as an expenditure). These interfund transfers are recorded by the receiving fund as equivalent to revenue.

As revenues to the general fund are received, say $101,000, they are recorded as follows:

Asset (cash, receivables, etc.)	101,000	
Revenue		101,000

At the end of the year, all of the revenue accounts are closed out against the estimated revenue amount (from recording the budget) with any difference increasing or decreasing the fund balance as follows:

Revenue	101,000	
Estimated revenue		100,000
Fund balance		1,000*

* Excess of actual revenue over budgeted revenue.

Assuming $85,000 of the liabilities were paid and recorded as follows:

Accounts payable	85,000	
Cash		85,000

---

[17] *Statement No. 1*, p. 13.

The balance sheet for the general fund would then reflect the following:

Assets	$16,000
Accounts payable	2,000
Reserve for encumbrances	10,000
Fund balance	4,000
Total liabilities and fund balance	$16,000

The principal financial statements for most governmental funds as opposed to proprietary funds are (1) the balance sheet, (2) the statement of changes in fund balance, (3) a statement of a revenue which compares actual to budgeted amounts by each source, and (4) a statement of expenditures and encumbrances which compares these to each of the budgeted appropriation items.

Illustration 13-1 gives an example in which the assumed estimated revenues could be compared to actual revenue and the appropriations (by type and amount) could be compared to actual expenditures and encumbrances.

Illustration 13-1

	Actual Revenue	Estimated Revenue	Effect on Fund Balance
Property taxes	$ 58,000	$ 60,000	$(2,000)
Sales taxes	23,000	25,000	(2,000)
Parking fees	14,000	10,000	4,000
Licenses and fines	5,000	6,000	(1,000)
	$100,000	$101,000	$(1,000)

	Appropriations	Expenditures and Encumbrances	Effect on Fund Balance
Salaries	$ 60,000	$ 62,000	$(2,000)
Utilities	20,000	21,000	(1,000)
Office supplies	10,000	8,000	2,000
Postage	5,000	4,000	1,000
Miscellaneous	3,000	2,000	1,000
	$ 98,000	$ 97,000	$ 1,000

Accounting Bases

With a governmental unit divided into many separate entities (accounting funds), different accounting bases are frequently used by different funds. *ASLGU* lists the accounting bases used by the various funds as follows:[18]

Accrual Basis	Accrual Basis (with some exceptions)	Modified Accrual
Commercial type funds: 1. Enterprise. 2. Intragovernmental service.	1. Capital projects. 2. Special assessment. 3. Trust and agency.	1. General. 2. Special revenue. 3. Debt service.

Generally the accrual basis is used whenever revenues and expenditures are clearly measurable and available for use. Some revenue such as from sales taxes, self-assessed income taxes, or fines are difficult to anticipate and measure (although for budget purposes an estimate must be made—often based on past experience). The modified accrual system uses the cash basis except for those items of revenue that are susceptible to accrual. The full accrual basis is used for commercial-type funds and includes some measurement of depreciation expense.

In addition, the account groups also have different accounting bases. The "general fixed asset group" is recorded at historical cost or at fair value at date received if the property is acquired by gift (with or without depreciation). The "general long-term debt group" is accounted for based on present value of future cash outflows for interest and for maturity of principals. This value can change with changes in interest rates.

FUTURE OF GOVERNMENTAL ACCOUNTING

Because of improper accounting in prior years, often by cities where management made little or no effort to follow the GAAFR rules, there has developed a great deal of interest in changing the so-called accepted accounting principles for governmental units.

The interest in changing these accounting principles centers on the idea that the accrual basis should be the only acceptable basis. Some would go so far as to require the recording of depreciation by any fund using depreciable assets. In addition, with one basis there should be little objection to a consolidated presentation of all of the separate entities (funds) comprising a governmental unit. This would then permit, in the consolidated statements (but not in the separate statements for each fund), the offsetting of interfund receivables and payables so that a governmental unit as a whole would not be overstating both assets and liabilities. In addition, interfund transfers recorded as expenditures and revenue could be offset so as not to show overstated revenue.

---

[18] *ASLGU*, pp. 13–14.

To illustrate the need for offsets, assume fund A, a general fund, receives money from issuing bonds and then transfers some of the proceeds to fund B in accordance with the budgets for the funds. This has been incorrectly recorded by some cities as follows:

Fund A:

Cash	1,000,000	
Proceeds from bond issue (bonds payable)		1,000,000
Expenditure* (transfer to fund B)	800,000	
Cash		800,000

Fund B:

Cash	800,000	
Revenue* (transfer from fund A)		800,000

* These titles, expenditures and revenue, are incorrect and should be recorded as "operating transfers."

In this case fund B incorrectly shows as *revenue* the $800,000 of debt incurred by fund A. While this does not comply with GAAP, consolidation of the funds would offset the expenditure and revenue amounts, thus no revenue could be reported as the result of borrowing. Note that if fund B had borrowed directly, there would have been no revenue recorded.

Some interfund transfers represent valid revenues and expenditures. For example, an enterprise fund (electric power station) might pay the general fund for property taxes and the general fund might pay this enterprise fund for some of the electricity used by the city. These are "quasi-external transactions" and represent valid revenues and expenditures for these funds just as they would if the electric power station were privately owned.

With many states and local units having legally established accounting requirements different from GAAP, it is difficult to enforce a set of standards created by an outside (professional) group. But if each governmental unit selling registered securities (bonds) on a public exchange were required to have an audit opinion by an independent CPA, pressure to comply with the professionally established standards could be greatly increased. This would make an evaluation of the credit worthiness of a governmental unit much easier and more reliable.

There is little doubt that accounting for governmental units will improve in future years. Only the nature of change appears to be in question.[19]

---

[19] For example, see *Experimentation Booklet,* "An Experiment in Governmental Accounting and Reporting by the AICPA State and Local Government Accounting Committee," September 1979.

A GLANCE AT THE FEDERAL GOVERNMENT[20]

It is perhaps interesting to take a brief look at something as large as our federal government, but its size is almost incomprehensible. Total revenues for 1980 are budgeted at $504.5 billion, and current service outlays are estimated at $536.1 billion, producing a deficit of $31.6 billion for the year.

Federal Revenues

The primary sources of federal revenues for years 1965 and 1980 were as shown in Illustration 13–2.

Illustration 13–2
REVENUES

	1965—Actual (national income basis)		1980—Estimated (current services basis)	
	Billions	Percentage	Billions	Percentage
Individual income taxes	$ 51.2	42.8	$229.6	45.5
Corporate income taxes	27.0	22.6	71.0	14.1
Social security taxes	24.6	20.6	161.2	32.0
Excise taxes	16.8	14.0	18.4	3.6
Other			24.2	4.8
Totals	$119.6	100.0	$504.4	100.0

Illustration 13–3 is an interesting way to visualize the change in tax sources and thus tax burdens. It projects the 1965 sources so as to obtain the 1980 total (which is 421.739 percent of the 1965 total) and then shows the shift in tax sources.

Illustration 13–3

	1965 Actual	1965 Amounts Times 4.21739	Less 1980 Estimate	Increase (Decrease)
Individual income taxes	$ 51.2	$215.9	$229.6	$ 13.7
Corporate income taxes	27.0	113.9	71.0	(42.9)
Social security taxes	24.6	103.7	161.2	57.5
Excise and other taxes	16.8	70.9	42.6	(28.3)
Totals	$119.6	$504.4	$504.4	–0–

---

[20] The data presented in this section was taken from *Special Analyses Budget of the United States Government* and does not include any revenue from a windfall profits tax on the oil industry.

Since the 1980 total is 421.739 percent of the 1965 total, each 1965 source was multiplied by this amount to produce the 1980 total revenue. The subsequent comparison with the 1980 estimates shows the change in sources for financing the government. This represents an enormous shift in tax burdens from corporations to individuals (primarily middle income wage earners through increases in social security taxes) in this 15-year period.

Even after adjusting the 1965 figures for change in purchasing power, there would be about a 200 percent increase in the real amount of federal revenues.

Federal Expenditures

Changes in the reporting systems for expenditures preclude a simple comparison of the categories for expenditures as was done with revenues. It is, however, interesting to note that expenditures were $1.2 billion less than revenues in 1965 and $31.6 billion more than projected revenues in 1980. Even though 1980 projected revenues had grown to over 400 percent of the 1965 revenues, expenditures had grown even more from $118.3 to $536.1 billion. Thus, projected 1980 expenditures are 453 percent of the 1965 expenditures.

As we have seen, there were enormous growths in social security revenues; however, the growth in expenditures for the OASDI (old-age, survivors, and disability insurance) portion of the social security program were even larger. This has been due in part to the adjustment in benefits for increase in the consumers price index. Thus, while the principal social security program, OASDI, used to operate in the black, it is currently operating at a deficit.

A GLANCE AT STATE AND LOCAL GOVERNMENTS[21]

With 50 different state revenue systems, plus about 80,000 local government units and districts, a glance at the aggregate picture is all we have time for.

State and Local Revenues

Total revenue for state and local governments during the 1976–77 fiscal year was $401 billion ($204 + state and $196 + local), or $338 billion when state and local intergovernmental revenues are removed so as not to double count. But this includes federal government transfers of

---

[21] The data presented in this section was taken from *Governmental Finances in 1976–77*, which is a publication of the U.S. Department of Commerce Bureau of the Census.

over $62 billion of federal revenue to the state and local governments through grants, revenue sharing, and so forth. For local units the primary revenue source is the property tax, and for states it is sales and income taxes.

State and Local Expenditures

At the state and local levels the largest categories of expenditures are for education, public welfare, highway, health, and hospitals. On average the state and local governments operated at a surplus for the 1976–77 fiscal year. Since World War II expenditures and employment by state and local government has been growing faster than that of the federal government (for which expenditures as we have just seen have been growing rapidly).

TAX ASPECTS OF FINANCING GOVERNMENTAL OPERATIONS

Taxation of Investors' Earnings

At the federal level, interest on federal bonds are fully taxable and as ordinary income, but the federal government does not tax the yield on most state or local bonds. With 50 states, taxation ranges from not taxing federal bond interest to taxing federal as well as other states and local governments bond yields, and a few states also tax their own state and local bond yields.

With ordinary income tax rates as high as 70 percent at the federal level, the "tax-free" nature of state bond interest is very appealing to some taxpayers. Thus, to someone in the top bracket this exclusion amounts to a substantial subsidy. The following illustrates this fact. Assume individual A in the 70 percent tax bracket invests $1 million in a state bond bearing 8 percent interest. Ignoring the state income tax (there are a few states without an income tax), the interest yield after tax would be $80,000 ($1 million × 8%) because it would not be taxed at the federal level. Now the question should be asked at what rate of interest would a U.S. corporation of equal risk as compared to the state have to pay to attract this $1 million of investment. A corporation would have to pay 26⅔ percent, or $266,667, in interest so that after paying a 70 percent tax the investor would have an $80,000 yield ($266,667 − 70%($266,667) = $80,000). The corporation would get to deduct this interest cost. Thus, aftertax cost of this interest is $144,000 ($266,667 × (1 − 46%)), which is significantly greater than the $80,000 cost to the state. Obviously, the growth in state and local bond issues have taken investment funds away from the public or corporate sector.

Use of Industrial Development and Mortgage Bonds

Some corporations have found a way to benefit from the tax-free nature of state and local bonds. Many communities have established industrial parks. These communities then build according to a corporation's specifications a plant facility using local community tax-free bonds to obtain the necessary funds. The plant is then rented to the corporation on a long-term lease with the lease-rental payments covering the interest and principal on the bond issue.

This is attractive to the community in that it helps in providing jobs for its local citizens (but perhaps at the cost of a better economic location for the national economy). It is also attractive to the corporation as long as this is less costly after tax than buying and depreciating the asset.

This same concept, using the tax-free nature of state and local bonds for community betterment, has led some large cities to issue their bonds and use the proceeds to provide mortgage money at reduced interest rates for people who will buy or build an inner city home. The federal treasury is really supplying the benefits because the interest revenue on the city bonds are tax-free while the interest on the mortgage payments to the city are tax deductible to the home buyer.

OTHER NONBUSINESS UNITS REQUIRING ACCOUNTING AND AUDITING SERVICES

Units of economic activity can no longer be classified as commercial or governmental, and profit or not-for-profit is perhaps not descriptive enough (e.g., a governmental unit could have profit and not-for-profit funds). There is a large, diverse, and growing sector of our economy which includes among other entities (1) voluntary health and welfare organizations, (2) employee health and welfare benefit funds, (3) hospitals, and (4) colleges and universities. For each of the above four groups the AICPA has prepared special industry audit guides.

A full-blown "nonbusiness" course should include coverage of each of the above in addition to governmental accounting. The fund system of accounting (with some significant differences) is one thing that these entities often have in common with governmental units.

REVIEW QUESTIONS

1. What items of accounting literature contain the generally accepted accounting principles (GAAP) for governmental units?
2. Why has it been difficult to enforce the use of GAAP in reports of governmental units?
3. Why is it difficult in governmental accounting to employ "cost-benefit" analysis in evaluating most governmental operations?

4. What are the eight common types of funds and two common account groups used in governmental accounting?
5. Prepare a comprehensive definition of a fund as used in governmental accounting.
6. When there is a conflict between the legal requirements and GAAP, which takes precedence and why?
7. What is an encumbrance and a reserve for encumbrances?
8. What is an appropriation and an allotment?
9. Why is a budget so significant to governmental accounting?
10. What accounting bases (e.g., cash basis) are used for governmental accounting and why?
11. At year-end how are receivables and payables from interfund transactions disclosed?
12. What precludes consolidation in financial reporting for governmental operations?
13. What is the difference between a special revenue fund and a special assessment fund?
14. What is the difference between the general long-term debt group and the debt-service fund?
15. What is an enterprise fund and how does it differ from an intragovernmental service fund?
16. What are trust and agency funds?
17. How do appropriations for the general fund and the capital projects fund differ?
18. How is depreciation reflected in governmental accounting?
19. In percentage of total federal receipts between years 1965 and 1980 which sources of federal revenue have increased and which have decreased and in terms of dollars which have increased and which have decreased?
20. Which source of federal revenue has grown the most between 1965 and 1980?
21. In terms of expenditures which has been growing faster since World War II (*a*) the federal government or (*b*) all state and local governmental units combined?
22. If an individual taxpayer in a 70 percent tax bracket could earn 10 percent on state and local bonds, what rate of interest would a corporate business with equal risk have to pay in order for this individual taxpayer to have an equivalent rate of return on the investment?
23. What is an "industrial development bond"?

PROBLEMS

Problem 1: City of Close

At the end of its fiscal year, 6/30/x3, the trial balance for the general fund of the City of Close appears as follows:

CITY OF CLOSE
Trial Balance
6/30/x3

Encumbrances	$ 15,000
Cash	44,000
Expenditures	465,000
Taxes receivable	80,000
Appropriations	(490,000)
Estimated uncollectible taxes	(10,000)
Estimated revenues	500,000
Due to Intragovernmental Service Fund	(4,000)
Revenues	(480,000)
Vouchers payable	(30,000)
Reserve for encumbrances	(15,000)
Fund balance	(75,000)
Total	–0–

Required:

1. Prepare a properly ordered trial balance.
2. Prepare the 7/1/x2 entry which recorded the budget.
3. Prepare the closing entries.

Problem 2: Transaction City

The general fund trial balance of Transaction City at 8/31/x4 appeared as follows:

TRANSACTION CITY
Trial Balance
8/31/x4

Cash	$ 40,000
Taxes receivable—delinquent	30,000
Estimated uncollectible delinquent taxes	(10,000)
Due to Intragovernmental Service Fund	(10,000)
Vouchers payable	(20,000)
Reserve for encumbrances	(5,000)
Fund balance	(25,000)
Total	–0–

With a new fiscal year beginning 9/1/x4, the following transactions took place in the new fiscal year:

1. The budget reflected estimated revenues of $400,000 and appropriations of $390,000.
2. Property was seized and sold for $10,000 to recover delinquent taxes of $5,000; the remaining $5,000 was returned to the former owner. This did not affect uncollectible taxes.
3. New property tax bills for $200,000 were mailed. This tax becomes delinquent if not paid by 12/31/x4. $5,000 was provided for uncollectible current tax.
4. Sales taxes of $150,000 were received in 19x4, as were $50,000 in fines and $4,000 in license fees.

5. Property taxes collected amounted to $180,000 of current year taxes and $8,000 of prior year's taxes.
6. Materials ordered last year with an anticipated $5,000 cost were received and actually cost $5,200.
7. Payrolls were paid at the end of each month and totaled $165,000.
8. Orders were placed for $150,000 of expenditure-type items. The orders received actually cost $145,000 but had been anticipated to cost $146,000; vouchers were properly prepared.
9. Vouchers paid amounted to $150,000.
10. The budgeted expenditure for $45,000 for interest and eventual bond retirement was paid.
11. Paid $30,000 to intragovernmental service fund and received a $25,000 billing for services.

Required:
1. Prepare the journal entries for these aggregate transactions for the fiscal year ending on 8/31/x5.
2. Prepare the closing entries.
3. Prepare a 8/31/x5 post closing trial balance.

Problem 3: City of Growth

On 1/1/x1 City of Growth received as a gift 5,000 acres of land to be used for an industrial park. The land had a fair value of $10,000,000, and there was a $1 million mortgage on the property. City of Growth immediately retired the mortgage payable from the proceeds of a $1,000,000 short term bond issue. These bonds were issued at face value. In addition, $50,000,000 of 8 percent 20-year-term bonds were issued on 1/1/x1 at face value to provide funds to build a new factory. A contract for a $50 million facility was signed. In year 19x1 the contractor billed $15 million for work on the contract. The City of Growth engineer approved this amount for payment less than 10 percent retention fee called for in the contract to ensure satisfactory work. The proper payment was made.

Required:

Record the effects in journal entry form in each fund or group of accounts affected.

Problem 4: City of Whatfore

You have been asked to establish a proper accounting system for the City of Whatfore. The bookkeeper has maintained only one fund, a general fund, in which all transactions have been recorded and a trial balance reflects the following:

CITY OF WHATFORE
Trial Balance
12/31/x1

Cash	$ 500,000	
Taxes receivable—current	150,000*	
Allowance for uncollectible current taxes		5,000
Expenditures from appropriations	750,000†	
Revenues		860,000
Donated land: For civic center building	100,000	
For recreational park	200,000	
Work in progress (civic center)	500,000	
Bonds payable (civic center)		800,000
Payable to contractor (civic center)		30,000
Retentions for contract fulfillment on civic center		50,000
Vouchers payable (for operating costs)		10,000
Excess resources over liabilities		445,000
Total	$2,200,000	$2,200,000

* $865,000 billed less $715,000 collected.
† For detail see 4 below.

1. The operating budget for the calendar year 19x1 was not recorded but it reflected estimated revenues of $850,000 and appropriations of $840,000. The unrecorded capital budget for the civic center was separate from the operating budget and reflected contracted construction costs of $750,000 to be funded entirely by new term bonds. $800,000 of 20-year, 10 percent term bonds were issued at par on 1/1/x1. In addition to the interest cost, the general fund budget provides for $50,000 in 19x1 to be invested for future retirement of the principal. Costs incurred to date show the center to be two-thirds completed, and $420,000 has been paid on the contract.
2. During year 19x1 there were orders placed for $460,000 of operating items and park equipment, but only $450,000 of this has been received; and the actual cost was $302,000 for operating costs and $152,000 for park equipment. Vouchers were prepared, and $444,000 was paid.
3. Interest payable in future years, through 12/31/x1, for civic center 10 percent term bonds which were issued on 1/1/x1 at face value, totals $720,000 at 12/31/x1. There has been no change in market interest rates in year 19x1.
4. An analysis of the expenditures reveals the following:

City of Whatfore operating costs	$302,000
Equipment for City of Whatfore recreational park	152,000
Purchase of land for an industrial park	128,000
Retirement of last series of serial bonds including $8,000 in interest	88,000
Interest on civic center bonds	80,000
	$750,000

5. The 1/1/x1 trial balance showed only:

Cash	$145,000	
Serial bonds payable		$ 80,000
Excess resources over liabilities		65,000
	$145,000	$145,000

Required:
1. For each of the eight common types of governmental funds and two groups of accounts, record in journal entry format the entries as they should have been made.
2. Prepare the closing entries for the general fund.

Index

A

Accounting concepts
  for asset acquisition, 98–104
  for taxable and purchase acquisitions, 328–30
  for tax-free and pooling combinations, 330–33
Accounting periods and methods, 169–70
Accounting Principles Board (APB)
  Opinion No. 1, 3 n
  Opinion No. 2, 3 n, 21, 22
  Opinion No. 4, 3 n, 21, 22
  Opinion No. 9, 245 n
  Opinion No. 10, 3 n
  Opinion No. 11, 3 n, 10, 21, 22, 47, 55, 88
  Opinion No. 16, 55, 273, 358
  Opinion No. 23, 3 n, 40–41, 64
  Opinion No. 24, 3 n, 41
  Opinion No. 25, 53, 54
Accounting theory, and the nature of income tax, 3–4
Accounts, self-balancing noncurrent groups of, 463–65
Acquisition
  accounting concepts of, 98–104
  from outside party, 219–24
  majority, 138–40, 145–49, 150–52
  100 percent, 135–38, 142–49
Add-on minimum tax on tax preferences, 6, 7 n
Advanced recognition entry, 171
Allocation
  of gains and losses, 224–25
  as problem in accounting for expenses, 4–18
  of purchase price in multiple asset acquisition, 109–14
Alternative minimum tax, 7 n
American Electric Power, 7 n, 42–43
Asset, fair market value (FMV) of, 96

Asset acquisition
  accounting concepts on, 98–109
  allocation of purchase price in multiple asset, 109–14
  of corporation, 96–98
AT&T, financial statements of, 61
Audit
  concepts, 466–67
  pad for anticipated deficiency on, 18–21

B

Bonds, as common stock equivalents, 246–53
Book equivalent of taxable income, 13, 14
Book value, possible combinations of, with fair value and cost, 155–58
Branch operations, taxability of income from, 291
Brother-sister corporation, 336, 336 n

C

Capital gain income, result of, in tax preferences, 6
Capital project funds, 458–59
Carryforwards, 45–50
Changing ownership interests
  through conversion of securities, 254–60
  through issuance of shares by subsidiary, 261
  through new share issues, 263–72
  through options, 261–63
  through sale of part or all of ownership interests, 279–82
  through treasury stock transactions, 272–78
Common stock equivalency test, 245
Common stock equivalents
  bonds as, 246–53
  preferred stock as, 243–45

483

Complex capital structures
  analysis of investments with both common and preferred stocks, 241–53
  distinguishing between debt and owner's equity, 239–40
  tax incentive, 240–41
Conglomerate operations, tiered corporate structure as logical outgrowth of, 289
Consolidation method of accounting for equity investments, 95–96
X Consolidated statements, preparation of
  combinations of book value, fair value, and cost, 155–58
  substitution under pooling of interest concept, 152–55
  substitution under purchase concept at date of acquisition, 127–40
  substitution under purchase concept subsequent to date of acquisition, 140–52
Consolidated tax returns, 39
Control systems, 467
  accounting bases, 471–72
  budgeting process, 467–69
  encumbrance accounting, 469–71
  use of agencies, 467
Conversions
  and decrease of ownership percentages, 254–58
  and increase of ownership percentages, 258–60
Convertible bonds, 246–53
  as owners' equity, 260
Corporate acquisition
  parties to, 325
  planning recorded value of corporate assets, 347–51
  pooling in theoretical perspective, 358–60
  reasons for, 325–27
  requirements for pooling of interests accounting, 340–46
  requirements for tax-free exchange, 333–35
  theoretical aspects of pooling, 335–40
  types of, with stock as compensation, 327–33
Corporate assets, planning recorded value of
  for financial reporting, 347–50
  for tax purposes, 350–51
Corporate combinations
  parties to, 325
  types of, with stock as compensation, 327–33
Corporate entity, change of percentage ownership in, 253–81
Corporate partners, 406–7

Corporate partnerships, 400
Corporations
  acquisition of, 96–98
  acquisition of chain of, 295–302
  as compared to partnerships, 396–97
Cost, possible combinations of, with book value and fair value, 155–58
Cost method of accounting for equity investments, 82–87

D

Debt
  distinguishing between, and owner's equity, 239–40
  gain on early extinguishment of, 228–29
  preferred stock as, 243
Debt acquisition, pathways for, 213–14
Debt service funds, 459–60
Debtor, sale of directly acquired debt to, 217–19
Deferral concept, 56–57, 172–97
Deferral entry, 171
Deferred income taxes, translation rules for, 377–78
Deferred tax accounts, in statement of financial position, 57
Deficiency, padding for anticipated on audit, 18–21
Depreciation
  changing methods of, 15–18
  result of, in tax preferences, 6
  timing differences due to, 17–18
Direct acquisition, from member issuing debt, 214–15
Directly acquired debt, disposal of, 216–19
Double-declining-balance (DDB) depreciation, 15

E

Earnings and loss ratios, in a partnership, 402–3
Earnings statement, required disclosure in, 57–60
Earnings statements accounts, translation of, 378
Economic reality, use of, as guidelines, 60–62
Encumbrance accounting, 469–71
Enterprise funds, 461
Equity investments
  business motivation for, 79
  categories of, 82–96
  tax motivations for, 79–82
Equity method of accounting
  for equity investments, 88–95

Equity method investments—*Cont.*
　impact on earnings under, when parent is selling affiliate, 206
Equity method earnings, 39–42
Erie-Lackawanna, 8 n
European Economic Community, 367

F

Fair market value (FMV), of asset, 96
Fair market value (FMV) allocation method, 109–11
Fair value, possible combination of with book value and cost, 155–58
Family partnerships, 398
Federal government, accounting for, 474–75
Fiduciary group of funds, 462–63
Fifo inventories, 377
Financial Accounting Standards Board (FASB)
　Interpretation No. 29, 41
　Statement No. 5, 18
　Statement No. 8, 374, 375–76, 377 n, 383
　Statement No. 9, 3 n
　Statement No. 12, 87
　Statement No. 20, 384–385
Financial disclosure of tax accounts, 54–60
Financial position accounts, translation of, 375–78
Fixed assets
　sale of depreciable, 180–89
　sale of nondepreciable, 172–75
Flow through method for investment tax credits, 21–23
Foreign company, use of equity method of accounting, 376
Foreign Corrupt Practices Act (1977), 367
Foreign country, operations located in, 373–75
Foreign currency, speculation in, 373
Foreign currency commitments, hedging on, 383–86
Foreign income taxes, 63–66
Foreign market, selling and buying in, 370–73
Foreign tax credit, 291
Foster Lumber Co., Inc., 46 n
Fund accounting system, development of, 466
Funds, standard governmental accounting system for municipality, 457–65
Funds concepts, 456–57

G

General fixed asset group, 363–64
General fund, 457–58

General long-term debt group, 464–65
Generally accepted accounting principles, effects of, on foreign operations, 374
General partners, 397
General price level accounting, on treatment of deferred tax accounts, 378
Good Hope Industries, Inc., 29
Government
　function of, 456
　tax aspects of financing operations of, 476–77
Governmental accounting, future of, 472–74
Governmental group of funds, 457–60
Governmental operations
　audit concepts, 466–67
　concept of stewardship, 465
　control system, 67–72
　development of fund accounting system, 466
　federal government, 474–75
　function of government, 456
　funds concept, 456–57
　future of, 472–74
　local government, 475–76
　standard accounting system for municipality, 457–65
　state government, 475–76
　tax aspects of financing, 476–77
　users of governmental reports, 465–66
Governmental reports, users of, 465–66
Gross change method for ascertaining amount of reversal, 15, 16, 18

H

Hartford Fire Insurance Company, ITT acquisition of, 352–58, 360
Hedging, use of forward exchange contracts for, 383–86

I

Income taxes
　accounting theory for, 3–4
　and allocation, 4–18
　carryforwards of investment tax credits, 49–50
　complexity of accounting for, 3
　deferral concept, 56–57
　deferred tax accounts in statement of financial position, 57
　deferred tax credits from timing differences, 46–49
　economic reality as guideline, 60–61
　equity method earnings, 39–42
　evaluation of accounting for, 60–63
　as expense, 3–4

Income taxes—*Cont.*
  financial disclosure of tax accounts, 54–60
  foreign taxes, 63–66
  liability concept, 56
  local taxes, 66–68
  nature of, and accounting theory, 3–4
  net operating losses (NOL), 42–45
  net-of-tax concept, 55–56
  padding for anticipated deficiency or audit, 18–23
  part permanent and part timing, 50–53
  provision for, 13–15
  reasons for electing NOL carryforward, 45–46
  required disclosure in earnings statement, 57–60
  state taxes, 66–68
  stock options, 53–54
Industrial development bonds, use of, 477
Intercorporate debt-transactions
  acquisition from outside party, 219–24
  direct acquisition from member issuing debt, 214–15
  disposal of directly acquired debt, 216–19
  minority interest aspects, 230
  pathways for debt acquisition, 213
  problem of allocating gains and losses, 224–25
  years subsequent to acquisition from outside party, 225–30
Intercorporate federal income tax allocation, 7–9
Intercorporate sales, from subsidiary to parent, 189–97
Intercorporate transactions
  accounting periods and methods, 169–70
  deferrals, 172–97
  effect of single entity concept, 169
  impact on earnings under equity method, 206
  offsets, 171–72
  restorations, 172–97
  subsidiary sales to parent, 197–99
Intergovernmental service funds, 461–62
International transactions
  current translation rules, 375–79
  effects of rate changes, 379–83
  effects of translation, 369–75
  hedging foreign currency commitments or exposed net asset or exposed net liability positions, 383–86
  investments and operations and need for translation, 368–69
  translation and investments in subsidiaries, 386–88
Interperiod federal income tax allocation, 9–18

Intraperiod federal income tax allocation, 5–7
Inventories
  fifo, 377
  intercorporate sales of, 190–97
  lifo, 377
  translation rules for, 377
Investment at book value of the underlying net assets, 127–30
Investment credit, 21–23
Investment at less than underlying book value
  majority acquisition, 138–40, 150–52
  100-percent acquisition, 135–38
Investment at more than book value of underlying net assets, 130–35
Investment at more than underlying book value
  majority acquisition, 145–49
  100-percent acquisition, 142–49
Investment at underlying book value, 140–42
Investments, analysis of, those with both common and preferred stock, 241–53
Investor's earnings, taxation of, 476
ITT, acquisition of Hartford Fire Insurance Company by, 352–58, 360

J–K–L

Joint ownerships, as compared to partnerships, 397
Liability concept, 56
Lifo inventories, 377
Limited partners, 397–98
Liquidation, of partnership, 440–45
Local government, accounting for, 475–76
Local income taxes, 66–68
Lower-of-cost or market method of accounting, 87–88

M

Majority acquisition
  investment at less than underlying book value, 138–40, 150–52
  investment at more than underlying book value, 145–49
Marketable securities
  indirect acquisition of, under purchase concepts, 298–302
  translation rules for, 376–77
Member, sale of directly acquired debt to another, 217–19
Mergers, in partnerships, 438–39
Minority interest, 230
  purchase of treasury shares from, 273–78
Modified FMV allocation method, 111–13

Monetary items, distinction of, between, and nonmentary items for foreign operations, 375
Mortgage bonds, use of, 477
Multiple corporations, 291
Municipality, standard governmental accounting system for, 457–65

N

Net change method for ascertaining amount of reversal, 15, 16–17, 18
Net monetary asset, 375
Net-of-tax concept, 55–56
Net monetary liability, 375
Net operating losses (NOL), 42–45
  carryforward, 45–50
Nonbusiness units, requirements of, for accounting and auditing services, 477
Nonrecognition of tax benefits concept, 41
Norfolk and Western Railway Company, 8, 8 n

O

Offset entry, 171
Offsets, 171–72
100 percent acquisition
  investment at less than underlying book value, 135–38
  investment at more than underlying book value, 140–45
Organization of Petroleum Exporting Countries, 367
Outsider, sale of directly acquired debt to, 216–17
Owner's equity
  distinguishing between, and debt, 239–40
  preferred stock as second class of, 241–43
Ownership, change in
  through conversion of securities, 254–60
  through issuance of new shares, 263–72
  through issuance of shares by subsidiary, 261
  through options, 261–63
  through sale of part or all of ownership interests, 279–81
  through treasury stock transactions, 272–78
Ownership, consideration of, 176–77

P

Pad for anticipated deficiency on audit, 18–21
Parent corporation
  acquisition of subsidiary with own stock, 292–95
  purchase of all of new issue by, 263–69
  purchase of half of new issue by, 269–72
  purchase of none of new share issues, 263
  purchase of treasury shares from, 277–78
  subsidiary sales to, 197–99
Part-pooling and part-purchase method, 337–40
Partner(s)
  death of, 438
  retirement of, 438
  types of, 397–98
Partnership agreement, 401–2
Partnerships
  accounting for, 395–420
  admission of new members, 407–20
    bonus or goodwill entry, 412–15
    premium paid by new partner, 409–11
    premium paid by old partner, 411–12
    purchase of existing partner's interest, 415–16
    purchase of part of each partner's interest, 416–20
    routes of, 407–9
  as compared to corporations, 396–97
  as compared to joint ownerships, 397
  as compared to proprietorships, 396
  concept of equality in, 400–1
  creation of, 401–5
  as form of business entity, 395
  general income tax aspects of, 395–96
  liabilities of, 433–34
  liquidations of, 440–45
  loans from partner to, 434
  loans to partner, 434
  operations of, 406–7
  sale of partnership interest, 435–38
  split-offs and mergers, 438–39
  tax aspects of partner's interests in, 399–400
  tax-free incorporation of, 446–47
  as tax shelters, 399
  termination, 435, 438–45
  tiered, 445–46
  types of, 398–400
Partner to partnership transactions
  impact of contributed, appreciated, or depreciated assets on earnings and loss ratios, 433
  potential for tax-free diversification, 430–31
  sales at gains, 427–30
  sales at losses, 431–33
Permanent differences, 12–13

Pooling concept
  acquisition of chain of corporations under, 295
  origin of, 335
  perfect case for, 336
  and prior years, 335
  reporting for tiered operations where subsidiaries are acquired under, 302–8
  theoretical perspective of, 358–60
  theoretical questions for, 336–37
Pooling of interests accounting
  absence of planned transactions, 344–46
  attributes of combining corporations, 340–41
  manner of combining interests, 341–44
Pooling of interests concept, 98–103
  partnership involved in, 407
  substitution under, 152–55
  translation following, 388
Preferred stock, 239–40
  as common stock equivalent, 243–45
  as debt, 243
  favorable tax treatment of, 246
  as second class of owner's equity, 241–43
Pretax accounting income, 10–12
Professional partnerships, 400
Proprietorships, 396
Proprietory group of funds, 460–62
Purchase acquisition, translation following, 387
Purchase concept, 103–4
  acquisition of chain of corporations under, 296–98
  illustration of, 104–9
  indirect acquisition of marketable securities under, 298–302
  reporting for tiered operations where subsidiaries acquired under, 308
  substitution under, at date of acquisition, 127–40
  substitution under, subsequent to date of acquisition, 140–52
Push-down accounting, 296 n

Q–R

Rate changes, effects of, 379–83
Reciprocal interests, 308–9
  recognition of, 309
  treasury stock treatment of, 309–12
Recording contributed aspects and liabilities in partnership, 403–5
Residual allocation method, 113–14
Restoration entry, 171
Restorations, 172–97
Revenue Act (1971), 22
Reverse acquisitions, 325, 325 n

S

Securities, change in ownership through conversion of, 254–60
Securities and Exchange Commission
  Accounting Series Release No. 96, 22
  Accounting Series Release No. 149, 57, 59
  Accounting Series Release No. 268, 239 n
  reporting requirements for foreign transactions, 367–68
  separate disclosure requirements of, for income tax categories, 6
Single entity concept, effects of, 169
Special assessment funds, 460
Special revenue funds, 458
Specific identification method of ascertaining amount of reversal, 15–16
Split-offs, in partnerships, 438–39
State government, accounting for, 475–76
State income taxes, 66–68
Statement of financial position, deferred tax accounts in, 57
Stewardship, concept of, 465
Stock-for-asset transaction, 325
Stock-for-stock combination, 325
Stock investments, accounting requirements for, 114–17
Stock option complexity, 53–54
Straight-line depreciation, 15
Subchapter S Corporation, 397
Subsidiary
  accounting for complex and changing capital structures within, 239–82
  sales of, to parent company, 197–99
Substitution at acquisition with 90 percent minimum ownership, 153–54
Substitution entry, 171
Substitution subsequent to acquisition with 90 percent minimum ownership, 152–55
Sum-of-the-years' digits (SYD) depreciation, 16

T

Tax credits, impact of, 21–23
Tax effects of transactions where intercorporate gain or loss is deferred, 177–180
Tax-free exchange, requirements for, 333–35
Tax planning
  and preferred stock, 246
  and sale of assets to partnership by partner, 429
Tax Reform Act (1969), 240
Tax shelters, partnerships as, 399, 445
Taxable income, 10–12

Temporal method, 369
Tiered operations
  acquisition of chain of corporations, 295–302
  acquisition with parent corporation stock, 292–95
  development of tiered structures, 289–92
  reciprocal interests, 308–12
  reporting for tiered chain of corporations, 302–8
Tiered partnerships, 445–46
Tiered structures
  configurations of, 289
  development of, 289–92
Timing differences, reversal of, 15–18
Translation
  current rules for, 375–78
  definition of, 368
  of earnings statements accounts, 378
  effects of, 369–75
  of financial position accounts, 375–78
  following pooling of interests, 388

Translation—*Cont.*
  following purchase acquisition, 387
  need for, 368–69
Treasury shares, purchase of, from parent corporation, 277–78
Treasury stock transactions, change in ownership through, 272–78
Triangular acquisition, 292, 294
  as family partnership, 398

U–W–Y

Undistributed earnings, accounting requirements for timing differences created by, 114–17
Uniform Partnership Act, 401
Working papers
  analysis of, 230–31
  attempts by IRS to obtain for pad accounts, 28–29
Years subsequent to acquisition from outside party, 225–29

This book is set VIP, in 10 and 9 point Palatino, leaded 2 points. Chapter numbers are 48 point Americana Bold and chapter titles are 18 point Americana Bold. The size of the type page is 27 × 46 picas.